THE RULE OF RECOGNITION AND THE U.S. CONSTITUTION

THE RULE OF RECOGNITION AND THE U.S. CONSTITUTION

EDITED BY

MATTHEW D. ADLER

KENNETH EINAR HIMMA

OXFORD
UNIVERSITY PRESS

OXFORD
UNIVERSITY PRESS

Oxford University Press, Inc., publishes works that further Oxford University's objective of excellence in research, scholarship, and education.

Oxford New York
Auckland Cape Town Dar es Salaam Hong Kong Karachi Kuala Lumpur Madrid Melbourne
Mexico City Nairobi New Delhi Shanghai Taipei Toronto

With offices in
Argentina Austria Brazil Chile Czech Republic France Greece Guatemala Hungary Italy
Japan Poland Portugal Singapore South Korea Switzerland Thailand Turkey Ukraine
Vietnam

Published by Oxford University Press, Inc.
198 Madison Avenue, New York, New York 10016

Library of Congress Cataloging-in-Publication Data

The rule of recognition and the U.S. Constitution/edited by Matthew D. Adler and Kenneth Einar Himma.
p. cm.
Includes bibliographical references and index.
ISBN 978-0-19-534329-8 ((hardback) : alk. paper)
1. Constitutional law—United States—Philosophy.
2. Jurisprudence—United States—Methodology. 3. Legal positivism.
4. Hart, H. L. A. (Herbert Lionel Adolphus), 1907–1992. Concept of law. I. Adler, Matthew D.
II. Himma, Kenneth Einar.
KF4552.R85 2009
342.7302—dc22

2009002782

---

1 2 3 4 5 6 7 8 9

Printed in the United States of America on acid-free paper

To Julia, Jonathan and Spencer

Matthew

To Maria Elias Sotirhos, and Angela and Maria Katinas

Kenneth

CONTENTS

ACKNOWLEDGMENTS

The editors are very grateful to Dean Michael Fitts, Professor Stephen Perry, the University of Pennsylvania Law School, and Penn's Institute for Law and Philosophy, for hosting and providing funding and facilities for a conference at which authors presented initial drafts of their chapters for this book; and to Anna Gavin, for her help in organizing the conference.

CONTRIBUTORS

Matthew D. Adler, Leon Meltzer Professor, University of Pennsylvania Law School

Larry Alexander, Warren Distinguished Professor, University of San Diego School of Law

Mitchell N. Berman, Richard Dale Endowed Chair in Law, University of Texas at Austin

Michael C. Dorf, Robert S. Stevens Professor of Law, Cornell University Law School

Richard H. Fallon, Jr., Ralph S. Tyler, Jr. Professor of Constitutional Law, Harvard Law School

Michael Steven Green, Professor of Law, College of William & Mary

Kent Greenawalt, University Professor, Columbia Law School

Kenneth Einar Himma, Professor of Philosophy, Seattle Pacific University

Stephen Perry, John J. O'Brien Professor of Law and Professor of Philosophy, University of Pennsylvania Law School

Frederick Schauer, David and Mary Harrison Distinguished Professor of Law, University of Virginia

Scott J. Shapiro, Professor of Law and Professor of Philosophy, Yale University

Jeremy Waldron, University Professor, New York University School of Law

Wil Waluchow, Senator William McMaster Chair in Constitutional Studies, Department of Philosophy, McMaster University

INTRODUCTION

MATTHEW D. ADLER AND KENNETH EINAR HIMMA

H.L.A. Hart, in *The Concept of Law*, offers a rule of recognition model of a legal system.[1] In any mature legal system, Hart claims, officials accept and practice a social rule of recognition that defines the system's ultimate criteria of legal validity. The rule of recognition provides the foundational rules for making, changing, and adjudicating the law, and imposes duties on officials to treat norms satisfying these criteria of validity as having the status of law. A legal system exists in a particular society at some point in time if (1) there is some rule of recognition *R* that has the status of a *social* rule among the contemporaneous officials of that society (i.e., officials accept *R* as binding, act consistently with its requirements, criticize officials who deviate from it, and accept such criticism as legitimate); and (2) citizens generally comply with the norms designated as law by virtue of satisfying the criteria of validity expressed in *R*.

This is, of course, just the barest thumbnail sketch of Hart's view. Scott Shapiro, in his chapter for this volume, provides a fuller picture of the rule of recognition model and reviews Hart's motivations for adopting it.[2]

Forty-five years after the publication of *The Concept of Law*, Hart's model remains the center for nearly all contemporary work in analytic jurisprudence—among both positivists who accept or build upon the model and antipositivists, such as Ronald Dworkin, who proceed in reaction to it. Despite its age, *The Concept of Law* retains its vitality as the font of all serious philosophical work about the nature of law—an area of legal theory that has seen a dramatic increase in the quantity and quality of scholarship over the last two decades.

Scholarship within contemporary positivism focuses on a number of different issues.[3] First, what is the nature of the social practice among officials that gives rise to the rule of recognition? Do the activities of officials amount to a social norm, a social convention, a "shared cooperative activity," the implementation of a plan, or some other kind of social practice? Second, to what extent is the

1. H.L.A. Hart, The Concept of Law (Penelope A. Bulloch & Joseph Raz eds., 2d ed. 1994).

2. *See* Scott J. Shapiro, *What Is the Rule of Recognition (And Does It Exist)?* (Chapter 9, this volume).

3. *See, e.g.*, Jules Coleman, The Practice of Principle (2001); Hart's Postscript (Jules Coleman ed., 2001); Matthew Kramer, Where Law and Morality Meet (2004); Andrei Marmor, Positive Law and Objective Values (2001); Joseph Raz, Ethics in the Public Domain (1994); Scott Shapiro, Legality (forthcoming); W. J. Waluchow, Inclusive Legal Positivism (1994).

content of the rule of recognition constrained by its function of guiding official or citizen behavior? "Inclusive" or "soft" positivists argue that the rule of recognition can incorporate moral criteria—a position that Hart endorsed in the Postscript.[4] "Exclusive" or "hard" positivists deny that the rule of recognition can incorporate moral criteria. Third, how can the normativity of law be explained by positivists? According to Hart, officials, in accepting the rule of recognition, adopt the "internal point of view" toward it: they take it as creating genuine reasons for action, indeed genuine obligations. But how can a mere social practice ever create genuine obligations? Fourth, to what extent is the methodology of jurisprudence itself necessarily normative? Hart explains that "[m]y account is *descriptive* in that it is morally neutral and has no justificatory aims."[5] But, given that the "internal point of view" accords normative force to law, can the jurisprudent's account of law really be successful if that account does not succeed in showing how law actually creates, or at least might be plausibly thought to create, genuine normative reasons?

The Hart/Dworkin debate also continues apace. In various writings, culminating in *Law's Empire* (1986),[6] Dworkin challenges the rule of recognition model. Regarding methodology, Dworkin insists—in contrast with Hart—that jurisprudence must be normative and that a norm can be law in the fullest sense only if it has genuine normative credentials. Regarding substance, Dworkin rejects Hart's claim that a legal system rests on official consensus about ultimate validity criteria. According to Dworkin, disagreement about the "grounds of law" is pervasive, and norms are validated as law not by application of a consensus rule of recognition, but by "constructive interpretation" of legal practices. Over the last twenty years, a number of jurisprudents sympathetic to Dworkin's views have pursued these themes.[7]

Despite the centrality of *The Concept of Law* to jurisprudential debates over many years, the book has been virtually ignored by United States constitutional theorists. To be sure, most constitutional theorists know the outlines of Hart's theory and are aware of the Hart/Dworkin debate. But there is very little scholarship that attempts to employ Hart's rule of recognition model to illuminate questions of U.S. constitutional theory. Conversely, few jurisprudents have seriously attempted to use the United States as a test case for the model. Does an examination of the actual functioning of the U.S. legal system vindicate the model, highlight aspects that need refinement, or suggest that the rule of recognition model is seriously flawed?

---

4. *See* HART, *supra* note 1, at 247–48, 25–54.

5. *Id.* at 240.

6. *See also* RONALD DWORKIN, TAKING RIGHTS SERIOUSLY (1977).

7. *See, e.g.*, SCOTT HERSHOVITZ, EXPLORING LAW'S EMPIRE: THE JURISPRUDENCE OF RONALD DWORKIN (2006); NICOS STAVROPOULOS, OBJECTIVITY IN LAW (1996).

This volume seeks to remedy these gaps, bringing together prominent jurisprudents and U.S. constitutional theorists to address the applicability of the rule of recognition model to the United States.

The first chapter reprints Kent Greenawalt's 1987 article, "The Rule of Recognition and the Constitution."[8] This important article is one of the few existing works attempting to identify the content of the rule of recognition in the United States. The article provides a rich discussion of various issues that Greenawalt confronted in the course of formulating a U.S. rule of recognition, some of which arise repeatedly in this volume. First, the U.S. rule of recognition may be substantially longer and more complicated than a simple reference to the 1787 Constitution (or the Amendment Clause thereof), in part because it may give independent effect to extraconstitutional sources of law, such as judicial precedent or official custom. Second, the rule of recognition must be formulated to take account of the special role of the Supreme Court in deciding constitutional issues. Third, different officials may well accept ultimate criteria that are sufficiently convergent to allow for a stable system, but that diverge in some respects—for example, on the question whether a long-accepted amendment to the Constitution is law by virtue of having been properly enacted, or would still be law even if it were shown that the amendment had not been properly enacted. Finally, disagreements about the appropriate methodology for interpreting the Constitution pose special difficulties for the rule of recognition account.

The remaining twelve chapters are new contributions specifically commissioned for this volume.

Richard Fallon and Michael Dorf are sympathetic to the rule of recognition model and demonstrate its utility within contemporary U.S. constitutional theory. Fallon responds to the claim, recently advanced by originalist scholars, that the Supreme Court's reliance on precedent in constitutional adjudication is illegitimate.[9] On the Hartian model, the legal status of interpretive methods, and indeed of the Constitution's text itself, ultimately rests upon official practice. In practice, judges and other officials *do* accept the text of the Constitution as supreme. But it has never been judicial practice to employ original meaning or the Framers' intentions as the sole basis for interpreting the text and to depart from prior precedent whenever the court would adopt a different reading of the text in a case of first impression. Indeed, every current Justice, including originalists such as Justices Scalia and Thomas, has explicitly accepted the authority of constitutional precedent; and no current Justice has suggested departing from long-standing precedents that are probably mistaken by originalist lights (such as the decisions permitting paper money and a Social Security system). Fallon argues that, given the rule of recognition framework, originalist scholars' attempts

---

8. 85 MICH. L. REV. 621 (1987).

9. *See* Richard H. Fallon, Jr., *Precedent-Based Constitutional Adjudication, Acceptance, and the Rule of Recognition* (Chapter 2, this volume).

to delegitimate precedent in the teeth of these social facts are misguided—or, more charitably, must be seen as proposals for legal change, rather than as claims about the current legal status of precedent. Fallon also suggests (as do Alexander and Schauer) that a critical social fact about the U.S. legal system is the fact of citizen acceptance of judicial review as legitimate—a social fact that tends to entrench judicial acceptance of precedent in constitutional adjudication, since the Court would risk public outrage if it overruled long-standing precedents.

Dorf uses the Hartian account to enrich our understanding of U.S. higher-law norms.[10] Constitutional scholars tend to assume that norms limiting legislative activity must be derived from the Constitution. But nothing in the rule of recognition account requires that. The extent to which the Constitution is supplemented by additional, extraconstitutional limitations on legislators is an empirical matter, resolvable only by examining the norms for legislation that officials in practice accept. Indeed, U.S. legal culture does implicitly recognize such limitations, as Dorf shows through a detailed examination of three cases—court packing, jurisdiction stripping, and voting in Presidential elections. In none of these cases is the relevant customary norm in any meaningful sense derived from the Constitution—although our practices are somewhat conflicted, officials being uncomfortable characterizing the norms as "extraconstitutional." Dorf points to work in social psychology that shows how formalized norms can "crowd out" informal ones, and suggests that the written Constitution may tend to "crowd out" extratextual elements of our rule of recognition.

Kenneth Himma, also sympathetic to Hart's model, addresses the problem of Supreme Court authority within the context of that model.[11] The basic jurisprudential observation that the content of the rule of recognition is defined by official practice, combined with the empirical observation that U.S. officials accept the Supreme Court's authority to settle constitutional issues, undercuts any simple attempt to formulate the U.S. rule of recognition in terms of the text of the Constitution. A U.S. official will typically treat as invalid a statute that the Court has struck down, even if the official believes the statute to actually comply with the Constitution. On the other hand, John Chipman Gray's notorious claim that the Supreme Court has unconstrained discretion to determine the content of U.S. law goes too far in the other direction, since it fails to recognize both limits on official willingness to accept Supreme Court constitutional rulings, and the fact that the Court itself looks to the Constitution in deciding how to rule. Himma therefore suggests that the ultimate validity criterion for U.S. law should be formulated along the following lines: "A duly enacted norm is legally valid unless declared unconstitutional according to what a majority of the Justices

10. *See* Michael C. Dorf, *How the Written Constitution Crowds Out the Extraconstitutional Rule of Recognition* (Chapter 3, this volume).

11. *See* Kenneth Einar Himma, *Understanding the Relationship between the U.S. Constitution and the Conventional Rule of Recognition* (Chapter 4, this volume).

decide is, as an objective matter, the morally best interpretation of the substantive norms of the Constitution."

Himma, in previous work, has pressed the point that a legal system such as that of the United States conforms to the model of exclusive rather than inclusive positivism.[12] Although the Bill of Rights may appear to give rise to a rule of recognition that incorporates moral criteria, if in fact official practice is to accept duly enacted statutes as valid until struck down by the Court, then validity criteria (for officials) are nonmoral, "source"-based criteria—namely, what Congress enacts and what the Court decides. Wil Waluchow, in his chapter for this volume, addresses this issue.[13] Waluchow acknowledges that there are features of legal practice in the United States and Canada that seem to support exclusive positivism, but he also describes features that cut against it. For example, an invalidated statute is often seen as being null ab initio, rather than merely being revoked by the Court. And the Bill of Rights (in the United States) and Charter of Rights and Freedoms (in Canada) are understood as containing norms that no legitimate government action may infringe, rather than merely grounds that the Supreme Court must look to in deciding when to change the law. Waluchow then attempts to reconcile the inclusivist and exclusivist positions by describing different senses in which a law might "exist" or be "valid."

Greenawalt, in the first half of a new chapter written for this volume, also engages Himma's views about the Supreme Court's role and about inclusive positivism.[14] Greenawalt argues that Himma overstates the Supreme Court's primacy in deciding constitutional issues. It is universally accepted that Supreme Court judgments are binding, but not that Supreme Court holdings are; and legislators feel free to rely on their independent readings of the Constitution in deciding not to enact a statute that would pass muster under the Court's constitutional doctrines. Further, Greenawalt argues that the normative standards that the Supreme Court itself applies in reading the Constitution are part of the ultimate validity criteria for U.S. law, even though nonjudicial officials may not always directly apply those standards. Greenawalt observes that this insight may support inclusive positivism. However, he also suggests that Himma's formulation of the Supreme Court's duty, namely as a duty to seek the "morally best interpretation" of the Constitution, papers over significant intrajudicial

---

12. Kenneth Einar Himma, *Making Sense of Constitutional Disagreement: Legal Positivism, the Bill of Rights, and the Conventional Rule of Recognition in the United States*, 4 J. L. SOC'Y 149 (2003); *Final Authority to Bind with Moral Mistakes: On the Explanatory Potential of Inclusive Legal Positivism*, 24 LAW & PHIL. 1 (2005).

13. *See* Wil Waluchow, *Four Concepts of Validity: Reflections on Inclusive and Exclusive Positivism* (Chapter 5, this volume).

14. *See* Kent Greenawalt, *How to Understand the Rule of Recognition and the American Constitution* (Chapter 6, this volume).

interpretive disagreements—for example, between originalists (who often rebel against the use of moral criteria) and nonoriginalists.

Larry Alexander and Frederick Schauer, in their coauthored chapter, engage the Court's constitutional role as part of a broader discussion of the social facts that undergird the U.S. legal system.[15] As a descriptive matter, they suggest, the U.S. legal system is best seen as having a multiplicity of rules of recognition. Justices who disagree about interpretive methodology in a case of first instance are following different rules of recognition. Citizens who know very little about constitutional interpretation are following yet a different rule of recognition, one that tells them to defer to the Supreme Court within very wide limits. As a normative matter, Alexander and Schauer ask how the value of "settlement"—the reduction of uncertainty—can be achieved in a society where different actors recognize different legal validity criteria. They point to features of U.S. practice that knit together these heterogeneous criteria and that allow reasonable stability: in particular, a general consensus about the existence of a Supreme Court and the rules for picking the Justices, plus a general consensus that the Supreme Court can settle constitutional controversies, at least on a case-specific basis. Finally, as a jurisprudential matter—and contrary to Hart—Alexander and Schauer argue for the necessity of citizen acceptance of some rule of recognition, if only one that instructs deference to more legally knowledgeable actors. A group of officials not accepted by citizens as legitimate would be no different from the "gunmen" Hart describes in his criticism of John Austin's account of law.

Matthew Adler, in prior scholarship, has pressed the multiple-rules-of-recognition view to the limit, arguing that law should be understood as "group-relative," and illustrating the idea using U.S. constitutional practice.[16] Throughout U.S. history, different groups have held competing views about the deepest questions of constitutional law—such as whether the text is the sole source of constitutional law; interpretive methods; the allocation of interpretive authority between the Court, legislatures, and the citizenry; and the nature of the federal system. This empirical observation prompts Adler to make a jurisprudential suggestion, namely that claims about constitutional law may be true only relative to one or another group, and not in an absolute sense. In the second part of his chapter, Greenawalt critically discusses the group-relative account. Greenawalt questions the utility of the account for purposes of empirical inquiry. It is not clear how groups would be defined—nor why we would posit a multiplicity of group conceptions of the Constitution, rather than a multiplicity of individual conceptions, to explain individual behavior. As for its utility in structuring normative inquiry, Greenawalt worries that the group-relative

15. *See* Larry Alexander and Frederick Schauer, *Rules of Recognition, Constitutional Controversies, and the Dizzying Dependence of Law on Acceptance* (Chapter 7, this volume).

16. *See* Matthew D. Adler, *Popular Constitutionalism and the Rule of Recognition: Whose Practices Ground U.S. Law?*, 100 Nw. U. L. Rev. 719 (2006).

framework will overemphasize the parochial rather than common interests of U.S. citizens.

While the chapters described to this point work within the rule of recognition framework, more or less, the remaining chapters are more critical. Adler's chapter closely examines argumentation by U.S. scholars and jurists about methods for interpreting the Constitution—methods such as textualism, originalism, "representation reinforcement," "minimalism," common law constitutionalism, substantive moral reasoning, and so forth.[17] Adler calls this body of argumentation constitutional interpretation (CI) discourse, and argues that the rule of recognition model of law and legal statements neither accurately describes CI-discourse, nor vindicates the statements that CI-participants characteristically make. The difficulty, Adler observes, is not merely that CI-participants disagree about interpretive methods. In addition, although CI-participants do often rely on social facts to defend interpretive methods, these tend to be facts about U.S. culture and tradition, about the Framers' intent, and about precedent—*not* the social fact that gives rise to a rule of recognition, namely contemporaneous official practice. However, Adler is equally skeptical about using a Dworkinian model to describe and vindicate CI-discourse, given Dworkin's questionable claims about the moral value of integrity. As for the group-relative framework, this framework certainly does allow CI-participants to argue for controversial interpretive methods and to rely upon a variety of kinds of social facts (as long as the method and the relevance of the facts are not controversial within the relevant group). But the framework fails to vindicate a very basic assumption of CI-discourse, namely that the United States has a single legal system rather than a multiplicity corresponding to different groups. In conclusion, Adler suggests, CI-participants may just be misguided in trying to make legal arguments for controversial interpretive methods and in presupposing that certain social facts, distinct from present official practice, are relevant to the legal status of interpretive methods.

Scott Shapiro presents a new account of the nature of legal systems, which sees each legal system as resting on a shared "plan."[18] (This account substantially modifies the "shared cooperative activity" based account of law, which Shapiro had pioneered.) The plan-based account, although different from the rule of recognition model in major respects, remains broadly Hartian in spirit—for example, in seeing social facts as the basis for law; explicating the unity of a legal system in terms of the fact that officials within the system are socially unified in a certain way; and denying that legal requirements necessarily generate genuine

---

17. *See* Matthew D. Adler, *Social Facts, Constitutional Interpretation, and the Rule of Recognition* (Chapter 8, this volume).

18. *See* Scott J. Shapiro, *What Is the Rule of Recognition (And Does It Exist)?* (Chapter 9, this volume). The plan-based account is more fully presented in Shapiro's forthcoming book, LEGALITY.

normative reasons for action. The account can be seen as an attempt to preserve these central Hartian insights without making implausibly strong claims about the extent to which officials "buy into" the legal system, intend to cooperate with each other, or share a consensus about ultimate validity criteria. The plan for a legal system allocates decision-making authority pursuant to the plan-designers' judgments about the relative trustworthiness of different types of officials and about political morality. As long as the members of a political community are currently in rough consensus about who the plan designers *are*, and as long as those designers indeed had common views about trust and political morality that they intended the plan to reflect, legal questions—for example, questions about interpretive methodology—can be both contestable among officials and citizens, yet also have a correct answer grounded in the plan-designers' views.

Mitchell Berman squarely rejects the rule of recognition model.[19] The model purports to derive validity criteria—necessary and sufficient conditions for the status of some norm or decision as law—from social practice. But it is impossible to derive such conditions from social practice, Berman argues. For example, every judicial decision involves a novel combination of circumstances (the parties' identities, the issues at stake, the particular process of adjudication, and so forth). It is only by arguing about the legal validity of a decision, after it occurs, that the community of lawyers resolves its validity. There is nothing in the antecedent social facts about the community that constitutes a conclusive test for the decision's validity. This insight suggests to Berman that law should be understood as an argumentative practice. Jurists' and scholars' views about constitutional interpretation, for example, will be reasonable or unreasonable, not correct or incorrect. Such an account, although very different from Hart's, is also not Dworkin's, because it denies Dworkin's "right answer" thesis. Finally, although the account has affinities to David Strauss's theory of common law constitutional interpretation,[20] the account is more general than Strauss's—applying to both constitutional and nonconstitutional matters—and does not necessarily yield Strauss's conclusions that precedent should be given substantial weight in constitutional adjudication and that the text of the Constitution should be downweighted.

Stephen Perry points to a crucial lacuna in *The Concept of Law*: Hart's failure to offer an analysis of social rules that are power-conferring rather than duty-imposing.[21] When Hart first introduces the notion of a rule of recognition, he

---

19. *See* Mitchell N. Berman, *Constitutional Theory and the Rule of Recognition: Toward a Fourth Theory of Law* (Chapter 10, this volume).

20. *See* David A. Strauss, *Common Law Constitutional Interpretation*, 63 U. Chi. L. Rev. 877 (1996).

21. *See* Stephen Perry, *Where Have All the Powers Gone? Hartian Rules of Recognition, Noncognitivism, and the Constitutional and Jurisprudential Foundations of Law* (Chapter 11, this volume).

recognizes that the fundamental secondary rules in a legal system will also include rules of change and rules of adjudication. These rules are power-conferring: they legally empower some body to change the law (for example, by enacting a statute) or to issue a judgment in an adjudicated case. But rules of change and adjudication fall by the wayside in Hart's subsequent discussion. Nor is this a mere oversight. Perry argues that Hart's noncognitivist analysis of internal legal statements—whereby an "assertion" of a legal duty is seen as an expression of the non-belief state of accepting the duty—has deep difficulty explaining what the assertion of a legal power consists in. The so-called Frege–Geach problem, which undermines noncognitivist analyses of *moral* statements, also calls into question noncognitivism about legal statements. Perry suggests that legal statements are best understood as genuine assertions of beliefs, and that a legal system rests upon a social practice that includes participants' beliefs about the moral legitimacy of the system. This view has multiple implications, including a possible rejection of the official-centric cast of Hart's view. *Pace* Hart, some degree of citizen belief in the moral legitimacy of a legal system may be a condition of its very existence—a point that, as we have seen, Alexander and Schauer also suggest.

Jeremy Waldron, like Perry, argues that *The Concept of Law* gives too little emphasis to the role of rules of change.[22] Indeed, Waldron suggests, the fundamental validity criteria for a legal system might consist *solely* in rules of change. For example, it is not unreasonable to think that Article I of the Constitution, together with the Bill of Rights, are part of the ultimate validity criteria for federal law. But note that Article I is a rule of change, empowering Congress to enact legislation, and that the Bill of Rights consists of Hohfeldian disabilities, limiting the legislative powers of Congress. One might object that our validity criteria must also include a separate duty-imposing rule, obliging judges to enforce statutes validated by Article I and the Bill of Rights; but this objection is mistaken, Waldron points out, because legal powers are, conceptually, capacities to change duties. Waldron also considers the possibility that the ultimate validity criteria for U.S. law must include a closure principle above and beyond Article I and the Bill of Rights: a principle that prohibits judges from enforcing anything *except* norms validated by the fundamental rules of change. But, as Dworkin's famous discussion of *Riggs v. Palmer* and the role of moral principles in adjudication shows, such a closure principle is not an element of every legal system as a conceptual matter, and may also be morally disadvantageous.

Michael Steven Green argues that Hart's account connects law too closely with social facts, and that Hans Kelsen's views are helpful in severing the link between legal statements and sociological assertions or presuppositions.[23]

22. *See* Jeremy Waldron. *Who Needs Rules of Recognition?* (Chapter 12, this volume).

23. *See* Michael Steven Green, *Kelsen, Quietism, and the Rule of Recognition* (Chapter 13, this volume).

According to Hart, an internal legal statement presupposes a certain kind of social fact: collective (official) acceptance of the ultimate validity criteria. But this model hamstrings our ability to make certain kinds of internal legal statements, namely statements that assert or presuppose the independence of legal validity from collective acceptance of the relevant validity criteria. For example, we may assert that the Constitution was valid law as of June 21, 1788, when it was ratified by the ninth state, New Hampshire, in accordance with the ratification procedure set out in Article VII—and that statutes enacted shortly thereafter, such as the Judiciary Act (1789), are fully valid law—even though general official and citizen acceptance of Article VII and the rest of the Constitution as supreme law may well not have occurred until 1790, when all thirteen states had ratified it, or even later. We say, or can say, not only that judges *now* are legally required to treat the Constitution and the Judiciary Act as law (even with respect to events between 1788 and 1790), but also that officials in 1789 *were* at the time legally required to treat these documents as law. Kelsen's view enables such assertions because, on that view, statements concerning the ultimate criteria of legal validity are fundamental, in the sense that they cannot be justified at all—neither by law, nor by social facts. Green is attracted to this view, but also recognizes its limitations. For example, it is difficult to make sense of the existence of multiple, separate legal systems except by virtue of social facts.

The special role of courts in legal systems; how to account for disagreement about the grounds of law; the connection between social facts and legal statements; whether citizens can be wholly alienated from a legal system; whether law is reducible to duties; whether law can incorporate moral considerations—these are hardly new issues for analytical jurisprudence. What this volume richly evidences, however, is the utility of engaging these issues with an eye to the actual features of a paradigmatic legal system, here the United States. Conversely, questions concerning the legitimacy of nonoriginalist constitutional interpretation, the scope of judicial review by the U.S. Supreme Court, the extent to which constitutional law is "just politics," the status of extratextual sources of higher law, the role of precedent in constitutional adjudication, and the viability of popular constitutionalism are the bread and butter of constitutional theory. This volume shows that constitutional theorists can make progress in answering these questions by explicitly bringing to bear an understanding about the nature of law and legal systems. Jurisprudence and constitutional theory are not alien enterprises. Whatever else this volume achieves, it demonstrates *that*.

1. THE RULE OF RECOGNITION AND THE CONSTITUTION[+]

KENT GREENAWALT*

I. INTRODUCTION

This chapter is about ultimate standards of law in the United States. Not surprisingly, our federal Constitution figures prominently in any account of our ultimate standards of law, and a discussion of its place is an apt jurisprudential endeavor for the bicentennial of the constitutional convention. Although, in passing, I offer some comments on constitutional principles, this chapter is not about how the Constitution—or, indeed, other legal materials—should be understood and interpreted. Rather, it attempts to discern the jurisprudential implications of widespread practices involving the Constitution and other standards of law.

The ambitions of this chapter are most easily explained in terms of its origins. For many years, I have taught students in jurisprudence courses the central themes of H.L.A. Hart's *The Concept of Law*.[1] Among the most important themes is the idea of a rule of recognition, which expresses a society's ultimate criteria for what counts as law. Rejecting John Austin's claim that commands of a sovereign are the ultimate standard of legality, Hart writes of a rule of recognition, a test accepted by officials for determining which normative standards are part of the legal corpus.[2] Each time I have asked students what the rule of recognition is in the United States, the answer has seemed more difficult and complex.

[+] Reprinted from *Michigan Law Review*, February 1987, Vol. 85, No. 4, Pp. 621–71. Except for a few very minor changes, this chapter is identical to the original article.

* University Professor, Columbia University, teaching at Columbia Law School. I am enormously grateful to H.L.A. Hart, whose careful critical comments on two previous drafts helped prevent confusion and imprecision and opened up avenues for examination. Also, I want to thank Bruce Ackerman, Meir Dan-Cohen, Stephen Massey, Henry Monaghan, David Morris, and Stephen Munzer who gave me helpful comments on earlier drafts, and Daniel Alter and Brad Theis, who provided research assistance. I also profited from discussion of the paper by the New York University Law and Philosophy Colloquium.

1. H.L.A. Hart, The Concept of Law (1961) [hereinafter The Concept of Law].

2. *See id.*, especially at 97–120.

My attempt to deal with this intellectual puzzle in a systematic way is the root of this chapter; I offer here a fairly comprehensive account of how one might try to state a rule of recognition for someplace in this country.[3] My aims in this respect are primarily analytical and pedagogical: to demonstrate what critical issues are and what approaches are needed to resolve them. My method is also pedagogical in a special way. I sometimes offer a first approximation for resolution of a particular problem, leaving aside complexities. Once those complexities are explored in a related context, I return to the original problem for a more complete resolution. This strategy has drawbacks for the resolution of any particular issue, but it permits a more logical unfolding of stages of analysis.

The analysis, which illuminates intriguing and rarely discussed features of the American legal order, certainly dispels any illusion that the rule of recognition for the United States can be reduced to any simple statement, such as, "The federal Constitution is our rule of recognition." I demonstrate that the rule of recognition will have a number of standards and be quite complex, omitting some of the federal Constitution but including aspects of state law and interpretive standards used by judges. Although I make tentative choices among alternative hypotheses about a rule of recognition, I do not undertake the extensive historical or legal research that would be needed to make fully considered judgments about every troublesome question.

In applying what Hart says to our complicated legal order, I have progressively grasped some of the effort's broader implications for Hart's own theory and for divergences between that theory and its main competitor. It was not until I had struggled with these matters for some time that I realized more was involved than applying Hart's basic theory to an extremely complicated legal reality. Aspects of that reality proved recalcitrant in the face of Hart's categories; the conceptual possibilities and relationships among standards proved richer than one would gather from *The Concept of Law*. At that point, the second ambition of this chapter emerged: to amplify Hart's basic idea of a rule of recognition so that it could apply without distortion to the United States. In the course of trying to discern the rule of recognition for the United States, I show, among other things, how uncertain the ultimate standards of law may be in a stable legal system; how the ultimate standards may shift unnoticed over time; how the precise relationship between the "ultimate rule" and "supreme criterion" may vary from the one Hart supposes; and how the interaction between acceptance and higher norms may have a level of complexity greater than he imagines.

For some time I supposed that I could rest with developing and applying to the United States a somewhat enriched account of Hart's approach, leaving for others the overall adequacy of such an account in light of challenges made to it,

---

3. I use the word "someplace" because, as will subsequently be made clear, the ultimate rule of recognition is different in each state.

most notably by Ronald Dworkin.[4] But I came to understand both that some of the problems with discovering the rule of recognition for the United States could not be resolved without reference to those challenges and that the concrete effort at application provided a valuable window for assessing important disagreements between Hart and Dworkin. Much of the best writing about Dworkin's disagreements with Hart over ultimate standards of law has been general and at a high level of abstraction.[5] Though something may be lost by concentrating on the details of a particular legal system, as this chapter does, attention to such details clarifies much of what is at stake by illustrating competing possibilities in a familiar context. The exercise of applying Hart's approach to the United States shows why one needs to draw from basic insights of both Hart and Dworkin to reach a satisfactory theoretical understanding about American law.

The chapter thus proceeds at three levels: (1) application to the United States of Hart's concepts regarding the rule of recognition; (2) enrichment of those concepts in light of this country's law and legal institutions; (3) evaluation of some strengths and weaknesses of this general approach to how ultimate legal standards are discerned, and a sketch of a fuller and more adequate account. The main body of the chapter is primarily addressed to the first level, though it involves comments of obvious relevance for the second level and lays the groundwork for discussion at the third. Only near the end of the paper do I draw together my conclusions about how Hart's theory requires amplification, and there I treat the relevant disagreements between him and Dworkin in a systematic way. In order to help the reader see how the details of application to the United States of the idea of a rule of recognition relate to the more abstract jurisprudential issues, I begin by briefly summarizing Hart's theory and the core of the challenge to it and by circumscribing the plausible range of disagreement.

Before embarking on that endeavor, I want to offer the reader, especially one not closely familiar with the relevant literature, two cautions. The first is that I employ terms like "rule of recognition" and "supreme criterion" in a technical way, following Hart's understanding because I am exploring the implications of his theory. I am not trying to defend the meanings he assigns as the only or best possible meanings of those terms. The reader who entertains different meanings will have to remember that my claims about application are only about the

---

4. *See, e.g.*, R. DWORKIN, TAKING RIGHTS SERIOUSLY 14–130, 338–53 (1978 ed.) [hereinafter TAKING RIGHTS SERIOUSLY]; R. DWORKIN, LAW'S EMPIRE (1986) [hereinafter LAW'S EMPIRE]; Dworkin, *A Reply*, in RONALD DWORKIN AND CONTEMPORARY JURISPRUDENCE 247 (M. Cohen ed. 1984) [hereinafter *A Reply*].

5. *See, e.g.*, J. RAZ, THE AUTHORITY OF LAW (1979); Coleman, *Negative and Positive Positivism*, 11 J. LEGAL STUD. 139 (1982); Postema, *Coordination and Convention at the Foundations of Law*, 11 J. LEGAL STUD. 165 (1982); Soper, *Legal Theory and the Obligation of a Judge: The Hart/Dworkin Dispute*, 75 MICH. L. REV. 473 (1977).

concepts Hart uses, not about every meaning that could be assigned to the key terms.

The second caution is that my effort here involves conceptual clarification. Insofar as theoretical clarifications dispel confusion, they may have some indirect practical influence, but I have no practical point to make here about how actors in the legal system should interpret the Constitution or other legal materials. Of course, it is possible that at some subconscious level practical aims are driving my attempt at theoretical understanding, and it is almost certainly true that no attempt at understanding the nature of social institutions is wholly compartmentalized from the social world one would like to see. But the reader who is looking for theory that has some meaty and straightforward practical significance, who is ill-disposed to conceptual elaboration for its own sake, is bound to be extremely disappointed by what follows and would be well advised to stop here.

II. HART'S CONVENTIONALIST ACCOUNT OF LAW AND THE NORMATIVE CHALLENGE TO IT

According to Hart, societies with advanced legal systems have criteria for distinguishing authoritative legal norms from norms that do not have legal status. These tests or criteria need not be understood by the general populace; they are employed by officials. To state for a particular society what the criteria of law are, and the hierarchy in which these criteria stand to each other, is to describe the standards that recognized officials now accept.[6] The reconstruction of the practices of officials tells us what the standards are for law in a society.

When societies experience revolution, sharp conflict may exist over who exercises official authority; and in some societies officials may be guided in their actual decisions by "authorities" (such as party officials) that they do not publicly acknowledge as having the power to determine what is valid law. As Hart does for the most part,[7] I shall disregard these possibilities and concentrate on a stable

6. At first glance, this account may seem to involve a troubling circularity, as officials determine what the standards of law are and they derive their official status from the law. The break in the circle is that one looks to the population at large to see who are recognized as officials. Ordinarily, people's judgments about who are officials may rely on certain assumptions about conformance with legal standards, such as election laws, but people need not understand the complex criteria judges and other officials use to determine what counts as law.

7. Hart discusses revolution in THE CONCEPT OF LAW, *supra* note 1, at 114–15. He suggests, *id.* at 68, that if an official habitually obeys someone else, that does not mean the person he obeys has legal authority; but Hart does not address a society in which the authority of those outside the legal hierarchy is generally acknowledged and has some legal support, as the authority of Communist Party members may be recognized in Communist countries.

legal order in which the criteria that officials purport to follow are those they generally do regard as authoritative.

In explaining the ultimate rule of recognition, Hart supposes that a question is raised about the validity of a local ordinance.[8] Americanizing the illustration, we might ask if what is claimed to be a housing regulation was adopted by the city council; if so, whether the city charter gave such power to the council; if so, whether the state legislature gave such power to the city government; if so, whether the state constitution gave such power to the state legislature; if so, whether the federal Constitution authorizes, or allows, the exercise of such power by the states. At each early stage in the process, we can refer to a higher standard that validates the lower standard for determining whether the rule counts as law. Finally, however, we reach a point at which the effect of a standard does not depend on a higher standard that we can refer to; all we can say is that this standard for determining law is accepted in the society. When we arrive at such a standard, we have reached the ultimate rule of recognition. That rule does not derive validity from a superior legal rule, it owes its status as law to its acceptance by officials.

Hart's discussion of the ultimate rule of recognition includes an account of a "supreme criterion," which is all or part of the ultimate rule:

> [A] criterion of legal validity or source of law is supreme if rules identified by reference to it are still recognized as rules of the system, even if they conflict with rules identified by reference to the other criteria, whereas rules identified by reference to the latter are not so recognized if they conflict with the rules identified by reference to the supreme criterion.[9]

Since Hart's phrase, "the rule of recognition," can be the source of confusion, we need to be clear about how he is using the term. First, "rules" are often thought of as imposing duties. The rule of recognition, which sets out criteria for identifying law, does not tell people in any simple way how to act, though it may be "duty-imposing" in the more complex sense of setting standards for how officials perform their functions.[10]

Second, nothing in the basic term "rule of recognition" necessarily suggests ultimacy; one could comfortably speak of the conferral of legal authority upon cities by a state legislature as a "rule of recognition," though the state legislature's power is itself derived from the state constitution. As a criterion courts would use to identify valid city law, the conferral of authority by the state legislature might be called a derivative rule of recognition. Hart, however, reserves the words "rule of recognition" to refer to ultimate standards for identifying law; in

8. *Id.* at 103–04.

9. *Id.* at 103.

10. *See* N. MacCormick, H.L.A. Hart 113–15 (1981); J. Raz, The Concept of A Legal System 198–99 (2d ed. 1980).

his terminology, a standard that can be derived from another legal standard is not part of the rule of recognition. To minimize possible confusion I follow him here, using other terms when I refer to derivative criteria.

Third, Hart is clear that the ultimate standards for identifying law may include quite separate strands. One might wish to speak of each of these as an independent rule, together comprising the ultimate *rules* of recognition.[11] Though Hart occasionally falls into using the plural "rules of recognition" in this way,[12] for the most part he intends the singular "rule of recognition" to include every ultimate standard for determining law in a particular political society. Again, for simplicity's sake, I adhere to his terminology.

Hart's account is conventionalist. What counts as law depends ultimately upon prevailing social practices, that is, what officials take as counting as law. If a judge or other official were to try to determine the law, he would implicitly employ the rule of recognition and what can be derived from it. If a sociologist were trying to describe the legal system, he would use the rule of recognition both to identify the corpus of law and to conceptualize how officials determine what is law. In calling the rule of recognition a social rule, Hart means more than that the rule expresses a convergence of perspectives officials happen to take about what is law. The constraints of the rule must be "effectively accepted as common public standards of official behaviour by [a system's] officials."[13] Part of the *reason why* officials use the rule is because they conceive of it as representing a shared social practice upon which expectations are built.

Hart usually speaks as if the main features of the rule of recognition and most of its applications will be reasonably straightforward. He clearly does not think the rule of recognition must include standards of morality, and it is probably fair to say that among the advanced legal systems in which he is primarily interested, Hart does not believe standards of morality will be among the rule's most important features.[14] For issues raised about the law that are not settled by reference to the rule of recognition or derivations from it, Hart talks as if a judge or other

---

11. *See* J. Raz, *supra* note 10, at 200.

12. *See, e.g.*, The Concept of Law, *supra* note 1, at 92.

13. *Id.* at 113. This aspect of the rule of recognition is explored in depth by Gerald Postema, *supra* note 5. On the notion of social rules, see N. MacCormick, *supra* note 10, at 29–44.

14. Moral standards, however, might figure into a full account of the authority of precedent or custom. That would be so if a precedent judged to have morally unacceptable applications had less force in some sense than other precedents or if a custom could have legal authority only if morally acceptable. Hart says that "reasonableness" is one test of whether a custom has legal status in England. The Concept of Law, *supra* note 1, at 46. Presumably one way in which a custom could be unreasonable would be by being morally reprehensible. Hart also says that in countries like the United States, the ultimate criteria of legal validity "explicitly incorporate principles of justice or substantive moral values." *Id.* at 199. Whether this observation is actually faithful to Hart's own account depends on

official has discretion, that is, a kind of legislative choice how to apply a vague standard to concrete facts or how to fill in an open gap in the rule of recognition itself or in one of the standards that derives from it.

Mainly addressing the role of judges in common-law systems, Ronald Dworkin has challenged the sharp distinction Hart draws between validity based on derivation from higher standards and the acceptance on which ultimate standards rest. Dworkin points out that, even in Hart's theory, the legal force of a particular claimed custom will depend partly on its acceptance.[15] More important, the vast number of principles, such as "no one should profit from his wrongdoing," that figure in adjudication depend not on prescription by a single authoritative act but on vague facts of institutional acceptance.[16] Since many of these "legal" principles will replicate or closely resemble moral principles, Dworkin's account draws a much less sharp distinction than Hart's between standards of law and moral standards. Further, Dworkin claims that the reach of legal duty extends to cases that are not resolved by any socially accepted rule of recognition; the judge deciding difficult cases must *as a matter of law* undertake (explicitly or implicitly) a complex exercise in interpretation, seeking to develop and apply the soundest theory of law.[17] Dworkin's writings make plain that though soundness is partly a matter of fit with legal materials, the judge interpreting the law will make important independent judgments of political and moral philosophy—independent in the sense of not being determined by the legal materials themselves.[18] The reason a judge employs a particular interpretive theory is because it seems soundest, not because it is socially accepted. In contrast to a conventionalist account, Dworkin offers a normative or interpretive account. The judge's final standards of what constitutes law are the best normative interpretive judgments he or she can make.

Subsequently, as I try to evaluate how well conventionalist and normative accounts apply to particular standards for determining law, I undertake a deeper analysis of distinguishing features of the two sorts of accounts. Here it is useful to make two preliminary points.

First, many of the specific questions that Hart's theory raises about the United States also arise if one tries to construct the most convincing normative account of what law is in this country. In a reconstruction of the basic structure of American law, the problems I raise largely transcend the debate over the nature of law's foundations, though how one tries to resolve the problems will depend partly on one's perspective about those foundations.

---

how the relation between the federal Constitution and the rule of recognition is conceptualized, a subject treated in Section IV *infra*.

15. *See* TAKING RIGHTS SERIOUSLY, *supra* note 4, at 41–43.

16. *Id.* at 39–44.

17. *See, e.g., id.* at 46–130; LAW'S EMPIRE, *supra* note 4.

18. *See especially* LAW'S EMPIRE, *supra* note 4, at 248, 255–63.

The second, more complicated, point is that a good many of Hart's crucial premises are left intact even if the normative challenge is fundamentally accurate. No one denies that certain kinds of legal norms require creation by nonjudicial bodies whose competence to legislate depends on conferral by authoritative legal norms. In most of the United States, for example, judges have no common-law power to create new crimes.[19] Though they may rely on principles to interpret legislative mandates, judges cannot declare behavior to be criminal just because it offends principles that the legal system embraces in some general way. Nor can courts create new taxes or authorize military conscription. These matters are left to legislatures, whose authority is conferred by federal and state constitutions. The validity of a great many legal norms can undoubtedly be traced in much the manner Hart envisions. Also, the legal order undeniably contains important principles of hierarchy: that federal law is superior to state law; that statutory law is superior to judicially created common law; and that constitutional law is superior to both statutory and common law. One aspect of this hierarchy is that rules of common law or interpretations of statutes that are based on principles can be overridden by subsequent legislative choice. In *Riggs v. Palmer*,[20] discussed by Dworkin,[21] the court held that a murderer cannot recover under the will of the person he murdered; but if the state legislature explicitly chose to allow such recovery, it could do so.

Even if it is true that, in deciding what the law is, judges look for the best interpretive theory rather than a socially accepted rule, it is also true that in any stable legal order there is bound to be a very great overlap in the content of what judges see as the best interpretive theories.[22] A convergence on many points will amount to a rule, or rules, for determining law that a sociologist could describe. Such is the situation in the United States, for example, in regard to the authority of the Constitution and the supremacy of legislation over the common law. Important theoretical questions about a legal order concern the nature and extent of these basic and agreed-upon standards.

At a deeper level, a normative account of how law is determined does not entirely escape dependence on convention. After all, every judge within a system takes as given certain basic materials that count as law; the judge who refers directly to the Articles of Confederation rather than the Constitution as a source of modern law is crazy. And Dworkin himself has argued that institutional support is critical to the status of principles. A plausible rendering of this understanding would be to say that even a normative account builds on many

---

19. *See generally* MODEL PENAL CODE § 1.5 comment (1985).

20. 115 N.Y. 506, 22 N.E. 188 (1889).

21. *See* TAKING RIGHTS SERIOUSLY, *supra* note 4, at 23–45; LAW'S EMPIRE, *supra* note 4, at 15–20.

22. *See* LAW'S EMPIRE, *supra* note 4, at 136–39.

conventionally accepted sources of law,[23] that the critical respect in which it differs from the conventionalist approach is in claiming that the binding standards for what counts as law extend well beyond what is conventionally accepted.

A normative theorist might resist this ingestion of conventionalism by asserting that nothing is law simply because it is conventionally accepted, that *any* accepted practice regarding the identification of law is in theory open to rejection or revision if it does not fit well with other standards for identifying law.[24] Nonetheless, any normative theorist would have to concede that some premises are so fundamental to our legal system, such as the primacy of the federal Constitution over conflicting state law, that a reasonable judge could not reject them. He would also have to concede that even were *every* particular standard for determining law theoretically subject to rejection, the bases for judging the overall coherence of a challenged practice with the entire law would be largely drawn from a wide collection of socially accepted practices. In sum, one cannot imagine any normative theory of law in which the law of a particular society could be identified wholly independently of socially accepted practices. Further, it would be highly surprising if these practices reflected *just* regularities of behavior and convergences of perspectives among officials and citizens. People and officials rely upon the expectations created by concordant practice. Thus, a plausible normative, or interpretive, alternative to the conventionalist approach to determining law must involve a claim more subtle than the view that convention plays no role at all.

Having endeavored to place Hart's account of the rule of recognition in its broader jurisprudential setting, I undertake to apply that account to the United States, using his views about Britain as a guide.

III. HART'S RULE OF RECOGNITION FOR BRITAIN: A STARTING POINT FOR INVESTIGATION OF THE UNITED STATES

When Hart focuses on the supreme criterion and the ultimate rule of recognition, he addresses the relatively simple situation of Britain—at a time preceding its adherence to the Common Market and to other European agreements that permit multinational bodies to disallow some of their national legal norms.[25] From his discussion of Britain we learn more precisely what Hart means by an

---

23. *See, e.g.*, Coleman, *supra* note 5; Postema, *supra* note 5.

24. In LAW'S EMPIRE, *supra* note 4, at 138, Dworkin suggests that some things in British and American legal systems may be settled as a matter of genuine convention, but he says "nothing *need* be settled as a matter of convention in order for a legal system not only to exist but flourish."

25. *See* Macarthys Ltd. v. Smith, [1979] 3 All E.R. 325, 328–29 (C.A.) (Denning, M.R., dissenting); Esso Petroleum Co. v. Kingswood Motors (Addlestone) Ltd., [1974] 1 Q.B. 142,

ultimate rule of recognition and a supreme criterion, and we prepare ourselves to tackle the more complicated legal terrain of the United States.

The supreme criterion, for Hart, is that what the Queen in Parliament enacts is law.[26] Any norm that emanates from other lawmaking authorities and is in conflict with parliamentary legislation must give way to the legislation. Perhaps a more exacting statement of the supreme criterion would include a temporal dimension, indicating that earlier legislation yields to subsequent legislation, but the basic standard of parliamentary supremacy is straightforward.

When we inquire what Hart conceives of as the ultimate rule of recognition in Britain, we must parse passages that lean in different directions. The problem arises over the legal status of custom and precedent. In one discussion, talking about the authority of parliamentary legislation "as the ultimate rule of recognition,"[27] Hart intimates that in Britain the supreme criterion and the ultimate rule of recognition converge. Yet a few pages earlier, he denies that custom and precedent "owe their status of law . . . to a 'tacit' exercise of legislative power."[28] Rather, their status comes from "a rule of recognition which accords them this independent though subordinate place."[29]

One conceivable way to interpret these passages in conjunction is to suggest that although particular pieces of customary law and precedent do not derive their status from parliamentary action or inaction, the criteria that give these norms authority have issued from Parliament in some way. Given Hart's analytical distinction between the ultimate rule and the supreme criterion, Parliament's power to alter or eliminate the legal status of custom or precedent is plainly not enough by itself to establish that the authority of these kinds of law emanates from Parliament; but perhaps when Parliament established courts, or circumscribed the jurisdiction of existing courts, it positively endorsed these forms of law. Hart, however, gives no hint that this is what he has in mind. More important, this version casts an unacceptable strain on his comment that custom and precedent have an independent place under the rule of recognition, which means that they do not depend on some exercise of power by a legislative body. Particularly because the passages that suggest otherwise address different issues, by far the most plausible rendering is that the ultimate rule does reach precedent and custom, that these are law in the United Kingdom because they are accepted

151; Chloros, *English Law and European Law: The Problem of Harmonization*, 36 Rabels Zeitschrift 601 (1972).

26. The Concept of Law, *supra* note 1, at 103–04.

27. *Id.* at 104.

28. *Id.* at 98.

29. *Id.*

as law by officials.[30] I shall take that as Hart's view when we address the more troublesome analogous questions about the United States.

IV. THE FEDERAL CONSTITUTION AND THE ULTIMATE RULE OF RECOGNITION AND SUPREME CRITERION

We are now ready to address the main subject of the chapter: What are the ultimate rule of recognition and supreme criterion for the United States? Many of the complicated questions center on the federal Constitution and its relationships to its own component parts and to state law. I deal with these questions first and then consider judge-made law and what I call interpretive techniques.

When first asked, many students suppose that the federal Constitution is the ultimate rule of recognition for the United States, or that the rule of recognition is that "whatever is in the Constitution is law." Before suggesting why either of these notions, unvarnished, is inadequate, I consider the supreme criterion of law for the United States.

A. A First Approximation: The Amending Clause as the Supreme Criterion

With one obvious minor qualification, some important edges of uncertainty, and a subtle point about institutional authority, the supreme criterion of law is rather easy to identify given prevailing assumptions about the American Constitution. A criterion of law is supreme, it will be recalled, if norms adopted according to it take precedence over norms adopted by any other procedure. The criterion about which that is true in the United States is the amending clause, article V, of the Constitution. A provision adopted according to its procedures for amendment has priority not only over state law, federal statutes, and federal judicial decisions, but also over what is in the original Constitution or in earlier amendments.

The obvious minor qualification to this conclusion concerns the constitutional rule, found in the amending clause itself, that no state may lose its equal vote in the Senate without its consent. That rule is not amendable by the ordinary amending process. An exact statement of the supreme criterion would have to cover this specially entrenched practice,[31] but I shall disregard this slight complication.

1. Edges of Uncertainty The edges of uncertainty concern conceivable restrictions on permissible amendments, appropriate procedures, the status of norms not adopted according to ordinary procedures, and the passage of time. In contrast

30. This interpretation has been confirmed by a February 7, 1986, letter from Professor Hart, which characterizes as a "slip" the reference to "what the Queen in Parliament enacts is law" as the rule of recognition.

31. Hart discusses unamendability briefly in THE CONCEPT OF LAW, *supra* note 1, at 71; *see also id.* at 242.

with India, where the supreme court has interpreted the constitution as barring amendments that are incompatible with the basic structure of the constitution or that infringe certain fundamental rights,[32] the dominant assumption in the United States is that amendments adopted in a procedurally proper manner are valid regardless of their substantive content.[33] Still, there may be limits. Perhaps an amendment cannot establish its own unamendability,[34] or change the amending clause, or repeal all or most of the Constitution at one fell swoop. In Hart's terminology, there is a limited "open texture" in the supreme criterion; neither the language of the amending clause nor the shared understandings of officials resolve the validity of every conceivable provision adopted according to the procedures of the amending clause.

Considerable doubts exist about what appropriate procedures are under article V. May states rescind ratifications?[35] Can Congress set a time limit on ratification, and, if so, must it do so in an amendment itself?[36] Does the time for ratification lapse if no limit has been set?[37] Under the yet-unused procedure by which a convention rather than Congress would propose amendments, can the convention's authority be limited to specific subjects if state legislative applications to Congress to call a convention are so limited?[38] Are all these matters genuine legal questions, or are they left to be decided by Congress on political grounds?[39]

---

32. *See, e.g.*, Golak Nath v. State of Punjab, 54 A.I.R. (S.C.) 1643 (1967); D.D. Basu, Constitutional Law of India 371–77 (3d ed. 1983).

33. *See, e.g.*, Dellinger, *Constitutional Politics: A Rejoinder*, 97 Harv. L. Rev. 446, 448 (1983); *cf.* L. Tribe, Constitutional Choices 13 (1985); Tribe, *A* Constitution *We Are Amending: In Defense of a Restrained Judicial Role*, 97 Harv. L. Rev. 433, 438–43 (1983) [hereinafter Tribe, *A* Constitution *We Are Amending*].

34. This question lies close to one discussed by Hart about Britain—whether a present Parliament could adopt legislation and preclude repeal. In The Concept of Law, *supra* note 1, at 145–47, Hart says that it is now clear that Parliament lacks this power, but that the related question whether it can entrench legislation against repeal by an ordinary legislative process remains open.

35. *See* Dellinger, *The Legitimacy of Constitutional Change: Rethinking the Amendment Process*, 97 Harv. L. Rev. 386, 421–27 (1983).

36. *Id.* at 406–11.

37. *Id.* at 424–27.

38. *See* Dellinger, *The Recurring Question of the "Limited" Constitutional Convention*, 88 Yale L.J. 1623 (1979). Article V also provides that Congress can provide for ratification by state conventions rather than state legislatures. I here disregard that alternative, used only in connection with the twenty-first amendment.

39. On Congress' role, compare Dellinger, *supra* note 35, with Tribe, *A* Constitution *We Are Amending*, *supra* note 33. The view that final determination is committed exclusively to Congress need not entail the view that the questions are not legal. One might think these are legal questions as to which the Court has no responsibility, that they are "political questions" only in the sense that judicial disposition is precluded.

Finally, there may be uncertainties as to whether provisions may become valid law though understood not to be adopted by prescribed procedures. Bruce Ackerman has suggested that the reference in the preamble of the Constitution to "We the People" and the specification of a convention alternative for proposing amendments evidence a kind of approval for constitutional reforms that, like the original Constitutional Convention, leap the bounds of prescribed procedures.[40] In this event, the Constitution itself might be viewed as conferring at least a quasi-legal status on some measures that would plainly be invalid if one asked only whether they were adopted according to set procedures. Whatever their status prior to endorsement, "new amendments" made by unprescribed means might become authoritative law if "promulgated" by Congress, published by the executive, or accepted over a period of time. If the Constitution can be validly amended by procedures that do not conform strictly with article V, but meet some standard of endorsement or of institutional support and public approval, the range of uncertainty about the supreme criterion is drastically increased.

The possible import of acceptance over time for "amendments" not properly adopted relates to the *continuing force* of amendments that were properly adopted. For these, the passage of time may diminish the legal significance of their having been adopted in accord with the amending clause. I return to this problem after I discuss the ratification clause.

2. Institutional Authority The subtle point about institutional authority with respect to the supreme criterion concerns the role of Congress and the executive in approval of amendments, and the relationship between various standards different officials might use to determine what counts as law. Exactly what authority the political branches have in settling the validity of amendments is now far from clear, but the leading case on the amendment process indicates that, at least in respect to many issues, Congress makes the final decision as to whether an amendment has been properly adopted.[41]

Before considering the jurisprudential implications of such a principle, I need to narrow a bit the assumption that I am making about the range and nature of authority that may be assigned to Congress. Perhaps courts would balk at acquiescing to a blatant usurpation by Congress accomplished through a

---

40. *See* Ackerman, *The Storrs Lectures: Discovering the Constitution*, 93 YALE L.J. 1013 (1984) [hereinafter Ackerman, *Storrs Lectures*]. He develops these themes at much greater length in B. ACKERMAN, DISCOVERING THE CONSTITUTION (forthcoming).

41. Coleman v. Miller, 307 U.S. 433 (1939). Four members of the Court indicated that Congress has undivided and exclusive control of the amendment process. 307 U.S. at 457 (Black, J., concurring). Three Justices in an opinion for "the Court" indicated that courts could not review congressional determinations about timeliness and the significance of prior rejection; that opinion has fairly broad implications for what is committed to Congress. 307 U.S. at 447–56.

purported promulgation of a constitutional amendment.[42] I am supposing only that within *some range* courts will take what Congress says as final. It is important that the position of the courts within this range is actually to assign final decision to Congress, not merely to give some deference to the judgment of Congress in the course of reaching an independent determination of whether an amendment has been properly adopted. Finally, the sort of judgment Congress is to make is important. I am assuming that, at least sometimes, Congress should make an essentially legal determination, one that will be followed by courts even if it is mistaken. I suppose therefore that the authority assigned to Congress is something more than the right to make some nonlegal political judgment about whether acceptance of proposed amendments would be desirable, and something more than the right to fill in the open texture of the process outlined by the amending clause.[43] The possibility I mean to examine is that, within a certain spectrum, Congress's determination as to whether an amendment has been properly adopted will be a determination controlled by legal standards and will also be a determination accepted as final by the courts. I want to inquire how we would state the supreme criterion for such cases.

From the point of view of Members of Congress viewing a proposed amendment that has something approximating the requisite number of ratifications but is not published by the executive or yet promulgated by Congress,[44] the supreme criterion is adoption according to the amending clause. Whether that process has been followed will determine a conscientious Member's decision whether to promulgate or let executive publication be effective, or instead refuse to treat the possible amendment as valid. The criterion for an amendment that the courts *actually use* will be different: whether a provision has been published

---

42. *See* Tribe, *A* Constitution *We Are Amending, supra* note 33, at 433.

43. The "political judgment" view supposes that legal standards require acceptance of ratification in some situations and preclude acceptance in others, but that in certain borderline instances Congress may make a determination based on the overall political wisdom of accepting ratification. In that event, the supreme criterion, properly understood, would indicate that in certain circumstances a proposed amendment may, but need not, be taken as having been ratified.

The "discretion to fill open texture" view is subtly different. It supposes that in certain situations the prescriptions of the amending clause, plus perhaps other relevant legal standards, are indeterminate in their coverage. In that event, someone must amplify the details of what counts as a proper ratification, and Congress is left this essentially legislative decision on how to fill in the gaps of existing legal standards (a type of "legislative" decision that is left to courts in most other areas of law).

44. Although *Coleman v. Miller* indicates that Congress is to decide matters of ratification, in actuality virtually all amendments have been published by the executive branch, since 1818 according to statutory authorization. *See* Dellinger, *supra* note 35, at 400–02. A view that assigns primary responsibility to Congress and purports to be in accord with historical practice must assume that Congress has implicitly accepted amendments that have been published by the executive without congressional involvement.

or promulgated as having been adopted in accord with the amending process.[45] How to characterize such a principle of judicial acceptance of congressional determination is troublesome. We might say either that the supreme criterion for Congress really is different from the supreme criterion for courts, or that the courts do not *apply* a supreme criterion that, in some sense, they recognize.

If Hart's notions of the ultimate rule and supreme criterion require that all, or virtually all, officials in their practical judgments really *use* the same standards for what counts as law, the theory indisputably requires emendation. For, once one thinks about this problem, one recognizes that many officials—most obviously lower-court judges and subordinate executive officials—are on many occasions expected to take as authoritative the judgments of other, often higher, officials as part of their final standards for what constitutes law.[46] Hart, in fact, recognizes the possibility that legal systems may place some subjects outside of judicial competence.[47] Although he does not explore the general significance for his theory of subordination and deference among officials, we must suppose that when Hart talks about official acceptance of an ultimate rule and a supreme criterion he does not mean that all officials use these directly in their decisions.

The important practical point is fairly straightforward. So long as the principles of authoritative determination are reasonably clear and settled, a legal order can operate quite smoothly even though many officials often do not themselves apply the ultimate rule and supreme criterion used by the highest relevant officials. We might conceptualize this conclusion by saying, with Joseph Raz, that within a legal order there may be "various rules of recognition, each addressed to different kind of officials"[48]; or we might understand the rule of recognition as the ultimate standards of law used by officials who are not simply accepting the judgments of other officials. With sufficient effort, either sort of conceptualization could fit reality. Given the pervasiveness of acceptance of judgments of higher officials, the latter course seems preferable; certainly it is more faithful to the overall spirit of Hart's treatment.

In any complete account, we should need to explicate situations that are intermediate between wholly independent judgment and complete acceptance of the judgment of another, situations in which one official body both gives considerable

---

45. This standard might also be used by subsequent Congresses, who would take initial promulgation or publication as determinative of validity. In that event, the *present validity* of an amendment may be determined for *all* official bodies by acceptance by Congress at a specific point in time.

46. I use the phrase "on many occasions" because in the typical situation it matters whether the higher authority has reached a judgment. If it has not, the subordinate authority may apply the same standards to a problem as the higher authority would. If the higher authority has spoken, the lower authority takes its judgment as conclusive.

47. THE CONCEPT OF LAW, *supra* note 1, at 71, 242.

48. J. RAZ, *supra* note 10, at 200.

deference to another official body and regards itself as authorized to reject that judgment if the judgment is very clearly mistaken. I address that problem when I discuss precedents and techniques of interpretation.

As far as the supreme criterion is concerned, I shall assume for the time being that the supreme criterion, with appropriate qualifications, is the amending clause. In the ensuing discussion, I do not usually complicate matters by referring to whatever special authority Congress may have with respect to the amending process.

B. The Original Constitution and the Ratification Clause

The tentative conclusion, qualified as it is, that the amending clause is the supreme criterion helps us to understand why the ultimate rule of recognition does not include[49] either the entire Constitution itself or the norm that whatever is in the Constitution is law. The amendments generally become valid law because they are adopted in accordance with the amending clause. The relationship between amendments and the amending clause is basically the same as that between particular laws and the authority of Parliament to enact laws. When one asks why a particular new amendment is valid law, one can take a step higher within the Constitution, to conformity with the amending process, to explain the amendment's validity. One need not simply refer to official acceptance of that amendment or of amendments in general. The new amendment itself does not need to be justified by an ultimate rule of recognition that rests on acceptance, because it emanates from a process that is prescribed in an authoritative legal document, the original Constitution.

These observations about the amendments and the amending clause leave us with three initial candidates for formulations that indicate how the Constitution relates to the ultimate rule of recognition:

(1) All or part of the ultimate rule is the Constitution itself, including the amending clause but excluding the amendments.
(2) All or part of the ultimate rule is: Whatever the Constitution contains that is not itself enacted according to another part of the Constitution is law.
(3) All or part of the ultimate rule is: Whatever has been adopted in accord with the ratification clause is law.

Before turning to these three possibilities, I will briefly address the language of the Constitution's preamble. It says: "We the people . . . do ordain and establish this Constitution . . . ." Reference to the people is not evidently presented as

49. My reason for using the phrase "does not include" is that some elements outside the federal Constitution turn out to be part of the ultimate rule of recognition.

a legal standard ordinary officials can use to determine what is valid.[50] Even if it is said that our country possesses a revolutionary heritage, and that we recognize the right of the people to overthrow an unjust government, the revolutionary principle is not a straightforward test of legality. Hart is always clear that the rule of recognition is a legal standard that judges and other officials can apply. Whatever "the people's" status as a matter of deep political philosophy, "the people" or "the people's will" is not part of the ultimate rule of recognition for the legal order in the United States.[51]

In considering the three possible formulations, I shall begin with the one involving the ratification clause of article VII, which states that upon ratification by nine states the Constitution becomes effective between those states. Since in proposing a new Constitution the members of the Constitutional Convention exceeded the authority conferred on them to propose amendments to the Articles of Confederation,[52] the chain of legal authority does not reach back prior to the Convention. In at least some sense, the main body of the Constitution owes its status as valid law to its ratification by the procedure the Constitution contains. It would not have become law for this country if the proposed Constitution had remained unratified. Does the main body of the Constitution, therefore, stand in the same relation to the ratification clause as the amendments stand in relation to the amending clause?

We need to consider three salient and related differences between the amending clause and the ratification clause. Unlike the amending clause, the ratification clause is a one-time-only matter. Were this not clear before the Civil War, it is now settled that a state that ratified the Constitution is not free later to withdraw. The second, more crucial, difference concerns the stage at which authoritativeness of the two clauses was established. The legal status of the amending clause preceded any amendments adopted pursuant to it. But the ratification clause had no status prior to the substance of what was to be ratified by it. And we cannot even be sure it was fully accepted as authoritative until officials accepted the Constitution as effective law. Conceivably, small states might have

50. I do not claim that a reference to "the people" could never be such a standard. We could imagine a society in which judges could treat as invalid norms that did not accord with the views of the people, or one in which judges could even use determinations of the views of the people as a basis for establishing new norms.

51. If Bruce Ackerman is right that the Constitution contains a kind of implicit approval of change in nonauthorized ways, *see* Ackerman, *Storrs Lectures, supra* note 40, then "We the People" could play some role in determining the legal status of such changes. Suitably interpreted, it might be used by officials to determine whether or not changes brought about in procedurally imperfect ways should be taken as authoritative nonetheless. Were this so, the statement in the text would need to be qualified.

52. As Ackerman notes, *id.* at 1017 n.6, an argument can be made that substantive changes as sweeping as those in the proposed Constitution were within the bounds of the Convention's authority; but the possibility of ratification by nine states clearly was not.

been favorably enough disposed to the Constitution to undertake the ratification process, but their officials might have hesitated to take the Constitution as governing law if major states like Virginia, Massachusetts, New York, and Pennsylvania had failed to ratify. It is at least possible that the ratification clause was not fully accepted as authoritative until after the Constitution was ratified by nine states.[53]

The third important difference between the ratification clause and the amending clause is closely tied to the second. The ratification clause cannot be viewed apart from the substance of the Constitution. The clause does not prescribe a general procedure for lawmaking; rather it indicates that a particular group of potential legal norms will become law when nine states ratify. Let us assume that prior to actual ratification officials in the states did accept that, if the Constitution was ratified in their state and eight others, it would become authoritative for their state. Following Hart's hierarchical chain, we might be tempted to say that the ratification process was accepted as one by which authoritative law could be made, and that the substantive provisions of the Constitution were valid because ratified by that process. But such a statement might be misleading in a way that a statement about acceptance of the authority of Parliament would not be. It would be misleading because we do not know whether the ratification clause would have been accepted if the Constitution had had a very different substance. Since no state was bound to participate in the constitutional union without its consent, the same principle of ratification by nine state conventions *might* have been widely accepted given very different substantive provisions, but we cannot be certain. All we can confidently say is that in the context of this Constitution the ratification procedure was accepted. Here the procedure for making law and the law to be made are intertwined in a way not contemplated by the usual model of a rule of recognition. This analysis suggests that the acceptance of the ratification clause cannot be regarded independently of the body of the Constitution; and that the legal authority of the original Constitution derives from a procedure whose significance is best understood in conjunction with the rest of the Constitution.

Whatever one concludes about the status of the ratification clause at the time of the Constitution's adoption, it almost certainly is not *now* any part of the ultimate rule of recognition. A judge might, to be sure, say that the Constitution is law because it was ratified—meaning that from the historical point of view we would not have the Constitution we do if the document had remained unratified. But no judge or other official would presently be likely to countenance a legal argument that an original state purportedly bound to comply with the Constitution

53. *See* J. Raz, *supra* note 10, at 138, criticizing Kelsen's concept of a basic norm that the makers of the original Constitution should be obeyed. Raz says a first Constitution can become law because it is part of an efficacious legal system, a fact that may not be determinable until after the Constitution is first issued.

had not ratified it properly. We may be hard put even to think of the kind of factual evidence that could cast an apparent ratification into question. Are we to say that ratification is now not mentioned as of *present legal significance* because everyone assumes that the ratification procedure was followed, but that ratification still lies in the background as part of the ultimate rule of recognition? Or are we to say that now the legal authority of the rest of the original Constitution is established by its continued acceptance and that the original ratification procedure is no longer directly relevant to tracing what counts as law?[54] The latter is almost certainly the more accurate modern characterization.

C. A Reprise—The Supreme Criterion and the Amending Clause

This conclusion about the ratification clause requires some reassessment of the relation of amendments to the amending clause. Whether any officials would look behind amendments of long standing to judge the validity of their ratification, or even the genuineness of executive publication, is highly doubtful. In contrast to the present role of the ratification clause, this point has practical significance. The reason is that serious questions can be raised about the original validity of the thirteenth and fourteenth amendments.[55] Both were proposed by Congresses devoid of representatives from seceding states. Ratification of the thirteenth amendment depended on the approval of southern states whose representatives were excluded from the Thirty-Ninth Congress, a combination of events that powerfully casts into question whether the southern governments could be legitimate enough to ratify the thirteenth amendment and illegitimate enough to have representatives properly excluded from the Congress that proposed the fourteenth amendment. The approval by southern states of the thirteenth amendment was achieved by strong presidential pressure, and approval of the fourteenth amendment was a requisite to being represented again in the Congress. Arguments about the invalidity of the amendments have failed in the courts,[56] but the Supreme Court generally is open to reexamining constitutional questions. Given earlier cases in which the Supreme Court has passed on the amendment process,[57] the diminished scope of the political question doctrine in

---

54. I put aside here the possibility that the manner in which the Constitution was ratified bears on how its provisions should be interpreted.

55. The problems are discussed in great depth in B. Ackerman, Discovering The Constitution, *supra* note 40; the fourteenth amendment issue is summarized in Ackerman, *Storrs Lectures, supra* note 40, at 1065–70; *see also* A. Kelley, W. Harbison & H. Belz, The American Constitution: Its Origins and Development 334–35 (1983).

56. *See, e.g.*, Maryland Petition Comm. v. Johnson, 265 F. Supp. 823 (D. Md. 1967), *aff'd*, 391 F.2d 933 (4th Cir. 1968); United States v. Association of Citizens Councils, 187 F. Supp. 846 (W.D. La. 1960); United States v. Gugel, 119 F. Supp. 897 (E.D. Ky. 1954).

57. These are summarized in Dellinger, *supra* note 35, at 403–05.

recent decades,[58] and the especially troublesome aspect of federal coercion of state approval, it is possible that the Supreme Court would review the validity of a modern amendment ratified in circumstances similar to those surrounding the two amendments.[59] Still, given the extent to which the Civil War amendments have become part of the fabric of our constitutional order, it is unthinkable that the Court would *now* consider an argument that they were not properly ratified. The *present* authority of these amendments may depend more on their acceptance for over a century than on their actual adoption by a process that may or may not now be thought to conform to what article V prescribes. Whatever the original source of authority of these constitutional standards may be, their present legal status, like that of provisions adopted under the original ratification clause, depends more directly on acceptance than on how they were adopted; and the same may be true of old amendments originally adopted in an uncontroversial manner.

Does this conclusion require a reformulation of the supreme criterion? That depends on exactly what question is asked. If the question is what present method of lawmaking, if any, is superior to all other sources of law in the society, the answer is law made according to the amending clause (and perhaps law made by procedures that are close enough to those prescribed in the amending clause). Putting aside the constitutional rule of equal state votes in the Senate, a modern amendment would take priority over all conflicting legal rules. For this question, no reformulation of the supreme criterion is needed. But if the question is what the source of authority is of that *body of law* that takes precedence over all others, then the answer needs to validate all unrepealed amendments. The present source of authority of that entire body of law may not be limited to actual adoption according to the amending clause and promulgation by the political branches, but may include continued acceptance of provisions as valid amendments. A criterion of law designed to account for the present legal status of the body of amendments may need to be expanded to include the way in which continued acceptance can supplant adoption by a specific procedure as the source of authority.

D. How the Rule of Recognition Reaches the Constitution

With these observations about the ratification and amending clauses, we can see that the status of old amendments in respect to the ultimate rule of recognition is less clear than I initially indicated. An amendment whose *present validity*

---

58. *See, e.g.*, Powell v. McCormack, 395 U.S. 486 (1969); Baker v. Carr, 369 U.S. 186 (1962).

59. It is probably unrealistic to imagine "similar circumstances" without supposing similar cataclysmic political events, in which case ordinary judicial doctrines might have little relevance; but what the Court might actually do in a similar setting is not critical to my main point here.

derives from adoption by a prescribed procedure does not depend directly on the ultimate rule of recognition. An "amendment" whose present authority rests on acceptance as an amendment may be part of the body of law that depends more directly on the ultimate rule.

We are now ready to reformulate and consider the remaining two candidates for how the Constitution relates to the ultimate rule of recognition:

(1) All or part of the ultimate rule is the Constitution itself, including the amending clause and any amendments whose present legal authority rests on acceptance, but excluding amendments whose present legal authority rests on their adoption according to the amending clause;
(2) All or part of the ultimate rule is: Whatever the Constitution contains, the present legal authority of which does not depend on enactment by a procedure prescribed in the Constitution, is law.

Which of these formulations is to be preferred? There seems no practical difference between saying that much of the Constitution is at least part of the ultimate rule of recognition and saying that at least part of the rule is that what the Constitution contains, with some qualifications, counts as law. Under either formulation, what is in the Constitution is authoritative law, and no reference to some definitive legal source higher than the Constitution establishes that.

From a conceptual perspective, the second formulation appears better, for two related reasons. First, saying that much of the Constitution is part or all of the ultimate rule is inelegant. It is difficult, though perhaps not impossible, to think of all the various parts of the original Constitution as a single complex rule for identifying what counts as law. We are more comfortable thinking of the Constitution as containing a substantial number of discrete rules. Moreover, while a sociologist might say that an ultimate source of legal authority is most of the provisions of the Constitution, it is awkward to think of officials as somehow accepting that set of provisions, when most officials, even judges, are not aware of all the relevant provisions. Second, it is not mere coincidence that the standards of the Constitution are accepted as law; they are accepted because they are part of the Constitution. A formulation for all or part of the rule of recognition that focuses on what the Constitution contains better expresses this reality than simply saying that the provisions of the Constitution are accepted as law. Such a formulation states a rule that judges or other officials may reasonably employ to decide if a standard counts as law.

There is one substantial worry about casting the ultimate rule in terms of what the Constitution contains counting as law. Recall that, in connection with the ratification clause, I urged that acceptance of provisions adopted according to that procedure could not be divorced from the substance of the provisions proposed. One might say the same thing about an ultimate rule that what the Constitution contains is law. *That rule* may be accepted only because much of what the Constitution contains is, and has been, regarded as substantively sound or desirable. But the worry here about a misleading separation of form from substance is much less telling than the same worry about the ratification clause, because a rule cast in terms of what the Constitution contains does not really suggest that very different provisions in the Constitution would also be accepted. So long as we understand that acceptance of a rule that what the Constitution contains is law cannot be detached from the substance of the constitutional provisions, a formulation in terms of what the Constitution contains seems most appropriate.

The discussion in this section permits us to draw some significant general conclusions. One concerns the relationship between the ultimate rule of recognition and the supreme criterion. In *The Concept of Law,* Hart assumes that the supreme criterion will be either part or all of the ultimate rule of recognition. The preceding analysis has demonstrated another possibility. That possibility would be most clearly realized if the ratification clause were now considered a critical part of the rule of recognition. The amending clause would be valid law because it was adopted according to the ratification clause; it, therefore, would not be part of the ultimate rule of recognition. The amending clause would remain the supreme criterion because norms adopted according to it would override other norms. Put more abstractly, the supreme criterion could derive its own authority from enactment in accord with the ultimate rule of recognition rather than constituting a part of that rule. Of course, if the ratification clause no longer has legal significance, the present legal status of the amending clause does not depend on it. However, the derivative character of the supreme criterion remains to a degree if the correct present formulation of the ultimate rule of recognition is in terms of most of what the Constitution contains. This is true because the amending clause then owes its authority to being among the materials this ultimate rule treats as legal.[60]

Three other significant conclusions are closely related to each other. First, what was once all or part of an ultimate rule of recognition could lose its significance over time in a stable legal order. That may well have happened in respect to the ratification clause. Second, at many points in time in stable legal orders it may be hard to say how ultimate a criterion for identifying law is, because no one really knows if a norm may be challenged as invalid under a procedure everyone has been pretty sure was followed. Hart, himself, clearly recognizes that the ultimate rule of recognition in a stable legal order can have gaps.[61] Also, in a discussion of England's relation to former colonies, he indicates how the ultimate rule

---

60. H.L.A. Hart drew my attention to this point in correspondence. The "derivation" is a little less sharp than if the ratification clause was critical under the ultimate rule, because, as indicated in the text, the substance of the Constitution is more closely intertwined with the idea that what the Constitution contains is law than with the idea that what is adopted in accordance with the ratification clause is law.

61. THE CONCEPT OF LAW, *supra* note 1, at 120.

can change in a stable system as a break is made with the past.[62] But he does not draw attention to the possibility that subtle shifts over time concerning how high one can go in the hierarchy of legal authorization can lead to deep uncertainties about where derivation stops and acceptance begins within well-operating legal orders. The third conclusion follows from the second. A stable legal order can operate quite well even if relevant officials have drastically different opinions about where derivation from higher norms stops and acceptance begins.[63] To give a specific illustration, if three Justices believe that the fourteenth amendment is valid because properly adopted, three believe it counts as valid for the Supreme Court because promulgated by Congress, and three believe it is authoritative because so long accepted, they agree on its legal status, the point of practical legal significance which is now so obvious it is not litigated.

I have explored the status of the federal Constitution in connection with original states. I assume that similar conclusions hold for the application of the Constitution in states admitted to the union, but this chapter does not work out that variation.

V. STATE LAW AND THE RULE OF RECOGNITION

Some reference to what is contained in the federal Constitution constitutes at least a crucial part of the ultimate rule of recognition. I now consider what, if any, standards outside such a reference are contained in the ultimate rule. Because a standard for determining law is part of the ultimate rule only if it is not derivable from a higher legal standard, any standard for law that is derivable from the federal Constitution is not part of the ultimate rule.

One fundamental question concerns the authority of state law. I shall begin to address that question by imagining that the status of some state statute is in question months after the original Constitution has been ratified. The statute has been passed in proper form, but a question has been raised as to whether the statute is within the authority of the state legislature to enact. We would initially look to the state constitution to see if it authorizes that kind of legislation explicitly or implicitly. Can we look yet higher to ascertain the source of the state constitution's legal authority? Certainly the federal Constitution sets limits on what state governments can do, so we need to examine whether the state constitutional authorization is *compatible* with the federal document and with federal legislation adopted under it. But the original federal Constitution does not actually confer power on the states; it only limits some powers they already have. The federal Constitution also does not settle the legal status of the state's constitution;

---

62. *Id.* at 117–18.

63. *See* Golding, *Kelsen and the Concept of 'Legal System,'* in MORE ESSAYS IN LEGAL PHILOSOPHY 69, 98–99 (R. Summers ed. 1971).

that depends upon the state constitution's having been adopted according to procedures that already had approved legal status within the state, or former colony, or upon the constitution's being accepted by officials as containing the highest law in the state. For any original state, therefore, the ultimate rule of recognition would include either the procedural mechanisms by which the state constitution was adopted, or a principle that much of what is contained in the state constitution is law.[64] Even as to *state law*, a reference to the federal Constitution would be a *part* of the ultimate rule of recognition, since federal law contained in or authorized by the federal Constitution sets negative limits on the overall authority of state law. But the positive authority of state law could not itself be *derived* from the federal Constitution.

The conclusion that, for original states within the federal union, the ultimate rule of recognition would not be limited to the federal Constitution but would include references to state law is not altered by adoption of the tenth amendment. That amendment does say that powers not delegated to the United States "are reserved to the States respectively, or to the people"; but this is an explication of an already implied restriction on federal powers rather than a conferral of powers on the states.[65] In a sense, the Constitution as a whole does, with the tenth amendment, outline the distribution of powers between state and federal governments, but that does not make the Constitution the legal source of state powers.

An argument might be made that this original conception has shifted over time, that—with the increase in federal power—officials now conceive of state authority as derived from the federal Constitution. Further, with respect to states joining the union after 1789, their admission might be said to represent federal approval of the exercise of state powers within the union. Nevertheless, the federal Constitution and federal statutes authorized by it remain essentially a negative restraint on state power, barring some subjects from state involvement, precluding many outcomes otherwise within state authority, and demanding a republican form of government.[66]

Even if the authority of the states to act within their domains was actually conferred by the federal Constitution, it would not follow that the ultimate rule of recognition could be limited to federal law. The reason is that a general conferral of power to act need not prescribe the form of government by which action is taken. The federal Constitution does not prescribe that all state authority must henceforth be exercised in accordance with an existing state constitution or *legal*

---

64. I include the words "much of" to take account of amendments in a manner similar to that applying to the federal Constitution.

65. *See* United States v. Darby, 312 U.S. 100, 124 (1941).

66. U.S. Const. art. IV, § 4. Some states when admitted to the union had special restraints placed on state law as a condition of admission. Certain western states, for instance, were precluded from having any law permitting polygamy.

successors to that constitution. We might imagine a state analogue to the national transition from the Articles of Confederation to the Constitution. A state convention is called with authority only to propose amendments to the state constitution. Instead it proposes a wholly new constitution and a method of adoption that differs from the method of amendment of the existing constitution. The proposed new constitution is "adopted" in the prescribed manner and all officials and citizens accept it as the authoritative state constitution. A sharp break in the chain of legal authority and a drastic shift in the standards for law within the state have occurred. Nevertheless, as long as a republican form of government and the federally vested rights of individuals have not been disturbed,[67] no violation of the federal Constitution has taken place. The possibility of such change shows that the present authority of particular state constitutions is not derived from the federal Constitution, but from acceptance or from creation by means accepted within the state. The rule of recognition for any location within the fifty states must include state as well as federal law.

VI. JUDGE-CREATED LAW: THE AUTHORITY OF PRECEDENT

I turn now to the more perplexing problem of the authority of courts to make law and the techniques by which they interpret legal materials. For clarity of analysis, I have, somewhat artificially, distinguished the authority of precedent, discussed in this section, from the interpretive standards courts use, discussed in the next section. Since interpretive standards circumscribe the meaning and force of precedents, these subjects are closely related, but it is helpful, initially, to regard precedents as legal rules created by courts, before attacking the complex questions about interpretive standards.

By talking of precedents as law made by courts, I do not mean here to presuppose any controversial position about judicial power. Hart's view, shared by most American legal philosophers in this century and probably still dominant, is that courts have in some cases a kind of legislative discretion;[68] as Cardozo put it, they legislate "between gaps."[69] That view has been challenged by Ronald Dworkin,[70] among others.[71] But even those who claim that there is a right answer

---

67. I am assuming that a formal break in the chain of legality would not be enough by itself for a citizen or official to mount a successful challenge under the due process clause of the fourteenth amendment. How one would describe the legal posture if revision did violate some vested rights, and federal courts recognized the legal effectiveness of the revision but required compensation for the violated rights, would be complicated.

68. *See* THE CONCEPT OF LAW, *supra* note 1, at 121–50.

69. B. CARDOZO, THE NATURE OF THE JUDICIAL PROCESS 113–14 (1921).

70. *See, e.g.*, TAKING RIGHTS SERIOUSLY, *supra* note 4, at 31–39.

71. *See, e.g.*, R. SARTORIUS, INDIVIDUAL CONDUCT AND SOCIAL NORMS 181–210 (1975).

to every legal case do not deny that if a highest court reaches the wrong answer, that answer can change the law. Mistaken precedents, if they are not too mistaken, are to be followed as law in future cases; and a related series of initially mistaken precedents can alter the law more generally.[72] That is enough to support the power of courts to create law in the sense I intend here.

In discussing the significance for a rule of recognition of the force of precedent, I shall begin with common-law precedents, discussed by Hart, and then consider precedent in legislative and constitutional interpretation.

A. Common Law

In describing Hart's account for Britain, I considered whether judicial power to generate common law by precedent derives from higher standards within the law, or rests on acceptance and is therefore grounded in the ultimate rule of recognition. I asserted that Hart's view is definitely that the power rests on acceptance and is covered by the rule of recognition. The same issue arises for the United States, but its dimensions here are significantly different because of our federal system, written constitutions, and "reception" statutes.

If I am right that the authority of state law is not wholly derivative from the federal Constitution, the status of judicial lawmaking power is a question for both the federal and state aspects of a rule of recognition. One possibility is that written constitutions authorizing the creation or continued existence of courts implicitly confer on the courts a traditional power to make law, even though the relevant provisions do not specify how courts are to decide cases or what the significance of their decisions will be. The argument to this effect is essentially the same as the argument that a simple statute creating courts or conferring jurisdiction approves traditional judicial power; but, since a constitution represents a more comprehensive and deliberate view about desired institutions than a limited statute, the argument of implicit endorsement has somewhat more power when it rests on a constitution. The argument is at its strongest when no courts existed in that jurisdiction before the constitution was adopted. That is true in respect to federal courts in the United States, which were authorized by article III and created by Congress in accord with that article.[73] Within states, courts are also typically authorized by constitutions and created by statutes, but many state courts predated statehood and some of these may have enjoyed a continuous existence up to the present.

---

72. Almost certainly the ways that courts formulate "correct" results also affect the law. That is a point little discussed by "law as discovery" theorists, but Dworkin briefly comments on the subject in LAW'S EMPIRE, *supra* note 4, at 248.

73. Judiciary Act of 1789, 1 Stat. 73.

Many states also have in their constitutions or statutes "reception" provisions that receive the pre-Revolutionary common law of England.[74] Further, a federal ordinance of 1787, which applied initially to the Northwest Territory and then to the states created out of that territory, gave judges within the territory "a common law jurisdiction."[75] The language of these provisions varies, but arguably they represent a more positive endorsement of judicial law-creating power than the mere setting up of courts.

If we follow Hart's approach to the ultimate rule of recognition, the capacity of the legislature or the makers of constitutions to *change* the nature of judicial power does not itself entail that the legal status of judicial decisions derives from implicit authorization. What is critical is whether the authority of precedent derives from some more positive implicit authorization or rather, as Hart assumes about Britain, rests on acceptance by officials. In the latter event, the authority of precedent is part of the ultimate rule of recognition; otherwise it is not. As Hart obviously supposes, claiming that the status of precedent is implicitly conferred simply by the statutory or constitutional creation, or continuation, of courts is somewhat artificial. And, even if the practice of giving *some* weight to prior decisions was thought to be inherent in the practice of courts or implicitly approved by legislative action, that would not mean that the full law-creating power that common law courts now have has been authorized legislatively. Whether such authorization has been given by reception statutes, especially those like the Ordinance of 1787 whose reference to a "common law jurisdiction" may include a traditional law-creating power, is more difficult.

Perhaps if one had to choose between authorization and acceptance as the basis for the law-creating power of judges in the United States, one might agree with Hart that acceptance is critical;[76] but the dichotomy that Hart assumes is itself somewhat artificial. Why can we not say that precedent has the status it does *both* because that status has been and is presently accepted by concerned officials *and* because higher lawmaking authorities have obliquely indicated their approval? If one were trying to explain to a new judge why common-law precedents count for a good deal, one would certainly say more about these higher lawmaking authorities than that they could have eliminated or altered judicial power and have chosen not to do so. Ordinary legislation dealing with courts does reflect a kind of implicit approval of present practices that bolsters those practices; and the support of many reception provisions is even stronger. It might be said that these implicit approvals only help explain why acceptance continues, but the point is that they help explain continued acceptance in a

74. *E.g.*, MD. CONST. Declaration of Rights art. V; N.C. GEN. STAT. § 4-1 (1986); VA. CODE ANN. §§ 1–18 (1979).

75. Northwest Ordinance of 1787, 1 Stat. 51 n.a.

76. One would have to review all the relevant legal materials in a particular state to make a considered judgment for that state.

special way, indicating that references up in the hierarchy of norms are supportive of a subordinate feature of the ultimate rule of recognition. If so, acceptance by officials and derivation from higher norms may intertwine here in a way that Hart's sharp distinction of derivation and acceptance does not suggest.

This is an insight that warrants generalization beyond the force of precedents. For example, it helps to show why the distinction between acceptance and derivation in respect to constitutional amendments is also misleading. At points in time, the legal status of particular constitutional amendments might rest *both* on continued official acceptance as constitutional standards *and* on adoption by the procedure prescribed under the amending clause.

Once we understand how acceptance and derivation intertwine in respect to the status of precedents, our attention is drawn to the various institutional aspects of a doctrine of precedent. In jurisdictions in which overruling of precedents is permitted, a particular precedent may carry more conclusive authority for a lower court, and perhaps for executive officials, than it carries for the court that has established it. And, since the operation of a legal system would be much more uneven if lower courts and executive officers felt free to disregard judicial decisions they thought unsound than if the courts rendering the decisions felt free to depart from them, the argument that the establishment of a hierarchy of courts and of separate branches of government implicitly points to affording authority to precedents may be strongest when one considers lower courts and executive officials. I will not repeat these observations in connection with precedent in statutory and constitutional interpretation, to which I now turn, but they apply in those contexts as well.[77]

B. Statutory Interpretations

Courts interpret legislation and reach controversial conclusions about the significance of statutory rules. Once a court interprets a statute to have a particular meaning, the court in a subsequent case will be hesitant to depart from that interpretation. That hesitancy represents the force of precedent in statutory cases. We might initially be inclined not to think of precedent in these cases as having any separate place in the rule of recognition, viewing the force of precedent here either as an adjunct of legislation itself or as an adjunct of the general common-law power of courts. But the subject cannot be disposed of so easily.

The legislature gets its power from the constitution, and if courts are plainly supposed to apply legislation to concrete cases, it follows that they will have to interpret statutes. That essential responsibility may be conferred implicitly by the constitution. But neither the constitution nor statutes tell courts how to do

77. There is a problem that deserves mention. When the highest court interprets statutory and constitutional materials, it might be argued that other officials accede to its decisions to avoid conflict, but do not necessarily concede that it has any genuine lawmaking power. *See also* note 80 *infra*.

their job of interpretation, beyond occasional legislative injunctions to construe a statute "liberally" or "according to the fair import of its terms." The status of precedents in statutory cases is not clearly approved in either constitutions or statutes. The argument that the status is implicitly approved by the creation and continuation of courts is less powerful than the similar argument in respect to common-law precedents—because the role of precedents in statutory cases is even now less striking and less well recognized, and would have been a matter of much slighter significance in previous eras.

The role of precedent in statutory cases does not follow ineluctably from the role of precedent in common-law cases, since one can imagine courts adhering to precedents in common-law cases but not doing so in statutory cases. Let us imagine there are settled standards—say the apparent force of the statutory language in context or the intent of the legislature[78]—for interpreting a statute that has not received a prior relevant interpretation. A system of law could work reasonably well if the same court in a subsequent case applied exactly the same standards, following a precedent only insofar as the intrinsic force of its reasoning was persuasive and insofar as its continued existence could reasonably affect judgment about the legislature's actual aim.[79] In such a system, precedents in statutory cases would have no inherent authority. Whatever the exact force of precedent in our system, I assume that precedents count for more than the power of their reasoning and what they tell a subsequent court about legislative aims. This *extra* force of precedent may have developed and been accepted easily because of the place of precedent in common-law cases, but it is analytically distinguishable.

Because an argument based on constitutional or legislative authorization is actually weaker in respect to the precedential force of statutory interpretations than in respect to common-law precedents, the lawmaking power of courts in statutory cases depends more clearly on acceptance than their lawmaking power in common-law cases. The rule of recognition for federal and state law must be formulated in a manner that gives this judicial power in statutory cases explicit recognition or that casts the general power to create law by precedent in terms plainly broad enough to include statutory cases.[80]

---

78. At a deep conceptual level there is controversy about appropriate standards for statutory interpretation, and each of these two candidates would require extensive explication to be defended; but the oversimplified supposition in the text is sufficient to make the relevant point about precedent.

79. If the legislature does not act contrary to a precedent, that may be some evidence (usually very weak) about what the legislature originally aimed to do, or about what the legislature *now* wants to do, or both.

80. One might try to avoid this conclusion by arguing that as far as statutes are concerned, the standard for what counts as law is statable quite independent of precedents, and the force of precedent merely reflects deference to the original deciding court. Because the power of precedent is so similar in common-law and statutory cases, this argument

C. Constitutional Decisions

What needs to be said about precedent in constitutional law resembles closely what I have said about precedent in statutory cases. There are some special "wrinkles," however, having to do with the weaker force of prior decisions in constitutional interpretation, the higher status of constitutional law, and the possibly unauthorized status of some constitutional adjudication.

Judicial opinions sometimes downplay the significance of precedent in constitutional adjudication, and it is generally supposed that, because of the difficulties of constitutional amendment, courts do and should feel freer to overrule constitutional decisions than statutory and common-law decisions, whose rules can be corrected by simple legislation. Does precedent have an independent place in constitutional law, or are highest-court judges always seeking to make a "best" interpretation of the Constitution—"best" not depending at all on what a previous majority happens to have said? Once the issue is put this way, the answer is clear. Most Supreme Court Justices give at least some weight to precedent; if the legal question is a close one and the prior decision has not caused any serious injustice, Justices will not overturn a prior holding even if they might have reached the contrary result in the original case. When a line of decisions becomes an important part of the fabric of the law, Justices will be even more hesitant to overrule prevailing doctrine, though that happens occasionally. Thus, precedents do matter in constitutional adjudication, and judges in cases posing new and difficult issues have a kind of lawmaking power.

On what basis does this power rest? Let us first assume that there is no doubt that courts are supposed to engage in substantive constitutional interpretation. As far as the federal courts and federal Constitution are concerned, such authority is fairly inferred from the Constitution in respect to constitutional challenges to state laws.[81] But the authority to interpret does not necessarily establish the status of precedents. A system of constitutional interpretation, like a system of statutory interpretation, could conceivably work if prior decisions had no independent force. Conferral of a power to interpret does not represent a judgment by those who made and approved the Constitution in favor of according force to constitutional precedents. Thus, this force neither rests directly on the Constitution nor follows

---

seems an evasion; but the problem does show how subtle the difference is between saying: (1) Official Body *A* has a law-creating power; and (2) Official Body *A* has no law-creating power but its determination about what the law is will be deferred to by other official bodies, including *A* at a later date. *See also* note 77 *supra;* notes 43–45 *supra* and accompanying text.

81. The supremacy clause of article VI requires state courts to treat federal law, including the federal Constitution, as the "supreme law of the land." If a claim is made that a state law violates the federal Constitution, a state court must interpret the federal Constitution to resolve the conflict. Because it would be senseless to have federal courts resolving such cases on a wholly different basis from state courts, federal courts must be supposed to have a similar authority, and duty.

inexorably from the force of precedents in common-law cases. The ultimate rule of recognition must include the force of precedents in constitutional cases.

Constitutional decisions have a higher status than both legislation and common law. Since officials generally treat a constitution as saying what the highest judges say it says, the power of courts to make constitutional law by decisions might initially be thought to be an aspect not only of the ultimate rule of recognition but also of the supreme criterion—that is, an aspect of the form of law that takes priority over all other forms of law.

That view would be mistaken, however. Because new constitutional amendments can override judicial interpretations of the Constitution, the legal force of constitutional interpretations is not part of the supreme criterion of law.

Any doubts about the courts' original constitutional authority to engage in substantive constitutional interpretation merely strengthen the conclusion that the force of constitutional precedents rests on acceptance. Although *Marbury v. Madison*[82] solidly established the power of the Supreme Court to pass on the constitutional validity of federal laws, some have argued, contrary to my own view, that the true purport of the federal Constitution was not to authorize such judicial determinations.[83] If the practice of judicial review of federal legislation lacked authority in the original Constitution, the development of the authority to interpret rested only on the acceptance of officials. Even in this case, it might be argued that more recent constitutional amendments presuppose such authority and therefore confer on it a kind of constitutional support. Here again, we would face a difficult problem about when derivation ends and acceptance begins; and a realistic resolution might claim that the present power to interpret the Constitution in challenges to federal laws rests on both acceptance and implied approval by higher lawmaking powers, the amenders of the Constitution. To summarize, so far as the authority to interpret rests on acceptance, the force of precedent also rests on acceptance; but even if the authority to interpret rests wholly or partly on implicit authorization by higher lawmakers, the force of precedent, as I have suggested, does not flow from that alone and is an aspect of our law because of acceptance.

VII. INTERPRETIVE STANDARDS

Our last subject for analysis is the interpretive standards judges use to resolve cases. When judges determine the significance of authoritative constitutional or

---

82. 5 U.S. (1 Cranch) 137 (1803).

83. I do not pause to analyze the intermediate possibility that courts could apply the Constitution, but that other branches, except in enforcing judgments, would not take judicial constructions as authoritative. I discuss the authority of Supreme Court decisions for the political branches in *Constitutional Decisions and the Supreme Law*, 58 U. Colo. L. Rev. 145 (1987).

statutory language or decide the reach of the common law, they employ techniques of reasoning and particular criteria of evaluation that are critical aspects of legal adjudication. Among these standards are notions like: "constitutional language should be interpreted in accord with the intent of those who framed and adopted it"; "penal statutes should be strictly construed"; and "no person should profit from his wrongdoing."

Dworkin's challenge to the whole idea of a rule of recognition rests largely on the place of such standards.[84] In brief, he claims that these standards are not typically given legal validity by a single authoritative act;[85] their status rests on more complicated facts of institutional acceptance and consonancy with other materials of the legal system. Dworkin suggests that an explanation of the authority and weight of many interpretive principles defeats any easy distinction between derivative validity and acceptance and shows that no straightforward standard indicates what principles count in the law and for how much.[86] He claims, moreover, that in respect to these matters judges do not even employ a commonly shared standard. Each relies on what seems to her the soundest approach, the one that best interprets the whole corpus of legal materials. Each judge makes essentially normative judgments; she does not try to ascertain some socially accepted rule and follow it. Here lies the heart of Dworkin's thesis that the criteria of law are normative, not conventional.[87]

Having this sketch in mind is helpful as we consider the status of interpretive standards. I will concentrate here on interpretive standards in constitutional cases, though, with slight modifications, the conclusions I draw apply to common-law and statutory interpretation as well.

For illustrative purposes, I will use an interpretive standard that can be drawn from Supreme Court cases establishing that wiretapping and electronic eavesdropping are practices covered by the fourth amendment.[88] The standard, roughly put, is that the concepts of "search" and "seizure" in the fourth amendment

---

84. *See, e.g.*, Taking Rights Seriously, *supra* note 4, at 14–130.

85. I say "typically" because statutes in this country do frequently contain some principles for their own construction.

86. *See, e.g.*, Taking Rights Seriously, *supra* note 4, at 41. According to Dworkin each interpretive principle counts for a decision one way or another, but each does not dictate the decision in every instance to which it applies. Thus, in a common-law case, a court might give some weight to the principle that a person should not profit from his wrongdoing and still allow the wrongdoer to win to his profit. How much weight to assign competing principles in context is an important aspect of adjudication.

87. The account given here is meant to be faithful both to Dworkin's earlier work and to his recent systematic statement in *Law's Empire, supra* note 4.

88. Berger v. New York, 388 U.S. 41 (1967); Katz v. United States, 389 U.S. 347 (1967). That constitutional interpretive standards cannot be excluded from a rule of recognition is emphasized by Richard Kay, who in fact accords them a more prominent place than I do. *See* Kay, *Preconstitutional Rules*, 42 Ohio St. L.J. 187 (1981).

should be flexibly interpreted in light of changing technologies and the evils the amendment was designed to prevent. It is evident that discrepancies in interpretive strategies can yield different conclusions about what the Constitution requires. Justice Black's more rigid approach to practices covered by the fourth amendment, for example, produced dissents in the wiretapping and eavesdropping cases.[89] Thus the determination of interpretive strategy is an important aspect of judgment about what the law provides.

Whether every standard of interpretation that constrains judges should be characterized as a "legal" standard is doubtful.[90] Some standards of interpretation, such as that ordinary words should be accorded their natural meaning absent some reason to do otherwise, are general and fundamental to all interpretation of language; but other standards are distinctly legal. Whether standards are distinctly legal or not, so long as judges are bound to follow them in deciding what the Constitution means, the standards need to be accorded some place among ultimate or derivative criteria for determining law. Perhaps general and fundamental standards for interpretation of language are already implicit in the idea that what the Constitution contains is law, but that could not be said for any distinctly legal standards whose status does not derive from the Constitution itself.

In considering the status of interpretive standards, I address the relevance of the Supreme Court's flexible approach to "search" and "seizure" for a new "X-ray vision" device that "sees" clearly through solid walls.[91] We might initially be inclined to say that whatever standards are now prevailing rest on acceptance and are part of the ultimate rule of recognition. But to speak in this manner could be doubly misleading. First, there is no guarantee that most Justices will adhere to the "dominant standards." Each Justice of the Supreme Court will actually employ a set of interpretive strategies that is at least subtly at variance with the strategies of any other Justice. And, as the next section explores, for some questions the "dominant" interpretive strategy may represent a composite of views. Second, how much weight a Justice will accord to a prevailing point of view because it occupies that status is an open question. Justices who do adhere to a dominant strategy need not do so because they take any prevailing standard as legally authoritative. A Justice who conforms to a dominant strategy might do so because he or she thinks it is normatively correct, regardless of what other judges now assume or have assumed.

The question of authoritative status is most sharply posed when there is some clear difference in interpretive approach, as might be perceived by a new Justice, Carolyn Gray, who is passing on the "X-ray vision" device and who thinks that Justice Black had the better of the argument in the original wiretapping and eavesdropping cases. We can very roughly imagine four possible positions. Justice Gray might feel constrained to accept prevailing interpretive standards as

89. *Berger*, 388 U.S. at 70, 78–81; *Katz*, 389 U.S. at 364–74.

90. *See* Soper, *supra* note 5, at 488–98.

91. The device mechanically achieves what Superman has always been able to do.

absolutely binding; she might consider the prevailing interpretive standard to be as binding as a clear line of constitutional precedents; she might suppose that the prevailing interpretive standard carries some weight, but less than would a clear line of precedent; or she might believe that whether a standard is prevailing or not carries no significance, her responsibility being to determine the best set of interpretive standards without deference to what past cases say or the rest of the present Justices think.

We can initially rule out the first possibility; all Justices believe it is sometimes appropriate to alter previously prevailing standards of interpretation. At least for many matters we can also rule out the last possibility. Most Justices suppose that it makes *some* difference what prevailing standards are. At least when an issue of interpretive strategy is regarded as close or a Justice is unsure of the correct strategy, he or she is likely to go along with a clear prevailing standard that has received majority support.

Generalizing between the second and third possibilities is complicated by the open-endedness of many relevant formulations of how judges should interpret, by different levels of interpretive standards, and by variations in the degree of firmness with which standards are settled; but we can say that prevailing interpretive standards typically exercise less constraint than clear precedents that establish rules of law. A Justice would feel freer to abandon the flexible approach to new technology in interpreting the fourth amendment than to overrule the cases applying the amendment to wiretapping and electronic eavesdropping. That a standard of interpretation prevails does make a difference, but even such a standard does not bind as strongly as authoritative constitutional or statutory materials or even as strongly as typical precedential rules of law.[92]

This analysis of standards of constitutional interpretation yields some important conclusions. *The Concept of Law* conveys the idea that the set of ultimate criteria for identifying law might vary in length from a sentence to a paragraph. Trying to state ultimate criteria that account for prevailing standards in constitutional, statutory, and common-law interpretation leads to difficulties in one of two directions. Either aspects of the criteria of recognition are cast in the simple circular and uninformative way that accepted standards of interpretation are part of the law,[93] or the standards themselves must be described. In the latter event,

---

92. Of course, since one critical question of constitutional law interpretation is how much of precedents on particular issues are to be taken as binding, and how the precedents themselves are to be interpreted, differences and uncertainties about standards of interpretation infect the significance and weight of precedents. Though Justices may generally agree that precedents count as law in some sense, they may differ considerably in their understanding of what that entails.

93. As Dworkin suggests in *A Reply*, *supra* note 4, at 248, Hart's discussion of a possible ultimate rule for international law is unsupportive of simple circular rules of recognition. *See* The Concept of Law, *supra* note 1, at 228–29.

the ultimate criteria might stretch to volumes and require constant alteration with every subtle shift in prevailing standards.

Another important conclusion concerns the relation between the prevailing standards and what an official within the system should do. Hart assumes that a sociologist's description of the ultimate rule of recognition will coalesce with the standards a loyal official would employ. But we can see that a follower of Justice Black who thought the majority's approach badly misguided might loyally continue to employ what she regarded as the best interpretive strategy for the fourth amendment even while recognizing that she was in the minority. If we thought a rule of recognition had to be accepted by virtually all officials as binding on all relevant officials, we might at this point say there is no rule of recognition that covers flexible or rigid interpretation of "search and seizure." If, on the other hand, we adopted the more modest notion that a "rule of recognition" can consist of presently prevailing ultimate criteria for identifying law, we might say that the generally accepted flexible approach is embraced by the ultimate rule. But we would then have to concede that the rule, in this respect, does not sharply constrain those who disagree with the flexible approach.

This point illustrates Dworkin's claim that judges developing complex interpretive strategies are not just seeking to ascertain what standards are now prevailing but what standards are best. However, Dworkin errs by not acknowledging *how* significant it may be for a judge whether an interpretive strategy is prevailing.[94] The same reasons of coordination that lead judges to join majority opinions that do not precisely represent their own views lead them to adhere to prevailing interpretive standards that are not exactly the ones they would have adopted.

Prevailing interpretive strategies, like precedents, affect the decisions of lower-court judges and nonjudicial officials. As I indicated with respect to precedents, the force of prevailing standards and the extent to which a principle of authoritativeness can be implicitly derived from constitutions and statutes may vary among different kinds of officials. I will not repeat that analysis here.

VIII. THEORETICAL LESSONS

The main effort of this chapter has been to apply Hart's theory regarding an ultimate rule of recognition to the United States. The insights generated by this effort allow enrichment of Hart's theory and illuminate some strengths and weaknesses of Hart's conventionalist account. In this final section, I recapitulate my major findings and comment on broader theoretical concerns.

---

94. *But see* LAW'S EMPIRE, *supra* note 4, at 248.

A. A Rough Approximation of the Rule of Recognition for Someplace within the United States

This whole exercise has demonstrated the immense difficulty of determining what the appropriate rule of recognition is in the United States. I shall here take the standpoint of a sociologist studying what counts as law within the American legal system and framing a rule of recognition with respect to the highest body that will determine a legal question. With qualifications indicated in the relevant sections, I have concluded that the supreme criterion of law is the amending clause of the federal Constitution, and that within one of our states the ultimate rule of recognition, cast in hierarchical order, is approximately this:

(1) Whatever is in the federal Constitution, that has not lost its legal force and does not derive its present legal force from enactment by a prescribed constitutional procedure, is law;
(2) On matters not clear from the text, the prevailing standards of interpretation used by the Supreme Court determine what the Constitution means,[95] and Supreme Court decisions interpreting the Constitution establish precedential law;[96]
(3) On matters not clear from statutory texts, the prevailing standards of interpretation determine what congressional legislation means,[97] and Supreme Court decisions interpreting that legislation establish precedential law;
(4) Prevailing standards of interpretation for common-law subjects determine federal law for those,[98] and Supreme Court decisions on such subjects establish precedential law;
(5) Whatever is in the state constitution (or whatever was adopted in accordance with an accepted constitution-making procedure), that has not lost its legal force and does not derive its present legal force from a procedure prescribed in the existing constitution, is law;

---

95. This formulation falls into the vice of circularity noted above. *See* note 93 *supra* and accompanying text. That vice could be avoided by extensive specification of prevailing standards.

96. I am unsure whether the power to make law by precedent is best folded into interpretive standards generally or treated independently. A more complete statement might have to include the place of precedents established by lower courts on issues not resolved by the Supreme Court.

97. The authority of the legislature itself is not included because that is derivative from the Constitution. I am assuming that most interpretive standards and the authority of precedent in statutory cases are not so derivative.

98. Despite the absence of a federal common law, there may be a "common law" for federal government contracts, for torts committed by federal officers, and for admiralty cases, among others. The federal "common law" in such cases can override conflicting state law.

(6) On matters not clear from the text, the prevailing standards of interpretation used by the highest state court determine what the state constitution means, and decisions of that court interpreting the state constitution establish precedential law;
(7) On matters not clear from statutory texts, the prevailing standards of interpretation used by the highest state court determine what state legislation means, and decisions of that court interpreting that legislation establish precedential law;
(8) Prevailing standards of interpretation determine the reach of the common law, and decisions of the highest state court establish common-law precedents;
(9) Customs meeting criteria of legal bindingness constitute customary law.

This summary attempts to state the standards of law that officials rely on that are not themselves derivable from some higher legal norm but rest on acceptance. The inclusion of custom here is of minor importance, but it incorporates a point made by Hart: certain customs may be established in a way that makes them legally binding before a court declares them to be so.[99] I have not reiterated all the complexities one would need to introduce to meet obvious objections to any formulations made in even this simple a way. The rest of this section, like the preceding sections, sheds some light on those complexities.

B. More General Possibilities

This chapter has demonstrated at least ten possibilities that are omitted or underdeveloped in Hart's account.

The first possibility is that, not only may a rule of recognition have gaps (a point Hart does emphasize), but there may also be deep uncertainty for someone tracing the legal status of a norm as to when one ascends above the authority of the last relevant higher legal norm and reaches the relevance of acceptance. Particularly when it has long been assumed that a higher norm does confer legal status on an important norm like a constitutional amendment, one may not know whether conformity with the higher norm remains crucial to the validity of the other norm.

The second possibility, closely related to the first, is that over time, in a perfectly stable legal order, the point of ultimacy may shift radically, despite the absence of any clear change at any particular stage. What was once law because adopted by a certain process may *now* be law because it has been so long accepted as law.

99. THE CONCEPT OF LAW, *supra* note 1, at 44–48, 98. I have omitted custom for federal law, though a custom might arise that would have legal effect in the limited areas of federal common law.

The third possibility, tied to the previous two, is that a system may be stable even if officials occupying the same position, say Supreme Court Justices, have variant notions of the point of ultimacy for the authority of some legal standards.

The fourth possibility is that differences in role may sharply affect what ultimate rules of recognition officials actually use. The working rule of recognition for highest court judges may look very different from the working rule of recognition for a police sergeant even when those working rules are fully compatible.

The fifth possibility is that some standards for what counts as law may be inextricable from what has been proposed as law under these standards. The point is clearest with respect to the original Constitution and a rule that what is adopted under the ratification clause is law, or a rule that what the Constitution contains is law; but it is also possible that other officials accept the results of judges' interpretive strategies only because they fall within a widely-tolerable range.

The sixth possibility is that as to some standards for authoritative norms, such as state constitutions, negative constraints on what they may provide come from one kind of higher norm, the federal Constitution, while positive endorsement of their status comes from either another higher norm, such as a prior procedure within the state for adopting a constitution, or from acceptance.

The seventh possibility is that the authoritative status of some norms, such as common-law rules and interpretive strategies established by judicial decision, depends both on oblique approval by higher norms and on acceptance.

The eighth possibility is that, as to some crucial and ultimate criteria of law, judges are not mainly asking what is generally accepted but are seeking the best possible criteria conceived in some other way. This possibility, urged by Dworkin, is most obviously realized with respect to interpretive criteria. This possibility shows that what a sociologist might describe as law within a society might not conform exactly with what any particular loyal official might take as law.

The ninth possibility is that the ultimate rule of recognition may be very long. If judges largely agree on correct interpretive standards but do not agree on a principle that prevailing standards should be followed, a noncircular statement of the ultimate rule may require specification of all relevant accepted standards.

The tenth possibility is that the supreme criterion of law need not be a part of the ultimate rule of recognition; rather it may be derived from that rule.

We may be confident that these possibilities are not restricted in their importance to the United States. If, for example, we reflected on Hart's own account of English law, we might find that he has not adequately explained the status of the principles courts use to interpret legislation and common-law precedents, that his clean dichotomy between legislative authorization and acceptance is too simple in respect to the status of common-law precedents, and that the present legal authority of ancient statutes rests on their having been accepted so long as law, not on the actual manner of their adoption.

C. The Virtues of Mixed Conventional and Normative Accounts of Law

Some of these possibilities can easily be incorporated into Hart's theory, but others pose serious difficulties. A number of them, the eighth most directly, raise the question as to whether judges who are seeking to determine the law exhaust the sources of law when they have ascertained whatever clear implications can be drawn from any higher legal norms and from any generally accepted ultimate norms of what counts as law. If we take a simplistic view of Hart's conventionalist account, we might conclude that when the answer these sources provide to a question is not reasonably evident, "the law" does not answer the question. Now, such a view might represent a satisfactory approach for a sociologist, but it is hardly adequate for a judge. Judges conceive of themselves as constrained by the law even when no widely accepted social rule includes such a constraint. At least to this degree, an approach with important normative elements provides a more compelling account of an insider's view than the simple conventionalist approach I have just sketched. Whether or not Dworkin's claim that the law provides an answer to every case is correct, and whether or not insiders suppose that the law provides such an answer, an account with critical normative elements can show why officials often consider themselves as legally bound even though no clear derivation from higher norms is possible and no socially established rule indicates they are bound in the way they suppose.[100]

An undiluted normative account, however, seems no sounder than a simple conventionalist account for explaining legal interpretation, unless it is rich enough to pay attention to the great importance of shared practices and conventions. As I suggested early in the chapter, a normative account must build from conventionally accepted standards of what obviously counts as law. Further, even on debatable matters such as interpretive strategies, it does matter what the prevailing view is in our system, and it matters because judges recognize the social advantage of employing shared standards. Prevailing standards, like precedents, ordinarily exert some normative force because they permit coordinated activity by officials and have generated reasonable expectations among citizens. A plausible normative account must accord convention its proper role, and it is difficult to imagine many legal systems for which this role will not be significant. A "descriptive" normative account, one that describes how officials behave, must indicate how far social acceptance does figure in the normative evaluations judges and other officials make; a "prescriptive" normative account must elaborate how far social acceptance should figure in normative evaluations for judges.

In trying to develop a satisfactory account of law that appropriately treats both normative and conventional elements, one can usefully distinguish an outsider's,

---

100. An account with normative elements may also handle more comfortably the ways in which higher norms can obliquely support practices without explicitly authorizing them.

or sociologist's, view from that of a participant who must actually decide what the law is. It is no coincidence that Hart, while emphasizing the "internal point of view" taken by officials, has been mainly interested in the former and Dworkin the latter. Because convention looms larger in a sociologist's view of law than a participant's, and normative elements are more central for a participant, Hart's focus has led him to stress convention, and Dworkin's focus has led him to concentrate on normative evaluation.

1. **The Sociologist's Account** I will start with the sociologist, who is interested in describing. He wants to differentiate law from other social phenomena. For a modern legal system, he wants to identify norms that are part of the system of norms administered by officials and backed by the state's coercive power. The sociologist's account of a society's law would include all the norms that are undeniably part of this system. Because he cares about norms that are *practically* part of this system,[101] his account of the standards by which law is identified would be based on the standards prevailing among the relevant officials. In respect to legal questions about which the relevant officials are uncertain or sharply divided, he might well say that the law is undetermined or not settled. What has been said so far about this "social fact" account of law is quite close to Hart's theory, but we need to pay attention to some complexities that show that this sociologist's account differs from the simple conventionalist account I sketched a moment ago.

First, we must recognize that a standard for determining law could be a "prevailing standard" without being generally shared, or even shared by a majority. A stark illustration is when a standard is applied by a key group in the center. For a period in the 1960s and 1970s, for example, a minority of Supreme Court Justices thought that communication could be punished by states as obscene only if it appealed predominantly to the prurient interest, was patently offensive, and was utterly without redeeming social value.[102] Some Justices to the "left" thought no speech could be punished as obscene[103] or that the appropriate standard was more "speech protective" than the threefold test;[104] some Justices to the "right" thought that the appropriate test was less "speech protective."[105] The "threefold" test was prevailing because its application by the Justices who

101. An outsider may, of course, be interested in reconstructing the basic values implied by legal materials and showing how practical administration has departed from these. Such an outsider may wish to give a more normative account of what constitutes the law. I am assuming that the typical social scientist has the interests ascribed to the sociologist in the text.

102. *See* Memoirs v. Massachusetts, 383 U.S. 413 (1966).

103. *See Memoirs*, 383 U.S. at 424–33 (Douglas, J., concurring); Ginzburg v. United States, 383 U.S. 463, 476–82 (1966) (Black, J., dissenting).

104. *See Ginzburg*, 383 U.S. at 497–501 (Stewart, J., dissenting).

105. *See Memoirs*, 383 U.S. at 441–55 (Clark, J., dissenting), 455–60 (Harlan, J., dissenting), 460–62 (White, J., dissenting).

accepted it determined the outcome of cases, although a majority of Justices did not accept or apply that test.

On more complicated interpretive matters, like the appropriate weight accorded to precedent, each Justice may apply an approach subtly different from that of every other Justice. In that event, the "prevailing standard," hard as it would be to formulate, might be a kind of distillation of a number of standards that would not itself track exactly the approach of any single official.

In an extreme case, the prevailing standard might combine elements actually rejected by every single official. Suppose, to oversimplify in a schematic way, that three Justices thought neither element *A* nor element *B* bore at all on whether a norm was law, three Justices thought element *A* was sufficient to make a norm law and that element *B* was irrelevant, and three Justices thought that element *B* was sufficient and element *A* irrelevant. The practical prevailing standard would be that, absent other lawmaking features, norms are law only if they combine elements *A* and *B*, even though this standard is at odds with the standard applied by every Justice.[106]

Employment of a "prevailing standard" approach would permit the sociologist to inform another person what criteria norms must satisfy to be treated as law within the system, and to predict the outcome of cases as to which application of a prevailing standard is clear.[107] For some genuinely novel issue, like the fourth amendment's application to the "X-ray vision" device, the sociologist might undertake substantial normative elaboration to decide how Justices adhering to given standards would treat this new issue. Insofar as the sociologist engages in a normative appraisal using prevailing standards, his effort will resemble that of actual Justices. But the sociologist is still not concerned with what interpretive standards Justices *should use* or with how they *should decide* genuinely doubtful cases. The sociologist's task remains descriptive.

Most clients of lawyers are mainly concerned with how the state's coercive power might be applied to their situations, not with how an ideal judge would decide. Although lawyers giving advice are certainly participants in the legal system, something very close to the sociologist's approach is the one they take in advising clients. About subjects for which no prevailing standard can be identified or the import of existing standards is uncertain, the lawyer as adviser is likely to say that the law is unsettled or unclear.

Beyond the fact that a prevailing standard need not be socially shared, the sociologist's account of law is modest in some other important respects. First, identification of relevant standards does not mean prediction of outcomes will necessarily be easy. Judges who agree on a standard of interpretation often disagree about its application to a particular case, especially when the standard is

106. *Cf.* National Mut. Ins. Co. v. Tidewater Transfer Co., 337 U.S. 582 (1949).
107. Subject, of course, to possible shifts in standards.

open ended. Second, prevailing standards may or may not include direct references to social morality or critical morality or to some vague combination or amalgam of these. There is no reason why an ultimate standard for law cannot include some moral criteria. Third, prevailing standards will shift subtly over time as new cases are presented and Justices change. None of these features is actually contrary to what Hart says, but *The Concept of Law* leaves the impression that the ultimate rule of recognition will be rather stable, will not refer to moral criteria much, and will allow a rather clear identification of what counts as law.

A fourth respect in which the sociologist's account is modest is the most important for an investigation of the adequacy of a conventionalist theory of law. The account as I have given it does not assert any particular explanation of why standards are prevailing. Indeed, once we see that a standard can be prevailing without being generally shared, we understand that not all prevailing standards need be conventionally accepted, that is, regarded as common standards for officials. But even among shared standards, acceptance by particular officials need not, as I have indicated in Section VII, rest on their acceptance by other officials. Suppose that, in a particular society, virtually everyone believed on religious grounds that Muslim officials should be guided by the Koran in their decisions. Each official might take the Koran as a standard for what counts as law, but not because other officials happen to do so. In an account that is conventionalist in a strong sense, officials apply standards *because* they are accepted as common public standards. The sociologist's identification of widely shared standards does not assure that the standards are accepted by officials because they are regarded in this way.

Hart's development of his "social rule" theory is primarily conceptual; but whether a society could have shared standards that do not rest on a conventional basis is an empirical, not a conceptual, question. I presently believe that in any society, at least any society with a moderate degree of cultural diversity, conventional elements will be very powerful in determining what counts as law; but shared standards, and *a fortiori* prevailing standards that are not shared, may extend well beyond what is accepted for primarily conventional reasons.

There are various tactics one might adopt to defend the notion that all law is based on convention, in the strong sense of being accepted for conventional reasons or derivable from what is accepted for those reasons. The simplest defense would be to claim that what is not settled by convention does not count as law, whatever other status it might have. This defense would not only sharply cut back on what the sociologist could count as law using the "prevailing standards" approach, it would deny the status of law to standards for determining law that every official uses for nonconventional reasons. That result is too strongly counterintuitive to make this defense plausible.

A second kind of defense is more promising. It concedes that standards for determining law are not all conventionally shared; but it claims that the exclusive source for developing those standards is conventionally accepted materials.[108] This approach is suggested by one reading of Dworkin's famous essay *Hard Cases*.[109] Starting with the agreed-upon materials of the law, i.e., undoubted legal rules and legal institutions, a judge constructs the justificatory theory that best explains these, and applies that theory to difficult cases. So long as necessary moral and political judgments required to construct the justificatory theory can be drawn from the materials themselves, and the best theory can be determined by "fit" with the materials alone, conventionally accepted materials might be the exclusive source of the standards for identifying law. This theory would be conventionalist only in a relatively weak sense, because it would concede that many prevailing standards for determining law are not themselves conventionally accepted.[110]

Is such a theory persuasive? Within any legal system, it will be an open question how much the standards for determining law are dictated in one way or another by conventionally accepted rules and practices. Even if one acknowledges that the undoubted legal rules and institutions rest on conventional acceptance, it does not follow that all decisions about standards to use in legal interpretation will flow from these materials. "Independent" moral and political judgments will come into play. That, indeed, is the position that Dworkin himself has consistently taken since *Hard Cases*,[111] and in his writings he has progressively emphasized the importance of these independent judgments.[112] If such judgments matter, official efforts to determine law will not rest exclusively on conventional materials even in this weaker sense.

A third defense of an ultimately conventionalist account is that even though judges may disagree about interpretive standards, and even though these standards may not be derivable from conventionally accepted materials, there may be conventional agreement on how judges should approach interpretive choices.[113] Suppose, for example, that all agree that each judge should try as best he or she can to fit a theory of justification to the clear legal materials. In that event, judges would agree conventionally on their responsibilities. One difficulty about this theory is that the "agreed-upon standard" might not be illuminating about actual criteria for determining law, since judicial disagreements would be so great. More importantly, perhaps, one could probably find an agreed-upon formulation

---

108. *See* Postema, *supra* note 5.

109. Taking Rights Seriously, *supra* note 4, at 81–130; *see also* R. Sartorius, *supra* note 71, at 181–210.

110. In Law's Empire, *supra* note 4, at 124–30, Dworkin suggests that "soft conventionalist" theories of this sort do not qualify as relevantly conventionalist.

111. *See, e.g.*, Taking Rights Seriously, *supra* note 4, app. at 340–42.

112. *See, e.g.*, Dworkin, *"Natural" Law Revisited*, 34 U. Fla. L. Rev. 165, 170–71 (1982); Law's Empire, *supra* note 4, at 255–56.

113. *See* Coleman, *supra* note 5, at 159.

only by moving to an extreme level of generality—e.g., judges should do what is right—or by using critical vague terms that would obscure genuine differences, such as whether judges legitimately inject their own views about moral and political philosophy into decisions. Further, even if judges do agree considerably on how they should approach hard interpretive questions, it is far from clear that they do so for exclusively conventional reasons. In sum, the attempt to preserve conventionalism by turning to the judge's tasks in resolving difficult problems is not convincing.

If we take the sociologist's perspective toward law, we may well preserve a "social fact" approach to law, one that refers to what is actually accepted and used in some sense; but the approach would not be fully conventionalist, that is, it would not claim that all of what is accepted as law is accepted because it has a conventional status.

2. The Participant's Account I turn now to an account of law for a judge or other participant who makes legal decisions. The judge is interested in making a correct normative decision about the law.[114] She is concerned with the standards that she should employ, not merely with the standards most judges happen to be using. What are the ultimate criteria of law for her? I will attend here to a Supreme Court Justice or other judge of a highest court, and I will disregard whatever principles of deference may exist to the determinations of the political branches, that is, principles that tell judges not to decide for themselves whether a norm is legal but to accept the judgment of someone else.

One possible position, suggested by Hart's analysis, is that what is law for the sociologist is congruent with what is law for the judge. What is unclear is not law until the judges settle a matter; then it becomes law either because judges have the prior authority to settle such things or because what the judges say in fact gets accepted by others as a correct statement of the law. There are two fundamental difficulties with this approach. One, already discussed, is that as they approach hard decisions judges typically do not conceive of the law as "running out."[115] The second difficulty is that judges often consider to be dispositive in hard cases the same sorts of "legal" considerations that yield clear answers to easy cases. Judges do not usually conceive of their function as being judicial up to a point, and then legislative. These are the essential points that have made Dworkin's attack on the rule of recognition seem so powerful, and they have force even if one does not think the law provides an answer to every case.

Let us suppose that disagreements between judges over interpretive strategies can occur because of differences of judgment over "fit" with the undoubted

---

114. I am omitting other participatory roles that connect to the judge's role. Starting from the interests of their clients, lawyers seek to persuade judges what standards to adopt. Scholars and other critics attempt, ordinarily from a noninterested perspective, to indicate what judges should do.

115. I believe that judges *sometimes* do perceive the law as running out.

legal materials, or because of differences of judgment about moral and political philosophy that are not determined by fit. Unlike Dworkin,[116] I think it is somewhat misleading for a judge to say "the law" really requires one answer rather than another, if the judge is aware that what distinguishes his answer from a competing one is an independent moral or political judgment that is not shared.[117] But if the judge thinks the difference concerns adequacy of fit with the legal materials, and all agree that fit is what counts, the judge rightly puts it that the law requires his answer. An account of law might draw such a distinction, but it would not track very well the experience of judges in deciding cases, because judges rarely distinguish precisely the input of independent judgment from fit.

From the judge's point of view, it may be most helpful to regard the standards for determining law as including every relevant standard the judge regards himself as bound to use in answering a legal question. In that event, the standards for determining law may include general standards for evaluative reasoning as well as distinctively legal standards. Since judges, like Justice Black adhering to his rigid fourth amendment approach, may well decide they are legally bound to do things that they know others do not assume they are legally bound to do, it may seem that an adequate account of law must be essentially normative.

Any such characterization, however, is substantially misleading if it implies that convention has little or no role. Officials are bound to adhere to much of what is conventionally established because they have explicitly or implicitly agreed to do so, because the justified expectations of citizens and other officials are based on established practices, and because officials' following established practices usually permits a more efficient resolution of social problems.

As I have suggested, the conventional aspects operate at three levels. What are taken as basic legal materials and institutions are matters of established social practice. A judge who swears to uphold the Constitution means our Constitution; he or she has promised to treat our Constitution and the organs of government created under it as authoritative in our legal system.[118] Insofar as the basic legal materials and institutions are the foundations for "fit" arguments, convention operates as the ground for much of the normative evaluation of judges. Finally convention operates directly at the level of interpretive practice when judges follow precedents and established interpretive standards that they would not have adopted, or join majority opinions whose approach is not exactly the one they would choose. Exactly how far judges do and should rely on convention is

---

116. *See* LAW'S EMPIRE, *supra* note 4, at 260–63.

117. A person who comes at the problem with different independent answers will hardly be reassured that "the law" requires an answer contrary to his simply because a majority of those who happen to be judges disagree with him.

118. Once officials promise in their oath of office to uphold the law, or implicitly undertake to do so by accepting their positions, the direct normative force of convention is supplemented by the normative force of promise.

difficult to say, and the right answers would obviously vary for different societies, legal systems, and stages of history. What one can confidently say about our legal system, and probably any modern legal system, is that conventional bases are very important ingredients in determinations of law.

How to conceptualize the view from inside is troublesome. One might say that since the judge is trying to determine the correct answer, and since factors other than convention may be relevant, we have a "normative account" which assigns a subsidiary place to convention. But this seems a little too neat. Suppose judges were trying to determine the correct answers, but they regarded themselves as entirely bound to adhere to what is conventionally established, and they thought that beyond what was conventionally established the law did not constrain them. Then we would have a fully conventional account of law. Suppose a single other normative factor were introduced that in some slight proportion of cases was determinative. Would we then need to shift to a "normative" account of law and away from a "conventional" one? If convention is almost entirely determinative of what counts as law, then saying that we have a largely conventional account, qualified by another factor, would seem more apt. If other normative factors are much larger in importance but convention is still absolutely critical, perhaps we can best speak of a mixed conventional and normative account. Whatever the label, we should recognize that the account of law for the inside participant makes existing social practice less decisive for what counts as law than it is for the sociologist's account.

IX. CONCLUSION

We have seen that Hart's rule of recognition theory requires substantial supplementation if it is to account for what insiders regard as law. Given the intertwining of judgments about the materials themselves, their moral and political implications, and the judge's independent moral and political assumptions, one needs to acknowledge that the boundaries of law are not the same as the boundaries of what is conventionally accepted. But if Hart's theory requires some revisions, it illuminates critical conventional elements in any satisfactory theory of law for the United States. Its basic outline, with additions and qualifications, remains a powerful explanatory account of how a sociologist might approach the law of a society, and of why an insider accords authoritative status to much that counts as law. Further, Hart's theory is an important beginning toward understanding how convention and normative judgments interact when a judge deals with interpretive techniques and other subtle aspects of law.

2. PRECEDENT-BASED CONSTITUTIONAL ADJUDICATION, ACCEPTANCE, AND THE RULE OF RECOGNITION

RICHARD H. FALLON, JR.*

According to Article VI of the Constitution of the United States, the Constitution is the "supreme Law of the Land."[1] Under the doctrine of stare decisis, however, the Supreme Court often adheres to past constitutional decisions that it believes to have been erroneous in the first instance. The question thus arises: How can the Court justify allowing judicial precedent to displace what it would otherwise regard as the dictates of the Constitution, notwithstanding the apparent mandate of Article VI that the Constitution should be supreme?

This question has current importance for two related reasons. First, although constitutional lawyers have long assumed that reliance on precedent is sometimes mandatory, even if the controlling precedent appears to have been decided wrongly,[2] this complacent assumption has recently come under strong attack. Especially prominent among the attackers are so-called "originalists," who contend that the only legitimate constitutional interpretation is that which accurately reflects the original intent or understanding of constitutional language. Second, once the originalist challenge is put on the table, it resonates strongly with the intuitions of many law students and much of the lay public. At first blush, many sophisticated people think it inherent in the nature of interpretation, or possibly law, that constitutional "meaning" cannot change as a result of past interpretive errors. Many students thus take the view that even if the Supreme Court has long got away with nonoriginalist, precedent-based decision making, deviations from original constitutional meanings cannot be justified as a matter of law.

---

* Ralph S. Tyler, Jr. Professor of Constitutional Law, Harvard Law School. I am grateful to Matthew Adler for comments and to Elizabeth Barchas for research assistance. Substantial parts of this chapter are adapted from my *Constitutional Precedent Viewed Through the Lens of Hartian Positivist Jurisprudence*, 86 N.C. L. Rev. 1107 (2008).

1. U.S. Const. art. VI, § 2, cl. 2.

2. *See, e.g.*, United States *ex rel.* Fong Foo v. Shaughnessy, 234 F.2d 715, 719 (2d Cir. 1955) ("Stare decisis . . . is significant only when a court feels constrained to stick to a former ruling although the Court has come to regard it as unwise or unjust."); Larry Alexander, *Constrained by Precedent*, 63 S. Cal. L. Rev. 1, 4 (1989) (noting that precedent controls a judicial decision only when it results in a decision different from that which a court would otherwise have reached); Frederick Schauer, *Precedent*, 39 Stan. L. Rev. 571, 575 (1987) (same).

In this chapter I shall respond to claims that the Supreme Court behaves lawlessly or violates the "supreme Law of the Land" whenever it follows erroneous past decisions, by invoking and applying H. L. A. Hart's famous assertions that the ultimate foundation for all legal claims lies in a "rule of recognition" and that the rule of recognition owes its status to "acceptance." The basic thrust of my argument will be that Article VI and other provisions of the written Constitution do not exhaust the pertinent American rule or practice of recognition; accepted rules or practices of recognition accord judicial precedent a sometimes authoritative status. In developing this argument, I shall explore whether Hart's account requires adaptation to provide an adequate explanation of American constitutional practice—which is famously argumentative and not obviously rule-bound—and, if so, what forms the adjustments ought to take. My ultimate goal will be to use Hartian positivist theory to illuminate American constitutional adjudication, and especially the role of precedent within it, while deploying American constitutional practice as a prism through which to examine some of Hart's ideas.

I. THE ORIGINALIST CHALLENGE TO PRECEDENT-BASED ADJUDICATION

Traditional thinking about American constitutional law includes two premises the conjunction of which could easily appear paradoxical: (1) the Constitution is the supreme law, which must prevail over all other purported sources of law,[3] and (2) the Supreme Court should, or may even be constitutionally required to, follow precedent in some cases in which doing so would conflict with the result that the Constitution would otherwise prescribe.[4] The appearance of paradox arises most vividly in constitutional theories such as originalism that have a clear gauge of what the Constitution would mean in the absence of precedent.

Although constitutional theories besides originalism can generate an appearance of paradox in judicial adherence to initially erroneous precedents, originalism is the theory that is most prominently deployed by critics to attack precedent-based adjudication at the present time. I shall therefore treat originalism as representative of the family of criticisms that I wish to confront, all of which seem to rest on the assumption that the very idea of a *written* constitution, entrenched against change except by supermajoritarian processes, would make no sense unless

---

3. *See* U.S. Const. art. VI, § 2, cl. 2.

4. *See, e.g.*, Dickerson v. United States, 530 U.S. 428, 443 (2000) (asserting that stare decisis "carries such persuasive force that we have always required a departure from precedent to be supported by some special justification" and treating the mere possibility of past error as an insufficient ground for reconsideration); Thomas R. Lee, *Stare Decisis in Historical Perspective: From the Founding Era to the Rehnquist Court*, 52 Vand. L. Rev. 647, 658 (1999) ("[M]embers of the modern Court have soundly rejected the perception of error as a basis for overturning precedent.").

based on the premise that constitutional language has a fixed and typically knowable meaning that binds judges irrevocably.

Despite having a clear criterion of constitutional meaning that is independent of past judicial precedents, first-generation originalists such as Judge Robert Bork and Justice Antonin Scalia grudgingly accepted the sometime authority of nonoriginalist precedent as a concession to brute practical necessity.[5] If tested against the original understanding of constitutional language, Judge Bork and Justice Scalia recognized, such mainstays of the legal, economic, and political order as paper money and the Social Security system might be unconstitutional.[6] It is seriously arguable, at the least, that the provision of Article I authorizing Congress to "coin Money"[7] was originally understood to preclude the alternative course of issuing greenbacks, and that no constitutional provision would originally have been understood to authorize creation of a social security system unimaginable in the eighteenth century. In cases such as these, Judge Bork and Justice Scalia maintained, the practical costs of returning to the original understanding might simply be too large to bear, and precedents must therefore be allowed to stand even if they could be shown incompatible with framing-era understandings.[8] Yet Judge Bork and Justice Scalia gave no clear explanation of how the preference for precedent over the Constitution's true meaning—as they understood it—could ever be constitutionally lawful. Apparently uncertain on this point, Scalia once characterized stare decisis as an exception to his originalist constitutional theory, not an aspect of it.[9]

More recently, a second generation of originalist theories has gone where Bork and Scalia refused to venture. According to Randy Barnett,[10] Gary Lawson,[11]

---

5. *See* ROBERT H. BORK, THE TEMPTING OF AMERICA: THE POLITICAL SEDUCTION OF THE LAW 155–59 (1990); ANTONIN SCALIA, A MATTER OF INTERPRETATION: FEDERAL COURTS AND THE LAW 138–40 (Amy Gutmann ed., 1997).

6. *See, e.g.*, BORK, *supra* note 5, at 155–58; *see also* Gary Lawson, *The Constitutional Case Against Precedent*, 17 HARV. J.L. & PUB. POL'Y 23, 33 (1994).

7. U.S. CONST. art. I, § 8, cl. 5.

8. *See, e.g.*, BORK, *supra* note 5, at 155 ("Whatever might have been the proper ruling shortly after the Civil War, if a judge today were to decide that paper money is unconstitutional, we would think he ought to be accompanied not by a law clerk but by a guardian."); JEFFREY TOOBIN, THE NINE: INSIDE THE SECRET WORLD OF THE SUPREME COURT 103 (2007) (quoting Justice Scalia as comparing his own judicial philosophy with that of Justice Clarence Thomas by observing that "I am an originalist, but I am not a nut").

9. *See* SCALIA, *supra* note 5, at 140.

10. *See* Randy E. Barnett, *It's a Bird, It's a Plane, No, It's Super Precedent: A Response to Farber and Gerhardt*, 90 MINN. L. REV. 1232, 1233 (2006) [hereinafter Barnett, *Super Precedent*]; Randy E. Barnett, *Trumping Precedent with Original Meaning: Not As Radical As It Sounds*, 22 CONST. COMMENT. 257, 258–59 (2005) [hereinafter Barnett, *Trumping Precedent*].

11. *See* Gary Lawson, *The Constitutional Case Against Precedent*, 17 HARV. J.L. & PUB. POL'Y 23, 30 (1994).

and Michael Paulsen,[12] the truly fundamental originalist premise is that the Constitution is the "supreme Law of the Land."[13] Once this premise is granted, they say, it follows that allowing precedent to prevail over what the Constitution would otherwise mean is inadmissible:[14] the objective public meaning of the constitutional text left no doubt on this score in 1789, and it leaves no doubt today.[15]

This challenge, with its appeal to constitutional first principles, holds the aura of profundity. When one casts off the blinkers of complacent traditionalism, how could adherence to judicial precedents that deviate from the true meaning of the supreme law—whether measured by the original understanding or some other criterion—possibly be other than judicial lawlessness and treason to the Constitution?[16]

II. MEETING THE ORIGINALIST CHALLENGE: ACCEPTANCE AS THE NECESSARY FOUNDATION OF FUNDAMENTAL LAW

In deploying their argument that initially erroneous precedent must always yield to the Constitution's plain or originally understood meaning, originalists cast themselves as defenders of the true Constitution who, almost uniquely, have the courage to place principle and the rule of law above policy preferences and expediency. In fact, insofar as originalists suggest that either current law or something inherent in the idea of law mandates their conclusions, their position reflects a jurisprudential mistake. The arguments that reveal the fallacies of originalist thinking trace to H. L. A. Hart's practice-based explication of the concept

12. *See* Michael Stokes Paulsen, *The Intrinsically Corrupting Influence of Precedent*, 22 Const. Comment. 289, 291 (2005).

13. U.S. Const. art. VI, § 2, cl. 2.

14. For originalist arguments to this effect, see, for example, Barnett, *Trumping Precedent*, *supra* note 10; Lawson, *supra* note 6; Paulsen, *supra* note 12. For textualist objections to precedent-based constitutional adjudication, see, for example, Akhil Reed Amar, *The Supreme Court, 1999 Term—Foreword: The Document and the Doctrine*, 114 Harv. L. Rev. 26, 68–78 (2000) (discussing areas in which doctrine has diverged from the Constitution's text and concluding that "the document is often more normatively attractive").

15. Professor Paulsen generalizes this argument by maintaining that if other constitutional theories are to maintain their integrity, they, too, must take the same hard stand against allowing precedent to play a decisive role in constitutional adjudication. *See* Paulsen, *supra* note 12, at 289–90.

16. One possible answer to this question would be that "clearly erroneous" precedents should be regarded as nonbinding and subject to judicial overruling, whereas "merely" erroneous precedents should be followed. *See* Caleb Nelson, *Stare Decisis and Demonstrably Erroneous Precedents*, 87 Va. L. Rev. 1 (2001). But modern doctrine does not rest on this distinction.

of law.[17] When originalist claims are examined through the lens of Hartian positivist jurisprudence, the originalists emerge not as principled defenders of our existing constitutional order, but as advocates of radical change.

A. The Social Facts Thesis and the Idea of a Rule of Recognition

The fundamental tenet of Hart's jurisprudence, as of legal positivism more generally, holds that the foundations of law necessarily lie in social facts that constitute a pertinent practice or practices. In this chapter, I shall offer some arguments supporting the proposition that law must be rooted in social facts, but I shall not attempt to lay out an exhaustive case. Rather, I shall assume that Hart successfully demonstrated "the social facts thesis" to be true—as I believe that he did.[18]

In developing and explicating the thesis that the foundations of law necessarily lie in social facts, Hart introduced the idea of a rule or rules of recognition.[19] By this terminology, he meant to refer to the criteria of legal validity by which officials, and especially judges, distinguish law from nonlaw. Some criteria of legal validity can be derived from other, more ultimate criteria. At some point, however, the chain of justification must end, and some criterion or criteria possess authoritative status simply because they are accepted as authoritative.

The illuminating power of Hart's idea of a rule of recognition, and especially of ultimate or nonderivable rules of recognition, comes into view if we ask why

---

17. *See generally* H.L.A. Hart, The Concept of Law (Penelope A. Bulloch & Joseph Raz eds., 2d ed. 1994).

18. The great traditional rival to positivism was the natural law tradition, classically rendered in the claim that an unjust law is "no law at all." *See* St. Thomas Aquinas, Summa Theologica Pt. II-I, Q. 95, Art. 2, Objection 4, *reprinted in* George C. Christie & Patrick H. Martin, Jurisprudence 166 (2d ed. 1995). Although I have nothing to contribute to the natural law/positivism debate, I am persuaded by the positivist position that the distinction between legality and morality is a useful one. More recently, the leading rival to positivism has been what has been described as Ronald Dworkin's "third theory" of law. *See, e.g.*, John Mackie, *The Third Theory of Law*, 7 Phil. & Pub. Aff. 3 (1977). Dworkin's theory expressly characterizes law as a "practice" that depends for its existence on the social facts necessary to constitute a practice, *see* Ronald Dworkin, Law's Empire 45–53 (1986), but it rejects Hartian positivism by claiming that law is inherently interpretive and that any interpretation necessarily has a moral component. *See id.* at 65–68. Although I find Dworkin's position to offer significant insights into American judicial practice, scholars of analytical jurisprudence appear increasingly to believe that his general attack on Hartian positivism was flawed and unpersuasive. *See, e.g.*, Brian Leiter, *Beyond the Hart/Dworkin Debate: The Methodology Problem in Jurisprudence*, 48 Am. J. Jurisprudence 17, 18–19 (2003) (advancing the view, shared by "many others," that Hart has emerged as the "clear victor" in the Hart/Dworkin debate). Without purporting to contribute to the Hart/Dworkin debate, I shall assume for purposes of this chapter that Hartian positivism survives Dworkin's attacks.

19. Although Hart occasionally uses the plural, *see, e.g.*, Hart, *supra* note 17, at 92, he more commonly uses the singular.

what we call the Constitution is, today, the law of the United States. The short answer is that the Constitution ultimately owes its status as law to the social fact that it, or at least some nonderivable part of it, is simply *accepted* as such within a relevant social practice or practices.[20] This is a point of fundamental importance: the fact that a provision was once intended or understood to have future binding force cannot suffice to make that provision law today unless a *current* rule or practice of recognition gives that intent or understanding legally controlling force.[21] The Articles of Confederation and the decrees of the British Parliament were once intended and understood to be binding law in part of the geographical territory that today is the United States. But Parliamentary decrees and the Articles of Confederation are no longer the law here because they have ceased to be recognized as such, regardless of whether the processes of their displacement were themselves legally valid under British jurisprudence, the Articles of Confederation, or the constitutions and laws of the former colonies in 1787, 1788, or 1789.[22]

B. Rules of Recognition and Nonoriginalist Precedent

Once it is recognized that the foundations of law necessarily lie in social facts involving contemporary acceptance, the claim that judicial precedent cannot establish valid law contrary to what otherwise would be the best relatively acontextual interpretation of the written Constitution immediately appears doubtful. Judicial recognition of precedent as establishing the binding law of the United States has been a central, widely accepted feature of our constitutional practice almost from the beginning.[23] Since then, the Supreme Court has invoked stare decisis with great frequency, seldom apologetically. So far as I am aware, no

20. *See* Frederick Schauer, *Precedent and the Necessary Externality of Constitutional Norms*, 17 HARV. J.L. & PUB. POL'Y 45, 51–53 (1994). It bears noting that rules of jurisdiction and hierarchy may bind lower court judges and some other officials to accept the Supreme Court's determinations, rather than to apply the same rule of recognition applied by the Court. *See* Kent Greenawalt, *The Rule of Recognition and the Constitution*, 85 MICH. L. REV. 621, 636 (1987) (reprinted as Chapter 1, this volume, at 15); Kenneth Einar Himma, *Making Sense of Constitutional Disagreement: Legal Positivism, the Bill of Rights, and the Conventional Rule of Recognition in the United States*, 4 J.L. SOC'Y 149, 162 (2003).

21. *See* David A. Strauss, *Common Law Constitutional Interpretation*, 63 U. CHI. L. REV. 877, 887 (1996).

22. Bruce Ackerman has argued—I believe persuasively—that the Constitution's ratification by "conventions" of the people, rather than by the legally regular processes of the states' legislatures, failed to satisfy the preexisting legal criteria in some of the states for valid enactment into law. *See* Bruce A. Ackerman, *The Storrs Lectures: Discovering the Constitution*, 93 YALE L.J. 1013, 1017 & n.6 (1984). For a contrary argument, see Akhil Reed Amar, *The Consent of the Governed: Constitutional Amendment Outside Article V*, 94 COLUM. L. REV. 457, 475–87 (1994).

23. *See* Lee, *supra* note 4, at 662–81.

Justice up through and including those currently sitting has persistently questioned the legitimacy of stare decisis or failed to apply it in at least some cases.[24]

Indeed, all of the current Justices, including the self-proclaimed originalist Justices Antonin Scalia and Clarence Thomas, have specifically and self-consciously accepted the authority of past judicial precedents that could not themselves have been justified under strict originalist principles. For example, in *Lucas v. South Carolina Coastal Council*,[25] Justice Scalia's opinion for the Court acknowledged that "early constitutional theorists did not believe the Takings Clause embraced regulations [as distinguished from total expropriations] of property at all," but relied on prior Court decisions to hold that the Takings Clause now restricts "regulatory as well as physical deprivations of property."[26] Similarly, in *West Lynn Creamery, Inc. v. Healy*,[27] Justice Scalia, joined by Justice Thomas, wrote an opinion in which he acknowledged that dormant Commerce Clause doctrine has no historical grounding but concluded that stare decisis mandated the doctrine's continued application, because the Court had "decided a vast number of negative-Commerce-Clause cases, engendering considerable reliance interests."[28] Justices Scalia and Thomas also joined an opinion that relied on precedent to subject federal affirmative action programs to strict judicial scrutiny in *Adarand Constructors, Inc. v. Pena*,[29] notwithstanding the total absence of any evidence that the pertinent constitutional provision, the Due Process Clause of the Fifth Amendment, was originally understood to bar racially discriminatory legislation.

It is also relevant that all of the Justices, again including the originalists, apparently converge in recognizing as currently valid, and show no wish whatsoever to reconsider, a number of past decisions that some scholars think would be difficult if not impossible to justify on originalist premises.[30] These include cases establishing that paper money is constitutional,[31] as is Social Security;[32] that the Equal Protection Clause bars race discrimination in the public schools;[33] that Congress has broad power under the Commerce Clause to regulate the national

---

24. *See* Richard H. Fallon, Jr., *Stare Decisis and the Constitution: An Essay on Constitutional Methodology*, 76 N.Y.U. L. Rev. 570, 582–83 (2001).

25. 505 U.S. 1003 (1992).

26. *Id.* at 1028 n.15.

27. 512 U.S. 186 (1994).

28. *Id.* at 209–10 (Scalia, J., concurring in the judgment).

29. 515 U.S. 200 (1995).

30. *See generally* Henry Paul Monaghan, *Stare Decisis and Constitutional Adjudication*, 88 Colum. L. Rev. 723, 729–39 (1988) (listing examples of prominent doctrines that are likely inconsistent with original understanding).

31. *See* Legal Tender Cases, 79 U.S. (12 Wall.) 457 (1871), *overruling* Hepburn v. Griswold, 75 U.S. (8 Wall.) 603 (1870).

32. *See* Helvering v. Davis, 301 U.S. 619 (1937).

33. *See* Brown v. Board of Education, 347 U.S. 483 (1954).

economy;[34] and that the Equal Protection Clause requires the distribution of voting rights on a one-person, one-vote basis.[35] Public officials besides the Justices, and indeed most of the American public, appear to share the Justices' assumption that past judicial rulings have settled these issues conclusively.

When the practices of constitutional law and adjudication are examined carefully, it thus seems impossible not to conclude that under the ultimate rules of recognition now existing in the United States, the Constitution that is either accepted or validated as law is a Constitution that is *somehow* compatible with results and practices that may well be inconsistent with the original understanding of constitutional language.[36] In so asserting, I need to acknowledge that the reasoning by which I have supported the validity of nonoriginalist precedents and precedent-based decision making may appear circular: it is lawful for Supreme Court Justices to treat precedent as controlling legal authority because the Justices long have regarded, and continue to regard, precedent as controlling authority. As I shall explain below, there is at least somewhat more to be said, involving other officials' acceptance of, and the public's acquiescence in, Supreme Court practice. But there is no way to escape the circle entirely once it is recognized—as Hart taught—that the foundations of law, and ultimate criteria concerning what is lawful, necessarily lie in contemporary social facts, not the efforts of past generations to control the future.[37]

C. Reconciling Originally Erroneous Precedent with the Constitution

Insofar as nonoriginalist or initially erroneous precedent is concerned, at least two conceptual accounts might explain the sociologically prevailing state of affairs. First, one might say that just as some of the Constitution (centrally including Article V, which prescribes methods of constitutional amendment) is law just because it is accepted as an ultimate rule of recognition,[38] nonoriginalist

---

34. *See* Gonzales v. Raich, 545 U.S. 1 (2005).

35. *See, e.g.*, Reynolds v. Sims, 377 U.S. 533 (1964).

36. For current purposes, I put to one side the important, much-debated question of whether the rule of recognition observed by officials is better characterized as a "social rule," *see* HART, *supra* note 17, at 55–61, 254–59; as a "convention" or "Lewis-convention," *see, e.g.*, Matthew D. Adler, *Popular Constitutionalism and the Rule of Recognition: Whose Practices Ground U.S. Law?*, 100 NW. U. L. REV. 719, 730–31 (2006) (explicating but not endorsing this view); as a "shared cooperative activity," *see, e.g.*, Scott J. Shapiro, *Law, Plans, and Practical Reason*, 8 LEGAL THEORY 387 (2002); as a "constitutive rule," *see* Andrei Marmor, *Legal Conventionalism*, 4 LEGAL THEORY 509, 521–27 (1998); or in some other terms.

37. According to the social facts view, the fact that the foundations of law lie in acceptance and that "what officials collectively and self-consciously recognize as constituting a valid law under a general criterion *is* a valid law" necessarily "rules out the possibility of officials, considered collectively, being generally mistaken about what counts as law." Himma, *supra* note 20, at 156.

38. *See* Greenawalt, *supra* note 20, at 642 (reprinted as Chapter 1, this volume, at 21).

precedent owes its lawful status directly to an accepted rule of recognition that accords some precedents a status superior to the written Constitution.[39] In other words, the pronouncement of Article VI to the contrary notwithstanding, the ultimate rule of recognition in the United States does not make the written Constitution "the supreme Law of the Land" in all cases. Although conceptually plausible, this effort to describe current legal practice in the United States fits poorly with the ways that lawyers argue cases and judges explain their decisions. Judges and Justices always purport to reconcile their rulings with the written Constitution and have never claimed authority to displace it.[40]

A second, and better, account asserts that the Constitution that owes its lawful status to accepted rules of recognition can sometimes accommodate nonoriginalist practices and decisions by being construed in light of nonoriginalist precedent. On this interpretation, the relationship between the Constitution and judicial precedent is harmonious, with precedent influencing how the Constitution should be interpreted or implemented, but never standing in a relationship of hierarchical priority.[41]

To put the thought in more expressly Hartian terms, the Constitution that is accepted as law under ultimate rules of recognition is not an irreducibly originalist Constitution. Indeed, among originalists' most fundamental errors is their failure to grasp this basic, Hartian positivist point. In contending that the acontextual meaning or original understanding of the Constitution is "the supreme Law of the Land," which must therefore necessarily prevail over judicial precedents reflecting contrary interpretations, originalists fail to acknowledge the foundational importance of *current*, rather than past, social facts in establishing ultimate criteria of legal validity. More often than not, originalist claims presuppose a bankrupt jurisprudential theory—a point to which I shall return below.

III. SOME PUZZLES ABOUT HARTIAN POSITIVIST JURISPRUDENCE

Although my argument so far has employed the central elements of Hart's framework to refute originalist claims, there is admittedly a good deal that is perplexing about the account I have just offered. Confronting a few of the perplexities will deepen understanding of the American constitutional order and,

---

39. *Cf. id.* at 654 (asserting that "the force of precedent. . . is an aspect of our law because of acceptance") (reprinted as Chapter 1, this volume, at 31); Steven D. Smith, *Stare Decisis in a Classical and Constitutional Setting: A Comment on the Symposium*, 5 AVE MARIA L. REV. 153, 168 (2007) (observing that "it would seem that stare decisis is legally secured on the same basis as the Constitution itself").

40. *See* Richard H. Fallon, Jr., *A Constructivist Coherence Theory of Constitutional Interpretation*, 100 HARV. L. REV. 1189, 1244 (1987); Strauss, *supra* note 21, at 899 (observing that "it is no part of our [constitutional] practice ever to 'overrule' a textual provision").

41. *See* Fallon, *supra* note 40, at 1245, 1260–62.

especially, of the role of precedent-based constitutional decision making by the Supreme Court. It may also generate some interstitial insights about the adjustments to or elaborations of Hartian positivist theory that might be necessary for it accurately to model the American system.

A. The Idea of Rules in Contexts of Disagreement

Perhaps the largest perplexity involves what exactly it means to say that all determinations of legal validity reflect "rules." As Ronald Dworkin—who rejects the notion that it even makes sense to talk of rules of recognition[42]—rightly emphasizes, the practice of constitutional interpretation is deeply argumentative.[43] Among its most striking features is that argument recurs, even among the Justices of the Supreme Court, about the criteria by which valid constitutional claims should be distinguished from invalid ones. If the Justices themselves disagree about the applicable rules of recognition, then how, Dworkin demands, can it be said that their conduct is rule-governed at all?[44] Confronting the same phenomena, Matthew Adler concludes that there are multiple groups applying diverse rules of recognition, with at most a partial overlap among them.[45]

As challenges such as these make clear, for the Hartian idea of a "rule of recognition" to fit the American legal system, the concept of a rule needs to encompass not just rules as defined by Dworkin—rigid dictates that either apply or do not and tolerate no accommodation of other considerations—but the whole range of standards, principles, and criteria of validity that officials use in resolving contested cases. When conceived in this way, the rule of recognition—or, perhaps more aptly, the rules or even the practices of recognition obtaining in the United States today—are rules only in the sense made famous by Ludwig Wittgenstein: references to the rule or rules of recognition mark the existence of broadly shared, often tacit understandings on the part of those at the center of constitutional practice (most notably Supreme Court Justices and judges, but also others, as I shall explain below) about how to "go on" in ways that will be acknowledged by others as appropriate or correct.[46] When the idea of a rule of recognition is conceptualized in this capacious sense, "the test of whether a man's actions are the application of a rule is not whether he can *formulate* it but

---

42. *See* RONALD DWORKIN, TAKING RIGHTS SERIOUSLY 39–45 (1977) (arguing that Hart's account of the rule of recognition as the "master rule" of a legal system is untenable).

43. *See* DWORKIN, LAW'S EMPIRE, *supra* note 18, at 3–4, 13.

44. *See id.*

45. *See* Adler, *supra* note 36, at 730–31. *Cf.* STANLEY FISH, IS THERE A TEXT IN THIS CLASS? THE AUTHORITY OF INTERPRETIVE COMMUNITIES 322 (1980) (explaining interpretive disagreement as resulting from multiple interpretive communities).

46. *See* LUDWIG WITTGENSTEIN, PHILOSOPHICAL INVESTIGATIONS para. 151–53, 179–83 (G.E.M. Anscombe trans., 1953); *see also* JULES L. COLEMAN, THE PRACTICE OF PRINCIPLE: IN DEFENCE OF A PRAGMATIST APPROACH TO LEGAL THEORY 81 (2001) (invoking the Wittgensteinian notion to explicate jurisprudential issues).

whether it makes sense to distinguish between a right and a wrong way of doing things in connection with what he does."[47] What matters is that those at the center of the practice of constitutional adjudication should regard their behavior as norm-governed, that their behaviors should be convergent, and that they should be open to persuasion that they have applied the rules wrongly.[48]

I am agnostic about whether it would advance jurisprudential analysis to develop a richer and more precise vocabulary than Hart's usage of the term "rule" provides—for example, by differentiating between (1) authoritative legal pronouncements such as the Constitution and the tax code and (2) the set of criteria or the "function"[49] then applied to those pronouncements to generate their legal meaning or content. Nevertheless, Hart seems to me to have been basically correct in inviting us to think of even the sharpest substantive and methodological disputes in constitutional law as bounded and shaped by widely shared normative understandings—many of which, admittedly, are more tacit than expressed. If disagreement is temporarily put to one side, the phenomenon of "easy cases,"[50] in which all or nearly all judges and lawyers concur in their judgments, strongly supports this conclusion. At the risk of laboring the obvious, there is no disagreement that the Constitution is law, that the tax code passed under the Constitution is law, that various forms of antisocial behavior are punishable by law, that punishments can be imposed only after judicial trials conducted in accordance with well-known procedures, and so forth. It is easy for those preoccupied with constitutional debates in the Supreme Court to lose sight of how overwhelmingly much of American law, including constitutional law, is settled beyond reasonable disagreement by accepted rules of recognition—including, as I have said, rules that mark some once-disputed issues (such as the validity of paper money and the Social Security system) as now resolved decisively.

Against the background of broad agreement, it should perhaps not be surprising that disagreements, even fundamental ones, should also occur. The most

---

47. PETER WINCH, THE IDEA OF A SOCIAL SCIENCE AND ITS RELATION TO PHILOSOPHY 58 (1958). Hart embraced Winch's account of rules and rule-following. *See* HART, *supra* note 17, at 289.

48. Stanley Fish argues that when the term "rule" is used in this loose a sense, it is either redundant or misleading, since competent practitioners will know how to "go on" in interpretive practice without reference to the "rules" that they are ostensibly supposed to follow. *See, e.g.*, Stanley Fish, *Fish v. Fiss*, 36 STAN. L. REV. 1324 (1984). In my view, however, in law—possibly unlike other practices that call for interpretation—there is a dialectical relationship between shared tacit understandings and attempts to articulate those understandings in propositional form. As a result, appeals to "rules," and arguments about them, inform judgments and can sometimes provoke reappraisals of what counts as "going on" correctly.

49. *See* COLEMAN, *supra* note 46, at 161–62.

50. *See* Frederick Schauer, *Easy Cases*, 58 S. CAL. L. REV. 399 (1985).

basic element of rule-following is simply "understanding":[51] one does not need to "interpret" when one knows immediately and unreflectively how to go on. Yet constitutional law has always, perfectly understandably, been thought to require "interpretation"—a reflective activity most naturally at home in contexts that give rise to doubt or uncertainty.[52] Indeed, the high stakes involved in many constitutional cases, especially in the Supreme Court, seem especially likely to trigger reflection and analysis that may actually exacerbate uncertainty. Then, as analysis deepens, it should not occasion surprise that second-order uncertainties and debates would arise about the processes that judges and Justices should follow in resolving disputed questions.

Based largely on the Justices' invocation of divergent criteria of legal validity when they disagree in contested cases, Dworkin and Adler conclude that there is no shared embrace of a single set of validity criteria, and thus that there are no agreed rules of recognition, even in "easy" cases. If everyone agrees that the tax code is law, that paper money is valid legal tender, or that the Equal Protection Clause forbids the states to segregate children in the public schools on the basis of race, it is only because an accidental overlap of different recognition criteria leads everyone to the same result.

But this conclusion seems to me to get things nearly backward. Judges and Justices of the Supreme Court know that the tax code is law, that paper money is constitutional, and that the Constitution forbids race discrimination in the public schools more certainly than they know how to articulate the criteria on which these judgments rest.[53] Insofar as judges, Justices, and law professors attempt to describe or articulate the standards that underlie their common judgments, they may misstate even their own implicit standards: there is often a gap between propositional knowledge and tacit knowledge,[54] with the latter outstripping the former. In addition, those trying to articulate the bases for shared judgments may go further awry insofar as their efforts implicitly or explicitly attempt to resolve cases in which others would reasonably disagree with them.

The lesson to be drawn, I think, is that agreements in judgment about what would count as "going on" correctly in identifying and applying the law are more fundamental than constitutional theorizing. Rules of recognition in the Hartian sense can manifest themselves in tacit knowledge and convergent behavior,

---

51. *See, e.g.*, Dennis Patterson, *The Poverty of Interpretive Universalism: Toward the Reconstruction of Legal Theory*, 72 Tex. L. Rev. 1, 20–21 (1993).

52. *See id.*

53. *See, e.g.*, Michael McConnell, *Originalism and the Desegregation Decisions*, 81 Va. L. Rev. 947, 953 (1995) (asserting that a constitutional theory would be "seriously discredited" if it did not support the correctness of the Supreme Court's decision in *Brown v. Board of Education*).

54. *See generally* Gilbert Ryle, The Concept of Mind 27–32 (1949) (emphasizing the importance of the distinction between "knowing how" and "knowing that").

notwithstanding disagreement about their precise propositional content. As invocations of the Hartian idea of rules or practices of recognition signal—however clumsily, given some of the connotations of the word "rule"—widely shared tacit understandings always set limits concerning, and sometimes uniquely determine, what can be said to be the law.

Dworkin and Adler are of course familiar with arguments such as this, and they have a response. Although judges and Justices notoriously disagree with one another in hard cases such as those involving abortion and affirmative action, disputants on all sides typically maintain that the contested questions have one right answer. The shared insistence on the existence of one right answer is telling, Dworkin and Adler maintain, because the phenomenon of disagreement makes it plain that *shared* standards do not generate a uniquely correct result, and thus demonstrates that the disputants must be appealing to different criteria of legal validity. And if they are doing so, the argument concludes, their behavior falsifies the Hartian positivist claim that law is a system of rules rooted in shared recognition criteria.

This is plainly a formidable objection to Hartian positivism, but there are at least three possible answers. First, in implicitly or explicitly claiming that there is a single legally correct answer to abortion or affirmative action disputes, judges and Justices may simply be in error.[55] Shared recognition criteria may determine the results in other cases, but not in these. Error by large numbers of judges and Justices on so important a point should not be ascribed lightly, but the alternative may require the imputation of error on even a larger scale. On Adler's view, it may be a mistake to think that we have a single legal system at all, rather than a multiplicity of sometimes overlapping legal systems constituted by the recognition practices of diverse groups.[56]

A second possibility is that judges and Justices asserting that shared legal standards determine one right answer in hard cases are simply following conventions of legal practice that call for them to claim there is one right answer even when there is not.

A third possibility, which I find the most plausible, is that in hard cases that are not uniquely resolved by widely shared substantive understandings, a tacitly recognized default rule confers upon judges and Justices—acting within conventionally recognized bounds of the legally plausible—a power to make determinations of what would be legally "best" in a sense that depends partly on moral or policy judgments.[57] This account recognizes that law is inherently a social

55. *See* Brian Leiter, *Explaining Theoretical Disagreement*, 76 U. CHI. L. REV. (forthcoming 2009).

56. *See* Adler, *supra* note 36, at 749.

57. *See* Himma, *supra* note 20, at 178 (asserting that "the Justices are practicing a recognition norm that requires the Court to ground its validity decisions in the best interpretation of the Constitution").

phenomenon, which could not exist in the absence of shared recognition criteria adequate to resolve nearly all actual and potential cases; it has the virtue of positing the existence of a single legal system rather than making the rules of recognition that constitute a legal system vary from group to group or even person to person; it acknowledges reasonable disagreement in hard cases; and it explains why judges in hard cases would claim that there is one best or right answer even if they must make controversial moral or policy judgments in order to do so.

B. Identifying a Practice and Its Practitioners: Whose Acceptance Matters?

In explicating the idea of a rule or rules of recognition, Hart thought the relevant practices were those of law-applying officials, especially judges.[58] Any application of Hartian positivist theory to the United States would undoubtedly need to emphasize the central role of Supreme Court Justices. But that emphasis should not be exclusive—a point that can perhaps usefully be brought out by asking whether it follows from a practice-based account that the constitutional law of the United States is whatever the Justices say it is. In the view of some, perhaps many, this would be a nightmare sufficiently frightening to inspire a flight to originalism, which promises to bind the Justices to unchanging law.

Hart himself rebuffed the suggestion that the Constitution means whatever the Justices say it means in terms that seem still largely correct:

> At any given moment judges, even those of a supreme court, are parts of a system the rules of which are determinate enough at the centre to supply standards of correct judicial decision. These are regarded by the courts as something which they are not free to disregard in the exercise of the authority to make those decisions which cannot be challenged within the system. . . . The adherence of the judge is required to maintain the standards, but the judge does not make them.[59]

Despite my basic agreement, I would differ from Hart with respect to a point of emphasis and would introduce a further, supplemental note of explanation. With respect to emphasis, it should be made explicit—as I have now argued at length—that although Supreme Court Justices are bound by legal rules, the pertinent rules either have a broader area of open texture than Hart's formulation might suggest or vest the Justices with considerable responsibility for making

58. *See* HART, *supra* note 17, at 256 (stating that "the rule of recognition . . . is in effect a form of judicial customary rule existing only if it is accepted and practised in the law-identifying and law-applying operations of the courts"); *see also id.* at 116 (asserting that the "rules of recognition specifying the criteria of legal validity and [the legal system's] rules of change must be effectively accepted as common public standards of official behaviour by its officials"). By contrast, Hart said, "[t]he ordinary citizen manifests his acceptance largely by acquiescence." *Id.* at 61.

59. *Id.* at 145–46.

practical judgments of great moment. It matters enormously who sits on the Supreme Court, where legal rules bind, but shared understandings often fail to determine ultimate conclusions.

With respect to supplemental explanation, I would maintain that even if the Justices might otherwise be disposed to deviate from ultimate rules of recognition, they would be constrained to at least some extent by others' practices of recognition. Although I shall not attempt to give a full account of the diversity of actors who have roles in constituting and supporting our present constitutional regime, the Justices' practices are clearly nested among, and are almost necessarily sensitive to, a variety of legal and political practices involving nonjudicial officials and ultimately the concerned public.[60]

The claim that the Justices' practices are sensitive to the practices of nonjudicial officials is most straightforwardly an empirical and predictive claim, supported by strategic speculations. Supreme Court decisions can be efficacious only insofar as they are accepted as legally legitimate by other public officials without whose cooperation judicial decrees could not be enforced. Justices who care about the implementation of their rulings thus have a reason to regard other officials' potentially defiant reactions as a constraint on their decision making.[61] Also pertinent to understanding the role of the Supreme Court in applying and sometimes adapting ultimate rules of recognition is the Court's need to maintain the support, acceptance, or at least acquiescence of a broader public within a structure of government that creates multiple levers of influence on the Court's size, its composition, and its jurisdiction.[62] Under these circumstances, Supreme Court Justices who want to maintain the long-term efficacy of their own rulings must recognize dominant public sentiment—typically as manifested through elections and the political branches—as a constraint on their authority to shape constitutional law, at least with respect to matters of high public salience.[63]

In describing the Supreme Court as constrained, I have thus far spoken in an empirical or strategic vein, without explaining how the constraints to which the Court is subject relate to legal norms. The problem here seems to me to be a deep one, in ways that the Wittgensteinian notion of a rule helps to bring out though not ultimately to resolve. Looking at the Supreme Court's long-term pattern of decisions, I surmise that the Justices have internalized a norm dictating that the Court must conduct itself in ways the public will accept as minimally lawful and practically tolerable: to count as the best legal interpretation, an interpretation must normally be likely to be accepted as valid and to be enforced by at least a critical mass of the nonjudicial officials normally counted on to implement

60. *See* Himma, *supra* note 20, at 154.

61. *Id.*

62. *See* Jack Knight & Lee Epstein, *The Norm of Stare Decisis*, 40 Am. J. Pol. Sci. 1018, 1021 (1996).

63. *See, e.g.*, Lee Epstein & Jack Knight, The Choices Justices Make (1998).

judicial decisions. Relatedly, the Court must normally avoid interpretations that would trigger a strong and enduring sense of mass public outrage that the Court has overstepped its constitutional powers.

The Court, I must emphasize, has never stated explicitly that such a rule exists. Moreover, the one opinion of which I know in which the Court suggested that public attitudes toward the Court should influence it—*Planned Parenthood of Southeastern Pennsylvania v. Casey*,[64] in which it said that it must consider public sensibilities in determining whether to overrule its most iconic precedents[65]—drew outraged protests from both commentators[66] and dissenting Justices.[67] Nevertheless, it is easy to point to cases, tracing as far back as *Marbury v. Madison*,[68] in which the Court has adhered to a rule (in the Wittgensteinian sense) of prudential avoidance of decisions likely to provoke executive branch defiance that would be backed by public opinion. Although *Marbury* spoke assertively of broad judicial power, Chief Justice Marshall's opinion in fact reached a result crafted to avoid a political showdown that the Court could not have won.[69] Since *Marbury*, the Court has exhibited a recurrent strand of prudential decision making in which it has seldom entered rulings that it could not expect federal officials, centrally including the President, to obey.[70] Although I cannot hope to capture the Court's complex practice in a propositional form that all would accept, it is both suggestive and important that the Justices' sense of how to "go on" in constitutional practice has seldom provoked sustained outrage by popular majorities or defiance by high officials.

Positing an internal connection between the rules of recognition applied by the Supreme Court and public practices of recognition of judicial decisions as constitutionally legitimate helps to explain why—as I have emphasized—it is virtually unimaginable that the Justices could ever renounce long-settled precedents around which public support and entrenched expectations have developed. A Supreme Court that held that paper money and Social Security were unconstitutional, that *Brown v. Board of Education* was wrongly decided, or that states need not adhere to one-person, one-vote principles would be rightly denounced

---

64. 505 U.S. 833 (1992).

65. *Id.* at 867.

66. *See, e.g.*, Michael Stokes Paulsen, *The Worst Constitutional Decision of All Time*, 78 NOTRE DAME L. REV. 995, 1031–38 (2003).

67. *See Casey*, 505 U.S. at 996–1001 (Scalia, J., concurring in the judgment in part and dissenting in part).

68. 5 U.S. (1 Cranch) 137 (1803).

69. *See, e.g.*, Richard H. Fallon, Jr., Marbury *and the Constitutional Mind: A Bicentennial Essay on the Wages of Doctrinal Tension*, 91 CAL. L. REV. 1, 16–20 (2003); *see also* BRUCE ACKERMAN, THE FAILURE OF THE FOUNDING FATHERS: JEFFERSON, MARSHALL, AND THE RISE OF PRESIDENTIAL DEMOCRACY 182–86 (2005) (discussing the political circumstances motivating the Court's opinion in *Marbury*).

70. *See, e.g.*, Fallon, *supra* note 69, at 16–20, 27–33.

by the public as committing grave constitutional errors—even if the Court could demonstrate compellingly that its rulings correctly reflected the original understanding. The gravamen of the complaint against the Court—which, again, is one that the Court is nearly certain never to trigger—would be that the Constitution that is the fundamental law of the United States is not an exclusively originalist one. Rather, it is a Constitution under which the Court can and sometimes must accept settled precedent around which strong reliance interests and settled expectations have developed. If the Justices were suddenly to abandon the long-accepted rules of recognition that validate some nonoriginalist precedents as legally authoritative, they would not be following the law, but attempting a political and jurisprudential revolution. There is reason to doubt whether the Court could get away with it.

IV. THE CRITICS' OBJECTION RESTATED—AND RE-ANSWERED

In response to my jurisprudential claims that the Constitution necessarily draws its meaning from the interpretive practices in which it is situated, and that what is accepted and enjoys the status of law in the United States today is a Constitution capable of being interpreted in light of judicial precedent, originalists might attempt either of two jurisprudential counterarguments. The first would merely apply a jurisprudential label to, and supply a historical pedigree for, the assumption that the original understanding of the words adopted by the Constitution's Framers and ratifiers fixes their meaning irrevocably. According to the "command" theory of law articulated by John Austin, the commands of the sovereign define the law.[71] Invoking this theory, originalists might say that in the case of the United States Constitution, the Framers and ratifiers are the relevant sovereign whose commands (as originally understood) therefore establish the Constitution's enduring meaning.[72] As H. L. A. Hart demonstrated, however, the command theory of law is a bankrupt jurisprudential theory. The commands of a would-be sovereign can count as law only insofar as they are accepted as such as a matter of sociological fact.

A second jurisprudential counterargument would be more subtle. Embracing Ronald Dworkin's claim that theories of law are necessarily "interpretive,"[73] it would concede that the foundations of law lie in the social facts of contemporary practice, but would claim that originalism offers the "best" account—as measured

71. *See* John Austin, *The Province of Jurisprudence Determined*, *in* JOHN AUSTIN, THE PROVINCE OF JURISPRUDENCE DETERMINED AND THE USES OF THE STUDY OF JURISPRUDENCE 13–14 (H.L.A. Hart ed., 1954) (1832).

72. *See id.*

73. *See, e.g.*, DWORKIN, LAW'S EMPIRE, *supra* note 18, at 87 (arguing that "[l]aw is an interpretive concept" and that disagreements among judges are "interpretive" disagreements).

by criteria of "fit" and normative attractiveness—of the interpretive approach that the norms of our current practice require.[74] An originalist who adopted this defense would begin by emphasizing that existing practice has an indisputable originalist strand, with many cases decided in accordance with the original understanding. An originalist who accepted Dworkin's interpretive theory of jurisprudence would then need to acknowledge that our current practice also includes nonoriginalist elements, but would insist that the best interpretation of our practice would characterize precedents claiming judicial authority to adhere to nonoriginalist decisions as "mistakes."[75]

Although surely imaginable, this purported "interpretation" of our existing practice seems to me to fail with respect to both of Dworkin's criteria of "fit" and normative desirability. I shall briefly discuss normative arguments in favor of originalism, and indicate why I think those arguments unpersuasive, below. With respect to fit, examples that I have cited already should suffice to show that too many strands of nonoriginalist decision making are too deeply entrenched in our existing constitutional practice for any theory that dismissed them as mere mistakes to qualify as a genuine interpretation of that practice, rather than a proposal for its reform.

V. PRACTICE WITHIN PRACTICES AND THE PHENOMENON OF METARULES

Despite originalism's implicit jurisprudential mistake in failing to acknowledge that the foundations of law lie in current practices of acceptance, originalists are right about one important point, which not only is crucial in understanding how our constitutional practice works, but also may require some loosening (which is not to say the abandonment) of the basic Hartian picture of a legal system. Many originalists shrewdly grasp, at least intuitively, that our existing practices of constitutional adjudication and argument have multiple facets or levels. Those practices are, moreover, reflexive and fluid: they permit and even invite arguments about what *ought* to count as good first-order constitutional arguments. Accordingly, within the practices by which American constitutional law is defined and in which it is embedded, no sharp boundary divides rules of adjudication from rules of legal change. Even the norms that constitute and the patterns of behavior that mark the rule of recognition can change, partly in response to second-order arguments about what the criteria of legal validity ought to be.

Exploiting the potential fluidity of current understandings, at least some originalist claims can be interpreted not as assertions about what current law requires, but as calls for now-prevailing rules of recognition to be changed for

74. *See id.* at 229–32.

75. *Cf.* Dworkin, Taking Rights Seriously, *supra* note 42, at 118–23 (discussing the need for legal theories to dismiss some past decisions as "mistakes").

the future so that interpretations supported by the original understanding of constitutional language would always prevail. What is more, originalists' arguments for adopting exclusively originalist rules of recognition require consideration and response (within broadly shared tacit understandings of the bounds of legitimate constitutional debate) in a way that an argument for interpreting the Constitution to accord with the teachings of, say, Plato, Hobbes, or Lenin would not.

To frame the point specifically in terms of the legal status of nonoriginalist precedent, those who argue for a rejection of the current doctrine of constitutional stare decisis advance a reform agenda, but one that can be supported by colorable arguments within the second-order rules or shared tacit understandings of our complex, multilayered constitutional practices. Second-generation originalist Randy Barnett seems to recognize as much when he laments that most judges and justices are not originalists[76] but then goes on to say that the goal of originalists should be to "achiev[e] a change in the law, however gradual."[77]

Assuming the burden of expressly normative argument, Barnett maintains that only through the adoption of an originalist rule of recognition could we get a "legitimate" Constitution, by which he means one that would deserve adherence.[78] According to him, a legal regime is legitimate only if it includes sufficient guarantees to ensure that the coercive exercise of governmental authority violates no one's rights.[79] Barnett believes that the written Constitution of the United States, as originally understood, satisfies this demand (as a result of the addition of provisions such as the Fourteenth Amendment that corrected earlier deficiencies). He further contends that the current legitimacy of an originally just Constitution requires that its meaning be entrenched against change through official interpretation.

Although I agree with Barnett that we have a Constitution that is "legitimate" in the moral sense,[80] my criteria for the ascription of legitimacy are less stringent than his. For me, it suffices that our imperfect Constitution passes a minimal threshold of justice and that unlawful deviations from it are unlikely to conduce to agreement on a better alternative. I also differ from Barnett in my conclusion that the moral attractiveness of our written Constitution, most of which was adopted in the eighteenth century, depends heavily on its adaptability under currently prevailing rules of recognition. It would not be a morally attractive

---

76. *See* Randy E. Barnett, *Scalia's Infidelity: A Critique of "Faint-Hearted" Originalism*, 75 U. CIN. L. REV. 7, 13–15 (2006).

77. Barnett, *Super Precedent*, *supra* note 10, at 1247.

78. *See* Barnett, *supra* note 76, at 16–19.

79. For a full statement of his views, see RANDY E. BARNETT, RESTORING THE LOST CONSTITUTION: THE PRESUMPTION OF LIBERTY (2004).

80. *See* Richard H. Fallon, Jr., *Legitimacy and the Constitution*, 118 HARV. L. REV. 1787, 1809–13 (2005).

Constitution if it dictated, for example, that paper money was unlawful and therefore worthless, that Social Security was unconstitutional, that voting need not occur on a one-person, one-vote basis, and so forth—or even if it made the constitutional status of such institutions and decisions depend on the uncertain outcomes of ongoing historical investigations. Among other things, to make constitutional validity turn entirely on historical research—in a context in which the Constitution is so hard to amend formally—would create enormous pressure for the Supreme Court to engage in less than candid analysis in order to guarantee publicly acceptable outcomes. I can think of no good reason to demand that the Justices cast themselves as historians and then create powerful incentives for them to falsify the historical record.[81]

I must acknowledge, however, that I am not entirely sanguine about relying on our Constitution's adaptability as a consideration important to its moral legitimacy. A more perfect constitution would probably occasion less need for judicial adaptation and could, accordingly, give judges and Justices less authority to change the fundamental law. My qualified defense of our current legal regime thus rests heavily on a Burkean sense that we are wiser to continue with the very old Constitution that we have—which has required adaptive interpretation to be workable and morally attractive—than to accept the hazards of attempting to design, reach agreement on, and implement a better constitution under current circumstances.

Although there is admittedly much more to be said in response to originalists' normative arguments, I shall go no further here, for the claims that I want most to establish in this chapter are far more empirical and analytical than they are normative. Most important for present purposes, I mean to be making an empirical claim, not a normative one, when I assert that our constitutional practice not only encompasses, but actually invites, second-order arguments about what the rules of recognition ought to be. I mean to make a similarly empirical claim when I say, further, that our current rules of recognition tolerate some judicial adaptations of the fundamental law, including ultimate rules of recognition.[82]

If I am correct on this point, the power that American law confers on judges and Justices seems to me to be quite startling. Within Hart's jurisprudential framework, it would of course always be the case that the rule of recognition

---

81. *See generally* David A. Strauss, *Originalism, Precedent, and Candor*, 22 CONST. COMMENT. 299 (2005) (arguing in favor of interpretive methodologies that encourage candor); David L. Shapiro, *In Defense of Judicial Candor*, 100 HARV. L. REV. 731 (1987) (asserting a judicial obligation of candid legal analysis).

82. A fully adequate conceptual account would need to root ultimate power-conferring rules authorizing legal change as much as ultimate rules of recognition in customary practice, with both existing among the same group. *See* Stephen J. Perry, *Hart on Social Rules and the Rule of Recognition: Liberating the Internal Point of View*, 75 FORDHAM L. REV. 1171, 1188–89 (2006).

would change if the recognition practices of relevant officials changed, irrespective of issues of legal authorization. But in the United States, I am suggesting, changes in ultimate rules of recognition may—in some cases—be less extralegally revolutionary than lawfully evolutionary.

If this claim is accurate, it has important implications concerning the legal status of nonoriginalist precedents. In thinking about the Supreme Court's power and sometime obligation to adhere to initially erroneous constitutional rulings, we need to acknowledge the contingency of the foundations on which current law and practices of recognition rest. Today it is unthinkable that paper money could be unconstitutional. But in a possible future world in which all financial transactions occurred via wireless networks, a declaration that greenbacks are unconstitutional might not be impossible. If a future government succeeded in creating a strong enough system of individual retirement accounts, it is not unimaginable that at some point a court might knock the last legs from under the Social Security system by ruling it constitutionally invalid. And if skin color ever came to seem as socially irrelevant as eye color, then the judicial validation of the 1964 Civil Rights Act might come to be seen as a legal mistake explainable only by the social pressures of the 1960s.

It is imaginable, of course, that changes such as these might only alter the status of certain precedents under criteria of legal validity that themselves remained unaltered. But the relevant contingencies run deeper. In a future world in which originalist methodology ceased to generate practically or morally untenable conclusions, originalism might take root and flourish. Or changed circumstances, currently unforeseeable, might provoke other adaptations in interpretive practice that are currently unthinkable. However stable current rules of recognition may appear to be, any sound theory of precedent in constitutional adjudication must acknowledge the inescapable possibility of change.

The image of an American legal system that incorporates debates about whether the rule of recognition should change into the very practices that define the rule of recognition is not inconsistent with Hartian legal positivism. Neither, however, is it the image that would spring most naturally into the mind of a casual reader of *The Concept of Law*.

3. HOW THE WRITTEN CONSTITUTION CROWDS OUT THE EXTRACONSTITUTIONAL RULE OF RECOGNITION

MICHAEL C. DORF*

I. INTRODUCTION

In the Postscript to *The Concept of Law*, H. L. A. Hart explains that the rule of recognition (RoR) "is in effect a form of judicial customary rule existing only if it is accepted and practiced in the law-identifying and law-applying operations of the courts."[1] Yet many scholars read the main text of *The Concept of Law*[2] to imply that the practices of government officials generally, and not only judges, comprise the rule of recognition.[3] Matthew Adler uses this ambiguity in Hart's theory to shed light on an important question in contemporary American constitutional theory: To what extent do and should the constitutional views of judges, elected officials, and the People themselves establish constitutional meaning?

---

* Robert S. Stevens Professor of Law, Cornell University Law School. For helpful suggestions, comments, and questions, I am very grateful to the organizers of and participants in the conference out of which this book grew, as well as to Sherry Colb, Trevor Morrison, Joseph Raz, Elizabeth Scott, Robert Scott, Emily Sherwin, and Jane Stapleton. Jordan Connors and Jessica Karp provided excellent research assistance.

1. H.L.A. Hart, The Concept of Law 256 (Penelope A. Bulloch & Joseph Raz eds., 2d ed. 1994).

2. *See id.* at 152.

3. *See* Matthew D. Adler, *Popular Constitutionalism and the Rule of Recognition: Whose Practices Ground U.S. Law?* 100 Nw. U. L. Rev. 719, 731–32 (2006) ("[Hart] is most straightforwardly read (and has generally been read by Hart interpreters) to say that this rule [of recognition] supervenes on official practice, nonjudicial as well as judicial."); *see also* Leslie Green, *The Concept of Law Revisited*, 94 Mich. L. Rev. 1687, 1700–02 (1996) (defining Hart's recognitional community as "elites"); Kenneth Einar Himma, *Making Sense of Constitutional Disagreement: Legal Positivism, The Bill of Rights, and the Conventional Rule of Recognition in the United States*, 4 J.L. & Soc'y 149, 152–56 (2003) ("It is important to realize that judicial officials are not the only participants whose behavior and attitudes figure into determining the existence and content of the rule of recognition."); Michael Steven Green, *Does Dworkin Commit Dworkin's Fallacy?: A Reply to Justices in Robes*, 28 Oxford J. Legal Stud. 33, 34 (2008) ("In H.L.A. Hart's theory . . . [s]omething is the law of a jurisdiction if it satisfies the criteria that the jurisdiction's officials (judges, legislators, sheriffs and the like) have accepted for enforcing norms."); Jeremy Waldron, *All We Like Sheep*, 12 Can. J.L. & Jurisprudence 180 (1999) (defining a recognitional community to include "legislators, judges, senior bureaucrats, etc.").

The answer, no doubt, is complex. For purposes of this chapter, however, I will accept that, in cases of conflict, judicial practices and interpretations prevail over the practices of other actors. That view finds strong support in both the pronouncements of the United States Supreme Court and the conduct of elected officials and private parties who, however reluctantly, accept the supremacy of Supreme Court interpretation in contested cases.[4]

Yet even if, as a descriptive matter, we accept at least this relatively weak form of judicial supremacy, we are left with puzzles about the RoR on matters that present no justiciable case or controversy, or as to which the judicially enforceable constitutional rule leaves the political branches substantial freedom of movement. Consider two illustrative questions: (1) Can the President be impeached and removed from office based upon "mere" policy disagreements between Congress and the President? (2) Can a Congress in which the President's party has a working majority in each house increase the size of the Supreme Court so as to allow the President to pack the Court with Justices in ideological sympathy with that party?

Although the issues are not entirely free of doubt, the courts probably would not interfere with such actions by Congress. As to question one, so long as Congress did not specifically *admit* that policy disagreements formed the basis for its action,[5] the outcome of impeachment proceedings in the House and Senate could not be appealed to the courts, because it would be deemed a nonjusticiable political question.[6] As to question two, the essentially unquestioned

---

4. Andrew Jackson is reported to have said, in response to the Supreme Court's ruling in *Worcester v. Georgia*, 31 U.S. (6 Pet.) 515 (1832), that "John Marshall has made his decision[;] now let him enforce it." JEAN EDWARD SMITH, JOHN MARSHALL: DEFINER OF A NATION 518 (1996) (suggesting the report is apocryphal). But in the most dramatic showdown in modern times, President Nixon accepted the Court's ruling in *United States v. Nixon*, 418 U.S. 683 (1974), which rejected his claim of executive privilege in documents and taped conversations. *See White House Statement on Complying with Decision*, N.Y. TIMES, July 25, 1974, at A20 ("While I am, of course, disappointed in the result, I respect and accept the Court's decision [in *United States v. Nixon*] and I have instructed [my chief counsel] to take whatever measures are necessary to comply with that decision in all respects." (quoting President Nixon)). Likewise, Vice President Al Gore, acting in his capacity as a Presidential candidate, strongly disagreed with the Supreme Court's ruling in *Bush v. Gore*, 531 U.S. 98 (2000), but accepted its authority. *See* Richard L. Berke & Katharine Q. Seelye, *Bush Pledges to be President for 'One Nation,' Not One Party; Gore, Conceding, Urges Unity*, N.Y. TIMES, Dec. 14, 2000, at A1 ("[T]he United States Supreme Court has spoken . . . Let there be no doubt. While I strongly disagree with the court's decision, I accept it." (quoting Al Gore)).

5. *Cf.* Powell v. McCormack, 395 U.S. 486, 549 (1969) (treating as a justiciable question whether a House member was entitled to his seat in Congress where the House admitted that he had the requisite qualifications under Article I).

6. *See* Nixon v. United States, 506 U.S. 224, 224 (1993) (finding that "[t]he language and structure of Art. I, § 3, cl. 6, demonstrate a textual commitment of impeachment to the Senate" and that therefore a challenge to the procedures used in impeachment is nonjusticiable).

acceptance of increases in the size of the Supreme Court during the nineteenth century[7] makes it extremely improbable that the Justices would invalidate a contemporary Court-packing plan, even if they found the issue justiciable. Indeed, in the one case in which the Justices ruled on the substantive validity of court reorganization, the Marshall Court acquiesced in a law eliminating lower federal court judgeships.[8]

In any event, because I use these examples merely to illustrate, I shall assume in the balance of this chapter that I have correctly predicted the judicial outcomes: (1) Congress can get away with impeaching and removing the President based on policy disagreements, because such an action does not give rise to a justiciable case or controversy; and (2) Congress can get away with packing the Supreme Court because doing so does not violate the Constitution, as it has come to be understood.

How should we characterize the *de facto* freedom given to Congress by the courts' (presumed) noninterference in these two examples? If Congress equates the Constitution with the judicially enforceable Constitution and regards the RoR as dependent solely on the practices of the courts (as per Hart's Postscript), then it will consider itself free to engage in policy-based impeachment and Court packing, limited only by prudential concerns. However, if Congress regards its own practices—where they do not conflict with any judicially enforced limits—as constitutionally obligatory and/or constitutive of the RoR, then it may have additional reasons of principle to refrain from policy-based impeachment and Court packing.

Consider the Clinton impeachment. In both the House and the Senate, arguments about whether President Clinton should be impeached and removed from office focused on whether his conduct amounted to one of the "other high crimes and misdemeanors"[9] (besides treason and bribery) for which impeachment and removal are permitted.[10] Admittedly, the ultimate vote closely tracked

---

7. *See* RICHARD H. FALLON, JR., ET AL., HART AND WECHSLER'S THE FEDERAL COURTS AND THE FEDERAL SYSTEM 35 (5th ed. 2003) (cataloging early changes in the size of the Court); Peter Nicolas, *"Nine of Course": A Dialogue on Congressional Power to Set by Statute the Number of Justices on the Supreme Court*, 2 N.Y.U. J. L. & LIB. 86, 89–90 n.10 (2006) (listing nineteenth-century laws that changed the number of Justices).

8. *See* Stuart v. Laird, 5 U.S. 299, 309 (1803) (upholding the repeal of the Judiciary Act and resulting elimination of federal judgeships); *see also* Michael W. McConnell, *The Story of* Marbury v. Madison: *Making Defeat Look Like Victory, in* CONSTITUTIONAL LAW STORIES 26, 31 (Michael Dorf ed., 2004).

9. U.S. CONST. art. II, § 4.

10. *See, e.g.*, 145 CONG. REC. S1105–1106 (1999) (statement of Sen. Cleland) (explaining his vote to dismiss impeachment on grounds that the President's conduct did not rise to the level of high crimes and misdemeanors); 144 CONG. REC. H11785 (1998) (statement of Rep. Schumer) ("[L]ying about an extramarital affair, even under oath, does not rise to the level of high crimes and misdemeanors as spelled out in the Constitution."); *id.* at H11796 (statement of Rep. Tom Campbell) (arguing that lying under oath "rises to the level of high crimes and misdemeanors").

party lines,[11] but that may only show that in politics, as in other realms, human beings suffer from confirmation bias.[12] It is not very plausible to suppose that the Republicans who sought to impeach President Clinton based on his testimony about the Lewinsky affair were thereby hoping to change any White House policy or were motivated by a desire to make Al Gore the President, as incumbency would have likely conferred advantages on Gore in the 2000 election. Nor is it plausible to suppose that they or the Democrats regarded their respective constitutional arguments as mere makeweights.[13] No one thought to impeach Clinton or any other President based on an offense—such as jaywalking—that could not remotely be described as a high crime or misdemeanor.[14] Then-Congressman Gerald Ford was wrong when he stated that an impeachable offense is whatever a majority of Congress says is an impeachable offense[15]—or if Ford was right, it was because a majority of Congress would never say that jaywalking is an impeachable offense.

To acknowledge that the Constitution can impose constraints on Congress and other political actors even in circumstances that give rise to no justiciable case or controversy is to believe in the possibility of what is sometimes called "the Constitution outside the courts."[16] We have good reasons to be interested in the question of whether to characterize our lawmaking system as one in which there is a substantial role for the Constitution outside the courts.

---

11. *See* Alison Mitchell, *Clinton Acquitted Decisively: No Majority for Either Charge*, N.Y. TIMES, Feb. 13, 1999, at A1 (displaying a chart of party-line impeachment vote, with no Democrats voting guilty).

12. *See* Albert H. Hastorf & Hadley Cantril, *They Saw a Game: A Case Study*, 49 J. ABNORMAL & SOC. PSYCHOL. 129 (1954) (describing a now-classic study in which partisans of Princeton and Dartmouth viewed the officiating of a football game differently depending on school allegiance).

13. *But see* Michael J. Klarman, *Constitutional Fetishism and the Clinton Impeachment Debate*, 85 VA. L. REV. 631, 655 (1999) (arguing that in the Clinton impeachment debate, "[c]onstitutional argument [was] principally a form of rhetoric deployed to enhance the status of those political values").

14. *Cf. id.* (recognizing that even in an extrajudicial setting, the Constitution is not indeterminate, and providing as an example the fact that in the Clinton impeachment, "both sides adhered to the explicit textual requirement that Senate conviction be by two-thirds majority").

15. *See* GEOFFREY STONE ET AL., CONSTITUTIONAL LAW 415–16 (5th ed. 2005) (quoting Ford's statement that "[a]n impeachable offense is whatever a majority of the House of Representatives considers it to be at a given moment in history").

16. *See, e.g.*, James E. Fleming, *Judicial Review Without Judicial Supremacy: Taking the Constitution Seriously Outside the Courts*, 73 FORDHAM L. REV. 1377 (2005) (reviewing some of the scholarship on the "Constitution outside the courts"); LARRY KRAMER, THE PEOPLE THEMSELVES: POPULAR CONSTITUTIONALISM AND JUDICIAL REVIEW (2004) (arguing that "the people" have a responsibility to interpret and enforce the Constitution); MARK TUSHNET, TAKING THE CONSTITUTION AWAY FROM THE COURTS 54–71 (1999).

We also might be interested in a related question, however: To what extent is our system one in which there is a substantial role for the RoR outside the courts? That is the question raised by Hart's language in the Postscript, which indicates that Hart himself came to think that there is no substantial extrajudicial role for the RoR[17]—but it is entirely possible that he misunderstood his own theory in so thinking.

If the RoR in the United States simply were the Constitution, then our answer to the Constitution-outside-the-courts question would dictate our answer to the RoR-outside-the-courts question. However, as Kent Greenawalt argues persuasively, the relation between various parts of the Constitution and the RoR is complex.[18] If one takes a certain austere view of the RoR, most provisions of the Constitution form no part of it. On such a view, the Amendment Clause of Article V and perhaps the Ratification Clause of Article VII are the only parts of the Constitution that are themselves part of the RoR in the United States. They are only *part* of the RoR, however, because one must look outside the Constitution itself for the rules and standards governing how amendments are recognized as having satisfied the criteria of Article V,[19] for the authority of state law, and for the authority of judicial precedents, among other things.

Admittedly, the austere view is not necessarily the best view. One might think that the original Constitution's Ratification Clause is no longer part of the RoR and that provisions of the Constitution that were enacted long ago no longer derive their authority from either the Ratification Clause or the Amendment Clause but directly from their acceptance by government officials[20]—although this view then reopens the crucial question of *which* government officials. Sorting out the precise relation between various bits of the Constitution and the RoR is thus a tricky business. We are therefore justified in thinking that answers to the questions of whether, and if so, to what extent, the Constitution operates outside the courts, do not fully answer the questions of whether, and if so, to what extent, the RoR operates outside the courts.

---

17. *See supra* note 1 and accompanying text.

18. *See* Kent Greenawalt, *The Rule of Recognition and the Constitution*, 85 MICH. L. REV. 621 (1987) (reprinted as Chapter 1, this volume).

19. *See* Coleman v. Miller, 307 U.S. 433, 450 (1939) (stating that "the efficacy of ratifications [of Constitutional Amendments] by state legislatures . . . should be regarded as a political question").

20. *See* Greenawalt, *supra* note 18, at 637–40 (arguing that "the legal authority of . . . the original Constitution is established by its continued acceptance and . . . the original ratification procedure is no longer directly relevant to tracing what counts as law") (reprinted as Chapter 1, this volume, at 16–19); Ernest Young, *The Constitution Outside the Constitution*, 117 YALE L.J. 408, 420–22 (2007) (arguing that "[t]he authority of [the Reconstruction] amendments . . . must stem from some combination of traditional acceptance and current agreement with the values they embody" rather than from compliance with Article V).

One might wonder, nonetheless, why we care about the RoR outside the courts (or, for that matter, inside the courts). Hart's theory, though influential among scholars and students of jurisprudence, is not law. Once we have determined the scope, if any, of the Constitution outside the courts, what practical difference could it make what conclusion we draw about the scope, if any, of the RoR outside the courts?

We can see the practical significance of the RoR-outside-the-courts issue by focusing on my question 2: Can Congress and the President pack the Supreme Court? As I explore in greater detail below, we have excellent textual and historical reasons to think that the Constitution poses no obstacle, justiciable or nonjusticiable, to Court packing. Nonetheless, we have very good reasons to think that Court packing is something that Congress and the President *just cannot do.* In other words, Court packing would violate a customary rule observed by Congress and the President. If the practices of government officials other than judges can contribute to the RoR, then the rule against Court packing is part of the RoR but not the Constitution.

To be clear, the crucial question here is not what we say about the RoR, or what Hart thought, or should have thought, but how we understand the system of government in the United States. To recognize that there are portions of the RoR that arise solely out of the practices of nonjudicial actors, and that are not part of the written Constitution, is to see past the blinders that the American love affair with our Constitution has placed upon us. It is to see that in addition to having a written Constitution, the United States also has a small-c "unwritten" constitution of the sort that figures in traditional accounts of the English constitution.[21] For clarity (if not felicity of language), I shall refer to the latter as the extraconstitutional Rule of Recognition ("eCRoR").

---

21. The canonical text is A.V. DICEY, INTRODUCTION TO THE STUDY OF THE LAW OF THE CONSTITUTION (8th ed. 1915). I use quotation marks around "unwritten" to alert the reader to two possible confusions. First, I do not mean here to enter the debate about whether, in interpreting the written Constitution, judges should rely upon values outside the document's text. *See* Thomas C. Grey, *Do We Have an Unwritten Constitution?*, 27 STAN. L. REV. 703 (1975) (arguing that they do and should). Second, I acknowledge that provisions of what I mean by the "unwritten" constitution may in fact be written down. *Cf.* Young, *supra* note 20, at 415 ("the overwhelming bulk of the 'constitution outside the Constitution' is, in fact, written down in statutes and regulations."). For example, the customary rule against Court packing is at least partly embodied in the statute currently fixing the number of Justices at nine. 28 U.S.C. § 1 (2000). Ernest Young accordingly prefers the term "extracanonical" to refer to provisions of the small-c constitution, but I shall use a distinct term to avoid the impression that Young and I are talking about the exact same set of norms. Although our projects are related, his extracanonical constitution necessarily includes much that I would regard as ordinary law, for Young is interested in identifying those extracanonical materials that play a role in constituting institutions of our government, even when they are not entrenched against amendment by ordinary democratic means. *See* Young, *supra*, at 413; *infra* text accompanying notes 88–90.

We can then inquire into the effect on the eCRoR of having a written Constitution. This effect, I argue later in this chapter, is substantial and not wholly benign. The written Constitution, I contend, can "crowd out" the eCRoR. Because of the widespread but mistaken belief that the Constitution alone grounds legal authority, political actors feel the need to search for a constitutional hook for arguments that customary rules should be obeyed.

The search for such hooks has two lamentable consequences. First, for some customary rules, there is no readily available hook, and as a consequence, political actors may be tempted to violate them. The rule against Court packing is a good example. President Roosevelt was emboldened to attempt his Court packing plan because he could make an excellent argument that it breached no constitutional barrier. Although a Congress controlled by his own party, to its credit, rejected the plan, there is at least a plausible story to be told in which the plan succeeded in inducing the "switch in time" in the meantime.[22] Periodically, other Presidents and members of Congress have attempted to interfere with judicial independence via means that violate no constitutional rule but arguably violate the eCRoR,[23] and these efforts can have similar *in terrorem* effects.

The written Constitution's crowding out of the eCRoR has another negative effect: Even when there is a textual hook for some customary rule, the hook may not be a perfect one, but its very existence induces defenders of the customary rule to invoke the hook rather than the custom. The debate over habeas corpus is illustrative. *Ex Parte Bollman* established that the federal courts only have jurisdiction to grant writs of habeas corpus if that jurisdiction is granted by Congress[24] (which is a plausible reading of the Madisonian compromise and the limited original jurisdiction of the Supreme Court), while *Tarble's Case* held that state courts cannot grant writs of habeas corpus against federal officers[25] (which is a plausible reading of the Supremacy Clause). Taken together, these precedents appear to

---

22. *See, e.g.*, William E. Leuchtenburg, The Supreme Court Reborn 132–62 (1995) (describing the Court-packing plan and congressional, judicial, and popular reactions); Robert L. Stern, *The Commerce Clause and the National Economy, 1933–1946*, 59 Harv. L. Rev. 645, 677–82 (1946) (arguing that the Court-packing plan "undoubtedly played a vital role" in inducing Justices to stop striking down New Deal measures); *see also* Barry Cushman, *Rethinking the New Deal Court*, 80 Va. L. Rev. 201, 201 n.1 (1994) (collecting sources attributing the "switch in time" to the Court-packing plan). *But see id.* at 208–28 (arguing that the Court-packing plan "is unlikely to have been the proximate cause of the Constitutional Revolution of 1937").

23. *See, e.g.*, Linda Greenhouse, *Judges as Political Issues*, N.Y. Times, Mar. 23, 1996, at A1 (reporting the Clinton Administration's threat to seek resignation of a judge after an unpopular search-and-seizure opinion); Neil A. Lewis, *Impeach Those Liberal Judges! Where Are They?*, N.Y. Times, May 18, 1997, at E5 (quoting Rep. Tom DeLay's suggestion that judges be impeached for "usurping the legislative function").

24. 8 U.S. (4 Cranch) 75, 83 (1807).

25. 80 U.S. (13 Wall.) 397, 409 (1871).

leave the decision whether to make habeas available to persons held by the federal executive entirely within the hands of Congress—even if Congress does not suspend the writ according to the terms of Article I, Section 9. Thus, before the Supreme Court's decision in *Boumediene v. Bush*,[26] it was plausible to argue (at least if one disregarded *INS v. St. Cyr*[27]) that, as Attorney General Gonzales testified to the Senate Judiciary Committee in January 2007, the Constitution contains no right to habeas corpus.[28] Plausible, that is, as a matter of interpretation of the written Constitution, but implausible as a matter of interpreting the customary rule that absent special circumstances such as the exigencies of battle, habeas must generally be available to test the legality of executive detention.

My claim that the existence of the written Constitution crowds out arguments rooted in the customs of nonjudicial government officials is an empirical claim. This chapter offers support for the existence of the phenomenon, but undertakes nothing like what would be needed to measure its full scope. Nor does the chapter examine whether the phenomenon occurs in other legal systems with written constitutions. For my present purposes, it shall suffice to call attention to the existence and to some of the consequences of crowding out in the United States. Accordingly, this chapter should be understood as attempting to raise consciousness.

The balance of this chapter proceeds in three sections. Section II is the heart of the chapter. It introduces the concept of crowding out in other contexts and then provides three principal examples of constitutional crowding out of the eCRoR, involving Court packing, jurisdictional gerrymandering, and the right to vote in Presidential elections. Section III explores practical, normative, and theoretical questions: Within Hart's framework, can we develop workable standards for identifying customary rules of recognition, and should we even try? Finally, Section IV concludes by calling attention to an earlier effort along these lines by Karl Llewellyn, asking whether my formulation of the issue has a chance of succeeding where his largely failed.

II. CONSTITUTIONAL "CROWDING OUT"

Behavioral scientists have shown how a formal system of external rewards and punishments can diminish intrinsic motivation to follow social norms. Formal

---

26. 128 S. Ct. 2229 (2008).

27. 533 U.S. 289, 301 (2001) ("[A]t the absolute minimum, the Suspension Clause protects the writ [of habeas] 'as it existed in 1789.'" (quoting Felker v. Turpin, 518 U.S. 651, 663–64 (1996))).

28. *Department of Justice Oversight: Hearing Before the Sen. Committee on the Judiciary*, 110th Cong. 52 (2007) (statement of Attorney General Alberto Gonzales) ("[T]he Constitution does not say every individual in the United States or every citizen is hereby granted or assured the right to habeas.").

incentives motivate people to act while they remain available, but they displace, or "crowd out," social norms.[29] A person who would otherwise feel obliged to honor a contract will feel less bound to do so if the contract contains material incentive provisions.[30] This phenomenon of crowding out has led some legal scholars to caution that formalization of legal norms may be less effective than expected, or even counterproductive, as it displaces social norms that would otherwise operate.[31]

The crowding-out literature thus suggests that critics of judicial review are right to worry that judicial enforcement of the Constitution reduces the likelihood that legislators will respect those aspects of the Constitution that are not judicially enforced. Judicial invalidation of legislation may come to be seen as a cost of doing business for legislators; if the cost is high enough, legislators will not enact laws they believe the courts will invalidate, but unconstitutionality as such will come to be less of a concern for the legislature.

We can also expect judicial enforcement of the written Constitution to crowd out the eCRoR. Because external sanction in the form of judicial invalidation only occurs for violations of the justiciable portions of the Constitution, crowding-out theory tells us that political actors will lose their motivation to comply with nonjusticiable portions of the Constitution as well as the eCRoR, which is also not subject to judicial enforcement.

Indeed, to the extent that the written Constitution itself—quite apart from its judicial enforcement—can be seen as a formalization of norms, it may crowd out

---

29. *See, e.g.*, Edward L. Deci, *Effects of Externally Mediated Rewards on Intrinsic Motivation*, 18 J. Personality & Soc. Psychol. 105, 114 (1971) (when money is used as an external reward for some activity, the subjects lose intrinsic motivation for the activity); Bruno S. Frey, *Institutions and Morale: The Crowding-Out Effect*, *in* Economics, Values, and Organization 437 (Avner Ben-Ner & Louis Putterman eds., 1998) (offering people compensation for living near a nuclear power plant increased their opposition to the plant); Uri Gneezy & Aldo Rustichini, *A Fine Is a Price*, 29 J. Legal Stud. 1, 5–8 (2000) (imposition of a fine for late pickup from daycare resulted in more lateness, as parents came to see the fine as a price that displaced the prior social norm against late pickups).

30. *See* Ernst Fehr & Simon Gachter, *Do Incentive Contracts Crowd Out Voluntary Cooperation?* (Univ. S. Cal. Cent. in Law, Econ. and Org., Research Paper No. C01-3, 2001), *available at* http://ssrn.com/abstract=229047.

31. *See* Margaret M. Blair & Lynn A. Stout, *Trust, Trustworthiness, and the Behavioral Foundations of Corporate Law*, 149 U. Pa. L. Rev. 1735 (2001) (worrying that a formal duty of loyalty can undermine the social basis for trust); Mark A. Cohen, *Norms Versus Laws: Economic Theory and the Choice of Social Institutions*, *in* Social Norms and Economic Institutions 95 (Kenneth J. Koford & Jeffrey B. Miller eds., 1991) (warning that formal laws may displace reputational rewards); Dan M. Kahan, *Trust, Collective Action, and Law*, 81 B.U. L. Rev. 333 (2001) (arguing that formal norms can signal the absence of social norms, and thus erode social norms); Robert E. Scott, *The Death of Contract Law*, 54 U. Toronto L.J. 369, 388–89 (2004) (explaining that formal contract terms crowd out informal norms of reciprocity).

the eCRoR. The empirical literature indicates that even symbolic rewards and punishments crowd out intrinsic motivation.[32] The ability of legislators to say plausibly that some controversial bill violates the Constitution may count as a symbolic demerit, so that bills that do not earn this demerit are seen as acceptable, even if they violate customary norms that form part of the eCRoR.

Whether even the nonjusticiable aspects of the Constitution crowd out customary norms in this way cannot, however, be answered by reference to the behavioral literature alone, because experimental evidence also shows that *verbal* rewards enhance rather than undermine intrinsic motivation.[33] If the ability to say that a bill satisfies or violates the Constitution only counts as a verbal reinforcement of legislative duty, it may not undermine legislators' incentives to abide by the eCRoR.

In any event, we need not speculate about how exactly the behavioral experiments bear on the relation between the Constitution and the eCRoR. We can instead look for direct evidence of constitutional crowding out in public debate.

The balance of this section explores three examples of customary norms that are not clearly derived from the Constitution. These examples do double duty: First, they illustrate the proposition that such customary but extraconstitutional norms exist. Second, they make plausible the causal claim that conventional accounts of the American constitutional structure tend to overlook such norms because conventional accounts tend to equate the RoR with the Constitution. Thus, the customary norms that comprise the eCRoR tend to be rendered invisible or to be shoehorned, sometimes awkwardly, into familiar constitutional categories. The formal Constitution (including judicial review) crowds out the eCRoR.

A. Court Packing

The written Constitution does not fix the size of the Supreme Court. Arguably, the guarantee to all Article III judges of life tenure and salary protection[34] forbids Congress from reducing the size of the Supreme Court by abolishing a seat on the Court that is occupied by an active Justice—although recent scholarship suggests that Congress could validly demote a Supreme Court Justice to a district or circuit court,[35] and having done that, Congress could then abolish the newly vacant

---

32. *See* Bruno S. Frey & Reto Jegen, *Motivation Crowding Theory*, 15 J. ECON. SURV. 589, 596 (2001) (citing a study reported in E.L. DECI & R. FLASTE, WHY WE DO WHAT WE DO: THE DYNAMICS OF PERSONAL AUTONOMY (1995), in which awarding a violin student gold stars for time spent practicing undermined her intrinsic motivation to learn new music).

33. *See id.* at 598.

34. U.S. CONST. art. III, § 1.

35. *See, e.g.*, Roger C. Cramton, *Reforming the Supreme Court*, 95 CAL. L. REV. 1313, 1333–34 (2007) (arguing that a judge's life tenure "may include . . . successive service that started in the Supreme Court and moved to a lower court or vice versa").

Supreme Court seat. Whatever the constitutional limits, if any, on *reductions* in the size of the Supreme Court, *increases* in the Supreme Court's size have occurred several times in the course of American history, and do not even arguably violate any specific constitutional rule.[36] If, say, Congress were to increase the size of the Supreme Court to eleven Justices, neither the Court itself, nor any member of Congress, could plausibly claim that in so doing it was acting unconstitutionally. Nonetheless, if, in increasing the Court's size, the President and Congress were principally motivated by a desire to shape judicial outcomes, it would be engaged in Court packing in violation of a strong customary norm.

As I explain in the next section, identifying the content and even the existence of a customary norm can be a difficult business. To borrow Hart's terminology, customary norms, no less than formal written norms, often have a core of settled meaning and an open-textured periphery.[37] The customary norm against Court packing is no exception. There might be circumstances in which expansion of the Supreme Court's size would not violate the norm. For example, a bipartisan effort to reorganize the judiciary as a whole, in which the number of Justices chosen was thought necessary to match the number of circuits, could qualify as expansion of the Court without the tainted motive of changing constitutional law along with the Court's membership. However, Court *packing*—in the sense of expanding the Court's size to obtain different outcomes in contested cases—violates the norm's core, as the reaction to President Franklin D. Roosevelt's Court-packing plan illustrates.[38]

In his March 9, 1937 Fireside Chat on Reorganization of the Judiciary, Roosevelt made no secret of his result-oriented motive, even as he offered the most transparent result-neutral fig leaf.[39] The Chat began with a warning that the progress the Administration had made in battling economic hard times was in jeopardy due to an intransigent Supreme Court, that "has been acting not as a judicial body, but as a policy-making body."[40] Professing nonetheless to value "an independent judiciary,"[41] and eschewing any desire to "pack the Court . . . with spineless puppets,"[42] Roosevelt stated that even an independent judiciary lacks authority "to amend the Constitution by the arbitrary exercise of

---

36. *See supra* note 7 and accompanying text.

37. *See* HART, *supra* note 1, at 124–47.

38. *See infra* notes 46–52 and accompanying text.

39. A transcript can be found among the documents of the Franklin D. Roosevelt Presidential Library, *available at* http://www.fdrlibrary.marist.edu/030937.html. Page citations below refer to the version reproduced as Address by the President of the United States, March 9, 1937, *in* 2 DOCUMENTS OF AMERICAN HISTORY 383 (Henry Steele Commager ed., 9th ed. 1973).

40. *Id.* at 384.

41. *Id.* at 385.

42. *Id.* at 386.

judicial power."[43] Conceding that amending the Constitution to expressly validate the New Deal would remedy the problem, Roosevelt proposed instead to add one Justice to the Court for each Justice over the age of seventy who had already served ten years as a judge.[44] His core justification barely disguised the plan's substantive aim:

> By bringing into the judicial system a steady and continuing stream of new and younger blood, I hope, first, to make the administration of all Federal justice speedier and, therefore, less costly; secondly, to bring to the decision of social and economic problems younger men who have had personal experience and contact with modern facts and circumstances under which average men have to live and work. This plan will save our national Constitution from hardening of the judicial arteries.[45]

The trope that relatively youthful Justices would bring a fresh perspective did not conceal Roosevelt's true aims, for no one imagined that Roosevelt would seek to fill one of the new seats with a youthful *critic* of the New Deal.

Accordingly, it is beyond serious argument that Roosevelt's scheme in fact sought to change the Court's jurisprudence by increasing its size. And understood in exactly that way, the Court-packing plan was forcefully rejected by a Congress controlled by the President's own party, in what has been characterized as "probably the most serious setback which the President suffered during his [first] eight years of office. . . ."[46] After explaining why the proposal would not achieve its stated neutral purpose,[47] the Senate Judiciary Committee Report proceeded to denounce it in language that both reflects and obscures the fact that the core vice of the proposal is its violation of the eCRoR.

The reaction to, and defeat of, Roosevelt's Court-packing plan may thus be seen as an archetype of the eCRoR. By spinning the Midnight Judges bill of 1801, the Jeffersonian reaction of 1802, and subsequent changes in the Court's size as motivated by administrative concerns,[48] the Report claimed that Roosevelt's proposal was unprecedented. "This is the first time in the history of our country," the Report stated, "that a proposal to alter the decisions of the court by enlarging its personnel has been so boldly made."[49] In other words, what Roosevelt had

43. *Id.* at 385.

44. *See id.*

45. *Id.*

46. Editor's Note on Reform of the Federal Judiciary 1937, *in* 2 Documents of American History, *supra* note 39, at 382.

47. *See* Adverse Report from the Committee on the Judiciary, *in* 2 Documents of American History, *supra* note 39, at 387, 387–88.

48. *See id.* at 389–90 ("Neither the original act nor the repealer was an attempt to change the course of judicial decision."); *id.* at 390 ("[I]n every instance after the Adams administration, save one, the changes were made for purely administrative purposes in aid of the Court, not to control it.").

49. *Id.* at 390.

proposed to do was *something that just isn't done.* It violated a customary norm obligatory on Congress even though not formally part of the Constitution.

Court packing is archetypal too in how it illustrates the warping effect of the written Constitution on government officials' recourse to the eCRoR. The Senate Judiciary Committee Report twice stated that the proposal was contrary to "the spirit of the" Constitution.[50] How so? By applying "force to the judiciary,"[51] the Court-packing bill would undermine judicial independence, separation of powers, the Constitution's grant of life tenure to the federal judiciary, and the difficulty of impeaching judges. The Report never quite stated that the Court-packing plan violated any particular provision of the Constitution, or even some congeries of provisions. Nonetheless, it concluded that the plan amounted to "an abandonment of constitutional principle," while "point[ing] the way to the evasion of the Constitution. . . . Under the form of the Constitution it seeks to do that which is unconstitutional."[52]

Thus, in the reaction to Roosevelt's Court-packing scheme we see the strong assertion of a customary norm, along with an attempt to shoehorn that norm—however awkwardly—into the Constitution. The episode illustrates both the force of the eCRoR and the tendency in the United States to associate it with the written Constitution.

B. Jurisdiction Stripping

Under the "Madisonian Compromise" of Article III, Congress was under no obligation to create lower federal courts, and because Congress would only "ordain and establish" such courts "from time to time," presumably it could eliminate the lower federal courts as well.[53] Although Article III does require a Supreme Court and prescribes its original jurisdiction, it expressly authorizes Congress to make "such Exceptions" to the Supreme Court's appellate jurisdiction as it wishes.[54] Thus, under the most straightforward reading of the text of Article III, Congress could abolish the lower federal courts entirely, and eliminate all appellate jurisdiction of the Supreme Court[55]—thereby ensuring that no federal court would

---

50. *Id.* at 387; 389.

51. *Id.* at 388.

52. *Id.* at 391.

53. U.S. CONST. art. III, § 1.

54. *Id.* art. III, § 3, cl. 2.

55. This is not the only possible reading. The Exceptions Clause might simply be read to mean that Congress can shift cases from the Supreme Court's appellate to its original jurisdiction. *See* Steven G. Calabresi & Gary Lawson, *The Unitary Executive, Jurisdiction Stripping, and the Hamdan Opinions: A Textualist Response to Justice Scalia*, 107 COLUM. L. REV. 1002, 1036–42 (2007). However, that reading would require overruling *Marbury v. Madison*, 5 U.S. (1 Cranch) 137 (1803), and can thus be regarded as off the table. The Supreme Court came very close to accepting Congressional omnipotence under the Exceptions Clause in *Ex Parte McCardle*, 74 U.S. (7 Wall.) 506 (1869) (dismissing a habeas claim for want of jurisdiction where Congress had revoked the provision of the habeas corpus act invoked by petitioner),

have the authority to resolve federal questions except in the narrow category of cases that happened to fall within the high Court's original jurisdiction. Or, if one thinks that the concept of an "exception" requires that there be some residuum not excepted, Congress would still be entitled to eliminate nearly all of the Supreme Court's appellate jurisdiction, perhaps leaving only patent cases, or some subset of patent cases.[56]

To be sure, it is possible to find support in other aspects of Article III—such as its extension of federal jurisdiction to "all Cases . . . arising under" federal law[57]—for an obligation on Congress to compensate for limitations on the high Court's appellate jurisdiction with grants to the lower federal courts of original jurisdiction. Justice Story advanced this theory in the early nineteenth century,[58] and a somewhat modified version of the theory has been offered more recently by Akhil Amar,[59] but these readings must grapple with the fact that they would render invalid the actual jurisdictional scheme in place from the Founding through the abolition of the amount-in-controversy requirement for federal district court jurisdiction in 1980.[60]

Accordingly, those who have argued that Congress could not strip the federal courts of jurisdiction to hear the most important federal cases have tended to make the point in ways that do not rely on any specific constitutional provision. For example, Henry Hart (not to be confused with H. L. A. Hart) argued that Congress could not wield its powers under the Exceptions Clause in a manner that "would destroy the essential role of the Supreme Court in the constitutional plan."[61] And what is that essential role? Relying on Founding Era sources as well as textual support such as the grant of life tenure and salary protection to federal judges, Lawrence Sager argues that Congress cannot eliminate the Supreme Court's ability to invalidate unconstitutional action by the states,[62] or, more

---

although *Ex Parte Yerger*, 75 U.S. (8 Wall.) 85 (1869) (finding an alternate source of jurisdiction over a similar habeas claim), casts some doubt on that view.

56. *See* Henry M. Hart, Jr., *The Power of Congress to Limit the Jurisdiction of the Federal Courts: An Exercise in Dialectic*, 66 Harv. L. Rev. 1362, 1364 (1953) (offering the patent example).

57. U.S. Const. art. III, § 2.

58. *See* Martin v. Hunter's Lessee, 14 U.S. (1 Wheat.) 304, 328–37 (1816).

59. *See* Akhil Reed Amar, *A Neo-Federalist View of Article III: Separating the Two Tiers of Federal Jurisdiction*, 65 B.U. L. Rev. 205, 238–59 (1985) (arguing that the constitutional text and the original understanding show that some Article III court must have the "last word on a federal question or admiralty issue").

60. *See* Federal Question Jurisdictional Amendments Act of 1980, Pub. L. 96-486, § 1, 94 Stat. 2369 (amending 28 U.S.C. § 1331 to eliminate the amount-in-controversy requirement for federal question cases); Fallon et al., *supra* note 7, at 320 (noting historical limitations on federal court jurisdiction); Lawrence Gene Sager, *The Supreme Court 1980 Term, Foreword: Constitutional Limitations on Congress' Authority to Regulate the Jurisdiction of the Federal Courts*, 95 Harv. L. Rev. 17, 53 n.105 (1981) (same).

61. Hart, *supra* note 56, at 1365.

62. *See* Sager, *supra* note 60 at 45–57.

tentatively, its ability to invalidate unconstitutional federal action.[63] Sager is especially confident that Congress could not engage in what is sometimes called "jurisdictional gerrymandering"[64]—that is, directing the outcome of constitutional cases through the pretense of jurisdictional statutes.[65]

Perhaps one or more of the restrictions on congressional power over federal court jurisdiction that Story, Amar, Hart, Sager, and others have inferred from Article III and other sources can indeed be said to be constitutional requirements, whether or not justiciable. But at the very least, extreme forms of jurisdiction stripping—complete elimination of the lower federal courts, severe curtailments of the Supreme Court's appellate jurisdiction, and jurisdictional gerrymandering—would violate a very strong customary norm. Sager essentially says as much when he observes that "[a]lthough proposals to neuter the federal judiciary—and in particular, the Supreme Court—have been seriously advanced and debated throughout our constitutional history, Congress has almost always repudiated such efforts."[66] Congress has, in other words, observed a customary norm forbidding jurisdiction stripping.

Consider a recent example. In response to bills that would engage in jurisdictional gerrymandering to prevent the federal courts from invalidating the Pledge of Allegiance and finding a constitutional right to same-sex marriage, Congressman Stark had this to say:

> These bills threaten the foundation of American government by stifling productive discussion of social issues and undermining our system of checks and balances. . . . [T]he function of the Judiciary is to review the constitutionality of laws. It is thus undemocratic and blatantly partisan to use a procedural trick to protect certain legislation from being questioned in court. Not only does this indirectly violate the Constitution by devaluing the Judicial Branch, it also renders the entire document meaningless since constitutionality is no longer a standard by which all laws must be judged.[67]

Congressman Stark's use of the phrase "the function of the Judiciary" could be taken to suggest agreement with the "essential functions" theory of Professor Hart, but the balance of these remarks show him—like his predecessors resisting Roosevelt's Court-packing scheme nearly seventy years earlier—somewhat flummoxed by his inability to settle directly on a constitutional provision that the

---

63. *See id.* at 57–60.

64. *See, e.g.*, Laurence H. Tribe, *Jurisdictional Gerrymandering: Zoning Disfavored Rights Out of the Federal Courts*, 16 HARV. C. R.-C.L. L. REV. 129 (1981).

65. *See* Sager, *supra* note 60, at 68–80.

66. *Id.* at 20.

67. *Introducing a Concurrent Resolution Recognizing the Independence of the Courts of the United States*, 152 CONG. REC. E1707-01 (2006) (speech of Hon. Fortney Pete Stark of California).

outrageous proposals violate. He is thus reduced to decrying jurisdictional gerrymandering as "undemocratic," "blatantly partisan," a "trick," and, most tellingly, an indirect violation of the Constitution. These remarks are typical of members of Congress who oppose jurisdictional gerrymandering. They weakly suggest that the practice may violate the Constitution, even as they struggle for the vocabulary to condemn the proposals for violating the eCRoR.[68]

C. Voting in Presidential Elections

Under Article II and the Twelfth Amendment, the President is chosen by the Electoral College, a body selected by processes adopted by the States "in such Manner as the Legislature thereof may direct. . . ."[69] In the early Republic, state legislatures commonly chose the electors themselves,[70] but over time, more and more states came to use elections, either on a winner-take-all basis (as is the practice in 48 states today) or on a district-by-district basis (as is the current practice in Maine and Nebraska,[71] and was apparently the method that James Madison thought most appropriate[72]). Nevertheless, as the Supreme Court reaffirmed in the aftermath of the contested 2000 Presidential election, the Constitution does not require states to hold any popular elections to choose its electors.[73] As the Court stated (without any dissent on this point) in *Bush v. Gore*[74]: "The individual citizen has no federal constitutional right to vote for electors for the President of the United States unless and until the state legislature chooses a statewide election as the means to implement its power to appoint members of the electoral college."[75]

Note that, in so stating, the Justices did not say that any constitutional right to vote in Presidential elections is protected only by the political process. In other words, a constitutional right to vote in Presidential elections is not protected by the Constitution outside the courts. It simply does not exist.

---

68. *See, e.g., Providing for Consideration of H.R. 2389, Pledge Protection Act Of 2005*, 152 Cong. Rec. H5388-04, H5391 (2006) (statement of Hon. Steny Hoyer) (decrying the proposed Pledge Protection Act as a "radical court-stripping bill" that is "unnecessary and . . . probably unconstitutional" because it would "intrude on the principles of separation of powers [and] degrade our independent Federal judiciary."); *id.* ("If we are a Nation of laws, we must be committed to allowing courts to decide what the law is.").

69. U.S. Const. art. II, § 1.

70. *See* McPherson v. Blacker, 146 U.S. 1, 29–34 (1892) (elaborating on early methods of choosing electors).

71. *See* Samuel Isacharoff et al., The Law of Democracy 244 (2d ed. 2001).

72. *See McPherson*, 146 U.S. at 29.

73. *See* Bush v. Palm Beach County Canvassing Bd., 531 U.S. 70, 76 (2000) (quoting McPherson, 146 U.S. at 25).

74. 531 U.S. 98 (2000) (*per curiam*).

75. *Id.* at 104.

Yet we have good reason to think that a customary norm now protects a right to vote in Presidential elections. To confirm the existence of this norm, consider what would happen were some state legislature to replace popular elections with direct legislative selection of electors. We need not engage in much speculation, because the Florida legislature nearly attempted just that in 2000. Both the aborted attempt and the reaction that ensued are instructive.

After the Florida Supreme Court had intervened in the Presidential election but before the U.S. Supreme Court had finally stopped the recount, Republican members of the Florida legislature were preparing a special legislative session to choose a set of delegates directly.[76] Even as sympathetic academics were assuring the country that the proposal was constitutional,[77] Florida Republicans tacitly acknowledged the customary norm that direct legislative selection of electors seemed to violate. Thus, rather than simply say that a state legislature has the unfettered prerogative to choose electors without popular elections—which is a true statement of constitutional law—Republicans defended the special session not as an alternative to voting but as a protection for it. As one Florida Republican state representative put the point: "Because there is no other way to protect our votes, I expect us to name our own delegates as soon as possible."[78] Likewise, Florida Senate President John McKay characterized the special session as simply an effort to "ensure that the voters of Florida are not disenfranchised."[79] Contending that George W. Bush had in fact won the state's election, and that the state high court's intervention was thus itself an effort to wrest control from the voters, Republicans portrayed the proposed special session as fully consistent with the customary norm. Even then, Florida Republican legislators were tentative throughout the postelection struggle, perhaps fearing that the public would judge them harshly if they appeared to take the election away from the voters.[80]

Critics of the planned Florida special legislative session also spoke the language of customary norms, even as they struggled with the fact that the norm at issue

---

76. *See* Jeffrey Gettleman, *For Florida Legislature, It's Full Speed Ahead to Name Electors*, L.A. Times, Nov. 29, 2001, at A25.

77. *See id.* (noting the support for the plan from Harvard Law Professor Einer Elhauge and Boalt Hall Law Professor John Yoo).

78. Gettleman, *supra* note 76 (quoting Republican state representative Johnnie Byrd).

79. David Firestone, *Contesting the Vote: The Overview; With Court Set to Hear Appeal, Legislators Move on Electors*, N.Y. Times, Dec. 7, 2000, at A1.

80. *See* Howard Gillman, *Judicial Independence Through the Lens of Bush v. Gore: Four Lessons from Political Science*, 64 Ohio St. L.J. 249, 255–56 (2003) ("Republican legislators in Florida were being pressured by legislative leaders to take the controversial step of challenging the Florida courts by appointing a new slate of Bush electors, but there was some grumbling about the need to take this course of action, and there was a public expression of hope that the Washington justices would make it unnecessary for them to go on record with that vote.").

here—a right to vote in Presidential elections—is not also a constitutional norm. For example, Georgetown Law Professor David Cole opined:

> It would be seen as an entirely illegitimate move to short-circuit the process that was set forth in the law before the election. . . .The important point is the election is supposed to be decided by popular vote. . . .Only in the highly unusual circumstances of that process failing should the Legislature step in and only if Florida risks not having a voice in the Electoral College. People would understand if there was no other recourse.[81]

Note that Cole apparently agreed with the Florida Republicans who thought a special session would be appropriate to preserve a role for voting, that is, for Florida sending some electors to Washington. But unlike the Republicans, Cole did not begin with the assumption that Bush had won the popular vote in Florida, and thus he saw the proposed legislative session as "entirely illegitimate" because an "election is supposed to be decided by popular vote." Supposed by whom or what? Cole did not say, but we can: A very firmly entrenched customary norm requires popular elections for the selection of a state's electors.

But even as critics of the Florida special legislative session unwittingly spoke the language of customary norms, they were stymied by the poverty of our eCRoR vocabulary. In American legal and political culture, constitutionality is so frequently assumed to be the ultimate test of legitimacy that those who would rely on the eCRoR are at a serious rhetorical disadvantage. The degree to which the Constitution crowds out the eCRoR leaves them either attempting to shoehorn the customary norm into constitutional arguments—as we saw in the cases of Court packing and jurisdiction stripping—or talking vaguely about fairness. Thus, Florida House Democratic leader Lois Frankel condemned the planned Florida special legislative session as "ultimately a partisan act that is unnecessary, unfair and unjust."[82] Even as she groped for a way to say that the special session would violate the customary norm requiring popular elections for President, Representative Frankel was reduced to making what sound like ordinary policy arguments.

D. The Extent and Causes of Constitutional Crowding Out

The foregoing examples vividly illustrate the characteristic features of constitutional crowding out: The existence of the written Constitution blinds judges, scholars, and, most importantly for my purposes, political actors, to the eCRoR. The central place of the written Constitution in American conceptions of government leads the relevant actors to try to fit customary norms onto the procrustean

---

81. Jay Weaver, *Dueling Electors? Race May Bring Unprecedented Legal Showdown: 2 Sets of Electors Could Emerge*, MIAMI HERALD, Nov. 30, 2000, at 25A.

82. Dana Canedy & David Barstow, *Contesting The Vote: The Legislature; Florida Lawmakers to Convene Special Session Tomorrow*, N.Y. TIMES, Dec. 7, 2000, at A35.

bed of the Constitution, often in awkward ways that undermine the customary norms' claim to fundamentality. And, where a practice that violates the eCRoR cannot plausibly be made to fit the Constitution, judges, scholars, and political actors lack the vocabulary to condemn the practice as repugnant to the eCRoR.

The principal examples I have given hardly exhaust the full range of customary limits on government action. We can readily imagine various actions that violate strong customary norms but not the Constitution. Suppose Congress were to repeal (rather than merely amend at the margins) the 1964 Civil Rights Act.[83] Or suppose that, absent any substantial new change in circumstances, in an effort to revitalize the New Orleans economy, Congress decided to move the capital from Washington, D.C. to the French Quarter (after a cession by Louisiana). There may be disagreement about whether any particular custom has normative force, or about how much normative force it has, but acceptance of any single one is sufficient to establish the existence of the eCRoR.[84]

Why do we so often fail to see the norms that comprise the eCRoR? My examples point to two culprits. First, the very writtenness of the Constitution distracts us from the eCRoR. Second, the practice of judicial review plays an important role in hiding the eCRoR.

These two effects reinforce one another. There was a brief time when it was possible for an American judge to argue that a duly enacted law, though inconsistent with no constitutional provision or doctrine, was nonetheless invalid as inconsistent with natural law.[85] But that time has long passed, so that today the judicially enforceable limits on government are *constitutional* limits. And, I want to suggest, the judicialization of our constitutional discourse casts a shadow onto extrajudicial deliberations: The understandable judicial habit of shoehorning eCRoR claims into constitutional claims misleads political actors into thinking

---

83. As Bruce Ackerman argues, the Civil Rights Act is "canonical" if not, strictly speaking, a constitutional requirement. Bruce Ackerman, *The Living Constitution*, 120 Harv. L. Rev. 1737, 1788–89 (2007). Similarly, William Eskridge and John Ferejohn treat the 1964 Civil Rights Act as a "super-statute." William N. Eskridge, Jr. & John Ferejohn, *Super-Statutes*, 50 Duke L.J. 1215, 1237–42 (2001).

84. For a list of candidate aspects of the eCRoR, see Keith E. Whittington, Constitutional Construction: Divided Powers and Constitutional Meaning 12 (1999). Whittington lists examples of what he calls constitutional "construction," an activity that, he says "elucidate[s] the text in the interstices of discoverable, interpretive meaning. . . ." *Id.* at 5. Constitutional construction is not entirely co-extensive with the eCRoR, however. Some of Whittington's examples of mere constitutional construction qualify as bona fide constitutional rules rather than extraconstitutional rules under both my view and the conventional view. *See, e.g., id.* (listing, *inter alia*, judicial review, judicial refusal to issue advisory opinions, and prohibition of racial exclusions from jury service as examples of construction).

85. *See* Calder v. Bull, 3 U.S. (3 Dall.) 386, 388–89 (1798) (arguing that "general principles of law and reason forbid" state laws interfering with certain individual rights).

that they too—when seeking the limits on their authority—must find them only in the Constitution.

III. PRACTICAL, NORMATIVE, AND THEORETICAL IMPLICATIONS

To recognize the existence in principle of merely customary norms that comprise the eCRoR is not to say that we can clearly identify criteria for distinguishing between such norms and other practices that lack this status. As Hart says of the RoR more generally, rules of recognition, like other legal rules, typically have a core of settled meaning and an open-textured periphery.[86] As I acknowledged above, there will be borderline cases—circumstances in which a customary norm appears to have developed but its eCRoR status may be plausibly contested.

Consider an example. Before 1940, was there really a customary norm forbidding Presidents from seeking a third term in office? Akhil Amar has argued that there was not,[87] but even if there was such a norm, how should we understand President Roosevelt's decision to seek a third term nonetheless? Did Roosevelt violate the norm? Did he—and the voters who returned him to the Presidency—change the norm? Did the very act of violating the norm also simultaneously change the norm? Did the adoption of the Twenty-Second Amendment convert what was previously a mere customary norm into part of the formal Constitution and thereby affirm that the pre-1940 practice was indeed normative? Or did it merely show that the pre-1940 pattern lacked the status of higher law? It is difficult to imagine good answers to such questions that are not largely stipulative—that is, answers that do not depend upon some set of controvertible definitions of the eCRoR, as well as changes to and violations thereof.

Accordingly, if we were interested in identifying aspects of the eCRoR that are enforceable by the courts, we would have good reason to doubt that judges possess the expertise and legitimacy to accomplish this task in the face of contrary decisions by elected officials. This is why Ernest Young worries that theories of constitutionalization without constitutional text face "'rule of recognition' problems."[88]

However, if the eCRoR is not enforceable by the courts (except to the extent that it is embodied in enforceable statutes, treaties, and the like), then the issues of judicial legitimacy go away. Young renders the courts irrelevant by bracketing issues of entrenchment. He identifies what he calls "extracanonical" provisions of our small-c constitution as those materials that play a role in literally "constituting" institutions of our government, even when they are not entrenched

86. Hart, *supra* note 1, at 147–48.

87. Akhil Reed Amar, America's Constitution: A Biography 433–35 (2005) (providing examples of earlier Presidents who seriously contemplated running for a third term).

88. *See* Young, *supra* note 20, at 454.

against amendment by ordinary democratic means.[89] If, as Young concedes, Congress can eliminate extracanonical parts of our unwritten constitution by an ordinary statute—repealing the statutory authority for the Federal Reserve system, say—then we don't need to worry about judicial legitimacy. The courts would have to accept congressional elimination of the Fed as an amendment to the small-c constitution accomplished by means appropriate to amending unentrenched but constitutive features of our constitutional system.

Young's project is important but it is not exactly my project. I want to know what aspects of the American system of government are deemed by the relevant government officials to be fixed by customary norms that are not themselves embodied in the norms of the upper-case-C Constitution. If the relevant officials thought that, even absent special circumstances, they could amend one of these norms—for example, the norm against Court packing—by ordinary legislation, that would mean that it was not in fact part of the eCRoR. So unlike Young, I cannot bracket the entrenchment question.

But neither do I have a rule-like answer to the entrenchment question. I cannot say, for example, that if a customary norm is part of the eCRoR, it can only be changed by a two-thirds vote of each house of Congress, or by a law that is warranted by the most pressing necessity. The imposition of such criteria would be both arbitrary and contrary to the very nature of a customary norm.[90]

Nonetheless, my account of the eCRoR avoids the legitimacy worry because it is an account for elected officials, not for courts. By calling attention to the eCRoR, I aim to strengthen the hand of those who would resist rash calls for radically transformative laws by giving them a vocabulary for resistance. In short, I want to elevate the utterance "you just can't do that" to a matter of principle.

To be sure, my aim here is principally descriptive. An account of American law that overlooks the eCRoR will not be a complete account. But the project also has normative content. It is conservative in the Burkean sense: Strengthening the hand of those who would resist changes to the eCRoR—even if only rhetorically—means erecting obstacles to fundamental change. And one will only favor erecting such obstacles if one thinks that, *ceteris paribus*, fundamental change is likely to do more harm than good.

---

89. *See id.* at 413 (aiming to "decouple the constitutive function of a constitution from the entrenchment function.").

90. The least convincing aspect of Bruce Ackerman's magisterial account of constitutional change outside the formal requirements of Article V has always been Ackerman's effort to identify formal criteria for distinguishing successful from failed constitutional moments. *See* BRUCE ACKERMAN, 1 WE THE PEOPLE: FOUNDATIONS 266–90 (1991) (identifying a four-stage gauntlet that informal amendments must run). *Cf.* Akhil Amar, *Philadelphia Revisited: Amending the Constitution Outside Article V*, 55 U. CHI. L. REV. 1043 (1988) (arguing for the permissibility of constitutional amendment by national referendum).

Space limitations prevent me from setting forth anything like a full defense of Burkeanism—or even Burkeanism in constitutionalism[91]—here. Instead, I shall simply point out that the same conservative impulse that drives my call for political actors to open their eyes to the eCRoR typically underwrites fidelity to the written Constitution as well.

Constitutionalism, as a restraint on legislative action, is almost necessarily conservative in the Burkean sense. It prevents legislators from changing the status quo in ways that they would otherwise prefer. We can see this point most clearly in debates about the Constitution outside the courts. When House member A resists House member B's call for some measure—say, opposing the impeachment of a President for lying about sex on the ground that, in A's view, this is not a high crime or misdemeanor—A asserts a limit on the House's freedom of action. In this instance, A will point to the written Constitution as the source of the limit, but by now we understand that, with the exception of recently enacted amendments, the underlying warrant for the authority of the Constitution itself is customary acceptance.[92]

Matters are somewhat more complicated with respect to the judicially enforceable Constitution. The Supreme Court sometimes invokes the Constitution to invalidate long-established practices, such as laws mandating racial segregation in public schools[93] or laws forbidding sodomy between consenting persons of the same sex.[94] In such cases, rather than impeding change, the Constitution itself acts as the agent of change. Constitutionalism in such cases cannot plausibly be described as conservative in the Burkean sense—which is not to say that the results in such cases cannot be defended on other grounds.

In any event, in focusing on the RoR outside the courts, I aim here to sidestep the contentious and long-standing debates about the proper methods of constitutional interpretation by the courts. With respect to legislative action, the argument for adherence to the eCRoR is as strong as the argument for adherence by legislators to the large-C Constitution, even when the latter is nonjusticiable. Indeed, the arguments are not only of equal strength; given the source of the large-C Constitution's authority, they are the *same* arguments.

Before concluding, it is worth pausing over what, from the Hartian perspective, might count as an oddity of the American legal system. According to Hart, a legal norm exists either because it is derivable from other legal norms or because it is directly accepted by governmental officials as ultimate. In the United States, however, government officials typically act under a kind of double false consciousness about which norms are derived and which are ultimate.

---

91. *See* Thomas Merrill, *Bork.v. Burke*, 19 HARV. J.L. & PUB. POL'Y 509, 511 (1996) (presenting the case for a Burkean conventionalist approach to interpretation, which "seeks out . . . [the] consensus view about the meaning in the legal community of today").

92. *See supra* note 20 and accompanying text.

93. *See* Brown v. Bd. of Educ., 347 U.S. 483 (1954).

94. *See* Lawrence v. Texas, 539 U.S. 558 (2003).

First, many government officials think that operative provisions of the original Constitution are valid because the document was ratified in 1789, and that amendments are valid because they were adopted in conformity with the procedure described in Article V. They thereby treat such provisions as nonultimate, instead treating the Ratification Clause of Article VII (which also validated Article V) as the ultimate RoR. But as Greenawalt and others have shown, this is a mistake. With the exception of recent amendments, operative provisions of the original Constitution are ultimate, deriving their authority directly from acceptance by government officials.

Second, as I have illustrated in this chapter, government officials sometimes regard provisions of the eCRoR either as not truly binding or as interpretations of various constitutional provisions (themselves ultimately validated via Article VII). This too appears to be a mistake. The norms against Court packing, jurisdiction stripping, and eliminating the right to vote in Presidential elections are valid (if I am right that they are valid) because they are ultimate norms directly accepted by government officials.

It is not entirely clear whether Hart's theory, as articulated by Hart himself, has room for the sorts of mistakes about ultimate authority that run rampant in the American legal system. But certainly nothing of importance in Hart's theory would be lost by admitting the possibility that government officials can be mistaken about the reasons why they accept any particular norm. Hart gives the example of a simple legal system in which Rex I and his successors legislate.[95] Certainly the example works equally well if, instead of assuming that acceptance of the Rex dynasty is an ultimate rule, we assume that the Rex dynasty and their subjects believe that Rex I was authorized to rule in virtue of what they mistakenly take to be his divine origins.

Likewise, we can give a descriptive account of the American legal system that is largely true to Hart's project even though many—probably most—government officials and ordinary citizens are mistaken about what rules are ultimate. That is not to say, however, that it makes no difference that Americans hold erroneous views about ultimate authority. Dispelling the mistaken belief that Article VII validates most constitutional norms would weaken the case for originalism in constitutional interpretation. Dispelling the mistaken belief that strong customary norms only have force if traceable to the Constitution would provide members of Congress and other political actors with the tools to resist radical change.

IV. CONCLUSION

I am hardly the first scholar to note the existence of the eCRoR. In one of Karl Llewellyn's few forays into public law, he argued that most of what he called the

95. Hart, *supra* note 1, at 52–66.

"working Constitution" "is hardly adumbrated in the Document."[96] In *The Constitution as an Institution,* Llewellyn gave as good an account as I can imagine of what makes some norm part of the RoR:

> The actors, and any non-actors in a position to block or modify action, must *feel* that the way or institution is not subject to abrogation or material alteration. They need not feel that it is right or wise . . . if they are clear that it is permanent. But in the normal case the two feelings coincide. This is intended to exclude . . . practices which, even though long-established, have not acquired in the relevant minds the intangible atmosphere of unquestioned rightness or of course of nature.[97]

If I am right that our elected officials continue to lack a vocabulary with which to invoke the eCRoR, then Llewellyn failed in his effort to call attention to our unwritten constitution over seventy years ago. Why would a contemporary effort fare better? It may not, but my account has a key tactical advantage over Llewellyn's. His conception of the working Constitution drew no distinctions between the written Constitution and the eCRoR, or between judicial and extra-judicial practice.

Throughout his article, Llewellyn equates the working Constitution with the written Constitution. He provides a nice example of a proposition that I would regard as a customary norm necessary to implement the customary right to vote in Presidential elections: that electors must vote their ticket, not their conscience. Llewellyn asks rhetorically: "Can any doubt that if [the Electoral C]ollege should today disregard their mandate, such action would be contrary to the Constitution?"[98] The short answer is of course we can doubt this. As a matter of the judicially enforceable large-C Constitution, there is a very good argument that voters have no direct recourse against faithless electors.[99] By failing to distinguish the Constitution from the eCRoR, Llewellyn stokes fears that acceptance of the latter would authorize judicialization of a wide swath of action that we now regard as committed to political actors.

Llewellyn compounds that impression by the way he talks about Supreme Court adjudication of cases arising under the Constitution. As a legal realist, Llewellyn sometimes affirmed the proposition that rules do not decide contested

---

96. K.N. Llewellyn, *The Constitution as an Institution*, 34 COLUM. L. REV. 1, 15 (1934).

97. *Id.* at 29.

98. *Id.* at 12.

99. *See* Ray v. Blair, 343 U.S. 214, 230 (1952) (assuming, *arguendo*, that there exists a "constitutional freedom of the elector . . . to vote as he may choose in the electoral college"). *See also* Robert W. Bennett, *The Problem of the Faithless Elector: Trouble Aplenty Brewing Just Below the Surface in Choosing the President*, 100 NW. U. L. REV. 121, 122 n.10 (2006) (citing scholarship supporting the constitutional freedom of electors to cast votes as they see fit).

cases, and in *The Constitution as an Institution* he applies the point to constitutional jurisprudence.[100] He writes that "a sane theory would utterly disregard a Documentary text *if any relevant practices existed* to offer a firmer, more living basis for the ideal picture."[101] Legislators, lawyers, judges, and scholars who did not share this strongly legal-realist view would have understandably balked at the notion that judges are warranted in disregarding the text in favor of their understanding of customary norms.[102] Llewellyn claimed that he was only putting into words what the Supreme Court already practiced,[103] but for those who disagreed as a descriptive matter, his prescriptions would have been too radical.

Resistors to radical legal realism would have dismissed Llewellyn's account entirely, and in doing so would have overlooked the very real phenomenon of the eCRoR to which *The Constitution as an Institution* attempted to draw attention. An account that builds on Llewellyn's astute observations about customary norms but jettisons his extreme rule-skepticism might fare better. That, at any rate, is the ambition of this chapter.

---

100. *See* Llewellyn, *supra* note 96, at 6–10.

101. *Id.* at 31.

102. *See, e.g., id.* at 33 ("To my mind, the judge who builds his decision to conform with his conception of what our institutions must be if we are to continue, roots in the deepest wisdom.").

103. *See id.* at 40.

4. UNDERSTANDING THE RELATIONSHIP BETWEEN THE U.S. CONSTITUTION AND THE CONVENTIONAL RULE OF RECOGNITION

KENNETH EINAR HIMMA*

Legal theorists specializing in constitutional theory have tended to regard positivism and other conceptual theories as irrelevant; the idea is that a theory of the concept of law cannot tell us anything that helps to solve substantive issues of constitutional theory.

There is something to this complaint. A theory of the concept of law merely fleshes out the metaphysical implications of the social commitments governing use of the concept-term "law," and tells us how to distinguish something that is law from something that is not. But knowing how to do this does not seem to help answer the normative questions typically asked by constitutional theorists: it will not help answer the question of how the constitution is properly interpreted or the question of who should decide what the constitution means.[1] About all an analysis of a concept can tell you is how to identify the things to which the concept applies, but our pre-theoretic understanding of the concept is usually, by itself, enough to do this. Judges and lawyers do this all the time without having a worked-out conceptual theory of law.

Still, there is at least one substantive non-normative issue worth pursuing—and I do so here. In particular, I attempt to determine how the Constitution and rule of recognition are related by examining the practices of officials. This will

---

* Professor of Philosophy, Seattle Pacific University. I am grateful to participants in the Conference on the Rule of Recognition at the University of Pennsylvania Law School. I am especially indebted to comments by Larry Alexander, Matt Adler, Wil Waluchow, Jeremy Waldron, Michael Dorf, Kent Greenawalt, Mitch Berman, Stephen Perry, Michael Green, and Richard Fallon. This work builds on analysis begun in two earlier papers: Kenneth Einar Himma, *Final Authority to Bind with Moral Mistakes: On the Explanatory Potential of Inclusive Legal Positivism*, 24 LAW & PHIL. 1 (2005); and Kenneth Einar Himma, *Making Sense of Constitutional Disagreement: Legal Positivism, the Bill of Rights, and the Conventional Rule of Recognition in the United States*," 4 J. L. SOC'Y 149 (2003).

1. Of course, there are some non-normative substantive issues that conceptual analysis can help resolve. For example, legal theorists disagree on whether arguments for interpretive principles are moral or legal in character. A conceptual analysis might help in resolving that disagreement; perhaps theorists are confused about where the line is between morality and legality. But, then, to answer the substantive normative questions that really matter—for example, how should we interpret the Constitution—one will have to engage in the appropriately normative analysis.

not solve any interesting issues of constitutional theory, but it entails that judicial supremacy extends further than is commonly assumed, making the morally normative issues associated with this practice in a democratic system of governance even more difficult.

I. CONCEPTUAL FOUNDATIONS OF POSITIVISM

A. The Concept of Validity Criteria

Fundamental to a conceptual analysis of law is the metaphysical thesis that, in any possible legal system, there are certain properties that *constitute* a norm as law (in exactly the way the instantiation of unmarriedness constitutes a man as a bachelor). Any norm instantiating the appropriate properties is, for that reason, a law in that legal system; any norm not instantiating the appropriate properties is, for that reason, not a law in that legal system.

One consequence of this idea is that in every conceptually possible legal system there exist necessary and sufficient conditions for a norm to count as law. If *S* is a legal system and *P* is a statement that describes the properties that constitute a norm as law,[2] then *P* states necessary and sufficient criteria of "legal validity" in *S* in the following sense:

> The Differentiation Thesis: In every conceptually possible legal system *S*, there is a set *CoV* (for "criteria of validity") such that, for every norm *n*, *n* is a law in *S* at time *t* if and only if *n* satisfies the criteria in *CoV* at *t*.

There are a couple of observations worth making here about the Differentiation Thesis. First, the Differentiation Thesis is a metaphysical thesis, and not an epistemological thesis. The Differentiation Thesis neither presupposes nor implies any claims about the extent to which the criteria of validity of a system can be identified. Second, the Differentiation Thesis implies nothing about the conceptual relations between law and morality. Legally valid content might—or might not—be necessarily constrained by moral principles or by the inherently interpretive character of law. Up to now, every conceptual theorist has assumed the Differentiation Thesis.

B. The Separability Thesis

Understood here, the Separability Thesis denies Augustine's claim that unjust norms cannot be law. While Augustine believed that law must conform to moral principles, the Separability Thesis claims there can be legal systems with validity criteria not including conformity to moral principles. In other words, there *can*

---

2. *P*, of course, might express a complicated list of properties that include disjunctions or conjunctions.

be both wicked legal systems and wicked laws—like Nazi Germany, apartheid South Africa, and the antebellum United States.

Thus construed, the Separability Thesis does not deny necessary relations between law and morality; it simply excludes one particular necessary relation between law and morality—namely, a necessary connection between the criteria for determining what counts as law and moral principles. Positivists have frequently recognized other necessary relations between law and morality. H. L. A. Hart claims law must include "the minimum content of natural [moral] law" for law to conduce to its conceptual purpose of guiding behavior. Joseph Raz argues that law makes possible forms of social cooperation not otherwise possible among non-angels and hence performs a distinctively moral task.

C. The Social Fact Thesis

The Social Fact Thesis asserts that what, in essence, distinguishes legal norms from nonlegal norms is that the former instantiate a property that makes reference to some social fact. The relevant social fact, then, is what ultimately explains the existence of a legal system and constitutes it as a social artifact.

On Hart's view, a legal system is brought into existence by the existence of a rule of recognition specifying recipes for making, enforcing, changing, settling, and adjudicating law that produce laws effectively regulating citizens' behavior. And, for Hart, there is a legal system in *S* when (1) officials in *S* practice the rule of recognition defining the criteria of validity and (2) citizens in *S* generally comply with first-order rules validated by those criteria. Properties (1) and (2) are the social facts that give rise to law and hence constitute law as an artifact.

D. The Conventionality Thesis

The Conventionality Thesis explains the content and authority of the validity criteria in every conceptually possible legal system in terms of a social convention practiced by the persons who function as officials. As it functions here, the term "convention" is used to pick out what Hart calls a "social rule," and not a coordination convention as David Lewis uses the term. Social rules have an "external aspect" and an "internal aspect." The external aspect consists in members of the group converging their behavior to a rule—so much so that it can be described as doing it "*as a rule*."[3] The internal aspect consists in members of the group converging on a critical reflective attitude that constitutes the social rule as *normative* in the sense that deviations from that rule are appropriately criticized.

On Hart's view, social rules can, but need not, establish duties. Duty-defining social rules or conventions have, according to Hart, the following features: (1) people in the relevant social group converge in their behavior on the actions

3. H.L.A. Hart, The Concept of Law 55 (Penelope Bulloch & Joseph Raz eds., 2d ed. 1994) (emphasis in original).

required by the rule, (2) people in the critical group manifest a reflective critical attitude by criticizing deviations from the rule, and (3) significant social pressure is brought to bear on persons to abide by the rule and avoid unexcused or unjustified deviations.

According to the Conventionality Thesis, law exists when there is a social rule of recognition that results in efficacious regulation of citizen behavior. As Hart puts the point, "those rules of behaviour which are valid according to the system's ultimate criteria of validity must be generally obeyed, and . . . its rules of recognition specifying the criteria of legal validity and its rules of change and adjudication must be effectively accepted as common public standards of official behaviour by its officials."[4]

While some positivists think that the rule of recognition is no more than a *judicial* custom, this is mistaken. The extent of a court's authority is limited, for example, by the acceptance of those officials who have authority to enforce the law. If officials decline to back a line of court decisions with the state's police power, then those decisions lack the normative consequences that law, as a conceptual matter, must have if it is to count as law in the positivist's sense of the word. Since the legal authority of the courts is constrained by the acceptance of other officials, the existence and content of the rule of recognition depend on the joint practices of both judges *and* other officials.

II. THE LOGICAL RELATIONSHIP BETWEEN THE CRITERIA OF VALIDITY AND THE SOCIAL RULE OF RECOGNITION

The terms "criteria of validity" and "rule of recognition" are not synonymous. Whereas the social rule of recognition is at least partly normative, as one would expect of rules, the criteria of validity are purely descriptive in character. Indeed, criteria of validity—that is, the criteria that distinguish law from nonlaw in a legal system—are usually expressed by biconditionals without any normative language:

> Criteria of Validity Schema: *X* is a law in *S* if and only if *X* conforms to the conditions set forth by the proposition *P*.

A statement with this form neither is a norm nor has the resources to provide reasons for action, because it lacks deontic language capable of providing such reasons.

In contrast, the rule of recognition is expressed in deontic terms describing or defining obligations and duties. Thus, recognition norms (alternatively referred to as "recognition rules") have the following form:

> Recognition Rule Schema: A president/legislator/judge has a duty (or ought) to perform *X* in the execution of her function as president/legislator/judge.

---

4. *Id.* at 113.

The Recognition Rule Schema, unlike the Criteria of Validity Schema, contains the logical resources—that is, deontic notions—to define and express duties.

The *purely descriptive* criteria of validity are extrapolated from a study of the *normative* recognition rules, particularly those that require certain acts as a precondition for creating law. Clearly, the recognition norms that directly define duties with respect to recognizing, creating, and adjudicating law, as well as those that confer the power to do so, will determine the properties a norm must have to have the status of law.

Although "rule of recognition" and "criteria of validity" are closely related, it is important to distinguish the two, because, as we will see below, there are some recognition norms defining duties pertaining to how the Court interprets the Constitution that are, strictly speaking, not part of the criteria of validity. The two terms are related without being synonymous.

III. IDENTIFYING THE CRITERIA OF VALIDITY AND RULE OF RECOGNITION: THE MODELING CONSTRAINT

Hart's view that the existence and content of the rule of recognition are determined by official practice entails that what officials self-consciously treat as validity criteria *are* the validity criteria. While individual officials—including judges—can presumably have mistaken beliefs about the validity criteria, it is simply not possible, on the Conventionality Thesis, for officials of the legal system, considered collectively, to be *generally* mistaken about some *social* validity criterion. If officials all self-consciously recognize and treat norms satisfying *N* as valid law and *N*'s authority rests on acceptance, then *N* determines a validity criterion in *S*. What officials collectively regard as the properties constituting norms as legally valid, as a conceptual matter, *are* the properties that are incorporated into the social rule of recognition defining the criteria of legal validity.

Each feature constituting a social rule is empirically observable. First, we can empirically ascertain convergence in behavior. Second, we can empirically ascertain that conformity to the rule is encouraged and that deviations are criticized. Third, we can empirically ascertain that the requisite social pressure is brought to bear on participants in the group to conform to the rule. Although it is possible to hide these features, legal systems, such as the United States, characteristically make no attempt to do so.

Accordingly, if Hart's Conventionality Thesis is true, then the project of identifying the validity criteria is empirical. The only way to identify the content of the social rule of recognition and the validity criteria is by empirical means. To identify the content of the validity criteria in any particular society, one must employ roughly the same sorts of empirical tools that are commonly utilized by sociologists to study the behavior of officials. Thus, according to what I will call the Modeling Constraint, a correct description of the validity criteria in a legal system *S* must express those properties that, as a matter of observable empirical fact, officials collectively recognize as giving rise to legally valid norms they are obligated to enforce.

IV. THE U.S. SUPREME COURT AND THE NATURE OF FINAL AUTHORITY

There are a number of controversial issues regarding the authority the U.S. Supreme Court has to decide constitutional issues. Theorists, for example, disagree about whether courts in a democratic society *should*, as a matter of political morality, have final authority to declare unconstitutional a duly enacted bill. Theorists likewise disagree about whether, as a descriptive matter of law, the Constitution grants the Court final authority over a particular class of issues.

At the outset, however, it is important to note that one matter is clear: the Supreme Court currently has final authority to decide at least some constitutional issues. Indeed, one could not plausibly deny, for example, that the Supreme Court has final authority on a variety of issues, including prayer in public schools, the constitutionality of the death penalty, the constitutionality of abortion restrictions, and so on.[5]

Such authority is limited, of course. For example, the Court lacks authority to override impeachment of government officials, nullify amendments, or decide "political questions." But the claim is not that the Court's authority is unlimited; it is rather that, at the very least, the Court has final authority to decide the constitutionality of Congressional enactments.

It need not be the case that courts have final authority or that the scope of this authority over the class of relevant issues is unlimited. It might be that such authority is spread over a number of official departments, or it might even be that the people have it. Likewise, it might be that there are just some issues over which no one has final authority. Nothing in any conceptual theory of law requires any particular person or official to have the last say.

A. The Capacity to Create Legal Obligations that Bind Other Officials of the System

A court has *authority* to decide a substantive legal issue only if its decision creates presumptive *obligations* on the part of other officials to accept its decision as law. To have authority is to be able to issue directives that are authoritative over some relevant class of individuals, and a directive is authoritative by virtue of its obligating the relevant class of individuals.

5. As we will see, even Ronald Dworkin concedes this. *See* RONALD DWORKIN, LAW'S EMPIRE 2 (1986).

A court's authority to decide a substantive issue of law is *final* if and only if there is no *official* agency with authority to overrule the court's decision. As Dworkin puts this uncontroversial point, "[an] official has final authority to make a decision [when her decision] cannot be reviewed and reversed by any other official."[6] Accordingly, if a court has final authority over a decision, then its decision creates an obligation that binds officials in the jurisdiction; since there is no possibility of reversal, the obligation is final.

One might characterize the people in a democracy as having final authority in the sense they can initiate amendments with the effect of overruling an official's holding and can elect officials who appoint judges. While this affords citizens some authority that would have to be reflected in a complete statement of the criteria of validity, officials practice a rule that invests some authority in official agencies such as courts and legislatures—and it is the content of this authority I am concerned with here.

The obligations created by the decisions of a court with final authority are legal, if not *morally legitimate*. This has a very important consequence: *insofar as a court has final authority to decide a substantive issue of law, it can legally bind officials in its jurisdiction, other things being equal, with either of two conflicting decisions on that issue*. For example, if a court has final authority to decide whether abortion rights can be restricted by legislation, then its decision creates legal obligations that bind other officials regardless of how the decision comes out—as long as the court reaches its decision in an acceptable way. Thus, the Supreme Court can legally bind other officials with a decision that is mistaken under the "correct" theory of interpretation (if such there be).

B. Final Authority and Scorer's Discretion

In his new chapter for this volume (Chapter 6), Kent Greenawalt notes that in baseball, there is a rule that a batter is out after three strikes; however, the umpire is the one who ultimately makes the decision. It would be a mistake, on his view, to think that there is a disjunctive baseball rule that states you are out either after three strikes or after the umpire calls you out, or to think that there is some kind of recognition norm authorizing the umpire to apply the three-strikes rule. Similarly, Greenawalt holds that it would be a mistake to characterize a recognition norm as conferring final authority on the Court.

This seems mistaken. The *rules of baseball* are distinct from, and do not include, recognition rules giving umpires decision-making authority, but some recognition rule on who makes the call is necessary. This is clear in the context of professional baseball, which contains a set of recognition rules that supplement the rules of baseball; the rules of baseball are *fundamental to the game*, but the recognition norms are fundamental to what norms will govern professional

6. Ronald Dworkin, Taking Rights Seriously 32 (1977).

baseball—and they include both the rules of baseball and the rule granting umpires authority to apply the rules of baseball.

There is another difference between the umpire's decisions and those of the Court considering the constitutionality of some enactment. An umpire might mistakenly call a ball strike three, but this does not involve striking down the rule that calls a batter out after three strikes. When the Court incorrectly strikes down some official rule, it nonetheless affects the status of the rule in a way that an umpire's mistakes do not—although the character of this effect is not yet clear.

C. Final Authority and the Criteria of Validity

While it is natural to think that the holdings of the court with final authority are legally binding because they establish the content of the law, this is not necessarily true. It is both logically and causally possible for officials to be legally bound to enforce the content of a norm lacking the status of law—something that frequently happens in disputes that implicate the law of some other nation, state, or jurisdiction.

But this is not how officials in the United States understand the constitutional holdings of the Court. Although officials and citizens might disagree with a holding by the Court, thinking it mistaken as a matter of interpretation, that holding is nonetheless treated and characterized as law. Even when a holding is widely thought mistaken, the state enforces the holding with the same coercive mechanisms used to enforce any other legal norm. The holdings of the Court establish the content of the law in the constitutional arena.

This should not be taken to mean that a Court holding declaring a statute unconstitutional invalidates the law in the sense that it removes a statute from the books or precludes a legislature from reenacting the very same law to challenge the Court to reverse itself (which happens quite frequently with *Roe v. Wade*).[7] An explicit repeal by the legislature is required to remove the statute from the books, but there is little reason for that body to expend the energy after a statute is declared unconstitutional. The legal effect of a declaration of unconstitutionality and a legislative repeal is the same: the statute creates no enforceable rights or duties. And the same is true of a reenactment—unless the Court reverses itself upon a subsequent legal challenge.

Officials and constitutional theorists disagree on how to characterize the effects of a declaration of unconstitutionality. Some theorists and judges argue that the effect of a declaration of unconstitutionality is to nullify the law. Indeed, in *Norton v. Shelby County*,[8] the Court declared, "an unconstitutional act is not a

---

7. *See, e.g.*, Matthew D. Adler & Michael C. Dorf, *Constitutional Existence Conditions and Judicial Review*, 89 VA. L. REV. 1105 (2003).

8. 118 U.S. 425 (1886). For a defense of this view, see Larry Alexander & Frederick Schauer, *On Extrajudicial Interpretation*, 110 HARV. L. REV. 1359 (1997). For its part, the Court has not always adhered to this view. *See* U.S. v. U.S. Coin and Currency, 401 U.S. 715, 741 (1971).

law; it confers no rights; it imposes no duties; it is, in legal contemplation, as inoperative as though it had never been passed." Similarly, in *U.S. v. Dickerson*, the Court stated, ". . . Congress may not legislatively supersede our decisions interpreting and applying the Constitution."[9] *Dickerson* invited "Congress and the States to . . . search for . . . other procedures which are at least as effective in apprising accused persons of their [rights]," but this was an invitation to cooperate with the other official bodies made at the discretion of the Court—and nothing in the notion of final authority precludes this.[10]

Others argue that such declarations might preclude state enforcement of the law by the parties to the decision, but go no further than that.[11] There are two different arguments here. First, such decisions do not "nullify" the law, because the statute would take effect without other action by the legislature if the Court were to reverse itself. Theorists making this argument also frequently claim that state officials, not party to the decision, should conform to such decisions to the extent of avoiding acts reasonably likely to be declared unconstitutional given the Court's stated view on the matter.

None of this makes much difference because the Court's declaration of a norm as unconstitutional clearly renders the norm unenforceable and hence as lacking the force that partly constitutes an enacted bill as *law*; norms of a system *S* that may not be legally enforced are not properly characterized as "law" or as having the status of "legal validity" or "legality." Legal norms are backed up by the police power of the state. Once this latter feature is removed, their status as "law," as far as positivism is concerned, has for all practical purposes been removed—regardless of whether such norms remain on the books.

Second, Court decisions create legal obligations binding parties to the case, but do not create general obligations to refrain from enforcing laws declared by the Court as unconstitutional.[12] But, as a matter of legal practice, other executive officials follow the holding and decline to enforce laws that are declared

9. 120 S. Ct. 2326, 2332 (2000).

10. *See* Michael C. Dorf & Barry Friedman, *Shared Constitutional Interpretation*, 2000 Sup. Ct. Rev. 61. Although Dorf and Friedman defend the normative claim that other political actors should be given some role in constitutional meaning, they claim the last word should belong to the Court. Indeed, they point out that "it is beyond doubt that the Court is assigned the primary role in determining the scope of constitutional rights," and thus seem to concede the "maximal" view of the Court's authority defended by Alexander & Schauer, *supra* note 8.

11. Edwin Meese takes this view. *See, e.g.*, Edwin Meese, *The Supreme Court of the United States: Bulwark of a Limited Constitution*, 27 S. Tex. L. Rev. 4555 (1986). Larry Kramer argues in *The People Themselves* that this sort of "departmentalism" was implied by *Marbury v. Madison* and that political morality requires a return to this understanding of the Court's role in interpreting and applying the Constitution relative to other political actors.

12. *See* Richard Fallon, *As-Applied and Facial Challenges and Third-Party Standing*, 113 Harv. L. Rev. 1321, 1339 et seq. (2000). For an opposing view, see Alexander & Schauer, *supra* note 8.

unconstitutional or laws with content that is sufficiently close to the law declared as unconstitutional that there is a strong probability it would be declared unconstitutional. This practice includes the President.

Although there are some constitutional scholars who believe there is no legal duty among such executive officials to refrain from enforcing such laws and who would presumably adopt this practice only as some sort of professional courtesy or out of prudential concern to keep their jobs, those scholars are concerned with a different issue than the positivist. These constitutional scholars are arguing a normative issue regarding the interpretation of the Constitution—namely, the issue of whether, under the proper interpretation of the Constitution and associated history, Supreme Court decisions *should* be construed as creating general obligations. This is a *normative* issue different from the purely *descriptive* issue with which the positivist is concerned—namely, whether the other executive officials converge on a social norm that requires them to refrain from enforcing laws declared unconstitutional by the Court. If, as seems clear, the answer is "yes," then officials are taking the internal point of view toward a recognition norm that creates a legal obligation to refrain from enforcing such laws.[13] That practice might change if and when constitutional theorists arguing the normative issue reach a general consensus that there is no such legal duty under the proper interpretation of the Constitution. But, until the practice itself changes, officials are treating Court holdings as legally obligatory—especially if they would criticize, as seems reasonable to hypothesize, incidents where other officials utterly ignore a holding and enforce a law identical to one declared unconstitutional by the Court. Constitutional theorists are concerned with the content of the proper interpretation of the Constitution and not the content of the rule of recognition, which are related but distinct rules.

From the standpoint of general jurisprudence, unconstitutional enactments are not properly characterized as "law" because they are no longer enforced as a general practice among officials and hence do not give rise to enforceable legal rights or obligations. This, at any rate, is how the terms "law" and "legal validity" should be understood here.

Indeed, lawyers are trained to regard the holdings of the court with final authority as establishing the content of the law. Every casebook in constitutional law in the United States contains excerpts from controversial Supreme Court cases that are widely considered mistaken. For example, there is not a comprehensive

---

13. *See* Larry Kramer, The People Themselves: Popular Constitutionalism and Judicial Review (2005). Kramer argues that the Supreme Court has usurped final authority, which should be taken back by the people. The descriptive claim, grounded in a comprehensive historical analysis, confirms that the official practice today confers final authority over the Constitution to the Supreme Court; the normative claim is that this is illegitimate. But the normative issue is not relevant for a positivist analysis of the content of the rule of recognition—although it is undeniably important.

casebook or treatise on constitutional law in the United States not containing an excerpt or discussion of the *Roe* case. It is taken for granted among legal practitioners, students, and officials of the legal system that, for better or worse, the Court's decision in *Roe* established the content of the "law" (in the sense explained above) on abortion in the United States.

U.S. officials, then, are practicing a recognition norm that requires them to treat the holdings of the court with final authority as establishing the content of the law on certain issues involving the Constitution—although this authority is, as we will see, limited in a number of ways. It is not just that officials happen to behave this way. Most, but not all, accept and practice this rule because they believe they are required to do so by fundamental principles governing the structure of the legal system. But some may accept the rule for purely prudential reasons (say, to get ahead), and may even believe it is not the best rule or required by such fundamental principles.

D. Final Authority and Official Disagreement

That officials are bound by a holding does not imply that they have to agree with it; it merely implies that they must comply with it with respect to acts within its scope. For example, as Greenawalt points out, a Senator might disagree with a holding that a legislative act is constitutional and vote against it believing it unconstitutional when it comes up for renewal. There is nothing in the claim that the Court has final authority to decide constitutional issues that implies that any official bound by a holding must *believe* it is correct.

Of course, some officials have sometimes publicly denied the Court's final authority. Most recently, John Ashcroft has done so. President Jefferson threatened to disobey the Court's holding in *Marbury v. Madison* if it went the wrong way. Perhaps the most significant example involves *Brown v. Board of Education.* The Court held that public schools should be desegregated with "all deliberate speed" to signal to the southern states that the Court would not enforce the decision immediately, as a way of preventing a widespread official rebellion in the south that would have caused the most serious crisis in the United States since the Civil War.

A couple of observations should be made here. First, these situations are too few and far between to justify doubt that the Court has final authority in deciding the constitutionality of a law. The situation regarding *Brown* might, however, have ultimately led to a rebellion and, given the resistance of southern officials, might have produced a period in which the social practice investing the Court with final authority broke down. Because the Court did not enforce its holding with mandatory desegregation orders until the culture in the southern states had changed significantly, we may never know what exactly the social practice was during that period.

Second, it is likely that most officials who suggested they would disobey a certain holding would have obeyed that holding if pressed to do so. It is one thing for an official to express that inclination and quite another to *act* on it. The consequences of breaching an entrenched social practice regarding the Constitution are grave enough to deter officials who believe the Court lacks such authority from acting accordingly. Talk is cheap.

Third, even if some officials occasionally acted on such a belief, it does not affect the analysis. A positivist could not hold that it is a necessary condition for the existence of a legal system that *all* the officials *always* converge in behavior and attitude on specific content. If positivism held this position, John Ashcroft's denial of the Court's final authority would, by itself, suffice to show that the United States has no legal system—and that is a *reductio* of any claim with this result. The most that a positivist can claim on this score is that enough officials converge often enough on the content of a recognition norm that they can effectively regulate the behavior of citizens.

Indeed, there is nothing in the idea that the Court has final authority that implies that a Justice who dissents from a holding must abandon his or her dissent the next time the issue comes up. On the abortion issue, Justice Scalia has indicated he will "continue to dissent from [the Court's] enterprise of devising an Abortion Code, and from the illusion that [the Court has] authority to do so."[14] This is not only consistent with the analysis offered up to this point; as we will see, it is arguably required of Scalia, given his views on the best theory of constitutional interpretation, by the recognition norm that the Justices converge in practicing.

The general practice is this: an official who refused to enforce some holding of the court with final authority, believing it mistaken and hence not law, would induce a cascade of criticism and a court order to enforce the holding. Insofar as these expectations are both institutional and normative, officials are practicing a recognition norm that makes certain court holdings determinative of the *content of the law*—a fact that determines the content of the criteria of validity.

But to the extent that officials are practicing a rule that constrains judges to decide substantive issues of law according to *N*, they will not enforce a decision that isn't putatively grounded in an attempt to satisfy *N*. There is considerable incentive for the other officials to enforce the holdings of the court with final authority; in our dangerous world, any sign of a breakdown between the various branches of government can have grave consequences for national security. Even so, there are probably limits to the cooperation of the other officials in the recognition norms they practice.[15] For this reason, the authority of the court to establish legal content will usually be circumscribed by second-order requirements—a requirement that will also find expression in a purely descriptive statement of the validity criteria.

---

14. Hodgson v. Minnesota, 497 U.S. 417, 480 (1990) (dissenting).

15. For example, I would guess that a court decision that was explicitly grounded in a coin-flip would precipitate a breakdown between that court and the other officials.

A judicial decision is sufficient, but not necessary, for legality because officials might treat a duly enacted norm as law for an extended period without a judicial challenge. If citizens are diligent in conforming to the norm, then the norm is fairly characterized as "law" even without an official affirmation by the court with final authority. This feature of legal practice complicates the task of summarizing the necessary and sufficient conditions for law—and the reader should understand, at the outset, that I have not resolved such issues.

E. Final Authority and Declarations that a Law Is Constitutional

So far I have focused on Supreme Court declarations that a law is unconstitutional; however, additional issues are raised by Court declarations that a law is constitutional. I have argued that officials are practicing a norm that creates a legal obligation to recognize a decision by the Court (within the limited scope of its authority) as establishing the content of the law—regardless of whether they think the decision is mistaken or not. This is exactly why the Court is fairly regarded, from the standpoint of identifying the content of the rule of recognition, as having final authority.

But it is important to be careful here. Just as a Court decision that one of the Justices believes mistaken does not preclude that Justice from dissenting the next time the issue comes up or require the Justice to change his or her vote, so too it does not require any official to enforce a law he or she believes, contra the Supreme Court ruling, is unconstitutional. As Frank Easterbrook points out, there is a long-standing practice among presidents to refuse to enforce statutes that they believe to be unconstitutional;[16] there might very well be a practice among officials, including presidents, not to enforce statutes they believe the Court has mistakenly declared to be constitutional.

This is not inconsistent with what has been said here. It is well established that officials responsible for the enforcement of what counts as law have considerable discretion with respect to whether or not to enforce something that formally has the status of "law." There are plenty of statutes on the books that have not been enforced for years out of a belief it would be inappropriate to do so, but that still formally count as law because they could be enforced as such in the absence of some court holding to the contrary. If the Supreme Court declares a law to be constitutional and the President believes this is mistaken, the President has legal discretion not to enforce that norm out of a belief that it is unconstitutional.[17] But the general thrust of the official practice is that it *can* be enforced

16. On this, see Frank Easterbrook, *Presidential Review*, 40 CASE W. RES. L. REV. 905 (1990); and Michael Stokes Paulsen, *The Most Dangerous Branch*, 83 GEO. L.J. 217 (1994), particularly 267 et seq.

17. Indeed, some theorists believe that the Constitution, properly understood, defines a legal duty on the part of the President not to enforce such laws. *See* Paulsen, *supra* note 16. But, again, this is a different issue from the one with which I am concerned here as

and hence counts as law—even if an official exercises discretion not to do so. The Court's decisions do not, on this analysis of final authority, legally obligate officials to enforce norms it declares constitutional.

V. THE RULE OF RECOGNITION AND THE CONSTITUTION

As may be evident from the preceding section, there is no straightforward relationship between rules of recognition and written constitutions. First, a legal system might not have a written constitution. Second, even if it does, officials might not view it as binding and ignore it. Third, a constitution's text must be interpreted, and there are many different theories of constitutional interpretation. To determine the role a written constitution plays in determining what counts as law, we have to observe all the relevant practices of officials in the system.

A. The Modeling Constraint and the Direct Incorporation Formulation

Many positivists have assumed the U.S. Constitution directly defines criteria of validity. Hart argues, for example, that the "criteria provided by the rule of recognition . . . may . . . be substantive constraints on the content of legislation such as the Sixteenth or Nineteenth Amendments to the United States Constitution."[18] Likewise, Brian Leiter states that "[a] rule is a valid rule of law in the United States if it has been duly enacted by a federal or state legislature and it is not inconsistent with the federal constitution."[19] On this view, the United States contains the following as a validity criterion:

> The Direct Incorporation Formulation (*DIF*): A duly enacted norm is legally valid if and only if it conforms to the norms of the Constitution.

DIF asserts that, for example, duly enacted norms that objectively violate the First Amendment are, for that reason, legally invalid.

In evaluating *DIF*, it helps to remember that officials frequently regard Supreme Court validity decisions as objectively mistaken. For example, the Court's holding in *Roe v. Wade* continues to be controversial thirty-five years after it was decided. Many people believe the *Roe* decision is *incorrect* as a matter of constitutional law and interpretation. While some believe *Roe* is inconsistent

---

a positivist. Paulsen is concerned with the normative issue of what the Constitution, properly interpreted, entails with respect to the President's legal obligations. I am concerned with the descriptive issue of identifying the content of the rule of recognition that is being practiced by officials. Much confusion will result from failure to distinguish these two issues.

18. HART, *supra* note 3, at 250.

19. Brian Leiter, *Legal Realism and Legal Positivism Reconsidered*, 111 ETHICS 278, 278–301 (2001).

with the Constitution's protection of a person's right to life, others believe it illegitimately created a new constitutional right. And such critics include congressional representatives, the attorney generals for several recent presidents, and Supreme Court Justices—the very officials whose practices determine the content of the validity criteria.

The problem for *DIF* is that officials characteristically treat such decisions as establishing what is legally valid—"legally valid" and "law" here being construed to express the idea that these decisions have the effect of creating, sustaining, or extinguishing enforceable legal rights and duties. Even when there is widespread disagreement among officials about whether a Supreme Court decision is "correct" as a matter of constitutional law, officials cooperate by treating the decision *as* the law. Enforcement agencies decline to enforce a law the Court has declared unconstitutional even if they think the decision mistaken. The relevant legislative bodies might reenact the law, but it has no legal effect. Other courts dismiss as a matter of law any action grounded in an enactment declared unconstitutional by the Court.

Despite the unending controversy about *Roe*, officials treat it as law. Every federal and state enforcement agency enforces *Roe* with whatever coercive mechanisms it uses to enforce any other law. Officials might sometimes attempt to enact rules that restrict abortion in some way, but they unfailingly obey the Supreme Court if it strikes down those rules as unconstitutional. Officials generally accept, however grudgingly at times, that they are bound by even Court decisions they believe are mistaken, and hence treat *Roe* as law—regardless of whether they believe it was correctly decided.

This is not happenstance; as a matter of legal practice, officials generally regard one another as under an institutional duty to defer to the Court's validity decisions that fall within the scope of the Court's commonly accepted authority. In *Arizona v. Evans*, for example, the Court declared that "[s]tate courts, in appropriate cases, are not merely free to—they are bound to—interpret the United States Constitution . . ., [but] they are *not* free from the final authority of this Court."[20] Though the Court has found other occasions to affirm its authority over other officials, such reminders are rarely needed because officials always converge on expecting one another to accept the Court's decisions as establishing the law.

This has an important consequence: such behavior indicates that officials are self-consciously practicing a recognition norm that confers upon the Court final authority to decide whether a duly enacted norm conforms to the substantive norms of the Constitution. Insofar as most officials regard themselves as bound by even mistaken Court decisions, it is because they are converging upon practicing a recognition norm that imposes a second-order duty to treat the Court's decisions as establishing the law (as the positivist understands that term).

20. Arizona v. Evans, 514 U.S. 1, 8–9 (1995).

Positivists and antipositivists agree on this. As Hart puts it, "[W]hen [the supreme tribunal] has said [what the law is], the statement that the court was 'wrong' has no consequences within the system: no one's rights or duties are thereby altered."[21] As Dworkin puts it, the Court "has the power to overrule even the most deliberate and popular decisions of other departments of government if it believes they are contrary to the Constitution, and it therefore has the last word on whether and how the states may execute murderers or prohibit abortions or require prayers in the public schools, on whether Congress can draft soldiers to fight a war or force a president to make public the secrets of his office."[22]

But this means that *DIF* is incorrect as an empirical description of the validity criteria in the United States. While *DIF* purports to validate all and only duly enacted norms that conform to the substantive guarantees of the Constitution, officials characteristically recognize and treat as law even those Supreme Court validity decisions they believe are mistakenly decided *as matter of constitutional law*. Since officials look ultimately to the Court's decisions—and not to the substantive guarantees themselves—as settling the issue of which duly enacted norms are legally valid, *DIF* is inconsistent with the empirical behavior of officials and violates the Modeling Constraint.

One might counter that what law *is* in the United States and what officials *enforce as law* come apart in cases where the Court makes a mistake in a validity decision, but this move is not available to a positivist. If the criteria of validity are determined by the empirical practices of officials, those norms officials collectively recognize as legally valid under a shared second-order recognition rule *are* legally valid. *DIF*, then, cannot be reconciled with official practice as required by positivism's Conventionality Thesis.

B. Legal Realism and the Supreme Court's Final Authority

Another natural view goes too far in the other direction. John Chipman Gray, for example, argues that the law is, as a conceptual matter, what the highest court says it is: "To quote . . . from Bishop Hoadly: 'Nay, whoever hath an absolute authority to interpret any written or spoken law, it is He who is truly the Law Giver to all intents and purposes, and not the person who first wrote and spoke them.'"[23] On this view, final authority to decide what the law is logically entails "absolute authority" that cannot be legally constrained in any way.

Accordingly, Gray infers the notorious claim that the law in the United States is what the Supreme Court says it is from the claim that the Court has final authority to decide the validity of duly enacted norms. Since, on this line of analysis, the

---

21. Hart, *supra* note 3, at 141.

22. Dworkin, *supra* note 5, at 2. Of course, many theorists believe that, as a matter of political morality, the Court ought not to have this authority. *See, e.g.*, Jeremy Waldron, Law and Disagreement (1999).

23. John Chipman Gray, The Nature and Source of Law 125 (1924).

Court has unlimited authority to shape constitutional content, the validity criteria in the United States include the following norm:

> Unlimited Discretion Formulation (*UDF*): A duly enacted norm is valid if and only if it conforms to whatever the Supreme Court decides is asserted by the substantive guarantees of the Constitution.

UDF makes the Court the standard and denies that the Constitution might genuinely constrain the Court in some way.

Hart explicitly rejects Gray's view as applied to the U.S. Constitution on the ground that the Court's legal authority over validity decisions is always constrained by the determinate meanings of the Constitution: "At any given moment judges, even those of a supreme court, are parts of a system the rules of which are determinate enough at the centre to supply standards of correct judicial decision."[24] On Hart's view, then, *UDF* overlooks the fact that the Court is legally bound to ground its validity decisions in the language of the Constitution, and that hence the Court is legally constrained to *interpret* the Constitution.

Hart is correct that there are limits to the range of constitutional interpretations that officials are prepared to accept as establishing what is and is not legally valid in all existing legal systems. For example, a Court decision invalidating a federal speed limit on the ground that it violates the Second Amendment right to bear arms would likely provoke a constitutional crisis unprecedented in U.S. history. Moreover, a Court decision invalidating the legality of paper money on an originalist theory would probably be ignored in practice and viciously criticized.

Taking Hart's remark above into account, it appears that, as an empirical matter, officials accept at least the following norm as constraining the Court's discretion:

> The Acceptability Constraint: The Supreme Court has a duty to ground decisions on whether a norm is legally valid in an interpretation of the Constitution that (1) can rationally be grounded in the text and (2) is pragmatically acceptable.

It seems clear that Hart is correct in thinking Justices are constrained by both the language of the Constitution and certain (difficult to specify) pragmatic considerations.

We are now in a position to ground in a positivist framework what is, among mainstream legal theorists, an uncontroversial conclusion about *UDF*. Insofar as the range of plausible interpretations defines a conventional constraint on the Court's discretion in making validity decisions, U.S. officials are, as an empirical matter, practicing a recognition norm that incorporates the Acceptability Constraint on the Court's discretion in making validity decisions. Since the

---

24. Hart, *supra* note 3, at 145.

Acceptability Constraint is a legal norm, it constrains the Court's decision making by imposing on Justices a *legal duty* to ground their validity decisions in the text of the Constitution. While the Justices presumably accept this norm, the other officials of the system can loosely be thought of as imposing it on them from the outside; thus, I will refer to this as an external constraint.

At this point, then, we can identify the beginnings of a recognition rule (and hence a legal norm) that defines the duties of officials to abide by Supreme Court decisions that satisfy certain constraints, and that is inconsistent with *UDF*:

> Final Authority (*FinAuth*): Officials in the United States have (1) a duty to treat as legally valid duly enacted norms upheld by the Court as conforming to an interpretation of the Constitution that satisfies the Acceptability Constraint and the Λ-Constraint, and (2) a duty to treat as not legally valid duly enacted norms struck down by the Court as not conforming to an interpretation that satisfies the Acceptability Constraint and the Λ-Constraint.

The locution "Λ-Constraint" serves as a variable for further empirical limits, if any, that officials accept on the Court's discretion. *FinAuth* is thus a schema, the details of which remain to be filled in.

In any event, the fact that *FinAuth* includes the Acceptability Constraint on the Court's discretion, by itself, shows that *UDF* violates the Modeling Constraint. Although the Acceptability Constraint defines an extremely modest legal constraint on the Court's discretion, the existence of *any* legal constraint on the Court's discretion is inconsistent with a statement of a validity criterion that asserts there are none. Thus, *UDF* violates the Modeling Constraint.

C. Identifying Other External Constraints on the Court's Discretion

It is reasonable to think there are other interpretive limits on the Court's discretion than just the Acceptability Constraint. Though we can't begin to understand the Constitution without understanding the ordinary meanings of its terms, those ordinary meanings cannot dictate a particular outcome in any validity case likely to be entertained by the Court. And this means that the Acceptability Constraint always leaves the Court free to choose either a "yes" answer or a "no" answer to the question of whether a particular duly enacted norm is legally valid.

Consider whether the Court should uphold a duly enacted norm that prohibits virtual child pornography. It is true that the Court cannot understand the First Amendment without understanding the ordinary meanings of such terms as "abridge" and "speech," but this does little to constrain the Court in reaching a particular outcome—for merely putting together the ordinary meanings of "Congress," "shall," "make," "no," "law," "abridging," "freedom," "of," and "speech" tells us almost nothing about whether the First Amendment prohibits a ban on virtual child pornography. Since the ordinary meanings of the First Amendment are indeterminate with respect to the permissibility of a ban on virtual child pornography, the Acceptability Constraint leaves the Court *entirely* free to uphold or to strike down the statute as it sees fit.

Although the Acceptability Constraint defines enough of a limit on the Court's discretion to refute the idea that *UDF* is a validity criterion, this limit really doesn't amount to much in determining the *outcome* of validity cases. There are always two logically possible outcomes in any case challenging the validity of a duly enacted norm: the Court can either uphold the norm or strike it down. While the Acceptability Constraint precludes a very large number of irrational interpretations of the constitutional text, it will leave in any "hard" case one rational interpretation that would justify upholding the norm and one rational interpretation that would justify striking it down, because, by definition, a case is "hard" when existing law fails to dictate a unique outcome. Given that any validity case likely to reach the Supreme Court is hard in this sense, it follows that the Acceptability Constraint will never eliminate a sufficiently large set of interpretations to rule out, as a logical matter, one of the two conflicting decisions. In essence, then, the Acceptability Constraint operates to constrain the Court in *justifying* its decisions in hard validity cases, but it does not operate to limit the *outcomes* available to the Court.

Existing legal practice is difficult to reconcile with the idea that the only limit on the Court's discretion is a duty to rationally ground its decisions in some plausible interpretation of the Constitution. The Court's validity decisions are always based on interpretative standards that demand considerably more than just a minimally rational connection to the ordinary meanings of the constitutional text. Each of the prevailing approaches to constitutional interpretation, such as evolutionism, originalism, and textualism, purports to identify the best interpretation of the text and hence one that is superior to any interpretation bearing only a minimal connection to ordinary meanings of the text.

This suggests that an accurate statement of the validity criteria must also take account of the role that these substantive interpretive standards play in constraining judicial determinations of what counts as law. As Kent Greenawalt points out:

> Whether every standard of interpretation that constrains judges should be characterized as a "legal" standard is doubtful. Some standards of interpretation, such as that ordinary words should be accorded their natural meaning absent some reason to do otherwise, are general and fundamental to all interpretation of language; but other standards are distinctly legal. Whether standards are distinctly legal or not, *so long as judges are bound to follow them in deciding what the Constitution means, the standards need to be accorded some place among ultimate or derivative criteria for determining law.*[25]

25. Kent Greenawalt, *The Rule of Recognition and the Constitution*, 85 MICH. L. REV. 621, 655–56 (1987) (reprinted as Chapter 1, this volume, at 33)(emphasis added).

Greenawalt believes that the rule of recognition and criteria of validity must acknowledge the role that legal principles of interpretation, like originalist or textualist standards, play in determining what counts as law in the United States.

Not surprisingly, Greenawalt's description of the validity criteria affords "prevailing" interpretive standards a prominent place in determining what counts as U.S. law. As he puts the matter in his own description of the U.S. rule of recognition: "On matters not clear from the text, the prevailing standards of interpretation used by the Supreme Court determine what the Constitution means."[26]

Of course, the prevailing standards themselves cannot wholly determine the result if the Court's mistaken interpretations bind, but Greenawalt explicitly acknowledges this: "officials generally treat a constitution as saying what the highest judges say it says."[27] Accordingly, Greenawalt should be interpreted as endorsing the following formulation:

> Prevailing Standards Formulation (*PSF*): A duly enacted norm is legally valid if and only if it conforms, on matters not clear from the text, to what the Supreme Court decides the Constitution means according to the prevailing standards of interpretation.

Although a step in the direction of adequately capturing the Court's authority with respect to deciding issues of constitutionality, *PSF* is at odds with the empirical practices of the other officials. As Greenawalt himself points out:

> [To] say that whatever standards are now prevailing . . . are part of the ultimate rule of recognition . . . could be misleading. . . . [A]ll Justices believe it is sometimes appropriate to alter previously prevailing standards of interpretation. . . .[28]

It is not just that Justices sometimes *believe* it is appropriate to alter those standards. Rather, the point is that the Court *has authority* to alter interpretive standards in making validity decisions; should the Court decide to interpret the Constitution based on the popular understanding, I would hypothesize that other officials would accept those holdings and enforce them. But if the Court is not legally bound by the "prevailing" standards, then it follows that the Court, as an empirical matter, has legal authority to depart from those standards.

This, however, poses a difficulty for *PSF*. If, as an empirical matter, the Court has authority to bind officials with validity decisions that explicitly depart from prevailing standards, it is because officials are practicing a norm that requires them to treat those decisions as establishing what is legally valid. But since, according to positivism, what officials collectively recognize as legally valid on the ground that it satisfies a general criterion *is* legally valid, it follows that the

26. *Id.* at 659 (reprinted as Chapter 1, this volume, at 36).
27. *Id.* at 653 (reprinted as Chapter 1, this volume, at 31).
28. *Id.* at 656–57 (reprinted as Chapter 1, this volume, at 33–34).

Court's departures from prevailing standards in making validity decisions establish what is legally valid. Since *PSF* holds that only those decisions that are grounded in prevailing interpretive strategies establish what is legally valid, *PSF* violates the Modeling Constraint and hence fails as a positivist description of a validity criterion in the United States.

By this time, the reader may have noticed a general problem in formulating *external* limits on the Court's discretion. While conspicuous features of our legal practice suggest that there are more stringent limits on the Court's discretion than just the Acceptability Constraint, we should expect that it will be very difficult to identify other external limits (i.e., limits primarily defined by the cooperation of officials outside the Court). After all, the limits of official cooperation have rarely, if ever, been breached by a Supreme Court validity decision. On the whole, U.S. officials nearly always treat the Court's decisions on constitutionality as establishing what is valid.

It is easy to surmise why this might be. As noted briefly above, a refusal on the part of other officials to treat as binding a Court decision would likely signal a breakdown between the various branches of government that would have profound consequences for the economic, psychological, and military constituents of national well-being.[29] A decision violating the Acceptability Thesis, of course, creates grave risks of its own since it suggests bad faith by the Court, which may itself be symptomatic of a general governmental breakdown; that is why it is reasonable to think other officials would balk at enforcing such decisions. The risks associated with a breakdown between the Court and other officials create a strong incentive for other officials to treat the Court's good faith decisions (i.e., those that satisfy the Acceptability Constraint) as binding—no matter how profoundly mistaken they may seem.

D. The Role of Moral Considerations in Constraining the Court

At this point, it would be helpful to attempt to determine where the Supreme Court Justices themselves draw the line with respect to what *they* are prepared to do. Given that it is the Court's obligations with which we are concerned, we might make more progress by attempting to identify the limits imposed by the standards that the Justices themselves accept as constraining the Court's discretion in constitutional cases. I will call such limits "internal" because the Justices seem to impose these limits on themselves.

Greenawalt's analysis, though problematic, indicates a very natural direction for the project of identifying internal limits on the Court's discretion and the recognition norms that express these limits. The Justices clearly employ a number

29. This might not have always been so and possibly will not always be so; perhaps, it should not be so. But, as an empirical matter, it is generally understood inside and outside the United States, by friends and foes alike, that Supreme Court decisions characteristically bind other officials.

of interpretive standards that constrain the discretion of the Court beyond the limits defined by the Acceptability Constraint. A Justice who accepts one of these standards, then, will regard herself as duty-bound to decide validity cases in accordance with the constitutional interpretations that satisfy that standard.

Nevertheless, the task of identifying the relevant recognition norm is complicated by the fact that Justices frequently disagree about which interpretative standards are appropriate. If, in contrast, each Justice regarded originalism as the only legitimate standard of constitutional interpretation, the Justices would be practicing a norm requiring them to decide validity cases on an originalist understanding. But this, of course, is not the case: while some Justices favor an originalist approach, others favor an approach that views the Constitution as a "living document"; still others favor a pragmatic approach, adopting elements of different strategies as circumstances warrant. Insofar as the Justices regard the Court's decisions as binding on the other officials regardless of which of these favored principles ultimately provides the justification, a description of the relevant recognition norm should not uniquely favor one of the interpretive principles.

It is worth noting that Justices routinely criticize one another for their choice of prevailing interpretive strategies. Originalists, for example, frequently criticize living-document theorists for inappropriately reading their political preferences into the Constitution, while living-document theorists criticize originalists for adhering to an understanding of constitutional text that lacks contemporary relevance. In every such case, however, the criticism is that the particular interpretation, even if plausibly grounded in some prevailing interpretive standard, is not grounded in what—in some sense—is the *best* interpretation of the Constitution.

This kind of criticism suggests that Justices are practicing a recognition norm requiring the Court to ground validity decisions in the best interpretation of the Constitution. The most coherent explanation for the fact that Justices criticize each other for failing to produce the best interpretation of the Constitution is that they regard themselves as bound by the best interpretation in making decisions and are practicing a norm that makes this the standard.

Something more, of course, should be said about the relevant sense of "best." What is "best" might, for example, be determined from a policy standpoint; or it might be determined from the standpoint of personal ambition. Thus, while the claim that the Justices regard themselves as under a duty to ground their validity decisions in the best theory of constitutional interpretation should seem eminently plausible, we cannot understand exactly what it amounts to without an explanation of what is meant by "best."

Somewhat surprisingly, we can look to the work of positivism's most influential critic for a theoretically viable account of the sense that is employed in the Court's validity practice. Dworkin makes a number of empirical claims about what judges "characteristically" do in deciding hard cases. Dworkin observes that judges, as a general matter, experience themselves as constrained by morally normative considerations of political legitimacy.[30] Hard cases of any kind, on his view, are typically decided on the strength of moral considerations—and not the sort of policy considerations that ground legislative decisions. Judges in this legal system take an interpretive attitude toward law that requires them to interpret the law in a way that shows it in the best moral light.

These empirical claims are quite plausible. Supreme Court opinions and dissents "characteristically" suggest that the Justices are trying to interpret the Constitution in a way that legitimizes the legal system and its official monopoly of the police power. These opinions and dissents frequently challenge each other's arguments and interpretive principles on grounds of political morality.

The range of interpretive strategies that might fall under the rubric of "morally best" is quite wide. For example, this rubric would embrace a purely result-oriented theory that simply attempts to reach the morally best outcome, regardless of all other considerations—including considerations of legitimacy having to do with democracy. It would also embrace Dworkin's own moral reading of the Constitution, which requires that putatively moral terms in the Constitution be interpreted as incorporating the corresponding moral norms. But it would also embrace purely historicist theories, like originalism, which *precludes recourse to objective morality* in deciding a case in favor of an interpretation based on a historical understanding of the terms; originalists, such as Scalia, typically believe that originalism is justified on the basis of considerations of moral legitimacy. Indeed, the "morally best" rubric would embrace consequentialist-driven interpretations—or, for that matter, any hybrid method consisting of various pieces of this. At the end of the day, it seems reasonable to think that Justices are all concerned to ground their decisions in the morally best interpretation of the Constitution (broadly understood to incorporate all the above strategies and theories of interpretation)[31]—and there are many different views about how to reach this.

In *Planned Parenthood v. Casey*,[32] for example, the Court argued that considerations of legitimacy required it to reaffirm *Roe*:

> [T]he Court's legitimacy depends on making legally principled decisions under circumstances in which their principled character is sufficiently plausible to be accepted by the Nation. . . . There is . . . a point beyond which frequent

30. Here it is important to remember that the notion of legitimacy is a moral notion that is concerned with the extent to which the state is morally justified in using its coercive force.

31. One might think that the notion of morality is being stretched, as Greenawalt suggests in his second contribution to this volume, beyond recognition. This is false. There is a wide range of morally normative theories of constitutional interpretation, some which allow recourse to moral norms in interpreting the Constitution, others of which prohibit it as being inconsistent with legitimate democratic considerations.

32. 505 U.S. 833 (1992).

> overruling would overtax the country's belief in the Court's good faith. . . . The legitimacy of the Court would fade with the frequency of its vacillation.[33]

In response, Justice Scalia argues that the majority's claim that "the Court must adhere to a decision for as long as the decision faces 'great opposition' and the Court is 'under fire' acquires a character of almost czarist arrogance."[34]

It is no accident that majority and dissenting Justices criticize each other in terms of what is legitimate. At a deeper level, the Justices' views on constitutional interpretation are usually based on normative views about moral legitimacy. Proponents of more conservative textualist and originalist approaches typically reject more liberal theories of constitutional interpretation as being inconsistent with moral principles emphasizing the legitimacy of majoritarian decision making. Scalia's disdain for living Constitution approaches is unmistakably moral in character:

> This is not to say that I take issue with [the claim] that the problem of judicial rewriting of democratically adopted texts is "deeply rooted in our history" and that "judges have exercised that sort of presumably *undemocratic authority* from the very beginning." To acknowledge that is simply to acknowledge that there have always been, as there undoubtedly always will be, *willful* judges who bend the law to their wishes. But acknowledging *evil* is one thing, embracing it is something else. . . .[35]

It is clear Scalia believes that Court decisions that modify the Constitution violate democratic ideals of legitimacy: allowing judges to "exercise undemocratic authority" is an "evil" that threatens "the existence of democratic government."

Liberal theorists are no less likely to ground their conceptions of what the Court is legally bound to do in substantive considerations of political morality. William Brennan rejected originalism as "arrogance cloaked in humility" and argued for an interpretative norm that protects the individual rights to which human dignity gives rise:

> In general, problems of the relationship of the citizen with government have multiplied and thus have engendered some of the most important constitutional issues of the day. As government acts ever more deeply upon those areas of our lives once marked "private," there is an ever greater need to see that individual rights are not curtailed or cheapened in the interest of what may temporarily appear to be the "public good."[36]

---

33. *Id* at 866.
34. *Id* at 999.
35. ANTONIN SCALIA, A MATTER OF INTERPRETATION 131, 132 (1997) (emphasis added).
36. Speech by Justice William J. Brennan, *reprinted in* THE GREAT DEBATE: INTERPRETING OUR WRITTEN CONSTITUTION 14, 19–20 (Federalist Soc'y eds., 1986).

Whereas Scalia's view of legitimacy emphasizes the significance of majoritarian decision making and hence requires a nonmoral, purely historicist interpretation of the Constitution, Brennan's view emphasizes the significance of respecting individual rights. Like Scalia, Brennan formulates the Court's legal duty in terms of protecting certain substantive ideals of political morality, and advocates interpreting the Constitution in light of evolving moral standards.

Such empirical observations suggest that the Justices are practicing the following second-order recognition norm:

> Duty to Find the Best Interpretation Standard (*DutBest*): Supreme Court Justices are legally obligated to decide the validity of duly enacted norms according to what is, as an objective matter, the morally best interpretation of the Constitution.

As their writings indicate, Justices attempt to (1) conform their behavior to a norm that obligates them to decide cases according to the morally best interpretation of the Constitution, and (2) take the internal point of view toward that standard as governing their behavior as officials.

The other officials also seem to take the internal point of view toward *DutBest*—although, strictly speaking, the only duties defined by *DutBest* are those owed by the Supreme Court. Like Supreme Court Justices, the other officials of the legal system tend to ground their views about how the Court ought to decide cases in standards of constitutional interpretation that are based on more general views about the Court's morally legitimate role in a democratic society. When other officials criticize mistaken Court decisions, such criticism is immediately grounded in these views about how to interpret the Constitution, and ultimately grounded in the underlying moral views about the scope of the Court's legitimate authority under democratic ideals. Accordingly, the attitude and behavior of both the Court and the other officials seem to converge on *DutBest*.

On the strength of such considerations, then, one might think that the objectively best interpretations of the constitutional norms directly define validity criteria. On this line of analysis, the following is a validity criterion in the United States:

> Objectively Best Interpretation Formulation (*OBIF*): A duly enacted norm is legally valid if and only if it conforms to what is, as an objective matter, the morally best interpretation of the substantive norms of the Constitution.

If officials in the United States accept *DutBest* as defining the Court's duties in making validity decisions, then *DutBest* must straightforwardly give rise to a validity criterion.

OBIF violates the Modeling Constraint by understating the Court's authority to bind other officials with its decisions. While the other officials will criticize the Court for not producing the objectively best interpretation, those officials will nonetheless continue to treat mistaken decisions as binding law. Since the Court thus has characteristic authority to bind other officials by either of two conflicting interpretations of the relevant provisions, a norm can be legally valid even if its content is, as a matter of fact, inconsistent with the objectively best interpretation of the Constitution. It follows, then, that the *objectively* best interpretations of the substantive provisions of the Constitution, if such there are, do not directly determine what counts as law in the United States—though it is true that they function to constrain the Court's decision making in validity cases.

E. The Court's Best Interpretation Formulation of the Relevant Validity Criterion

Given that officials will accept *any* Supreme Court decision that satisfies the Acceptability Constraint and is grounded in what a majority of Justices take to be the morally best interpretation of the Constitution, it appears that the relevant recognition norms are the Acceptability Constraint and *DutBest*, and therefore that the relevant recognition norm defining the duties of officials in the United States should be formulated to fill in the Λ-Constraint as follows:

> Final Authority (*FinAuth*): Officials in the United States have (1) a duty to treat as law duly enacted norms until struck down by the Court as failing to conform to what the Justices collectively have decided is, as an objective matter, the morally best interpretation of the Constitution that satisfies the Acceptability Constraint; and (2) a duty to treat as not being law those duly enacted norms that are struck down by the Court as not conforming to what they collectively take to be the interpretation that is, as an objective matter, the morally best interpretation that satisfies the Acceptability Constraint.

FinAuth coheres more tightly with empirical legal practice because it acknowledges that officials will accept the Court's decisions about what is the morally best interpretation of the Constitution.

Accordingly, a more accurate statement of the ultimate validity criterion will look something like this:

> Court's Best Interpretation Formulation (*CBIF*): A duly enacted norm is legally valid unless declared unconstitutional according to what a majority of the Justices decide is, as an objective matter, the morally best interpretation of the substantive norms of the Constitution.

Again, it should be emphasized that there are many issues to which the Court's authority does not extend, such as issues that involve political questions—but the Court has final authority to decide whether an issue is a political question. If, on the one hand, the Court declines to address an issue on the ground that it decides it is a political question, this is consistent with *CBIF*. If, on the other, it mistakenly decides a case that presents a political question, then officials are bound by that holding—which is also consistent with *CBIF*.

Though admittedly vague, *CBIF* and *FinAuth* better model the facts of the Court's validity practice than do any of the other formulations we have considered.

Like *PSF* and *UDF* but unlike the other proposed formulations, *CBIF* and *FinAuth* are consistent with the empirical fact that, in any hard validity case, the Court can go either way with its decision and bind other officials. Further, like *OBIF* but unlike all the other formulations, *CBIF* and *FinAuth* cohere with the empirical fact that the Justices and the other officials accept *DutBest* as defining a second-order duty on the part of the Court to decide validity cases in accordance with the morally best interpretation of the Constitution.

While it is surely possible to improve on this formulation, any minimally adequate formulation will look more like *CBIF* and *FinAuth* than like any other we have considered—including *DIF*. First, since (1) what officials recognize as law *constitutes* law and (2) U.S. officials characteristically treat as law even mistaken Court decisions on the content of the substantive norms of the Constitution, the criteria of validity in the United States must reflect the Court's discretionary authority to shape the content of those norms. Second, since (1) the legal authority of the Court is constrained by the standards officials jointly accept as limiting what the Court can do in validity cases and (2) U.S. officials accept certain standards limiting the Court's authority in interpreting the Constitution, the criteria of validity in the United States must acknowledge that there are limits on the Court's discretionary authority in validity cases. Thus, if positivism is correct, then a correct description of the relevant validity criterion must acknowledge both the fact that the Court has some discretionary authority to shape the content of the Constitution *and* the fact that there are limits to this authority.

5. FOUR CONCEPTS OF VALIDITY
Reflections on Inclusive and Exclusive Positivism

WIL WALUCHOW*

I. THE STATE OF PLAY

In a well-known passage from *The Concept of Law*, H. L. A. Hart makes the following remark:

> The law of every modern state shows at a thousand points the influence of both the accepted social morality and wider social ideals. . . . In some systems, as in the United States, the ultimate criteria of legal validity explicitly incorporate principles of justice or substantive moral values. . . .[1]

How is one to interpret the provocative claim made in Hart's second sentence? Providing a plausible answer to this question has been one of the main projects of modern positivism, and has led to the development of two different streams within that theory. Those who defend versions of "inclusive legal positivism" often point to the phenomenon Hart describes as illustrating a crucial fact that no viable legal theory can deny: that there is nothing in the nature of law that rules out the possibility that consistency with a moral norm might serve among the conditions for legal validity within a particular legal system. In Hartian terms, there is nothing in the very nature of law that rules out the conceptual possibility that a rule of recognition—whose existence and content are purely contingent matters of social fact—might, as a matter of further social fact,

---

* Senator William McMaster Chair in Constitutional Studies, Department of Philosophy, McMaster University. I would like to thank the participants in the Rule of Recognition and the U.S. Constitution conference for their helpful comments on an earlier version of this chapter. Of particular note were the insightful suggestions of the editors and conference organizers, Matthew Adler and Kenneth Himma. I also wish to acknowledge a debt of gratitude to the members of my 2008 McMaster graduate seminar in legal theory. Helping them to work their way through contemporary debates surrounding the forms and limits of modern legal positivism has helped me sort out my own thinking on these matters. I need to acknowledge a special debt of gratitude to Matthew Grellette, who persuaded me of the usefulness of distinguishing between what he calls "existence" and "validity" conditions of law, and of the need to develop a theory that does justice to the insights of both inclusive and exclusive legal positivism. My distinction between *validity as existence* and *systemic legal validity* owes a great deal to Matt's thoughts on these matters. In many ways, this chapter is but a footnote to his initial insight.

1. H.L.A. Hart, The Concept of Law 203–04 (Penelope A. Bulloch & Joseph Raz eds., 2d ed. 1994).

include conformity with one or more moral norms among its conditions for legal validity.[2]

Defenders of "exclusive positivism" vehemently oppose all such readings of Hart's suggestion and of the practices it purports to describe. They argue that consistency with a moral norm simply cannot, as a conceptual matter, figure among the conditions for legal validity, and that Hart made a serious mistake in suggesting otherwise.[3] These exclusive positivists proclaim the "sources thesis," which holds that the conditions for legal validity must focus exclusively on factors that have nothing to do with the merits (moral or otherwise) of the norm in question, in order to avoid conflating questions of law and morality which it is the business of law to separate for us. The validity of a norm always depends exclusively on whether, for example, it has the appropriate source in precedent or congressional legislation. To think otherwise—that is, to think that legal validity could in some way be tied to moral conditions—would force one to deny a number of key features of legal practice. Not the least of these is the law's claim to be a legitimate authority, one of whose primary tasks is to regulate and guide our conduct in ways that allow us to avoid the controversial moral and political questions that dog modern political societies.[4]

So exclusive positivists thoroughly reject the inclusivist account of Hart's observation about the American rule of recognition. That rule *does not,* because it *cannot,* recognize consistency with moral norms specified in the American Constitution and its constituent Bill of Rights as a condition of validity for American laws. But we seem to have a problem here. The American Bill of Rights, as it has been interpreted and applied over the years in adjudicating constitutional disputes, *does* seem to permit citizens to challenge legal validity on moral grounds. For example, the Due Process Clause is widely regarded as specifying a constitutional test of fairness. And it does seem that this standard of fairness serves as a norm consistency with which is among the criteria for legal

---

2. *See, e.g.*, W.J. WALUCHOW, INCLUSIVE LEGAL POSITIVISM (1994); JULES COLEMAN, THE PRACTICE OF PRINCIPLE (2001); MATTHEW KRAMER, WHERE LAW AND MORALITY MEET (2004).

3. *See, e.g.*, JOSEPH RAZ, THE AUTHORITY OF LAW (1979); Leslie Green, *Legal Positivism, in* THE STANFORD ENCYCLOPEDIA OF PHILOSOPHY (Edward N. Zalta ed., Spring 2003), *available at* http://plato.stanford.edu/archives/spr2003/entries/legal-positivism/; Scott Shapiro, *On Hart's Way Out*, 4 LEGAL THEORY 469 (1998) and *Law, Morality and the Guidance of Conduct*, 6 LEGAL THEORY 127 (2000); ANDREI MARMOR, POSITIVE LAW AND OBJECTIVE VALUES (2001); Michael Guidice, *Unconstitutionality, Invalidity, and Charter Challenges*, 15 CAN. J. L. & JURISPRUDENCE 69 (2002), and *The Regular Practice of Morality in Law*, 21 RATIO JURIS 94 (2008).

4. *See, e.g.*, RAZ, *supra* note 3, and Shapiro, *supra* note 3. For an overview of the debates between inclusivists and exclusivists, see my *Legal Positivism, Inclusive versus Exclusive*, in ROUTLEDGE ENCYCLOPEDIA OF PHILOSOPHY (Edward Craig ed., 2001), *available at* http://www.rep.routledge.com.

validity within the American legal system—just the kind of possibility contemplated by Hart and other inclusive positivists.

Now it might appear that this seemingly undeniable fact is fatal to exclusive positivism. But appearances can be deceiving, and it is here that things get very tricky indeed. Contrary to what one might initially have thought, exclusive positivists are actually quite happy to acknowledge a thoroughly robust role for norms of political morality in the kinds of constitutional cases Hart mentions. They simply dispute the inclusive positivists' *theoretical account* or *interpretation* of this feature of legal practice, and the consequences, for legal theory, that their account is said to entail. The American rule of recognition does not, via the Due Process Clause, specify fairness as a condition of legal validity. Rather, it specifies a moral condition under which judges are legally required to exercise what Joseph Raz calls a "directed power"[5] to *change* the law. On this reading, the Bill of Rights specifies moral conditions under which judges are obligated to invalidate what was, till the judicial act of striking it down, perfectly valid law—perfectly valid because, up till that particular point in time, the law satisfied all the relevant source-based criteria. It was, for example, duly enacted by Congress, met with the requisite approval from the executive branch, and so on. In other words, the American rule of recognition does not, by way of its Bill of Rights, establish consistency with the norms of fairness as a fundamental test for legal validity. On the contrary, the fundamental rules involved in these scenarios are examples of what Hart calls "rules of change."[6] The Bill of Rights specifies moral conditions the application of which triggers the legal obligation of a judge to exercise her Hohfeldian power to *alter* the state of valid law. If an existing law violates due process, then the judges are mandated to change it, by invalidating it, or otherwise restricting its application. The end result? The existence and content of valid laws still depend exclusively on their sources—including judicial acts of "striking down"—even though moral norms can and do figure prominently in legal decisions to eliminate or otherwise change laws via a system's rules of change.

Despite its undoubted appeal as a sophisticated theoretical account of an important aspect of legal practice, I remain troubled by the exclusivist's directed-powers account of constitutional challenges.[7] The main source of my discomfort

---

5. *See* JOSEPH RAZ, *The Inner Logic of the Law*, *in* ETHICS IN THE PUBLIC DOMAIN: ESSAYS IN THE MORALITY OF LAW AND POLITICS 242 (rev. ed. 1996).

6. *See* HART, *supra* note 1, at 95–99.

7. Henceforth, I will use the phrase "constitutional challenge" to refer to the kinds of cases to which Hart makes reference—cases in which norms of political morality are invoked in applying an instrument like the American Bill of Rights to address in some way the legal validity of some other norm, for example, a statute. I say "in some way" so as to remain neutral as to whether the judge is deciding whether the norm is already invalid or whether it is in need of invalidation.

lies in the tendency of this account to run up against key aspects of constitutional challenges—including how legal actors conceive what they are doing when they argue or decide constitutional cases. These aspects of legal practice sit uncomfortably with the directed powers account. On the other hand, I am equally troubled by certain implications of the rival inclusive account of constitutional challenges. It too sits uncomfortably with a different set of key aspects of legal practice that seem equally undeniable.

These conflicting sources of discomfort are nicely reflected in a recent exchange between Ken Himma and Matthew Kramer over the question whether modern legal systems actually do include rules of recognition containing moral criteria for legal validity. According to Himma, the following is how an inclusive positivist would have us understand the American or Canadian rule of recognition: *"A duly enacted . . . norm is law if and only if it conforms to the substantive norms of the Constitution (properly interpreted)."*[8] In Himma's view, this is not, as a matter of empirical fact, the rule actually in play in American and Canadian judicial practice.[9] On the contrary, American and Canadian judges follow a rule of recognition more like the following: *A duly enacted norm "is law, other things being equal, until declared inconsistent with the best interpretation of the Constitution that comports with due regard for precedent by the highest court to consider the constitutionality of [the norm]."*[10] Himma takes it to be an empirical fact that American and Canadian legal actors engage in practices better described by this second rule. They have adopted a practice of always deferring to judicial *interpretations* of the moral norms cited in their Bill and Charter of Rights respectively, and it is consistency with these precedents, not the specified moral norms themselves, that serves as a condition of legal validity. Of course, the existence of such precedential interpretations is always a matter of social fact of the kind exclusive positivism points to as an eligible source of law. In all these legal systems, including the American one with its constitutional Bill of Rights, moral norms do not serve the role Hart and other inclusive positivists say they do: they do not serve as conditions for legal validity.

---

8. Kenneth Einar Himma, *Final Authority to Bind with Moral Mistakes: On the Explanatory Potential of Inclusive Legal Positivism*, 24 Law & Phil. 1, 18 (2005) (emphasis added). Himma's formulation is restricted to federal norms, but I have taken the liberty of widening it to encompass all laws within the U.S. legal system, on the understanding that the U.S. Constitution applies to all laws within the United States. I do not believe that this adversely affects any of the arguments made in this paper.

9. Himma is happy to acknowledge the conceptual possibility of genuinely inclusivist criteria. He nevertheless insists that no contemporary societies, in which there tend to be deep disagreements about the requirements of morality, actually include any such criteria. According to Himma, there is insufficient convergence of belief and official action to sustain a conventional rule of recognition containing any such criteria.

10. Himma, *supra* note 8, at 24 (emphasis added). Again, I have taken the liberty of widening the formulation so that it encompasses all laws within the U.S. legal system.

Matthew Kramer, a card-carrying inclusive positivist, is unhappy with Himma's rendering of matters, and sets out to defend a distinctive role for the relevant moral norms that is consistent with Himma's empirical observations. His claim is that the kind of deference Himma describes is fully compatible with an otherwise decisive role for the relevant norms of political morality (not the judges' interpretations of them) in constitutional challenges. These legal systems remain as illustrations of the inclusive possibility Hart seemingly brought to our attention, that "[i]n some systems, as in the United States, the ultimate criteria of legal validity explicitly incorporate principles of justice or substantive moral values."

My principal aim in this chapter is not to explore the Himma/Kramer debate so as to determine which of the two has the better argument. Rather, I wish to use it as a springboard to what is, I hope, a richer understanding of the relevant conceptual landscape. As will become clear, I think that each of the two disputants has highlighted points of significance that no one concerned to understand the nature of law can safely ignore. My aim is to use their dispute as a means of bringing into relief something that is becoming increasingly clear, at least to me: Each side of the inclusive/exclusive debate highlights and explains important aspects of legal practice for which no plausible theory of law can fail to account—and does so reasonably well. On the other hand, each side does a less than stellar job of highlighting and explaining other important aspects of legal practice for which no plausible theory can fail to account. This is a situation we should endeavor to avoid if at all possible. We can begin to do so, I shall argue, if we acknowledge that there are in fact crucially different notions of validity at play in these debates—and that we need a (more inclusive?) theory of law that finds room for all of them.

II. THE HIMMA/KRAMER DISPUTE

As observed at the outset, Hart asserts that conformity with constitutionally recognized norms of justice counts among the conditions for validity within the American legal system. According to Himma, this claim is empirically false. What is in fact doing all the work in such constitutional cases are not the norms of justice, but the courts' decisions about them. "[A] moral norm *N* cannot function as a necessary or sufficient condition of legality if the rule of recognition grants a court general legal authority to bind officials with either of two conflicting decisions on whether a proposition is law in virtue of satisfying *N*."[11] The powers of courts to introduce precedent-setting—and hence law-determining—interpretations of the recognized moral norms renders the latter of no legal force

11. Himma, *supra* note 8, at 2.

or effect. Whether, in truth, a duly enacted law, *R*, violates *N* is legally irrelevant. Before the courts become involved (if they ever do) in the question of *R*'s validity, *R* is valid because it was duly enacted, and its having been duly enacted means that it satisfies all the relevant source-based criteria of validity. Of course, once the courts become involved with the question whether *R* is consistent with *N*, their judgment about *R*'s conformity with *N* now determines its validity. What ultimately matters at that point is whether the highest court to have addressed the question of violation has ruled that *N* has been infringed. If it determines that *R* is inconsistent with *N*, then *R* is invalid; if it rules that *R* is consistent with *N*, then *R* is valid. The court's *decision* about *N*, not *N* itself, is what ultimately determines validity. Hence, sources continue to do all the work; moral merit plays no role at all.

Matthew Kramer is understandably unhappy with this result and sets out to show that the relevant moral norms can and do continue to play a decisive role in matters of legal validity arising in constitutional cases. Kramer's analysis is multifaceted and subtle, but his main points seem to be the following. First, having the power to bind someone with a mistaken decision does not mean that one is at liberty or has the authority to do so:

> If someone is legally empowered to accomplish a certain alteration in legal relations but is not legally at liberty to do so [because, e.g., she must do so only when *N* is actually in conflict with a putatively valid legal norm, *R*, but there is, in fact, no such conflict between *N* and *R*], then she does not have the discretion or authority to do so. She *can* accomplish the alteration, but she *may* not; that is, she cannot *permissibly* accomplish it. Yet, according to Himma, the Supreme Court is in precisely such a situation in connection with its erroneous law-ascertaining judgments.[12]

In other words, even when legal officials are bound by a superior court's mistaken interpretations of *N*, it remains true that the judges in that superior court—so long as they are not bound by an interpretation of *N* issued by a court superior to them—are required to apply *N* in making their decisions regarding the legal validity of *R*. *N* itself serves, at least for them, as a criterion of validity. The fact that they are in this way bound is evidenced by a number of factors, not least of which is that legal actors, including those who are bound by the superior court's decision on the relevant constitutional question, will nevertheless consider it quite appropriate to criticize (or praise) the court's decision on whether *R* is in conflict with *N* and is therefore unconstitutional. And, importantly, those who engage in criticism will do so on the ground that the court *got the law wrong*, that what the court took to be valid (or invalid) was in actual fact not valid (or invalid) at all:

> Because the officials' denunciations and commendations of the Court's rulings share an underlying orientation toward that guiding principle [e.g.,

12. KRAMER, *supra* note 2, at 127.

> fairness], they sustain the existence of a duty on the Court to ascertain the law in accordance with that principle's requirements. Even when the denunciations and commendations are inapposite in their specific bearings, their justificatory foundations establish the standard which the Court is obligated to meet.[13]

In short, criticism or condemnation of a Court's interpretation or application of *N* presuppose that conformity with *N* serves as the relevant criterion of validity. Otherwise, there would be no logical or legal basis for criticism, or praise for that matter.[14]

A second key point of criticism leveled by Kramer draws on the fact that criteria of validity within rules of recognition are often multiple in number and ranked in relation to one another. Certain doctrines of federal paramountcy supply one obvious example of this feature.[15] When a rule duly enacted by a state or provincial legislature requires a result that conflicts with another rule enacted by the federal legislature, legal systems often regard the latter as taking precedence over the former. When they do so, this is because enactment by federal legislatures is, in that system, taken to be a criterion of validity that overrides enactment by state or provincial legislatures. Much the same, Kramer suggests, can be true when one turns to the role of moral criteria of validity. Here, judicial interpretations of a constitutionally recognized moral norm, *N*, can take precedence over *N* itself. In other words, if a rule, *R*, *in fact* infringes moral norm *N*, but a court has *ruled* that *R* is consistent with *N*, then the court's ruling on the question of consistency takes precedence. *R* is actually legal valid, despite its conflict with *N*. According to Kramer, this is exactly how the American rule of recognition works. "[T]he validating and invalidating effects of the Incorporationist criteria in the American Rule of Recognition are indeed [as Himma argues] superseded by any Supreme Court decisions that run contrary to those effects."[16] But importantly, for Kramer, "they are superseded only within the precedential purviews of the decisions. Beyond the precedential scope of each of those decisions, the moral principles [such as *N*] absorbed into the law by the Incorporationist criteria will have retained their force as legal standards to which the conduct of everyone within the jurisdiction is subject."[17] There is here, Kramer adds, "no

13. *Id.* at 130–31.

14. One is reminded here of Leibniz's objection to the divine command theory of morality. Supposing that the standards of morality or perfection are determined by God's commands robs us of the ability to praise God for commanding the right things. How, Leibniz asks, can one praise an agent for making the right choices if there is no standard against which to measure those choices *save the choices that are in fact made by that agent?*

15. This is my example, not Kramer's. But I think it provides a clear example of the kind of ranking he has in mind.

16. KRAMER, *supra* note 2, at 135.

17. *Id.*

across-the-board displacement; there are only piecemeal displacements."[18] *R*'s actual conflict with *N* means that *R* is invalid, but only till such time as the court rules to the contrary. After the ruling the superior criterion kicks in, rendering *R* no longer invalid. But *N* continues to work as a criterion of validity on all other matters not subject to the court's mistaken interpretation of it. In this respect, the legal force of *N* is analogous to the force that state or provincial rules often have when they run up against the requirements of a paramount federal statute. On some doctrines of federal paramountcy, the state or provincial rule remains valid and determines results in all cases in which there is no conflict with the federal law.[19]

So according to Kramer, one can retain a vital role for moral criteria for validity even after one has fully accommodated Himma's insightful observations. That role may be more limited than, or different from, that initially contemplated by defenders of inclusive positivism, but it is an important one nevertheless. But is this in fact an accurate reading of Kramer's position? I must confess to a degree of puzzlement on this question. Consider the following scenario:

1. *R* is a "duly enacted" rule that satisfies all the relevant source-based criteria of validity;
2. *R* is in fact inconsistent with moral norm *N*, the norm of fairness to which the Due Process Clause makes reference;
3. No court has ever ruled on whether *R* is consistent with *N*; and
4. There have, therefore, been no erroneous court rulings on *N* that "displace" the effect of *N* on *R*.

Is *R* valid law on Kramer's rendering of matters? In light of the quotations cited above (notes 16–18), it would seem that *R* is *not* valid, owing to its actual conflict with *N*. And this is precisely what one would expect an Inclusive Positivist to say. Kramer himself sums up this view nicely when he says:

> Inclusive Legal Positivism, as understood [here], consists in the following thesis: it can be the case, though it need not be the case, that a norm's consistency with some or all of the requirements of morality is a precondition for the norm's status as a law in this or that jurisdiction. . . . Insofar as a threshold criterion of that sort does prevail in any particular legal system, then some degree of moral worthiness is a necessary condition for the legally authoritative force of each norm that is validated as a law within the system.[20]

---

18. *Id.*

19. This is precisely how the Canadian paramountcy doctrine operates. *See* Peter Hogg, Constitutional Law of Canada 113–14 (2d ed. 1985).

20. Kramer, *supra* note 2, at 2.

According to Kramer's interpretation of American law, it would seem, *R* can be duly enacted by Congress and yet be legally invalid owing to its actual conflict with a moral norm, *N*, which (1) has been incorporated into the law as a moral benchmark for validity, and (2) has not been subject to the "piecemeal displacement" brought about by erroneous judicial interpretations of *N*. To be sure, *R* will cease to be invalid should a court later rule erroneously in its favor—that is, mistakenly rule that *R* is in fact consistent with *N*. But till such time as that ruling takes place, *R* is *in fact* legally invalid.

Now it is at this point that the inclusive account runs squarely up against apparent facts of legal practice to which defenders of exclusive positivism are apt to draw our attention: barring unusual circumstances, it is likely that rule *R*, which is said to be invalid owing to its conflict with *N*, will nevertheless be *accepted and practiced as valid law* till such time as a court declares it to be invalid. And of course this is something that may never occur. A court may never in fact have the opportunity to issue a ruling on *R*'s validity because, for example, no one has seen fit (for any number of reasons, perhaps financial) to issue a constitutional challenge. Even if such a challenge does eventually occur, and the court does in fact rule that *R* is invalid, the point remains: despite its objective inconsistency with *N*, *R* will likely be accepted and practiced as valid law, perhaps for decades, till such time as the court issues its ruling.[21] And if law is, as the positivists insist, ultimately a matter of social fact—of social practice—then there is a strong inclination to say that *R* *was* actually valid law till the point of the court's ruling, and that it would have remained valid law if no such ruling had ever occurred. In short, *R* *is* law if it is *accepted and practiced* as law. This important point is one to which Kramer seems rightly sensitive.

> Himma . . . has repeatedly pointed out that norms duly adopted through legislative or judicial or administrative procedures are legally valid before any subsequent adjudicative pronouncements on their validity. Until those norms are challenged in the courts—if in fact they ever are challenged—they

---

21. I say only that it will *likely* be accepted and practiced as valid law because citizens and government actors—say administrative bodies charged with implementing *R*—may well refuse to accept or apply it in the firm belief that *R* violates *N* and is therefore constitutionally invalid. In fact, in some instances, courts and other government actors will continue to act in the belief that the law under which they act is valid (or invalid) even after a superior court has ruled otherwise. See, for example, *Cooper v. Aaron*, 358 U.S. 1 (1958), where the state of Arkansas refused to act on the belief, endorsed by the U.S. Court of Appeals for the Eighth Circuit and, ultimately, the U.S. Supreme Court, that the U.S. Constitution required the abandonment of segregated schools. Cases of "non-compliance" with a superior court's rendering of a constitutional norm are highly controversial. But they do seem to occur, and they should give one pause in accepting Himma's claim that mistaken judicial interpretations of validity criteria always trump those criteria themselves. On this broader issue, see MARK TUSHNET, TAKING THE CONSTITUTION AWAY FROM THE COURTS (1999).

> are routinely treated by officials as law *and are therefore properly classified as laws.*[22]

He later adds:

> Himma rightly contends that the status of a norm as a law in the United States need not derive from the fact that the norm has been or would be deemed a law by the Supreme Court Justices in the event of a challenge to its constitutionality. A duly adopted norm's status as a law antecedes any such ruling by the Court, and continues until the norm is deemed unconstitutional by the Court or by an unappealed lower-court judgment—or until the norm is rescinded, of course.[23]

If I have him right, then, Kramer's position, as expressed in these particular passages, would appear to be this. Any rule, *R*, once duly adopted through appropriate legislative, judicial, or administrative procedures and employed as a valid basis for asserting legal rights, claims, and so on, is legally valid—at least till such time, if such a time ever comes about, that a court rules that *R* is inconsistent with *N*. And this is true even if, as an objective matter of fact, *R* is *not* consistent with *N*. In other words, if *R* is accepted and practiced as valid law, then it is in fact valid law—notwithstanding any inconsistency between *R* and moral validity criterion *N*, and notwithstanding any future ruling a court might make as to *R*'s consistency with *N*. But how can this be if, as Kramer also wants to insist, moral criteria can—and if the legal practices are right *do*—determine validity till such time as a court determines otherwise? If no paramount criterion of validity renders *R* invalid—which is supposed to happen only when a court (perhaps mistakenly) rules on whether *R* is consistent with *N*—then *N*, the subordinate criterion, is supposed to be the one in play. And if it is in play, then should not the legally correct answer be that, despite its being accepted and practiced as law, *R* is *in fact legally invalid*? Can a dyed-in-the-wool inclusive positivist accept anything else while remaining faithful to the main tenets of his theory?

Something has obviously gone wrong here. But what? Perhaps the most obvious answer is that I have simply misunderstood Kramer's subtle arguments, a not altogether implausible hypothesis. In suggesting that "norms duly adopted through legislative or judicial or administrative procedures" are legally valid till a court decides otherwise, perhaps Kramer meant something quite different from what I took him to mean. I took him to mean that *R* is valid if it satisfies all the requisite *source-based* criteria—for example, it received the requisite number of votes in Congress, was not vetoed by the executive, and so on. These, of course, are exactly the kinds of criteria favored by exclusive positivists as fully determinative of validity, and just the kinds of criteria that inclusive positivists deny are

---

22. KRAMER, *supra* note 2, at 139 (emphasis added).
23. *Id.*

sufficient for validity in systems such as one finds in the United States. According to inclusive positivists, a "duly adopted" rule can be legally invalid in the United States if it in fact fails to comport with the substantive moral provisions of the American rule of recognition. And if one wants to add that this will be so only till a court rules otherwise, so be it. But one does, it would seem, at the very least have to insist that till such a ruling takes place, violation of the substantive moral provision renders the "duly adopted" rule legally invalid—a legal fact that courts are duty-bound to recognize when they consider a constitutional challenge. And so it is natural to read Kramer as denying what appears definitive of the kind of theory to which he purports allegiance. So I am led to suspect that perhaps I have got Kramer wrong. Perhaps we are to read the phrase "duly adopted through legislative or judicial or administrative procedures" as encompassing the fulfillment of more than source-based criteria. On this alternative reading, a rule "*duly* adopted" is one that meets *all* the appropriate criteria for validity—both source based and merit based. If so, then Kramer will have remained faithful to his inclusivist credentials, but at the cost of denying the truth of at least some of Himma's empirical observations—and he does seem to want to grant Himma those observations about American legal practice.

As noted earlier, my principal aim is not to determine which of our two disputants, Himma or Kramer, is right or has the better argument. I'm more interested in using their dispute to bring to light some key lessons we might draw from their lively exchange. That a legal theorist of Kramer's talent should reach a point where he has either abandoned his inclusive positivism without being aware of it, or has couched his defense in words that strongly suggest he has done so, may give one reason to pause and take stock. In particular it may lead one to suspect that current debates surrounding inclusive and exclusive positivism have hit a brick wall, and that we need to find terms of engagement that better reflect the insights each side brings to the table. The remainder of this chapter represents a tentative step in such a direction.

III. LEGAL PRACTICE: SOME KEY OBSERVATIONS

Let's begin with some observations about legal practice, many of which figure prominently in the Himma/Kramer exchange. First, some facts that appear to favor exclusive positivism:

1. Notwithstanding its actual conflict with a constitutionally recognized moral norm, *N*, a duly adopted rule, *R*, will routinely be *accepted and practiced as valid law* till such time, if such a time ever comes, as *R* is judged by a court to be inconsistent with *N*.
2. Notwithstanding its actual conflict with a constitutionally recognized moral norm, *N*, a duly adopted rule, *R*, will routinely (continue to) be

accepted and practiced as valid law if the highest court to consider the issue rules that *R* does not in fact conflict with *N*.

3. Notwithstanding an *absence* of conflict with a constitutionally recognized moral norm, *N*, a duly adopted rule, *R*, will routinely *not* be *accepted and practiced as valid law* if a court rules that *R* actually conflicts with *N*.

A few observations. First, it should be stressed that propositions 1–3 represent only what is routine or typical. There are notable exceptions in each case. For instance, government bodies could refuse to implement a rule, *R*, in the firm belief that it is constitutionally invalid (proposition 1). With respect to proposition 3, *Cooper v. Aaron* illustrates the possibility that a government body can act (or at least propose or attempt to do so) in the firm belief that *R* is valid, despite a court's opinion to the contrary. Second, in calling a rule "duly adopted" I mean that it meets all the requisite nonmoral, source-based requirements for validity.[24] Third, the practices described as routine in propositions 1–3 are fully consistent with the sources thesis because, in the scenarios described, what counts toward establishing the legal validity of a rule, *R*, are nonmoral facts of legal practice, including the decisions of courts with respect to the validity of *R*. And finally, the described practices are fully consistent with the directed powers account of constitutional norms such as the due process provision. On this account, recall, a conflict between *R* and *N* does not mean that *R is* invalid; it means that judges are duty-bound to exercise their power to invalidate *R*, that is, to *make* it invalid.

Now some facts that appear to favor inclusive positivism.

4. Bills and charters of rights are generally taken to contain, and are expressed in terms that strongly suggest that they contain, paramount (moral) conditions of legal validity that have decisive legal force independently of, indeed even when in conflict with, court decisions.
5. In some legal systems, once a court has held that rule *R* infringes *N*, *R* will, for most legal purposes, be treated as though it never were valid law.
6. Constitutional instruments like the American Bill of Rights are generally understood to describe rights that no legitimate (i.e., valid) government action—including the actions of a court—may infringe. They are not taken to describe (mandatory) grounds for changing valid law.

A few observations. Propositions 4–6 reflect widespread beliefs regarding the nature of constitutions. One of the primary roles of a constitution is to specify legally recognized limits on the powers of government authorities with respect to the creation and/or recognition of valid law. Among other things, a constitu-

---

24. It is worth stressing that a rule can be *accepted* as having met all the requisite source-based requirements yet fail to do so, a fact highlighted by Matthew D. Adler and Michael C. Dorf in *Constitutional Existence Conditions and Judicial Review*, 89 VA. L. REV. 1101 (2003). We will explore the significance of this point later.

tion enshrines the thought that governments are inherently fallible—a thought that Les Green claims is integral to the positivist enterprise and upon which I will have more to say below.[25] A constitution does this by specifying limitations on the powers of government to introduce or recognize legally binding rules. Failure to observe the prescribed limits is, in many systems, not just a ground for criticizing the government morally or politically, or a reason why the government should mend its ways by changing the law. On the contrary, failure to observe the prescribed limits—conditions on the valid exercise of the relevant Hohfeldian power—is routinely taken to result in a nullity. It is a failure on the part of the government to effect the desired change to the legal landscape by introducing a new, valid, legal norm into the system.

This is arguably the case in the United States. As the U.S. Supreme Court stated in *Norton v. Shelby County*, "[a]n unconstitutional act is not a law; it confers no rights; it imposes no duties; it affords no protection; it creates no office; it is, in legal contemplation, as inoperative as though it had never been passed."[26] Adler and Dorf argue that many provisions of the American Constitution have just this effect because they contain "existence conditions" for valid law. For example,

> . . . Article I, Section 7 sets forth existence conditions for legislation. If the piece of paper that Smith calls a statute is actually a bill that passed the House but not the Senate, or a bill that the President vetoed, or just a piece of paper on which Smith typed words seeming to grant him rights, then Judge Jones "enforces" Article I, Section 7 by refusing to treat Smith's piece of paper as a statute.[27]

Some constitutions *explicitly* recognize this power-limiting, and hence existence-determining, role of constitutionally recognized validity norms. They do so by explicitly stating that any product of an attempt to exercise valid government power that violates the relevant constitutional norm is for legal purposes a nullity. It is a failed attempt, an attempt that is, as the Canadian Constitution puts it, "of no force and effect." Some systems give further concrete expression to this claim by requiring, in any case in which a ruling of nullity figures, further steps that presuppose that particular reading of the decision. For example, if the impugned rule, *R*, is a criminal code provision under which the appellant had earlier been charged and found guilty, the result will not be taken to be purely prospective. Rather, the decision will be that the appellant is not guilty of the alleged crime—he is not guilty because *R* was not a valid law establishing a legal

25. *See* Leslie Green, *Positivism and the Inseparability of Law and Morals*, 83 N.Y.U.L. Rev. 1035 (2008).

26. 118 U.S. 425, 442 (1886).

27. Adler & Dorf, *supra* note 24, at 1145.

duty to which he stood in breach.[28] Some constitutions go even further than this and provide legal remedies for those invalidly charged or held liable in such circumstances. The Canadian Constitution Act, Article 24 (1), specifies that "[a]nyone whose rights or freedoms, as guaranteed by this Charter, have been infringed or denied may apply to a court of competent jurisdiction to obtain such remedy as the court considers appropriate and just in the circumstances." Why, one might reasonably ask, would a legal remedy be thought appropriate in these circumstances if the exclusive positivist's directed powers account of constitutional challenges is correct? After all, on that account, *R*—because it was "duly adopted"—did indeed exist as valid law before the court's decision to invalidate it because of its conflict with a constitutional norm, *N*. Hence *R* presumably did determine valid legal obligations that the appellant would have to have violated when he did what he did. Recall again that on the directed powers account of constitutional challenges, a duly adopted rule, *R*, is legally valid until such time as the court exercises its directed power to invalidate it. So *R* existed as valid law between the time of its adoption and the time a court took the legal step of rescinding it because of its conflict with *N*. And so it did in fact impose the legal duties it claimed to impose.[29]

All these features of legal practice highlighted in propositions 4–6 incline one toward thinking that constitutionally recognized moral norms determine validity in systems such as one finds in Canada and the United States.[30] And this leads one in the direction of inclusive positivism and the claim that more than sources count in establishing legal validity. The moral norms upon which the Courts draw in justifying their decisions regarding validity, appropriateness of remedy, and so on, are what really count in constitutional cases, not what the courts *say* about those norms.

So, we seem to be in a bit of a fix. We seem to have a serious tension between apparent facts favoring the exclusive side (1–3, which henceforth I will call *exclusive facts*) and apparent facts favoring the inclusive side (4–6, which I will call *inclusive facts*). One way round the difficulties surrounding this tension is to continue to deny one set of facts and insist that belief in them stems from misunderstanding, conceptual confusion, or the effects of misleading language. To be sure, an exclusive positivist might say, the law often expresses itself very

28. *Cf.* WALUCHOW, *supra* note 2, Chapter 5.

29. For further discussion, see *id.*

30. I say only that they "incline" toward this thought because there are, to be sure, other possible explanations one might give regarding why, for example, remedies might be thought appropriate—explanations that are consonant with exclusive positivism. For example, it might be argued that remedies are appropriate because *R*, though legally valid, was inconsistent with the defendant's *moral* right—say, his moral right to due process. Whether such a reading does full justice to the thought that *legal* remedies are appropriate even though *illegal* acts on the part of the defendant took place is a question I will leave unaddressed.

loosely and misleadingly in ways that support inclusive facts. But none of this can be taken literally. What must be going on is better understood in terms of the directed powers account. One inclined toward inclusive positivism might, on the other hand, argue that her opponent would have us buy into a theory that misstates, indeed misconceives, the crucial role played by constitutions in limiting the valid exercise of government power. He has failed to account for the fact that failure to observe a condition for the valid exercise of a Hohfeldian power of law creation must, as a sheer conceptual matter, be a nullity. Consider this parallel, the inclusive positivist might suggest. When I fail to observe the conditions for the valid exercise of my legal power to create a will, I will not, despite my efforts, have succeeded in creating a valid will. The change in the legal landscape of rights, duties, and so on that I had attempted to bring about will not have occurred. In short, my efforts will have resulted in a nullity. The same must be true when we turn to the exercise of public powers of law creation. When a legislature fails to observe a condition for the valid exercise of its power to create valid law, it will have failed in doing what it set out to do—failed to create new valid law. The attempt to bring about a change in the legal status quo will not have occurred, resulting, once again, in nullity. As Hart recognized long ago, "nothing which legislators do makes law unless they comply with fundamentally accepted rules specifying the essential law-making procedures."[31]

Each of the two strategies outlined in the preceding paragraph is of course possible. Indeed, they are the ones that positivists have tended to pursue when debating among themselves. But both are, I suggest, ultimately unsatisfying. And the reason is one to which I have already drawn attention: each side in these debates has highlighted facts of importance that any plausible theory of law should be prepared to accommodate, but has done so only at the cost of underplaying, or distorting our understanding of, the important facts stressed by the other side. So my question is this: Can we somehow fashion a theory that does not leave us with the sense that something of importance has been ignored, downplayed, or mischaracterized? Can we fashion a theory that does justice to both sides? Perhaps we can, but only, I suspect, if we acknowledge different notions of *existence* and *validity* at play in these long-standing debates. Those who stress exclusive facts have one set of ideas in mind, while those who highlight inclusive facts have something else in mind. Each, however, is on to something of importance.

IV. FOUR CONCEPTS OF VALIDITY

In an early discussion of the topic, Joseph Raz introduces us to some important notions that are often at play in disputes concerning the existence and validity

---

31. H.L.A. Hart, *Positivism and the Separation of Law and Morals, reprinted in* ESSAYS IN JURISPRUDENCE AND PHILOSOPHY 48, 59 (1983).

of laws. If we pay close attention to these notions, we might begin to see a way round the current impasse between inclusive and exclusive positivism. Let's begin by noting that Raz, following Kelsen, identifies the existence of law with its validity.[32] To say that a law *is valid* is to say that it *exists*—and vice versa. A law is valid, however, only if it "conforms to tests of validity laid down by some other rules of the system that can be called rules of recognition."[33] If it does not conform to these tests—which for an exclusive positivist like Raz will all be source-based—then it is not legally valid and hence does not exist. Furthermore, to say that a rule is legally valid is to say that it is *systemically valid*—that is, that it ought to be obeyed because it is part of an effective legal system and because of "the need to have effective law and the justified authority of those who make it."[34] So a law is legally valid (i.e., exists) only if it is systemically valid and is for that reason something to which I am *justified* in conforming my behavior—if it actually has the normative consequences for me that it purports to have and hence "ought to be obeyed." And it is crucial to observe that the "ought" here is a full-blooded moral ought. "In following Kelsen," Raz writes, "we have adopted the natural law view on the meaning of 'validity.'"[35] Of course, to say that any such law is legally, and hence systemically, valid, and therefore morally ought to be obeyed, is not to say that it is *morally* valid by virtue of its content. "Moral validity is presumably established by argument and the way to argue that a rule is morally binding or valid is to show that it is justified, that the requirements and restraints it imposes ought to be observed. Here validity and justification seem particularly close."[36]

So (for our purposes at least) the bottom line for Raz appears to be this: if I morally ought not to obey a rule, *R*, then it cannot be legally valid. And if *R* is not legally valid, then it is not systemically valid and does not *exist*. It does not exist *even when it is accepted and practiced as valid law* within the particular legal system in question—that is, even when it is in fact followed. But can this be right? A law that is accepted and practiced as valid law does seem to *exist* even if I ought not to obey it. To deny this seems to flout the positivist's social thesis, the claim that the existence of law depends, ultimately, on facts of social practice. If a rule, *R*, is accepted and practiced as law, then regardless of whether that acceptance is misguided or misplaced, and whether, morally, I ought not to obey *R*, the fact remains that we do seem to have the existence of valid law despite its lack of merit.

Or do we? So far I have been stressing Raz's "natural law" understanding of legal validity, according to which to say that *R* is legally valid is to commit to the claim that it ought morally to be obeyed for the reasons Raz outlines. But let's

---

32. RAZ, *supra* note 3, at 146.
33. *Id.* at 150–51.
34. *Id.* at 152.
35. *Id.* at 150.
36. *Id.*

turn our attention now to another of Raz's claims—one that card-carrying positivists at least since Hart have embraced: "the legal validity of a rule is established not by arguments concerning its value and justification but rather by showing that it conforms to tests of validity laid down by some other rules of the system which can be called rules of recognition."[37] As Raz notes, "normally" these tests concern a rule's source—that is, they have to do with, for example, legislative enactment or the laying down of the rule by judges. But Raz does not note at this juncture something that I think needs to be stressed: these source-based tests of validity, in their very nature as criteria or tests of validity, are such that one can attempt but fail to satisfy them.[38] Should any such failure occur, then, as a sheer conceptual matter, the result must be invalidity. In the case of something like legislative enactment, invalidity must amount to a nullity. These kinds of failures to observe source-based conditions are perhaps not an everyday occurrence, but they do occur.[39] One particularly striking example is to be found in the *Manitoba Language Case*, where the Canadian Supreme Court determined that over a century's worth of Manitoba legislation was legally invalid because the legislature had failed to meet a constitutionally recognized condition of legal validity—passage of laws in both official languages. Though the Court ruled that Manitoba legislation was legally invalid, it drew on rule of law values to justify a temporary suspension of invalidity. The purpose of the suspension was to give the legislature enough time to translate all existing statutes into French.[40]

What this case illustrates—and what those who point to inclusive facts are keen to stress—is that rules can be accepted and practiced as valid law, and yet *fail actually to be valid* because they fail to comport with relevant tests of validity. And this point is not restricted to moral criteria of validity; it applies to source-based criteria just as well—a fact nicely illustrated in the *Manitoba Language Case*, and the many other cases in American law canvassed by Adler and Dorf. Such cases all seem to illustrate an absolutely crucial point that is too often overlooked: the fact that *R* is accepted and practiced as valid law, and can in that sense be correctly said to *exist*, does *not* entail that *R* actually satisfies all the relevant criteria of validity and is therefore *valid* law. Yet if we are happy to accept this point as it applies to source-based criteria of validity, then what possible reason could one have for denying that the same might be true when we turn to non-source-based criteria, such as conformity with the norms of fairness contemplated in the Due Process Clause of the American Constitution? Why must failure to meet this type of condition for validity be ruled out as conceptually impossible?[41]

---

37. *Id.* at 150–51.

38. Otherwise, we are left with something analogous to what Hart, in his discussion of rule skepticism, called "scorer's discretion." *See* HART, *supra* note 1, at 141–47.

39. *See* Adler & Dorf, *supra* note 24.

40. Re Manitoba Language Rights, [1985] 1 S.C.R. 721

41. I am assuming here that arguments like Raz's authority argument and Shapiro's guidance argument can be satisfactorily answered, as I think they can. For a brief outline

We are now in a position to consider some potentially helpful distinctions. They stem from (and partially reflect) the Razian thoughts summarized above, and from my earlier analyses of the dispute between Kramer and Himma.

Four Concepts of Legal Validity

1. Legal Validity as Existence (or Acceptance)

R is officially accepted and practiced in legal system *L* as a norm that fully satisfies all systemic criteria of legal validity (both pedigree- and merit-based) included within *L*'s rule(s) of recognition.

2. Systemic Validity

R is officially accepted and practiced in legal system *L* as a norm that fully satisfies all systemic criteria of legal validity (both pedigree- and merit-based) included within *L*'s rule(s) of recognition, and does, as a matter of objective fact, satisfy all such systemic criteria of validity.

3. Systemic Moral Validity

R is officially accepted and practiced in legal system *L* as a norm that fully satisfies all systemic criteria of legal validity (both pedigree- and merit-based) included within *L*'s rule(s) of recognition; does, as a matter of objective fact, satisfy all such systemic criteria of validity; and "has the normative consequences [it] purport[s] to have"[42] because it is the product of a legal system that (1) fulfills "the need to have effective law" and (2) issues from "a justified authority."[43]

4. Moral Validity

R is morally justified on its own terms, that is, independently of its membership in *L*.[44]

A few words of explanation, beginning with legal validity as *existence*. It's probably fair to say that most modern positivists have, without giving it much thought,

---

of these arguments and some of the responses that have been made to them, see my *Legal Positivism, Inclusive versus Exclusive, supra* note 4.

42. Raz, *supra* note 3, at 150.

43. *Id.* at 152.

44. It is, in other words, the morally ideal or best rule for the particular circumstances in question—the one that we would choose to adopt if we were unconstrained by prior legal/political practice. A rule that has been duly chosen in accordance with democratic procedures might, for example, not be the optimal rule from the point of view of ideal morality. But it may, because of its democratic pedigree and because it is morally tolerable, nevertheless have systemic moral validity. I suspect that many if not most statutory laws fall into this category. Legislators tend not to be Platonic Guardians, nor do they labor under conditions and procedures that lead to the same decisions as would be made by Plato's ideal legislators.

simply followed the lead of Kelsen and Raz in treating validity and existence as equivalent notions when applied to law. To say that a law exists is to say that it is valid, and vice versa. And if, in light of our exclusive facts, one is inclined to say that any rule, *R*, that is accepted and practiced as law undeniably exists as law, then one will be led to say that *R* must be legally valid so long as it is accepted and practiced as valid law. This will be one's interpretation of the social thesis—that in the end law is a social institution that, as Raz puts it, "regulates is own validity."[45]

But if one takes these initial steps, then one will be led to deny that a legal system, *L*, could treat *R* as though it satisfied *L*'s very own criteria of validity and yet be wrong about that fact. And then one will be led to a conception of validity that reduces law to little more than scorer's discretion—that treats the law as though it were, on this ground at least, infallible or incorrigible. Just as a goal is, in Hart's imaginary game of scorer's discretion, whatever the scorer *says* it is, a valid law will be whatever legal officials *say* is valid. And this will be so even in those cases where the law fails to fulfill its very own criteria of validity—even when, to use the second of our four concepts of validity, the law is not, in actual fact, *systemically valid*.

However, if we separate validity as existence (or acceptance) from systemic validity, then we can intelligibly say that such laws—though they *exist* because they are accepted as a valid basis for asserting legal rights, claims, and so on (and are, in that very special sense of the term, legally valid)—are not, in another very important sense of the term, really valid at all. Because they fail to meet the system's very own internal criteria of validity, they cannot be *systemically* valid. And one can add, for good measure, that because they lack systemic validity, it cannot be true that they ought to be obeyed because of their status as valid law. A law that fails to meet the system's own criteria for legal validity ought not to be obeyed on the ground that it is valid law if it is not really valid at all.

This is not, of course, to say that, morally speaking, one is therefore at liberty to disobey the law in question. There might be good moral reasons—for example, reasons resting on the rule of law values cited by the Canadian Court in *The Manitoba Language Case*—for conforming with an existing but systemically invalid law. But the important point to stress at this juncture is that these *moral* reasons do not rest on the fact that the law in question is one that is systemically valid—that is, one that derives its moral justification and call upon our behaviour from its place within a system that meets the needs invoked in our third concept of validity, *systemic moral* validity. Any law that fails to be systemically valid is automatically disqualified from having any such status.

This last point is an important one that natural lawyers have long been keen to stress. Aquinas tells us that laws that are unjust are not really laws at all; they are acts of violence which no one is bound to obey. But Bentham's talk of terrorist

45. RAZ, *supra* note 3, at 150–51.

language notwithstanding, Aquinas is keen to add that we may nevertheless be required (in his view, by the natural law itself) to conform our behavior to the unjust law, if such conformity is the only way to avoid "scandal and disturbance." The same point can easily be made in the terms introduced here: a law, *R*, which exists but is systemically invalid may be such that we ought, morally, to conform our behavior to it nevertheless. But our reasons for conforming with *R* will *not* lie in its possession of systemic moral validity. If *R* is not systemically valid because, for example, it was not enacted in both official languages, then our reasons for behaving in accordance with *R* cannot stem from its being a systemically valid law, because it is not. Our reasons will stem, as the Canadian Supreme Court recognized, from other factors, such as the rule of law values upon which the court relied in justifying its suspension of (systemic) invalidity.

Finally, we come to the fourth concept of validity—*moral* validity. That a law exists does not mean that it is morally valid or justified. In other words, that a law is accepted and practiced as valid law in no way entails that it is morally good or justified on its own terms. In this sense, its existence is indeed one thing, its merit or demerit another. So existence does not entail moral validity.[46] Neither does *systemic* validity. That a rule, *R*, satisfies all recognized tests of systemic validity in no way entails that *R* is morally good or justified. This can, of course, very easily happen if the system in question contains no moral criteria whatsoever. But even when it does, moral validity does not necessarily follow. The demands of morality are often much wider (and more stringent) than the moral conditions recognized in a rule of recognition. This is especially so when those moral conditions have been subject to the kind of piecemeal displacement Kramer describes. *R* might therefore meet all the legally acknowledged moral tests of systemic validity and yet flagrantly violate another of morality's demands. Finally, that a law possesses *systemic moral* validity does not entail its moral validity. A system of law can be fully justifiable—that is, *as a system*, it can meet the moral need to have effective law and possess the justified moral authority it necessarily claims to have[47]—and yet bring into existence systemically valid laws that are highly deficient morally. To be sure, a system most of whose laws were seriously lacking in this regard would not, Hobbes notwithstanding, be likely to possess systemic moral validity. But it is clear, I take it, that the existence of some number of morally deficient laws is fully compatible with the systemic moral validity of each and every law within the system. Allegiance to a legal system need not depend on its moral perfection.

46. As we have just seen, it does not entail systemic validity either.

47. I am here following Raz's lead once again in endorsing the view that a legal system necessarily claims justified moral authority. For Raz's views on this, see RAZ, *supra* note 3, Chapters 1 & 2. For a contrary view, see KRAMER, *supra* note 2, *passim*, but especially 216–22.

V. A RETURN TO KRAMER AND HIMMA

So how does all this help us understand the debate between Kramer and Himma, and more broadly the disputes between inclusive and exclusive positivists? Very briefly, it helps as follows.

Himma (rightly) points out that American and Canadian legal practice routinely recognize judicial interpretations of accepted moral conditions of validity as overriding those moral conditions themselves. From this he concludes that these systems are not ones in which actual conformity with moral provisions such as we find in the Due Process Clause functions as a necessary condition of legal validity. We can now see, I hope, the respects in which Himma's inference may be warranted—as well as the respects in which it may not. A rule, *R*, that conflicts with a recognized moral condition, *N*, can no doubt *exist* as valid law (validity as existence or acceptance) till such time as a court determines that the conflict exists. But this in no way entails that *R* will be valid in the sense of satisfying the system's very own conditions of validity—that is, it is not to say that *R* will be systemically valid. What Himma's analysis fails to accommodate fully is the law's *fallibility*. It fails to fully appreciate that the failure of *R* to meet the system's very own tests of validity (moral or otherwise, I might add) must mean that *R* is, in one very important sense of the term "validity," not valid at all. And it is invalid not because it violates some independent, free-floating requirement of morality. It is invalid because it fails to meet the legal system's very own tests of validity—tests that the system, perhaps fully aware of its own moral fallibility, has decided to adopt as a condition of systemic validity. The test is not whether *R* is *accepted* as meeting the system's test; the test is whether R actually *does* meet that test. Otherwise, as Kramer correctly notes, and as I have stressed in my references to scorer's discretion, Himma's analysis leads to a very unpalatable version of extreme rule-skepticism—a version according to which our legal rules are valid if and only if their judicial interpreters say they are. If we are to avoid this kind of rule-skepticism, then we are going to have to acknowledge the point upon which Hart and Green insist—that the law is inherently fallible. Whatever one thinks of the various distinctions discussed above, they do serve to highlight a crucial point that has hitherto been underappreciated: the fallibility of law is not limited to its moral shortcomings. Law can go wrong in any number of ways, not the least of which is its failure to observe its very own conditions for systemic validity. Finding a place for systemic validity as well as existence, moral validity, and systemic moral validity allows us to keep this crucial point front and centre.

Turning now to Kramer, we can see how his identification of existence and validity—an identification inherited from his positivist predecessors Kelsen and Raz—may have led him to the tensions evident in his reply to Himma.[48] On the

48. It must be added that Kramer is by no means alone in presupposing this identification. I myself have consistently done so in the past. *See, e.g.*, WALUCHOW, *supra* note 2.

one hand, Kramer is keen to maintain a significant role for moral conditions of validity of the kind stressed by Hart and other proponents of inclusive positivism, a position to which he seemingly continues to be committed. In light of this element of his thinking, Kramer is led to agree with Hart that a condition of validity can include consistency with moral norms. On the other hand, he is equally keen to accommodate Himma's empirical claims about the (typically) decisive force, within systems such as one encounters in Canada and the United States, of judicial determinations under such moral norms. This wish to accommodate leads Kramer to focus on the role of multiple criteria of validity, and on the ways in which these can be ranked against each other in a manner that allows consistency with a nondisplaced moral norm to function as a decisive criterion of validity. So far so good: such accommodation seems perfectly compatible with inclusive positivism and with Hart's claims about the role of moral criteria. It's when Kramer takes his next step that trouble looms large. As observed earlier, Kramer is happy to concede Himma's claim that, despite its actual conflict with a constitutionally recognized moral norm, *N*, a "duly adopted" rule, *R*, can, because it is "routinely treated by officials as law," be "*properly classifiable as [a] law*."[49] But how can this be, we were led to ask, if inclusive positivism is true? How can *R* be valid law if, in truth, it fails to satisfy a moral condition of its validity where that condition has not been "displaced" by a paramount judicial decision regarding its content?

We are now, I hope, in a better position to solve this puzzle. If *R* is indeed accepted and practiced as valid law, it does (as Kramer and Himma agree) seem to *exist* as law, and can in that limited sense of the term be said to have legal validity. And it does so even though it lacks *systemic* validity, that is, even though it fails to meet a still-dispositive condition of its validity recognized by the legal system—still dispositive because that condition has not been displaced by a mistaken judicial decision. *R* will, of course, also lack *systemic moral* validity because it lacks systemic validity, since possessing systemic validity is a necessary condition of possessing that further property. It will not be a rule that one ought to obey because it is systemically valid *and* because it is the product of an existing system of law that meets the further moral conditions specified by Raz. One can say all these things so long as one is careful to recognize that different concepts of validity are at play in these descriptions, and so long as one is careful not to let them run into one another.

49. Kramer, *supra* note 2, at 139 (emphasis added).

6. HOW TO UNDERSTAND THE RULE OF RECOGNITION AND THE AMERICAN CONSTITUTION

KENT GREENAWALT*

I. INTRODUCTION

Two decades ago I published an article that focused on how someone guided by the theory of H.L.A. Hart's *The Concept of Law*[1] should understand the content of the rule of recognition for the United States.[2]

As my work on the article evolved, I came to realize that the effort (1) showed respects in which certain of Hart's general assumptions about rules of recognition needed supplementation or revision, and (2) shed light on challenges to his basic theory that at the apex of each legal system lay a set of criteria for determining law that owed their status to broad acceptance by high officials. The article in its final form had three connected but separate objectives: to portray the rule of recognition for a locale within the United States; to show respects in which Hart's own account definitely requires clarification, revision, or expansion; and to draw conclusions about the fundamental disagreement over whether an acceptance-based theory of the ultimate sources of law is convincing.

The 2008 conference for which this chapter was written provided an opportunity for me to revisit this topic in light of some recent writing, in particular claims that the practice that judges (at least for the most part) have the last word about what counts as law strongly affects how we should understand a rule of recognition, that in some deep sense citizens may be the final authorities about constitutional principles, that perhaps different groups in society have different rules of recognition, and that official adherence to a rule of recognition in society may be based on an understanding that is not, as Hart indicates in the Postscript to his book's second edition, a convention—according to which officials adopt the rule largely because they know that other officials are accepting the rule.

Because my 1987 article appears in this book, I will not summarize its analysis and conclusions here. Subject to any qualifications in the remainder of this chapter, I still believe it presents a persuasive version (though perhaps not the

---

* University Professor, Columbia University, teaching at Columbia Law School.

1. H.L.A. HART, THE CONCEPT OF LAW (1961). The second edition, to which subsequent citations are given, was published in 1994 (Penelope A. Bulloch & Joseph Raz eds.).

2. Kent Greenawalt, *The Rule of Recognition and the Constitution*, 85 MICH. L. REV. 621 (1987) (reprinted as Chapter 1, this volume).

only persuasive version) of how best to understand the crucial premises of Hart's account as they apply to the United States. It may help, however, to clarify one point and to add an observation the original piece omits.

The clarification is this. If the rule of recognition is complex and in some features is adhered to only by some judges (and other officials), whereas other judges (and other officials) employ competing understandings, the dominant approach (as suggested in my "sociological" account of what judges do) will, it follows, not necessarily be based on a consensus. There is not a consensus if some judges regard themselves as justified in deviating from the dominant approach. Thus, the account I offer does not follow Hart's assumption that in ordinary circumstances a consensus will support all the elements of the rule of recognition.

The additional observation concerns an aspect of U.S. federal–state relations. Related to a point I did make—that limits on state constitutions come from federal law, but the internal authority of state constitutions comes from acceptance within states—is a distinction between a state's range of power and the authority of its internal governing structure. At least for states created by the U.S. Congress after adoption of the Constitution, one may believe that the powers they possess are conferred by federal law,[3] but the structures mandated by their state constitutions nevertheless depend on acceptance within the states.[4]

The clarification about judicial disagreement serves to reemphasize a theme of my original piece. If, in fact, judges actually employ somewhat variant interpretive standards, as they undoubtedly do in the United States, can we speak about ultimate criteria of law on which officials agree? This is a puzzle that any positivist account of law must seek to solve in some way—a puzzle that figures prominently in the remainder of this chapter.

II. THE AUTHORITY OF HIGHEST JUDGES TO DECIDE CASES THAT DECLARE THE LAW FOR OTHER OFFICIALS

In what follows, I focus on three related problems that may seem to threaten Hart's basic approach. These problems bear both on the relative persuasiveness of competing positivist accounts and on the plausibility of legal positivism in any version. One of the problems is that most officials often accept the determinations of other officials about what counts as law. The second problem is that even

---

3. However, as one might think the authority of old amendments to the Constitution now rests on their long acceptance as part of our law rather than on the form of their adoption, one might also think all state powers now rest on their long acceptance rather than any original conferral by Congress.

4. One other minor addition to my original article is that one should include binding customs as they affect federal common law.

American officials occupying the same formal position, most notably Supreme Court Justices and judges on the highest state courts, disagree significantly about how exactly to interpret statutes and the federal and state constitutions. The third problem is highlighted by claims that citizens occupy a more significant role in deciding what counts as fundamental law than they are accorded by Hart, but the problem concerns various groups of officials as well: should we speak of multiple rules of recognition applied by different groups, rather than a single unifying rule?

In this section, I concentrate on officials, putting citizens to the side. In developed legal systems that we know, other officials generally accept judicial determinations about the law as binding, and judges of inferior courts accept determinations of the highest court. Nonjudicial officials and lower court judges accept these determinations even if they think they were strikingly mistaken. Sharp dissent with the U.S. Supreme Court's decision in *Roe v. Wade*[5] establishing a constitutional right of women to have abortions is one example.

Kenneth Himma has argued strongly that the rule of recognition for the United States must take this reality into account, and indeed give it prominence.[6] Once we do that, he contends, we will significantly revise Hart's version of a rule of recognition, in a manner that preserves legal positivism against Ronald Dworkin's assertion that no positivist rule of recognition explains how judges determine what is law,[7] and that also reveals as mistaken, for legal systems with which we are familiar, the theory of inclusive legal positivism that the rule of recognition itself may incorporate moral standards.

This chapter was written to respond to two previous articles by Himma. His contribution to this book adheres to the basic position of those two pieces, clarifying the content of some of his assertions and disavowing claims he has not been making. When in respect to my positions certain of the passages in his new essay are particularly relevant, I indicate that in footnotes.

After briefly outlining Himma's approach, I note certain nonessential points about constitutional interpretation in his presentation that I suggest involve mistakes or misleading categorizations, or rest on dubious empirical grounds. I then lead up to an examination of Himma's crucial claims in a somewhat oblique way, focusing on illustrations that embody some but not all of the characteristics of his central case, in order to tease out just which factors are needed to render

5. 410 U.S. 113 (1973).

6. Kenneth Einar Himma, *Making Sense of Constitutional Disagreement: Legal Positivism, the Bill of Rights, and the Conventional Rule of Recognition in the United States*, 4 J.L. Soc'y 149 (2003) [hereinafter *Making Sense*]; *Final Authority to Bind with Moral Mistakes: On the Explanatory Potential of Inclusive Legal Positivism*, 24 Law & Phil. 1 (2005) [hereinafter *Final Authority*]; *Understanding the Relationship between the U.S. Constitution and the Conventional Rule of Recognition* (Chapter 4, this volume) [hereinafter *Understanding*].

7. The most complete account of Dworkin's theory is in Law's Empire (1986).

his thesis plausible. Finally, I indicate why I reject the way in which he handles the phenomena he describes.

Himma matches empirical reality against a basic premise of Hart's theory, and concludes that a description of the content of the rule of recognition must take account of the acceptance by other officials, including lower-court judges, of the U.S. Supreme Court's ability to declare the law, indeed to make law, even when other officials regard their decisions as misguided. In Himma's view, a full version of what officials take as legally valid must also recognize that executive officials take Congressional enactments adopted according to proper procedures as valid until a court declares otherwise, and that lower courts must make their own constitutional interpretations until a court above them settles an issue. My examination of Himma's central thesis takes these important nuances into account, but they are not crucial for my critique.

Himma assumes that the Supreme Court's power to make law is not derivable from some superior law,[8] so it properly falls within the scope of the ultimate rule based on official acceptance—that is, it is part of the rule of recognition as Hart understands it. The Court's authority is not unlimited; it must give a minimally plausible interpretation of the relevant constitutional or statutory provision, and it must at least appear to be striving for a best interpretation. (Himma's first piece refers to a best *moral* interpretation; in the second piece, without altering his own position, he leaves that issue open). Himma offers various formulations of what a rule, or part of a rule, of recognition might look like. One is what he calls the Court's Best Interpretation Formulation (CBIF):

> A duly enacted norm is legally valid if and only if it conforms to what the Supreme Court takes to be the morally best interpretation of the substantive protections of the Constitution.[9]

Another version is:

> A proposition is law if the court with final authority holds that it represents the best interpretation of the relevant legal materials that comports with the existing institutional history.[10]

---

8. This turns out to be a somewhat complicated issue. The original U.S. Constitution, art. VI, cl. 2, definitely contemplates judicial review of claimed state violations of its provisions, and the Constitution as a whole arguably contemplates federal judicial review of federal legislation and executive action. Judicial review alone need not entail acceptance by other officials of declarations of law, but one might draw such an acceptance out of judicial review plus the understood powers of common law courts.

9. *Making Sense*, *supra* note 6, at 186. I think it is doubtful, in fact, whether if the justices of the Court engaged in isolated departures from Himma's conditions of minimal plausibility and apparent efforts at best interpretation, others would reject the law they declared. *See* MATTHEW KRAMER, WHERE LAW AND MORALITY MEET 123 (2004).

10. *Final Authority*, *supra* note 6, at 13.

Both these formulations capture what Himma takes to be three crucial features. Each is descriptive, not deontic; it tells us what officials in the society take as valid law, not what anyone *should* do. Each rule, as formulated, is something officials agree upon. And each formulation shows—and this is the critical point—that actual conformance with the Constitution is not a criterion of legal validity. It is true, Himma writes, that the formulations draw on an accepted duty of Justices of the Supreme Court to decide constitutional cases according to the best interpretation of the Constitution,[11] and that Justices will take the internal point of view toward this standard, trying to arrive at the best interpretation they can; but this standard is "a second order norm defining the Court's duty,"[12] which "does not directly define a validity criterion."[13]

That the basic "rule" is descriptive and agreed upon by officials shores up the positivist notion that official acceptance (not moral soundness) determines law, against Ronald Dworkin's theory of adjudication. That the criterion for valid law does not include *actual* compliance with moral standards consigns to irrelevance the inclusive legal positivist theory that ultimate criteria of law may themselves include moral criteria.[14] That a legal system could incorporate such criteria remains a conceptual possibility, but one with no bearing on the main legal systems of our world.

For me, the most fundamental aspects of the puzzles Himma has raised are how one best relates judicial responsibilities to the roles of other officials, and how one picks the level of generality for conceptualizing a rule of recognition. Before attacking these questions, I want to clear away what I take as certain nonessential features of Himma's account.

Himma remarks that officials of a "legal system, considered *collectively*" cannot, under Hart's theory, "be generally mistaken about some validity

---

11. In one passage, Himma states that the first formulation I have quoted "is simply an extrapolation from . . . recognition norms [about the Supreme Court's duty to reach a best interpretation and the Court's final authority]—and not a recognition norm itself." *Making Sense*, *supra* note 6, at 194. I do not think my conclusions would differ if we focused on these two recognition norms in combination. I believe, partly from reading *Understanding*, *supra* note 6, at 98, that in Himma's sense a rule of recognition is partly normative, while a criterion of validity is purely descriptive; and that his point is that a descriptive criterion of validity is extrapolated from norms about the Court's duty and authority. In the same way a passenger's descriptive sense of when a train will arrive could be based on a timetable that tells those operating the train what schedule to keep.

12. *Making Sense*, *supra* note 6, at 193, 195.

13. *Id.* at 197.

14. Hart himself believed that ultimate criteria of law could "explicitly incorporate principles of justice or substantive moral values" and that the legal system of the United States did so. HART, *supra* note 1, at 204. In his Postscript, he treats his position as one of "soft positivism." *Id.* at 250–51.

criterion."[15] This is correct for those criteria that rest on acceptance, but I do not think it is right about criteria that are themselves derived from higher criteria. If a state legislature with indisputable authority confers definite authority on a city council to legislate a particular norm, and the council does so, the failure of the great majority of relevant executive officials to see that the norm is valid law, or even to recognize that the council possesses that kind of lawmaking authority, does not deprive the enacted norm of validity.[16]

Himma's claim in his first piece that Justices have a duty to make the best *moral* interpretation is confusing, because the content of "moral" is so open ended. Himma rightly sees that every theory of constitutional adjudication must in some respect reach beyond what "the law" (in some narrow sense) settles to broader considerations about faithfulness to basic premises of our system, the appropriate role of judges, and what citizens in a polity like ours deserve. If any reference of this kind counts as "moral," then Justice Scalia's argument that desirable limits on judicial power are best served by a form of originalism, qualified by moderate respect for precedent, is "moral"—even though it explicitly purports to exclude moral evaluations by judges in individual cases, perhaps the heart of Dworkin's theory. And if one focuses on evaluations in individual constitutional cases, many (perhaps all) Justices think consequential considerations sometimes count, considerations arguably excluded by Dworkin's original claims that judges must rely on principle, not policy[17]—a distinction to which Himma refers in discussing moral evaluation.[18] One can preserve a thesis that officials generally agree that Justices must make the best moral evaluation only by adopting a sense of "moral" that includes every conceivable relevant reason of political philosophy, and by allowing that a broad range of consequentialist considerations might sometimes be relevant.[19] Because Himma treats Justice Scalia's

15. *Making Sense, supra* note 6, at 155. For a slightly different formulation, see *Understanding, supra* note 6, at 99.

16. Hart does not suppose that nonenforcement affects a derived norm's legal validity, *see* HART, *supra* note 1, at 103–10; and I do not believe confusion about proper derived authority would change this. *See id.* at 256 for the comment that laws adopted by criteria set by the rule of recognition are valid before any occasion for their practice has arisen. If officials *accept* as legally valid a particular norm or method of lawmaking that they believe to be derived but that clearly was *not* authorized, the analysis may well differ. That norm might be law because accepted.

17. A central, early piece by Dworkin on this subject is *Hard Cases*, 88 HARV. L. REV. 1057 (1975). My views about the distinction as I then understood it are in *Policy, Rights, and Judicial Decision*, 11 GA. L. REV. 991 (1977). My sense of a shift by Dworkin to a view that any considerations relevant to claims of right may count as reasons of principle is expressed in a book review of A MATTER OF PRINCIPLE and LAW'S EMPIRE, 84 J. PHIL. 284 (1987).

18. *Making Sense, supra* note 6, at 179.

19. Insofar as justices disagreed about the status of consequential considerations, they would *agree* only that they should try to make a best interpretation that might or might not include these.

approach as one based on "moral legitimacy,"[20] and consistently acknowledges that due regard for precedent is one part of a best interpretation,[21] it is clear that his own view of "moral" is indeed broad.[22] But such a widening of "moral" makes it nearly an empty vessel, save only for its assertion that something beyond narrow legal evaluation is called for.[23]

By far the most disturbing nonessential aspect of Himma's thesis is his apparent assumption about the deference of nonjudicial officials to judicial decisions.[24] On this subject, we need to draw a threefold distinction among (1) enforcement of judgments, (2) acceptance as law if a conflict with the judiciary would arise from nonacceptance, and (3) acceptance as law if no such conflict would result from nonacceptance. That a legal system would be seriously undermined if judgments were not enforced is clear. Although the Supreme Court has asserted over the last fifty years that its declarations of constitutional law are authoritative, that position has been contested at various times in American history, even for issues as to which legislative or executive nonacceptance of judicial "law" would generate a conflict with the judiciary. Lincoln's claim that the *Dred Scott* decision should not be taken as establishing a valid constitutional principle is a notable example, and Ronald Reagan's Attorney General mounted a challenge to the Court's sweeping assertions of authority.[25]

About the third category, I believe not only that other officials *need not* take the Court's statements as the final word about constitutional principles, but also that this is widely understood.[26] For example: Congress authorizes a form of antiterrorist surveillance to last for five years. By a 5–4 margin, the Supreme Court upholds it against plausible assertions that it violates the Fourth Amendment. Without any relevant change in social conditions, the act comes up for renewal. A Senator opposes it on the ground that despite what the Supreme Court has said, the surveillance is unconstitutional.[27] If Congress declines to

---

20. *Making Sense, supra* note 6, at 181–83.

21. *See* especially *id.* at 183, n.45.

22. Himma explicitly adopts a view of moral considerations that is very broad in *Understanding, supra* note 6, at 115–20.

23. Nothing I have said here is meant to deny that moral considerations in a narrower sense are sometimes important. I make only the obvious point that these considerations are often in competition with other considerations.

24. In *Understanding, supra* note 6, at 100–05, Himma indicates that he accepts much or all of what this and the next two paragraphs assert, but (rightly) does not see those features as undercutting his main claims.

25. Edwin Meese, U.S. Att'y Gen., The Law of the Constitution, Address at Tulane University (Oct. 21, 1986), *in* 61 TUL. L. REV. 979 (1987). My much more academic response is in *Constitutional Decisions and Supreme Law*, 58 U. COLO. L. REV. 145 (1987).

26. Greenawalt, *Constitutional Decisions, supra* note 25, at 158.

27. I am omitting another subtlety. The Court's constitutional test may be based on deference to the legislature. Its decision could actually *be consistent* with a judgment by a legislator that the law is unconstitutional.

reenact the law, no conflict with the Court arises. Something similar may be true if there *would otherwise* be a conflict, but legislators are highly confident that changes in the composition of the Court will alter the result of an earlier case. Yet another variety of nonconflict is when legislators vote for a measure because they disagree with the Court's narrow interpretation of one provision (say, the degree to which Section 5 of the Fourteenth Amendment authorizes Congressional efforts to implement that amendment's Equal Protection Clause) but are sure their new statute will be sustainable under another provision (say, the Commerce Clause).

Himma's analysis seems to disregard features of our legal system[28] according to which courts accept as final the constitutional judgments of other officials (such as impeachment by the House of Representatives and conviction by the Senate, and perhaps the validity of constitutional amendments), or consider matters outside their domain (as under the political question doctrine), or grant decisions of another branch great deference (determining not whether constitutional standards have been met, but whether a plausible (or rational) *argument* may be made that they have been met).[29]

Despite these quibbles, Himma undoubtedly is right that in the vast majority of circumstances, other officials take the Supreme Court's decisions as establishing the law; they behave as if what the Supreme Court has declared as law is law, and they refer to it as law. What should we make of this phenomenon in respect to criteria of law?

If we think about sports referees and subordinate executive officials, we quickly see that we would not always identify the way in which officials understand what counts as authoritative with a rule of recognition for determining law. For Himma's thesis to achieve a degree of persuasiveness, one or more extra elements are needed, as I believe he recognizes.

In major league baseball, with some simplification, there are four umpires; each has authority to decide plays within his domain.[30] The first-base umpire decides whether a batter is safe or out based on whether he reaches the base before the first baseman, with foot touching the base, catches the baseball. Television replays occasionally show mistakes. Following Himma, we might say that other officials take the umpire's call as authoritative if it reasonably approximates which event occurred first—that is, if, though possibly mistaken, it fell

---

28. However, see *supra* note 24 for his clarifications in *Understanding*.

29. In what was once the most important article in the literature about constitutional decision, James B. Thayer advanced the thesis that this was always the Court's role in reviewing federal statutes. *See The Origin and Scope of the American Doctrine of Constitutional Law*, 7 HARV. L. REV. 129, 144 (1893).

30. In fact, it may be that the umpire in chief for the day or the crew as a whole can override a decision. In reality, this happens only when the umpire making the original call acknowledges uncertainty about its correctness.

within a normal range of accuracy or error.[31] However, were we asked about the rule for determining "safe" or "out," would we not revert to the basic standard the umpire making the call is indisputably required to use? How officials treat possible mistakes would help tell us what count as final decisions, but would not be part of the fundamental rule for what makes a runner safe (or would be a *subordinate* part of such a rule).[32]

Because Himma responds to this illustration in his contribution to this book,[33] it is worth saying a bit more about what I take it to show. I am not claiming that one can go easily from the baseball example to conclusions about law and the Supreme Court. What the example highlights is that if a basic substantive rule is simple and recognized by all, we would not state a rule of recognition in a form that would refer only to how applications of the rule (some mistaken) are treated, relegating the basic rule itself to at most a secondary status. I have suggested that one might take the fundamental rule of recognition here[34] as the basic rule that the crucial decision-makers, the umpires, use—either omitting for that purpose how others treat umpire mistakes in applying the rule *or* regarding authority to have even mistaken decisions count as a subordinate part of the fundamental rule. If I understand Himma, he rejects, even with this illustration of a simple substantive rule, any notion that as far as professional baseball (and I suppose any baseball in leagues with official umpires) is concerned, we could state a fundamental rule of recognition that omitted umpire authority to bind with mistaken decisions. He does suggest, however, that the recognition norms would include not only umpire authority to apply rules but also the (substantive) rules of baseball—an approach that apparently differs from my second option only in not characterizing recognition of umpire authority as subordinate. (This difference will loom as important when we turn to the legal system.)

With infrequent exceptions, lesser executive officials follow what their bosses tell them about the law. Personnel delivering mail, police on the beat, sanitation workers, firefighters, social workers, and teachers do not generally try to figure out the law for themselves. They fulfill their duties in line with what their supervisors tell them is legally permitted and legally required. On occasion, they may make legal judgments about subjects their supervisors have not addressed, but with that exception, their *practical* criterion of legal validity is what their bosses

31. We might include an assumption that the umpire was doing his best.

32. *See infra* text preceding note 34 for a clarification of the status of the relevant rule.

33. *Understanding, supra* note 6, at 101–02.

34. Strictly speaking, on Hart's account, since the rules about "safe" and "out" are contained in official rules of baseball, they may owe their status to acceptance of the authority of those who lay down the official rules, and thus may be derived rather than part of a rule of recognition. (On the other hand, it might be said that this rule was accepted long before there were official rules and could not have been altered by any official body, given how basic it is to the game.) All this is irrelevant to the point of the illustration.

tell them. Something similar is true for lower courts in relation to higher courts, except that much more frequently they must decide without direction from above.

This distinction between how bosses and subordinates identify what is law need not cause ripples in a legal system. Indeed, were subordinates to use the same criteria as the boss after the boss has spoken, not infrequently disagreeing with the boss about how the criteria apply, that could make a legal system unworkable. No doubt when Hart talks about the rule of recognition being accepted by officials, he fails to distinguish higher officials from subordinates; but if nothing more were involved than the fact that subordinates accept the judgments of their bosses, we should consider the crucial criteria for legal validity within the system as those the highest officials use.

It is perhaps this understanding that has led some, including Hart in the Postscript,[35] to identify judges as *the* officials who determine the rule of recognition, implicitly treating them as the highest officials for deciding the content of the law. Were one to follow this line rigorously, one would need to take account of those aspects of American constitutional law as to which judges do not determine content, rather leaving authoritative decision to another branch (as with the impeachment process).[36] But Himma's objection to this strategy of focusing dominantly on judges flows in the opposite direction, based as it is on the idea that the ultimate rule must take into account how other officials respond to judicial decisions they take as final.

Three important aspects distinguish the reality Himma addresses from the umpire and the subordinate executive officials. Most relevant "other officials" are not subordinates of judges; they are members of independent branches of government that possess the legal authority to pick judges and (with help from the states) amend the Constitution. Furthermore, those other officials typically (though not always) treat what the Supreme Court says about constitutional law as *the* law, not just as a superior's judgment about the law that a subordinate should follow. Other officials recognize that the Supreme Court can *establish* law, even when it makes mistakes. This is partly a matter of recognizing that, given the doctrine of precedent, decisions can affect the course of future law

35. HART, *supra* note 1, at 256, 258.

36. In my original piece, my attempt to incorporate this feature into Hart's approach led me to suggest that the rule of recognition would track "the ultimate standards of law used by officials who are not simply accepting the judgments of other officials." Greenawalt, *supra* note 2, at 636 (reprinted as Chapter 1, this volume, at 15). KRAMER, *supra* note 9, at 108–09, challenges this approach as obfuscating how lower-tier officials are guided by their rule of recognition. I believe one could defend my original approach as the best conceptualization to focus on Hart's main concern, but I agree with Kramer (and Himma) that a more complete account of legal systems would include a description of what lower court judges and nonjudicial officials take as law.

even for Justices who believe those decisions were mistaken in the first instance. Relatedly, sophisticated officials recognize that many constitutional cases that come before the Court are difficult, that the correct way to decide *and* the correct way to declare the law (if there is a correct way) are arguable, and that Justices often disagree, making it difficult for other officials to know if a decision and prevailing opinion are mistaken. All this helps to confirm a sense that the Supreme Court has the authority or discretion to declare law in more than one way—to *create* constitutional law. Accordingly, acceptance of that law creation needs to be part of the ultimate rule of recognition.

It is worth pausing for a moment over the terms "authority" and "discretion." Matthew Kramer has urged that judges have the *duty* to arrive at a best interpretation, even though they have the *power* to create law by a less than best interpretation.[37] My sense is that Kramer fails to take into account the degree to which terms like authority and discretion are responsive to the range and difficulty of choice, even when we assume one answer is really best. We need to recall that Himma is mainly concerned about *declarations of law*, not just the results of cases. Often, a court might state the relevant law in scores of different ways; that choice is not either/or. If we believe it extremely rare that the Supreme Court will come up with the very best declarations of law, it is misleading to suggest that they are consistently failing to perform their duty.[38] Terms like "discretion" and "authority" better capture how we regard choice under these conditions.[39]

Suppose, to take an artificial example that differs from dog shows, talent contests, and beauty pageants in having a definitely ascertainable best answer, that musical judges are asked to pick as a winner the one of fifty equally talented child pianists who hits the most correct notes of a Beethoven sonata. All make a significant number of mistakes, the judges diverge significantly in who they think succeeded best, and the chances of picking the "right" winner are slight. In these circumstances, we think of a duty to try to pick correctly, but not a duty to pick correctly (since that is so difficult). And I think we would speak comfortably of the judges as having a kind of discretion and authority to choose (even if repeated playbacks of each performance compared with Beethoven's score could, in theory, tell us who made the least mistakes). Ideas of discretion and authority to choose seem even more obviously apt if we have no reliable way—even in theory—to identify "best" answers.

---

37. KRAMER, *supra* note 9, at 126–28.

38. Kramer talks of the court as "not legally at liberty to exercise that power." *Id.* at 127. It is odd to speak of the court as having only one chance in one hundred of doing the one thing it is "at liberty" to do.

39. My thoughts about this are much more fully developed in Greenawalt, *Discretion and Judicial Decision: The Elusive Quest for the Fetters That Bind Judges*, 75 COLUM. L. REV. 243 (1975).

Up to this point, I am sympathetic with Himma's endeavor. It is reasonable to include as one aspect of the rule of recognition the acceptance by other officials of declarations of law by the highest court. But the way Himma does this is not convincing. Less importantly, even if we put aside nuances concerning judicial abdication and the instances when legislative or executive action based on a view contrary to the Court's judgment will create no conflict with the judicial branch, the manner in which other officials accept the Court's declarations as law can be complex. If I am asked whether the Free Exercise Clause protects the use of peyote in worship services, I will equivocate: "The Supreme Court has said that it does not, but I continue to believe that, properly interpreted, it does, and that this principle is important enough that *Employment Division v. Smith*[40] should be overruled as soon as possible." A member of Congress or the President may take a similar view, and this can affect legislative measures,[41] executive policy, and subsequent appointments to the Court. Thus, official acceptance of the Court as establishing constitutional law can be less than unqualified.

My more important objection is to Himma's assigning the Court's implicit duty to reach a best interpretation to a secondary position, treating it as other than a criterion of legal validity.[42] It may be that if one were making discrete empirical inquiries about what judges and other officials do, and discrete normative inquiries about what they should do, the "secondary position" would make no difference; but it definitely makes a difference to how we conceptualize law, and that itself may affect how people understand certain empirical and normative issues.

Let us grant that Himma is right (with the qualifications I have mentioned) about the criteria that other officials apply to decide whether the Court has established law, and also that he is right, descriptively, that other officials agree Justices should do the best they can to reach best interpretations and that the Justices agree they should seek best interpretations. Each Justice then regards himself or herself as under a responsibility to reach the best interpretation (qualified, I would say, by a willingness to join a majority opinion that comes close if no majority can be garnered for the best interpretation). Why is this only a second-order duty? If we ask what counts as law in the system, are not the criteria the final deciders use at least as important as (if not more so than) the criteria that the officials who defer to the highest deciders are using? And, as Kramer points out, lower court judges and other officials may use the same criteria as the

40. 494 U.S. 872 (1990).

41. Such views undoubtedly did influence passage of the Religious Freedom Restoration Act, in which Congress responded to the *Smith* decision. The Court in turn struck down the Act's application to the states, but has applied it to the federal government.

42. If one wanted, with Himma, to say that criteria of legal validity must be purely descriptive, one would say the recognized duty underlies the descriptive criterion as a Supreme Court Justice would see it.

highest court, except insofar as the highest court has declared the law, and thus displaced the use of those criteria.[43]

If one lifts the criteria Supreme Court Justices use out of the secondary (indirect) position to which Himma assigns them, his rejection of inclusive positivism and of a Dworkian approach fails.[44] The inclusive positivist can say it is highly plausible that the Justices agree that standards that are moral (in a narrower sense than Himma's) count for what is law under the Constitution.[45] This is clear for specific provisions like the ban on "cruel and unusual punishment," and it may well be true more generally. Dworkin's basic claim that Justices do not agree about much that goes into constitutional interpretation also emerges unscathed from Himma's particular challenge.

This observation brings us back to the length of the rule of recognition (or any relevant theoretical analogue that rejects that concept). If we focus on the part of the rule of recognition that does not concern acceptance by other officials of Supreme Court declarations, and aim for a high enough level of generality, we can come up with a formulation that reflects near-universal acceptance among officials, including all Supreme Court Justices: "Given what weight should be accorded precedents and whatever accommodations they should reach to achieve majority opinions, Supreme Court Justices should render the best interpretations possible in constitutional cases." We could treat this, or a reformulation cast in descriptive terms about what officials do accept, as part of a rule of recognition, one that satisfies the requirement of official agreement about the ultimate bases of law. But that formulation papers over a wide range of disagreement about how to make a best interpretation, leaving it open to a nonpositivist to argue that the crucial criteria for law are not agreed upon and do not depend entirely on what officials do, but require normative judgments. In this light, the debate between positivists and opponents who reject the idea that any rule of recognition captures what counts as law seems largely to come down to the degree of specificity one insists on for criteria of law.

The question about specificity is closely related to questions about the ranges of agreement and disagreement. A formulation about "best interpretation" may be unrevealing about substance, but in the United States all officials also agree

43. KRAMER, *supra* note 9, at 134–37. Whether officials in other branches do (and should) use the same criteria is a complicated question addressed more fully in the next section.

44. What is crucial is whether criteria are part of the rule of recognition itself, not whether they are primary or secondary. Kramer suggests that criteria that incorporate moral norms are "subordinate" to those that obligate officials to treat Supreme Court decisions as binding. *Id.* at 136. I disagree with this classification, but it is adequate to establish the claims made in the text.

45. My earlier skepticism about how many standards should count as moral does not reflect doubt that standards that are undoubtedly moral sometimes are relevant for constitutional and other judicial decisions.

about the overarching legal authority of the Constitution, about judicial review, and about many other matters. Perhaps it is enough to speak of a single rule of recognition when there is wide agreement about most important matters, even if there is disagreement about subtle details at the periphery.[46] Against this view it might be said that in the United States some persistent disagreements about constitutional interpretation are far from minor, and that, in any event, even subtle disagreements about ultimate criteria of law show we do not have a single rule of recognition.

As my earlier article suggests, it helps to distinguish empirical (or sociological) from normative (or participant-centered) inquiries.[47] If one asks how Justices *should* interpret the Constitution, one understands that the range of disagreement is significant, making it impossible to reduce best interpretations to actions that officials have taken up to that time and will take on that occasion. If, on the other hand, one asks what are the criteria for law that reflect the practices of a society, one can refer to a distillation of standards that are then prevailing, recognizing that a standard may be prevailing even if not accepted by a majority of Justices, or by one Justice. The history of Supreme Court adjudication includes various areas of law in which a minority in the middle has determined results, and it is conceivable that a combination of factors could determine results, although no single Justice thought that exact combination was dispositive.[48]

One might fairly conclude that a positivist theory can and should underpin an empirical approach, but that some nonpositivist theory will be needed to account for the normative task of judges, particularly if one wants to reach beyond vague generalities to more nuanced criteria. On this understanding, if a friend asks a Supreme Court Justice who believes *Employment Division v. Smith* was wrongly decided and should be overturned whether the First Amendment protects the use of peyote in worship services, the Justice might respond, "According to prevailing doctrine, the answer is 'No,' but were the issue to come before the Court the correct normative answer would be 'Yes.'"

---

46. Hart makes clear that the rule of recognition need not completely determine results, that it sets "only the general conditions which correct legal decisions must satisfy. . . ." HART, *supra* note 1, at 258. *See also* KRAMER, *supra* note 9, at 106, who defends a positivist approach while acknowledging that in most systems officials "will likely diverge from one another in their understanding of the details of their Rule of Recognition."

47. *See* Greenawalt, *supra* note 2, at 662–70 (reprinted as Chapter 1, this volume, at 39–46).

48. If three justices think that factor A makes law and that B is irrelevant, two justices think factor B makes law and A is irrelevant, and four justices think neither factor nor both together make law, only when (in the absence of any other law-making feature) A and B are joined will five justices vote that law exists, though no justice thinks the combination is what makes law.

III. THE CHALLENGE OF POPULAR CONSTITUTIONALISM, BASES FOR ACCEPTANCE OF THE LEGAL ORDER, AND THE POSSIBILITY OF MULTIPLE RULES OF RECOGNITION

In two wide-ranging articles, Matthew Adler has posed a number of central questions about how one might best conceive application of rule of recognition theory to the American Constitution and legal order.[49] To a certain extent, his questions overlap with ones Himma discusses, but they also raise problems unlike any we have yet considered. The central overlapping concern is the reality that various persons in dissimilar roles apply different standards for what counts as law. This reality leads Adler to question whether within the United States we can sensibly speak of one canonical group as the reference point for the legal system's rule of recognition. He offers as an alternative a group-relative account that includes not only groups of officials but also citizens and other residents. Various groups, he claims, may recognize different rules of recognition. This account significantly reforms Hart's approach, which supposed that either the body of officials (the theme of the original *Concept of Law*) or judges (as proposed in the Postscript) agree upon standards for determining law that constitute a uniform rule of recognition, and, further, that it is their understanding that matters. Adler also challenges any notion that whatever agreement obtains about what counts as law is conventional in some relatively narrow sense.

Although much of what Adler suggests is persuasive, I see matters more as ones of degree than as stark alternatives among which one must choose. I will first try to clarify the scope of the crucial problem Adler identifies about people employing different standards for what counts as law, before analyzing his major claims.

We have already noted that different officials use different practical standards for what counts as law. Subordinates typically accept what their superiors say about the law.[50] Legislative and executive officials typically take judicial decisions about the law as authoritative. If the courts have not spoken, legislators typically give some consideration to the constitutionality of proposed legislation; chief executives may treat unconstitutionality as the basis for a veto. Executive officials consider the constitutionality of possible actions, such as techniques of interrogation,

---

49. Matthew D. Adler, *Popular Constitutionalism and the Rule of Recognition: Whose Practices Ground U.S. Law?*, 100 Nw. U. L. Rev. 719 (2006) [hereinafter *Popular Constitutionalism*]; Matthew D. Adler, *Constitutional Fidelity, the Rule of Recognition, and the Communitarian Turn in Contemporary Positivism*, 75 Fordham L. Rev. 1671 (2006) [hereinafter *Constitutional Fidelity*].

50. Some subordinates make their own independent legal judgments about issues that their supervisors have not faced; others, such as ordinary firefighters and sanitation personnel, may rarely be in that position. Of course, all (or virtually all) officials do need to assess factual circumstances to decide whether they fall within legal requirements.

the legitimacy of which is not resolved by judicial decisions or addressed clearly by statutes; and these officials usually apply statutes that are enacted in proper form until those laws are declared unconstitutional by courts, although they may decline to enforce a law or devote fewer resources to enforcement because of constitutional doubts.[51]

These various nuances could be fitted into a fully coherent pattern, so long as everybody who is relevant agrees about when officials should make independent judgments rather than accepting the judgments of others, agrees about *whose* judgment should be accepted *when*, and agrees that officials making independent judgments should use the same basic criteria.[52]

I have suggested that, were these conditions met, we could say either that the ultimate criteria for law are those that the highest body uses when it makes its determinations,[53] or that an *ultimate* rule should include both the criteria judges and other officials use when they make independent judgments and the ways in which various officials accept the judgments of others.[54]

A further complexity we have examined is that final judgment about some matters is not assigned to the Supreme Court. It has been generally assumed that the constitutional issues involved in the impeachment process, and particularly what behavior meets the constitutional requisite of "Treason, Bribery, or other high crimes and misdemeanors," is left to Congress.[55] Something similar may be true about what the Supreme Court has labeled political questions, such as whether a state has a "Republican form of government" and whether a President's commitment of military forces has violated the constitutional mandate that declaring war is up to Congress. On the military engagement issue, there may, as Adler points out,[56] be no single final decider, leaving the possibility that the President and Congress may remain at odds. *If* all the branches decided constitutional questions according to the same criteria as Supreme Court Justices, this additional complication would create little conceptual difficulty. The ultimate

51. Although a pattern of following Supreme Court decisions about the law is relatively settled for the executive branch, how far the national executive will follow one or more federal courts of appeals opinions outside of their geographical areas is far from uniform.

52. That is, it would be agreed that legislators and executive officials should make independent judgments about constitutionality in essentially the same as the way courts make such judgments, although they would not be expected to engage in the exhaustive research and defense in written opinions that appellate courts provide.

53. On this view, nonjudicial officials accepting judicial views and subordinate officials accepting the views of superiors are subsidiary matters not well captured in an ultimate rule of recognition.

54. A third possibility is Himma's suggestion that the fundamental rule is about what most officials will take as law from the body making final decisions about the law, with whatever constraints that involves on how that body renders its determinations.

55. U.S. Const. art. II, § 4.

56. *Constitutional Fidelity, supra note* 49, at 1685–86.

rule for what counts as law when officials make independent decisions would remain undisturbed.

Does it matter if the criteria of decision are different for different officials when they are making constitutional judgments? I shall focus on Congress and the Supreme Court, but one might engage in a similar analysis involving the executive. On precisely the same topics the judgments of Congress might be more or less rigorous than those of the Justices. When Thayer urged judicial restraint, or minimalism, he assumed that legislators should decide whether, on balance, a proposed law is constitutional; courts should ask only whether one might rationally defend its constitutionality. Thayer explicitly drew the logical inference: the same individual, without any change in his understanding, could consistently vote against a bill in Congress on the ground that it is unconstitutional and, after being appointed to the Supreme Court, vote to uphold the measure.[57]

In modern times, the reverse degree of appraisal may be more common. Congress adopts a law that many members think may or may not be constitutional; they decide to leave that question to the courts. The Supreme Court's examination is more exacting. (The Court also uses certain standards of evaluation, such as "strict scrutiny," that may be viewed as resulting in the invalidation of certain measures that are actually constitutional according to a more refined (impractical) standard, because most measures of that sort are not constitutional and it is difficult for courts to identify the relatively few that are all right. Thus, some rare acceptable forms of racial classification may be struck down because most forms are bad.).

If different kinds of officials use different standards, we now face two additional problems with saying that the substantive criteria in a rule of recognition depend on standards used by the final decider. For constitutional issues left to one final decider, the ultimate interpretive standards that determine legal status will differ from what those standards are for constitutional issues that are left to another final decider. (For example, Congress might be originalist about grounds for impeachment; the Supreme Court might accept an evolving Constitution.) And a theorist would need to explain what happens if the final decider, say the Supreme Court, is neither accepting the judgment of Congress without review (in which event the Court would not be final decider) nor deciding on balance whether a statute is constitutional, but doing something in between, such as according great deference to the judgment of Congress as Thayer recommended.

Even with all the nuances I've introduced so far, the system could be fully coherent. All officials could conceivably agree on who decides what and on the appropriate standards each group should be using.[58] That cannot be said once we invoke further complexities.

57. Thayer, *supra* note 29, at 144.

58. One might doubt whether the system was fully coherent for issues without any final decider to settle disagreements between branches about ultimate criteria or their applications.

Suppose officials disagree about the appropriate ultimate criteria for discerning law, either in respect to their own independent judgments or when they reflect on how other kinds of officials should make their judgments. We know, of course, that Supreme Court Justices do disagree sharply about many interpretive matters, and the same is true of members of Congress who address constitutional issues. Further, other officials disagree about the criteria Justices should use. If most members of Congress had a significantly different view from most Supreme Court Justices about standards the members should use *and* about standards the Justices should use, and Congress legislated accordingly, the view of the final decider (the Court) would not be effective unless and until some court decided an issue. Thus, the effective legality of many measures might depend on the fortuity of a judicial challenge, even as to the kinds of issues for which judicial authority was unquestioned.

Ronald Dworkin's approach to this reality is to deny the existence of a rule of recognition, on the basis that officials, especially relevantly judges, do not agree on ultimate criteria of law. One positivist response is that officials *do* agree on such things as the authority of the Constitution and the responsibility of judges to give it the best interpretation they can. As I suggested in the previous section, one may believe that the comparative attractiveness of these accounts depends largely on what level of generality one thinks is illuminating, and on whether one is more interested in empirical description or normative guidance.

A final complexity is even more disturbing. People may disagree about who has final authority to decide various issues. Some issues may be resolved by the Supreme Court, only to have the President and Congress respond by making appointments intended to change those resolutions, by removing court jurisdiction over particular subjects, by failing to renew legislation, and so on.[59] If agreement is lacking about who counts as the final authority and standards of judgment are likely to differ (as they inevitably are, among relevant groups), the effort to identify a single set of substantive criteria for determining law and a single group whose judgments will determine that set seems fated to fail. This is the heart of the problem Adler faces, and it leads him to posit that multiple recognitional communities accept multiple rules of recognition. Very importantly, he does not limit this conclusion to officials. He notes that one way to understand popular constitutionalism is to conceive of groups of citizens or residents as relevant groups, in this respect.

Adler's take-off point in the longer of his two articles is recent discourse about popular constitutionalism, the idea that at bottom the opinions of citizens do

59. The practices mentioned in the sentence in the text do not *necessarily* show disagreement about respective authority. Everyone could agree that the Supreme Court's judgments count as final and as the law for many purposes, but that various responses by the Congress and President are appropriate. I am relying partly on the fact that debates on these subjects do touch significantly on what respect the Supreme Court should be given.

and should count a great deal for what is constitutional law within the United States. He initially offers a helpful distinction between what he calls shallow judicial supremacy or shallow popular constitutionalism, on the one hand, and deep judicial supremacy or deep popular constitutionalism, on the other.[60] Someone who argues that although judges are the final arbiters of constitutional meaning they should give great weight in their determinations to the opinions of citizens is a shallow popular constitutionalist and a deep judicial supremacist. A theorist who contended that judges should pay no attention to popular opinion but that if they stray too far from any acceptable course, popular rejection should occur and that rejection should be taken by other officials (and Justices in subsequent cases) as a basis for disregarding what the Court has said, would be a shallow judicial supremacist and a deep popular constitutionalist.

This categorization is somewhat oversimple because it fails to address degrees of deference, percentages of subjects, and numbers of occasions for citizen nullification. With respect to shallow theories, there could be a great spectrum of judicial attention to popular opinion, ranging from a lot to none. As for deep theories, suppose someone believes judges have the last word about the law, except for one particular subject (e.g., abortion), or except where their disregard of popular opinion reaches truly outrageous proportions (which occurs about once a century), in which event popular opinion should more directly determine constitutionality. Would a reservation for an isolated topic or for very extreme situations be enough to make one a deep popular constitutional theorist? As with shallow theories, deep theories could differ in important degrees.[61]

According to Adler, the debate over what role our legal institutions imply for official consideration of a popular sense about the Constitution is a debate about the law; the disagreement over deep theory is unresolvable in legal terms,[62] although considerations of morality and political theory may favor one side or the other.[63] Again, the dichotomy seems less sharp than Adler makes it. Arguments among shallow theorists are certainly not going to be resolvable in some straightforward fashion, or indeed in any fashion based on fit with what are undoubtedly authoritative laws and institutions. Judgments of political theory—about what makes liberal democracies legitimate, and about appropriate relations of citizens to officials—as well as more standard moral claims about rights

60. *Popular Constitutionalism*, *supra* note 49, at 725–29.

61. Since Adler begins by positing various groups with perspectives on constitutional principles, it may seem that this differentiation about who has the final word is either/or, rather than a matter of degree. But my point is that one might adopt the perspective of a certain group only for some limited subjects or for really extreme abuses. These are different kinds of degree from points on a spectrum, but nonetheless they are aptly seen as matters of degree.

62. *Popular Constitutionalism*, *supra* note 49, at 728–29, 801–02.

63. *Id.* at 729.

and desirable consequences, will figure in the contentions at the shallow level. And arguments about authoritative laws, especially the Constitution and the institutions it sets up, will figure in arguments at the deep level, though they *may* figure less decisively.

Someone might respond that citizens have a different perspective from judges, and that we cannot expect persons from fundamentally different perspectives to agree on who shall have the ultimate word on constitutional legality. Such a claim might or might not be descriptively accurate,[64] but even were it true empirically it would not resolve who *should* set the standards of ultimate legality. Adler is not a relativist about morality. He assumes that there is a correct answer to moral questions, and presumably this includes questions of political theory about what are desirable responsibilities under an already established structure of fundamental law. If we had to choose between deep judicial supremacy and the alternative, I do not see why there would not be a correct answer to that question. Indeed, Adler indicates one kind of correct answer—that both approaches in their most robust forms are "wrong," because his multiple group approach is more sound descriptively and normatively.[65]

Adler builds from his stroll into the domain of popular constitutionalism to a broad theory that different groups of officials and citizens may have different theories of how the Constitution should be understood, and that these groups may not concede final authority to resolve all foundational matters[66] to the Supreme Court or to anyone else. Of course, the different theories contain significant overlapping components, but we should acknowledge that our system is made up of multiple groups of reference, multiple recognitional communities, and that these actually accept different rules of recognition. As a practical matter, the legal system may function with reasonable stability,[67] but we should abandon any notion that various perspectives fit neatly into a coherent unity about who should finally decide on what subjects and about how they should decide. Adler has come up with one plausible version of how a positivist theory might treat the complex reality of the American constitutional order, but do we need to choose between a multiple-group–multiple-rule theory and a single-group–single-rule theory?

One issue is overlap, and its degree. If the overlapping agreement were huge and disagreement slight and at the edges, we would not be likely to rush to a

64. We could learn from an empirical inquiry that citizens, or scholars who wish to assign authority to citizens, do have a fundamentally different attitude than the deep judicial supremacists, and that reasoned discourse has proven incapable of bridging the gap (something undoubtedly true about competing religious perspectives, one or more of which may nonetheless contain more truth than its competitors).

65. *Id.* at 798.

66. *Id.* at 783.

67. *Id.* at 782–83.

theory about multiple recognitional groups. My sense of the empirical reality is roughly this. Most groups of officials and most citizens accept the Supreme Court's resolution of standard constitutional issues in much the way Himma supposes. The disagreements arise either over a few isolated, fundamental and controversial issues, such as the constitutional right to have an abortion, or over a string of discrete decisions that together reflect a highly controversial philosophy, such as older decisions that struck down social welfare legislation as violating substantive due process or more recent decisions that consistently granted procedural rights to criminal defendants. A theory needs to be faithful to the range of overlapping agreement, which itself will vary significantly over time. The thesis about multiple recognitional groups may implicitly understate the degree to which officials do agree and citizens acquiesce.[68]

Another issue for a group theory is how to define the groups. Adler rightly sees that not just any collection of individuals can count as a relevant group, and he notes departmental roles, partisan positions, regional affiliations, and federal or state connections as some distinguishing features of significant groups of officials.[69] But I wonder whether we have any truly satisfactory way to say who counts as a relevant group for this purpose. To take an illustration obvious for lawyers, Supreme Court Justices themselves have very different views about how the Constitution should be understood and about the interpretive strategies they should follow. One might conveniently divide the Court (most of the time) into two or more blocs, but some divisions about interpretation cut across the common divisions. May we not be left to say that each Justice is a relevant group? If we generalize the point, we may not find an agreed-upon set of criteria for determining law, even among easily classifiable groups. Rather *some* touchstones are widely shared among members of all groups, with the degree of sharing increasing as one focuses on smaller and more cohesive groups, but within even those smaller groups shared assumptions are complemented by divergent individual judgments founded on attempts at "best interpretation." Thus, as one moves from officials as a whole, or officials plus citizens, toward individual assessment, the degree of consensus will increase, but the "group," however defined, will form no obvious stopping point as one moves from the entire collectivity to individuals.

How to categorize citizens (or residents), whether one looks at them as an entirety or in subgroups, presents particular difficulties. Most citizens will not usually care much, or have definite views about, foundational standards of law. When they become concerned, it will be substantially because disturbed officials have persuaded them to a position, or at least have supported their initial disquiet over particular rulings (say, about school prayer, desegregation, or abortion).

68. Citizens may acquiesce even if they do not self-consciously understand and endorse.

69. *Id.* at 753–59.

And for any constitutional issue, citizens who have an opinion are sure to disagree. No one, I think, would say that a bare majority of citizens with an opinion should carry the day on a constitutional issue against the reflective view of most Justices and other officials. So it is hard to say just how citizens as a comprehensive group should be conceived. Matters may be simpler with discrete subgroups that share positions in common over time.

Adler offers his group approach as valuable for both empirical and normative purposes. If one is trying to understand how a legal system actually operates, one useful approach is to inquire how different significant groups believe fundamental constitutional adjudication should proceed—with respect to both what substantive standards should control and who should have the last word. In this descriptive endeavor, one would not necessarily require agreement among members of a group. One could report the dominant view of Republicans in Congress, or officials in the Deep South, or evangelical Christians, much as I have suggested one might take the prevailing view within the Supreme Court as the present standard for how judicial interpretation *does* proceed.

The relevance of different groups for normative analysis is more elusive. One could view certain kinds of group membership as kinds of commitments or involvements that affect how one *should* perceive the standards of law. But against this is the notion that everyone should be asking what are the best standards for the whole society, not what benefits any particular group. In that event, particular group membership *would* affect people's views, but membership would not carry genuine normative force.

Adler definitely offers one response to this possibility, and some of his comments might be taken as offering another. He believes that members of different groups may have attachments that affect what is the normatively best outlook for them. Connected to this claim, he develops an independent thesis about the bases on which officials accept fundamental criteria of law. Before considering this independent thesis, and how group participation might affect a normative approach to criteria of law, I shall briefly consider a different possible ground for assigning normative significance to group membership.

One might suppose that a fairly tight connection exists between the moral authority of law and the desirable manner of understanding criteria of law; in that event, the moral authority of law for various groups should affect their normative appraisal of what counts as law.[70] There may be some connection of this sort, but I do not think it is tight.

Imagine a society composed of discrete groups with widely different cultural premises and ideas of how to arrive at moral judgments. Each group is fearful that officials belonging to other groups will decide constitutional cases in light of

---

70. Some passages in *id.* at 775–78 may suggest such a position, but they left me uncertain whether Adler was taking it. Communications between us since I wrote the draft of this chapter have indicated that he is not asserting this position.

their moral judgments. All groups agree on a basic constitution that mandates strict originalism in interpretation and that itself forbids moral evaluation in constitutional interpretation. Although judges might not be able to rule out every consideration of political theory in their construction of a strict originalist approach, conscientious judges would try hard in individual cases not to give weight to what seemed morally right according to their own moral assessment. The actual laws, formulated in terms that did not use moral criteria, would still cover many activities—such as intentional homicide—regarded as morally wrong by all groups. The law as a whole might well have authority, of an epistemic or coordinative kind, for citizens; and for officials the law would certainly have whatever moral authority goes with their consent (explicit or not) to undertake official responsibilities. In this example, the kind of moral authority the law would possess would have little bearing on the manner in which judges and other officials would determine criteria for law.

By contrast, we can imagine a legal system that, as a whole, carries no genuine moral authority for citizens. The governing authority might be a foreign power that lacked any legitimate justification for invading. Even local residents who are officials, coerced or bribed to serve by their invaders, might realize that the system has no moral claim on them.[71] Nonetheless, those who are rendering interpretations of the law might well be guided by moral standards, as were many liberal judges in the old Union of South Africa (though not usually acknowledging that relevance). In short, the nature of a legal system's moral authority does not bear very directly on what are the best criteria for discerning law within that system.

Adler definitely suggests that the quality of one's participation in a group can affect one's best normative approach, a claim connected to his independent thesis about the nature of adherence to a rule of recognition. Regarding adherence, Adler convincingly explains alternatives that lie between a strict conventionalist reading of the rule of recognition and Dworkin's notion that each judge employs a somewhat different theory for identifying law.

(In the discussion that follows, I put aside a possibility that Hart omits and Adler does not discuss, namely, that some differences over fundamental criteria—such as whether old constitutional amendments now count as law because they were adopted by the amendment process or because they have been accepted for so long—may fail to produce any differences in legal result. On such matters, judges and other officials have hardly any reason to achieve a common view, or even to identify how their views differ from those of others.)

A strict conventionalist reading understands convention along the lines that David Lewis developed—people accept a practice because it is accepted by others, and they, if they thought about it, would understand that their continued

71. This is a considerable simplification, because *if* the invader carries on the aspects of ordinary law that preceded the invasion, those aspects might carry moral authority.

acceptance depends on the continued acceptance of others.[72] Thus, an individual would stop speaking English if everyone around her shifted to French and no longer understood English.[73] Hart's Postscript indicates that official acceptance of the rule of recognition rests at least partly on convention in this way.[74] Adler notes that a number of legal positivists have recently been attracted to the idea that officials are engaged in a kind of shared cooperative activity, an exercise in which one's coordination with the behavior and views of others is important but may take place without an assumption that one will definitely follow a radically different strategy if one's cohorts decide to do so.[75] Adler notes that in the original *Concept of Law,* Hart wrote of a social rule of recognition—a rule shared by officials, but not one necessarily grounded in efforts to coordinate nor one that each official would necessarily abandon if others did.[76]

Adler asks the simple question whether we would consider something to be a legal system if virtually all officials accepted a rule of recognition in a manner he calls "group-insensitive." In other words, each official would adhere to that rule whatever other members of the group did. In fact, it is not too hard to imagine such a system. An esteemed religious prophet might lay down a law as ordained by God. Believing officials would accept the criteria of law as compelling, and would understand their approach not to depend on what other officials did.[77] (I put aside here whatever group sensitivity would be entailed by subordinate officials accepting legal judgments of their superiors.) I fully agree with Adler that this would be (could be) a system of law; it is thus not crucial to the existence of a legal system that acceptance of criteria for law be group-sensitive.

Although the possible existence of such a legal system does not in itself establish the relevance of group-insensitive acceptance for our system of law, it raises the question how American officials generally regard adherence to the Constitution. Is adherence based on the wide acceptance of other officials and vulnerable to a shift in their positions? We might ask a number of different questions about the great

---

72. *See* David K. Lewis, Convention: A Philosophical Study (1969).

73. I add the point about understanding because in two-language households one parent may well continue to speak a language not actually spoken by her spouse and children.

74. Hart, *supra* note 1, at 255–56, 266–67. In indicating that *part* of the reason officials comply is the adherence of other officials, Hart leaves open whether compliance would cease if other officials shifted their practice. Thus, it is doubtful whether "convention" as he uses the word is the same as that of Lewis.

75. *Constitutional Fidelity, supra* note 49, at 1683–86.

76. *Id.* at 1688. Adler also writes of the possibility that officials together might *constitute* the rule of recognition. *Popular Constitutionalism, supra* note 49, at 735–36. I think this possibility could coexist with all sorts of reasons why officials observe a practice and with all sorts of circumstances in which they would cease to do so. Thus, I omit this possibility from the discussion.

77. Adler provides a religious illustration in *Constitutional Fidelity, supra* note 49, at 1678.

majority of crucial officials and ultimate criteria for determining law: (1) Do officials have a consistent, coherent view? (2) What do they perceive as having caused them to reach their view (or views)? Do they consider that the practice of officials generally (perhaps like the religious teaching of parents) has led them to the view they have? (3) What do they perceive as the justification for that view, the reason(s) why they should adhere to it? (A person who acknowledged that parental influence led him to particular religious beliefs might defend the beliefs in wholly other terms.) (4) What would be the effect of actual changes in the positions of other officials, and, if most officials' views were group-sensitive to some degree, how great would the shifts have to be to alter their views? (Someone who would adhere to the Constitution if sixty percent of officials ceased to acknowledge it might not adhere if ninety-nine percent of officials shifted to a different basis for law.) (5) What is the considered understanding of officials about what shifts by other officials *should* cause them to change their views? Under the assumptions developed by Lewis, participants in a convention *would* actually shift if enough others shifted and they now understood (on reflection) that it would make no sense to stick with a practice out of line with the vast majority of what others do.[78] We should recognize that what *would* actually cause officials to alter their views might differ from what they themselves would *predict* about that, and from their belief about what they *should* do if the circumstance arises.

Suffice it to say that, among most high officials, allegiance to the Constitution would probably not be regarded as highly sensitive to moderate shifts among other officials. And at a more mundane level, we see that Supreme Court Justices may stick to a fundamental strategy of interpretation over extended periods of time despite realizing they are in a small minority. (Although Justice Scalia now enjoys the support of some colleagues, one can be fairly confident he would not abandon his version of originalism even were he the only Justice using it.) In summary, what Adler treats as the strict conventionalist approach among officials about ultimate criteria of law cannot be a requisite of every developed legal system, and it is an implausible account of the American legal system.[79]

No doubt many aspects of ultimate standards of law are accepted by officials at least as a social rule, or social norm; on whatever basis, they agree widely about what they and other officials should do. In this broad sense, they follow a social rule—one that guides their own behavior and their approval and criticism of others—even if their adherence does not depend on its continuing acceptance by fellow officials.

---

78. However, any discrete number of people could maintain an old practice *among themselves*, for example, speaking Welsh.

79. Because Hart writes that adherence by other officials is only part of the reason officials accept ultimate criteria, see *supra* note 74, I think it is unclear how far his position in the Postscript is actually at variance with Adler's.

Adler spends substantial time considering the legal system as involving a somewhat intermediate category, shared cooperative activity. In such systems, each participant's activities are guided by the aim to cooperate with other participants; he tries to mesh his effort with theirs, but the various participants need not all adhere to the same practice or standard in the manner of a strict convention. In developing this model, legal theorists have drawn from the work of Michael Bratman, who posits "mutual responsiveness," "commitment to the joint activity," and "mutual support" as aspects of such cooperation.[80] Relying especially on Scott Shapiro's elaboration, Adler doubts that all three elements are essential for legal officials, and writes of a "proto" shared cooperative activity.[81] These puzzles about precise requisites are not crucial for our purposes, and I disregard them.

Adler explores the relation between the "social cooperation" approach and the question of whether we should think in terms of one or many recognitional groups and rules of recognition. In brief, his claim is that cooperation may exist within groups defined in various ways that does not exist among all officials together or among all officials and citizens.

This insight is undoubtedly correct, but it does not follow that moving to the multigroup hypothesis about the rule of recognition illuminates more than it misleads. Let us consider first the empirical issue. *Degrees* of cooperation among people vary hugely across the different groups and within the discrete groups, however the groups are defined. Virtually all officials are trying to contribute to a useful, legitimate government under the overarching umbrella of the federal constitution. (This, of course, was not true at the time of secession.) Officials cooperate more closely and more completely with others who work with them in similar roles and with others who share broadly similar political views. As far as citizens are concerned, it is hard to see them as cooperating with the broad group of other citizens (except in obeying the law, conforming to basic tenets of social morality, and voting in national elections). Particular groups of citizens do engage in close cooperation and may share a particular view of some aspects of criteria of law. Adler mentions the Amish who, among other things, share a particular view about religious liberty.[82] And occasional situations may arise that are so dispiriting that a majority of citizens have a view about some fundamental constitutional issue that differs from that of the Supreme Court. (Perhaps during the Depression most citizens had a sense that the Supreme Court was unduly interpreting the Constitution to defeat social welfare legislation.)

80. MICHAEL BRATMAN, FACES OF INTENTION 94–95 (1999).

81. Scott J. Shapiro, *Law, Plans, and Practical Reason*, 8 LEGAL THEORY 387 (2002).

82. *Popular Constitutionalism*, *supra* note 49, at 761–62. Adler discusses religious groups and public interest groups as collections of citizens who cooperate with respect to visions of constitutional authority.

The social cooperation approach applies more forcefully to officials than to citizens, but given some degree of cooperation among differently placed officials and widely overlapping ideas about ultimate criteria of law, we would need an empirical investigation of the degrees of cooperation and of similar views about ultimate criteria of law within the named groups, as compared with the cooperation and views of officials at large, to provide a persuasive basis to conclude that *the most perspicacious* categorization is in terms of recognitional groups. Nonetheless, it is undoubtedly true that some differences in understanding ultimate criteria of law and final authorities could well be connected to group perspectives.

If we turn to the normative inquiry, A's cooperative endeavor with B could possibly give her a normative reason to align herself with B's perspective more than C's. In this manner, the degree of cooperation within groups, as opposed to cooperation beyond one's own group, could affect the position one *should* take about ultimate criteria of law. (To take two simple illustrations, I have more reason to reach accord with members of my family or the Columbia Law School faculty than with members of other families or faculty from other schools.) But the problem here involves both subtly varying degrees of cooperation and the particular issue at stake—ultimate criteria of law. Given that all officials are, or should be, cooperating to some degree, it is plausible to suppose that in determining what should be regarded as the ultimate criteria of law and who should be the final authorities, this broader cooperation should make much more difference than narrower group attachments.

Adler apparently thinks that whether one focuses on consequentialist or nonconsequentialist values, group membership makes a difference.[83] However, for a consequentialist approach that sees law as serving epistemic and coordinative purposes, one's position in a group should not be a *basis* to calculate what is in the best interest of the society at large or one's group (although group membership inevitably will *affect* one's understanding). Does group membership nevertheless make a difference in the weight one appropriately assigns to the interests of the group itself, as is true of my illustrations about family and law school faculty? For various groups of officials, it is difficult to see why they should be self-consciously promoting their own welfare, and doubtful whether the particular interests of a narrow group of constituents should be given priority when they are considering ultimate criteria of law. If one puts aside whose particular interests will be served, it is possible that things will work best for everyone with respect to ultimate criteria if members of smaller groups try hard to coordinate with one another on that subject; disagreements within groups might be more harmful than disagreements between people not connected in this way. But such a conclusion is not obvious, and it may be plausible only for groups defined in

83. *Id.* at 775–81.

some ways and not for those defined in others. Citizens may be more justified than officials in strongly favoring good consequences for groups they belong to and care especially about, but these attachments may have little payoff in terms of general views about ultimate criteria of law.

For nonconsequentialist theories, group affiliation of some kinds may be more evidently relevant, as illustrated by consent.[84] If I align myself with a group, cooperating with other members, I may be committed to give their views more weight than those of outsiders; Adler suggests that South Carolina officials may "have a promissory duty to support the South Carolina conception of the Constitution."[85] But for state officials within the United States, the general, shared commitment to the federal constitution would seem to count for more than state connections when it comes to discerning ultimate criteria for federal law.[86]

A positivist can describe what are the prevailing norms for determining law within a society—even if those norms may not reflect agreement on many details—whether for empirical description he takes a single (broad) group approach or a multigroup approach. Whether the positivist can capture the normative duties binding officials rendering interpretations depends upon the generality with which he is willing to settle. He can say, "Judges and other officials should make the best interpretations possible, taking into account degrees of coherence with past practices, what other officials in similar roles are willing to accept, and what superior officials may have concluded, and they should also accept the best possible allocation of roles among different governmental departments and between government officials and the citizenry." But this general formulation papers over all the actual, reasonable disagreements judges and other officials have on these topics. It is this reality that, in part, makes attractive an approach that for normative purposes does not posit a single uniform rule of recognition. The multiple group approach is a way station, but it still does not quite encompass the reasonable range of disagreement, and it could have the effect of diverting normative inquiries from their most appropriate course by focusing the attention of those making decisions on their narrower group affiliations rather than on more broadly shared commitments.

IV. CONCLUSION

My original article summarizes how one might apply Hart's theory about the rule of recognition to the American constitutional order, and identifies a number of qualifications to the basic theory that such an effort requires. In this chapter,

84. *Id.* at 781.

85. *Id.*

86. Of course, conceptions within a state about the state constitution would be more important than the views of outsiders.

I have considered how we should conceptualize the reality that other officials accept the ability of the highest court to declare law and that various groups in society may perceive both different ultimate criteria of law and different authorities for settling those criteria. I have accepted the notion that a complete rule of recognition would account for the practices of various officials who accept the judgments of others about what counts as law, but I have resisted the idea that this inclusion supplants or renders subordinate the place of criteria used by final deciders. I have agreed that the standards many high officials use to discern law do not fit the pattern of conventions in a strict or narrow sense; acceptance of those standards could be significantly group-insensitive. I have acknowledged that different groups in society may have somewhat variant views about ultimate criteria of law and who should determine those, but I have indicated skepticism about whether focusing mainly on groups (rather than on officials as a body or on individuals) is the most illuminating way to approach ultimate criteria of law. My skepticism about the group approach is stronger with respect to normative evaluation than with respect to empirical inquiry, though it may be that Adler or other scholars can develop in more detail just how various group affiliations should affect normative judgments about foundational constitutional premises.

7. RULES OF RECOGNITION, CONSTITUTIONAL CONTROVERSIES, AND THE DIZZYING DEPENDENCE OF LAW ON ACCEPTANCE

LARRY ALEXANDER AND FREDERICK SCHAUER*

In this chapter we take up the question of the nonlegal foundations of any legal system and, in particular, H. L. A. Hart's notion of the ultimate rule of recognition—the master rule that pedigrees the other rules governing what officials and citizens are legally obligated to do.[1] Initially, we shall raise but not necessarily resolve several questions about Hart's own account of the rule of recognition. But even though we leave those questions largely unresolved, we shall come away from this discussion with a sufficiently firm grasp of the idea of a rule of recognition to proceed to the second section of the chapter. In that section we look at the United States Constitution—and the practices that have developed regarding its interpretation and enforcement—through the lens of the idea of an ultimate rule of recognition. And when we do so, we shall encounter some foundational questions about constitutional law and interpretation: Does the rule of recognition

* Larry Alexander is Warren Distinguished Professor, University of San Diego School of Law. Frederick Schauer is David and Mary Harrison Distinguished Professor of Law at the University of Virginia.

1. H.L.A. HART, THE CONCEPT OF LAW (Penelope A. Bulloch & Joseph Raz eds., 2d ed. 1994). It is important at the outset to stress that our goal here is not Hartian exegesis. We are concerned with the basic question of the nonlegal (or extralegal) foundation of any legal system, and thus with an issue also associated with Hans Kelsen's idea of a *Grundnorm*. HANS KELSEN, THE PURE THEORY OF LAW (Max Knight trans., 1967); KELSEN, INTRODUCTION TO THE PROBLEMS OF LEGAL THEORY: A TRANSLATION OF THE FIRST EDITION OF THE REINE RECHTSLEHRE OR PURE THEORY OF LAW (Bonnie Litschewski-Paulson & Stanley L. Paulson trans., 1992); Kelsen, *The Constitutional Function*, 25 JURID. REV. 214, 222 (1980). For important and relevant commentary, see JOSEPH RAZ, *Kelsen's Theory of the Basic Norm*, *in* THE AUTHORITY OF LAW: ESSAYS ON LAW AND MORALITY 122 (1979); LARS VINX, HANS KELSEN'S PURE THEORY OF LAW: LEGALITY AND LEGITIMACY (2007); George Christie, *The Notion of Validity in Modern Jurisprudence*, 48 MOD. L. REV. 1049 (1964); Julius Stone, *Mystery and Mystique in the Basic Norm*, 26 MOD. L. REV. 34 (1963). There are fundamental differences between Kelsen and Hart, not least the fact that Hart's ultimate rule of recognition is a social fact while Kelsen's *Grundnorm* is a foundational or transcendental understanding; but for our purposes what both Hart and Kelsen (and others) have identified and what they share is more important than how they differ, or whether the idea we work with here is or is not an accurate rendition of what either of them believed.

in the American legal system change over time, and if so, how does this occur?[2] Has the Constitution itself changed other than by organic processes—processes prescribed by the Constitution itself[3]—and, if so, how? If interpreters employ different methodologies in interpreting the Constitution, is there one constitution, or are there several (overlapping) constitutions?[4] And if the latter, how is stability achieved? If the Supreme Court (or some other governmental body with final interpretive authority)[5] misinterprets the Constitution, what is the legal status of such a misinterpretation, and why? And finally, given that one function of a constitution is to entrench the "rules of the game," and given that any entrenched rule will suffer from over- and under-inclusiveness with respect to its background purposes,[6] how is it possible for officials and citizens to accept as binding the ultimate rule of recognition and the constitutional and subconstitutional rules it pedigrees?[7]

Our enterprise in this chapter is primarily conceptual and descriptive rather than normative. We shall be attempting to identify the rule of recognition in the United States. Or rather, we shall be attempting to identify the multiple rules of recognition in the United States, for we believe that actual American recognitional practices are multifaceted. There is also, however, a normative element in our chapter, for we maintain that settlement for settlement's sake is an important legal, social, and moral value, and yet our existing recognitional practices inevitably put settlement at risk.

I. THE HARTIAN RULE OF RECOGNITION

Hart introduces the notion of a rule of recognition in Chapter 5 of *The Concept of Law,* and more fully elaborates it in Chapter 6.[8] The ultimate rule of recognition

---

2. *See* Frederick Schauer, *Amending the Presuppositions of a Constitution, in* RESPONDING TO IMPERFECTION: THE THEORY AND PRACTICE OF CONSTITUTIONAL AMENDMENT 145 (Sanford Levinson ed., 1995).

3. U.S. CONST. art. V.

4. Matthew D. Adler, *Popular Constitutionalism and the Rule of Recognition: Whose Practices Ground U.S. Law?,* 100 NW. U.L. REV. 719 (2006); Matthew D. Adler, *Constitutional Fidelity, the Rule of Recognition, and the Communitarian Turn in Contemporary Positivism,* 75 FORDHAM L. REV. 1671 (2006).

5. When governmental branches other than the Supreme Court are given final interpretive authority over a constitutional issue, the issue is called a "political question." For recent discussion of political question doctrine, see Louis Michael Seidman, *The Secret Life of the Political Question Doctrine,* 37 J. MARSHALL L. REV. 441 (2004); Rachel Barkow, *More Supreme Than Court? The Fall of the Political Question Doctrine and the Rise of Judicial Supremacy,* 102 COLUM. L. REV. 237 (2002).

6. *See* LARRY ALEXANDER & EMILY SHERWIN, THE RULE OF RULES: MORALITY, RULES, AND THE DILEMMAS OF LAW (2001); FREDERICK SCHAUER, PLAYING BY THE RULES: A PHILOSOPHICAL EXAMINATION OF RULE-BASED DECISION-MAKING IN LAW AND IN LIFE (1991).

7. *See* ALEXANDER & SHERWIN, *supra* note 6, at Ch. 4.

8. HART, *supra* note 1, at 92–93, 97–120.

sits at the apex of the legal system's rules, among which are also some number of nonultimate rules of recognition. Whereas all other legal rules achieve their status as legal rules by being validated (recognized) by higher-level rules, the ultimate rule of recognition cannot be validated in that manner; there is no higher-level legal rule available for its validation. The ultimate rule of recognition instead achieves its status by virtue of the fact of its acceptance by officials[9] as a rule with which they (and ordinary citizens) are obligated to comply.[10] The obligation here is a strong one, and sanctions for violations of it are appropriate.[11]

Hart tells us two things worth mentioning about his conception of the ultimate rule of recognition. The first is that for a legal system to exist, only the officials need accept the ultimate rule of recognition as obligatory.[12] Ordinary citizens need not so accept it, at least so long as the lower level rules it pedigrees are generally efficacious. That is, a legal system exists if officials accept an ultimate (or "master") rule of recognition, and if citizens generally obey the rules it validates.

Second, Hart is agnostic about the reasons that officials need to have for accepting a rule of recognition.[13] He suggests that it is not a necessary condition

---

9. It is widely believed that acceptance by *officials* rather than by citizens is necessary for an ultimate rule of recognition to exist. *See* Kenneth Einar Himma, *Understanding the Relationship between the U.S. Constitution and the Conventional Rule of Recognition* (Chapter 4, this volume); Stephen Perry, *Where Have All the Powers Gone? Hartian Rules of Recognition, Noncognitivism, and the Constitutional and Jurisprudential Foundations of Law* (Chapter 11, this volume); Scott J. Shapiro, *What Is the Rule of Recognition (And Does It Exist)?* (Chapter 9, this volume).Yet although this official-centered understanding of acceptance of the rule of recognition is indeed what Hart maintained, *see infra* text accompanying note 12, it is more accurate to understand the relevant recognitional community as that which has the power to interpret and enforce the law. Insofar as it is a contingent feature of some legal systems that what citizens understand the law to be just *is* the law by virtue of that citizen understanding, then citizen acceptance is a necessary part of the ultimate rule of recognition.

10. The factual existence and character of the ultimate rule of recognition is what distinguishes it from the somewhat similar idea of a *Grundnorm* in the work of Hans Kelsen. *See supra* note 1. Whereas a *Grundnorm* is a fiction—a Kantian transcendental understanding that allows the legal scientist to comprehend and make sense of the idea of law—the Hartian rule of recognition is undeniably real.

11. That is, if a rule is validated by the rule of recognition, officials are *justified* in threatening and imposing sanctions for its violation.

12. HART, *supra* note 1, at 112–14.

13. *Id.* at 198–99. Hart's suggestion here is in some tension with his own claim elsewhere (*id.* at 39) that theorists such as Austin—JOHN AUSTIN, THE PROVIDENCE OF JURISPRUDENCE DETERMINED (1995)—and Holmes—Oliver Wendell Holmes, *The Path of the Law*, 10 HARV. L. REV. 457 (1895)—vastly overestimated the importance of coercion in explaining legal obligation, and equally underestimated the importance of the "puzzled man" (as opposed to the "bad man"), the person who genuinely wants to know what the law is so that he can obey it, without regard to what will happen to him if he does not. Hart is commonly taken to have put on the agenda of legal philosophy the problem of normativity—the question of *how* the law creates obligations. *See, e.g.*, JULES COLEMAN, THE PRACTICE OF

for the existence of a legal system that the officials accept the rule of recognition for moral reasons, and that they may accept it instead for prudential reasons, for reasons of tradition, or even out of unthinking habit. All that is required for a rule to be the master rule of recognition of a legal system is that the officials regard themselves (and others) as obligated to follow it.

There are many questions one can ask in response to the Hartian view. With respect to Hart's belief that citizens need only (generally) obey the pedigreed rules but need not accept the ultimate rule of recognition and its progeny as obligatory, how in such a case is Hart's picture of a legal system different from the Austinian picture—the legal system as a coercive "gunman writ large"—that Hart expressly rejects?[14] After all, the officials are only "officials" because there is a rule of recognition that validates the rules declaring them to be officials; and the rule of recognition, in turn, is only the rule of recognition because they (the officials) treat it as such. So they are only "officials" from their point of view, not from the point of view of the citizens who do not accept the officials' rule of recognition.[15] To the latter, the "officials" may appear no different from a gang of muggers. If the citizens obey the officials solely out of fear but consider, say, a government-in-exile to be the legitimate government[16]—they accept a rule of recognition that validates the government-in-exile and its decrees—why should we conclude the officials' rule of recognition and its pedigreed rules to be the legal system governing the citizens? Would not such a conclusion be more in accord with Austin's gunman conception of a legal system? If only the judges and legislators—who are "officials" only by virtue of the rules *they* (and perhaps the 101st Airborne and the FBI) accept—need accept the rule of recognition in

---

PRINCIPLE 86–94 (2001); JOSEPH RAZ, ETHICS IN THE PUBLIC DOMAIN 280–81 (1994). But Hart's brief suggestion in these pages implies that a legal system resting entirely on coercion could still count as a legal system, a view with which at least one of us is in substantial sympathy. *See* Frederick Schauer, *Positivism Through Thick and Thin*, *in* ANALYZING LAW: NEW ESSAYS IN LEGAL THEORY 65 (Brian Bix ed., 1995); Frederick Schauer, *Critical Notice*, 24 CAN. J. PHIL. 495, 500 (1994).

14. Hart, *supra* note 1, at 80. *See also id.* at 112–14.

15. *See* Adler, *Popular Constitutionalism*, *supra* note 4, at nn.56–57.

16. This is by no means solely a hypothetical question, and indeed there is a substantial literature applying largely Kelsenian ideas and language to the question of which legal system "exists" when two different legal systems both purport to govern the same physical terrain, as has occurred with respect to, for example, Rhodesia, Pakistan, Bangladesh, and Uganda. *See* F.M. Brookfield, *The Courts, Kelsen, and the Rhodesian Revolution*, 19 U. TOR. L.J. 326 (1969); R.W.M. Dias, *Legal Politics: Norms Behind the Grundnorm*, 26 CAMBRIDGE L.J. 233 (1968); J.M. Eekelaar, *Principles of Revolutionary Legality*, *in* OXFORD ESSAYS IN JURISPRUDENCE: SECOND SERIES 23 (A.W.B. Simpson ed., 1978); Michael Steven Green, *Legal Revolutions: Six Mistakes About Discontinuity in the Legal Order*, 83 N.C. L. REV. 331 (2005); J.W. Harris, *When and Why Does the Grundnorm Change?*, 29 CAMBRIDGE L.J. 103 (1971). Additional discussions in this vein are cited in Tayyab Mahmud, *Jurisprudence of Successful Treason: Coups d'Etat & Common Law*, 27 CORNELL INT'L L.J. 49, 52 n.9 (1994).

order for its pedigreed rules to be the legal system governing the rest of the populace, then Hart's view begins to resemble only a more nuanced version of Austin's. And if even the officials might accept the rule of recognition for entirely prudential reasons—such as fear of the king or aspirations to higher office—does not much the same conclusion follow?

With respect to the reasons for which the officials accept the rule of recognition, is it really possible to accept a rule as *obligating* oneself and others—and obligating them in a way that makes sanctions for disobedience warranted—and yet not accept the rule for moral reasons? Can we, say, self-interestedly consider ourselves "obligated"? Can we consider *you* "obligated" if our reasons for doing so are not based on our moral views?[17] Isn't this just what Hart sought to avoid in distinguishing being *obliged* from being obligated?[18] Because legal and moral obligation occupy the same terrain—they both purport to tell us what we are strongly "obligated" to do, and they are always capable of conflicting—then, if "ought" implies "can," and if one cannot obey both of two conflicting obligations, one of the obligations must be either overridden or spurious.[19] And if moral obligations are always overriding—because they take into account all reasons—it is difficult to understand how one could accept a rule as obligatory for oneself as well as others without accepting it for moral reasons.

We raise these questions about Hart's account of the rule of recognition not to resolve them, and neither to praise nor bury Hart, but because having them in mind will help illuminate issues about the Constitution of the United States and the judicial practices involved in interpreting it. The possibility that many citizens do not recognize the officials as "officials" and regard them perhaps as illegitimate usurpers of, say, a government-in-exile—even though the rules the

---

17. Hart, as is well known, drew a distinction between *having an obligation* and *being obliged*, the latter being somewhat closer to the situation we find ourselves in when a gunman says "your money or your life." HART, *supra* note 1, at 79–88. The distinction is important, but it is not entirely clear that the language marks it as much as Hart supposed. It is far from a linguistic error to say that we were obligated to hand over our money to the gunman, or that we are obliged to treat our fellow human beings with respect.

Even more important is the question whether creating an obligation in Hart's sense is a necessary condition for the existence of a legal system. It is true that the Austinian account cannot explain legal obligation in Hart's sense, but is it true that an organized state-dominated coercive system (Zimbabwe comes to mind as we write this, and there are certainly others)—the gunman writ large—is not properly described as a legal system? Insofar as gunmen writ large control the coercive and regulatory apparatus of some nation states, there appears to be some tension between the view that legal obligation (in Hart's sense) is a necessary feature of all legal systems and at least one of the core commitments of legal positivism.

18. *See supra* note 17.

19. *See* Larry Alexander & Frederick Schauer, *Law's Limited Domain Confronts Morality's Universal Empire*, 48 WM. & MARY L. REV. 1579 (2007).

officials recognize as legally valid are generally obeyed, if only out of fear of sanctions—suggests that to the extent that Hart's views depart from Austin's, a follower of Hart could accept the idea that several different and conflicting legal systems might simultaneously purport to govern the same people. And although we believe the recognitional practices in the United States produce a single, unified legal system at the federal level, we also believe that this unity overarches a multiplicity of "Constitutions" in terms of substance. That unity and the settlement it represents is a morally valuable achievement, but it is nevertheless the case that legal obligations occupy the same terrain as moral ones, and that officials have moral commitments underlying their recognitional practices that pose a perpetual threat to undo the unity and settlement achieved by those recognitional practices.

II. THE U.S. CONSTITUTION AND THE RULE OF RECOGNITION

So what does American constitutional law and practice look like through the Hartian lens? First, what is the (ultimate[20]) rule of recognition that constitutional law and practice imply?

On one account, Michael Green's, the rule of recognition is—or was originally—the ratification process as described in Article VII of the Constitution.[21] This appears to follow from the fact that compliance with Article VII—which specifies how the Constitution is to be adopted[22]—is what validated the rest of the Constitution and resulted in its *being* the Constitution. Because Article VII is part of the Constitution that it validated, it looks as if Article VII validates itself. This is misleading, however; although Article VII's text is in the document, its status as the (original) rule of recognition is external to the document and rests on its acceptance as the validating rule, not on its validation by having been ratified in accord with its terms. In other words, the charitable interpretation of Green's claim is not that Article VII *is* the rule of recognition, but rather that Article VII *reports* or *describes* the rule of recognition, although even this reformulation is still open to the claim that the content (but not necessarily the exact

---

20. Although in the interests of linguistic economy we often in this chapter use the phrase "rule of recognition" as roughly synonymous with what Hart designates as the "ultimate" rule of recognition, it is important to note that rules of recognition—a variety of secondary rules—need not be ultimate. The rules in Article I of the U.S. Constitution delineating how a bill becomes a law, for example, are rules of recognition, although they are plainly not ultimate rules of recognition.

21. *See* Michael Green, *Legal Revolutions: Six Mistakes About Discontinuity in the Legal Order,* 83 N.C. L. Rev. 331 (2005).

22. "The Ratification of the Conventions of nine States, shall be sufficient for the Establishment of this Constitution between the States so ratifying the Same," U.S. Const. art. VII.

wording) of Article VII was the product of a still more ultimate rule of recognition specifying how the procedures for accepting the Constitution were themselves to be created.[23] (We omit from further consideration here the preexisting sovereignty of the states and the limited authority of the federal government, the only government the Constitution itself establishes; these items complexify the rule of recognition of the United States in ways that are irrelevant to our purposes here.)

The Rule of Recognition and Interpretive Methodologies

If Article VII was the original rule of recognition—and if the entire Constitution, including Article VII, became the rule of recognition once adopted—then Article VII "recognized" (validated) "this Constitution." But then what makes "this Constitution" *this* Constitution? Suppose that each of several officials employs a different methodology of constitutional interpretation. One is, let us say, an originalist of an intentionalist stripe.[24] Another is an original-meaning textualist such as Justice Scalia.[25] Still another is a current-meaning textualist somewhat closer in interpretive views to John Hart Ely than to Justice Scalia.[26] A fourth looks to the values presupposed by the text and asks what interpretation best realizes those values.[27] And so on. Not only will each of these officials assign different meanings to the Constitution; in a very real sense, each official is interpreting

---

23. It is probably the case today that the Constitution, including Article VII, is accepted as a whole, but not because the procedures described in Article VII were actually complied with in its ratification. That is why we use the phrase "*was* the product" rather than "*is* the product." A rule of recognition or recognitional practice is always premised on its *current* acceptance by the relevant recognitional group. And although it is possible that the Constitution is accepted today because of the ratification process in 1788, it is more probable that its contemporary acceptance rests on other grounds and would not be upended by a discovery that the ratification process was inconsistent with the specifications of Article VII—just as it is unlikely that contemporary acceptance of the Fourteenth Amendment as valid law depends on its ratification having been in compliance with Article V (the article setting forth the constitutional amendment processes).

24. As is, for example, RAOUL BERGER, GOVERNMENT BY JUDICIARY: THE TRANSFORMATION OF THE FOURTEENTH AMENDMENT (2d ed., 1997). For discussion of intentionalism, see LARRY ALEXANDER & EMILY SHERWIN, DEMYSTIFYING LEGAL REASONING 141–59 (2008); GREGORY BASSHAM, ORIGINAL INTENT AND THE CONSTITUTION (1992).

25. *See* ANTONIN SCALIA, A MATTER OF INTERPRETATION: FEDERAL COURTS AND THE LAW (Amy Guttman ed., 1997).

26. JOHN HART ELY, DEMOCRACY AND DISTRUST (1980). *See also* Frederick Schauer, *An Essay on Constitutional Language*, 29 U.C.L.A. L. REV. 797 (1982).

27. It should be noted that this "moral reading" of the Constitution is logically dependent on there being some other interpretive methodology with which it works in tandem. The Constitution has to have some meaning independent of the evaluative interpretation in order for there to be something to give an evaluative interpretation *of*. Otherwise, evaluative interpretation reduces all constitutional meaning to the Spike Lee injunction,

a different constitution. And this is because, in part, the interpretive methodology of each of these officials requires her to interpret different raw material.

But is this all we mean by saying that each is interpreting a different "Constitution"? To illustrate our idea, consider further what several of the interpretive methodologies noted above imply about their respective objects.

The originalist-intentionalist, for example, views the Constitution as a set of instructions authored by a specific group of people—instructions on "how to build a government and assign and limit its powers"—and he views his task as one of trying to ascertain what instructions the authors intended to convey.[28] If the best evidence of those instructions—the text—is vague, ambiguous, or otherwise indeterminate, the interpreter seeks whatever other evidence he can find that bears on what instructions were intended. The task for the originalist-intentionalist is basically no different from that of an American parent trying to assemble a child's toy made in some foreign land, the instructions for which are perhaps written in poor English and accompanied by imperfect illustrations. The parent has no clue how to go about assembling it in the absence of instructions. So what he attempts to do is figure out from the text and diagrams what those instructions are.

Similarly, the originalist-intentionalist wishes to know what instructions the constitutional authors intended to convey.[29] The marks on the parchment may be the starting point of the inquiry and the best evidence of the correct answer to it, but it is the intended instructions that are the ultimate quarry—perhaps because, like the toymaker, the constitutional authors were wiser than the interpreter; because of the virtues of the process by which the constitutional authors were selected; or because of some combination of these reasons.

The textualist, on the other hand, views the Constitution as consisting in the meaning its words would convey if they had been written in standard English (as it existed at a specific point in time, which for Justice Scalia is 1787, 1791, or 1868, while for John Ely it might have been today—we leave aside how one picks the year by which to gauge the standard English meaning, or how one determines

---

"Do the right thing." *See also* Adam M. Samaha, *Dead Hand Arguments and Constitutional Interpretation*, 108 COLUM. L. REV. 606, 650–51 (2008).

28. *Cf.* Richard A. Posner, *Legal Realism, Legal Formalism, and the Interpretation of Statutes and the Constitution*, 37 CASE W. RES. L. REV. 179 (1987).

29. There is an important difference between two types of originalist-intentionalist views. In one, the originalist-intentionalist views the intentions of the original drafters as *authoritative* for reasons of democratic theory. In the other, someone like the toy-assembler, but also someone like some legal interpreters, views the instructions as authoritative in a Razian service-conception sense (see, most recently, Joseph Raz, *Revisiting the Service Conception*, 90 MINN. L. REV. 1003 (2006)). There is a big difference, therefore, between deferring to the Framers (whether it be their language or their mental states) because we think they were smart and deferring to them because we think they were (and remain) legitimate.

that the marks *are* standard English rather than an idiolect, a code, or a foreign language.). Leaving aside the problems of multiple meanings in standard English and of whether to treat the punctuation as standard as well, the result is a constitution whose instructions are not necessarily those of its actual authors but are those that hypothetical authors employing the standard English[30] of a certain era would have conveyed.

The commonality between these different constitutional interpreters and their different methodologies is that they both start with the same piece of parchment and the same marks that are to be found on it. In doing so, however, they are looking at quite different material, and thus, in a real and important sense, they are looking at different constitutions. That can be seen by asking how these different interpreters—the originalist-intentionalist and the texualist—would translate the parchment and its marks for a non-English-speaking audience. The originalist-intentionalist would ask how best to convey the authors' intended instructions to that non-English audience. The textualist, on the other hand, would ask how best to translate standard English into another language. The two translations could be quite different because they are translating different material, and the multiplicity and diversity of objects (sets of words) to be interpreted is exactly why, for each interpretive methodology, there is a distinct and different constitution.[31]

---

30. Which could encompass standard technical English, which we do not take as oxymoronic. There *was* a standard meaning of "habeas corpus" (yes, we know that the phrase is Latin and not English) in 1787, just as there were standard meanings of "bill of attainder" and "letter of marque and reprisal," even though these were at the time technical terms of art unknown to the 1787 equivalent of the man on the Clapham omnibus. When we refer to standard (or plain) meaning, therefore, we are not necessarily referring to ordinary meaning.

31. The point about different interpretive methods entailing different objects of interpretation—as dissonant as that might sound at first—is, we are convinced, correct. The point is best illustrated by considering how the one common object—the parchment in the National Archives—would be translated by the different methodologies into, say, French. The intentionalists would give it one translation, the textualists another, the "living constitution" folks yet another, and so on. More radically, one who claimed that the Constitution was really the spaces between the pen marks, and that these spaces were letters in an exotic language, would give it still another. (That would still count as "interpretation" of the parchment in the National Archives.) If French students of U.S. constitutional law each had a different textbook, each authored by a different interpreter of these kinds, then the French versions of the Constitution in the backs of their books would be quite different one from another. So although there is one parchment, there are different constitutions corresponding to these different interpretive methodologies.

Think of it this way: Suppose a document has an ambiguous term *X*, which could mean *A*, *B*, or *C*. Suppose proponents of different interpretive methodologies would each interpret *X* differently: one as *A*, one as *B*, etc. Now suppose each was asked to translate

We believe it relatively uncontroversial that the nine Justices of the Supreme Court employ different methodologies in interpreting the Constitution—perhaps there are even nine methodologies (or more, if each Justice employs different methodologies at different times[32]). If that is so, and if it is also true that the rule of recognition for each Justice consists in the Constitution ratified in accordance with Article VII plus the Justice's interpretive methodology, then does the United States have one rule of recognition or many rules of recognition? And if a rule of recognition identifies an entire legal system, the question can be rephrased: does the United States have one legal system or many?

If what we have said about interpretive methodologies is correct, the answer would appear to be that the United States has many legal systems—at least as many legal systems as there are "constitutions," the number of which is the number of different interpretive methodologies. But that answer, although correct in one sense, is incorrect in another. For the actual rule of recognition—the recognitional practices—do not identify merely the document ratified in 1788 in pursuance of its Article VII plus a single interpretive methodology, but identify rules of settlement among competing methodologies—or among competing constitutions, if you will—as well.

Imagine that officials in the United States accept two rules of recognition—or, more precisely, engage in a recognitional practice with two principal aspects. The first recognitional rule or aspect is the one we have thus far described—it recognizes as supreme law the Constitution in the National Archives, plus some

---

the document into French, which has a term for *A*, a term for *B*, and a term for *C*, but no term for *X* itself. Each would produce a different document in French.

Notice that both the originalist-intentionalist and the textualist agree that it is the Constitution's semantic meaning that is authoritative, even if they disagree about the best account of that semantic meaning. They reject, for example, that it is the original parchment that is authoritative, or the particular marks and spaces found thereon. That is why, despite their interpretive disagreement, both the originalist-intentionalist and the textualist agree that "the Constitution" as it appears in a particular casebook is the same as "the Constitution" in the National Archives, and the same as "the Constitution" translated into Spanish, Finnish, Braille, or Esperanto. It is less clear, however, what the referent is for "the Constitution" for those who would "interpret" it to be "the best it could be," such as RONALD DWORKIN, FREEDOM'S LAW: THE MORAL READING OF THE AMERICAN CONSTITUTION (1996); RONALD DWORKIN, LAW'S EMPIRE (1986); SOTIRIOS A. BARBER, ON WHAT THE CONSTITUTION MEANS (1984); JAMES E. FLEMING, SECURING CONSTITUTIONAL DEMOCRACY (2006); SOTIRIOS A. BARBER & JAMES E. FLEMING, CONSTITUTIONAL INTERPRETATION: THE BASIC QUESTIONS 155–56 (2007). To interpret "it" implies an "it" to be interpreted, an "it" that either has a meaning or does not. If it has a meaning, then it means what it means. It cannot be better than it is. *See supra* note 27.

32. Although it is possible that a metamethodology allowing the selection of different methodologies at different times—*cf.* PHILIP BOBBITT, CONSTITUTIONAL FATE (1982)—is itself just another methodology, and perhaps reduces to simply a "do the right thing" methodology.

range of interpretive methodologies (which will vary from Justice to Justice). The second aspect of the rule of recognition establishes a decision rule for settling controversies among the Justices regarding what the Constitution requires and permits. This aspect of the rule of recognition is probably something like the following: "Determinations endorsed by a majority of Supreme Court Justices shall count as having been authorized by 'the Constitution' so long as the Justices were trying in good faith to ascertain constitutional meaning employing an interpretive methodology that they sincerely believe to be authorized by 'the Constitution.'"[33] This settlement rule of recognition may apply only to the case before the Court—that is, it may have only res judicata effect. Alternatively, it may have stare decisis effect and bind all officials in all cases that fall within the scope of the Court majority's interpretation.[34] Moreover, it may even bind the Court itself with varying degrees of strength.[35] What is significant, however, is that resolution of the strength and scope of the settlement rule of recognition will itself be determined by a majority of the Justices.

In short, the rule of recognition for the Justices in a case of first impression (and for other officials until the Court decides[36]) is the National Archives Constitution plus whatever constitutional interpretive methodology or methodologies the Justices hold in good faith. Once the Court decides, however, the rule of recognition incorporates that decision. In this way, settlement is achieved, and the anarchical tendencies produced by differing interpretive methodologies

---

33. Larry Alexander, *Originalism, or Who is Fred?*, 19 HARV. J. L. & PUB. POL'Y 321 (1995).

34. This is, more or less, the position taken in, for example, Larry Alexander & Frederick Schauer, *On Extrajudicial Constitutional Interpretation*, 110 HARV. L. REV. 1359 (1997); Larry Alexander & Frederick Schauer, *Defending Judicial Supremacy*, 17 CONST. COMM. 455 (2001). And this position is in contrast to the positions of those who are, to put it mildly, less concerned with settlement, such as the so-called "departmentalists"—for example, Michael Stokes Paulsen, *The Most Dangerous Branch: Executive Power to Say What the Law Is*, 83 GEO. L.J. 217 (1994); Gary Lawson & Christopher D. Moore, *The Executive Power of Constitutional Interpretation*, 81 IOWA L. REV. 1267 (1996)—and those who these days ride under the banner of "popular constitutionalism," for example, LARRY KRAMER, THE PEOPLE THEMSELVES: POPULAR CONSTITUTIONALISM AND JUDICIAL REVIEW (2004); MARK V. TUSHNET, TAKING THE CONSTITUTION AWAY FROM THE COURTS (1999). *See also* Larry Alexander & Lawrence B. Solum, *Popular? Constitutionalism?*, 118 HARV. L. REV. 1594 (2005).

35. *See* Alexander & Schauer, *supra* note 34; Gary Lawson, *The Constitutional Case Against Precedent*, 17 HARV. J. L. & PUB. POL'Y 23 (1994); Lawson & Moore, *supra* note 34; Schauer, *supra* note 2; Kurt Lash, *Originalism, Popular Sovereignty, and Reverse Stare Decisis*, 93 VA. L. REV. 1437 (2007) (distinguishing among various types of erroneous Supreme Court constitutional precedents in terms of how binding they should be on the Court itself).

36. And for other officials even after the Court decides, according to the departmentalists and the popular constitutionalists. *See supra* note 34.

and differing results reached using the same methodology are averted.[37] Depending on the strength and scope of the settlement rule of recognition—do decisions of the Court have only res judicata effect or do they also have stare decisis effect, and if so, against which officials and with what strength vis-à-vis overrulings?[38]—the American legal system will be more or less unified and stable.[39]

If, contra Hart, citizens as well as officials must accept the rule of recognition, must citizens actually accept the rather complex rule of recognition we have just described? Many citizens—perhaps most—are unaware of the content of the Constitution, not conversant in the vocabulary of interpretive methodologies, and only dimly aware of the decisions of the Supreme Court.[40] It is preposterous to suppose that they either accept or do not accept the complex rule of recognition. On the other hand, most citizens do not view the deliverances of the legal system as they would the orders backed by threats of muggers. So does this vindicate Hart's restriction of acceptance to officials?

We think not. We think rather that ordinary citizens do accept the rule of recognition—not in the way a sophisticated legal analyst would, but in an indirect, mediated way. Citizens remain for the most part blissfully ignorant of the Court, the contents of the Constitution, interpretive methodologies, stare decisis and res judicata, and, indeed, almost all of the subsconstitutional corpus juris. But they trust other bodies—the legal profession, elected officials, the press, and

---

37. This point has been emphasized by both Larry Alexander, *supra* note 33, and Ken Himma. *See* Kenneth Einar Himma, *Making Sense of Constitutional Disagreement: Legal Positivism, the Bill of Rights, and the Conventional Rule of Recognition in the United States*, 4 J.L. SOC'Y 149 (2003); Kenneth Einar Himma, *Final Authority to Bind with Moral Mistakes: On the Explanatory Potential of Inclusive Legal Positivism*, 24 LAW & PHIL. 1 (2005).

38. As a descriptive matter, Supreme Court rulings appear to have only weak strength against subsequent overrulings. *See* JEFFREY A. SEGAL & HAROLD A. SPAETH, STARE INDECISIS: THE IRRELEVANCE OF PRECEDENT ON THE U.S. SUPREME COURT (1995); Henry Monaghan, *Taking Supreme Court Opinions Seriously*, 39 MD. L. REV. 1 (1989); Frederick Schauer, *Has Precedent Ever Really Mattered in the Supreme Court?*, 24 GA. ST. L. REV. 381 (2007).

39. In this way, acceptance of the rule of recognition for the law of the United States—the Constitution plus the settlement rule of recognition—can be in one sense "group-independent" and in another sense "group-sensitive." *See* Adler, *Constitutional Fidelity*, *supra* note 4, at 1685, 1694–95. A Supreme Court Justice may hold to his or her interpretive methodology in the face of its rejection by the other Justices. Such a Justice in a very real sense recognizes a different constitution than the others recognize. Nevertheless, she may also accept as the supreme law of the land decisions by a majority of the Justices with which she disagreed because they were inconsistent with her interpretive methodology.

40. *See, e.g.*, Daniel Kurtzman, *Seven Dwarfs Better Known Than Supreme Court Justices* (Aug. 16, 2006), *available at* http://politicalhumor.about.com/b/2006/08/16/seven-dwarfs-better-known-than-supreme-court-justices.htm (detailing the results of a survey which showed that three times as many people could name two of the seven dwarfs as could name two Supreme Court Justices).

so on—to inform them of any constitutional coup d'état. They assume that the Supreme Court Justices and other officials are adhering in good faith to the rules of the game, whatever those rules might be. In addition, the deliverances of the legal system of which they are aware, although not always to their liking, are not so oppressive or unjust that they perceive any reason to withhold their allegiance.[41] After all, ordinary citizens, although they have their opinions about what justice requires and which policies are good, also count settlement and stability as preconditions for these desiderata. That is why rules of recognition that provide settlement of moral controversies can be remarkably hardy, even in societies where there is profound moral disagreement.[42] The United States Constitution, so long as it is interpreted other than as equivalent to "whatever I want it to be," will have some elements in it that everyone will find objectionable or at least suboptimal. But at the same time, everyone might conclude that, warts and all, the Constitution is better than any other set of rules *that everyone will accept*.[43]

III. THE RULE OF RECOGNITION, ENTRENCHMENT, AND SUPREME COURT GOOD FAITH

Rules settle moral controversies precisely by being more determinate than the controverted moral principles themselves.[44] If moral principles were uncontroversial in content and application, Spike Lee's law—"Do the right thing"—would be sufficient by itself.[45] There would then be no need for constitutions, statutes,

---

41. Jeffrey L. Yates & Andrew B. Whitford, *Part I: Bush v. Gore's Legacy: The Presidency and the Supreme Court After Bush v. Gore: Implications for Institutional Legitimacy and Effectiveness*, 13 STAN. L. & POL'Y REV. 101, 118 (2002) (finding that the Supreme Court is excluded from most of the public outrage following the decision, and proposing that the Supreme Court's legitimacy does not rest on any one case, but on a long-term assessment of its decisions); Erwin Chemerinsky, *How Should We Think About Bush v. Gore?*, 34 LOY. U. CHI. L.J. 1, 4–5 (2002) (stating that the Supreme Court was able effectively to end public debate because it enjoys a robust popular legitimacy); John C. Yoo, *In Defense of the Court's Legitimacy*, 68 U. CHI. L. REV. 775, 777 (2001) (finding that *Bush v. Gore* did little to undermine the legitimacy of the Supreme Court, even in the face of withering criticism from the legal community, partly because it was seen as an authoritative decision about the rules of elections, and not a moral judgment); David A. Strauss, *Legitimacy and Obedience*, 118 HARV. L. REV. 1854 (2005).

42. *See* ALEXANDER & SHERWIN, *supra* note 6, at Ch. 3. *See also* Samaha, *supra* note 27, at 661–64.

43. *See* ALEXANDER & SHERWIN, *supra* note 6, at Ch. 3.

44. *See id.* at Ch. 2. *See also* BRAD HOOKER, IDEAL CODE, REAL WORLD: A RULE-CONSEQUENTIALIST THEORY OF MORALITY 11–13 (2000); Larry Alexander, *Pursuing the Good—Indirectly*, 95 ETHICS 315 (1985).

45. *See* ALEXANDER & SHERWIN, *supra* note 6, at Ch. 1; Larry Alexander, *"With Me, It's All er Nuthin'": Formalism in Law and Morality*, 66 U. CHI. L. REV. 530, 549 (1999).

administrative orders, or judicial rulemaking, because none of these could improve upon doing the right thing—what could? And by hypothesis, everyone would know the right thing to do in all circumstances. If some lacked motivation to do the right thing, others would know the right thing to do in response.[46]

Of course, the content and application of "the right thing" are and realistically will remain enormously controversial. Authoritative rules settle what to do in the face of that controversy, and by their formality, simplicity, and determinacy avoid the huge moral costs of moral controversy.[47] Instead of being told "do the right thing," the rule subject is told "in circumstance *C*, do *X*," where *C* and *X* are relatively easy for rule subjects to comprehend and ascertain—at least easier to comprehend and ascertain than the direct moral desiderata themselves. Just as the minimum age provision in Article II eliminates virtually all controversy about how old someone must be in order to serve as President by substituting the far more easily ascertainable "age of thirty-five years" for the more controversial and less ascertainable "of sufficient maturity and experience to manage the responsibilities of the Presidency," so too do authoritative interpretations of even the vaguer clauses of the Constitution do the same thing. It is not without interest that police officers reading warnings from a "*Miranda* card" are pretty much reading the words of a Supreme Court opinion, and most Supreme Court decisions similarly, although in less stark fashion, settle what might otherwise be a larger social disagreement.[48]

When authoritative rules are morally necessary to achieve settlement and thus avert the moral costs of moral controversy, they admittedly achieve these moral gains at some moral cost of their own. Because rules simplify, they will undoubtedly prove to be over- and under-inclusive with respect to the background moral goals they are meant to achieve.[49] What the rules require will consequently turn out in many cases not to be "the right thing." But if the rule subject in those cases ignores the rule and opts for the right thing, the rule collapses into the Spike Lee rule. If the rule subject follows the rule where the rule departs from what is morally best, the subject will not be doing the right thing, which to the subject will seem irrational.[50]

---

46. *See* Alexander, *supra* note 45, at 549.

47. *See* ALEXANDER & SHERWIN, *supra* note 6, at Ch. 2; Alexander, *supra* note 45, at 540–48.

48. *See* Miranda v. Arizona, 384 U.S. 436 (1966) (setting forth constitutionally based procedures for police interrogations); Grutter v. Bollinger, 539 U.S. 982 (2003) (deciding controversy over racial preferences in higher education). Compare these decisions with Morse v. Frederick, 127 S. Ct. 2718 (2007), criticized precisely for providing neither settlement nor guidance in Frederick Schauer, *Abandoning the Guidance Function: Morse v. Frederick*, 2007 SUP. CT. REV. 205.

49. *See* ALEXANDER & SHERWIN, *supra* note 6, at Ch. 2; SCHAUER, *supra* note 6, at Ch. 2.

50. ALEXANDER & SHERWIN, *supra* note 6, at Ch. 4.

Thus, it may well be that there are rational reasons to create and enforce rules that the subjects of those rules will perceive, from their lights, to be irrational. This may appear paradoxical, but this paradox, which one of us has called "the asymmetry of authority"[51] and the other has called "the gap,"[52] applies to all legal rules, including constitutional rules and even to the rule of recognition itself. There will frequently be reasons—moral ones—for those in authority to create rules that limit the decisional moral freedom of the subjects of those rules, but there will always be a reason—a moral one—for the rule subject (from the rule subject's perspective) to ignore a legal rule where the rule's requirements depart from the subject's own vision about what the right thing to do is.

One thing that helps mitigate this dilemma is publicity. If everyone is aware of the moral benefits of settlement, then they are likely to be averse to undermining the rules and the settlement they achieve. Public refusals to follow the rules will undermine others' reasons for abiding by them and hence undermine settlement. What might appear to be "the right thing"—violating the rule—may, because of its effects on rule-following generally, turn out to be "the wrong thing." For that reason, officials will be—or at least ought to be[53]—prone to follow rules when their failure to do so will be easily detected.

Given how little the public knows about the Constitution, about constitutional interpretation, and about the debates over stare decisis in constitutional cases—and given how controversial these matters are among the elites to whom the public looks for monitoring the Court[54]—the Justices of the Court will have a great deal of cover should they wish to do the right thing as they perceive it in the guise of deciding constitutional cases. It is true that they may be unlikely to conclude that the Constitution permits presidential terms of five years or three senators per state (or none), even if they believe such arrangements would be optimal. As Ricky Ricardo would have said, they would have too much "splaining" to do.[55] But when it comes to clauses that appear less rule-like, or when it comes to deciding whether to follow a precedent or to follow the text, it is easy for a Justice to put forward his or her policy preferences as consistent with the rule of recognition. Moreover, it will be even more tempting to do so if the Justice suspects that other Justices are doing so.

---

51. SCHAUER, *supra* note 6, at 128–34; Frederick Schauer, *Imposing Rules*, 42 SAN DIEGO L. REV. 85 (2005).

52. Larry Alexander, *The Gap*, 14 HARV. J. L. & PUB. POL'Y 695 (1991).

53. As an empirical matter, what we believe desirable in this respect may be a far cry from existing American political practice. *See* Frederick Schauer, *Ambivalence About the Law*, 49 ARIZ. L. REV. 11 (2007).

54. And perhaps given how little the public actually cares (which is not the same as saying that they should not care) about most of the matters the Supreme Court decides. *See* Frederick Schauer, *The Supreme Court, 2005 Term. Foreword: The Court's Agenda—and the Nation's*, 120 HARV. L. REV. 4 (2006).

55. *I Love Lucy* (1951).

Notice, however, that when the Justices pick and choose interpretive methodologies and theories of stare decisis in a purely result-oriented way, there will be no real rule of recognition other than "whatever five Justices of the Supreme Court decide."[56] And because the Supreme Court itself (that is, the institution we recognize as the Supreme Court) is a product of the National Archives Constitution and an interpretive methodology that is tied to originalism rather than any notion of a "living Constitution"—the requirements of Article III have not "evolved"—the Justices cannot destabilize the Article VII Constitution without threatening their own existence as an institution.[57]

Yet, the existence of the Court and adherence to (at least most of) its deliverances seem quite secure. What explains this? The rule of recognition in the United States turns out to be an enormously complex matter.[58] Those parts of the original Constitution that are quite rule-like, including those designating how Supreme Court Justices are selected, testify to the originalists' Constitution's continued place in the rule of recognition. But that Constitution has been supplemented by "whatever five Justices decide"—so long, that is, as what they decide is not too loopy. And the opportunity and temptation this provides for Justices to tailor their views on interpretation, the role of precedent and the like would lead one to predict that the Justices will adapt their interpretive methodologies to achieve what they think is right, just, and good public policy—so long, that is, as they believe they can get away with doing so. And because every change in interpretive methodology implies a change in the object of interpretation, the Constitution—or large parts of it—will be constantly changing, and changing other than in accordance with the originalists' Constitution's Article V amendment process.

We said earlier that such non-Article V changing of the Constitution by five Justices of the Supreme Court will not be publicly viewed as a constitutional coup d'état so long as the public believes the Supreme Court Justices are in good faith trying to interpret *the* Constitution rather than legislating the supreme law of the land from the bench.[59] We probably should relax this requirement to some extent. For it may be true that the public accepts the constitutional deliverances of the Court so long as it either (1) believes the Justices are trying in good faith to interpret the Constitution or (2) is happy with the substance of Supreme Court

56. In his concurrence in Brown v. Allen, 344 U.S. 443, 540 (1953), Justice Robert Jackson quipped, "we are not final because we are infallible, but we are infallible only because we are final." *See also* Kenneth Einar Himma, *Understanding the Relationship between the U.S. Constitution and the Conventional Rule of Recognition* (Chapter 4, this volume); authorities cited in note 37 *supra*.

57. *See* Green, *supra* note 21, at nn.121–24, for a similar point.

58. *See* Kent Greenawalt, *The Rule of Recognition and the Constitution*, 85 MICH. L. REV. 621 (1987) (reprinted as Chapter 1, this volume).

59. *See also* Green, *supra* note 21, at nn.125–34.

decisions. When members of the public are unhappy with the substance of a constitutional decision, they will nonetheless accept it as authoritative if they believe the Justices felt themselves bound to decide as they did by their good faith interpretation(s) of the Constitution. And they probably will accept it even if they learn that the Justices disagree about interpretive methodologies and thus about what the Constitution *is* (its originally intended meaning, its meaning in standard English, and so on). Moreover, they probably will accept a substantively obnoxious decision that is inconsistent with the Constitution if it is consistent with precedent—for they will probably accept the controversial case for making Supreme Court constitutional precedents as authoritative as the Constitution itself. What is unlikely to be accepted is a substantively obnoxious decision that the public perceives to fail all these conditions.

This is perhaps well illustrated by reference to the strong negative reaction by large parts of the public to decisions like *Roe*.[60] Many people detest the substantive outcome in *Roe*. Within that large group is a smaller group that believes *Roe's* outcome was not compelled by the Constitution as properly interpreted.[61] And within that group is a smaller group that denies that *Roe's* outcome was compelled by Supreme Court precedents. But it is doubtful that there is a sizeable subgroup within that group that believes the Supreme Court majority did not in good faith believe that the outcome was compelled (or at the very least permitted) by either the Constitution as they in good faith believed it should be interpreted, or by precedents that they in good faith believed must be followed. If there is a subgroup of *Roe* opponents who believe that the Court in *Roe* was not acting in good faith along any of these dimensions, then that subgroup will believe the Constitution has been overthrown by a few judicial usurpers and their apologists.[62] But as we interpret the actual rule of recognition in the United States, most people, including most opponents of *Roe*, believe that *Roe* is consistent with the rule of recognition, even if it is a misinterpretation of the Article VII Constitution and Supreme Court precedents. And what is true of *Roe* is perhaps even more true of *Bush v. Gore*.[63]

---

60. Roe v. Wade, 410 U.S. 113 (1973) (overturning on substantive due process grounds Texas's law criminalizing most abortions).

61. Of course, some—perhaps many—who believe *Roe's* outcome was not compelled (or even permitted) by the Constitution actually like the outcome on policy grounds. *See* John Hart Ely, *The Wages of Crying Wolf: A Comment on Roe v. Wade*, 82 YALE L.J. 920, 921–22 (1973).

62. Michael Paulsen, perhaps. *See* Michael Stokes Paulsen, *Paulsen, J., Dissenting, in* WHAT ROE V. WADE SHOULD HAVE SAID: THE NATION'S TOP LEGAL EXPERTS REWRITE AMERICA'S MOST CONTROVERSIAL DECISION (Jack M. Balkin ed., 2005).

63. 531 U.S. 98 (2000) (overturning an order by the Supreme Court of Florida requiring a manual recount of votes cast in one Florida county, on the ground that the Florida Supreme Court failed to identify and require standards for vote counting and thereby violated the Equal Protection Clause of the Constitution).

IV. CONCLUSION: IT'S TURTLES ALL THE WAY DOWN

Our conclusions about the effect of Supreme Court decisions on public consciousness and political decision making are empirical suppositions, and as such they may very well be mistaken. And even if they are not mistaken now, they may become mistaken in the future. But our central argument does not rest on debatable empirical premises. Rather, our principal claim is that the nonlegal foundations of any legal system have profound implications for thinking about American constitutional law. These implications do not depend on resolution of jurisprudential debates about Hart's conception of the rule of recognition or Kelsen's of the *Grundnorm*. Instead, they flow from the unavoidable dependence of law on the nonlegal environment in which it exists, not simply to decide how law should be interpreted, and not simply to evaluate the extent to which law will be effective, but more broadly to determine just what is to count as law and what is not.

Once we appreciate the unavoidable and dizzying fragility of a legal system's nonlegal foundations, we discover that the security and stability that constitutionalism is alleged to bring depends less on constitutionalism itself than on the preconstitutional understandings that make constitutionalism possible. Some such understandings will make constitutionalism more stable than others, and thus will serve settlement and consistency values more than others. We believe such values are important, but we recognize that others may not share these beliefs. But even those who place less importance on settlement and stability than we do cannot escape confronting the extent to which their constitutional values and commitments depend as well on nonlegal and nonconstitutional concerns. That will provide little solace to lawyers and judges, but it will be a useful reminder that constitutionalism of any sort resides not in a constitution, but in the preconstitutional commitments that make any form of constitutionalism possible.

8. SOCIAL FACTS, CONSTITUTIONAL INTERPRETATION, AND THE RULE OF RECOGNITION

MATTHEW D. ADLER*

How do participants in the United States legal system argue about constitutional interpretation? Constitutional scholars and leading jurists have long been preoccupied with elaborating different possible interpretive methods, such as an original-intent approach, an original-meaning approach, John Hart Ely's representation-reinforcement method, Cass Sunstein's "minimalism," the "structure and relationship" approach defended by Charles Black, and so forth.[1] I want to shift the discussion a level up. What is the structure of argumentation *about* the different possible approaches?

For short, I will call an argument or statement in favor of some approach to interpreting the U.S. Constitution a constitutional interpretation (CI) argument or statement, and the total body of such statements "CI-discourse." Someone who participates in this discourse is a "CI-participant."

Oddly, constitutional scholars have given little attention to the semantics of CI-discourse. There are scores of books and hundreds of law review articles contributing to CI-discourse, but very little scholarship that analyzes the discourse itself.[2]

Several related puzzles about CI-discourse are worth reflecting upon. One is differentiating between legal and nonlegal arguments for interpretive methods. It is certainly possible to advance a nonlegal argument for some interpretive method—for example, to argue that some method has a favorable moral status,

---

* Leon Meltzer Professor, University of Pennsylvania Law School. Many thanks to Mitch Berman, Michael Dorf, Kent Greenawalt, Alon Harel, Ken Himma, Matt Lister, Stephen Perry, and Kevin Toh, for their written comments; to the other authors in this book, for helpful discussions at a University of Pennsylvania Law School conference where initial chapter drafts were discussed; and to participants in workshops at the University of Texas Law School and the law faculty of Queen's University, where I presented an initial draft.

1. Prominent scholarly and judicial discussions of constitutional interpretation are analyzed in Section III. For references to other scholarship on constitutional interpretation, see CONSTITUTIONAL THEORY: ARGUMENTS AND PERSPECTIVES (Michael Gerhardt et al. eds., 3d ed. 2007).

2. The few extant discussions of CI-discourse include Richard Fallon, *How To Choose a Constitutional Theory*, 87 CAL. L. REV. 535 (1999), with commentaries by Michael Dorf and David Strauss, *see* 87 CAL. L. REV. at 581, 593; and PHILIP BOBBITT, CONSTITUTIONAL FATE (1982); CONSTITUTIONAL INTERPRETATION (1991).

while leaving open the question of its legal status. However, as we shall see, CI-participants often claim, explicitly or implicitly, that some interpretive method has a favorable *legal* status—by which I mean either the minimally favorable status of being legally permitted, or some more strongly favorable status, such as being legally required, or supported by a legal presumption, or supported by the balance of legal considerations.

But what exactly is the structure of a legal—as opposed to nonlegal—argument for an interpretive method? What is the feature of an interpretive method that CI-participants see as conferring a favorable legal status upon that method? And are CI-participants correct on this score? What is the feature of an interpretive method that actually *does* make it legally permitted, required, or otherwise favored?

Another puzzle concerns the role of *social facts* in CI-arguments. As we shall see, CI-arguments often point to social facts as part of the grounds for the favorable legal status of some interpretive method. By social facts, I mean facts about the behaviors, utterances, or mental states of some group of individuals in the United States, either past or present. It turns out that three kinds of social facts figure repeatedly in CI-arguments: facts about the Framers' intent, facts about judicial precedent (that is, facts about judicial behavior, utterances, or mental states), and facts about our constitutional culture or tradition.

But does the nexus between an interpretive method and certain social facts indeed function to establish that the interpretive method is legally permitted, required, or otherwise favored? If so, how do social facts play this role? Does the nexus between an interpretive method and certain social facts indeed function to establish that judges or other actors have a genuine reason to employ the interpretive method? If so, how do social facts play *this* role?

As an exemplar of CI-argument, consider Thomas Grey's famous article, "Do We Have an Unwritten Constitution?"[3] Grey argues for nontextualism—for "[c]onstitutional adjudication going beyond the norms implicit in text and original history."[4] He is quite explicit in distinguishing between the question whether nontextualism is normatively attractive in some nonlegal sense (what he calls "the question of practical wisdom"[5]), and the question of its legal status. "Even if this mode of judicial review [nontextualism] produces good results in the eyes of some beholders, and even if it is not intrinsically unjudicial, there remains the question whether in our Constitution we have actually granted this large power to our judges."[6] And Grey makes clear his intention to argue that nontextualism is *legally* favored. He writes:

> In resolving this issue of legal authority, there seems to me only one plausible method of inquiry. We must apply the conventional and accepted categories

---

3. 27 Stan. L. Rev. 703 (1975).
4. *Id.* at 714.
5. *Id.*
6. *Id.* at 715.

> of legal argument—original understanding, judicial precedent, subsequent history, and internal consistency—and see if they support judicial review that goes beyond [textualism].
>
> I believe that when these tests are applied, constitutional adjudication of the sort objected to by Mr. Justice Black and the other proponents of the pure [textualist] model will be seen to be a lawful and legitimate feature of our system of judicial review.[7]

Grey's appeal to "original understanding," "judicial precedent," and "subsequent history" is, I suggest, quite remarkable. Understand that Grey is not proposing "original understanding," "judicial precedent," or "subsequent history" as first-order interpretive methods that judges should employ in reading the text of the Constitution. Constitutional scholars and jurists make such proposals all the time, and no one would be surprised by them. Rather, he is proposing "original understanding," "judicial precedent," and "subsequent history" as *second-order criteria for choosing among interpretive methods.*

In the remainder of the article, Grey adduces facts about precedent, original understanding, and U.S. constitutional culture and tradition to argue in favor of nontextualism. He labors at length to show the inconsistency between textualism and Supreme Court case law in areas such as substantive due process, the application of the Bill of Rights to the states, and the application of equal protection norms to the federal government. He concludes: "[A]n extraordinarily radical purge of established constitutional doctrine would be required if we candidly and consistently applied the [textualist] model. Surely that makes out at least a prima facie practical case against the model."[8]

Grey claims that the Framers were nontextualists:

> For the generation that framed the Constitution, the concept of a "higher law," protecting "natural rights," and taking precedence over ordinary positive law as a matter of political obligation, was widely shared and deeply felt. An essential element of American constitutionalism was the reduction to written form—and hence to positive law—of some of the principles of natural rights. But at the same time, it was generally recognized that written constitutions could not completely codify the higher law. Thus in the framing of the original American constitutions it was widely accepted that there remained unwritten but still binding principles of higher law.[9]

Finally, Grey points to an ongoing tradition of invoking fundamental, unwritten rights, starting with the Framers, continuing with the antislavery constitutionalists, then the *Lochner*-era proponents of liberty of contract, and ending

---

7. *Id.*
8. *Id.* at 713.
9. *Id.* at 715–16.

with contemporary commitment to the rights of privacy, voting, travel, and other unwritten rights. "[This] is the modern offspring, in a direct and traceable line of legitimate descent, of the natural rights tradition that is so deeply embedded in our constitutional origins."[10]

Can we "make sense" of the appearance of social facts about precedent, Framers' intent, and U.S. constitutional culture and tradition in Grey's article and the other places in CI-discourse where these social facts appear? To put the question more precisely: can we develop a framework for CI-discourse that (1) *describes*, with reasonable accuracy, the sorts of arguments that Grey and other CI-participants are actually making; and that (2) *vindicates* characteristic features of CI-discourse, namely the CI-participant's assertion or presupposition that some interpretive method is legally favored; that social facts contribute to the legally favored status of this method; and that judges and other actors have a genuine reason to employ the legally favored method?

A full analysis of these questions would require a comprehensive survey of jurisprudentially plausible accounts of law and legal discourse, seeing how well each one functions to describe and vindicate CI-discourse. Such an analysis is beyond the scope of this chapter. Rather, I begin at the beginning: with H.L.A. Hart's rule of recognition account.[11] This account is the foundation for all contemporary work on the nature of law in the Anglo-American philosophical tradition, both by positivists, who build upon Hart's account, and by Dworkinians, who proceed in reaction to it.[12]

The rule of recognition model includes a semantics for legal statements. According to Hart, legal systems always include committed participants, who take the "internal point of view" toward a rule stating ultimate criteria of legal validity (the rule of recognition). In that state of mind, committed participants make "internal" legal statements. Notably, as we shall see, internal legal statements assert or presuppose a certain kind of social fact: namely, the fact that present officials in the society accept the rule of recognition.

The rule of recognition account of the semantics of legal statements—for short, "RoR semantics"—might seem to be a promising framework for CI-discourse in the United States. Reference to social facts is both a characteristic feature of CI-discourse and a pivotal element of RoR semantics. For Hart, it is the social fact of official acceptance of the rule of recognition, together with

---

10. *Id.* at 717.

11. *See* H.L.A. Hart, The Concept of Law (Penelope A. Bulloch & Joseph Raz eds., 2d ed. 1994).

12. Ronald Dworkin's jurisprudential views are most comprehensively stated in Law's Empire (1986). The reader unfamiliar with contemporary jurisprudential debates might begin by reading Jules L. Coleman, The Practice of Principle: In Defence of a Pragmatist Approach to Legal Theory (2001); and the chapters in Hart's Postscript: Essays on the Postscript to The Concept of Law (Jules Coleman ed., 2001).

general efficacy of the legal duties flowing from the rule of recognition, that gives rise to a certain kind of social reality: a legal system. The difference between a genuine and a spurious legal position (right, duty, power, etc.) is just that the genuine position has the right nexus, direct or indirect, to the rule of recognition. And the difference between a legal statement and some other type of normative statement is (in part) that a legal statement makes reference to the fact of official acceptance of the rule of recognition.[13]

However, as I will show in this chapter, RoR semantics does not accurately describe CI-discourse, nor does it help vindicate various characteristic aspects of CI-discourse. One key problem, which should already be evident, is that the *kinds of social facts* that figure in CI-discourse are different from those that figure in RoR semantics: not facts about a present official consensus, but rather facts about precedent, culture/tradition, and Framers' intent. Another problem, which is not apparent from the Grey article but will emerge below, is the *heterogeneity* of appeals to social facts in CI-discourse. Some CI-participants, such as Grey, appeal to precedent, Framers' intent, *and* culture/tradition. But some CI-participants appeal only to one or two of these kinds of facts, and some to none. More strikingly, some CI-participants explicitly disclaim reliance upon precedent; some explicitly disclaim reliance upon Framers' intent; and some explicitly disclaim reliance upon culture/tradition.

Section I of this chapter discusses the various dimensions for evaluating a candidate semantics for some normative discourse, such as CI-discourse. Section II explicates RoR semantics. Section III reviews a sample of CI-discourse and discusses how social facts figure therein. Section IV analyzes whether RoR semantics describes or vindicates CI-discourse reasonably well, and reaches a negative conclusion.

Section V looks beyond the rule of recognition model, in an initial and exploratory way. The fact that RoR semantics fails to describe and vindicate CI-discourse does not necessarily indicate a flaw in RoR semantics and, more generally, Hart's account of law. Reaching that conclusion, based on the analysis in this chapter, would be premature. We should be open to the possibility that CI-discourse is a misguided body of argument—at least to the extent that participants argue for the favorable legal (rather than merely moral) status of controversial interpretive methods, and for the role of certain social facts in buttressing this status. CI-participants may just be *incorrect* to think that an interpretive method can be legally favored absent a current official consensus supporting the method, and that facts about precedent, Framers' intent, or culture/tradition provide legal support for interpretive methods, absent a current official consensus that such facts play this role. In short, we should be open to an "error theory" of CI-discourse—a theory that says that some of the assertions or presuppositions characteristic of CI-discourse are, in fact, systematically false.

---

13. *See infra* Section II.

To be clear, this chapter does not embrace an error theory of CI-discourse. Section V merely suggests, in a preliminary manner, why various alternatives to RoR semantics—such as successor positivist frameworks, Dworkinian semantics, and group-relative semantics—may also have difficulty in both describing and vindicating CI-discourse.

I. SEMANTIC FRAMEWORKS

CI-discourse is normative. CI-participants *recommend* interpretive methods. This chapter will consider whether RoR semantics provides a satisfactory semantics for CI-discourse. At the threshold, then, we need to think about the criteria for evaluating a candidate semantics for some normative discourse.

Scholarship in metaethics on the semantics of moral statements is helpful in this regard.[14] One proposed semantics for moral discourse is *cognitivist*. According to a cognitivist semantics, a moral statement asserts the speaker's belief in some proposition. Cognitivists note that the surface grammar of moral statements is propositional—speakers ascribe the property of "rightness" or "goodness" to actions or outcomes. Cognitivists also note features of moral discourse most readily explained by a propositional semantics, for example: (1) the fact that speakers sometimes disagree with each other, which is most readily explained as a conflict of beliefs—that is, one speaker believing some moral proposition which another disbelieves; and (2) the fact that speakers make deductive inferences from moral premises to moral conclusions, in accordance with the norms of propositional logic, again most readily explained if moral statements express beliefs in propositions.

Noncognitivists deny that a moral statement is an assertion of the speaker's belief in some proposition. Their position is that moral statements express some non-belief state, such as an emotion, a commitment, or a plan. They ask cognitivists to explain the link between moral statements and motivation. Normally, when a speaker makes a sincere moral statement, she is motivated to behave consistently with that statement. But beliefs, without more, don't motivate.

Noncognitivists also ask cognitivists whether moral statements—if they indeed express propositions—can possibly be true. What are the properties of "rightness" and "goodness"? Some cognitivists respond to this challenge by arguing that moral properties are nonnatural properties. Others claim that moral properties are natural properties. Still others adopt an error theory of moral discourse. John Mackie, the most famous expositor of this approach, combines a cognitivist moral semantics with an ontology that denies the existence of moral

14. For an overview, see ALEXANDER MILLER, AN INTRODUCTION TO CONTEMPORARY METAETHICS (2003).

properties. Mackie takes the position that moral statements assert propositions which, however, are never true.[15]

Drawing from this scholarship on moral semantics, I will take the following approach to thinking about CI-statements. A "semantics" offers a model or framework for some target discourse, such as some normative discourse. This model characterizes the target discourse as consisting in one or more kinds of speech acts. The model can be *evaluated* along different dimensions. I will mention three (there may be others). One dimension is descriptive: the model can be better or worse in describing the statements that the participants in the target discourse are actually making. Another dimension is explanatory: the model can be better or worse in explaining why the participants are making these statements.

Another dimension, for lack of a better word, is the dimension of *vindication*. Roughly speaking, what I mean by this is whether speech acts that conform to the model tend to be made by speakers who are logical, rational, and accurate in their view of the world. One aspect of vindication has to do with the *truth* of those factual statements that the model licenses. Insofar as the semantics licenses statements where speakers express their beliefs, are those statements generally true or untrue?

I don't have a grand theory about which dimensions "matter" more in evaluating a candidate semantics for some discourse. It seems to me that different scholars will focus on different dimensions, depending on their interests. For example, a sociologist developing a semantics for legal discourse may not care at all about the dimension of vindication, while a legal scholar who is both trying to get a handle on the semantics of legal discourse, and participating herself in legal discourse, *will* presumably care about the dimension of vindication. Presumably she doesn't want to develop a framework for her own arguments that will lead her to make false claims.

A Dworkinian or Davidsonian[16] about these matters might insist that a candidate semantics is a failure unless it vindicates the target discourse sufficiently. I don't take that position. The sociologist might deny the existence of moral properties (on the ground that such properties have no role in our best scientific theories of the physical and social worlds), but construe moral statements as expressing beliefs in moral properties (on the ground that such beliefs best explain the deductive inferences that participants in moral discourse

15. *See* John Mackie, Ethics: Inventing Right and Wrong (1977); Miller, *supra* note 14, at 111–27.

16. Donald Davidson famously argued for a principle of "charity" in interpretation—roughly, that interpreters should strive to interpret statements so as to make them true. *See* Simon Evnine, Donald Davidson (1991). There are affinities between this view and Ronald Dworkin's idea in *Law's Empire* that interpretation seeks to make its object the best it can be. *See* S.L. Hurley, Natural Reasons: Personality and Polity (1989).

make)—ending up with an error theory of moral discourse. Error theories of other areas of discourse remain live options in the relevant scholarly literatures.[17] For example, it is surely the case that a scholar can study and theorize about religious discourse without herself believing in God.

I focus in this chapter on the problem of describing and vindicating CI-discourse, given that my own interests are jurisprudential (to understand when some interpretive method is genuinely legally favored) and normative (to understand when judges and other actors genuinely have a reason of some kind to employ an interpretive method). I emphatically do *not* mean to suggest that any scholar studying CI-discourse must have this combination of aims.

II. HART'S SEMANTICS OF LEGAL STATEMENTS

Hart's *The Concept of Law* sets forth a model of a legal system, involving the familiar notions of an ultimate criterion of legal validity—the rule of recognition—toward which officials take the "internal point of view"; derivative legal rules validated by the rule of recognition; and general efficacy of the valid conduct-regulating rules.[18]

One part of Hart's model is a semantics for legal statements. He distinguishes between "internal statements" and "external statements," the former being made by those who take the internal point of view toward the rule of recognition.[19]

Participants in CI-discourse accept, or seem to accept, the normative force of the U.S. Constitution; they seem to be doing something like taking the internal point of view toward it, or toward a rule of recognition validating it. It is therefore Hart's model of internal legal statements, rather than his model of external legal statements, that seems a more promising candidate to describe and vindicate CI-discourse, and that shall be my focus in this chapter.

Recent scholarship by Kevin Toh has dissected *The Concept of Law* and Hart's other writings in great detail, and has argued persuasively that Hart's semantics for internal legal statements were *noncognitivist*.[20] Stephen Perry and Scott Shapiro reach the same conclusion.[21] Toh offers the following gloss on Hart: "In making an

17. On error theories, see Brian Leiter, *Explaining Theoretical Disagreement*, 76 U. Chi. L. Rev. (forthcoming 2009).

18. *See* Hart, *supra* note 11, at 78–117.

19. *See id.* at 102–03.

20. *See* Kevin Toh, *Hart's Expressivism and his Benthamite Project*, 11 Legal Theory 75 (2005).

21. *See* Stephen Perry, *Hart on Social Rules and the Foundations of Law: Liberating the Internal Point of View*, 75 Fordham L. Rev. 1143 (2006); Stephen Perry, *Where Have All the Powers Gone? Hartian Rules of Recognition, Noncognitivism, and the Constitutional and Jurisprudential Foundations of Law* (Chapter 11, this volume); Scott J. Shapiro, *What is the Internal Point of View?*, 75 Fordham L. Rev. 1157 (2006).

internal legal statement, according to [Hart], a speaker (i) displays his acceptance of a particular norm as the rule of recognition of his legal system; and (ii) presupposes that this rule of recognition is generally accepted by the officials of his community."[22] According to this framework, what the speaker making an internal legal statement explicitly expresses is not some belief—for example, a belief that the rule of recognition is binding, or legitimate, or anything like that—but rather a non-belief state of accepting or being committed to the rule of recognition.

So we have a substantial problem, right off the bat, in using Hart's model of internal legal statements as the semantics for CI-discourse. All things considered, it seems that noncognitivism does a pretty poor job of describing and vindicating moral discourse. And these deficits would presumably carry over to a noncognitivist semantics for other kinds of normative discourse, such as legal discourse. For example, legal speakers make deductive inferences about which legal positions (rights, duties, etc.) exist. Such inferences can be correct if "assertions" of legal positions are genuine assertions, expressing beliefs in propositions, but they are very difficult to see as correct otherwise. Indeed, Stephen Perry has argued at length that the best semantics for legal discourse is cognitivist.[23]

However, it is not too difficult to reformulate Hart's semantics along cognitivist lines. This cognitivist reformulation is meant as a friendly amendment—one intended to bolster the ability of RoR semantics to describe and vindicate U.S. legal discourse, in particular CI-discourse.

What exactly should the reformulation be? One key aspect of Hart's model of a legal system, obviously, is the way in which it rests upon a social practice. According to Hart, officials in any legal system instantiate a special kind of social practice vis-à-vis the system's rule of recognition: they accept it, comply with it, criticize officials who deviate from it, and accept such criticism as legitimate. For short, I will call this practice official "acceptance" of the rule of recognition.

The social practice foundational to a legal system, according to Hart, is a *contemporaneous official* practice. *The Concept of Law* makes crystal clear that the rule of recognition is the norm stating ultimate validity criteria that is accepted by officials, and that the rule of recognition need not be accepted by citizens. Nor, it seems, is the rule of recognition merely accepted by judges; rather, officials in general, including legislators and other nonjudicial officials as well as judges, necessarily accept it.[24] As for the rule's temporal features, Hart's discussion of the emergence of new legal systems suggests that the rule of recognition for a

---

22. Toh, *supra* note 20, at 112–13.

23. *See* Perry, *Hart on Social Rules* and *Where Have All the Powers Gone?* both *supra* note 21.

24. On the official-centric cast of the rule of recognition, see Matthew D. Adler, *Popular Constitutionalism and the Rule of Recognition: Whose Practices Ground U.S. Law?*, 100 Nw. U. L. Rev. 719, 729–37 (2006).

legal system at some time *T* is the ultimate criterion of legal validity accepted by officials at *T*.[25]

Internal legal statements, according to Hart, make reference to the fact that officials accept the rule of recognition. Internal statements do not explicitly state this fact, but neither do they ignore it. Rather, Hart says, an internal legal statement *presupposes* the social fact of official acceptance of the rule of recognition.[26]

A second key aspect of a legal system, according to Hart, is the foundationalist character of legal reasoning. There is an ultimate criterion of legal validity, the rule of recognition, which "can neither be valid nor invalid,"[27] and subordinate legal rules, which are validated by derivation from the rule of recognition. And, although Hart is not fully explicit about this point, *The Concept of Law* seems to say this: a speaker who makes an internal statement asserting a legal duty or some other legal position pursuant to a subordinate rule presupposes that this subordinate rule can be derived from the rule of recognition.[28]

I therefore suggest the following cognitivist reformulation of Hart's semantics, which retains the central idea that an internal legal statement makes reference to a special kind of social fact, and incorporates Hart's foundationalist picture of legal reasoning. It also preserves the normative character of internal legal statements—the critical difference from external statements. I will henceforth drop the term "internal" and refer to internal legal statements simply as "legal statements."

RoR Semantics for Legal Statements

A legal statement:

1. Asserts the existence of some legal position (a duty, right, liberty, etc.) (*legal character*);
2. asserts or presupposes that the legal position has normative force, providing genuine reasons for action for the holder of the position and/or those who hold connected positions (*normative character*);
3. asserts or presupposes that this legal position can be derived from an ultimate criterion of legal validity, the rule of recognition (*foundationalism*);
4. asserts or presupposes that the rule of recognition is generally accepted by present officials (*social fact: present official acceptance*);
5. asserts or presupposes that the duties derivable from the rule of recognition are generally complied with by citizens as well as officials (*social fact: general efficacy*); and

25. *See* HART, *supra* note 11, at 117–23. This is consistent with Hart's sociological aims. The fact that officials accept some rule at *T*, as opposed to the fact that they accepted some rule at a previous time, is more explanatory with respect to official behavior at *T*.

26. On the presuppositions of an internal statement, see HART, *supra* note 11, at 104, 108–09; Toh, *supra* note 20, at 88, 112–13.

27. HART, *supra* note 11, at 109. On the rule of recognition as the ultimate legal criterion, see generally *id.* at 105–08.

28. *See id.* at 102–03, 108.

6. asserts or presupposes that the combination of (3), (4), and (5) is part of the grounds for (1) and (2) (*nexus between social facts and legal and normative character*).

The reader might wonder why someone who has engaged in normative deliberation under favorable epistemic conditions and then makes an internal legal statement would ever assert or presuppose (6). How could a rational, well-informed speaker ever believe that the mere social facts of official acceptance of the rule of recognition and general efficacy could furnish genuine normative grounds for anyone to comply with the rule of recognition or with legal positions derivable from it?

I should note that Hart's own interests were not to vindicate the normative cast of legal discourse[29]; but, in any event, there are plausible answers to the question just raised. As various post-Hartian positivists have noted, the social fact of official practice might solve a coordination problem, or generate reliance interests.[30] Or, official practice might have epistemic authority, furnishing evidence of what some individual has genuine normative reason to do.

Hart scholars might also object that RoR semantics is not *Hart's* semantics. Why go through the exercise of applying it to CI-discourse? The answer is that Hart's actual semantics, just in virtue of being noncognitivist, will fail to function as a good model (given my interests) of CI-discourse. The question I want to ask is this: If we drop that feature of the semantics, and use a cognitivist semantics which in other respects is as close as possible to Hart's, can we do a decent job describing and vindicating CI-discourse?

III. A SAMPLE OF CI-DISCOURSE

This section examines a sample of twenty-four instances of CI-argument by legal scholars or judges, to see how social facts figure therein. A CI-argument defends or criticizes an "interpretive method," by which I mean some view either about the sources of constitutional law (i.e., whether the 1787 text as amended is the exclusive source or, if not, what the additional sources are) or about the approach that judges and other actors should use to interpret those sources.

I selected the sample as follows. I limited myself to post–New Deal examples. I also limited myself to books, articles, and speeches, which provide the fullest discussion of interpretive methods, rather than judicial opinions, which sometimes do defend a method but are invariably briefer.

I began by choosing the most famous and influential instances of CI-argument. I then supplemented this initial list with additional texts so that my sample included at least one defense of each of the interpretive methods that has

---

29. *See infra* Section IV.D.

30. *See, e.g.*, Coleman, Practice of Principle, *supra* note 12, at 87–100.

substantial current support. Finally, so as to be sure that the sample was not overly weighted toward scholars rather than judges, I added all the examples I could find of post–New Deal Supreme Court Justices providing extended defenses of some interpretive method in books, articles, or speeches.[31]

The sample is:

- Bruce Ackerman, *We the People*, vol. 1 (*Foundations*) (1991)
- Alexander M. Bickel, *The Least Dangerous Branch: The Supreme Court at the Bar of Politics* (2d ed. 1986)
- Charles Black, *Structure and Relationship in Constitutional Law* (1969)
- Hugo LaFayette Black, *A Constitutional Faith* (1969)
- Robert H. Bork, *The Tempting of America: The Political Seduction of the Law* (1990)
- William J. Brennan, Jr., "The Constitution of the United States: Contemporary Ratification" (1985)
- Stephen Breyer, *Active Liberty: Interpreting Our Democratic Constitution* (2005)
- Ronald Dworkin, *Law's Empire* (1986)
- John Hart Ely, *Democracy and Distrust: A Theory of Judicial Review* (1980)
- Felix Frankfurter, "Some Observations on the Nature of the Judicial Process of Supreme Court Litigation" (1954)
- Ruth Bader Ginsburg, "Speaking in a Judicial Voice" (1992)
- Thomas Grey, "Do We Have an Unwritten Constitution?" (1975)
- Learned Hand, *The Bill of Rights* (1958)
- Richard H. Fallon, Jr., "A Constructivist Coherence Theory of Constitutional Interpretation" (1987)
- Robert H. Jackson, *The Supreme Court in the American System of Government* (1955)
- Michael J. Perry, *The Constitution, the Courts, and Human Rights: An Inquiry into the Legitimacy of Constitutional Policymaking by the Judiciary* (1982)
- Richard A. Posner, "Against Constitutional Theory" (1998)
- William H. Rehnquist, "The Notion of a Living Constitution" (1976)
- Antonin Scalia, "Originalism: The Lesser Evil" (1989)
- John Paul Stevens, "The Bill of Rights: A Century of Progress" (1992)
- David A. Strauss, "Common Law Constitutional Interpretation" (1996)
- Cass R. Sunstein, *One Case at a Time: Judicial Minimalism on the Supreme Court* (1999)

---

31. Readers whose primary expertise is not U.S. constitutional law may not know who the Supreme Court Justices and lower court judges on this list are. The Justices are Hugo Black, Brennan, Breyer, Frankfurter, Ginsburg, Jackson, Rehnquist, Scalia, and Stevens. The lower court judges are Bork, Hand, and Posner.

— Herbert Wechsler, "Toward Neutral Principles of Constitutional Law" (1959)
— Keith E. Whittington, *Constitutional Interpretation: Textual Meaning, Original Intent, and Judicial Review* (1999)[32]

The sample certainly cannot be thought to be representative of CI-discourse in general (which includes discourse by private citizens and nonelite officials). At most, the sample is representative of CI-discourse by legal elites. The desire to find full discussions of interpretive methods, for comparison in detail to RoR semantics, pushed me in this direction. I have focused on the most influential CI-discourse by scholars and jurists, in the hope that an instance of CI-discourse is influential just because it exemplifies what scholars and jurists see as an appropriate CI-argument.

So the sample is just a first stab at understanding the state of CI-discourse. If the findings prove of interest, more research may be warranted.

In this section, I first confirm that most CI-participants in my sample do indeed typically seek to defend some interpretive method as having a favorable *legal* status. Then, I describe the social facts that the authors in the sample explicitly rely upon, or explicitly disclaim reliance upon.

To be sure, the RoR template, as I have reconstructed it, provides that a speaker making a legal statement may either explicitly assert *or* presuppose (without explicit assertion) the social fact of present official acceptance of the rule of recognition. It would be very difficult to compactly summarize the social facts that the authors presuppose without explicitly asserting, and I do not attempt to do that here. The next section discusses whether the RoR template accurately describes CI-argument, and that section is sensitive to the possibility that authors are presupposing, without asserting, relevant social facts.

What emerges from the sample is the following. First, many authors explicitly rely on social facts in arguing for interpretive methods—in particular, social facts within one or more of the three categories of judicial precedent, Framers' intent, and what I shall term "culture/tradition" facts. Further, although I will not belabor the point in the description below of particular CI-arguments, a reading of these sources shows that authors who rely on social facts to support interpretive methods explicitly or implicitly do so in order to support the favored legal status of the interpretive method (not just to assert that the interpretive method is favored in some nonlegal sense).

---

32. Stevens's essay was published as a chapter in THE BILL OF RIGHTS IN THE MODERN STATE, at 13 (Geoffrey R. Stone et al. eds., 1992). The remaining items on this list other than books were published as articles in the following journals. Brennan: 19 U.C. DAVIS L. REV. 2. Frankfurter: 98 PROC. AM. PHIL. SOC. 233. Ginsburg: 67 N.Y.U. L. REV. 1185. Grey: 27 STAN. L. REV. 703. Fallon: 100 HARV. L. REV. 1189. Posner: 73 N.Y.U. L. REV. 1. Rehnquist: 54 TEX. L. REV. 693. Scalia: 57 U. CINCINNATI L. REV. 849. Strauss: 63 U. CHI. L. REV. 877. Wechsler: 73 HARV. L. REV. 1.

I do not find a single instance in which an author explicitly relies upon present official practice to support an interpretive method. Some authors appeal to present or past-and-present citizen practices, which include the practices of present officials (who are a subset of citizens) but also include the practices of nonofficial citizens.

Finally, the pattern of appeal to social facts in the sample of CI-discourse is heterogeneous. Some authors explicitly rely upon social facts within all three categories. Others rely upon some but not all categories. And for each category there are some authors who disclaim reliance upon social facts within the category.

A. Legal Arguments

Characterizing CI-argument as legal or non-legal is, concededly, a subtle matter. To begin, it may well be the case that a legal argument draws on moral considerations. Indeed, Dworkin (although not Hart) takes the position that a legal argument is just a special variety of moral argument. So the test for distinguishing between legal and nonlegal CI-discourse is not whether the argumentation draws on moral considerations, but whether its aim is to establish that an interpretive method has a favorable legal status or merely a favorable status in some nonlegal sense—one that does not in turn entail a favorable legal status.

Further, CI-participants sometimes make *both* legal and nonlegal arguments. To give one example: Rehnquist argues that the "living Constitution" approach to constitutional interpretation, that is, nontextualism, "misconceives the nature of the Constitution, which was designed to enable the popularly elected branches of government, not the judicial branch, to keep the country abreast of the times"[33] and that it also "ignores the Supreme Court's disastrous experiences when in the past it embraced contemporary, fashionable notions of what a living Constitution should contain."[34] The first quoted passage seems to make a legal argument for textualism. Presumably Rehnquist is not appealing to the Constitution's nature and how it was designed (Framers' intent) to show merely that textualism has a favored nonlegal status. But the second quoted passage could well be a nonlegal argument, seeking to show that textualism has better consequences than nontextualism.

However, virtually none of the CI-participants in my sample advance *solely* nonlegal arguments. Virtually all argue, inter alia, that one or another interpretive method has a favorable legal status. Sometimes this is explicit, as in Grey's claim that nontextualism is a "lawful and legitimate feature of our system of judicial review"[35]; or Wechsler's claim that courts, *qua* "courts of law," have "the

33. Rehnquist at 699.
34. *Id.*
35. Grey at 715.

duty when a case is properly before them" to adjudicate constitutional claims using neutral principles.[36]

Often, the legal character of CI-argument is implicit, but clear. For example, Scalia argues for originalism along the following lines:

> The principle theoretical defect of nonoriginalism . . . is its incompatibility with the very principle that legitimizes judicial review of constitutionality. . . . Central to [*Marbury*'s argument for judicial review] is the perception that the Constitution, though it has an effect superior to other laws, is in its nature the sort of "law" that is the business of the courts—an enactment that has a fixed meaning ascertainable through the usual devices familiar to those learned in the law. If the Constitution were not that sort of a "law," but a novel invitation to apply current societal values, what reason would there be to believe that the invitation was addressed to the courts rather than to the legislature?[37]

It is very hard to see Scalia, here, as merely arguing that originalism has good moral credentials without necessarily having good legal credentials. Clearly, Scalia's intention is to show that originalism is *legally* favored (indeed, legally required).

Bork, Whittington, and Hugo Black argue, along lines similar to Scalia, that textualism or originalism is entailed by the status of the written Constitution as higher law. Although none of these authors say explicitly that judges have a legal duty to employ textualism or originalism, that seems clearly implicit.[38]

As we shall see in a moment, a number of scholars (such as Ackerman, Dworkin, Ely, Fallon, Strauss, and Michael Perry) defend interpretive methods with reference to our culture and tradition. Although it is certainly possible to make a nonlegal argument based on culture and tradition, the particular manner in which these scholars draw on culture/tradition makes clear that their aim is to show that some method is legally favored.[39] For example, Strauss observes: "The common

---

36. Wechsler at 19.

37. Scalia at 854.

38. *See* Bork at 139–60; Whittington at 15–16 (clarifying that his aim is to provide two arguments for originalism, one based on the existence of a written Constitution, and a second, based on "popular sovereignty," that "does not depend on the prior acceptance of the current constitutional system"); *id.* at 47–109 (providing first argument); Hugo Black at 7–10.

39. *See infra* Section III.D. Dworkin defends his favored approach to constitutional interpretation by engaging in constructive interpretation—which, for him, is just the hallmark of a legal argument. Fallon also says explicitly that he is engaging in constructive interpretation. Strauss seems to be engaged in an approach close to constructive interpretation and, in any event, it is clear (as the quotation immediately below shows) that Strauss intends to provide a legal argument for common law constitutionalism. The extent to which Ackerman, Ely, and Perry are inspired by Dworkin is less clear, but in any event Ackerman and Ely (as the quotations at Section III. D will show) clearly do not intend to

law is the most distinctive feature of our legal system. . . . We should expect that the common law would be the most natural model for understanding something as central to our legal and political culture as the Constitution."[40] And he continues: "Perhaps common law constitutionalism is not the best we could do if we were writing on a blank slate. But unless our current practices are to be rejected wholesale, the common law model is . . . the best way to understand what we are doing."[41] To argue that some interpretive method is the best understanding of our legal practices, even though it might not be the best method to set up ab initio, is surely just to argue that the method is legally favored (indeed, not just permitted, but legally required, or at least favored in a stronger sense than permissibility).

Without belaboring the point, I suggest that all the other authors in the sample can be seen as arguing for the favorable legal status of an interpretive method, with only a few possible exceptions.[42] One is Posner, who may be read

---

provide merely moral arguments for their favored methods. As for Michael Perry, he makes clear that he is concerned with the "legitimacy" rather than "soundness" of noninterpretive review. *See* Perry at 4–5. And, by "legitimacy," Perry pretty clearly seems to mean legal rather than merely moral legitimacy. He writes that if "interpretive review. . . is authorized by the constitutional text. . . the practice is legitimate. Indeed, if mandated and not merely authorized by the text, the practice is obligatory." *Id.* at 12.

40. Strauss at 887.

41. *Id.* at 888.

42. Breyer argues at length that his "active liberty" approach to constitutional interpretation is supported by Framers' intent. *See* Breyer at 21–34. He also argues that it "helps make sense of our Constitution's structure." *Id.* at 6. Bickel says explicitly that the grounding of an interpretive method in precedent provides support for the method. *See* Bickel at 48. And his book describes, at length, how courts have followed his favored method (bringing "principle" to bear in constitutional adjudication, while also exercising the passive virtues).

It would be unusual to draw upon these sorts of considerations—the structure of the Constitution, Farmers' intent, judicial precedent—to make a nonlegal argument for some conclusion about what judges or other actors ought to do.

Stevens draws on Framers' intent to support courts' use of a common-law process to expand the scope of constitutionally protected liberties. Further, he explains that this reliance on Framers' intent is meant to show that judicial expansion of liberty has not merely been "progress," but that such progress has been achieved "by legitimate means." *See* Stevens at 34–36.

Ginsburg draws on Framers' intent to argue for an approach to constitutional interpretation whereby judges achieve progress via a dialogue with legislatures, *see* Ginsburg at 1185–86, 1208, and also embeds this approach in a theory of the good judge, *see, e.g., id.* at 1209.

Frankfurter argues that an interpretive approach to the Due Process Clause that allows its meaning to evolve over time flows from the nature of law. *See* Frankfurter at 234–35. He also appeals to Framers' intent: the Constitution "was designed for a developing nation." *Id.* at 235–36 (internal quotation omitted).

as skeptical about the very possibility of judicial duties apart from the promotion of good consequences.

Another, perhaps, is Sunstein, who argues that "minimalism" promotes deliberative democracy,[43] but also states that "the American constitutional system aspires . . . to a system of deliberative democracy."[44] The latter statement suggests that Sunstein's intention is to defend the *legal* status of minimalism by appealing to a value, deliberative democracy, which not only is a moral value but also has legal force in our system. Similarly, Jackson argues that an activist approach to constitutional adjudication is undemocratic and "promising of [no] permanent good to the country,"[45] but also argues that for judges to depart from a restrained approach would be a "usurpation" of judges' limited powers under the Constitution.[46] Finally, Charles Black explains that he admires "structure and relationship" reasoning because:

> [W]here a fairly available method of legal reasoning, by its very nature, leads directly to the discussion of practical rightness [as does structure-and-relationship reasoning], that method should be used wherever possible. It is the best wisdom of every system of law to seek and to cleave unto such intellectual modes.[47]

Black's position seems to be that structure-and-relationship reasoning is at least legally permitted by virtue of being morally advisable.

In short, although some parsing of the texts is certainly required, there is little doubt that a very substantial fraction of CI-discourse aims to show the favorable legal status of some interpretive method.

B. Explicit Reliance upon Precedent

Supreme Court case law is often discussed in CI-discourse. I would not infer from the sheer fact that a CI-participant discusses precedent that she views an interpretive method's grounding in precedent as support for the method; she may be discussing precedent just to illustrate the method. But a substantial

---

Hand famously argues that "[f]or myself it would be most irksome to be ruled by a bevy of Platonic Guardians," *see* Hand at 73, which might seem like simple moral disapproval of expansive judicial review; but his basic argument for limited review proceeds from the text of the Constitution, rather than moral considerations. "I have been. . . trying to say what is the measure of judicial intervention that can be thought to be implicit, though unexpressed, in the Constitution." *Id.* at 67.

Brennan argues that judges should make substantive value judgments, and that doing so is required "[t]o remain faithful to the content of the Constitution." Brennan at 6.

43. *See, e.g.*, Sunstein at xiv.

44. *Id.* at 24.

45. Jackson at 58, 61.

46. *Id.* at 61. *See also id.* at 79.

47. Charles Black at 23.

number of CI-participants go beyond merely discussing precedent, and explicitly take the position that the grounding of an interpretive method in precedent is support for the method. Grey does so, as we have seen. Similarly, Bickel in *The Least Dangerous Branch*, criticizing Hand's defense of extremely limited judicial review, writes: "There is a great deal to be said . . . for a theory that is able to accommodate . . . more of what the Court has done in fact than Judge Hand was able to accept."[48] And much of *The Least Dangerous Branch* attempts to show that the Supreme Court has acted consistently with Bickel's favored approach to constitutional adjudication, namely, a dual approach whereby courts both apply "principle" and employ various "passive virtues" so as to respect democratic values.[49]

Other CI-participants make culture/tradition arguments for their favored methods, and quite explicitly include judicial decisions as one element of culture/tradition. Strauss argues for an incrementalist "common law" approach to constitutional interpretation that countenances departures from the text and from Framers' intent. His overall strategy is two-pronged: to show that "it is the common law approach, not the approach that connects law to an authoritative text, or an authoritative decision by the Framers . . . that best explains, and best justifies, American constitutional law today."[50] Strauss therefore describes various aspects of our constitutional "practice" that are inconsistent with textualism or a Framers' intent methodology. This "practice" includes, as one component, judicial precedent:

> There are a number of specific aspects of our practice of constitutional interpretation that are well-settled, and that lie at the core of how constitutional law operates in our society, but that are difficult to justify under any theoretical approach [other than Strauss' favored approach]. These puzzles concern not just how the courts interpret the Constitution but how the Constitution is received in the society as a whole.[51]

Fallon, similarly, looks to the practices of "judges, lawyers, and other constitutional interpreters" to defend his "constructivist coherence" approach to constitutional interpretation.[52]

Ackerman, in *We the People*, defends a "dualist" view of constitutional change and interpretation that assigns judges a "preservationist" role: judicial interpretation of the original text plus formal as well as informal amendments. The overall

---

48. Bickel at 48.

49. See *id.* at 69–72, 199–200, for a general statement of the dual approach. Bickel's discussion of the case law is at 111–272.

50. Strauss at 879. *See also id.* at 888 (explaining that his aim is to identify the interpretive method that best describes and justifies our practices).

51. *Id.* at 880.

52. *See* Fallon at 1239. *See also id.* at 1248 (explaining that "judicial opinions" as well as "briefs [and] scholarly articles" in fact engage in constructivist coherence reasoning).

strategy of *We the People* is to show that all the actors in the U.S. system—judges, officials, and citizens—have acted consistently with "dualism" since 1787.[53] As part of this overall strategy, Ackerman makes substantial efforts to show that judges have more or less successfully executed their "preservationist" role.[54]

C. Explicit Reliance upon Framers' Intent

Many authors rely on Framers' intent in arguing for an interpretive method. This includes authors whose favored method is textualist or originalist. For example, Rehnquist argues against the notion of a "living Constitution" on multiple grounds, including the fact that

> it misconceives the nature of the Constitution, which was designed to enable the popularly elected branches of government, not the judicial branch, to keep the country abreast of the times. . . .
>
> It seems to me that it is almost impossible, after reading the record of the Founding Fathers' debates in Philadelphia, to conclude that they intended the Constitution itself to suggest answers to the manifold problems that they knew would confront succeeding generations.[55]

Similarly, Bork, in a chapter section entitled "the original understanding of original understanding," argues that originalism "corresponds to the original understanding of the place of courts in our republican form of government" and that "[t]he structure of government the Founders of this nation intended most certainly did not give courts a political role."[56] Hugo Black's defense of textualism also appeals to Framers' intent.[57] Ackerman, an idiosyncratic originalist, relies upon the Federalist Papers' commitment to "dualism" as part of his broader culture/tradition argument for "dualism."[58]

However, many CI-participants who defend some *non*textualist or *non*originalist interpretive method also rely on Framers' intent to defend their favored method—either as a separate basis for justifying the interpretive method, or as one component of a broader culture/tradition argument. Grey, strikingly, falls into the

53. *See infra* Section III.D.

54. *See, e.g.*, Ackerman at 60–61 (stating that he aims to show that judges have fulfilled a preservationist role). Among other things, Ackerman's arresting claim that the Constitution was informally amended during the New Deal, expanding national power and removing constraints on economic regulation, essentially relies on the content of post-1937 judicial doctrine. The claim would be completely implausible if the Supreme Court's Commerce Clause and substantive due process case law had not changed so radically around 1937.

55. Rehnquist at 699.

56. Bork at 153–54.

57. *See* Hugo Black at 10, 19.

58. Ackerman at 165–99.

first category. So do Ginsburg, Stevens, Breyer, and Frankfurter. Ginsburg argues that the Supreme Court can "reinforce or signal a green light for a social change" through a "temperate brand of decisionmaking," as exemplified by the gender discrimination cases (as contrasted with *Roe v. Wade*.)[59] And in partial support of this interpretive method, she writes: "What I hope to convey about courts . . . is in line with the founders'—Madison's and Hamilton's—expectation."[60] Stevens, defending a common-law approach to constitutional interpretation, writes:

> I firmly believe that the Framers of the Constitution expected and intended the vast open spaces in our charter of government to be filled not only by legislative enactment but also by the common-law process of step-by-step adjudication that was largely responsible for the development of the law at the time this nation was conceived.[61]

Breyer, in the course of defending an interpretive method centered around the concept of "active liberty," spends fourteen pages arguing that the Framers valued "active liberty" and designed the Constitution to promote it.[62] Frankfurter defends a view of due process that permits its content to evolve over time by noting, inter alia, that the Constitution was designed "for a developing nation."[63]

Ely is a nonoriginalist who invokes Framers' intent as part of a broader appeal to culture/tradition. Ely rejects originalism or traditionalism as interpretive methods, arguing instead for a nonoriginalist methodology centered on the goal of representation reinforcement. But, in arguing for representation reinforcement, Ely appeals to our tradition of valuing democracy—starting at the beginning, with the Framing:

> We have as a society from the beginning, and now almost instinctively, accepted the notion that a representative democracy must be our form of government. The very process of adopting the Constitution was designed to be . . . more democratic than any that had preceded it.[64]

Ely goes on to support this assertion by citing passages from the *Federalist* papers.[65]

D. Explicit Reliance upon Culture/Tradition

Philip Bobbitt, in his classic study of judicial styles of constitutional reasoning, includes a separate category of "ethical" argument: "Ethical constitutional arguments

---

59. Ginsburg at 1208.
60. *Id.* at 1185–86.
61. Stevens at 35–36.
62. Breyer at 21–34.
63. Frankfurter at 235–36 (internal quotation omitted).
64. Ely at 5.
65. *See id.* at 5–6.

do not claim that a particular solution is right or wrong in any sense larger than that the solution comports with the sort of people we are. . . ."[66] A good example is the Supreme Court's (intermittent) reliance on tradition in defining the scope of substantive due process rights.[67]

"Ethical" arguments, in Bobbitt's sense, also play a substantial role at a different level of constitutional discourse—the level of CI-discourse. I will call these "culture/tradition" arguments, and will define them inclusively: as arguments that appeal to the practices and understandings of a group of U.S. actors not limited to judges or Framers. The temporal scope of these arguments is heterogeneous: some give priority to present practices,[68] while others make reference to both present and past practices without priority for the present. I will include both types under the heading of culture/tradition arguments.

A substantial number of CI-participants make culture/tradition arguments (including scholars who would reject a traditionalist or conventionalist approach to interpreting the Due Process Clause or other parts of the Constitution). Dworkin, obviously, does so: he argues that his favored method of constitutional interpretation, a nonoriginalism that protects substantive rights,[69] emerges from a "constructive interpretation" of our preinterpreted constitutional practices. As I read Dworkin, these preinterpreted practices are the shared present understandings, among all citizens, about the content of the law. [70]

Fallon, explicitly relying on Dworkin (with some minor disagreements), defends his "constructivist coherence" approach to constitutional interpretation as a "theory of our practice of constitutional interpretation [that is] neither purely descriptive nor purely normative."[71] Strauss, as already noted, defends a common-law approach to constitutional decision making by arguing that it "best

66. Bobbitt, Constitutional Fate, *supra* note 2, at 94–95.

67. *See, e.g.*, Washington v. Glucksberg, 521 U.S. 702, 720–21 (1997); Collins v. City of Harker Heights, 503 U.S. 115, 125–27 (1992); Moore v. City of East Cleveland, 431 U.S. 494, 503–04 (1977). I say "intermittent" because important elements of the substantive due process case law, in particular the protection for abortion and contraception rights and the decision in *Lawrence v. Texas*, 539 U.S. 558 (2003) protecting homosexual sex, are difficult to square with a traditionalist interpretive approach.

68. I place in this category Dworkin (for reasons discussed in Adler, *Popular Constitutionalism, supra* note 24, at 737–45) and Strauss. Strauss at various points speaks of interpreting our "current practices" or our practices "today." *See* Strauss at 879, 887, 888. For Strauss (as I read him), prior judicial decisions are relevant to constitutional interpretation, as a matter of our practices, because it is our *present* practice to look to these decisions.

69. *See* Dworkin at 355–99.

70. *See* Adler, *supra* note 24, at 737–46.

71. Fallon at 1233. On Fallon's intention to engage in constructive interpretation, see generally *id.* at 1231–37. For his disagreement with Dworkin, see *id.* at 1233 n.206, 1235 n.213.

explains, and best justifies, American constitutional law today."[72] Strauss tries to distance himself from Dworkin,[73] but the substance of his strategy for CI-argument, like Fallon's, seems pretty close to Dworkinian constructive interpretation.

Other CI-participants who rely upon culture/tradition arguments include Ely, Michael Perry, and Ackerman, as well as Grey (already discussed). Ely's *Democracy and Distrust* is oriented around the countermajoritarian difficulty. "[R]ule in accord with the consent of a majority of those governed is the core of the American governmental system."[74] The book begins with a lengthy statement of the countermajoritarian difficulty; criticizes extant interpretive methods on various grounds, including their countermajoritarian cast; and defends representation reinforcement on the grounds that it is workable in the hands of judges, consistent with the text of the Constitution, and consistent with majoritarian democracy. Notably, as Michael Dorf discusses in an incisive treatment of *Democracy and Distrust*, Ely does not present a straight moral argument for majoritarian democracy.[75] Ely notes in a footnote that "I have suggested that the appeal of democracy can best be understood in terms of its connections with the philosophical tradition of utilitarianism,"[76] but does not in fact present a utilitarian case for democracy.[77] Instead, he argues that majoritarian democracy is rooted in our traditions, both the Framers' original design and later practice, concluding that: "Our constitutional development . . . [has] substantially strengthened the original commitment to control by a majority of the governed. Neither has there existed among theorists or among Americans generally any serious challenge to the general notion of majoritarian control."[78]

Michael Perry defends what he calls "noninterpretive," that is, nonoriginalist review in the area of human rights by invoking what he calls the "religious" element of American culture/tradition—"a basic, irreducible feature of the American people's understanding of themselves."[79] This "religious self-understanding has generally involved a commitment . . . to the notion of moral evolution."[80] And "[n]oninterpretive review . . . has enabled us, as a

72. Strauss at 879. *See also id.* at 888.

73. *See* Strauss at 888 n.35, 896.

74. Ely at 7.

75. Michael C. Dorf, *The Coherentism of Democracy and Distrust*, 114 YALE L.J. 1237 (2005).

76. Ely at 187 n.14.

77. Instead, Ely goes on in the footnote to say that "nothing in the ensuing analysis depends on this claim." *Id.*

78. *Id.* at 7. *See also id.* at 54, 59 (arguing that interpretive approaches that allow judges to make substantive judgments are inconsistent with the views of "our society" about the existence of objective moral principles and about the role of judges).

79. Perry at 97.

80. *Id.* at 99.

people, to keep faith with . . . our religious understanding of ourselves as a people committed to struggle incessantly to see beyond . . . the imperfections of whatever happens at the moment to be the established moral conventions."[81] In short, Perry roots noninterpretive review in a deep American tradition of looking beyond current moral conventions.[82]

Ackerman's *We the People* very clearly refrains from making a straight moral argument for "dualism." Instead, the thrust of the book is to show that American political practice, from the Framing up to the present, has more or less conformed to the dualist template. He stresses that the book is "anti-utopian":

> We have been searching for the spirit of *this* Constitution, not some better one. The ultimate question is not whether this Constitution meets the standards of our highest moral ideals . . . but whether it is good enough to warrant respectful and conscientious support.[83]

The aim of *We the People* is "to capture the spirit of the existing historical enterprise"[84]—to describe the "development [of dualism] through three constitutional regimes, by reflecting upon its source in the revolutionary tradition, and by exploring the way it continues to control normal and constitutional politics in America."[85] Ackerman specifically identifies at least one aspect of dualism that, he believes, is truly a feature of it—given our traditions—but is morally flawed: the fact that dualism does not allow constitutional rights to be entrenched.[86]

E. Explicit Reliance upon Officials?

Do participants in CI-discourse ground arguments for an interpretive method in the practices of officials? I find no instance where a CI-participant cites the current practices of the totality of officials. For that matter, I find no instance where a CI-participant cites the past practices, or the past-and-present practices, of the totality of officials.

CI-participants do occasionally cite facts about individual officials to support an interpretive method. For example, President Lincoln's constitutional views and activities are discussed approvingly by several CI-participants,[87] and Ackerman

---

81. *Id.* at 101.

82. Admittedly, Perry waffles somewhat on the question whether he sees the nexus between the method of noninterpretive review and our tradition of moral evolution as affirmative support for the method. *See id.* at 99, 101–02, 106, 125.

83. Ackerman at 296.

84. *Id.* at 321.

85. *Id.* at 296. For other places where Ackerman suggests his enterprise is to reconstruct our practices, see, for example, *id.* at 3–6, 22–24.

86. *See id.* at 13–15, 319–22.

87. *See* Stevens at 23; Bickel at 65–69.

discusses a number of other Presidents.[88] Very occasionally, a CI-participant will explicitly discuss the practices of a subset of officials (for example, Ackerman's discussion of the role of the Republican Party in spearheading a constitutional moment during the Reconstruction period).[89]

What about appeals to culture/tradition? The thrust of a culture/tradition argument is to appeal to widely shared practices. The large group of individuals whose behaviors and mental states constitute these practices presumably *includes* all or many present officials. But the CI-participants in my sample who make culture/tradition arguments pretty clearly intend to refer to the behaviors and mental states of nonofficial citizens as well.

Dworkin, on my reading, is a "deep popular constitutionalist": it is the shared present understandings of citizens generally, not just officials, that are the data for constructive interpretation.[90] Strauss argues that common-law constitutionalism best fits "how the Constitution is received in the society as a whole."[91] Fallon defends his constructivist-coherence approach by engaging in an interpretation of the practices of lawyers, including both officials and nonofficial lawyers.[92] Grey, in noting the grounding of nontextualism in post-Framing history, points to the natural rights views of the antislavery movement (a paradigmatic citizen constitutional movement).[93] Ely describes the acceptance of majoritarian democracy among the American citizenry, not just American officials: "Neither has there existed among theorists or among Americans generally any serious challenge to the general notion of majoritarian control."[94] Michael Perry stresses the "religious" self-understanding of the "American people," not just American officials.[95] Ackerman points to the popular mobilization during the 1860s and 1930s as examples of "higher lawmaking" leading to constitutional amendments. The fact that citizens, in these instances, conformed to the "dualist" template is an important part of his argument that our traditions are dualist.[96]

88. *See, e.g.*, Ackerman at 67–86.

89. *See id.* at 45–46.

90. *See* Adler, *supra* note 24, at 737–45.

91. Strauss at 880.

92. On Fallon's focus on lawyers, see Fallon at 1193 (discussing opinions, briefs, and scholarly argument as elements of our legal culture); 1248 (same); 1239 (citing facts about "judges, lawyers, and other constitutional interpreters" as evidence for his approach).

93. *See* Grey at 716.

94. Ely at 7.

95. *See* Perry at 97, 98, 101, 106.

96. *See, e.g.*, Ackerman at 48 (noting that the "process of interbranch struggle and popular mobilization made the elections of 1866 and 1936 decisive events in constitutional history").

F. Non-reliance upon Social Facts

Some authors explicitly rely on all three categories of social facts I have outlined here, while some explicitly rely only on one or two, and others on none.[97] Most strikingly, for each category of social fact, there are authors who *disclaim* reliance upon it.

A number of authors stress the inconsistency of their favored interpretive methodology with precedent. These authors go beyond simply indicating that some prior case law is inconsistent with their preferred method. Rather, these CI-participants show that large amounts of existing case law are inconsistent with some interpretive method, which they nonetheless view as legally favored. Such a discussion implicitly seems to indicate the CI-participant's belief that the absence of a link between precedent and a method does not undermine its favorable legal status.[98] For example, Hugo Black criticizes much due process and First Amendment case law as inconsistent with textualism.[99] Bork lambastes the Warren, Burger, and Rehnquist courts as all "display[ing] a strong affinity for legislating policy in the name of the Constitution."[100]

Nor is this counterprecedential posture limited to originalists or textualists. Hand argues for very limited First Amendment and due process review, and states: "I am well aware that the [Court's] decisions do not so narrowly circumscribe the power of courts to intervene" under these provisions.[101] Posner, defending a pragmatic and empirically sensitive approach to constitutional decision making, works through the *VMI* and *Romer* cases as examples of how "the Court does not base its constitutional decisions on fact,"[102] which he views as pervasive. Charles Black, in *Structure and Relationship*, stresses throughout the book the unfortunate fact that constitutional case law generally (if not invariably) *fails* to engage in structure-and-relationship reasoning: "What can be asserted is that our preference for the particular-text style has been a decided one, leading . . . to the failure to develop a full-bodied case-law of inference from

97. Prior sections discuss all the CI-participants who I read as explicitly relying on precedent, on Framers' intent, and on culture/tradition.

98. Of course, a CI-participant who discusses the inconsistency of her favored interpretive method with precedent might take the view that this inconsistency is prima facie grounds against the method, but that other considerations on balance favor the method. However, one would think that a CI-participant who believes that precedent is indeed prima facie grounds for a method would try to explain away the troubling (by her lights) inconsistency between her favored method and precedent by explaining that precedent is *merely* prima facie grounds. None of the CI-participants I am about to cite say that—which suggests that they don't believe precedent supports the legal status of a method *at all*.

99. Hugo Black at 23–63.

100. Bork at 101.

101. Hand at 67.

102. Posner at 12.

constitutional structure and relation. . . ."[103] Wechsler takes aim at much case law—most famously, *Brown v. Board of Education*—for failing to rest on neutral principles.[104]

There are also examples, albeit fewer, of authors explicitly disclaiming reliance on Framers' intent or culture/tradition. Whittington quite clearly abjures the relevance of Framers' intent at the level of choosing an interpretive method: "Bootstrapping ourselves into originalism by turning to the founders to authorize such a methodology has been justly criticized."[105] Bickel also disparages originalism, both as an interpretive method and as a higher-level tool for choosing among methods.[106]

As for culture/tradition: it is quite plausible to read Charles Black as claiming that not only judges, but also the broader legal tradition, generally fails to engage in structure-and-relationship reasoning. At several points, Black uses the term "legal culture"—presumably meaning some set of practices broader than judges'. "[T]he method of inference from structures, status, and relationship is relatively little attended to in our legal culture."[107] Wechsler's attack on the Supreme Court for being unprincipled is clearly targeted against nonjudicial actors as well. He says explicitly, "this type of *ad hoc* evaluation is, as it has always been, the deepest problem of our constitutionalism, not only with respect to judgments of the courts but also in the wider realm in which conflicting constitutional positions have played a part in our politics," and proceeds to provide examples of unprincipled stances taken by officials and citizens.[108]

IV. RoR SEMANTICS AND CI-DISCOURSE

RoR semantics is a framework for *legal* statements. Some CI-participants may be making *nonlegal* arguments for interpretive methods. A mismatch between RoR semantics and their arguments is hardly noteworthy. However, many CI-participants claim that some interpretive method is legally favored. A mismatch between RoR semantics and *legal* arguments for interpretive methods *is* noteworthy, and will be the focus of my discussion here. In particular, I will claim that RoR semantics (1) does not, in general, accurately describe the legal statements that CI-participants are making; and (2) does not even minimally vindicate some of the assertions that are characteristic of CI-discourse.

103. Charles Black at 8.
104. *See* Wechsler at 20–35.
105. Whittington at 49. *See also id.* at 3.
106. Bickel at 16. *See also id.* at 98–110.
107. Charles Black at 93. *See also id.* at 7–8.
108. Wechsler at 12.

A key point, for both parts of the analysis, will be that Hart's rule of recognition model makes the content of the rule of recognition, the ultimate criterion of legal validity, a matter of *consensus* among current officials. I first discuss this point; then discuss the sense in which interpretive methods, and the relevance of social facts to interpretive methods, is controversial in the United States; and then turn to the issues of description and vindication.

A. The Rule of Recognition as a Consensus Rule

Hart sees the rule of recognition as a special kind of social rule: a social rule among officials stating ultimate legal validity criteria. In general, according to Hart, a social rule exists in a group only if there is some normative standard that group members generally accept.[109]

In particular, then, the existence of the rule of recognition involves official consensus on some ultimate standard of legal validity. Hart writes: "[W]hat is crucial to [the existence of a legal system] is that there should be a unified or shared official acceptance of the rule of recognition containing the system's criteria of validity."[110] He repeatedly characterizes the rule of recognition as being accepted by officials as a "common standard."[111] Hart explains that "unity among officials" is "normally presupposed when internal statements of law are made within the system."[112] He discusses the case of South Africa, in which the legislature and a special appellate court that it created disagreed with the ordinary courts about the legislature's competence, and notes that, had the legislature continued to pursue its views in the teeth of the ordinary courts', "the normal conditions of official, and especially judicial, harmony, under which alone it is possible to identify the system's rule of recognition, would have been suspended."[113]

To be sure, Hart does not require the ultimate criterion of legal validity to be a matter of consensus among *citizens*. But he *does* require it to be a matter of consensus among *officials*. As Les Green puts the point, "for Hart, the only consensus necessary for law is a consensus of elites,"[114] namely officials.

It is also important to understand that Hart does not make official consensus a necessary condition for the truth of every legal proposition. A *derivative* legal proposition, which is not itself part of the rule of recognition, can be true by direct or indirect application of the rule of recognition, even though officials aren't in consensus with respect to that proposition. For example, officials might disagree about where the boundary line between two cities lies; but if there is a statute on the books that specifies the boundary, and if the statute is

---

109. *See, e.g.*, HART, *supra* note 11, at 57.
110. *Id.* at 115.
111. *See id.* at 116–17.
112. *Id.* at 122.
113. *Id.*
114. Leslie Green, *The Concept of Law Revisited*, 94 MICH. L. REV. 1687, 1702 (1996).

valid by derivation from a rule of recognition that officials commonly accept as the ultimate criterion of validity, and if no official believes that her view of where the boundary lies is part of the ultimate criterion, *then* the legal boundary will indeed be a particular line on the map even though many officials deny that this particular line is the boundary.[115] However, on the Hartian model, a legal proposition cannot be itself part of the *ultimate* criterion of legal validity unless officials are in consensus with respect to that proposition.

Hart does discuss the possibility of indeterminacy in the rule of recognition: the rule of recognition, like every rule, will have some open texture.[116] The case of a consensus rule of recognition, which is generally accepted but has some open texture, is different from the case of official controversy about ultimate legal standards. Hart himself seems to view official controversy about the rule of recognition as more pathological than consensus on an open-textured rule.[117] Still, one might try to domesticate the controversy case, using Hart's notion of indeterminacy, and say the following: where some legal proposition is accepted by some officials as an ultimate legal truth, but rejected by others as a legal truth, then the proposition is indeterminately true[118] (unless the proposition is determinately true by derivation from some other proposition that officials generally accept as ultimate). For short, call this the "indeterminacy refinement" to the rule of recognition model.

So, in thinking about the legal status of methods for constitutional interpretation and about the legal relevance of social facts to interpretive methods, under the rule of recognition model, we should be sensitive to the possibility of truth by derivation, and sensitive to the possibility of indeterminacy. Still, even with these nuances in the picture, the rule of recognition model says the following: if some present officials deny that an interpretive method is legally favored,[119] then the method cannot be determinately legally favored as an ultimate legal matter. Similarly, if some present officials deny that certain social facts are legally relevant to the status of interpretive methods, then those facts cannot determinately possess such relevance as an ultimate legal matter.

B. Constitutional Controversy in the United States

At the outset, it should be stated that current U.S. officials do share a consensus on many legal and, specifically, constitutional matters. For example, they share

---

115. *See* COLEMAN, THE PRACTICE OF PRINCIPLE, *supra* note 12, at 116–17 (discussing the possibility of judicial disagreement about the application of a consensus rule of recognition).

116. *See* HART, *supra* note 11, at 123, 147–54, 251–52.

117. *See id.* at 122–23.

118. Neither true nor false.

119. Since to be legally favored, in my terms, is to be at least permissible, to deny that a method is favored is just to take the position that it is impermissible.

a consensus (it appears) about the existence of various legal institutions (the President, the Supreme Court, the Congress), and about which natural persons belong to key roles in these institutions. They also share a consensus (it appears) that the text of the 1787 Constitution, as amended, is one key source of higher law. But they lack consensus, I suggest, about two key matters.

First, there are a plurality of interpretive methods that are currently controversial among officials—that are both supported by a substantial number of officials and opposed by a substantial number of officials. Interpretive methods that are currently controversial among officials include, I suggest, the following: nontextualism, which supplements the text of the Constitution with nontextual sources of constitutional law; textualism, which views the text of the Constitution as the exclusive source of constitutional law; originalism, which looks to original meanings or intentions as the sole basis for interpreting that text; and nonoriginalism, in all its variants, which uses some approach other than looking to original meanings or intentions to interpret the text or other sources (for example, representation reinforcement, or protecting moral rights, or implementing judicial doctrine as it has developed over time).

The interpretive methods that are controversial among officials include, in particular, all the methods defended by CI-participants in my sample. How do I know that? To begin, each CI-participant in my sample defends a method that is controversial within the sample itself, and more generally among constitutional scholars. Why mount a lengthy defense of some interpretive method (as participants in my sample do) if the method is universally accepted? One doesn't observe long books or articles arguing that the 1787 text is one source of constitutional law.

To be sure, it is possible for certain matters to be controverted by legal scholars but not officials generally; and I haven't attempted to systematically investigate official beliefs about constitutional interpretation. However, the sample includes jurists as well as scholars, and is plausibly representative of CI-discourse by elites (including prominent officials and judges), not just elite scholars.

Further, Supreme Court constitutional decisions have long been a heated topic of general public debate in the United States.[120] This public debate has often involved general questions about the appropriate role of courts in constitutional decision making, with many citizens and officials favoring a more expansive role, and many others a more limited role. It is therefore, I believe, quite implausible to think that current officials are in consensus concerning whether the text of the Constitution is the sole source of higher law, and concerning whether the text should be read using an originalist methodology or, alternatively, some particular variant of nonoriginalism.

---

120. *See, e.g.*, Adler, *supra* note 24, at 753–65 (describing controversial controversies among officials and citizens).

Second, the relevance of the social facts of precedent, Framers' intent, and culture/tradition to the legal status of interpretive methods is controversial within my sample. As we have seen, there are some CI-participants who rely on precedent to defend an interpretive method, but others who fail to rely on precedent or even argue for an interpretive method in the teeth of precedent; and the same is true for Framers' intent and culture/tradition. More generally, the legal relevance of each of these types of social facts is controversial within constitutional scholarship.[121] And it seems very plausible, then, that their relevance is controversial among current officials: that some but not all officials believe that an interpretive method is bolstered by its grounding in precedent, in Framers' intent, and in culture/tradition.

C. Does RoR Semantics Accurately Describe CI-Discourse?

RoR semantics, as I have reconstructed it in Section II, models a legal statement as consisting in a specified package of assertions or presuppositions. To ask whether RoR semantics accurately describes CI-discourse is to ask whether CI-participants are actually making these specified assertions or presuppositions when they are defending interpretive methods as legally favored. Of course, this may be a matter of degree. RoR semantics might accurately describe few, some, many, or all instances of CI-discourse, or it might describe none at all.

My sample suggests that RoR semantics accurately describes few, if any, instances of CI-discourse. The key problem is this: A CI-participant who defends an interpretive method as legally favored, and who does so in a manner consistent with RoR semantics, must be asserting or presupposing that the interpretive method is contained in, or derivable from, some ultimate criterion of legal validity that is generally accepted by present officials. But CI-participants generally do not seem to be saying this.

To begin, let me note that CI-participants never *assert* the existence of a present official practice supporting some interpretive method. I cannot find a single instance in my sample where a participant does so. Some CI-participants do explicitly assert the existence of practices that *include* present official practice, namely by making culture/tradition arguments. Such arguments cite either present or past-and-present citizen practices, both of which include official practices (since officials are citizens). However, culture/tradition arguments are, themselves, hardly a universal feature of CI-discourse. Many CI-participants in my sample do not make such arguments.

---

121. For scholarly controversy about the role of precedent in constitutional interpretation, see Richard H. Fallon, Jr., *Precedent-Based Constitutional Adjudication, Acceptance, and the Rule of Recognition* (Chapter 2, this volume). Concerning the role of Framers' intent, see Daniel A. Farber, *The Originalism Debate: A Guide for the Perplexed*, 49 OHIO STATE L.J. 1085 (1989) and Mitchell Berman, *Originalism is Bunk*, 84 N.Y.U L. Rev. 1 (2009). Concerning tradition, see LAURENCE H. TRIBE & MICHAEL C. DORF, ON READING THE CONSTITUTION 97–109 (1991).

The obvious response by Hartians, at this juncture, is to suggest that participants in CI-discourse are *presupposing* rather than *asserting* some present official practice. Hart is crystal clear that the fact of present official acceptance of the rule of recognition may merely be presupposed, rather than asserted, by legal statements.

But there is a further difficulty: a substantial number of CI-participants explicitly assert social facts other than present official practice, in particular precedent, Framers' intent, or culture/tradition, in supporting the legal status of an interpretive method. How are these explicit assertions consistent with RoR semantics?

The foundationalist character of RoR semantics creates a dilemma, here. Consistent with that framework, a social fact can only be asserted in legal argument in two ways: (1) the speaker is asserting the social fact of present official acceptance of the ultimate criterion of legal validity; or (2) the speaker is asserting a social fact that she believes to be legally relevant, directly or indirectly, *by application* of the ultimate criterion of legal validity.[122] References to precedent, Framers' intent, and culture/tradition in CI-discourse do not fit under the first prong. So if RoR semantics is to describe CI-discourse, these assertions must somehow be made to fit under the second.

In some instances, it is unproblematic to think of social facts figuring in legal argument by application (direct or indirect) of an ultimate criterion of legal validity. Here's an example. Imagine a society in which there is a written constitution, and present officials accept that the constitution should be interpreted using a Framers' intent method. A judge in this society, consistent with RoR semantics, could decide a constitutional case by (1) presupposing the present official practice; (2) referencing some provision in the written constitution; and (3) explicitly asserting what the Framers intended by that provision.

But a key feature of CI-discourse, one I have tried to stress, is that the social facts of precedent, Framers' intent, and culture/tradition come into play in this body of legal statements *at the level of choosing an interpretive method*, not at the level of deciding particular cases. The best available strategy for describing this phenomenon, consistent with RoR semantics, is to imagine an ultimate criterion of legal validity that includes certain social facts (precedent, Framers' intent, culture/tradition, or some combination thereof) as the *triggering condition* for the legal validity of a candidate interpretive method. That is to say, the ultimate criterion of legal validity has something like the form: "Judges should decide constitutional cases using method $M1$ if $M1$ is best supported by SF; judges

122. Strictly, there is a third possibility, namely that a legal statement is asserting the fact of general efficacy, that is, the fact of general citizen compliance with legally valid conduct rules; but I will ignore that possibility, since clearly CI-participants are not referring to Framers' intent, precedent, or culture/tradition to show that U.S. law is generally complied with by citizens.

should decide constitutional cases using method *M2* if *M2* is best supported by *SF*; judges should decide constitutional cases using method *M3* if *M3* is best supported by *SF*; . . .," where *SF* is some stipulated social fact or combination of social facts.[123]

Indeed, Kent Greenawalt, in his illuminating attempt to formulate a rule of recognition for the United States, concludes that the best candidate for our rule of recognition is a rule with this sort of triggering-condition structure: specifically, one that makes Supreme Court precedent the triggering condition for the legal validity of an interpretive method. "[T]he ultimate rule of recognition," he writes, "is approximately this":

1. Whatever is in the federal Constitution . . . is law;
2. On matters not clear from the text, the prevailing standards of interpretation used by the Supreme Court determine what the Constitution means. . . .[124]

Does this triggering-condition strategy work? The key difficulty, here, is that current U.S. officials are not in consensus with respect to the legal relevance of the sorts of social facts cited in CI-discourse. Current U.S. officials do not agree that precedent, Framers' intent, culture/tradition, or some combination thereof, are the triggering condition for the legal validity of an interpretive method.[125]

Now, one could try to make CI-discourse consistent with RoR semantics by offering an error theory of that discourse with respect to the truth about present

---

123. A different strategy is to argue that there is a rule of recognition, *R+*, that does not merely make some particular social facts the triggering condition for interpretive methods. Instead, the relevance of different social facts is itself conditional on further facts. *R+* has the structure: "Under conditions *C1*, judges should decide constitutional cases using whichever method is best supported by social fact(s) *SF*; under conditions *C2*, judges should decide constitutional cases using whichever method is best supported by *SF**;. . . .; under conditions *C+*, social facts are irrelevant to the choice of interpretive methods and judges should use method *M1*; under conditions *C++*, social facts are irrelevant to the choice of interpretive methods and judges should use method *M2*;. . . ." However, I see no evidence that *R+* describes the views of any actual U.S. officials, let alone the totality, and so will not pursue the implausible strategy of seeing CI-participants as presupposing official consensus on *R+*.

124. Kent Greenawalt, *The Rule of Recognition and the Constitution*, 85 MICH. L. REV. 621, 659 (1987) (reprinted as Chapter 1, this volume, at 36). Ken Himma gives Supreme Court decisions a yet more substantial role in functioning as a component of the rule of recognition. *See* Kenneth Einar Himma, *Understanding the Relationship between the U.S. Constitution and the Conventional Rule of Recognition* (Chapter 4, this volume).

125. In particular, Greenawalt's and Himma's proposals are problematic as attempts to formulate a rule of recognition for the United States because it is controversial, among U.S. officials and citizens, whether the Supreme Court has any legal role in shaping constitutional law above and beyond its role of deciding particular cases. *See* Adler, *supra* note 24, at 724, 760–61, 784 (discussing challenges to *Cooper v. Aaron*); Fallon, *supra* note 121 (discussing challenges to the role of precedent in constitutional adjudication).

official practice. One could say this: CI-participants *do* presuppose the fact of present official acceptance of precedent, Framers' intent, culture/tradition, or some combination thereof as the triggering condition for interpretive methods. So CI-statements *do* fit the template of RoR semantics. It's just that their presupposition about present official practice is incorrect.

But the absence of official consensus about which (if any) social facts are the triggering condition for the legal validity of interpretive methods is surely evident to CI-participants, at least the sophisticated participants in my sample. For each category of social fact (precedent, Framers' intent, culture/tradition), there are some who assert it but others who fail to rely upon that type of social fact or explicitly downplay its relevance. Are we to assume that this lack of consensus, within CI-discourse, is somehow opaque to CI-participants—that we are aware of it, examining their discourse, but they are not? A more plausible description of the beliefs of CI-participants is that they do not believe themselves to be in consensus about the relevance of social facts to the legal validity of interpretive methods, and therefore do not believe officials to be in consensus either. If CI-participants do not believe officials to be in consensus about the status of precedent, Framers' intent, or culture/tradition as the triggering condition for the legal validity of interpretive methods, then these participants cannot be *presupposing* that consensus when they rely on precedent, Framers' intent, or culture/tradition to justify an interpretive method.

Note that what I earlier called the "indeterminacy refinement"[126] to the rule of recognition model doesn't help the Hartian here. If some officials believe that certain social facts are the triggering condition for interpretive methods, but other officials deny that these social facts bolster the legal status of interpretive methods, then the relevance of those facts to the methods will, at most, be indeterminate.[127] CI-participants who are aware of the official controversy, and who are making legal statements consistent with the Hartian model, will not take the position that the social facts at issue provide *determinate* support for some interpretive method. But, in practice, CI-participants who rely on precedent, Framers' intent, or culture/tradition to argue for various interpretive methods do seem to think that these facts provide determinate support for the methods.

D. Does RoR Semantics Vindicate CI-Discourse?

Before we turn to the question at hand, several preliminary points are in order.

First, where there are a variety of kinds of assertions characteristic of some target discourse, it may be possible to vindicate some but not all of the assertions.

---

126. *See supra* text accompanying note 118.

127. More precisely, it will be indeterminate unless determinately relevant by application of a rule such as *R+*. *See supra* note 123. But there is no official consensus on a rule such as *R+*, and CI-participants surely don't believe otherwise.

Second, the extent to which we can vindicate a particular kind of assertion characteristic of a target discourse is itself a matter of degree. Imagine that some participants in moral discourse assert that a particular behavior is morally good (assertions which we understand as ascribing the property of moral goodness to the behavior), and that other participants make contradictory moral assertions (which we understand as ascribing the property of moral badness to the behavior). It is impossible, in this case, to vindicate all the assertions: a behavior cannot be both morally good and morally bad. However, we might aim to vindicate some of the assertions—to show that there really are properties of moral goodness and badness, and that the behavior possesses one or the other property. By contrast, a moral "error theorist" such as Mackie will claim that the discourse cannot be vindicated at all.[128] She will claim that there are no moral properties, and that the moral speakers are universally mistaken in presupposing the existence of such properties and ascribing them to behaviors.

Third, we might ask about Hart's own aims in developing his rule of recognition account. To what extent did Hart himself hope to vindicate the claims that participants in a legal system typically make?

Pretty clearly, Hart did not aim to show that law creates genuine reasons, moral or other. He writes in the Postscript:

> My account is *descriptive* in that it is morally neutral and has no justificatory aims: it does not seek to justify or commend on moral or other grounds the forms and structures which appear in my general account of law, though a clear understanding of these is, I think, an important preliminary to any useful moral criticism of law.[129]

However, it would be a mistake to think that Hart did not aim to vindicate legal statements at all. Hart may have been a skeptic about the moral force of law, but he was certainly not a skeptic about the existence of law itself. Hart thought of a legal system as a genuinely distinctive way in which a society might be organized, built upon a special kind of social fact: official acceptance of a rule of recognition. Because this distinctive kind of social organization can arise, legal rules and legal positions can actually exist; and, where they do, an assertion of their existence, and of their grounding in social fact, will be true. Indeed, *The Concept of Law* argues at length that the rule of recognition model, by contrast with Austin's model, is able to vindicate characteristic beliefs and assertions of participants in legal systems—for example, concerning the persistence and continuity of law, the existence of legal powers as well as duties, the existence of customary law, and limitations on legislative authority.

---

128. *See supra* Section I.

129. Hart, *supra* note 11, at 240.

With these preliminaries tucked away, we can ask: how well does RoR semantics, and more generally Hart's rule of recognition model of a legal system, vindicate CI-discourse?[130]

Because the interpretive methods characteristically defended by CI-participants are *controversial*, as I've discussed, RoR semantics and the rule of recognition model do not even minimally vindicate CI-participants' characteristic assertion that some interpretive method is legally favored. According to the rule of recognition model, if some officials deny that an interpretive method is legally favored, the method cannot *be* determinately legally favored as an ultimate legal matter. The indeterminacy refinement allows that a controversial method might be indeterminately legally favored. But this refinement doesn't do much to vindicate CI-discourse, because CI-participants are asserting that one or another method is *determinately* favored, not merely indeterminately so.

The RoR framework does allow that an interpretive method, albeit controversial, might be determinately legally favored if the method is derivable by application of the ultimate criterion of legal validity, rather than being part of that criterion. But, as a matter of the actual facts of social practice in the United States, it is very hard to believe that there is a "deep" rule of recognition that is universally agreed upon by present officials, the application of which will yield any of the controversial interpretive methods defended by CI-participants. Try to formulate that rule!

Further, RoR semantics and the rule of recognition model fail to even minimally vindicate the reliance by CI-participants on the social facts of precedent, Framers' intent, and culture/tradition to argue for the legal status of interpretive methods. U.S. officials do not, in fact, accept an ultimate criterion of legal validity that makes certain social facts the triggering condition for the legal status of interpretive methods.[131] Therefore, given the rule of recognition model of a legal system, an assertion or presupposition by a CI-participant that precedent, Framers'

---

130. The careful reader might object here that the question whether a semantic framework vindicates a target discourse should be reserved for frameworks that sufficiently well describe the discourse. Since RoR semantics doesn't describe CI-discourse very well, as shown in the preceding subsection, why does the question of vindication even arise? In response to this possible question, let me note that the difficulty discussed in this subsection consists in the fact that CI-participants assert that various interpretive methods are legally favored, and that various social facts bolster the legal status of interpretive methods, but that both claims are falsified by the rule of recognition model of law because there is insufficient official consensus. Perhaps this is better seen as a mismatch between Hart's model of law (which specifies when law, legal rules, and legal positions genuinely exist) and CI-discourse, rather than as a failure of Hart's model of legal *statements*, RoR semantics, to vindicate CI-discourse. In any event, it is certainly a mismatch between *The Concept of Law* and CI-discourse, and one that bears note.

131. Nor do they accept a more recondite rule such as *R+*. *See supra* note 123.

intent, or culture/tradition determinately bolsters the legal status of an interpretive method will be *incorrect*.

Finally, does the RoR framework vindicate the normative cast of CI-discourse? As just mentioned, Hart's aims in *The Concept of Law* were not normative. Hart conceptualized a certain kind of human activity, law, which involves normative statements and judgments; but *The Concept of Law* did not aim to characterize the kinds of considerations that constitute genuine normative reasons. It is therefore perfectly consistent with RoR semantics and the rule of recognition model to believe that judges have a genuine normative reason (for example, a moral reason) to follow one or another interpretive method. And it is perfectly consistent with RoR semantics and the rule of recognition model to believe that certain social facts strengthen a judge's normative reason to employ some interpretive method. For example, it is perfectly consistent with these frameworks to think that the Framers were epistemic authorities with respect to the normative bona fides of interpretive methods; that precedent has epistemic authority; or that considerations of stability and reliance give judges genuine reasons not to depart from tradition.

So adopting RoR semantics and the rule of recognition model does not mean adopting an error theory with respect to CI-participants' characteristic assertion that judges have a genuine normative reason, perhaps bolstered by social facts, to employ some interpretive method. But adopting RoR semantics and the rule of recognition model *does* have the upshots that (1) CI-participants are systematically mistaken in thinking that one or another controversial interpretive method is determinately legally favored; and that (2) CI-participants are systematically mistaken in thinking that the nexus between an interpretive method and social facts such as precedent, Framers' intent, or culture/tradition determinately buttresses that method's legal status. In short, there are real costs in adopting RoR semantics and the rule of recognition model for our ability to vindicate CI-discourse.

V. CAN WE DEVELOP A "BETTER" MODEL THAN RoR SEMANTICS?

Can we develop a "better" model of CI-discourse than RoR semantics? I have stressed that the "goodness" of a scholarly model, such as RoR semantics and, more generally, models of law and legal systems, depends on the scholar's aims and interests. A model may describe very well what legal participants are doing and saying, but explain little of it. It may describe only some of what they say and do, but explain quite well what it does describe. A model may describe and explain beautifully, but provide an error theory of legal practice, which sees participants as systematically mistaken in various important ways.

If our aim is simply to describe CI-discourse, then clearly we can do better than RoR semantics. Consider the following framework for legal statements: A legal statement (1) asserts the existence of some legal position; (2) asserts or presupposes that the position has normative force; and (3) may, but need not, assert or presuppose that some social fact is part of the grounds of (1) or (2). This framework *perfectly* describes each and every case in which a CI-participant argues that some interpretive method is legally favored. Because the framework is so permissive in its stipulated components of legal discourse, it has no trouble matching what CI-participants are saying. Of course, the framework explains nothing (Why do CI-participants rely on certain facts, or characterize certain methods as legal?); nor does it help to vindicate anything they say.

What if our aim is to both describe and vindicate CI-discourse? Here, improving on RoR semantics becomes more difficult. The fact that RoR semantics fails to vindicate CI-discourse *may* just be one upshot of the fact that CI-discourse is relatively intractable to vindication.

I emphasize "may" because it is impossible to reach clear conclusions without systematically analyzing CI-discourse through the lens of a variety of plausible jurisprudential theories. Of course, "plausible" is itself relative to our aims. So I guess the real test for whether the failure of RoR semantics to describe and vindicate CI-discourse is the "fault" of RoR semantics, or of CI-discourse, would be something like this: Take accounts of law that do pretty well in describing and vindicating legal discourse in various domains. In that sense, they are "plausible." Then apply them to CI-discourse in particular. If they all fail to vindicate characteristic assertions by CI-participants, then the conclusion should be that CI-participants are, indeed, systematically mistaken in those assertions.

I of course lack the space to undertake this analytic exercise here. However, a very preliminary stab at examining CI-discourse through the lens of non-Hartian theories suggests no easy solution to the puzzle of how interpretive methods can be genuinely legally favored in the teeth of official disagreement, and how certain social facts can bolster the legal status of some interpretive method in the teeth of official disagreement about the relevance of those facts.

Some post-Hartian positivists reject Hart's view that the rule of recognition is a social rule in the sense he describes, and instead argue that ultimate criteria of legal validity emerge from a shared cooperative activity (SCA) among officials.[132] On this view, officials are committed to working together to maintain a unified system of rules. Officials may not all have the same conception of what that unified system should be; but they all intend to develop such a system and, in particular, to "mesh" their competing conceptions of legal validity in a cooperative manner.

---

132. I discuss the SCA view in Adler, *supra* note 24, at 750–65; and Matthew D. Adler, *Constitutional Fidelity, the Rule of Recognition, and the Communitarian Turn in Contemporary Positivism*, 75 FORDHAM L. REV. 1671, 1682–87 (2006). Scott Shapiro, who was central to the development of this view, has recently adopted a different view. *See* Scott J. Shapiro, *What Is the Rule of Recognition (And Does It Exist)?* (Chapter 9, this volume).

Whatever the virtues of the SCA account, it does not actually seem to explain how a controversial proposition can be part of the ultimate criterion of legal validity. Some officials believe that *P* is an ultimate legal proposition; others believe that *Q*, which contradicts *P*, is an ultimate legal proposition. The officials are cooperative, and committed to working through their disagreement about *P* versus *Q*—but until they actually do that, and come to consensus one way or the other, how can either *P* or *Q* really be determinately true?

Further, as I have argued at length elsewhere, the SCA account does a questionable job of describing actual constitutional practice in the United States, because it is doubtful that officials are as cooperative as the model requires. Officials holding competing constitutional conceptions may well lack an intention to mesh their views with each other. Thus, to the extent that an SCA-based semantics stipulates that legal statements assert or presuppose that officials are cooperative, that semantic framework will fail to describe CI-discourse very well.[133]

Both Hart's view and the SCA view posit a single, canonical "recognitional community" of officials, whose practices give rise to law. I have previously suggested a different view: that the truth of legal statements might be relativized to various official or citizen groups.[134] This "group-relative" account does not make general official or citizen consensus a necessary condition for the determinate truth of ultimate legal propositions. If a group accepts some ultimate criterion of legal validity (and if norms validated by this criterion are sufficiently effective in shaping behavior, within or outside the group), then the components of that criterion will be ultimate, determinate legal truths, relative to the group—whether or not these propositions are accepted by nonmembers. In particular, if a group accepts an interpretive method, or the proposition that certain social facts are relevant to the legal status of an interpretive method, then CI-discourse that defends the method or adduces such facts, relative to this group, will be vindicated—even if the interpretive method, or the relevance of the facts, is controversial outside the group.

However, there is a very important way in which the group-relative account fails to vindicate CI-discourse. Thinking of propositions of constitutional law as being true or false in a relative rather than absolute sense is deeply revisionary. To be sure, we all recognize that constitutional requirements may change over time, and that the corpus of constitutional law may have areas of fuzziness and indeterminacy; but the notion that there are a very large number of distinct bodies of constitutional law in the United States at a given point in time (corresponding to each separate group) is deeply unfamiliar. CI-participants, in particular, do not assert that controversial interpretive methods are legally

133. Assuming CI-participants understand that officials are not very cooperative.

134. *See* Adler, *supra* note 24.

favored relative to one or another group. Rather, they assert that these methods are legally favored, period. There is a sense in which, even for the group-relative framework, a noncontroversial proposition can be true in an absolute sense (namely, because it will be true relative to all groups). But the framework sees as mistaken the characteristic attempt of CI-participants to assert that some interpretive method, or the relevance of some social fact, is part of the single system of constitutional law that binds all of us, even though some of us fail to accept the method or the relevance of the fact.

Finally, what about Dworkin's conception of law, "law as integrity"? One of Dworkin's chief criticisms of Hart has long been that the rule of recognition model ties law too tightly to consensus.[135] Legal propositions can be both controversial and true, Dworkin emphasizes—and "law as integrity" explains how. A legal proposition is true if and only if it is validated by the constructive interpretation of the preinterpreted legal data that is best, all things considered, in both fitting the data and being morally justified. Current community (specifically, citizen) consensus determines what the preinterpreted data is, but not what the best constructive interpretation is.[136] Note further that, for Dworkin, legal argument is not straight moral argument, but rather a mixture of certain social facts (the preinterpreted data) and moral considerations.

In both these senses, law-as-integrity seems to be a promising framework to describe CI-discourse. But are CI-participants actually engaged in anything like constructive interpretation? Some are—for example, Ackerman, Ely, Fallon, Grey, Michael Perry, and Strauss, all of whom ground interpretive methods in culture/tradition facts in a manner not too distant from constructive interpretation. It is less clear whether the pervasive reliance on Framers' intent to buttress interpretive methods is consistent with the "law as integrity" model. Since current citizens do not agree that Framers' intentions are legally relevant, it is hard to see why their intentions have much weight in determining which interpretive method to adopt, under the law-as-integrity model.[137] Dworkin himself has been a vigorous critic of the reliance on Framers' intent in constitutional argument.[138]

A deeper difficulty with relying on Dworkin's law-as-integrity model to describe and vindicate CI-discourse is that the model rests on a problematic moral view. *Law's Empire*, a work of normative theory, revolves around the claim

---

135. *See, e.g.*, DWORKIN, *supra* note 12; RONALD DWORKIN, TAKING RIGHTS SERIOUSLY (1977).

136. *See* Adler, *supra* note 24, at 737–45 (defending this reading of Dworkin).

137. Perhaps Framers might be taken as epistemic authorities with respect to various moral considerations. But surely Framers are not epistemic authorities with respect to constructive interpretation, because constructive interpretation synthesizes morality with present practices, and the Framers, who died long ago, know nothing of present practices.

138. *See, e.g.*, DWORKIN, *supra* note 12, at 355–99.

that there exists an independent moral value, "integrity," which is distinct from the various moral considerations that a substantial number of moral theorists have long argued for—equality, overall welfare, fairness, rights not to be harmed and other deontological rights, democracy, or due process. Dworkin's defense of this novel value is based on our intuition that the state should speak with one voice, and on a putative link between integrity and associative obligation. In a political community where members accept the value of integrity, by identifying the content of law through constructive interpretation, the conditions for associative obligation arise and law will genuinely have prima face moral authority. Those conditions are that members believe they possess—or behave as if they believe they possess—special responsibilities to each other flowing from an equal concern for each others' well-being.

Denise Réaume has provided a devastating critique of Dworkin's argument for integrity.[139] Among other things, Réaume points out that Dworkin's conditions for associative obligation amount to a kind of moral bootstrapping. The conditions mean that members of a community who sincerely believe and act upon a flawed egalitarian ideology owe *genuine* prima facie moral duties to each other just by virtue of this social fact. Dworkin limits the counterintuitive implications of this claim by stipulating that the community must not be too unjust, but, even so, the claim is startling and troubling. Consider a theocracy that provides for its citizens' material needs, and affords them some rights of political participation, but requires them to engage in religious observance in service to a nonexistent deity, to whom the regime and citizenry genuinely believe all citizens to be equally subject. Do these edicts have genuine moral authority for the citizens? Or consider a society with a system of ethnically based occupations. Members of different ethnic groups hold each other in equal regard but sincerely believe that different groups are specially suited for different occupations. Laws limit the occupational choices of each group's members. Do the citizens have a prima facie moral obligation to comply with these misguided laws?

In short, although Dworkin's law-as-integrity model, with its methodology of constructive interpretation, does describe CI-discourse somewhat more accurately than RoR semantics, relying on that model to vindicate CI-discourse is problematic—because doing so means accepting Dworkin's novel and (I believe) implausible claim that integrity is a genuine moral value.

VI. CONCLUSION

Constitutional scholars have paid surprisingly little attention to the structure of their own arguments. When scholars and jurists defend some controversial

139. *Is Integrity a Virtue? Dworkin's Theory of Legal Obligation*, 39 U. TORONTO L. REV. 380 (1989).

method for interpreting the Constitution—such as originalism, textualism, common law constitutionalism, representation reinforcement, and so forth—they typically seek to show that the method is legally required, permitted, or otherwise favored, and often draw on various kinds of social facts to strengthen the argument. An important puzzle, worth more scholarly attention than it has received, is how to "make sense" of these features of constitutional argument.

This chapter has argued that Hart's rule of recognition model of legal statements doesn't resolve the puzzle. That model is neither particularly accurate in describing what proponents of interpretive methods say, nor particularly helpful in vindicating their characteristic assertions and presuppositions. Whether a different model of law can do a better job, in these respects, is an open question.

9. WHAT IS THE RULE OF RECOGNITION (AND DOES IT EXIST)?

SCOTT J. SHAPIRO*

One of the principal lessons of *The Concept of Law* is that legal systems are not only comprised of rules, but founded on them as well. In sharp contrast to Bentham and Austin, who had insisted that the sovereign makes all of the rules, Hart argued instead that *the rules make the sovereign*.[1] For as Hart painstakingly showed, we cannot account for the way in which we talk and think about the law—that is, as an institution that persists over time despite turnover of officials, imposes duties and confers powers, enjoys supremacy over other kinds of practices, resolves doubts and disagreements about what is to be done in a community, and so on—without supposing that it is at bottom regulated by what he called the secondary rules of recognition, change, and adjudication.

Given this incontrovertible demonstration that every legal system must contain rules constituting its foundation, it might seem puzzling that many philosophers have contested Hart's view. In particular, they have objected to his claim that every legal system contains a rule of recognition. More surprisingly, these critiques span different jurisprudential schools. Positivists such as Joseph Raz, as well as natural lawyers such as Ronald Dworkin and John Finnis, have been among Hart's most vocal critics.

In this chapter, I would like to examine the opposition to the rule of recognition. What is objectionable about Hart's doctrine? Why deny that every legal system necessarily contains a rule setting out the criteria of legal validity? And are these objections convincing? Does the rule of recognition actually exist?

This chapter has five sections. In Section I, I try to state Hart's doctrine of the rule of recognition with some precision. As we will see, his position on this crucial topic is often frustratingly unclear. Hart never tells us, for example, what kind of rule the rule of recognition is: is it a duty-imposing or power-conferring rule? Nor does he identify the rule of recognition's audience: is it a rule practiced only by judges or by all legal officials? I also explore in this section whether the United States Constitution, or any of its provisions, can be considered the Hartian rule of recognition for the U.S. legal system.

---

* Professor of Law and Professor of Philosophy, Yale University. Thanks to Matt Adler, Daniel Halberstam, Scott Hershovitz, and the participants in the "Rule of Recognition and the U.S. Constitution" conference for very helpful comments on an earlier version of this draft.

1. I once heard Jeremy Waldron describe Hart's inversion of Austin in this way.

In Section II, I attempt to detail the many roles that the rule of recognition plays within Hart's theory of law. In addition to the function that Hart explicitly assigned to it—namely, the resolution of normative uncertainty within a community—I argue that the rule of recognition, and the secondary rules more generally, also account for the law's dexterity, efficiency, normativity, continuity, persistence, supremacy, independence, identity, validity, content, and existence.

In Section III, I examine three important challenges to Hart's doctrine of the rule of recognition. They are: (1) Hart's rule of recognition is under- and over-inclusive—that is, some rules that are part of a particular legal system are not so considered by his account, and, conversely, some rules that his account deems to be part of a legal system are not in fact so; (2) Hart cannot explain how social practices are capable of generating rules that confer powers and impose duties, and hence cannot account for the normativity of law; and (3) Hart cannot explain how disagreements about the criteria of legal validity that occur within actual legal systems, such as in American law, are possible.

In sections IV and V, I address these various objections. I argue that although Hart's particular account of the rule of recognition is flawed and should be rejected, a related notion can be fashioned and should be substituted in its place. The idea, roughly, is to treat the rule of recognition as a shared plan that sets out the constitutional order of a legal system. As I try to show, understanding the rule of recognition in this new way allows the legal positivist to overcome the challenges lodged against Hart's version while still retaining the power of the original idea.

I. THE RULE OF RECOGNITION: AN INTRODUCTION

Hart formally introduced the rule of recognition in Chapter 5 of *The Concept of Law*. There he considered a community that does not have a legal system, and then invited the reader to ponder the various social problems that would arise in that group and how the introduction of certain rules (among them being the rule of recognition) would resolve these difficulties.

In a prelaw society, Hart supposed, all rules are customary ones.[2] In other words, a rule exists within such a group if, but only if, it is accepted and practiced by most of its members.[3] Hart then considered what would happen should some doubt or disagreement arise within the group about proper behavior. (Imagine that some members believe that a person should be able to take two mates, whereas

2. H.L.A. Hart, The Concept of Law 91 (Penelope A. Bulloch & Joseph Raz eds., 2d ed. 1994).

3. For Hart's theory of social rules, see *id.* at 54–56, 86–88. For an excellent description of Hart's theory, see generally Joseph Raz, Practical Reasons and Norms 49–58 (2d ed. 1992).

others think that the limit should be one.) Since the only property that the group's rules share is their acceptance by the group, there will be no other common mark to which members can point (e.g., an inscription in some authoritative text, declaration by some official, etc.) in order to resolve their controversy.[4]

Hart claimed that this normative uncertainty would be unproblematic in a small group united by bonds of kinship and inhabiting a stable ecological niche.[5] Presumably, relatively few doubts and disagreements would arise in such groups, and those that did could be overcome through either head-counting to determine the existing custom or some combination of persuasion, deliberation, and negotiation. However, as groups expand and become more heterogeneous, or when environmental conditions are highly fluid, uncertainty will likely proliferate and these techniques will become more costly or less effective. And given that the need for dispute resolution is bound to be great within such groups, the insecurity engendered by these doubts and disagreements will be distressing, perhaps even crippling.

Normative uncertainty is not the only problem facing such groups; customary rules also possess a "static character" that renders them defective tools for regulating all but the smallest human communities.[6] Suppose there is sudden need for the group to act in a certain manner—for example, to increase the amount of grain that each family contributes to communal storage as a result of drought. The simplest and quickest response would be for some members of the group to deliberately change the rules—for example, to amend the tithing rules. However, in a group governed solely by custom, this option is unavailable. Their rules cannot be changed at will: customary rules vary only through a slow process of growth and decay. The urgent need of the group to respond to the drought, therefore, will likely go unmet.

Finally, Hart considered the "inefficiencies" associated with this simple regime of customary rules.[7] Suppose there is a clear rule about how land is to be acquired. It is accepted custom, say, that the first person to stake his claim is the rightful owner. What happens, though, when there is factual disagreement about who is the first claimant? Since the regime contains no mechanism for determining the satisfaction or violation of any of the rules, the attempt to settle who actually staked the claim first will likely be costly and could even turn ugly.

Hart suggested that the fundamental rules of legal systems solve the various defects of prelegal, customary societies. Legal systems address the problem of uncertainty by providing a rule that determines which rules are binding. By referring to this rule about rules—what Hart termed the "rule of recognition"—normative questions can be resolved without engaging in deliberation, negotiation,

4. Hart, *supra* note 2, at 92.

5. *Id.*

6. *Id.* at 92–93.

7. *Id.* at 93–94

or persuasion.[8] If there is a doubt about, say, how many mates are acceptable, the rule of recognition can direct the parties to the authoritative list of rules on the rock in the town square, the past pronouncements of the village elder, the practice of other villages, and so on, to determine the answer.

The static character of customary norms is overcome by what Hart called a "rule of change."[9] A rule of change confers power on a person or institution to create, modify, or extinguish rules, and may also specify the procedures to be used in exercising that power. Since the rule of change empowers certain persons or bodies to amend the rules, behavior may be shifted in the desired direction through the exercise of legal authority. A group facing a drought can, for example, deliberately change the tithing rules and hence address the dire circumstances in an expeditious manner.

Finally, the problem of inefficiency is solved by what Hart called a "rule of adjudication."[10] This rule confers the power on certain bodies to apply the rules—that is, to determine whether a rule has been satisfied or violated on a particular occasion—and specifies the method to be followed in adjudication. In our example of first claimants, the body identified as the authoritative adjudicator would have the power to determine which person first claimed the land and hence who is the rightful owner of the property.

We are now in a position to state Hart's doctrine of the rule of recognition in a more abstract manner. According to Hart, every legal system necessarily contains one, and only one, rule that sets out the test of validity for that system. The systemic test of validity specifies those properties the possession of which by a rule renders it binding in that system. Any norm that bears one of the marks of authority set out in the rule of recognition is *a law of that system*, and officials are required to recognize it when carrying out their official duties.

In the course of setting out the criteria of legal validity, the rule of recognition also specifies orders of precedence among sources of law. In the United States, for example, the rule of recognition mandates that federal law trumps state law, federal constitutional law trumps federal statutory law, and constitutional amendments made in accordance with Article V trump earlier constitutional provisions.[11] Hart called tests such as the one set out in Article V "supreme" criteria of legal validity, because they specify those legal rules that are not trumped by any other possible rule.[12]

The most salient property of the rule of recognition is that it is a *secondary* rule. It is a rule about the validity of other rules (i.e., the "primary" rules). The rule of recognition is also a *social* rule. It is "social" in two different senses. First,

8. *Id.* at 94.

9. *Id.* at 95.

10. *Id.* at 97.

11. *See, e.g.*, U.S. CONST. art. VI, § 2 and U.S. CONST. art. V.

12. HART, *supra* note 2, at 106.

the rule of recognition exists and has the content it does because, and only because, of certain social facts.[13] In particular, its existence and content is determined by the fact that members of a group take the internal point of view toward a standard of conduct and use it to evaluate the validity of norms and the behavior that falls within their purview.[14] Second, the rule of recognition is social in the sense that it sets out a *group-wide* standard. Members of this group do not accept this rule "for their part only," but rather treat the standard it sets out as the official way in which the law is to be determined in their community.[15]

Because the rule of recognition is a social rule, it is capable of being an *ultimate* rule.[16] It is ultimate in the sense that it does not exist in virtue of any other rule. Its existence is secured simply because of its acceptance and practice. The primary rules of the legal system, by contrast, are not ultimate, because they exist in virtue of the rule of recognition. The rule of recognition validates, but is not itself validated.

Some Complications

Stating the basic idea behind Hart's doctrine of the rule of recognition is easy enough; formulating the doctrine with greater precision, however, is surprisingly difficult. For example, what is the basic form of the rule of recognition? Astonishingly, Hart was vague on this critical point. Hart often characterized the rule of recognition as a *test* of what the law is in a particular legal system.[17] Thus, he described the British rule of recognition as "whatever the Queen in Parliament enacts is law."[18] On this interpretation, then, the rule of recognition has the following canonical form: "Any norm that bears properties (*A*1, . . . , *A*m), (*B*1, . . . , *B*n), . . . , (*C*1, . . . , *C*o) is a law of system *S*."

Treating the rule of recognition simply as a test of legality, however, fits uncomfortably within the Hartian framework, which famously acknowledges only two types of legal rules, namely, duty-imposing and power-conferring.[19] On their face at least, tests are neither. The scientific criterion that states that a substance is acidic if its pH is lower than 7, and the linguistic test that defines a "bachelor" as an unmarried male, do not confer powers or impose duties. Is it possible, then, to understand the rule of recognition as either a power-conferring or a duty-imposing rule?

---

13. *Id.* at 110.

14. On Hart's account of the internal point of view, see Scott J. Shapiro, *What is the Internal Point of View?*, 75 FORDHAM L. REV. 1157 (2007).

15. HART, *supra* note 2, at 115–16.

16. *Id.* at 107–08.

17. *See, e.g.*, *id.* at 100–01.

18. *Id.* at 107. *See also id.* at 68: "In the simple society of Rex it may be the accepted rule . . . that no law of Rex shall be valid if it excludes native inhabitants from the territory. . . ."

19. *See id.*, ch. 3. *See also* JOSEPH RAZ, THE AUTHORITY OF LAW 92 (1979).

I think that the first option cannot be Hart's position. For if we suppose that the rule of recognition in Britain is, "The Queen in Parliament has the power to create British law," we inadvertently convert Britain's rule of recognition into its rule of change. Moreover, the rule of recognition can validate certain types of customs, and since customs need not be (and usually are not) created through the exercise of legal authority, the rule that validates them cannot be power-conferring.

The only alternative, then, is to treat the rule of recognition as a duty-imposing rule. The rule of recognition, on this account, imposes a duty on officials to apply rules that bear certain characteristics.[20] In our British example, it requires members of the British legal system to apply the rules enacted by the Queen in Parliament. In the United States, the rule of recognition requires, at least in part, all federal and state officials to apply those rules that regulate interstate commerce, and have been enacted by a majority of both houses of Congress and signed by the President (or have been enacted by a supermajority of both houses after veto by the President).

This interpretation of Hart's doctrine, however, might raise the following concern: why does Hart present the rule of recognition as a test when in reality it is a duty-imposing norm? The answer, I believe, is that, according to Hart, the law consists of all the norms that legal participants are under a duty to apply in their official capacities. In other words, the rule of recognition sets out the criteria of legal validity, and hence picks out the set of legal rules for a particular legal system, because *the law of a particular system just is the set of rules that officials of that system are under a duty to apply, and the rule of recognition sets out the content of this duty.*[21]

If this interpretation of Hart's doctrine is correct, it follows that the vast majority of the text of the U.S. Constitution does not set out the U. S. rule of recognition. Article I, Section 8, for example, begins: "The Congress shall have Power To lay and collect Taxes, Duties, Imposts and Excises, ..."[22] This provision formulates part of the federal rule of change insofar as it confers power on Congress, rather than imposing a duty on officials. Articles V and VII are also part of the rule of change, for both provisions confer power on state legislatures and conventions to ratify and amend the Constitution and specify the procedures to be used. Similarly, most of Article III is best understood as part of the federal rule of adjudication, for it confers power on the Supreme Court—and on any lower federal courts that Congress should happen to create—to decide

20. *See also* Raz, *supra* note 19, at 93; Neil MacCormick, H.L.A. Hart 21 (1980). Raz reports that Hart confirmed his acceptance of this interpretation. *See* Joseph Raz, The Concept of a Legal System 199 (2d ed. 1980).

21. For a similar interpretation, see Raz, supra note 19, at 93.

22. U.S. Const. art. I, § 8.

certain cases, as well as partially specifying the method that courts should follow when engaged in adjudication.

If the rule of recognition imposes duties on legal officials, we might wonder *which* officials. Sometimes, Hart made it appear as though the rule of recognition applies to *all* officials. He wrote: "There are therefore two minimum conditions necessary and sufficient for the existence of a legal system. On the one hand, those rules of behavior which are valid according to the system's ultimate criteria of validity must be generally obeyed, and, on the other hand, its rules of recognition specifying the criteria of legal validity and its rules of change and adjudication must be effectively accepted as common public standards of official behavior by its *officials*."[23] Other times, Hart focused exclusively on judges. "[I]t is the case that this rule of recognition. . . is not only accepted by him but is the rule of recognition actually accepted and employed in the general operation of the system. If the truth of this presupposition were doubted, it could be established by reference to actual practice: to the way in which *courts* identify what is to count as law and to the general acceptance of or acquiescence in these identifications."[24]

One resolution of these conflicting statements is that the rule of recognition is directed at courts, while the rules of change and adjudication are directed at the official parties who are empowered by these rules. On this interpretation, the text of the U.S. Constitution has no provision that explicitly sets out the duty-imposing portion of the U.S. rule of recognition, at least as it pertains to federal judges,[25] given that Article III only *empowers* courts to decide cases that arise under constitutional and federal law but does not *mandate* that they decide cases according to these rules. The closest the text of the Constitution comes to imposing duties on federal judges is the requirement that all federal and state officials take an oath to support the Constitution.[26] Requiring judges to take an oath to support the Constitution is not quite the same as requiring them to support the Constitution. Nevertheless, even though not overtly mentioned in the text, it is part of federal constitutional law that judges are under such a duty because official practice takes this as a given.

While the proposed interpretation harmonizes with much of what Hart explicitly said, and is in keeping with the views of some of his contemporaries,[27] it nevertheless saddles Hart with a problematic position. To think that the law consists only of those rules that courts are under a duty to apply appears inconsistent with

23. HART, *supra* note 2, at 115–16 (emphasis added).

24. *Id.* at 108 (emphasis added). See also Hart's description of the rule of recognition in the Postscript as a "*judicial* customary rule," at 256.

25. The Supremacy Clause of Article VI, § 2 does impose such a duty on state judges.

26. U.S. CONST. art. VI, § 3.

27. *See, e.g.*, SALMOND ON JURISPRUDENCE 41 (Glanville Williams ed., 11th ed. 1957) ("The law consists of the rules recognized and acted on by courts of justice."), *quoted in* RAZ, *supra* note 20, at 190.

various justiciability constraints, such as the so-called "political question" doctrine in the United States—according to which federal courts will refuse to apply certain legal rules when doing so would resolve a political question.[28] Even though courts are not under a duty to apply certain constitutional rules in such cases, no one seriously doubts that these rules are law.

II. THE ROLES OF THE SECONDARY RULES

To be sure, there are many more questions we could ask about the particularities of Hart's doctrine; indeed, much of recent Anglo-American legal philosophy has concerned itself with debating the exact nature of the rule of recognition.[29] Fortunately, these details need not concern us. For now at least, we should have a firm enough grasp of Hart's theory to be able to understand the challenges to it and assess their cogency.

Before I go on to examine these various objections, however, I would like to spend a bit more time exploring the various roles that Hart thought the rule of recognition, and the secondary rules more generally, play in a legal system. As I hope to show, the rules of recognition, change, and adjudication are absolutely indispensable for making sense of a whole range of legal phenomena. This being the case, our puzzle will deepen: how can anyone sensibly reject Hart's doctrine and deny the existence of the rule of recognition?

A. Resolution of Normative Uncertainty, Dexterity and Efficiency

In Section I, we saw one role that the rule of recognition plays in all legal systems, namely, the resolution of normative uncertainty. According to Hart, the rule of recognition resolves doubts and disagreements within a group about which primary rules to follow. It does this by picking out properties of primary rules the possession of which marks such rules as binding.[30]

---

28. *See, e.g.*, Baker v. Carr, 369 U.S. 186 (1962).

29. On whether the rule of recognition may incorporate moral criteria of legality, compare Jules Coleman, *Negative and Positive Positivism, in* MARKETS, MORALS AND THE LAW 3 (1988); WILFRED WALUCHOW, INCLUSIVE LEGAL POSITIVISM (1994); and Matthew Kramer, *How Moral Principles Enter Into Law*, 6 LEGAL THEORY 83 (2000) with Scott Shapiro, *On Hart's Way Out*, 4 LEGAL THEORY 469 (1998); on whether the rule of recognition is a conventional rule, compare ANDREI MARMOR, POSITIVE LAW AND OBJECTIVE VALUES, Chs. 1 and 2 (2001) and Gerald Postema, *Coordination and Convention at the Foundations of Law*, 11 J. LEGAL STUD. 165 (1982) with Julie Dickson, *Is the Rule of Recognition Really a Conventional Rule?*, 27 OXFORD J. LEGAL STUD. 373 (2007) and Leslie Green, *Positivism and Conventionalism*, 12 CAN. J. L. & JURIS. 35 (1999).

30. The rule of recognition, of course, does not resolve *all* normative uncertainty. It only resolves those doubts and disagreements that arise in cases regulated by the norms that it happens to recognize.

We also saw that the rule of change advances the dexterity of the law. When in place, the law has the ability to adapt nimbly to changed circumstances. Those designated by the rule of change need not wait for custom to evolve; rather, they have the power to deliberately alter the rules and thus enable the group to meet the urgent challenges they face.

Finally, the rule of adjudication promotes the efficiency of the law. In a group fortunate to contain such a rule, disputes concerning the satisfaction or violation of a norm need not drag on and ripen into feuds. When an empowered adjudicator determines that a rule has been broken, this decision is supposed to settle the disagreement. The judgment is authoritative and is to be supported by the social pressure that law typically brings to bear.

B. Normativity, Continuity and Persistence

According to Austin, legal sovereignty is created by asymmetrical habits of obedience: the sovereign is the one who is habitually obeyed by the bulk of the population and who habitually obeys no one else. Hart effectively showed that habits of obedience cannot create sovereignty. First, habits are not "normative"—that is, they are incapable of generating rights or obligations all by themselves.[31] Second, habits cannot establish the "continuity" of legal authority: Rex I's successor, Rex II, will be the sovereign from the moment he takes office even though Rex II has yet to be the object of habitual obedience.[32] Third, habits cannot establish the "persistence" of law: Rex I's laws will be legally valid after his death despite the fact that the dead cannot be habitually obeyed.[33]

Instead, Hart argued, sovereignty is created by rules, not habits. Rules are normative: they are capable of conferring rights and imposing duties. Moreover, rules can account for the continuity of legal authority: Rex II has the power to legislate from the moment of Rex I's death because the legal system contains a secondary rule of change giving him the power to do so. Finally, rules can explain the persistence of law: Rex I's rules are valid even after his death because the rule of recognition requires judges to apply all the rules made by past kings.

C. Supremacy and Independence

In addition to resolving normative uncertainty and accounting for the dexterity, efficiency, normativity, continuity, and persistence of law, Hart also showed that the secondary rules can be used to explain two properties shared by modern state legal systems: supremacy within a system's borders and independence from other systems. In contrast to Austin's account, according to which these properties arise from the asymmetry in habitual obedience—that is, Rex is supreme because he is habitually obeyed and habitually obeys no one else, and his regime

31. HART, *supra* note 2, at 60.

32. *Id.* at 53.

33. *Id.* at 62.

is independent because he habitually obeys no one else—Hart credited the rule of recognition. In Rex's kingdom, the rule of recognition requires all officials to privilege Rex's will, and hence renders his power supreme above all others.[34] The independence of Rex's legal system is established in a similar manner. Since the rule of recognition refers to Rex's enactments, those of his subordinates, and no one else's, the system formed will have a separate existence from all other legal regimes (which have their own rules of recognition).[35]

At the same time, Hart's account of sovereignty does not imply that the sovereign is necessarily "above the law."[36] In a constitutional regime, the secondary rules will typically limit the supreme and independent powers of the sovereign. Although the American people are sovereign in the United States and have the power to amend the Constitution, the Constitution nonetheless limits their power to do so, both by making certain provisions unalterable and by prescribing an extremely onerous procedure that must be followed before an amendment is ratified.[37]

D. Identity

Hart also pointed out that secondary rules are necessary to distinguish legal systems from other collections of norms, such as games, religions, corporations, clubs, etiquettes, popular moralities, and so on. According to Hart's famous dictum, law is best understood as "the union of primary and secondary rules."[38] Thus, a legal system differs from etiquette because the latter consists solely of primary rules, whereas the former also contains rules about these rules. Hart does not claim, of course, that the union of primary and secondary rules completely distinguishes legal systems from all other normative systems. The rules of corporations, for example, contain secondary rules as well. There are rules about who can change the rules of the corporation and which rules corporate officers are required to recognize when doing their job. Yet, corporations are not legal systems. The postulation of secondary rules is at best only *partially* constitutive of the identity of law.

E. Validity, Content, and Existence

In contrast to prelegal societies that are governed purely by custom, legal systems can, and typically do, contain some rules that are not themselves practiced by members of the group. Jaywalking, for example, is prohibited in New York City even though almost everyone does it. On Hart's account, the rule prohibiting

34. *Id.* at 106
35. *Id.* at 121.
36. *Id.*
37. *See, e.g.*, U.S. Const. art. V.
38. This phrase is the title of Chapter 5 of Hart's The Concept of Law.

jaywalking exists because it is validated by the New York City rule of recognition that requires legal officials to heed rules enacted in similar fashion.

For Hart, then, the rule of recognition secures the existence of all primary rules. As long as a rule bears the characteristics of legality set out in the rule of recognition, it exists and is legally valid. Indeed, Hart claimed that the concept of *validity* is used precisely in those contexts where the existence of rules does not depend on their being practiced.[39] To say that a rule is valid is to express a judgment that it is binding because it passes the test of some other existing rule, and not because it is accepted by its audience from the internal point of view.

Aside from establishing the validity of all the primary legal rules, the rule of recognition determines the membership, or content, of particular legal systems. On Hart's account, the rule of recognition of *S* determines all and only the laws of *S*.[40] Thus, the New York State Statute of Frauds is not simply binding *according to* New York law—it is *part of* New York law.

Finally, the rule of recognition secures the existence of legal systems. According to Hart, a legal system exists for a group *G* if and only if (1) the bulk of *G* obeys the primary rules, *and* (2) officials of *G* accept the secondary rules of recognition, change, and adjudication from the internal point of view and follow them in most cases.[41] Thus, even if it turned out that most of the citizens of Rhode Island obey most of the rules of Roman law, it would not be true that Roman law still exists today, given that the Rhode Island State officials would not be following the secondary rules of the (extinct) Roman legal system.

III. THREE OBJECTIONS

Having set out Hart's doctrine of the rule of recognition, I would like to rehearse three important objections that philosophers have lodged against it. The first challenge concerns Hart's claim about the content of a legal system, while the second and third relate to his claim that the rule of recognition is necessarily a social norm. As we will see, these objections do not challenge Hart's general thesis that the law rests on secondary rules. Rather, they seek to undercut his specific claims about the nature of these rules. Whether these challenges are successful will be taken up in the last two sections of the chapter.

A. First Objection: Under- and Over-Inclusiveness

Any theory that purports to characterize a legal system's content must ensure that, for every system, it specifies *all* and *only* those norms that belong to that

39. *Id.* at 108–10.
40. *Id.* at 95, 103.
41. *Id.* at 113–17.

system. The theory will fall short, therefore, to the extent that it is either under- or over-inclusive. The first objection is that Hart's theory fails in both these respects.

Recall that on Hart's theory, the content of a legal system is established by that system's rule of recognition. The New York Statute of Frauds is part of New York law, and not, say, New Jersey law, because the statute is valid according to the New York, and *not* the New Jersey, rule of recognition.

It is important to see that on Hart's account the rule of recognition can characterize the content of a legal system only because it is *one* rule. Suppose, for example, the Governor of New York issues an executive ruling. Hart would say that this executive order is part of New York law because it is endorsed by the same rule of recognition that validates the Statute of Frauds. The unity of New York law, therefore, is secured by the unity of New York's rule of recognition.

As John Finnis and Joseph Raz have objected, however, Hart does not explain what makes the rule of recognition *a rule*, as opposed to *rules*, of recognition.[42] Why think that the rule that validates executive orders of the Governor is the same one that validates the regulations enacted by the New York State Legislature? Hart, it seems, is able to establish the content of the law only by helping himself to the *oneness* of the rule of recognition. But without establishing the unity of the New York rule of recognition, he cannot show why the Governor's orders ought to be included within the set of New York law. Indeed, on Hart's own theory of rule-individuation, according to which rules that guide different audiences ought to be considered separate rules, many of the provisions of a Hartian rule of recognition do not properly belong to the same rule.[43] In any complex system, different officials will be under duties to apply different rules. When this is so, there will be multiple rules of recognition and hence the rules that they validate will not be part of the same legal system.[44]

Hart's theory is not only underinclusive, but overinclusive as well. For it can easily be shown that Hart's rule of recognition transforms the law into a vortex

---

42. *See* John Finnis, *Revolutions and Continuity of Law*, *in* OXFORD STUDIES IN JURISPRUDENCE 44, 65–69 (Brian Simpson ed., 2d Series 1973); RAZ, *supra* note 19, at 98 n.32.

43. *See* HART, *supra* note 2, at 38–42.

44. At one point, Hart sought to establish the unity of the rule of recognition by claiming that any rule of recognition that sets out multiple criteria of legal validity will also contain a provision determining the order of precedence in cases of conflict. "The reason for still speaking of 'a rule' at this point is that, notwithstanding their multiplicity, these distinct criteria are unified by their hierarchical arrangement." H.L.A. Hart, Book Review, 78 HARV. L. REV. 1281, 1293 (1965) (reviewing LON FULLER, THE MORALITY OF LAW (1964)). I must confess to not understanding Hart's argument. Why is the mere fact that a rule ranks certain criteria sufficient to incorporate those criteria into the rule? Furthermore, it is not clear how Hart would explain the unity of a rule of recognition that set out multiple sources of law but did not contain a conflict-resolution provision.

that sucks the rules of other normative systems into its voracious maw. As Joseph Raz argued, judges are often under an obligation to apply laws of other jurisdictions in conflict-of-law cases.[45] In contract litigation involving a New York plaintiff and New Jersey defendant, a New York court may be required to apply the New Jersey Statute of Frauds. On Hart's treatment of the rule of recognition as a duty-imposing rule, however, the New Jersey law would automatically become incorporated into New York's law because judges would be under a legal obligation to apply it in certain cases. But this is clearly wrong: New York law does not annex New Jersey law simply because there are occasions when New York officials are required to apply the rules adopted by New Jersey officials.

B. Second Objection: Social Rules Are Normatively Inert

Hart criticized Austin's theory of sovereignty by pointing out that habits are not "normative," that is, that they are incapable of conferring rights and imposing duties. The legal power of the sovereign, therefore, cannot be explained simply by noting that others are in a habit of obeying him or her. But as Ronald Dworkin pointed out, it is unclear how Hart's theory dodges the same bullet.[46] After all, the secondary rules of a legal system exist if, but only if, they are accepted and practiced from the internal point of view. The rule of recognition, for example, need not be morally acceptable—it need only be followed. But how does the mere fact that certain judges *think* they should follow certain rules, and *act* on this judgment, make it the case that any other judge *ought* to do so as well? If mere habits cannot impose duties and confer powers, neither can mere practices.

According to Dworkin, Hart's account conflates a "social" with a "normative" rule. When we assert the existence of a social rule, Dworkin claims, we are simply indicating that most members of the group accept the rule.[47] In merely recognizing the practice, we are not thereby endorsing it. A group, for example, may seriously frown on interracial marriage, and we may describe this racist practice by stating that in this group there is a (social) rule against miscegenation.

A "normative" rule, on the other hand, necessarily provides reasons for action. If we criticize someone for violating the rule against smoking indoors, we are not simply asserting that most others do not smoke indoors and would criticize others for doing so. Rather, we are identifying the ground of our criticism: smoking indoors is wrong *because* there is a (normative) rule against it.

In order to account for the sovereign's right to rule and the judicial duty to apply the law, Dworkin concluded, it is not enough to postulate the existence of

45. RAZ, *supra* note 19, at 97–98. Hart appears to have recognized this problem. *See* H.L.A. Hart, *Kelsen's Doctrine of the Unity of Law, in* ETHICS AND SOCIAL JUSTICE 195–96 (Howard Kiefer & Milton Munitz eds., 1970).

46. *See* RONALD DWORKIN, *The Model of Rules II, in* TAKING RIGHTS SERIOUSLY 46 (1978).

47. *Id.* at 50–51.

social rules. The mere fact that judges treat certain rules as valid is not dispositive as to whether they *ought* to do so. Only normative rules are *normative*—only they can confer rights and impose duties.

This second challenge to Hart's doctrine, therefore, does not deny that there are secondary legal rules that impose duties and confer powers. Rather, it asserts that these rules are not social in nature. For if secondary rules are to have normative power, they cannot exist simply because they are accepted from the internal point of view and followed in most instances. On this view, secondary rules can confer rights and impose duties only when they are also grounded in moral facts—namely, those that create a moral duty for judges to apply certain rules and confer moral legitimacy on persons to change and apply those rules.

C. Third Objection: The Incoherence or Insincerity of Disagreements about the Ultimate Criteria of Validity

On Hart's theory, the rules of recognition, change, and adjudication derive their content solely from consensus. The rule of recognition in the United States, for example, validates rules enacted by Congress and signed by the President that regulate interstate commerce because most judges/officials take the internal point of view toward such a test.

Yet, as Ronald Dworkin has famously argued, this account of the criteria of legal validity is seriously flawed.[48] For if it were correct, widespread disagreements about such criteria would be highly problematic. Since the criteria of legality are supposedly fixed by consensus, any pervasive disagreement about their content would indicate the *absence* of consensus, and hence the absence of a fact of the matter over which disagreement could be had.

The most obvious examples of disagreements over the criteria of legal validity are disputes about interpretive methodology. Many judges, for example, think that the proper way to interpret provisions of the U.S. Constitution is via the meaning that the public would associate with the provision at the time of its ratification (a view often called "public-meaning originalism"). Others believe that constitutional provisions should be interpreted in light of current social mores, even if these attitudes contradict the original public meaning of the provision in question (a view often called "living constitutionalism").

As Dworkin correctly points out, the dispute over originalism is best understood as a dispute about the criteria of legal validity.[49] Originalists believe that

---

48. *See generally* RONALD DWORKIN, LAW'S EMPIRE, Ch. 1 (1986). I discuss this third objection in greater detail in Scott J. Shapiro, *The 'Hart-Dworkin' Debate: A Short Guide for the Perplexed, in* RONALD DWORKIN 22 (A. Ripstein ed., 2007).

49. DWORKIN, *supra* note 48 at 29–30. Although Dworkin does not talk about "criteria of legal validity," but instead about the "grounds of law," the former can be defined in terms of the latter. On this point, see Shapiro, *supra* note 48, at 40–41. Not all theorists agree with Dworkin that disagreements about interpretive methodology are disputes about the criteria of legality. *See, e.g.*, Kenneth Einar Himma, *Understanding the Relationship*

the criteria of legal validity in the United States are originalist in nature: a rule of constitutional law is valid only if it corresponds to the original public meaning of a constitutional provision. Living constitutionalists, on the other hand, deny this characterization. Moreover, this disagreement over interpretive methodology is both prevalent and common knowledge: everyone knows that this disagreement is widespread, and everyone knows that everyone knows that this disagreement is widespread.

However, if Hart is right about the rule of recognition, the disputants are either insincere or incoherent. If judges do not in general agree about the correct way to interpret a constitutional provision, then there can be no correct way to do so. It follows that taking a position on such interpretive matters amounts to political chicanery, confused thinking, or both.[50]

---

between the U.S. Constitution and the Conventional Rule of Recognition (Chapter 4, this volume) and *Making Sense of Constitutional Disagreement: Legal Positivism, the Bill of Rights, and the Conventional Rule of Recognition in the United States*, 4 J.L. SOC'Y 149, 162 (2003).

50. In his defense of Hart, Brian Leiter accepts this very conclusion. *See* Brian Leiter, *Explaining Theoretical Disagreement*, 76 U. CHI. L. REV. (forthcoming 2009). According to Leiter, the test of a theory is how well it fits the *totality* of the data. If Hart's account does a better job than Dworkin's in accounting for the whole range of legal phenomena, as Leiter believes it does, we must conclude that disagreements about interpretive methodology are indeed either confused or insincere. Leiter's methodological point is clearly correct: no jurisprudential theory can be expected to validate *every* intuition that lawyers have about the practice in which they engage. Yet, I think that Leiter underestimates the theoretical importance of this data point. The idea that the criteria of legality are determined by consensus is not just one aspect of the practice among many; on Hart's account, it is *the fundamental ground rule of law*. What ultimately makes it the case that some rule is a binding legal rule is that it is validated by some standard accepted by officials of the group. And herein lay the problem for Hart: the prevalence of disagreements about the criteria of legality, and the complete absence of criticism for engaging in them, strongly suggests that competent legal practitioners do not follow the ground rules that Hart claims they do. To be sure, this evidence is not dispositive. It is possible that legal experts are so confused about the practice in which they are engaged that they are simultaneously committed to mutually incompatible sets of fundamental ground rules. Sometimes they act on Hartian ones; other times they act on Dworkinian ones. Yet, as a methodological matter, any theory that flouts the principle of charity so brazenly should be severely penalized. Alternatively, legal experts may not be confused about their practice but are simply acting insincerely. The problem with this explanation is that it is hard to understand why anyone would dare try this strategy. If the fundamental ground rule of law precludes controversial interpretive methodologies, then the mere advancement of one would automatically result in a charge of duplicity. While Leiter is right that many legal practitioners who engage in theoretical disagreements are thought to be acting in bad faith, no one, except for the Hartian positivist, thinks they are acting in bad faith *merely because* they are engaged in theoretical disagreements. Rather, their motivations are called into question because the methodologies they advocate just so happen to produce the political results they favor.

Dworkin concludes that the criteria of legal validity are determined not by social facts alone, but by moral facts as well. The virtue of such a position is that it can establish the possibility of such fundamental disputes: disagreements about the criteria of validity, on Dworkin's view, reflect the fact that officials disagree about the moral value of law and/or its relation to practice.

IV. SHARED PLANS

This chapter began with a puzzle, namely, how any theorist could object to Hart's doctrine of the rule of recognition. The solution I hope should now be apparent. Critics of Hart's doctrine do not deny either that the law is founded on rules or that the notions of legal authority and obligation are rule-based concepts. No one is proposing a return to Austin. Rather, these objections focus on the specific nature of the fundamental legal rules. Critics deny that there is a rule of recognition in Hart's particular sense, which is to say a unitary duty-imposing norm that sets out the criteria of validity whose existence and content derive from consensual practice among legal officials.

In the remainder of this chapter, I would like to respond to these objections. In this section, I will suggest that the key to answering them involves reconceiving the secondary rules of a legal system as elements of a much larger shared plan that sets out the constitutional order of a legal system. The function of this plan is to guide and organize the behavior of legal officials through the specification of the roles that each is to play in the collective activity of legal regulation. I will then argue that the rule of recognition should be identified with *all* of the norm-creating and norm-applying parts of this shared plan. These provisions determine the content of a particular legal system, and also play all of the other roles that Hart ascribed to his version of the rule of recognition. In Section V, I try to show how this reconceptualization helps to resolve the above objections.

A. Second-Order Uncertainty

To motivate my account of the secondary rules as constituting the major elements of a shared plan, I would like to return to Hart's creation myth, which was set out at the beginning of section I. In his recounting, Hart dwells on the doubts and disagreements that arise in prelegal communities concerning the obligations of private parties.[51] Call this "first-order" uncertainty. According to Hart, the rule of recognition is needed to resolve these sorts of doubts and disagreements, which it accomplishes by picking out the primary rules that members of the group are obligated to follow.

---

51. *See, e.g.*, HART, *supra* note 2, at 91 ("the rules must contain in some form restrictions on the free use of violence, theft and deception. . .").

We can imagine another type of uncertainty, one that concerns not private behavior, but rather the legitimacy of public officials to settle first-order uncertainty. Call this "second-order" uncertainty. In Hartian prelegal communities, it is highly likely that second-order doubts will be as common as first-order ones. Just as group members can be uncertain as to whether a person is permitted more than one mate, they can have doubts and disagreements about whether, say, Rex gets to answer that question. Some members of the community, for example, might object to this proposed royal allocation of power and insist that the will of the majority be respected on these sorts of issues; the aristocracy, on the other hand, might be inclined to trust such power to one of their own. Still others might think that choosing mates is an individual and inviolable right that even democratic majorities cannot eliminate.

In such groups, the most obvious source of second-order uncertainty will be differing views about political morality. Since many people disagree about the natures of justice, equality, liberty, privacy, security, and the like, they are bound to disagree about the proper form that government ought to take.

But there is another reason, often overlooked by legal theorists, for why issues of institutional design are bound to lead to normative uncertainty. Political questions about who should have power and how they should exercise it are intimately connected to questions of *trust*. Legal systems are constituted by delegations of awesome power to individuals—power that can be, and often has been, exploited to devastating effect. Conferring authority on those of ill will not only endangers mundane political objectives but more importantly, and ominously, provides a fertile environment in which tyranny and anarchy can grow. The need to discriminate between the trustworthy and the untrustworthy, therefore, will always be a central and pressing concern of legal design.

Because proper institutional design ought to track correct judgments of competence and character, disagreements about the latter will induce disputes about the former. And disagreements about trust are likely to arise within political communities because questions of who is trustworthy to do what—like issues of political morality—are highly complex and contentious.

B. Settlement

As I have argued, Hart neglected to recognize an important type of normative uncertainty that would take hold in a prelegal community. In groups not linked by bonds of kinship, belief, or value, doubts and disagreements would arise between the members not only as to what is to be done, but also as to who has the authority to resolve these sorts of questions.

Recognizing the prevalence of second-order as well as first-order uncertainty is imperative, for the resolution of the latter cannot be had without the resolution of the former. In other words, public officials can resolve the doubts of, and disagreements between, private parties only if members of the group are not uncertain about the identity of the public officials. If Rex intends for everyone to increase the amount of grain tithed, the group must know that they are supposed to listen to Rex before that intention can be fulfilled.

Thus, if a legal system is to resolve first-order questions about what private parties should do, it must be able to settle second-order questions first. But like the resolution of first-order uncertainty, settling complex and contentious questions of institutional design on an improvised, ad hoc basis, or through the forging of communal consensus, will likely be unachievable, or attainable only at a prohibitive cost. Even when questions of political power are not based on complex and contentious issues of moral principle and social psychology, they are often generated by massive coordination problems that defy spontaneous or consensual solutions.

Legal systems are able to function effectively, I would suggest, because they resolve questions relating to the proper moral goals of the system, the competence and goodwill of legal actors, and how to coordinate behavior in pursuit of the proper goals *via the system's secondary rules.* In particular, some rules settle the content and contours of official duty, whereas others determine the scope of legislative, judicial, and executive powers. These secondary rules resolve second-order uncertainty in an economical fashion. Instead of requiring members of the community to deliberate, negotiate, bargain, or simply guess about the proper distribution of political power, they can appeal to the secondary rules of the system in order to resolve some of their doubts and disagreements.

Insofar as the task of the secondary rules is to determine the roles that legal officials of a particular system are to play, we might see them as constituting parts of a much larger plan shared by those officials. The constitutional law of a system, in other words, represents *a plan for governance*. Like all plans that regulate collective activities, the function of this shared plan is to guide and organize the shared activity of legal officials. It seeks to overcome the enormous complexity, contentiousness, and arbitrariness associated with arranging a system of social regulation. Because reasonable (and unreasonable) people can have doubts and disagreements about which social problems to pursue and about who should be trusted to pursue them, it is essential to have a mechanism that can settle such questions, creating a mesh between legal officials and channeling them all in the same direction.

The shared plan of a legal system, therefore, must settle questions of political morality by determining which goals and values a particular system should pursue and realize. It must determine whether and when equality trumps efficiency, security trumps privacy, the minority trumps the majority, faith trumps science, tradition trumps innovation, and so on. These choices are normally manifested in the constitutional order, such as when a system that prizes democratic participation makes provisions for voting, representation, elections, and some protection for public deliberation, or when a theocratic system empowers clerics to decide matters of principle and policy and minimizes the degree to which secular forces can affect the direction of the law.

Likewise, the shared plan of a legal system must allocate power and authority on the basis of certain judgments of competence and character. Indeed, different constitutional configurations normally reflect these differing assessments of trustworthiness. Individuals who are judged to be less trustworthy are accorded fewer powers and subjected to greater scrutiny than those who are judged more dependable. Because power normally tracks trust, it is useful for many purposes to conceptualize the distribution of rights in a legal system as a distribution of trust, or, as I will call it, an "economy of trust." Monarchies, for example, can be understood as based on radically inegalitarian economies of trust, where only royalty is trusted to set the terms of social cooperation. By contrast, democracies are based on more egalitarian economies, where trust is widely distributed to its citizens. Systems of absolute legislative supremacy dole out greater trust to legislators than ones with judicial review. Regimes with unitary executives distrust committees to make decisions and hence grant a monopoly of trust to one person, whereas those with plural executives are more suspicious of individuals with large concentrations of power and hence disperse trust over a greater number of persons.

To say that a legal system's shared plan resolves second-order normative uncertainty is not to claim, of course, that it resolves *all* such uncertainty. Plans, as Michael Bratman has emphasized, are typically partial: they settle certain questions about what is to be done, but leave other issues undecided.[52] My initial decision to go to Mexico for vacation settles the general issue of destination but not the specifics of the journey. Plans are meant to be filled in over time as the future becomes clearer and the time for action approaches. Similarly, a constitution might confer the right to free speech, thus establishing that there is such a right, without setting its exact scope, weight, or content. These questions are typically delegated to other bodies, such as courts, to decide. Constitutional adjudication, therefore, should be understood as a form of social planning, where the system's shared plan is filled in over time and thus rendered more complete and informative.

C. Sharing a Plan

According to what I will call the "planning theory of law," legal activity is best seen as structured by a shared plan. The function of this plan is not only to resolve first-order uncertainty about the obligations of private parties, but also to resolve second-order uncertainty about the rights and responsibilities of legal officials. The secondary rules of a legal system are thus seen as constituents of this shared plan, imposing and conferring law-creating and law-applying duties and powers.

---

52. Michael Bratman, Intention, Plans, and Practical Reason 28–30 (1987).

In claiming that officials of a particular legal system always share a plan of governance, I have been tacitly presupposing an account of plan sharing. In the interest of full and fair disclosure, therefore, let me briefly sketch out such an account. What must obtain before we can say that a group shares a plan? On the account that I favor, a group shares a plan when: (1) the plan was designed, at least in part,[53] for the group so that they may engage in some joint activity; (2) the members of the group commit to do their parts within the plan; and (3) the members commit to not interfere with the others doing their parts.[54] My friend and I, for example, share a plan to cook together because we designed the plan for ourselves so that we may cook a meal, each accepts our parts, and each is committed not to undermining the other's efforts.

On the planning theory, therefore, we can say that the constitutional law of New York State is the shared plan that structures legal activity in New York because: (1) the New York State Constitution was developed in 1938 by the New York State Constitutional Convention Committee so that a collection of individuals who meet certain qualifications could create and apply rules for the people of New York State; (2) those individuals intend to play the roles set out in the State Constitution and the remaining parts of the State's constitutional law; and (3) those individuals are committed not to interfere with others playing their respective roles. Those who accept New York State's constitutional law (in the sense of (2) and (3)) are members of the New York State legal system, and act together with all others who accept the same rules.[55]

Notice that sharing a plan, and hence acting together according to that plan, does not require that the participants care at all about the success of that plan, or even intend that their actions contribute to its success.[56] Legal officials may be

53. On the importance of the qualification that a shared plan need only be designed "in part" for the group that shares it, see *infra* note 55.

54. Because a plan that is completely secret cannot be shared, we should also add that a shared plan must be at least "publicly accessible"—that is, that the participants, if they wished to do so, could discover the parts of the plan that pertain to them and to others with whom they are likely to interact. In the interest of brevity, I have omitted this condition in the discussions that follow.

55. By claiming that all legal systems are structured by a shared plan, I do not mean to suggest that all legal systems have been designed in advance. Historically, certain fundamental aspects of legal systems have arisen purely through custom. The model of plan sharing I set out in the text above accounts for these cases by requiring only that the shared plan be designed "at least in part" with the group in mind. Groups may share plans, in other words, even though parts of their plans have not been planned for the group. A plan is shared if at least *some* part of the plan was designed for the group and group members see the nonplanned parts as means to carry out the ends of the shared activity. Thus, the shared plan of a legal system may contain many customary parts, so long as it also contains noncustomary parts and the officials see the customary parts as *subplans* of these noncustomary parts.

56. I previously argued that legal officials act together only if most intend to contribute to the creation and maintenance of a unified system of norms. Scott J. Shapiro, *Law, Plans*

completely alienated from their roles; judges may apply the law simply in order to advance their careers, to avoid criminal sanctions, or to pick up their paychecks. As long as the fundamental rules of the system were designed (at least in part) for individuals like them, the officials intend to do their part and not to interfere with other officials doing their parts, and they act on their intentions, we may say that they share a plan and act together in governing their community.

V. RESPONSES TO OBJECTIONS

In this section, I would like to show how the planning theory of law can help address the three objections to Hart's doctrine we examined in Section III. While the solutions I offer blunt the main force of the canvassed challenges, it will quickly be apparent that not every aspect of Hart's doctrine of the rule of recognition, or of his theory of legal obligation and authority, can be salvaged in the process. The objections show that Hart's particular jurisprudential vision is flawed, but the responses offered suggest that his basic positivistic picture of law and its fundamental rules remains viable.

A. Shared Plans and the Content of Legal Systems

According to our interpretation of Hart, the rule of recognition is a unitary norm that imposes a duty on officials to apply certain rules that bear certain characteristics. It follows that, on such an account, the law of a particular system consists of all the norms that this rule obligates officials to apply. The first problem with this view, as we have seen, is its under- and overinclusiveness: some rules that are part of the same legal system are not considered so by Hart's account, and, conversely, some of the rules that are considered part of the same legal system are not in fact part of it.

These problems would be alleviated, I would like to suggest, if we widened our lens so as to privilege not only the duties of courts but also the powers of legislators. On this proposal, the rule of recognition in the United States should be identified with *all* of the constitutional provisions that allocate rule-creating powers and impose rule-applying duties.[57] A rule is a law of the United States, therefore, if it was created in accordance with, and its application is regulated by,

---

and Practical Reason, 8 LEGAL THEORY 387, 419–21 (2002). I now believe this condition is too strong. On the revised view set out in the text above, legal officials need have no intention to contribute to the existence of their legal system. In order to engage in the shared intentional activity of legal regulation, there must at least be a shared plan (which does not require intentions to contribute to the goals of the plan) and the members of the group must act on that plan.

57. Clearly, the rule of recognition will no longer be an ultimate rule on this conception, although a portion of it will be.

American constitutional law.[58] Congressional statutes are thus part of the American legal system because they were created by Congress and the President in accordance with articles I and II and federal and state officials are under a duty to apply these laws in their official capacities.

My suggestion that the rule of recognition be identified with the norm-creating and norm-applying provisions of a system's constitutional order is not meant to exclude ordinary legislation from being part of the criteria of validity. In the United States, for example, statutory provisions such as the Judiciary Act of 1789 and the Administrative Procedure Act are bona fide elements of the rule of recognition.[59] Even though they are not formally part of the U.S. Constitution and hence not entrenched from revision, they nevertheless confer powers to create rules and impose duties to apply them, and hence should be understood as partially constituting the criteria of validity for the U.S. system.

To see how this proposal solves the problem of underinclusiveness, let us return to the case where the New York State Legislature and Governor each create a rule. According to the planning theory, two rules are part of the same system if they are created in accordance with, and their application is regulated by, the system's shared plan. Since these two rules were each created in accordance with, and their application is regulated by, New York State constitutional law, it follows that they are both part of New York State law, which is the correct result.

Another virtue of this proposal is that it does not transmute rules of one system into the rules of another merely because one group is under a duty to apply the other's rules. For two enacted rules to be part of the same system they must have been created according to the power-conferring provisions of the same shared plan. Thus, even though the shared plan that structures New York legal activity requires that the rules of New Jersey be applied in certain instances, New Jersey officials do not share this plan with New York officials, and hence the New Jersey rules have not been enacted pursuant to the same plan as the New York rules.

It will surely be objected that my account—which identifies the rule of recognition with the rule-creating and rule-applying portions of a system's shared plan—marks no advance over Hart's, for I have given no justification for supposing that the shared plan that structures legal practice is *one* shared plan rather than many shared plans.

Two responses are in order. First, there is a very good reason to suppose that the fundamental rules that set out the rights and responsibilities of legal participants are all part of the same shared plan. Because the shared plan is a group

58. Customary rules, which are not created through the exercise of legal power, are part of a U.S. legal system merely if officials are under a constitutional obligation to apply them.

59. *See generally* Ernest Young, *The Constitution Outside the Constitution*, 117 YALE L.J. 408 (2007).

plan, it should be individuated according to the group whose conduct it is supposed to guide. And since the fundamental rules of a legal system are designed, at least in part, for the group of officials of that system, it is natural to treat them as forming one plan, not many. Thus, the rules that empower the Governor of New York and the rules that empower the New York State Legislature are subplans of the same plan, because each was conceived as defining the role of part of the group that creates and administers the laws of New York.

Secondly, and more importantly, although the account I sketched of a legal system's content requires that there be one shared plan, it is possible to relax this requirement without changing the essentials of the approach. Thus, we could say that a law is a member of a legal system if it was created in accordance with, and its application is regulated by, a *set of plans* that the relevant official group shares. We can further stipulate that a group shares a set of plans if and only if: (1) each plan of the set was designed, at least in part, for that group so that they may engage in a joint activity; (2) the members of the group accept the parts of the plans that apply to them; and (3) the members of the group commit to not interfere with the parts that apply to others.

On the planning theory, therefore, the content of a legal system does not depend on the unitary nature of its shared plan. Rather, it ultimately depends on the fact that someone conceived of officials *as a group* and developed a set of instructions for them so that they may govern a community. The *normative* unity of law, we might say, depends on the *social* unity of officials. Whether we treat the instructions addressed to this group as forming one plan or many is, in the end, immaterial.

B. The Normativity of Law

As I have argued, Hart's theory is unable to accurately characterize the content of a legal system, because it focuses too narrowly on a small part of the constitutional structure. On Hart's myopic view, it is immaterial that congressional legislation has been enacted in accordance with articles I and II, insofar as these provisions are power conferring, not duty imposing. This, we have seen, is a mistake. Legislation counts as law of a particular system in part because it was created in accordance with the shared plan that structures the collective activity of legal regulation. Articles I and II are major parts of the American plan of governance, and hence are essential for characterizing the content of American law.

Yet, one might object that our solution to the first objection precludes us from responding to the second objection. Since shared plans are social norms—they exist and are shared by a group if and only if they have been designed at least in part with the group in mind and are accepted by each member of the group—they raise the same difficulty that the secondary rules raised for Hart, namely, the problem of normativity. How, for example, can anybody have legal authority to impose obligations simply because certain of their cronies authorize them to have such a power and members of the community acquiesce? Similarly, how can judges be under a legal obligation to apply certain rules just because other judges plan to do so as well? To generate normative relations of legal authority and obligation, the objection goes, a group needs more than social facts—it needs *moral facts* as well.

The proper response to the second objection, I believe, is to concede that the shared plans that constitute legal practice do not necessarily confer rights and obligations. What they do always succeed at doing, however, is to confer *legal* rights and *legal* obligations, which may or may not coincide with actual rights and obligations. And as long as one can show that shared plans are capable of generating legal rights and obligations, then the planning theory is able to account for the normativity of law.

In order to explain what I mean, let us begin with a basic question: when we attach the word "legal" to terms like "obligation," "right," "wrong," "authority," and so on, what are we doing? One possible answer is that "legal" acts as an adjective modifying the noun phrase that follows. A legal obligation is an obligation that is *legal*, namely, one that arises from the operations of legal institutions. On this interpretation, then, a legal obligation is an obligation that one has because of the law.

According to a second interpretation, the word "legal" acts as a modal operator that qualifies the normative statement in which it is embedded. To say that one has a legal obligation, for example, is simply to assert that *from the legal point of view* one has an obligation. Statements of legal obligation, on this interpretation, are perspectival assertions. Regardless of whether one believes that the law has created actual obligations or has existing authority to do so, when one claims that another has a legal obligation, one is making an assertion from the point of view of the law. From the law's perspective, it has the actual authority to impose actual obligations.

What, then, is the legal point of view? It is not necessarily the perspective of any particular legal official; indeed, the law's conception of itself may be accepted by no official. The legal point of view, rather, is the perspective of a certain normative theory. According to that theory, those who are authorized by the norms of legal institutions have moral legitimacy, and, when they act in accordance with those norms, they generate a moral obligation to obey. The legal point of view of a certain system, in other words, is a theory that holds that the norms of that system are morally legitimate and obligating.[60] Thus, communism is the point of view of communist legal systems, individualism the point of view of laissez-faire capitalist systems, democratic theory the point of view of democratic systems, and so on.

---

60. On the legal point of view, see RAZ, *supra* note 3, at 170–77 and RAZ, *supra* note 19, at 140–43. Although my treatment of the legal point of view and legal statements differs in several important respects from Raz's, my thinking on these matters is heavily indebted to his seminal work in this area.

The normative theory that represents a system's point of view may, of course, be false from a moral perspective—that is, the legal point of view may not coincide with the true moral point of view. Those authorized by legal institutions to act may be morally illegitimate, and their actions may generate no moral obligations to obey. The point of view of a particular legal system may be like the phlogiston theory of combustion: a scientific theory that aimed to be true but missed the mark. In short, the legal point of view always *purports* to represent the truly moral point of view, even when it fails to do so.

I would like to suggest that when we say that the law necessarily has the power to confer legal rights and impose legal obligations, we are using the word "legal" in the second, modal sense. We are *distancing* ourselves from our normative assertions, claiming only that from the legal point of view the law's activities are reason giving. On this second interpretation, it is easy to see how even morally illegitimate shared plans can confer legal rights and impose legal obligations. For to ascribe legal authority to a body in a particular legal system is to assert that, *from the point of view of that legal system*, the body in question is morally legitimate:

(1) *X* has legal authority over *Y* in system *S* $\leftrightarrow$ From the point of view of *S*, *X* has moral authority over *Y*.

The point of view of that legal system, in turn, will ascribe moral legitimacy to a body if and only if its norms confer legal power on that body. Since on the planning theory the legal norms that confer legal authority are subplans of the system's shared plan, the legal point of view will ascribe moral legitimacy to a body when its shared plan authorizes that body to so act:

(2) From the point of view of *S*, *X* has moral authority over *Y* $\leftrightarrow$ The shared plan of *S* authorizes *X* to plan for *Y*.

It follows from (1) and (2) that a body will have legal authority in a particular legal system if and only if the system's shared plan authorizes that body to so act:[61]

(3) *X* has legal authority over *Y* in system *S* $\leftrightarrow$ The shared plan of *S* authorizes *X* to plan for *Y*.

Contrary to the second objection, then, accounting for the normativity of law does not require showing that the secondary legal rules are always capable of creating rights and obligations. One must only demonstrate how the existence of the secondary rules necessarily ground normative judgments made from the legal point of view. As we have seen, the shared plan of a legal system renders true certain perspectival judgments even if the shared plan happens to be morally

61. *X* will have legal authority over *Y* in *S* only when *S* is a generally efficacious system. I am assuming throughout, however, that S is generally efficacious given that general efficacy is a necessary condition of its existence as a legal system.

illegitimate. For a body has legal authority in a system, and thus the ability to impose legal obligations, if and only if the shared plan authorizes it, and a shared plan authorizes such a body if and only if certain social facts obtain.

C. Law and Disagreement

According to the third objection, Hart's doctrine of the rule of recognition must be flawed because it cannot account for pervasive, well-known and sincere disagreements about the ultimate criteria of legal validity. As Dworkin pointed out, widespread disagreements about the content of the rule of recognition are inconsistent with the consensus that supposedly generates its content. Thus, if legal participants are neither hopelessly confused about legal practice nor opportunistic liars, the criteria of legal validity cannot be determined by judicial agreement about those very criteria.

One reaction to Dworkin's objection (Dworkin's reaction, in fact) is to deny that the ultimate criteria of legality can *ever* be determined by existing official consensus.[62] This response, I think, would be too hasty, for one extremely appealing aspect of Hart's theory is how it discounts the importance of what Woodrow Wilson once called the "literary Constitution" in favor of the "Constitution in operation."[63] By privileging current social practice, Hart's theory is able to account for the legality of actions that would otherwise be very difficult to justify. For example, the Supreme Court has held that the Due Process Clause of the Fifth and Fourteenth Amendments should be interpreted substantively, as well as procedurally. Under so-called "substantive" due process analysis, government must not only provide fair procedures for the adjudication of legal claims, but must also ensure that the individuals involved are afforded certain basic rights. To say the very least, this interpretation is quite strained. As John Hart Ely once quipped, "there is simply no avoiding the fact that the word that follows 'due' is 'process'. . . . 'Substantive due process' is a contradiction in terms—sort of like 'green pastel redness.'"[64] Despite its apparent absurdity, this interpretation of the text is now legally correct. It is so because most everyone currently accepts that the Constitution confers a right of substantive due process on individuals. End of story.

---

62. Another reaction is to claim that there can be multiple inconsistent rules of recognition in a particular system, each one determined by the subgroup that accepts it. For this possibility, see Matthew Adler, *Popular Constitutionalism and the Rule of Recognition: Whose Practices Ground U.S. Law?*, 100 NW. U. L. REV. 719 (2006).

63. WOODROW WILSON, CONGRESSIONAL GOVERNMENT 30 (Johns Hopkins Univ. Press, 1981) (1885). As American constitutional theorists would now put the point, Hart discounts the big-C Constitution (the document) in favor of the small-c constitution (that is the practice of constitutional law). On this distinction, see e.g., David A. Strauss, *The Irrelevance of Constitutional Amendments*, 114 HARV. L. REV. 1457, 1459–60 (2001).

64. JOHN HART ELY, DEMOCRACY AND DISTRUST 18 (1980).

Present consensus, therefore, should be seen as a sufficient condition for determining the ultimate criteria of legal validity. What Dworkin's critique of Hart shows, I believe, is that it cannot be a *necessary* condition. In some instances, there may be a fact of the matter as to whether a certain test is legally proper despite the lack of agreement on such a question.

It is important to see that this acknowledgment is consistent with the core positivistic claim that the existence and content of the rule of recognition are determined by social facts alone. Specific agreement on the criteria of validity counts as a social fact for these purposes, but such consensus is only *one kind* of social fact. It is possible that the rule of recognition will be determined by social facts other than agreement on its existence or content. It is this possibility I would now like to pursue.

Let us devote our attention to American-style legal systems, that is, legal systems that have developed through a self-conscious process of constitutional design. In any such regime, there will usually be an existing agreement on at least three constitutional matters: (1) the system's basic institutional arrangements; (2) those empowered to affect its structure (which we might call its "constitutional designers");[65] and (3) its authoritative texts. Since present consensus is a sufficient condition for determining the existence and content of a shared plan, these agreements partially specify the shared plan of that legal system. In order to figure out the remainder of the system's shared plan, an interpreter must ascertain the proper way to interpret the authoritative texts that set it out.

Of course, a consensus might exist in this system about which interpretive methodology ought to be used, in which case the agreed-upon methodology would indeed be legally authoritative for such a regime. Yet what does the interpreter do when she works within a system, like the one in the United States, in which there is no official accord on interpretive methodology?

The proposal is that the proper way to interpret these texts can be derived by focusing on the *reasons* that the system's constitutional designers had for adopting its basic institutional arrangements, and figuring out which interpretive methodology would best harmonize with these reasons. In particular, the interpretive methodology that best furthers the designers' shared goals, values, and judgments of trustworthiness is the proper one for interpreting the authoritative texts and hence for revealing the content of the system's shared plan.

An example may help motivate this procedure. Consider a regime in which the constitutional designers hold a very distrustful view of the competence and character of officials. As a result, they aim to create a certain legal framework

---

65. In the American system, for example, the constitutional designers ordinarily include Congress, the President, state legislatures, constitutional conventions, and federal courts. While there is not universal agreement about the entire roster of constitutional planners (e.g., are We the People designers?), I believe there is a list that one could draw up that would command sufficient consensus among American jurists.

for coping with such problems: they intend to diffuse authority through the system, forbid executive and judicial officers from legislating, set up lengthy waiting times before legislation can be passed, enforce sanctions for abuse of discretion, and so on. They also draft a constitution that sets out these rights and duties in very clear and precise language. Suppose further that after ratification, there is a general consensus among officials about the basic constitutional rules of the regime. That is, everyone accepts that executive and judicial officers are forbidden from legislating, that there are lengthy waiting times before legislation may pass, that sanctions should imposed for abuses of discretion, that certain individuals have the authority to alter these arrangements, and so on.

In contrast to the jaundiced views of the designers, however, the officials who must interpret the constitution think of themselves as eminently trustworthy. They believe that the constraints placed upon them by the constitutional designers are unnecessary and impede their valuable work. Hence, when they interpret the texts that set out the rules of the system, they use their liberal views about their own trustworthiness and assume large degrees of discretion in interpretation: they read grants of power broadly; interpret constraints narrowly; ignore legislative texts when the texts give a result with which they mildly disagree; refuse to defer to the interpretation of regulations by the appropriate administrative agencies; and so on.

The obvious difficulty with this mode of proceeding is that the very point of having designers design the constitutional order is undone by the actions of the interpreters. The shared plans that set out the distribution of rights and responsibilities are supposed to resolve second-order uncertainty in general, and questions of trust in particular. However, if the interpreters are authorized to use their own judgments of trustworthiness in order to determine the interpretive method, and to use that method to interpret legal texts, then they defeat this aim. Whenever the designers want to constrain discretion, the interpreters can widen discretion; when the designers want to widen discretion, they can constrain discretion. It is the interpreters' views that ultimately determine the system's economy of trust, not the plan or the designers. Here, Bishop Hoadly's famous dictum is apt: "Nay, whoever hath an absolute authority to interpret any written or spoken laws, it is he who is truly the Law-giver to all intents and purposes, and not the person who first wrote or spoke them."[66]

Thus, if the shared plan of a legal system is to resolve political issues relating to goals, competence, and character, its content cannot depend in any way on the goals that the system morally ought to pursue or on the competence and character that legal officials truly possess. And since the content of a shared plan depends on the correct way to interpret the texts that set it out, the proper way to

---

66. Benjamin Hoadly, Bishop of Bangor, "Sermon Preached Before the King," (1717), *quoted in* John Chipman Gray, *The Nature and Sources of Law* 125 (2d ed. 1921).

determine interpretive methodology cannot depend in any way on which goals are morally best or on the actual trustworthiness of officials.

As the above example suggests, determining proper interpretive methodology cannot be a "protestant" affair.[67] The fatal defect of this approach is that it is self-defeating. It makes no sense from an organizational perspective to empower the designers of legal systems to control the system's authority structure and the content of its legal texts, but not its interpretive method—for any attempt to resolve second-order uncertainty through the process of institutional design and legislative drafting would be defeated at the stage of interpretation. Those questions of morality and trust that were settled at ratification would suddenly be reopened during implementation. And, by allowing interpreters' views on morality and trust to determine the interpretive method and how much interpretive discretion they should be allowed, the implementers would be able to substitute their attitudes for those of the designers.

It is easy to see, I think, that the same logic that excludes moral and psychological truths as the determinants of proper interpretive methodology necessitates that the judgments of those who are deemed the appropriate designers for constitutional matters should control. For if their assessments about, say, trustworthiness do not control the proper way to interpret texts that set out shared plans, they cannot control the distribution of political power, and hence resolve second-order uncertainty—which is the very point of having them fashion shared plans in the first place. If the constitutional designers are distrustful of officials, interpreters must take these judgments as given for the purposes of legal interpretation, lest they arrogate to themselves too much power from the legal point of view. Conversely, trusting attitudes should lead to greater interpretive discretion; otherwise, legal participants will preclude themselves from pursuing the objectives that they were entrusted to serve.

D. Determining Interpretive Methodology: The Case of Originalism

According to the planning theory, the proper interpretive methodology for a legal system that has been (1) self-consciously planned (2) by a group of agreed-upon constitutional designers is the procedure that best furthers the goals and values that the system has been designed to serve in light of the attitudes of trust that motivated the distribution of political power. Needless to say, the relationship between the shared ideology of constitutional designers regarding goals, competence and character, and proper interpretive methodology is highly complex. Setting out the many complex links that exist between them is clearly beyond the scope of this chapter.[68] But I would be remiss if I did not give the reader an approximate sense of how the procedure works in practice.

---

67. On the "protestant" attitude toward the law, see DWORKIN, *supra* note 48, at 413.

68. I explore these relationships in detail in SCOTT J. SHAPIRO, LEGALITY (forthcoming).

Roughly speaking, the planning theory requires that interpretive discretion track systemic judgments of trustworthiness: an interpretive methodology that requires for its effective implementation a high degree of competence or moral character will be inappropriate for systems designed in accordance with distrustful views of human nature; instead, hermeneutic procedures that are easier to apply and less subject to abuse—perhaps ones that defers to plain meaning, instead of purpose—would be more fitting.

Indeed, popular arguments for theories of constitutional interpretation that privilege the Framers' intentions can be seen on the model that I have presented: the American legal system, in one way or another, is distrustful of individuals, and the best way to deal with this distrust is to confine legal interpretation to original understanding. For example, in *A Matter of Interpretation*, Justice Antonin Scalia argues that constitutional provisions ought to be interpreted in accordance with the original meaning of the text, rather than with an "evolving sense of decency." A judge living today should not, for example, interpret the Eighth Amendment according to the meaning that she assigns to the term "cruel" if that meaning diverges from the late-eighteenth-century understanding, for such evolutionary methodologies flout the fundamental function of constitutions.

> It certainly cannot be said that a constitution naturally suggests changeability; to the contrary, its whole purpose is to prevent change—to embed certain rights in such a manner that future generations cannot readily take them away. A society that adopts a bill of rights is skeptical that "evolving standards of decency" always "mark progress," and that societies always "mature," as opposed to rot.[69]

On Scalia's view, then, the purpose of constitutions is to prevent untrustworthy future generations from rescinding rights that the present generation has deemed proper. But, he argues, granting judges the power to interpret the constitutional text in accordance with changing conceptions of morality would effectively permit future generations to change the constitution and thereby defeat its raison d'être. Scalia, therefore, argues for originalism by noting the distrustful nature of the American constitutional order, and then claiming that living constitutionalism is inconsistent with this economy of trust.

Likewise, opposition to such views can be understood on the planning theory, for a standard rejoinder to the originalist claims of distrust is to argue that the American constitutional order is not nearly as wary of courts as these originalists suggest. Opponents point to the fact that the Constitution often eschews concrete and particular language in favor of setting out broad statements of moral principle, such as when it prohibits "cruel" punishment, mandates "due" process,

69. Antonin Scalia, A Matter of Interpretation 40–41 (1997).

and guarantees "equal" protection of the law. This would seem to indicate that the Framers trusted future generations to use their moral judgment in determining which state action is acceptable. As Dworkin has argued: "Enlightenment statesmen were very unlikely to think that their own views represented the last word in moral progress. If they really were worried that future generations would protect rights less vigorously than they themselves did, they would have made plain that they intended to create a dated provision."[70] Thus, some form of living constitutionalism would best harmonize with the distribution of trust and distrust manifested in the American constitutional order.

As this brief discussion indicates, although the planning theory requires deference to planners' attitudes about goals, values, and trust, it is not a version of originalism. First, originalism is an interpretive methodology, whereas the planning theory sets out a decision procedure for adjudicating *between* interpretive methodologies. The planning theory may, of course, recommend originalism in certain circumstances, specifically in situations where the designers' attitudes of trust demand this. But, as we just have seen, it is entirely possible that attending to the designers' trust attitudes requires that the original understanding of certain textual provisions be ignored.

Second, originalism focuses on *original* intent, that is, on the attitudes of those who framed particular texts. The planning theory, on the other hand, does not privilege the views of the system's original constitutional designers. Because legal systems always contain mechanisms for revision, the constitutional designers change as the structure of the system changes. The designers of the present American system include not only the Framers and ratifiers of the Constitution of 1787, but also the numerous agents that have changed the complexion of the system over the past two hundred years. Moreover, the constitutional designers who are relevant for determining interpretive methodology are those singled out by the present consensus in the legal community. This *present* consensus determines which *past* consensus to heed. The idea, once again, is that it is irrational for a group to treat a set of agents as designers whose role is to resolve second-order uncertainty, and at the same time not to privilege their attitudes about appropriate goals, values, and trust when trying to figure out how to interpret their instructions. Protestant practices, I have argued, are self-defeating and therefore cannot represent proper legal reasoning.

E. Social Facts without Total Consensus

The advantages of the planning theory, I believe, are considerable. Chief among them is that, insofar as official consensus is not necessary for the determination of interpretive methodology, the planning theory is able to account for the possibility of disagreements about the ultimate criteria of validity. Participants in

---

70. *Id.* at 124.

a practice can disagree over proper interpretive methodology because they disagree about the demands imposed by particular methodologies, the goals and values of the system, its economy of trust, or which methodology best harmonizes with such ideologies.

In order to secure this result, as well as to respond to the other objections, we have seen that the planning theory departs from Hart's doctrine in several important respects: it treats all of the norm-creating and norm-applying provisions of a system's constitution, instead of merely a portion thereof, as its rule of recognition; denies that the secondary rules always confer rights and impose duties (as opposed to *legal* rights and duties); and deems present official consensus merely sufficient, but not necessary, for the determination of the criteria of legality.

Nevertheless, I think that the planning theory is at least Hartian in spirit, if not in letter. First, like Hart's theory, the planning theory does not require that the fundamental rules of a legal system be morally desirable. The shared understandings of a legal community and the system's animating ideology may be ethically odious, scientifically backward, or both. Nevertheless, these considerations are taken as settled and are thus used to determine the ultimate criteria of legal validity.

Second, like Hart's theory, the planning theory ultimately grounds the secondary rules in facts about the behaviors and attitudes of groups. After all, that a group of constitutional designers shared a certain ideology regarding goals, values, and/or trust is a *social fact*. Similarly, that a legal community presently shares an understanding about the identity of those designers, and the basic structure and texts they have created, is also a social fact. The shared plan of any legal system, then, is a social rule because its existence and content is determined by social facts alone.

Finally, both Hart's rule of recognition and the planning theory's shared plan play the same role—namely, the resolution of normative uncertainty. One could argue, in fact, that this concurrence on function is the most important one, insofar as any account that shares this equivalence is required to share the other properties as well. As I claimed in section IV, doubts and disagreements concerning second-order questions of political morality are bound to be as socially confounding in communities governed by law as first-order questions that concern private obligations. A rule of recognition that exists simply in virtue of its moral desirability, however, cannot and will not resolve such disputes—for those who have doubts or disagree about who has legitimate authority would first have to know, or agree about, the moral facts and which marks of authority those moral facts pick out. By hypothesis, these parties neither know nor agree about these very issues.

By contrast, a rule whose existence and content was determined by social facts alone could resolve such doubts and disagreements. One would not have to know whether one was truly entitled to rule; one would simply have to know who was designated by the shared understandings or practices of the relevant legal participants, and work from there.

VI. CONCLUSION: THE EXISTENCE OF THE RULE OF RECOGNITION

So, does the rule of recognition exist? Well, it all depends on what the rule of recognition is. If we take the rule of recognition in a very minimal manner—as the test of legal validity for a particular legal system—then everyone agrees that such a rule exists. Even "Law as Integrity" is a rule of recognition in this anodyne sense.

On the other hand, if we construe the rule of recognition as Hart did—as a duty-imposing convention among officials—then I think we must conclude that the rule of recognition does not exist. For as we have seen, such a rule cannot accurately characterize the content of a legal system, impose duties or confer powers, or exist in the face of disagreement about its content.

Finally, if we take the rule of recognition of a legal system to be constituted by the norm-creating and norm-applying provisions of its shared plan, then I believe that it does exist. Like Hart's rule of recognition, this norm is always at least partially constituted by official convergence on certain standards of conduct; but in contrast to Hart's account, total convergence is not necessary. As long as there is present agreement among officials on the constitutional designers, the authoritative texts, and the basic structural rules of the constitutional order, as well as past consensus among the constitutional designers about the goals and values the institution is to serve and the degree of trust warranted of members of the community, then the raw materials are available from which proper interpretive methodology may be divined and, in turn, the remainder of the rule of recognition ascertained.

It no doubt follows from this account that there must be sufficient consensus about the content of the legal system in question in order for there to be a proper interpretive methodology to find. At the very least, there must be ample shared understandings about who are the constitutional designers of the system, and about the basic institutional structure and authoritative texts they have created. These happy convergences provide the preinterpretive materials that form the heart of the system's economy of trust, and from which the determination of interpretive methodology must proceed. Without them, the procedure cannot get off of the ground.[71]

Lack of consensus, of course, does not preclude actors from *arguing* about appropriate interpretive methodology. As long as disputants think that there is such convergence, or at least act as though they do, each side can fashion, against this assumed common ground, coherent arguments for originalism, interpretivism, pragmatism, or whichever "ism" they support. The absence of presupposed consensus merely precludes either side from being correct. Their hermeneutical disputations may be filled with sound and fury, but from the legal point of view

---

71. I leave it as an open question whether there is another procedure that will determine interpretive methodology in the absence of the convergences mentioned in the text.

they signify nothing. In these cases at least, I believe that Hart's description of fundamental constitutional controversies is correct: "Here, all that succeeds is success."[72] A misguided legal argument, or covert political argument, may catch on and be taken as true by the legal community. Should this happen, the embraced political position will be transformed into a true legal conclusion, and the plan that they all share will shift accordingly.

72. Hart, *supra* note 2, at 153.

10. CONSTITUTIONAL THEORY AND THE RULE OF RECOGNITION

Toward a Fourth Theory of Law

MITCHELL N. BERMAN*

This chapter advances one argument and pitches one proposal. The argument is that Hart's theory of law does not succeed. On Hart's account, legal propositions are what they are—that is, they have the particular content and status that they do—by virtue of their satisfying necessary and sufficient conditions that are themselves established by a special sort of convergent practice among officials.[1] Drawing on debates within U.S. constitutional theory, I argue that law cannot be produced in this way.

If my argument is sound, and therefore Hart's account is not, it remains to determine what the correct theory of law is. My proposal, then, will be to view law as an argumentative practice. Of course, put so generally, this notion will hardly be controversial: no contemporary jurisprudential theories are likely to deny *tout court* that law incorporates a dimension of practice or that it involves argument. While I cannot fully articulate, let alone successfully defend, a distinctive practice-based theory of law in this short space, I will endeavor to say enough to escape vacuity, to distinguish my argumentative account from Dworkin's, and to nourish hope (much short, I'm afraid, of confidence) that the image dimly glimpsed can be realized.

This business is conducted over six sections. Section I identifies the more pressing and persistent questions of U.S. constitutional theory that might be productively advanced by attention to the "What is law?" question. These questions, it claims, closely connect to the familiar struggle to explicate the difference between law and politics. Section II explains how Hart's account of law as predicated on an ultimate rule of recognition (RoR) answers the question of the distinction between law and politics, and argues that the implications of that answer for the persistent interpretive questions of American constitutional theory are sufficiently dubious to justify some skepticism about the RoR account itself. Taking seriously the possibility that the RoR is infirm, Section III offers a diagnosis.

---

* Richard Dale Endowed Chair in Law, The University of Texas at Austin. I am grateful to Scott Shapiro for patient and helpful early discussions about Hart's account; to Matt Adler, Les Green, Mark Greenberg, Ken Himma, and Jerry Postema for insightful comments on a previous draft; to conference participants for very useful reactions; and to Guha Krishnamurthi for excellent research assistance.

1. H.L.A. Hart, The Concept of Law (Penelope A. Bulloch & Joseph Raz eds., 2d ed. 1994). *But see infra* note 13.

On Hart's account, the RoR establishes (directly and indirectly) the criteria that conclusively validate legal norms and propositions. But, Section III argues, the very notion of conclusive legal validation cannot be maintained on conventionalist premises. Insofar as Hart conceives of the RoR as a mechanism that creates the criteria of validity (CoV), the fact that it cannot perform this function suggests that there is no RoR in Hart's sense.

Notice that the upshot of Section III is only to reject the RoR as a means to generate CoV, not to take issue with the more general Hartian vision of law as the product of a social practice. Indeed, I believe that this component of Hartian positivism is correct. Accordingly, the next two sections combine to sketch an affirmative account of law as an argumentative practice. Drawing heavily on recent work by Gerald Postema, Section IV introduces the idea in admittedly tentative and telegraphic fashion. Section V adds some flesh to the bones by contrasting the account I favor with Dworkin's theory of law as integrity. Roughly, an account of law as an argumentative practice differs from Dworkin's theory in conceiving of law as a social practice that constitutes, rather than discovers, legal norms. Against Hart, the account claims that the social practice constitutes legal norms not by converging on a set of conditions of legal validity, but by generating and strengthening norms of reasoned argumentation. Section VI returns to the beginning by drawing from this account some implications for debates within constitutional law and theory.

I. THE PERSISTENT QUESTIONS OF CONSTITUTIONAL THEORY

In investigating whether the RoR model contributes to constitutional theory, we can proceed on either of two paths, starting from either of two points of departure. One possibility is to keep explicating, elaborating, or refining the RoR until implications are drawn whose relevance to American constitutional theory seem obvious or at least promising. An alternative is to begin by identifying particular questions that arise within American constitutional theory, tease out what answers Hart's account would provide, and assess their value or persuasiveness.

The latter approach seems clearly the more sensible. Indeed, it is the approach more faithful to Hart's own methodology in *The Concept of Law.* Hart did not inquire into the nature or concept of law as though it were a matter of abstract philosophical interest. To the contrary, he insisted,

> the best course is to defer giving any answer to the query "What is law?" until we have found out what it is about law that has in fact puzzled those who have asked or attempted to answer it, even though their familiarity with the law and their ability to recognize examples are beyond question. What more do they want to know and why do they want to know it?[2]

---

2. HART, *supra* note 1, at 5.

To this question Hart had an answer. Most speculation about the nature of law throughout history, he contended, was provoked by three questions: "How does law differ from and how is it related to orders backed by threats? How does legal obligation differ from, and how is it related to, moral obligation? What are rules and to what extent is law an affair of rules?"[3] Hart claimed that his theory of law proved its worth by supplying answers to these questions.

Without opining on whether Hart's account achieved the success he claimed for it, it is striking for present purposes that these are not prominent questions of American constitutional theory.[4] Of course, American constitutional theorists expend energy on a large number of questions, many of which are of a parochial vein wholly unlikely to lead, either directly or by degrees, to the question "What is law?" To put the point from the other direction, no further advances or refinements in general jurisprudence are apt to offer much help in answering questions concerning, for example, how best to understand particular amendments, or federalism, or the state action doctrine.

But some questions that occupy American constitutional theorists show potential to bring us into fruitful contact with the work of general jurisprudents or with accounts of the nature or concept of law. Consider, for illustration, three sets of questions that interest constitutional theorists today:

> *Popular constitutionalism:* Do (can) popular practices and understandings help determine constitutional meanings "directly" or do they function only insofar as courts or other officials (choose to) take them into account?[5]
>
> *Metadoctrinalism:* Much of the courts' output in constitutional cases consists of "tests" and "frameworks" that are not most plausibly understood—even by the judges themselves—as "interpretations" of the Constitution, or as statements of "constitutional meaning." Is this permissible? Are these "decision rules" law? What about the meanings that they are intended to implement? Do judicial decisions announce two types of law?[6]
>
> *Extrajudicial constitutional obligations:* Most everyone agrees that the executive and legislative branches have obligations of constitutional fidelity. But in circumstances where the relevant constitutional norm is unlikely to be enforced by the courts, how, exactly, should we think about that obligation? Some people

---

3. HART, *supra* note 1, at 13.

4. This is not to insist that issues that occupy contemporary constitutional theorists share nothing in common with these three questions. My claim—which is not essential to my argument, and which I therefore assert without defense—is that to assimilate constitutional theorists' concerns to those that motivated Hart would be more forced than natural.

5. *See, e.g.*, Matthew D. Adler, *Popular Constitutionalism and the Rule of Recognition: Whose Practices Ground U.S. Law?*, 100 NW. U. L. REV. 719 (2006).

6. *See, e.g.*, Mitchell N. Berman, *Constitutional Decision Rules*, 90 VA. L. REV. 1 (2004).

refer to it as a moral obligation, or an obligation of conscience. Is that to say it is not a legal obligation? Or are there different types of legal obligation, depending on the prospects of enforcement by agents of the legal system?[7]

I hope that these questions convey the flavor of the puzzles of American constitutional theory that a contemporary theorist of law proceeding in a Hartian mode might aim for his or her account to help resolve. None is as central, urgent, or long-standing as the three questions that motivated Hart's inquiry. However, the focal concern of constitutional theory is. Very generally, it is the question of how constitutional meaning, content, or law derives from, or relates to, the constitutional text, and it arises with a piquancy not found in the realms either of common law (where there is no canonical text to interpret) or of statutory law (where the distance to traverse between text and its meaning or content is typically much shorter). Thus did Chief Justice Marshall memorably urge in *McCulloch* that "we must never forget that it is a *constitution* we are expounding."[8]

Because constitutions do not "partake of the prolixity of a legal code," Marshall further observed, questions regarding their meaning or significance are "perpetually arising, and will probably continue to arise, so long as our system shall exist."[9] In meeting the challenge that Marshall foresaw, American legal culture has come to recognize a variety of argumentative modalities (as Philip Bobbitt termed them)[10] for deriving constitutional law in the face of the nontransparency of constitutional text: the ordinary or plain meaning of the text, the expectations or semantic intentions or purposes of the Framers or ratifiers, the original public meaning, post-ratification historical practice, judicial precedent, constitutional structure, prudence, ethics, and others.

The variety of recognized argumentative modalities raises at least two profound questions for American constitutional theory—questions at the retail and wholesale level:

Retail constitutional interpretation: What is the constitutional law, and how ought we (or judges alone) identify it, when different modalities point in different directions? How, on a case-by-case basis, ought the interpreter to adjudicate among competing interpretive considerations?

Wholesale constitutional interpretation: Are the argumentative modalities presently in use valid or legitimate? Consider, for example, frequently voiced contentions that the Constitution must be interpreted in an originalist mode, or that judicial adherence to precedents the judges deem incorrect is inconsistent

7. Questions of this sort are explored in important recent work by Trevor Morrison. *See, e.g.*, Trevor W. Morrison, *Suspension and the Extrajudicial Constitution*, 107 Colum. L. Rev. 1533 (2007).

8. McCulloch v. Maryland, 4 Wheat. (17 U.S.) 316, 407 (1819).

9. *Id.* at 407, 405.

10. *See generally* Philip Bobbitt, Constitutional Fate (1982); Philip Bobbitt, Constitutional Interpretation (1991).

with their obligation of fidelity to the Constitution as the supreme law of the land. Are arguments of this sort to change existing judicial interpretive practice possibly correct *as a matter of law*, or are they necessarily evaluable only from a perspective, external to law, of political morality?[11]

These questions, or ones broadly like them, have engaged constitutional theorists since the founding. They gain their urgency from the worry that, if no good answers are forthcoming, then the interpretation and enforcement of the Constitution involves the exercise of will rather than judgment—inverting Alexander Hamilton's claim in *Federalist* 78—rendering potentially illegitimate the exercise of constitutional review by unelected federal judges. To put the concern more simply: is the choice among reasonably contested interpretations of the Constitution a matter of law or of politics, and what is the difference? The question of the relationship between law and politics may be felt especially keenly in the domain of American constitutional theory, but is not unique to it. The American legal realists, for example, obsessed over the distinction but paid relatively little attention to constitutional law and theory. If the test of Hart's account of law is its ability to shed light on "aspects of law which seem naturally, at all times, to give rise to misunderstanding,"[12] it should provide an answer to the law/politics question that is of some use to American constitutional theorists.

II. THE RULE OF RECOGNITION AND THE DISTINCTION BETWEEN LAW AND POLITICS

The fundamentals of Hart's account of law are too familiar to warrant extensive recapitulation. In crude outline, and skipping past subtleties and ambiguities that will not affect my basic argument, a legal system is a complex union of primary and secondary rules in which the primary rules of obligation are generally obeyed and in which the secondary rules of recognition, change, and adjudication are accepted by officials from the internal point of view, which is to say that they are regarded as public common standards of correct behavior. In turn, the content of the law is the set of norms that satisfy the system's criteria of legal validity—criteria that may be established in part by other (higher) legal norms but that find ultimate validation in a criterion or criteria that exist only by virtue of a convergent recognitional practice among judges.[13]

---

11. See the illuminating discussions in this volume by both Matt Adler and Dick Fallon. Matthew D. Adler, *Social Facts, Constitutional Interpretation, and the Rule of Recognition* (Chapter 8, this volume); Richard H. Fallon, Jr., *Precedent-Based Constitutional Adjudication, Acceptance, and the Rule of Recognition* (Chapter 2, this volume).

12. HART, *supra* note 1, at 6.

13. In correspondence, Les Green has objected that the convergent practice that interested Hart was that which identified legal *sources*, not the practice that determined rules

The implications of this account for the law/politics question are straightforward. Law exists only to the extent validated by criteria ultimately derivable from a convergent practice among officials. When norms validated in this way underdetermine the answer to any putatively legal question, judges can furnish a legal resolution only by exercising a "legislative" discretion.[14] Roughly, then, law exists only within the space defined by criteria validated by convergent official behavior and attitudes of acceptance. To be sure, because the RoR is a social rule, and because all rules have "open texture" and thus penumbras of vagueness, just where its borders lie will be contestable. Nonetheless, when agreement regarding the governing CoV runs out, lawmaking begins.

Answers to the constitutional theorists' questions of constitutional interpretation follow directly. Recall that what I have called the retail questions arise when argumentative modalities already legitimated by practice yield different conclusions regarding what the (constitutional) law is. Theorists following Hart often conclude that part of the CoV in the United States reads something like this: a norm is law if it is traceable to the plain meaning of a Supreme Court decision purporting to interpret the Constitution, or to the plain meaning of the text of the Constitution not supplanted by a Supreme Court decision.[15] If neither a candidate norm nor its negation can be validated in this way, then it might possibly be validated if it conforms with other settled argumentative modalities, such as the original semantic intentions of the Framers or ratifiers, or their expectations, or stable historical nonjudicial practice, or the demands of conventional principles of justice, or the like. But—and here's the critical point—a norm cannot be validated in this way when customary modalities of this sort conflict. (Otherwise, if norm *N* accords with, say, the Constitution's original meaning, and $-N$ accords

---

or principles for deriving *content* from those sources. For this reason, Green also resists my characterization of Hart's account, *supra* text accompanying note 1. I agree that Hart's focus was on the problem of identifying sources. In my view, however, that was not because he had—or even took himself to have—adequate basis for bracketing the step of content derivation, but because he naively failed to appreciate the importance of this step for a theory of law. In any event, and because it would be foolhardy to debate Hart exegesis (or reconstruction) with Green, two points warrant emphasis. First, as an empirical matter, I am fairly confident that my reading of Hart is shared by the great majority of constitutional theorists who seek to derive lessons for American constitutional law from work in general jurisprudence. (After all, doubts about the identity of legal sources constitute a very small part of constitutional theorists' concerns.) It is therefore an account—even if not, exactly, Hart's—that must be taken seriously by those who would hope that general jurisprudence can illuminate debates in constitutional theory. Second, on Green's reading, Hart's account is patently incomplete as a theory of law, and therefore demands to be either supplemented or replaced.

14. HART, *supra* note 1, at 135–36.

15. *See, e.g.*, Kent Greenawalt, *The Rule of Recognition and the Constitution*, 85 MICH. L. REV. 621, 659–60 (1987) (reprinted as Chapter 1, this volume, at 36–37).

with, say, historical practice, then both *N* and –*N* would be the law.) And regardless of whether these interpretive standards align (or are thought to align) more often than one might expect,[16] they will pull apart in a large portion of cases that reach the Supreme Court and that engage the attention of constitutional theorists. When they do, Hart's account suggests, a judicial choice among the candidate meanings is one of lawmaking. Insofar as lawmaking is the stuff of politics, it might seem to follow that the choice is political, not legal.

Now, in the Postscript, Hart takes some pains to avoid this conclusion, deeming it "important that the law-creating powers which I ascribe to the judges to regulate cases left partly unregulated by the law are different from those of a legislature."[17] But his conviction that this must be so is more evident than the strength of his arguments for it, which are grounded in his account of law. The first difference Hart adduces between the law-creating powers of judges and legislatures—that the "judge's powers [are] subject to many constraints *narrowing his choice* from which a legislature may be quite free"—is more asserted than argued for; and the second—that judicial lawmaking authority is interstitial—says little or nothing about the character of judicial lawmaking when it occurs, merely restating that it does occur only in limited cases. So despite Hart's insistence that judicial lawmaking discretion is quite different from legislative discretion, the precise difference seems, at the end, to elude even Hart himself: the judge, he concludes, "must not [exercise his lawmaking powers] arbitrarily: that is he must always have some general reasons justifying his decision and he must act *as a conscientious legislator would* by deciding according to his own beliefs and values."[18] The law/politics divide emerges even more clearly with respect to the wholesale interpretive questions: arguments to alter present interpretive practices—to rule out accepted moves or to rule in presently excluded ones—are not arguments of law, but necessarily of politics (or of political morality).

For the moment, let us put aside the wholesale questions. (We will pick them up again in Section VI.) The principal objection to the retail conclusion is well known: it does not cohere with what judges say they are doing in hard cases of constitutional law, or with what many of us take to be the phenomenology of judging. On this latter point, moreover, academic constitutional theorists need not merely take actual judges' reports of their felt experiences as gospel; we reflect as well on our own experiences of "playing judge," as it were—of trying, that is, to resolve difficult constitutional questions for ourselves from as disinterested a posture as we are able.

Of course, this is not a decisive objection. Hartians respond that the rhetoric and phenomenology mislead, that participants who genuinely believe there to be

---

16. *See* Richard H. Fallon, Jr., *A Constructivist Coherence Theory of Constitutional Interpretation*, 100 HARV. L. REV. 1189 (1987).

17. HART, *supra* note 1, at 273.

18. *Id.* at 273 (emphasis added).

law in hard cases are mistaken and that others know there is no law but falsely claim otherwise to serve personal or systemic ends.[19] That could be. But claims of widespread error or disingenuousness naturally come with a heavy burden of proof, so we ought not to toss aside these objections to Hart too readily. We'd have greater confidence in doing so were we persuaded that Hart's apparent position—namely, when the RoR is indeterminate, there is no law and judges are free (perhaps required) to make it—had resulted from more sustained and careful engagement with problems of constitutional interpretation.

However, no present-day reader of *The Concept of Law* can fail to be struck by Hart's casual, even innocent, treatment of the subject. As Kent Greenawalt critically observed in his penetrating analysis of what the Rule of Recognition in the United States might be, "*The Concept of Law* leaves the impression that the ultimate rule of recognition will be rather stable, will not refer much to moral criteria, and will allow rather clear identification of what counts as law."[20] Although Hart devotes a short section to "uncertainty in the rule of recognition,"[21] the discussion suggests both that uncertainty will reign only at the margins and that, once an indeterminacy is identified, it is likely to be authoritatively resolved by judicial decision fairly quickly. Hart seems not to contemplate precisely what American constitutional law bears out—namely, that debates over ultimate interpretive standards can constitute a mostly stable feature of the legal order.

That Hart was operating with an unrealistic picture of American constitutional practice is strongly suggested by his initial presentation of the legal realist challenge to formalist confidence in the breadth and bindingness of legal rules:

> Skepticism about the character of legal rules has not . . . always taken the extreme form of condemning the very notion of a binding rule as confused or fictitious. Instead, the most prevalent form of skepticism in England and the United States invites us to reconsider the view that a legal system *wholly*, or even *primarily*, consists of rules. . . . In very simple cases this may be so; but in . . . most important cases there is always a choice. The judge has to choose between alternative meanings to be given to the words of a statute or between rival interpretations of what a precedent "amounts to." . . .
>
> If so much uncertainty may break out in humble spheres of private law, how much more shall we find in the magniloquent phrases of a constitution such as the Fifth and Fourteenth Amendments to the Constitution of the

---

19. Although arguments of this sort are advanced frequently, they are developed most fully in Brian Leiter, *Explaining Theoretical Disagreement*, 76 U. Chi. L. Rev. (forthcoming 2009).

20. Greenawalt, *supra* note 15, at 665 (reprinted as Chapter 1, this volume, at 42).

21. Hart, *supra* note 1, at 147–54.

> United States[?] . . . In view of all this, is not the conception of law as essentially a matter of rules a gross exaggeration if not a mistake?[22]

Hart presents this skeptical challenge as one he intends to meet; he will answer that last question in the negative. And yet given the vagueness of the constitutional text and the wide variety of practice-legitimated argumentative modalities, the argument of *The Concept of Law* more plausibly *vindicates* the skeptic's claims about the U.S. Constitution than undermines them.

My point is not to criticize Hart. I have said that worries about the legal or political character of constitutional interpretation have been with us for over 200 years. And that is true.[23] But such concerns have exploded over the past two generations. Indeed, one wishing to date the start of the modern obsession with problematics of constitutional interpretation could do worse than choose the publication of Alexander Bickel's *The Least Dangerous Branch* in 1962. Because a fuller appreciation of the difficulties of constitutional interpretation and the implausibility of official consensus regarding how content derives from text has flowered only since *The Concept of Law* first saw print, it is not surprising that Hart evinced what must strike today's readers as an incomplete grasp of the subject. But it would be foolish to deny that this significant change in the understandings and concerns of (one set of) legal theorists might reasonably affect our current evaluation of the adequacy of Hart's account. Better to recognize, with Gray, that "our attempts at classification are necessarily provisional and temporary" and that "the one certain prophecy . . . is that the classification which approves itself . . . at the beginning of the twentieth century will surely *not* be the one which will prevail at its end."[24]

In sum, the answers to their questions that flow from the Hartian account strike most constitutional theorists as facially implausible, and the arguments Hart marshaled for those conclusions are too weak and cavalier to instill confidence.

III. CHALLENGING THE CRITERIA OF VALIDITY

Attention to problems of American constitutional theory provides reason to doubt Hart's account of law. But can it do more than that? Can it help us to see what about the Hartian account is mistaken? I think it can.

A principal function of the RoR is to establish the CoV, the "feature or features possession of which by a suggested rule is taken as a *conclusive affirmative*

---

22. *Id.* at 12–13.

23. For an examination of debates in the early republic, see Larry D. Kramer, The People Themselves: Popular Constitutionalism and Judicial Review (2004).

24. John Chipman Gray, The Nature and Sources of the Law 4 (1921).

indication that it is a rule of the group."[25] In a complex legal system, the CoV likely take the form of a disjunctive set of complex sufficient conditions, such that *X* is law if *C1*, or *C2*, or . . . *Cn*. Although it is notoriously difficult to articulate, consistent with the Hartian account, the complete set of the ultimate CoV in the United States, our earlier, very brief discussion suggests what is ordinarily accepted as at least a sufficient condition of legal validity—call it *C1*:

> *C1*: a norm is law if it conforms to the plain language of the holding of a non-overruled Supreme Court decision.[26]

Thus, if the Supreme Court announced in *Jones* that "*P* is the law," then *P* is the law; the legal validity of *P* is conclusively validated by *C1* plus the Supreme Court decision in *Jones*.

The problem, however, is that even this seemingly uncontroversial formulation of just a single criterion that partially constitutes the CoV is not secure. Suppose that *Jones* was decided by a coin flip or by astrological divination or by alectryomancy (divination through the peckings of grain by birds), or that the majority in *Jones* accepted bribes to decide as they did or are manifestly insane. If any of these facts obtain (or are believed to obtain), one might reasonably doubt whether *P* is the law, notwithstanding its ostensible validation by a non-overruled Supreme Court decision. Put another way, it is an open question whether officials will treat *P* as law, notwithstanding its conformity with *C1*. Therefore what we had taken to be a sufficient condition of legal validity—essentially, conformity with a non-overruled Supreme Court decision—turns out to be defeasible. And if a putatively sufficient condition isn't, then it surely follows that there can be no set of validity criteria.

That's the quick objection to the CoV—much too quick, you might think. We have already remarked upon Hart's own acknowledgement that the RoR, like all rules, has an "open texture." Perhaps, then, these examples challenge not the idea of CoV, but only the too-casual formulation offered above of what some portion of the CoV in the United States in fact is. On this view, *C1* is incomplete or insufficiently nuanced. A more accurate condition, the argument would run, would be something like this:

> *C1**: a norm is law if it conforms to the plain language of the holding of a Supreme Court decision that (1) has not been overruled and (2) was not reached in palpably inappropriate or unfair ways.

---

25. Hart, *supra* note 1, at 94 (emphasis added).

26. To be more precise, one might add conditions like the following: ". . . and does not violate any other non-overruled Supreme Court decision or the plain language of the constitutional text not already displaced by a decision of a high court." For purposes of my present argument, we can safely put qualifications of this sort aside.

All of my examples designed to destabilize the CoV by challenging *C1* are simply cases that are either excluded by this more careful statement of *C1*—that is, *C1**—or, at worst, fall within its vague periphery.

Unfortunately for Hart, I do not think that this rebuttal succeeds. It is true that a rule could be *posited* that would force my challenging cases into the vague periphery, leaving norms with respect to which the CoV *do* fulfill their function of providing conclusive legal validation. But the CoV are not posited, they are inferred from social practice. And this substantially constrains our ability to reformulate the criteria to accord with what we anticipate would make good sense. Ken Himma observes that the decision of a high court establishes the law "as long as the court reaches its decision in an acceptable way."[27] My claim is this: if the high court had not previously reached its decision in a way that officials convergently deemed unacceptable, then it is not clear on Hartian premises where Himma's (sensible) qualification to the CoV can come from.

A fanciful hypothetical can illustrate. Let us continue to assume that *Jones* announced "*P*." But now suppose that the defendant in *Jones* was Sylvester McMonkey McBean, and that a post-*Jones* litigant were to challenge the legal validity of *P* by proposing that a Supreme Court decision cannot validate a norm if it involved a party named after a character from Dr. Seuss.[28] Just as Hartians might seek to resist the force of my hypotheticals involving coin flipping, bribe taking, or insane Justices by contending that *C1* is less accurate than *C1**, I am now imagining that somebody proposes to replace *C1** with *C1***:

> *C1***: a norm is law if it conforms to the plain language of the holding of a Supreme Court decision that (1) has not been overruled, (2) was not reached in palpably inappropriate or unfair ways, and (3) did not involve any party named after a Dr. Seuss character.

Of course, this is a ridiculous argument, one we can bet will not persuade a court or anybody else. But the instant question is not whether it will win; the question is whether Hartians are entitled to the proposition that *C1*** is not a criterion in the system and therefore that a norm is law so long as it satisfies *C1** (or something like it).

I maintain that Hartians are not entitled to this proposition. Inferring rules from practices always confronts the problem of inductive generalization. But the challenge here is one step greater. If the issue of how the presence in a lawsuit of amusingly named parties bears on the Supreme Court's power to make law has not yet arisen, there can be no convergent practice on point, and the contours of the CoV, as they bear on the question, are as yet undetermined. Put another way, if the conditions of legal validity are established by convergent behavior, then

---

27. Kenneth Einar Himma, *Understanding the Relationship between the U.S. Constitution and the Conventional Rule of Recognition* (Chapter 4, this volume, at 101).

28. *See* DR. SEUSS, THE SNEETCHES AND OTHER STORIES (1961).

there is no fact of the matter that can allow us to choose between *C1*** and *C1**. But if that's true, then it's also true that we cannot choose between *C1* and *C1**. More generally, because novel legal arguments cannot be ruled in or out by preexisting practice, there cannot exist any set of criteria that provide the *conclusive* validation that Hart assumes.

To be sure, we have reached this conclusion via bizarre hypotheticals involving corrupt or nutty judges and oddly captioned cases. But challenges to the CoV arise in the real world. For example, does a Supreme Court decision establish law under the following unprecedented combination of circumstances: it (1) purports to resolve a contested presidential election (2) in a manner that accords with the apparent political preferences of the majority Justices (3) by reference to arguments that those same Justices have rejected in other cases, (4) while disavowing that the decision will have precedential significance? Hartians would be entitled to an affirmative answer were *C1* true. However, as we have seen, hypotheticals involving decision by coin flip or by divination powerfully suggest that *C1* is not true. And it is more than doubtful that there exists any criterion of validity established by past practice that more specifically addresses this particular concatenation of circumstances. If the Hartian account is correct—if a norm is law only if validated by criteria that are themselves produced by convergent official practice—then it would seem to follow not merely that *Bush v. Gore* presented a hard case for the Justices that required the exercise of legislative discretion (a conclusion that Hartians would have no trouble embracing), but that the decision announced by *Bush v. Gore* was not law. Some readers will not resist that conclusion either. But notice that what's doing the work in driving that conclusion does not depend upon the *content* of circumstances (1) through (4). The argument depends only on the fact of an unusual combination of circumstances. Yet every case involves unusual, indeed unprecedented, circumstances, wanting only for someone with either the perspicuity or the whimsy to point them out for us.

To see the challenge yet more clearly, it is worth briefly comparing this critique of Hart's understanding of CoV with Dworkin's criticism of Hart for endorsing the erroneous view—one that cannot accommodate the existence of "theoretical disagreements" about law—that "the very meaning of the word 'law' makes law depend on certain specific criteria."[29] As Hart and many others have rightly objected, Dworkin's discussion of the "semantic sting" mischaracterizes its target: Hart's theory is of the concept of law, not the word. However, in an endnote that responds to this very objection, Dworkin contends that his criticism regarding Hart's inability to explain theoretical disagreements applied equally to semantic theories of law and to "accounts of the 'truth conditions' of propositions of law."[30] Addressing this endnote, Hart insists in his Postscript that "even

29. RONALD DWORKIN, LAW'S EMPIRE 31 (1986).
30. *Id.* at 419.

if the meaning of such propositions of law was determined by definitions or by their truth conditions this does not lead to the conclusion that the very meaning of the word 'law' makes law depend on certain specific criteria."[31] But if my analysis above is correct, then Hart's response is nonresponsive. Dworkin is claiming that his criticism of Hart goes through so long as Hart espouses a criterial theory either of the word "law" *or* of propositions of law. I am arguing, consistent with Dworkin's assertion, but on distinct grounds, that Hart's theory is infirm precisely because it advances a criterial account of the validity of legal propositions (and because the criteria are said to arise from conventional practices).[32]

Given the intended force of this critique, two points deserve emphasis. First, I am not construing Hart's notion of CoV idiosyncratically or uncharitably. Contemporary jurisprudents agree that the Hartian criteria of validity comprise a set of necessary and sufficient conditions that a candidate norm must satisfy for it to qualify as a legal norm. Indeed, Ken Himma argues in this volume that a criterial view of what distinguishes law from nonlaw is shared by all jurisprudents. Labeling the claim "that in every conceptually possible legal system there exist necessary and sufficient conditions for a norm to count as law" the "Differentiation Thesis,"[33] Himma declares not only that it was held by Hart, but that it is shared by "every conceptual theorist."[34] I am floating a dissent. My argument to this point suggests that the Differentiation Thesis is false: a proposition of law is never *conclusively* validated; it is always provisional, always potentially subject to invalidation by a new consideration that existing practice cannot decisively rule out. At the risk of belaboring, my claim is not that the line demarcating valid legal norms is not sharp; Hart clearly acknowledges as much. My claim is that norms that all participants would characterize as uncontroversially legally valid—the norms that are to law much as your family's Toyota Camry is to vehicle—do not enjoy that status in the way Hart proposes, that is, by virtue of satisfying a series of tests that existing practice has certified as the finite and conclusive set.[35]

Second, my criticism of Hart's criterial account of legal propositions dovetails with the arguments from Section II. The divide between law and politics, or (if

31. HART, *supra* note 1, at 247.

32. One might reasonably debate just how distinct my argument is from other arguments in Dworkin's corpus. As Jerry Postema helpfully pointed out to me, it bears similarity to "the argument from controversy" in "The Model of Rules II." *See* Ronald Dworkin, *The Model of Rules II, in* TAKING RIGHTS SERIOUSLY 46 (1977). But where Dworkin appears to rely heavily on circumstances in which judges *already* divide over some aspect of the RoR, *see id.* at 61–63, my argument cuts more deeply in emphasizing that we need not await disagreement. That novel circumstances continually arise threatens the idea of conclusive validation even before any disagreement actually materializes.

33. Himma, *supra* note 27, at 96.

34. *Id.*

35. HART, *supra* note 1, at 103.

you prefer) between law and nonlaw, that Hart's theory entails but that many American constitutional theorists believe ill captures hard cases, depends upon the premise that some norms and propositions are conclusively validated as law, such that judicial discretion of a legislative cast occurs when courts are asked to choose among candidate norms or propositions none of which is so validated. So if CoV established in a Hartian way cannot provide what they promise, then the Hartian distinction between law and nonlaw seems no longer supportable. In short, we can now surmise that the Hartian theory of law reaches dubious conclusions about U.S. constitutional interpretation precisely because it rests on a dubious conception of legal validity.

IV. TOWARD A THEORY OF LAW AS ARGUMENTATIVE PRACTICE

I observed in Section II that the Hartian answer to the hard cases of constitutional law rests on a law/nonlaw distinction that constitutional theorists resist. Taking this resistance seriously, I argued in Section III that the Hartian account is in fact untenable because it assumes CoV that it cannot deliver. Possibly, though, the preceding analysis does more than undermine Hart; perhaps it points us as well in a more promising direction.

Return to the contrasting hypotheticals already discussed: it is submitted that the Supreme Court's declaration that *P* does not validate *P* as law because, in the first instance, the decision was reached by divination and, in the second, it involved a party with a bizarrely funny name. I have argued that the RoR cannot distinguish the two cases. Yet many of us are confident that the first decision is not law (notwithstanding *C1*), whereas the second, ceteris paribus, is. And why this is so is not mysterious. As persons already well socialized into Anglo-American legal practice, we grasp reflexively that the fact that a judicial decision was reached by numerology is a good argument against its validity while the fact that it involves funny names is not.[36] And this observation suggests a more general jurisprudential possibility worth pursuing—namely, that *law is an argumentative practice*.

36. To anticipate a critical idea developed in the next section, you might be tempted to explain this difference by reference to a deeper or more fundamental consideration: a judicial decision sets forth the law only so long as it rests on rational considerations—considerations that, for example, are well suited to ascertaining what a text "really means" or to providing moral justification for the exercise of coercive power. A decision produced by divination violates this condition whereas the fact that a party has an odd name does not. But this proposal might be too quick. After all, some contemporary constitutional theorists believe that it is irrational to interpret the Constitution in accordance with, say, the application intentions of the framers, but they would not thereby deny that a Supreme Court decision that relied on such considerations set forth the law. So we should not quickly gallop past the much thinner explanation in text.

Because this idea, stated so baldly, will appear obvious or uninteresting, it is worth attending to the common observation that "law" is ambiguous as between a type of system or institution on the one hand, and a type of norm, rule, or proposition on the other. Hart himself was not always as clear as he might have been regarding which of these referents of "law" he had in mind. More often, though, he used the term "law" to mean *legal system*. He took the concept of a legal system as analytically primary, and sought to explain law-as-norm as some sort of output or component of the legal system. But law-as-system and law-as-norm (or law-as-proposition) do not exhaust the guises of law with which jurisprudence might be concerned. Law refers to an entire domain of social life. Unmodified, the term can refer to the institution or system of law (legal system), or to the rules or norms of law (legal rules), or to the practice or activity of law (legal practice), or to other aspects or features of the domain.[37] Without advancing a view regarding what hierarchy among these more or less distinct concepts obtains for different purposes, I suggest that contemporary jurisprudence has not paid sufficient attention to the practice dimension of law and to the argumentative or discursive character of that practice.[38]

That the practice dimension of law could assume a more central position within jurisprudential thinking emerges more clearly when today's views are contrasted with the traditional common law attitude. As Gerald Postema has recently shown in a powerful and important series of essays, when common law jurists spoke of law as far back as the fourteenth century, law-as-practice was at least as salient to them as law-as-norm. "While common lawyers recognized statutory law and other 'constitutions' issuing from the monarch or monarch-in-Parliament, still the law in its fundament was understood to be not so much 'made' or 'posited'—something 'laid down' by will or nature—but rather, something 'taken up,' that is, used by judges and others in subsequent practical deliberation."[39] At least by the seventeenth and eighteenth centuries, it was "orthodox common law jurisprudence" that "the *law* is to be found in the accumulated experience recorded in the books and memories of common law jurists, not in

37. Compare Hart's discussion of railways. HART, *supra* note 1, at 16.

38. Gerald Postema, on whom I rely at length, is a prominent exception. So too is Dennis Patterson. *See* Dennis M. Patterson, *Book Review—Law's Practice*, 90 COLUM. L. REV. 575 (1990); Dennis M. Patterson, *Law's Pragmatism: Law as Practice and Narrative*, 76 VA. L. REV. 937, 940 (1990) (advancing a "view of law as practice and narrative discourse"). Patterson's particular take on law-as-practice is too philosophically nuanced and rich to allow for a quick summary. To note just one difference between his account and mine, though, I will not agree with his claim that "law is an activity and not a thing." *Id.* As the text indicates, I take law to be activity in addition to thing (proposition, norm).

39. Gerald J. Postema, *Classical Common Law Jurisprudence (Part I)*, 2 OXFORD U. COMMONWEALTH L.J. 155, 166 (2002).

any theory or articulation of this experience. Law is practice, not a theoretical representation of it."[40]

The common law tradition viewed law-as-practice not only as on a par with law-as-norm, but as explanatorily prior to it:

> It was the general practice of the courts, not the specific decisions or reasoning in a given case or line of cases, that established the propositions of law. The law emerged from the course of argument exemplified in the cases so reported, but it was not laid down by the courts. The recorded cases offered authoritative evidence of the forms and usages of the courts and hence of the law. These records taught students modes and contexts of argument rather than settled rules and criteria by which to authenticate them.[41]

One of a positivist cast of mind, especially one reared in an age that sees law's paradigmatic form as statutory, is apt to conceive of law-as-norm as an output of politics that it is the task of law-as-practice to enforce. A natural lawyer likely sees law-as-norm as a feature of the world or of the human condition that law-as-practice aims to discern. In contrast, the common law tradition, Postema teaches, viewed law-as-practice as the organizing fabric of the legal order from which law-as-norm emerges. This perspective—what Postema calls "common law conventionalism"—

> reorients thinking about the nature of law dominated by positivist and natural law conceptions. Its theoretical point of departure is not a set of norms, prescriptions, or propositions of law, but rather a practice of common practical reasoning. Rather than a metaphysical thesis, it urges a methodological thesis, a point about order of explanation and understanding, not an ontological point about the ultimate order of being.[42]

Moreover, legal practice produced or generated legal propositions in a manner appropriately labeled *legal* because it relied upon, indeed embodied, "artificial reason"—a distinctive habit of mind and argumentation that respected constraints and emphases different from the all-things-considered reasoning that might prevail outside the confines of the practice.[43] "The philosopher and theologian are not suited for this task, . . . for it is not an enterprise of discovery,

40. Gerald J. Postema, *Classical Common Law Jurisprudence (Part II)*, 3 OXFORD U. COMMONWEALTH L.J. 1, 6 (2003).

41. Postema, *supra* note 39, at 161.

42. Gerald J. Postema, *Philosophy of the Common Law*, *in* THE OXFORD HANDBOOK OF JURISPRUDENCE AND PHILOSOPHY OF LAW 589, 602 (Jules Coleman & Scott Shapiro eds., 2002).

43. Postema identifies six defining features of artificial reason: it was pragmatic (not theoretical), public-spirited (not parochial), contextual (not abstract), local (not global or systematic), discursive and forensic (not solitary or introspective), and common or shared (not individual or hidden).

through exercise of abstract reason, of general practical principles, but rather an enterprise of judging particular cases through a grasp of concrete relations and arrangements woven into the fabric of common life."[44] For Coke and Hale, "the artificial reason of the common lawyer was regarded as a disciplined and informed *practice* of reasoning, and if reason understood in this way was thought to legitimate doctrines, rules or decisions of common law, this was only because they survived critical scrutiny in a *process of reasoning and disputation*."[45] In short, the artificial reason that defined legal practice was: first, not a way to discover legal norms, but rather a way to *constitute* them; and second, a creative activity distinct from paradigmatically positivist modes of law-creation.

Karl Llewellyn was heir to the same tradition in insisting that "practice . . . is the bony structure of a legal system."[46] For Llewellyn, argues Dennis Patterson, "[t]ruth, that is legal truth, is the product neither of the correspondence of sentences with 'the world' (objectivism) nor is it simply what judges decide it will be (relativism). Truth in law is a function of three elements: training, tradition, and creativity."[47] Thus, "it is the practice that is the ultimate source of legal meaning. Practice or 'way of acting,' not rule or principle, is primary."[48]

This thumbnail sketch of the common law tradition relies to an inordinate degree on the work of a single contemporary scholar. This might seem to leave me hostage to the accuracy of Postema's characterization of common law practice and jurisprudential understandings. I should emphasize, then, that it matters little to my argument whether the picture I've drawn from Postema is faithful to history. I have invoked that picture solely to convey a flavor of what a dynamic, practice-based account of law could look like. And the key idea, to repeat, is that legal norms are the product of the identification, evaluation, and acceptance or endorsement of arguments by participants within a structured practice. Legal norms and propositions are ultimately traceable to social practices, just as in Hart's account. But the social practices converge, not on criteria that have the capacity to furnish conclusive legal validation, but on norms of reasonable and persuasive argumentation. We might call this view "law-as-argumentative-practice" to signal that it is a species within the law-as-practice genus. In modest shorthand, I will refer to it as "law-as-argument."

The remaining question, accordingly, is whether a theory of law broadly along the foregoing lines can be rendered coherent and plausible. The answer could well be no even if the preceding sketch adequately captures self-understandings of the common law tradition. Then again, the answer could be yes even if it

44. Postema, *supra* note 40, at 9.

45. *Id.* at 3.

46. KARL N. LLEWELLYN, MY PHILOSOPHY OF LAW 181, 187 (1941), *quoted in* Patterson, *Law's Practice, supra* note 38, at 593.

47. Patterson, *Law's Practice, supra* note 38, at 593.

48. *Id.* at 577.

doesn't. While cashing out this promissory note will ultimately require many more details than I can provide here, I will make a down payment by flagging the most obvious, and perhaps the most formidable, challenge to law-as-argument—namely, that it might seem to confuse a theory of law with a theory of adjudication, and also threatens to ignore the more general distinction between metaphysics and epistemology upon which the jurisprudential distinction rests. We need something like the law/adjudication distinction, this argument goes, even to make sense of law-as-argument. Without the idea that a legal norm preexists argumentation about it (argumentation that frequently culminates in, but is not reducible to, judicial resolution),[49] the practice itself seems aimless. For unless we believe that legal norms exist in some form independent of or antecedent to actual embodied argumentation, it is unclear to what end the arguments are directed, and how we can sensibly characterize a judicial determination of the law as wrong.

In fact, the common law tradition largely did ignore these distinctions.[50] Still, and again, my goal is not to unearth seventeenth-century understandings, but to acknowledge and begin to address one twenty-first-century objection. How law-as-argument might successfully respond to this central challenge will emerge more clearly when we detour to consider the most prominent contemporary alternative to Hartian positivism, Dworkin's interpretive theory of law.

V. DISTINGUISHING DWORKIN

Dworkin's theory of law is too complex and contains too many moving parts to permit concise yet complete summary. Very briefly, though, it views law as the set of principles that collectively best fit and morally justify the institutional history of the community's legal system. Believing that there exist correct answers of moral principle, Dworkin concludes that there are also right answers to questions of law. Where Hart claims that there is no determinate law so judges must make it (i.e., in the hard cases not covered by criteria of validity derived from a convergent practice of rule-following by officials), Dworkin claims that there is

---

49. An account of law as practice embraces the contributions of all legal actors, including the practicing bar, legal academics, and executive officials; it is not limited to judges.

50. Blackstone's comment that the only way to prove that a particular maxim is a rule of the common law "is by showing that it hath been always the custom to observe it," was, claims Postema,

> not merely epistemic. He makes a claim about the mode of existence of common law. Law exists insofar as it is regularly taken up, used in deliberation and argument, and followed in practice. The law, as common lawyers conceived of it, was not a structured set of authoritatively posited, explicit directives, but of rules and ways implicit in a body of practices and patterns of practical thinking.

Postema, *supra* note 39, at 167.

law, which it is the judges' task to discover. Because Dworkin challenges Hart on precisely the point that, we have seen, leaves constitutional theorists troubled with the RoR, and because he writes with American constitutional law and practice squarely in mind, it is unsurprising that his work has proven more congenial to American constitutional theorists than has Hart's—even while more contemporary general jurisprudents follow a broadly Hartian than Dworkinian line.

This section cannot undertake a lengthy analysis or critique of Dworkin. Its more modest objective is to clarify how law-as-argument differs from the Dworkinian theory of law as integrity and to say a few words to bolster the former's credentials. Let me acknowledge at the outset that, even if I succeed in what I attempt, it will fall far short of a decisive argument against Dworkin.[51] John Mackie memorably dubbed Dworkin's account the "third theory of law."[52] The ambition of this section is not yet to displace or defeat that third theory but to put law-as-argument on the table as a candidate fourth theory.

The most significant difference between law-as-argument and law-as-integrity traces to Dworkin's embrace of (what Himma calls) the Differentiation Thesis.[53] Section III argued that CoV could not emerge from conventional means, as Hart envisions. But it did not contend that legal propositions could not be conclusively validated, so long as the validity conditions were established in ways not similarly dependent on social convention. Dworkin satisfies this constraint, explicitly rejecting Hartian conventionalism in favor of a view that validates law

51. The existing literature does not want for criticisms of Dworkin's theory. Among other things, critics dispute his methodological claim that law—in both concept and content—must be identified by the process of "constructive interpretation," which aims to show legal materials and institutional practices in their best light; and they challenge his related conceptual claim that the point or function of law is to justify the use of governmental coercion. Many also object to the justificatory role that Dworkin ascribes to the political ideal of "integrity"—roughly the state of affairs in which legal rights and duties can be intelligibly imagined as having all been "created by a single author—the community personified—expressing a coherent conception of justice and fairness." DWORKIN, *supra* note 29, at 225. I am sympathetic to these criticisms and find it additionally revealing that, although Dworkin has won more influence among American constitutionalists than has Hart, one would have to search hard, and perhaps in vain, for an adherent who does not broadly share Dworkin's liberal egalitarian political values. At bottom, then, Dworkin's theory of law is too heroic and partisan to win widespread acceptance among jurisprudents or constitutional theorists.

52. John Mackie, *The Third Theory of Law*, 7 PHIL. & PUB. AFF. 3 (1977).

53. At the same time, there are similarities. For example, Dworkin has emphasized that "[l]egal practice, unlike many other social phenomena, is *argumentative*." DWORKIN, *supra* note 29, at 13. This particular superficial similarity, however, is just that. Dworkin's point was merely that, due to its argumentative nature, legal practice cannot be adequately understood from the external perspective of history or sociology; accounts of it must also attend to the internal perspective of participants in legal culture.

by reference to putatively objective moral facts.[54] Yet more strikingly, he concludes that morality's contribution to the content of law ensures that there are legally right answers to (virtually) all questions of law. In terms that resonate with what I have supposed is the principal challenge to law-as-argument, Dworkin responds to those who deny his right-answer thesis:

> They say there are no right answers but only different answers to hard questions of law, that insight is finally subjective, that it is only what seems right, for better or worse, to the particular judge on the day. But this modesty in fact contradicts what they say first, for when judges finally decide one way or another they think their arguments better than, not merely different from, arguments the other way; though they may think this with humility, wishing their confidence were greater or their time for decision longer, this is nevertheless their belief.[55]

Similarly, he says, someone who reaches a judgment in an evaluative or argumentative practice "thinks he has been driven by the truth, not that he has chosen one interpretation to wear for the day because he fancies it like a necktie."[56]

In contrast, law-as-argument denies that there need be a contradiction between the beliefs (1) that discrete arguments one accepts are better than those one rejects and (2) that there is no right answer to the bottom-line question of law at issue. It denies Dworkin's starkly binary view of the attitude or phenomenology of reaching judgments. It contends that there is a middle ground: one can think of oneself as driven neither by truth nor by choice, but by *argument*. Thus, whereas legal propositions just are, for Dworkin, what the balance of (mind-independent) reasons dictates, on the law-as-argument model they exist as the product, not of reasons, but of reason*ing*. They depend on what actual participants in the practice treat *as* reasons, through the discursive practice of crafting, deploying, evaluating, and weighing arguments.

The plausibility of this middle ground derives from two central features of legal practice. First, legal practice is open to a great many incommensurable considerations. Law is a forum for adjudication among arguments sounding in such disparate material as welfare, rights, justice, harm, tradition, stability, predictability, consistency, democracy, separation of powers, security, fairness, and

54. Precisely what Dworkin means by "objective" is notoriously slippery. It is not critical for my purposes to attribute to him any particular metaphysical thesis. As this section will endeavor to explain, the key point will be to deny Dworkin's effort to conceptualize or constitute law by reference to reified reasons—whatever their supposed ontological status. Law-as-argument insists that legal norms are constituted by actual arguing practice, that is, by the reasoning of participants in the practice. (I am grateful to Jerry Postema for encouraging me to clarify this point.)

55. DWORKIN, *supra* note 29, at 10.

56. *Id.* at 77.

much else besides. Surely some of these values and disvalues can be reduced to the same currency, but not all can be. So we can agree with Dworkin that a participant would believe that there are right answers to such questions as which legal solution better corresponds to what the drafters of the law intended or better promotes the good of wealth-maximization. But that doesn't entail that she also believes there is a right answer to the bottom-line question of how disparate considerations are better weighed against one another or stitched together to realize law. Indeed, I venture that most participants would have no clear sense of the metaphysics that could possibly make an answer uniquely correct.

Second, legal practice is an intensely practical enterprise, not a theoretical one. Because it requires participants to act on their judgments about law, it requires that they actually *reach* judgments, not just that they continually move toward them (as philosophy permits). It also requires that they reach those judgments within time constraints. To make this possible, legal practice structures reasoning in an "artificial" way, by, inter alia, protecting favored reasons with varied and implicit burdens of proof. Many reasons are accepted or entrenched not to render them beyond challenge, but to direct that they ought to be followed *until* being challenged and successfully dislodged. A participant is always entitled to urge a revision to settled ways of constituting law—settled canons of statutory interpretation, or modalities of constitutional argument, or ways of treating concurring opinions—but never (or rarely) required to give deeper reasons for going on as before. For these two reasons, perhaps among others, the principal touchstone for legal practice as we know it is not truth but reasonableness. Participants frequently defend a solution as being more reasonable than another, but rarely as being truer. And what is more reasonable is partly constituted by the structure and content of the practice.

Given law's commitment to practice-informed norms of reasonableness, the value and sense of the argumentative practice does not require participants to believe that a right answer preexists the activity of reasoning. What it requires instead are such things as an internalized sense of continuity with the practice or custom and a commitment to both accept and act on the conclusions that the successful arguments dictate, and to reason in consistent fashion in other cases. In this way, arguments serve a valuable function in constraining and disciplining decision making, to promote predictability and a certain distance from first-order views of policy and political morality—if not *im*partiality, then mitigated partiality.

Some scholars have intimated that to dispute the existence of right answers undermines the intelligibility of the "practice of giving reasons"—that we need to maintain a belief in the objectivity of the answers that the practice yields in order to sustain the practice itself.[57] It is this that I wish to deny. Skepticism that

57. *See, e.g.*, Brian Leiter, *Objectivity, Morality, and Adjudication, in* Objectivity in Law and Morals 66, 88 (Brian Leiter ed., 2001).

claims within an argumentative dialectic can be objectively true need not cause us to repudiate the discourse so long as we continue to view it as useful or valuable for human ends. A society needs to resolve disputes. Law serves this dispute-resolution function. We could imagine that law could assume a form other than as argumentative practice. Legal practice could be the reading of entrails. But it is true that, for us, legal practice is argumentative. And, while that might not be inevitable, it is surely no accident for creatures constituted roughly as we are. We can recognize that propositions of law (and perhaps of morality too) are the dynamic product of practice-constrained argumentation, and that the arguments, hence the propositions, are responsive to reason, without, I think, taking a position on whether such a mode of existence is perspicuously classified as objective or true.

I speculated at the end of Section IV that the greatest challenge for a theory of law-as-argumentative-practice is to explain how it can be sensible to continue to make judgments in realms one believes are not directed toward, and validated by, facts of the matter. Deploying Dworkin as a foil, I have sketched an outline of how I'd hope this challenge to be met. If that outline can be filled in successfully—if something like this concept of law-as-argument is correct[58]—then it offers a middle way between Hart and Dworkin. Judges aren't merely *discovering* law because it does not always exist prior to the argumentative activity; law *emerges from* the activity but does not always preexist it. But judges are not *creating* law, and surely not in the same sense that lawmakers do who are engaged in a political practice. Against Dworkin: arguments do not reveal what is already so, they make it so. Against Hart: law is established by practice-constrained argument, not by will. Put otherwise, the way that law-as-proposition or law-as-norm is made by law-as-practice is sufficiently dissimilar from the way that it is made by politics so that the conflation of the two methods is more obscuring than illuminating, more false than true.

VI. IMPLICATIONS FOR CONSTITUTIONAL THEORY

We can now spin out a few implications of an account of law as argumentative practice for the problems of retail and wholesale constitutional interpretation introduced in Section I.

---

58. I mean "correct" in a weak sense consistent with Raz's caution that "[t]here is no uniquely correct explanation of a concept, nothing which could qualify as *the* explanation of the concept of law. There can be a large number of correct alternative explanations of a concept. Not all of them will be equally appropriate for all occasions. Appropriateness is a matter of relevance to the interests of the expected or intended public, appropriateness to the questions which trouble it, to the puzzles which confuse it." Joseph Raz, *Two Views of the Nature of the Theory of Law: A Partial Comparison*, *in* HART'S POSTSCRIPT: ESSAYS ON THE POSTSCRIPT TO THE CONCEPT OF LAW 1, 10 (Jules Coleman ed., 2001).

First, to advance and engage arguments legitimated by practice is to do law. To affirm a particular norm or proposition as one of constitutional law is to assert the conclusion of an argument. Such norms and propositions are inescapably dynamic and contestable. Although Bobbitt's menu of extant argumentative modalities is too parsimonious, the fundamentals of his account of constitutional practice are, I believe, correct. There is no sharp divide between easy and hard cases; all constitutional questions can be arrayed upon a continuum. In some cases, the arguments on one side are so weighty and so little appears on the other side (perhaps nothing at all) that it is comfortable and nearly costless to treat the obvious resolution of argument as simply "the right answer." To take the customary example, it is unproblematically unlawful for any person not yet thirty-five to become president, not because there is a set of conditions that make this conclusively the case, but because those of us acculturated into the practice of constitutional law see a weighty argument in favor of it, envision little or nothing that can be said against it, and believe that other participants share these twin assessments. Similarly, even those of us who would have assessed arguments differently than did the Supreme Court in a recent case, and thus would have reached a different conclusion, agree that the Supreme Court's conclusion that *P*, and not our contrary conclusion that not-*P*, is law because the practice recognizes the fact of the Court's announcement of *P* as an extraordinarily weighty reason for *P*—weighty but, as Section III argued, not conclusive. Harder cases arise with respect to those questions of law for which more arguments appear "on point," lead in different directions, and have less well-settled weights. But, so long as we take ourselves to be operating within the practice and remain responsive to its argumentative norms, we do not cross a barrier (even a vague one) that separates law from nonlaw.

With respect to wholesale interpretation, the practice-based account suggests that arguments to revise more or less settled practices need not (as Matt Adler's analysis seems to assume)[59] be classified according to a neat dichotomy—either as claims regarding what the law already requires or as extralegal arguments grounded in political morality. Because the argumentative practice of law is so richly textured, it accommodates first-order arguments about what the law is as well as second-order arguments regarding the considerations that should shape and determine what the law is. As Postema explains about the common law:

> Intricately interwoven into the activity of adjudicating particular disputes by application of rules of law were the activities of articulating and justifying those rules. To the common lawyer's mind, these three activities—articulating standards, showing them to be reasonable and sound, and applying them to particular cases—were not three separate processes, but rather interrelated moments of a single process of discursive reasoning.[60]

---

59. *See* Adler, *supra* note 11.

60. Postema, *supra* note 39, at 167; see also the discussion of "meta-rules" in Fallon, *supra* note 11.

This means, for example, that arguments to pay more (or less) attention to original understandings, or to the text, or to judicial precedents, need not be extralegal arguments of political morality. They are, or can be, legal arguments. But to say that does not mean that there exists a proposition of law that requires these outcomes; it means that these are legitimate moves within, not external to, the practice.

All that said, two further comments about wholesale interpretation are warranted. First, a reader versed in contemporary interpretive debates might see an affinity between the argument put forth—which, after all, owes a substantial debt to the view that Postema has termed "common law conventionalism"—and David Strauss's theory of "common law constitutional interpretation."[61] According to Strauss, the dominant contemporary approaches to constitutional interpretation—textualism and originalism—are grounded in a broadly Austinian jurisprudential tradition that views law as the command of the sovereign. The principal historical competitor to that vision of law, Strauss observes, is the common law tradition that locates law in evolving understandings. And, he argues, "it is the common law approach, not the approach that connects law to an authoritative text, or an authoritative decision by the Framers or by 'we the people,' that best explains, and best justifies, American constitutional law today."[62]

Because I find so much of Strauss's analysis illuminating and persuasive, I will highlight two differences between his account of constitutional interpretation and law-as-argument as I conceive it. The first concerns jurisprudential grounding. Strauss's account is presented as a theory of constitutional interpretation designed to compete with alternative approaches within American constitutional theory and practice. In contrast, any lessons for constitutional interpretation that flow from law-as-argument are the byproduct of an account designed to offer an alternative to Hart and Dworkin. Common law constitutionalism is a descriptive and normative account of American constitutional practice. Law-as-argument is a conceptual account of the nature of law. Given the route I have taken to reach law-as-argument, it is no surprise that the account bears implications for U.S. constitutional theory. But whereas Strauss contrasts the common law method that he thinks suitable for American constitutional interpretation with methods more suited for statutory interpretation, law-as-argument aspires to be a theory of law that applies even to statutory departments. This is because legal practice has an inherent diachronic aspect and because there exists an ineliminable gap between legal texts and legal propositions and norms. It may well be that the argumentative dimension of law is less salient when the practice grapples with ordinary statutes, but from a jurisprudential perspective law-as-argument does not disown statutory law.

---

61. *See* David A. Strauss, *Common Law Constitutional Interpretation*, 63 U. Chi. L. Rev. 877 (1996).

62. *Id.* at 879.

Second and more importantly, because law-as-argument is more general, it takes no position on certain features of American constitutional practice that Strauss observes and extols. In particular, Strauss valorizes the undeniable empirical fact that a substantial portion of the norms and propositions of contemporary American constitutional law derive from judicial precedents and relate only tenuously to the constitutional text. Consequently, Akhil Amar had Strauss directly in his sights when arguing that courts should be less deferential to previous judicial statements of constitutional law and should instead rework constitutional law to better accord with the text.[63] But judicial precedent and constitutional text are just two modalities of constitutional argument, and there is nothing about law-as-argument that necessarily privileges the former over the latter. Thus, were Amar to convert more participants to his argumentative style or predispositions, that would merely amount to a development within American constitutional argumentative practice; it would not threaten or undermine law-as-argument. Put another way, (David) Straussians would have to resist a greater shift toward Amarian textualism by making arguments from within the practice, not by drawing forth any supposed entailments from law-as-argument as an account of law.

The point, in short, is that law-as-argument, as an account of law, does not entail any particular partisan position within the wholesale debates of constitutional interpretation. It accommodates participants whose sensibilities run in, for example, Straussian, Amarian, and originalist veins. It is tolerant and capacious—but not to a fault. Its limits appear when we shift attention from those who espouse originalist sensibilities to those who advocate "originalism," that is, the thesis that constitutional law, correctly understood, just is the original meaning of the constitutional text (or the intentions of those who drafted or ratified it, or something of this sort). I have challenged this claim elsewhere.[64] It is enough here to observe that, insofar as originalists argue that some original feature of the constitutional text conclusively determines what the law is, they are flirting (at the least) with the Differentiation Thesis. As we have seen, such a position will have to be defended on a nonconventionalist theory of law. Hart will not help them. Nor will law-as-argument.

VII. CONCLUSION

Contemporary jurisprudents differ regarding the extent to which advances in general jurisprudence are likely to contribute insights to more parochial departments of law. On one reading, Hart himself seemed to believe that advances in

---

63. *See* Akhil Reed Amar, *The Supreme Court, 1999 Term—Foreword: The Document and the Doctrine*, 114 Harv. L. Rev. 26 (2000).

64. Mitchell N. Berman, *Originalism is Bunk*, 84 N.Y.U. L. Rev. 1 (2009).

our very general and abstract understanding of the nature or concept of law should have something to contribute to theoretical questions that arise within, or are provoked by, a domain of law. Of course, he did not think that general jurisprudential inquiry could tell us what the law of any jurisdiction is or should be. Rather, he appeared to have assumed a point of contact between the somewhat more abstract questions about law that percolate upward from law practice and the somewhat more concrete implications for law that flow downward from the philosophy of law. On Hartian assumptions, then, attention to U.S. constitutional theory can serve as a partial proving ground for his own theory of law.

I have argued that Hartian positivism does not emerge whole from this encounter because the criteria of validity that it believes are necessary to conclusively validate legal norms cannot arise from a convergent social practice. That is this chapter's most important and distinctive claim. As a secondary and more tentative matter, the chapter adumbrates an account of law that might better fit the experience of U.S. constitutional law and the insights of American constitutional theorists. This alternative account views the practice dimension of law as primary. "Law, on this view, is a matter of convention, but it is a convention of a special sort, namely a practiced discipline of practical reasoning."[65] But, of course, Hart—and Dworkin too, for that matter—understood that law is a type of practice. For a practice-based view along the foregoing lines to qualify as a genuinely distinct theory of law, it will eschew both the Hartian premise that legal norms are conclusively validated by a set of necessary and sufficient conditions, and the Dworkinian claim that such norms are determined by facts of the matter that exist independent of, and guide, the reasoning of flesh-and-blood (non-Herculean) participants in the practice.

---

65. Postema, *supra* note 42, at 601.

11. WHERE HAVE ALL THE POWERS GONE?
Hartian Rules of Recognition, Noncognitivism, and the Constitutional and Jurisprudential Foundations of Law

STEPHEN PERRY*

I. INTRODUCTION

Hart famously maintains in *The Concept of Law* that "the key to the science of jurisprudence" can be found in what he calls the union of primary and secondary rules.[1] Secondary rules are meant, very roughly, to be the foundational rules of a legal system, whereas primary rules make up what might loosely be referred to as the system's "regular" laws. Hart discusses three specific kinds of secondary rules in *The Concept of Law*, which he calls rules of change, rules of adjudication, and rules of recognition.[2] A rule of change "empowers an individual or body of persons to introduce new primary rules for the conduct of the life of the group, or of some class within it, and to eliminate old rules."[3] A rule of adjudication "empower[s] individuals to make authoritative determinations of the question whether, on a particular occasion, a primary rule has been broken."[4] A rule of recognition "specif[ies] some feature or features possession of which by a suggested rule is taken as a conclusive affirmative indication that it is a rule of the group,"[5] which means in this context that it is a primary rule of the relevant legal system. Hart also characterizes a rule of recognition as "a rule for conclusive identification of the primary rules of obligation."[6] He comes to call the identifying features specified by the rule of recognition criteria of legal validity, or simply criteria of validity, and he refers to the primary rules themselves as legally valid (or simply valid) rules of the system in question. Criteria of validity typically look

---

* John J. O'Brien Professor of Law and Professor of Philosophy, University of Pennsylvania Law School. The title is offered with apologies to Pete Seeger. I would like to thank the participants in the Conference on the Rule of Recognition and the U.S. Constitution for helpful comments on an earlier draft. I am particularly indebted to Matt Adler for his insightful observations and questions.

1. H.L.A. Hart, The Concept of Law 81 (Penelope A. Bulloch & Joseph Raz eds., 2d ed. 1994).

2. *Id.* at 91–99.

3. *Id.* at 95.

4. *Id.* at 96.

5. *Id.* at 94.

6. *Id.* at 95.

to such sources of law as legislative enactment, judicial doctrines of precedent, and certain customary practices within some segments of society.

When Hart first introduces the distinction between primary and secondary rules, he suggests that what distinguishes the two types of rule is a difference in their normative character: secondary rules are said to be power conferring, whereas primary rules are duty imposing.[7] Neither of these characterizations can, however, be correct.[8] To see that primary rules cannot be regarded as exclusively duty imposing in nature, it is sufficient to point out that primary rules are simply valid rules of the relevant system, and as such they can certainly impose obligations, but they can also create powers, rights, privileges, immunities, liabilities, and so on. So long as a primary rule counts as valid according to one of the criteria of validity specified by the rule of recognition—for example, it was properly enacted by a legal system's legislature—it can be of any normative character whatever.

So far as secondary rules are concerned, rules of change and rules of adjudication are, quite evidently, power-conferring rules, and Hart's discussion of them clearly acknowledges as much. A rule of change confers powers to modify old rules and introduce new ones; in other words, it confers powers to legislate, or, more generally, powers to make law (for example, through the invocation by courts of a doctrine of precedent). Rules of adjudication confer the various powers to apply the law and, more generally, to settle disputes, which we typically associate with courts. Rules of recognition, however, cannot be understood as power conferring. Hart's initial characterization of a rule of recognition makes it sound as though it simply sets out a list of criteria of validity: rules of recognition "specify some feature or features" possession of which by other rules shows that those other rules have legal validity.[9] A list, however, is not a rule, power-conferring or otherwise; a list, considered simply as a list, has no normative character at all. For reasons that I will examine at greater length in Sections II and III, it becomes abundantly clear that Hart regards rules of recognition not as power conferring in character but rather as duty imposing. More specifically, he regards a rule of recognition as a rule that imposes on the officials of a given legal system a duty to apply and enforce the rules that the rule of recognition identifies as legally valid rules for that system.

7. *Id.* at 81.

8. It has often been remarked that Hart draws this important distinction in a number of different and ultimately inconsistent ways. *See, e.g.*, JOSEPH RAZ, THE AUTHORITY OF LAW 177–79 (1979); NEIL MACCORMICK, H.L.A. HART 103–06 (1981); P.M.S. Hacker, *Hart's Philosophy of Law, in* LAW, MORALITY, AND SOCIETY: ESSAYS IN HONOUR OF H.L.A. HART 1, 19–21 (P.M.S. Hacker & Joseph Raz eds., 1977); Stephen Perry, *Hart's Methodological Positivism, in* HART'S POSTSCRIPT: ESSAYS ON THE POSTSCRIPT TO THE CONCEPT OF LAW 311, 311 n.4 (Jules Coleman ed., 2001).

9. HART, *supra* note 1, at 94.

As Hart's discussion of secondary rules in general proceeds, it becomes increasingly clear that he regards rules of recognition as theoretically predominant among the three types of secondary rules he initially identifies, and indeed rules of change and rules of adjudication largely drop out of the picture altogether. The only secondary rule that remains standing, so to speak, is the rule of recognition, which Hart repeatedly refers to as the *ultimate* rule of a legal system.[10] Thus when Hart says that law is a combination of primary and secondary rules, one could be forgiven for thinking that what he means in the end is that law is a combination of a duty-imposing rule of recognition on the one hand, and the various rules that are identified by the rule of recognition as valid on the other hand. Thus, despite the fact that at one point Hart explicitly characterizes secondary rules as power-conferring by their very nature, the view he eventually appears to settle on is that the most fundamental element in the foundational arrangements of a legal system is a rule that is duty-imposing.

In this chapter I will argue that Hart's doctrine of the rule of recognition is flawed in two distinct but ultimately related ways. The first error is to conceive of the foundations of law as necessarily consisting of a rule that is *constituted* by a pattern of behavior and an associated normative attitude, which Hart calls the internal point of view. The second error is to emphasize the role of duty in the foundational arrangements of law, rather than the role of normative power. These two errors come together, in ways that I discuss in Section II, to unjustifiably restrict the scope of what Matthew Adler calls the "recognitional community"—that group of persons whose conduct plays a role in defining the content of the law in particular legal systems—to officials, and indeed not just to officials in general but to judges. As Adler points out, there are plausible views of American constitutional law in particular, generally known as popular constitutionalism, that accord at least some role in defining the content of constitutional law to citizens as well as to courts and legislatures. It is one of the conclusions of this chapter that there is no good reason, grounded either in jurisprudence or in abstract constitutional theory, to rule out in advance versions of popular constitutionalism as viable theories of American constitutional law.

In Section III of the chapter I show why Hart is mistaken, in his general discussion of the theoretical foundations of law, to privilege duty-imposing rules over power-conferring rules. I further show that this error, as well as the error of treating the foundational norm of every legal system as not just related to but actually constituted by certain kinds of social facts, ultimately have their source in Hart's adoption of a particular version of ethical noncognitivism. In Section IV I explore, in a preliminary fashion, certain further considerations that suggest that—even within the framework of Hart's own theory of law—first, power-conferring rules should perhaps be privileged over duty-imposing rules, and second, Hart might be mistaken in thinking that every legal system necessarily

10. *Id.* at 105–10.

contains a rule of recognition, in his sense of a *general* rule that imposes a duty on all officials (or on all judges) to apply all the other laws of the system.

Finally, in Section V I suggest that, while Hart was absolutely correct to emphasize the importance to legal theory of what he calls the internal point of view, his understanding of this notion was mistaken in two respects. The first was to regard the internal point of view as an attitude of *endorsing* the law as obligatory, rather than as involving a *belief* that the law possesses normative (meaning moral) powers. The second mistake was that he treated the internal point of view as a constitutive element of what he took to be the foundational element of every legal system, namely, the rule of recognition. Both these mistakes flow from Hart's adherence to noncognitivism. Once we abandon noncognitivism and embrace a properly cognitivist account of law's normativity, we are in a position to see that the most important theoretical feature of law is not the fact that officials endorse a certain duty-imposing norm as obligatory, but rather the fact that legal systems claim to possess legitimate moral authority. As Joseph Raz has often emphasized, to say that a legal system claims moral authority is to say that its officials and, typically, many other participants within the system *believe* that the system's institutions have extensive moral powers to change the normative situation of those who are subject to its laws. To properly understand the theoretical foundations of law we must therefore emphasize belief rather than endorsement, and power rather than duty. To envisage the theoretical foundations of law along these lines permits us better to appreciate Hart's own insight that the introduction into society of rules conferring legislative and adjudicative powers "is a step forward as important . . . as the invention of the wheel."[11] At the same time, to reject the idea that the most important foundational element of law is a duty-imposing norm that is simply *constituted* by certain kinds of social facts makes it possible to formulate much more nuanced views about the relationship between social facts and the normativity of law than Hart's own doctrine of the rule of recognition permits. Any proposed modifications of the doctrine that are sufficient to rectify its flaws will depart sufficiently from the spirit of Hart's views as to make the continued use of the term "rule of recognition" misleading at best.

II. SOCIAL RULES AND THE PROBLEM OF THE RECOGNITIONAL COMMUNITY

As is well known, in *The Concept of Law* H. L. A. Hart sets out existence conditions for a certain kind of customary or "social" rule, and then characterizes both the concept of law and the existence of legal systems by reference to a special

11. HART, *supra* note 1, at 41–42.

instance of just such a rule. The special instance of a social rule that plays this foundational role in every legal system is, of course, the rule of recognition.

Simplifying somewhat, a social rule is, according to Hart, a complex social practice that consists of a general and regular pattern of behavior among some group of persons, together with a widely shared attitude within the group that this pattern is a common standard of conduct to which all members of the group are required to conform. To use the rule is to conform one's individual conduct to the relevant pattern, and to accept the rule is to adopt the attitude that the pattern is a required standard of conduct both for oneself and for all other members of the group. To adopt this attitude is to take up what Hart calls the internal point of view, which is the point of view of someone who is concerned with rules "[not] merely as an observer who does not himself accept them, [but rather] as a member of the group which accepts and uses them as guides to conduct."[12] The existence of a Hartian social rule consists in these very facts of acceptance and use, which is to say that the rule is *constituted* by the regular pattern of conduct and the internal point of view that accompanies it. That a person has adopted the internal point of view toward a rule is typically indicated by, inter alia, the use of normative language such as "ought," "must," "right," and "wrong,"[13] and, in cases where "the general demand for conformity [to the rule] is insistent and the social pressure brought to bear upon those who deviate or threaten to deviate is great," by the use of the terms "obligation" or "duty."[14]

A rule of recognition is a social rule in just the sense characterized in the preceding paragraph, and according to Hart such a rule lies at the foundation of every legal system. The rule of recognition is a complex social practice that holds among those persons in a society whom we would intuitively recognize as its officials. The normative character of the rule of recognition, like all Hartian social rules, is requirement-imposing, which in the case of law means that it is duty- or obligation-imposing.[15] More particularly, it imposes a duty on officials to apply other rules that can, in accordance with criteria set out by the rule of recognition, be identified as valid law. The existence of a rule of recognition is, according to Hart, a necessary condition of the existence of a legal system. Since the rule of recognition, like other social rules, cannot exist unless a sufficiently large

---

12. *Id.* at 89.

13. *Id.* at 56–57.

14. *Id.* at 86–87. Hart adds that the use of the expressions "duty" and "obligation" is typically accompanied by two other characteristics, which are, first, that "[t]he rules supported by this serious pressure are believed to be necessary to the maintenance of social life or some highly prized feature of it," and second, that "it is generally recognized that the conduct required by these rules may, while benefiting others, conflict with what the person who owes the duty may wish to do." *Id.* at 87. For purposes of this chapter, I use the terms "obligation" and "duty" more or less interchangeably.

15. *Cf.* Raz, *supra* note 8, at 92–93.

number of people in the requisite group adopt the internal point of view, and since, for Hart, the requisite group is a society's officials, it follows that a legal system cannot exist unless most if not all of its officials adopt the internal point of view. By the same token, according to Hart, a legal system can exist even if no one besides its officials adopts the internal point of view.

A central difficulty with Hart's doctrine of the rule of recognition has been aptly labeled by Matthew Adler as "the problem of the recognitional community."[16] A central role of the rule of recognition is, according to Hart, to enumerate or define the criteria of legal validity, which determine which other norms are to count as laws or legal norms within the relevant legal system. As was noted earlier, Hart famously limits the scope of the rule of recognition to a legal system's *officials*. It is true that, for Hart, one of the "two minimum conditions necessary and sufficient for the existence of a legal system" is the system's general efficacy, but all this means is that the system's laws are generally complied with by the citizenry; it does not matter what each individual citizen's reasons for compliance are. The other minimum condition, by contrast, is more demanding, and applies to officials only: "[the system's] rules of recognition. . . and its rules of change and adjudication must be effectively accepted as common public standards of behavior by its officials."[17] This means, among other things, that officials must actually be guided by the rule of recognition in making their official decisions.[18] As Adler points out, the fact that Hart limits the scope of the rule of recognition to officialdom *necessarily* precludes various forms of popular constitutionalism—for example, Bruce Ackerman's notion that the citizenry is from time to time decisively involved in defining constitutional understandings[19]—unless the constitutional role of the citizenry is itself recognized by official practice.[20] In other words, Hart's restricted understanding of the rule of recognition necessarily rules out all versions of popular constitutionalism that claim, whether explicitly or implicitly, that the appropriate recognitional community includes, in one form or another, citizens as well as officials.

Les Green correctly observes that, for Hart, "the only consensus necessary for law is a consensus of elites," and that this truth "is a direct and potent consequence

---

16. Matthew D. Adler, *Popular Constitutionalism and the Rule of Recognition: Whose Practices Ground U.S. Law?*, 100 Nw. U. L. Rev. 719, 725 (2006).

17. Hart, *supra* note 1, at 116.

18. Hart is at pains to emphasize that officials can accept the rule of recognition for many reasons besides moral reasons. *See id.* at 203.

19. Bruce Ackerman, We The People: Foundations (1991). For other versions of popular constitutionalism, see, for example, Jeremy Waldron, Law and Disagreement (1999); Mark Tushnet, Taking the Constitution Away from the Courts (1999); Larry D. Kramer, The People Themselves: Popular Constitutionalism and Judicial Review (2004).

20. Adler, *supra* note 16, at 720–29.

of the fact that law is an institutionalized normative system."[21] He notes that Dworkin's understanding of Hart's view as involving a master rule that is accepted by a general community such as "the people of California"[22] is not only a "fantasy" but also an "abstraction," meaning a legal concept that itself stands in need of explanation.[23] Finally, Green observes that, for Hart himself, the social "advance" that accompanies the institutionalization of officialdom brings with it costs as well as benefits. As Hart wrote in a famous passage:

> In an extreme case the internal point of view with its characteristic normative use of legal language ("This is a valid rule") might be confined to the official world. In this more complex system, only officials might accept and use the system's criteria of legal validity. The society in which this was so might be deplorably sheeplike; the sheep might end in the slaughterhouse. But there is little reason for thinking that it could not exist or for denying it the title of a legal system.[24]

Jeremy Waldron points to this same passage to make a point similar to Green's:

> It is not just a matter of semantic scruple to deny that law is necessarily moral. And it's not just a pragmatic issue either: a matter of keeping one's conceptual ammunition dry. It is a matter of normative sociology: considering what positive law actually is, its existence in a society raises a real and serious prospect that it will be used to facilitate injustice and to confuse and mystify many of those who are subject to that injustice and who have no choice but to live their lives under its auspices.[25]

Green and Waldron are of course correct to emphasize that, for Hart, law involves a sociologically very significant divide between officials and its subjects, that this divide has potentially serious social costs as well as potential benefits, and that the existence of this divide is no doubt at least part of the reason that Hart limits the recognitional community to officials. But there is another, more straightforward reason why Hart imposes this limitation—and when viewed from a certain perspective it is, in fact, a much deeper reason—that is very much a matter of keeping one's conceptual ammunition dry. Recall that, for Hart, social rules are *constituted* by the behavior and attitudes of the relevant group. Because the existence on a shared and widespread basis of the internal point of view is one of the

21. Leslie Green, *The Concept of Law Revisited*, 94 MICH. L. REV. 1687, 1702 (1996).

22. Rather interestingly, Dworkin mistakenly interprets Hart as holding what in effect amounts to a version of popular consitutionalism, since he suggests that for Hart the rule of recognition is a "fundamental master rule" that is accepted "by the community as a whole." *See* RONALD DWORKIN, LAW'S EMPIRE 34 (1986).

23. Green, *supra note* 21, at 1700–01.

24. HART, *supra* note 1, at 117.

25. Jeremy Waldron, *All We Like Sheep*, 12 CAN. J. L. & JUR. 169, 181 (1999).

constitutive elements of the rule of recognition, Hart was *forced* to restrict the group whose practice is said to comprise the rule to persons who could, in fact, be generally expected to have adopted the internal point of view. As a practical and empirical matter, this group is essentially limited to officials. If the relevant group were extended to include citizens generally, then because many and perhaps even most citizens may have adopted the external rather than the internal point of view,[26] Hart would face the embarrassment of having to treat states that most people would unhesitatingly regard as having legal systems as not, in fact, having them; such states would not have a rule of recognition, and hence would not have law. On the other hand, again because the internal point of view is partly constitutive of the rule of recognition, Hart is very naturally led to the view that, so long as a given political regime is efficacious in the sense that most people generally comply with its directives, it is still a legal system even if *no one* other than its officials adopts the internal point of view. Even granting the sociological points that Green and Waldron emphasize, it is far from clear that such a regime has the full conceptual *bona fides* that would entitle us to call it a legal system. At the very least, I think we are often inclined to agree with John Finnis that many such regimes are not properly characterized as "central cases" of legal systems.[27] I will return to this point in Section V.

In fact, Hart's characterization of a social rule boxes him into an even narrower conceptual corner than is involved in limiting the rule of recognition to officials. The rule of recognition, like all Hartian social rules, is obligation- or duty-imposing,[28] which means that, normatively speaking, it is a rule that imposes a duty to apply and enforce the valid rules of the relevant legal system. This point is underscored by Hart's constant comparisons of the rule of recognition to the scoring rule of a game, which imposes a duty on the scorer to apply and enforce the game's rules.[29] In the legal case the recognitional community is thus most naturally limited not to officials generally, but to officials who have a duty to apply and enforce the system's primary rules. It is often remarked that as Hart's discussion in *The Concept of Law* proceeds, he speaks less frequently of officials generally, and focuses more and more on judges in particular. In the Postcript to the second edition, Hart writes that "the rule of recognition . . . is in effect a form of judicial customary rule existing only if it is accepted and practiced

---

26. Hart defines the external point of view as, essentially, the viewpoint of someone who conforms his behavior to the rules of the system for purely prudential reasons, and not because he or she has adopted the internal point of view. *See* HART, *supra* note 1, at 89.

27. JOHN FINNIS, NATURAL LAW AND NATURAL RIGHTS 9–11 (1980).

28. Strictly speaking, Hartian social rules are, as a class, requirement imposing, but in the legal context they will always be obligation imposing. *See supra* note 14 for discussion of the further features of a rule that are, according to Hart, necessary to turn a requirement-imposing rule into a duty- or obligation imposing rule.

29. HART, *supra* note 1, at 102.

in the law-identifying and law-applying operations of the courts."[30] This is no accident, because the officials of a legal system who are primarily charged with applying and enforcing the law are, of course, judges. Thus the fact that Hart characterizes social rules as necessarily constituted by the behavior and attitudes of the members of the relevant group, together with the further fact that Hartian social rules are, normatively speaking, always duty imposing, almost inevitably forces Hart to adopt what has been called a "judicial supremacy" understanding of the recognitional community.[31] Thus, despite the fact that Hart vigorously rejects the American realist thesis that the law or the constitution "is what the courts say it is,"[32] his restriction of the recognitional community to judges entails that there is a sense in which this claim turns out to be true within his own theory of law, and Hart explicitly acknowledges as much.[33]

The feature of Hartian rules of recognition that restricts their scope to recognitional communities consisting solely of judges might seem at first glance to align quite naturally with American constitutional practice, given the centrality to that practice of the doctrine of judicial review. This is, however, too simplistic a view of the matter, as Matthew Adler has shown by distinguishing between what he calls "shallow" and "deep" versions of judicial supremacy. Shallow judicial supremacy is a claim "about the structure of constitutional decisionmaking."[34] Thus the shallow judicial supremacist will endorse *Cooper v. Aaron*,[35] in which the U.S. Supreme Court held that the propositions of constitutional law propounded in its opinions are legally binding on all nonjudicial officials and not merely on the parties to the case at hand. The shallow judicial supremacist

---

30. *Id.* at 256. *See also id.* at 116: "[The ultimate rule of recognition], if it is to exist at all, must be regarded from the internal point of view as a public, common standard of correct judicial decision, and not as something which each judge merely obeys for his part only."

31. *See, e.g.*, Kenneth Einar Himma, *Making Sense of Constitutional Disagreement: Legal Positivism, The Bill of Rights, and the Conventional Rule of Recognition in the United States*, 4 J. L. Soc'y 149 (2003); Kenneth Einar Himma, *Final Authority to Bind with Moral Mistakes: On the Explanatory Potential of Inclusive Legal Positivism*, 24 Law & Phil. 1 (2005); Kenneth Einar Himma, *Understanding the Relationship between the U.S. Constitution and the Conventional Rule of Recognition* (Chapter 4, this volume).

32. Hart, *supra* note 1, at 141.

33. "It is, of course, possible that behind the shield of the rules which make judicial decisions final and authoritative, judges might combine in rejecting the existing rules and cease to regard even the clearest Acts of Parliament as imposing any limits on their decisions. If the majority of their rulings were of this character and were accepted this would amount to a transformation of the system parallel to the conversion of a game from cricket to 'scorer's discretion.'" *Id.* at 146. In fact a judicial transformation of the legal system along the lines Hart here contemplates would not necessarily involve its conversion to a completely discretionary system, since the judges might collectively simply replace the old set of rules with a new set.

34. Adler, *supra* note 16, at 798.

35. 358 U.S. 1 (1958).

might also be expected to maintain that the Supreme Court should be fairly nondeferential toward other branches of government.[36] Deep judicial supremacy, on the other hand, involves a claim about the recognitional community that is associated with the rule of recognition. Thus, according to the deep version of judicial supremacy, "the constitutional role of nonjudicial actors is necessarily defined by judges."[37] While it may be that the courts, including in particular the Supreme Court, have adopted doctrines that defer to the views of other institutional actors in various circumstances—for example, various "rational basis" tests or the "political question" doctrine—all such limitations on judicial supremacy "must ultimately be legally justified by appeal to judicial practice."[38] According to Adler, one's "deep" theory can focus on judges, officials, the people, or some mixture of these groups as comprising the appropriate recognitional community, and he further argues that any one of these views can be combined with any of a range of "shallow" theses about whose views of constitutional doctrine should legally prevail. Thus the shallow judicial supremacist will, as already noted, endorse *Cooper v. Aaron*, whereas the shallow popular constitutionalist will at a minimum reject *Cooper* and will perhaps also endorse the view that judges or legislators should under certain circumstances defer to popular constitutional views.[39] Employing Adler's terminology, the problem with Hart's restricted understanding of the recognitional community is that it permits only "shallow" understandings of popular constitutionalism, and necessarily rules out all "deep" versions. In other words, it rules out all versions in which the recognitional community itself is composed, at least in part and for some purposes, of citizens as well as of officials.

If one adopted a sufficiently loose definition of what kinds of social practices are capable of constituting a rule, or if one treated the rule of recognition as

---

36. Adler, *supra* note 16, at 798.

37. *Id.* at 725.

38. *Id.* at 725. I am not sure that Adler should define deep judicial supremacy by reference to a notion of *legal* justification, as opposed to the simple descriptive idea that it is the practice of judges, and judges alone, that defines both the scope of the rule of recognition and the content of the law. Of course, considerations of principle and policy can enter, as a matter of essentially external rather than legal justification, to defend claims that a particular legal system ought to adopt one understanding of the recognitional community rather than another. For present purposes, however, this is a minor point.

39. Adler characterizes Ken Himma as a scholar whose "deep" theory regards officials generally, and not just judges, as the appropriate recognitional community, but who nonetheless embraces shallow judicial supremacy because the rule of recognition requires, according to Himma, that all nonjudicial actors defer to the Supreme Court on matters of constitutional interpretation. Adler, *supra* note 16, at 800, discussing Himma, *Making Sense of Constitutional Disagreement*, *supra* note 31. Adler himself argues that, at least from a moral perspective, it might be appropriate to acknowledge the existence of a "heterogeneity" of recognitional communities. Adler, *supra* note 16, at 729.

essentially just a list of criteria of legal validity that can in some, possibly quite loose, sense be "accepted" by a group of persons, then Adler might be correct that theorists (and perhaps the law itself) could choose among a range of recognitional communities, and that this choice could be made by reference to a variety of policy- or principle-based rationales. It is important to emphasize, however, that Hart did not himself see the matter that way. Because he treated the internal point of view as in part constitutive of the rule of recognition, he had to limit the recognitional community to persons who could be expected to have adopted the internal point of view, and that meant, essentially, officials. And because he treated the rule of recognition as a duty-imposing rule—more specifically, a rule imposing a duty to apply the law—he had to further limit the recognitional community to officials who indeed can plausibly be said to have such a duty, and the most important class of such officials is judges. For these reasons, Hart was committed to the view that deep judicial supremacy is true of all legal systems: according to Hart this is, in effect, a conceptual truth about law. However, as I shall argue in the remainder of this chapter, an appropriate theoretical characterization of the foundations of law should not force us to privilege the theoretical status of judges over that of, say, legislators. Nor should an appropriate theoretical characterization of the foundations of law force us, as a matter of pure jurisprudence, to exclude from the outset some version of "deep" popular constitutionalism.

III. THE RELATIONSHIP BETWEEN POWER-CONFERRING AND DUTY-IMPOSING RULES

As we have seen in preceding sections, Hart says that law is the union of primary and secondary rules. Primary rules are just the regular laws of the legal system; they are rules that possess the property of legal validity. Secondary rules are the fundamental or foundational rules of a legal system. They do not possess the property of validity, but exist only as complex social practices among officials. Hart points to three specific types of social rules, namely rules of recognition, rules of change, and rules of adjudication. Rules of recognition are duty imposing, whereas rules of change and rules of adjudication are power conferring. The rule of recognition is said to be a special case of a social rule. Hart analyzes the notion of a social rule, which he also calls a customary rule, in some detail, by specifying a set of existence conditions for such rules. Since social rules are, in their nature, duty imposing,[40] Hart's analysis of a social rule is a general account of how duty-imposing rules can exist simply as social practices. The rule of recognition has, in effect, two functions: it provides a list of criteria that determine

40. This is a slight oversimplification. *See supra* notes 14, 28.

which other rules are primary or valid rules of the system; and it imposes on officials concerned with the application of laws—and, more particularly, on judges—a duty to apply the system's valid laws.

At this point it is helpful to recall the second of the two minimum conditions that Hart says are necessary and sufficient for the existence of a legal system: "[the system's] rules of recognition specifying the criteria of legal validity and its rules of change and adjudication must be effectively accepted as common public standards of behaviour by its officials."[41] Hart here states that not just the duty-imposing rule of recognition, but also the power-conferring rules of change and rules of adjudication, must be accepted as "common public standards of behaviour by [the system's] officials." Given Hart's detailed analysis of duty-imposing social rules in general, and of rules of recognition in particular, as customary practices, it would make sense to expect that he would likewise regard the other two kinds of fundamental secondary rules as being themselves, in some appropriate sense, customary practices in their own right. For purposes of further discussion, let me focus on the case of rules of change.[42] In the context of English law, for example, it certainly makes sense to think of Parliament, which is the primary and ultimate body exercising legislative power in England, as having evolved as a matter of custom over time.[43] Furthermore, despite the fact that Parliament has changed its own character by means of many legislatively based modifications over the years, it still seems correct to say that, in Hartian terms, Parliament and its associated powers exist because of the complex customary practices of officials generally, including legislators in particular. The situation in American law might at first glance seem to be more complicated because of the existence of a written constitution, but here too the same basic point would seem to hold. Consider, for example, the Amending Power in Article V, the "Powers Granted to Congress" in Article 1, Section 8, and the "Powers Forbidden

---

41. Hart, *supra* note 1, at 116.

42. It is of course possible to imagine a marginal case of a legal system that does not possess a rule of change at all, and in which all the primary rules that the rule of recognition obligates judges to apply are preexisting customary rules that hold among the population at large or among some segment of the population (for example, the rules of the old law merchant). But we do not have a central case of a legal system in anything like the modern sense until there exists some person or body that is capable of enacting new rules, which means, in Hartian terms, that the system contains at least one rule of change.

43. I am using the term "custom" in a loose and intuitive sense here, in what I take to be the spirit of Hart's own reference to practices that are "effectively accepted as common public standards of behaviour by. . . officials." *Id.* at 116. Thus I am not using the term in the strict sense that Hart elsewhere adopts when he simply *defines* a custom as a social rule in his sense. MacCormick, in an interesting discussion that seems to rely on a similarly loose understanding of custom, describes a hypothetical historical process out of which modern rules of change and rules of adjudication might have emerged from much simpler and more purely customary practices. *See* MacCormick, *supra* note 8, at 118–19.

to Congress" in Article 1, Section 9. As Kent Greenawalt pointed out in his classic article "The Rule of Recognition and the Constitution," the most plausible characterization of the current situation is that "the legal authority" of the original Constitution minus the ratification clause "is established by its continued acceptance and that the original ratification procedure is no longer directly relevant to tracing what counts as law. . . ."[44]

Hart tells us that there will be a very close connection between rules of change and rules of recognition, "for where the former exists the latter will necessarily incorporate a reference to legislation as an identifying feature of the rules, though it need not refer to all the details of procedure involved in legislation."[45] This point is well illustrated, and better so than Hart perhaps intended, by his paradigmatic example of a rule of recognition, namely, "What the Queen in Parliament enacts is law."[46] This statement is best conceived not simply as a rule of recognition, but rather as a complex statement of two quite different rules. The first, which could be rephrased as something like "The Queen in Parliament has the power to enact valid law for all the Queen's subjects," is a rule of change.[47] The second, which could be rephrased along the lines of "The courts (and other law-applying officials) have the duty to apply all and only laws that meet such and such criteria of validity, including, in particular, the criterion of having been enacted by the Queen in Parliament," is a rule of recognition.[48] Normatively and

---

44. Kent Greenawalt, *The Rule of Recognition and the Constitution*, 85 MICH. L. REV. 621, 640 (1987) (reprinted as Chapter 1, this volume, at 19).

45. HART, *supra* note 1, at 96.

46. *Id.* at 107.

47. This statement of the rule is of course a first approximation only, because sophisticated legal systems regulate their own character and content and so can, by the enactment of valid laws or the adoption of appropriate constitutional changes, modify in various, often quite complex ways the makeup of the legislature, its rules of procedure, and so on. But the same point of course also holds true of the rules governing, say, the jurisdiction and procedures of the courts, even though the rule of recognition only exists, for Hart, as a customary practice among judges. A similar point would presumably hold of the fundamental rules of adjudication. Perhaps the most appropriate characterization of the situation in all three cases is to say that fundamental customary practices can change over time, and sometimes such changes have legal sources. But just as it is true for changes in the rule of recognition that, as Hart says, "all that succeeds is success" (HART, *supra* note 1, at 153), presumably a parallel point also holds of changes in the fundamental power-conferring rules of change and adjudication that are no doubt constituted by the customary practices of many kinds of officials, and not just judges. As MacCormick correctly observes, "[w]e have to reconsider the content and mutual relationship of rules of change, rules of adjudication, and rules of legislative change. We have to see how such rules can develop in interaction with each other as an historical process." MACCORMICK, *supra* note 8, at 120.

48. Raz observes that the logical form of a rule of recognition is "All law-applying officials have a duty to apply all and only laws that satisfy the following criteria:. . . ." RAZ, *supra* note 8, at 93 n.29.

conceptually, these are distinct rules. That Hart could so readily run them together suggests, among other things, first, that he did indeed conceive of rules of change and rules of recognition as having within legal systems a similar and equally fundamental status, and second, that he probably implicitly conceived of the most fundamental rule of change as being, like the rule of recognition, customary in character.

If the foregoing is correct, however, there would appear to be an omission in Hart's theory of law, which is his failure to offer an explicit analysis of the character of fundamental power-conferring rules that would correspond to his analysis of the rule of recognition. I have suggested that for Hart rules of change are, like social rules, best understood as themselves customary in nature (and a similar point would presumably hold for rules of adjudication).[49] What is apparently required, then, is an account of how customary rules can be power-conferring and not just duty-imposing. But even if it is a mistake to suggest that rules of change and rules of adjudication are, within the framework of Hart's theory, best understood as customary in nature, it nonetheless remains puzzling why Hart did not offer *some* account of the theoretical character of fundamental power-conferring rules. This is particularly puzzling given his statement earlier in *The Concept of Law* that "the introduction into society of rules enabling legislators to change and add to the rules of duty, and judges to determine when the rules of duty have been broken, is a step forward as important to society as the invention of the wheel."[50] Later he makes a similar point when he writes that "the simple idea of orders, habits and obedience cannot be adequate for the analysis of law," and that "[w]hat is required instead is the notion of a rule conferring powers. . . on

---

49. I defend this view at greater length in Stephen Perry, *Hart on Social Rules and the Foundations of Law: Liberating the Internal Point of View*, 75 FORDHAM L. REV. 1171, 1184–89 (2006). At one point, Joseph Raz writes that "All the laws of a legal system, except the rule of recognition the existence of which is a matter of social practice, are valid; they exist in the system because they satisfy some criterion of validity." RAZ, *supra* note 8, at 95. This would appear to suggest that the most fundamental rules of change and rules of adjudication are, contrary to Hart's own suggestion, not secondary rules at all but mere primary rules, meaning valid rules of the system. It is, however, difficult to see what criterion of validity could establish the validity of fundamental rules of change and adjudication other than some conception of custom. In that case, however, it is not clear why we would not speak of them as theoretically on a par with the rule of recognition, as indeed Hart does when he first introduces the three distinct categories of secondary rules, rather than speaking of them as rules that are merely valid. The more plausible intuitive view of the matter is precisely the one that Hart initially offers, namely, that we have three distinct kinds of secondary rule, where "secondary rule" is best understood as referring to a customary practice of some sort that is part of the foundational arrangements of a legal system.

50. Hart, *supra* note 1, at 41–42.

persons qualified in certain ways to legislate by complying with a certain procedure."[51]

To get a better sense of why this gap in Hart's account exists, we need to take a step back so as to be able to appreciate that a form of noncognitivist metaethics informed every aspect of his theory of law, and indeed virtually every aspect of his philosophizing about normative matters generally. To see this, it will be helpful to begin by focusing on Hart's notion of the internal point of view, which serves two particularly important and related roles in Hart's theory of law. The first role, as we saw earlier in Section II, is to specify one of the constitutive elements of the complex social practice that comprises a legal system, and, more particularly, to specify the element that permits us to say that law is not just a social practice, but a normative social practice. The second role is to explain the normative dimension of the meaning of such statements as "It is the law of Pennsylvania that everyone has an obligation to do *X*."[52] John Austin and Jeremy Bentham had maintained that law could be explained as a general habit of obedience, and that the concept of obligation could be reduced to the non-normative concepts of threat and sanction. Hart argues very persuasively, and to the satisfaction of virtually all of his successors in jurisprudence, that neither of these reductive analyses has any hope of success, precisely because they omit the normative dimension of, respectively, the practice of law and the concept of obligation. In each case, the remedy that Hart proposes to cure the defect is the internal point of view. Habits and rules both involve regular patterns of behavior, but rules also involve, and are partly constituted by, a characteristic normative attitude: those who accept the rule regard the pattern of behavior as a common and binding standard of conduct, and the characteristic attitude that marks this acceptance is itself partly constitutive of the rule.

It will be helpful to elaborate more fully on the role of the internal point of view in Hart's analysis of the meaning of legal statements. As Raz has pointed out, Hart's noncognitivist commitments lead him to analyze normative statements as having both a cognitivist and a noncognitivist dimension. Thus the meaning of a legal statement made from the internal point of view—for example, "It is the law of Pennsylvania that everyone has an obligation to do *X*"—involves, according to Raz's account of Hart's semantics, a kind of hybrid, "stating how things are under the law, while endorsing or expressing an endorsement of the

51. *Id.* at 77.

52. Scott Shapiro suggests that the internal point of view serves four distinct roles in Hart's theory of law, of which these are but two. The others are to specify a particular kind of motivation that the law can provide, and to offer an account of the intelligibility of legal practice. Scott Shapiro, *What is the Internal Point of View?*, 75 FORDHAM L. REV. 1157, 1158 (2006).

law at the same time."[53] On this view, all internal legal statements have truth conditions that derive from the general social practice that constitutes the rule of recognition. There is thus an ascertainable fact of the matter as to whether or not Pennsylvania has a law to the effect that everyone has an obligation to do *X*, and we can ascertain what the facts are by looking, for example, to the past activities of Pennsylvania's legislature. However, the meaning of the *normative* aspect of an internal legal statement has nothing to do with whether the residents of Pennsylvania do or do not, in fact, have an obligation to do *X*. It consists, rather, in the expressed endorsement of the relevant standard of conduct as obligatory for all those who fall within the standard's scope. This endorsement is expressed through the adoption of the internal point of view, which consists not of a belief that the law gives rise to obligations, but rather of an attitude of accepting the law as obligatory.[54] Attitudes, unlike beliefs, cannot be true or false. Thus, although Hart is not strictly speaking a reductivist about legal normativity—since he is not trying to reduce normative concepts to non-normative concepts as his positivist predecessors were—there is nonetheless a certain affinity between his view and theirs, since his noncognitivist explanation of normativity does not involve an account of how law might actually or potentially give rise to true obligations.

Once one sees this latter point, much else about Hart's general theory of law begins to fall into place. Despite Hart's rejection of his predecessors' sanction- and

53. Joseph Raz, *Two Views of the Nature of Law: A Partial Comparison*, 4 LEGAL THEORY 249, 251 (1998). To the best of my knowledge, the noncognitivist aspect of Hart's understanding of the meaning of normative statements was first noticed by Raz. *See* Joseph Raz, *The Purity of the Pure Theory*, 138 REVUE INTERNATIONALE DE PHILOSOPHIE 441, 447–48, 454 (1981); Joseph Raz, *H.L.A. Hart (1907–1992)*, 5 UTILITAS 145, 147–49 (1993). Hart explicitly states that he accepts a noncognitivist analysis of legal statements. H.L.A. HART, ESSAYS ON BENTHAM 158–60 (1982). Kevin Toh makes a careful and detailed case for the view that Hart is a norm-expressivist, meaning that he adopts an expressivist semantic strategy in combination with noncognitivism to explain the meaning of statements containing normative terms. Kevin Toh, *Hart's Expressivism and his Benthamite Project*, 11 LEGAL THEORY 75 (2005). Scott Shapiro appears to offer a similar view of Hart's semantics. Shapiro, *supra* note 52, at 1168–70. Although nothing turns on the point for present purposes, Raz does not appear to regard Hart's noncognitivism as a form of norm-expressivism, suggesting instead that it grows out of J. L. Austin's theory of performative utterances that can have various kinds of illoctionary force. *See, e.g.*, Raz, *H.L.A. Hart (1907–1992)*, *supra*, at 149. Austin's most complete statement of his theory of performative utterances is to be found in J.L. AUSTIN, HOW TO DO THINGS WITH WORDS (1962).

54. It is important to emphasize that, according to Hart, one can adopt the internal point of view toward the rule of recognition for nonmoral as well as for moral reasons, from which it follows that he does not regard the noncognitivist, normative dimension of legal statements as necessarily involving moral endorsement of the law. *See* HART, *supra* note 1, at 203.

prediction-based theories of law,[55] he nonetheless shared their commitments to naturalism and empiricism. These commitments are reflected in his noncognitivism, which in turn permits him to offer a certain kind of weak explanation of the normativity of both social rules like the rule of recognition and internal legal statements like "It is the law of Pennsylvania that X." The essence of this explanation is that one who adopts the internal point of view does not, as Kelsen would have it, express a *belief* in the reason-givingness of a norm but rather expresses, as Raz describes Hart's view, "an attitude of willingness to be guided in a certain way."[56] In further keeping with his commitments to naturalism and empiricism, Hart is interested in rules not as a source of reasons for action,[57] but rather as a certain kind of complex social practice that can explain the existence of law in purely empirical terms and in a way that lends itself to description that is wholly value-neutral. The need for rules that can explain law as a complex but nonetheless self-contained form of social practice leads Hart to treat the internal point of view, which is the upshot of his weak explanation of normativity, as a constitutive element of the rule of recognition. As we have seen in Section II, the fact that the internal point of view plays this constitutive role is the ultimate explanation for Hart's limitation of the recognitional community to officials. As we shall further see in the current section, Hart has no plausible noncognitivist analysis of power-conferring rules that would correspond to his analysis of duty-imposing rules. He therefore had no practical choice but to make a duty-imposing rule—namely, the rule of recognition—the most important theoretical element in his account of the foundations of law. As we have further seen in Section II, it is the duty-imposing character of the rule of recognition that forces

55. But note the following observation by Raz: "[Hart's noncognitivist position] led Hart to emphasize not people's views about what ought to be done, but their willingness to criticize and put pressure on those who fail to do so. His is, therefore, a sanction theory of rules and duties. The existence of social rules does not depend on the existence of institutionalized sanctions characteristic of the law. But it does depend on diffuse critical reactions that Hart treated as nebulous sanctions rather than as merely the expression of people's judgements about their duties and their and others' conformity to them." Raz, *H.L.A. Hart (1907–1992)*, *supra* note 53, at 149.

56. Raz, *The Purity of the Pure Theory*, *supra* note 53, at 454. Raz also makes the following, related observation: "[Hart] is not specifically interested in the descent of normative force from one norm to another. Validity indicates just membership in a system established in a certain way. It has little to do with binding force." *Id.* at 458. This observation makes complete sense in light of Raz's further remark that "[i]f the judicial practices which according to Hart establish the existence of the rule of recognition were also to endow it with normative status this could only be in virtue of yet another norm which would itself become the ultimate rule of the system." *Id.* It is worth pointing out that Shapiro takes Hart's doctrine of the rule of recognition to be a solution, and a successful one at that, to precisely this "chicken and egg" problem of ultimate authority. *See* Scott Shapiro, *On Hart's Way Out*, 4 LEGAL THEORY 469 (1998).

57. *See infra* note 96.

Hart to further restrict the recognitional community not just to officials generally but to law-applying officials and, more particularly, to judges.

With these points about Hart's noncognitivism in mind, let us return to the question of the theoretical status, within Hart's theory, of fundamental power-conferring rules such as a rule of change. I suggested earlier that the most natural understanding of such rules is that they are customary in nature, like the rule of recognition. But Hart's noncognitivism makes it difficult to offer a precise analysis of a customary power-conferring rule that would parallel his analysis of duty-imposing customary rules (i.e., social rules). If one thinks that normativity is appropriately explained by reference to a certain kind of attitude of endorsement, then the general contours of the account that one will be inclined to offer of the existence conditions of duty-imposing customary rules seem intuitive enough. One will point, as Hart does, to the fact that under certain circumstances everyone in a group tends to behave the same way, and one will also point, as Hart does, to the fact that this regular pattern of behavior is accompanied by a "critical reflective attitude" that disposes persons to endorse the pattern as a binding standard of conduct, to criticize behavior that deviates from the pattern, and so on. But how would one go about offering a parallel analysis of the existence conditions of a power-conferring customary norm? Given that Hart's noncognitivism has its origins in J. L. Austin's theory of performatives,[58] one might begin by pointing to the fact that legislators make legislative utterances with the intention of effecting a certain kind of change in the world, namely, a change in the normative situation of their subjects. We can think of a lawmaking act as an assertion made under certain formalized circumstances that is meant to have illocutionary force; more specifically, it is an assertion that is uttered precisely with the intention of changing the normative situation of others.[59] Perhaps one might then characterize the power-conferring rule itself as the general practice, on the part of appropriately designated persons, of routinely engaging in lawmaking acts of this kind.

The difficulty to which this sketch of an account of customary power-conferring rules would seem to give rise, however, is that it is difficult to find an appropriate analogue to the internal aspect of a duty-imposing rule.[60] As has already been noted, someone who exercises (or purports to exercise) a power to change the

---

58. *See supra* note 53. Hart explicitly characterizes lawmaking acts in terms of Austinian performatives in ESSAYS ON BENTHAM, *supra* note 53, at 260.

59. Raz defends the very plausible view that a person has a power to effect a normative change if there is sufficient reason for regarding an intentional action on his or her part as effecting such a change, and if the justification for so regarding the action is that it is desirable to enable persons to make such normative changes by means of such acts. *See, e.g.*, RAZ, *supra* note 8, at 18. MacCormick apparently takes the view that one can only exercise a power by invoking a power-conferring rule. *See* MACCORMICK, *supra* note 8, at 73–74. It is far from evident that this is so, however; it is possible to offer accounts of normative powers that are not rule- or practice-based.

60. I offer a more lengthy discussion of the difficulties that would face a noncognitivist account of customary power-conferring rules in Perry, *supra* note 49, at 1192–95. As I note

normative situation of another can normally be expected to have an intention to effect just such a normative change. This intention is, in addition, presumably normally accompanied by a belief that there is some fact of the matter about what the other person's current normative status is, as well as a belief that one's action has succeeded (or not) in changing that status. This combination of mental states—an intention to change the normative situation of another, together with various beliefs about the other's current and future normative status—are simply not equivalent to, or in any obvious way redescribable as, attitudes of endorsement. The most straightforward analysis of the practice of exercising a normative power would thus appear to be cognitivist in nature.[61] I do not mean to deny that there might be responses that a sophisticated noncognitivist could offer to this apparent difficulty. But the fact that there is clearly a difficulty to be faced could well explain why Hart did not even attempt to offer a precise analysis of the character of customary power-conferring rules that would be analogous to his noncognitivist analysis of customary duty-imposing rules.

I have been discussing Hart's failure to offer any analysis in *The Concept of Law* of the notion of a power-conferring rule, and the possible strategy for rectifying this failure that I have been considering so far would involve analyzing power-conferring rules as a distinct type of customary rule in their own right. There is, however, another possible strategy for rectifying this omission, which would involve analyzing all power-conferring rules as duty-imposing rules. Hart does, in fact, propose at least a partial reductive analysis along these lines in the following passage from his later work *Essays on Bentham*:

> [T]he general recognition in a society of [a] commander's words as peremptory reasons for action is equivalent to the existence of a social rule. Regarded in one way as providing a general guide and standard of evaluation for the conduct of the commander's subjects, this rule might be formulated as the rule that the commander is to be obeyed and so would appear as a rule imposing obligations on the subject. Regarded in another way as conferring authority on the commander and providing him with a guide to the scope or manner of exercise it would be formulated as the rule that the commander may by issuing commands create obligations for his subjects and would be regarded as a rule conferring legal powers upon him.[62]

---

there, such an account would probably face a version of the Frege–Geach problem that I discuss later in the text.

61. Note that this is so whether or not the exercise of the power is assumed to involve the invocation of a power-conferring rule. *See supra* note 59.

62. Hart, *supra* note 53, at 258. In this passage Hart describes a simple rule of change that takes the form of a conditional duty-imposing customary rule, in which the custom holds for the society at large. But in a more sophisticated society, in which not everyone adopts the internal point of view, the custom will have to be limited to officials, for reasons that I discussed in Section II.

Hart here makes the suggestion that a certain kind of duty-imposing social rule is, in effect, equivalent to a power-conferring rule. In the example the relevant rule is not simply a practice of officials (or of a sole "commander" like Rex), but is rather a society-wide practice of treating the commander's word as binding. Members of the larger society regard themselves, in effect, as bound by the practice in a conditional rather than a categorical way; the content of the duty is conditioned on the say-so of the commander, who for that reason can be regarded as doing something that is functionally or perhaps even logically equivalent to exercising a power when he tells his subjects to do this or to do that.

Ingenious as this suggestion is, there are a number of reasons for thinking that it cannot rectify the omission in the argument in *The Concept of Law* that I have been discussing.[63] The only such reason that I will discuss here concerns various difficulties that arise when we inquire how a "commander" like Rex conceptualizes his own normative practice of issuing obligation-imposing directives (or, more generally, how legislators conceptualize their lawmaking practices to themselves). Notice, to begin, that Hart is clearly correct when he claims that there can be duty-imposing social rules in his sense that are conditional in nature. Notice further, though, that the type of event that triggers the conditional rule need not be the command of a commander, but could be almost anything: if the harvest is good, we must have a harvest festival; if we triumph in battle, we must have a great victory celebration and ritually kill all our prisoners. In the latter case, for example, there will be a Hartian social rule if, on the occasion of triumphing in battle, the members of the group generally hold a great victory celebration, adopt the internal point of view toward the practice of holding such a celebration, criticize one another for not taking part in the ritual killing of prisoners, and so on. Hart is thus correct that there could be a general conditional social rule that makes obligatory conduct dependent on the intentional say-so of a commander. If, whenever Rex tells his people to do *X*, they in fact generally do *X*, endorse the doing of *X*, criticize one another for not doing *X*, and so on, then it seems unproblematic to say that we have, at least from the perspective of Rex's subjects themselves, a Hartian social rule that is both conditional and general, and in which Rex's commands are, in Hart's phrase, "content-independent." This latter point means that members of the group treat a practice as obligatory simply on the say-so of Rex, regardless of what the content of his say-so is. If Rex says do *X*, they do *X*. If Rex says don't do *X*, they don't do *X*.

Consider, however, how Rex himself must conceptualize his own practice of issuing commands or directives. Unless the relevant social rule is understood as a Kelsenian direction to judges to apply sanctions under various circumstances—a possibility that Hart very forcefully rejects in Chapter 3 of *The Concept*

63. I discuss at greater length the various difficulties that this strategy faces in Perry, *supra* note 49, at 1196–1200.

of Law[64]—then presumably Rex most naturally thinks of himself as being guided by a rule such that, if he acts in certain ways, his subjects will come under an obligation to do such and such. Thus, if Rex tells his subjects to do *X*, he thinks of himself as doing something that places them under an obligation to do *X*. Presumably he does *not* think of himself as doing something such that when he tells his subjects to do *X*, he is simply causing them all generally to do *X*, to endorse *X* as required behavior, to criticize one another for not doing *X*, and so on. In other words, Rex must formulate the rule to himself in the form of an internal legal statement, which will presumably take something like the following, conditional form: "If Rex utters the words 'Do *X*' under such and such circumstances, then his subjects have an obligation to do *X*." But because the formulation of the rule as an internal statement must be conditional in nature, any attempt to understand its meaning in noncognitivist terms will run into a version of what has come to be known as the Frege–Geach problem. In its general form, this problem concerns the fact that normative predicates are used in various contexts where they are not actually being asserted, whereas the basic noncognitivist analysis of the meaning of normative expressions applies to their use in assertions.[65] The most commonly stated version of the problem concerns the antecedent clause in conditional statements that are used as premises in deductive arguments.[66] In the present case, however, the problem is not with the antecedent clause of a conditional statement, but rather with the consequent clause. In the statement "If Rex says do *X*, Rex's subjects have an obligation to do *X*," the proposition "Rex's subjects have an obligation to do *X*" is not being asserted, and is therefore not straightforwardly amenable to a noncognitivist analysis of the kind that Hart proposes for statements of obligation that are categorical.

I of course do not mean to suggest that there are no responses to such difficulties that could be offered on behalf of Hart, and the literature on noncognitivism and expressivism offers many technical resources that might be drawn on

---

64. HART, *supra* note 1, at 35–38.

65. *See* Peter T. Geach, *Ascriptivism*, 69 PHIL. REV. 221 (1960); Peter T. Geach, *Assertion*, 74 PHIL. REV. 449–65 (1965). Both articles are reprinted in GEACH, LOGIC MATTERS (1972). Interestingly, one of Geach's primary targets in the first of these articles was an early article of Hart's, in which Hart offers an ascriptivist analysis of attributions of action and responsibility. H.L.A. Hart, *The Ascription of Responsibility and Rights*, 49 PROC. ARISTOTELIAN SOC'Y 171–94 (1948–49). As Kevin Toh points out, Hart states in the Preface to *Punishment and Responsibility* that Geach's criticism is justified, and that he no longer considers its main contentions to be defensible. Toh, *supra* note 53, at 102, discussing H.L.A. HART, PUNISHMENT AND RESPONSIBILITY v (1968). Toh goes on to express the view that "the apparent inconsistency between Hart's disavowing of his acriptivism and. . . his adherence to expressivism can[not] be eliminated."

66. Consider an argument of the following form: Premise (1) If A, then B; Premise (2) A; Conclusion: B. The difficulty is that "A" is being asserted in premise (2) but not in premise (1).

for these purposes.[67] My main concern, rather, is simply to point out that the noncognitivist aspect of Hart's views gives rise to more serious difficulties for his theory of law than perhaps has been appreciated in the past. There is, however, a much broader point at issue here than the technicalities of the Frege-Geach problem. Even if a power-conferring rule is formulated as a conditional duty-imposing rule, legislators must still think of themselves as being guided by a rule such that, if they act in certain ways, their subjects will come under an obligation to do such and such. This means, among other things, that they must have some concept of the power-conferring rule, so as to be able to invoke it when engaged in the relevant illocutionary act.[68] In that case, however, the practice of legislators among themselves cannot be regarded as a conditional social rule in Hart's sense and nothing more. Legislators must formulate the rule to themselves in the form of an internal legal statement, and in performing law-making actions that invoke the rule they must do this—and must conceive of themselves as doing this—with the specific intention of imposing obligations on others (or changing their normative situation in some other way). In fact, from this point of view, it is not clear what has been gained by reformulating the power-conferring rule as one that conditionally imposes duties. Under either formulation, legislators must think of themselves as engaging in acts that are undertaken with the intention of changing someone's normative situation, and not simply as engaging in acts that have the effect of triggering the antecedent clause of a conditional rule. But to engage in an act with the intention of changing someone's normative situation is, at least in this kind of case, precisely to engage in the act with the intention of exercising a normative power. The supposed reduction of a power-conferring rule to a duty-imposing rule thus cannot, it would seem, completely eliminate the concept of a power.[69]

---

67. For proposed solutions to the Frege–Geach problem, see, for example, SIMON BLACKBURN, SPREADING THE WORD 181–223 (1984); ALLAN GIBBARD, WISE CHOICES, APT FEELINGS 83–102 (1990); Simon Blackburn, *Attitudes and Contents*, 98 ETHICS 510 (1988). As Toh points out, the viability of these proposals remains controversial. Toh, *supra* note 53, at 102.

68. Notice that, in the case of duty-imposing, categorical social rules, it is *not* strictly necessary that those whose general behavior and attitudes comprise the rule must have a concept of the rule; it would appear to be sufficient to meet Hart's existence conditions for such rules that members of the relevant group generally conform their behavior to the relevant pattern of conduct, adopt the attitude that the pattern of conduct is a required or obligatory standard, are disposed to criticize departures from the pattern, and so on. As Hart writes: "The use of *unstated* rules of recognition, by courts and others, in identifying particular rules of the system is characteristic of the internal point of view. Those who use them in this way thereby *manifest their use of them* as guiding rules. . . ." HART, *supra* note 1, at 102 (emphasis added).

69. Raz has suggested to me in a private communication that it is plausible to think that any normative change is a conditional or unconditional change in the circumstances

Even if solutions to the technical difficulties of reducing power-conferring rules to duty-imposing social rules can be found, analogues of those solutions may be available to a defender of the Kelsenian view that all laws are, at bottom, directives imposing obligations on officials to apply sanctions. It is worth pointing out in this regard that Hart's vigorous rejection of the Kelsenian thesis that power-conferring rules are best understood as "fragments" of such directives appears, after all, to rely principally on the general claim that power-conferring rules are, quite simply, distinct in their normative character from duty-imposing rules. In rejecting the Kelsenian approach Hart adverts to what he calls "the variety of laws,"[70] by which he means the apparently irreducible normative diversity that we find among the kinds of rules that figure both in regular law and in the foundational arrangements of legal systems.[71] In *Essays on Bentham*, in the course of a discussion of a proposal by Bentham to reduce all legal powers to conditional commands, Hart rejects Bentham's specific proposal but, as we have already seen, nonetheless explicitly considers the general possibility that all power-conferring rules might be reduced to conditional, duty-imposing rules. But even though he leaves the technical question open, Hart nonetheless forcefully reiterates his view that power-conferring laws "guide those exercising such powers in ways strikingly different from the way in which rules imposing duties guide behavior," adding that "power-conferring rules are distinct in their normative function from duty-imposing rules" and that "[t]o represent them as fragments of duty-imposing rules is to obscure their distinct normative character."[72] The basic intuition that Hart expresses here, to the effect that power-conferring rules are quite simply and irreducibly distinct from duty-imposing rules, is surely sound. We should be guided by that instinct, and not give in to the reductivist temptation that Hart himself appears ultimately to have resisted.

It is important to emphasize that the main impetus for treating the project of reducing power-conferring rules to duty-imposing rules as theoretically worthwhile would be that one accepted some version of Hart's semantic noncognitivism. Even if technical solutions turn out to be available to the Frege–Geach problem and to whatever other technical difficulties that such a reductivist project faces, we surely do much better if we take the law's normative claims at face value and adopt a cognitivist theory of the meaning of legal statements. Not only will we then be in a much better position to appreciate Hart's insight that the

---

under which there is a duty. Plausible as that suggestion is, it simply does not follow that every kind of norm, including power-conferring norms, can be reduced to conditional or unconditional duty-imposing norms.

70. *Id.* at 26–49.

71. *See id.* at 41: "[P]ower-conferring rules are thought of, spoken of and used in social life differently from rules that impose duties, and they are valued for different reasons. What other tests for difference in character could there be?"

72. HART, *supra* note 53, at 219.

introduction into society of rules conferring legislative and adjudicative powers "is a step forward as important . . . as the invention of the wheel,"[73] but we will also be in a position to develop a much richer variety of jurisprudential theories. If we take seriously the law's claim to have the systematic capacity to change our normative situation, then we can ask such questions as whether the law ever does possess such a capacity, and what the justification for its possessing such a capacity might be. Although Hart's critique of the sanction- and prediction-based theories of his positivist predecessors was an essential move for the advancement of jurisprudence, his own theory of law is severely limited, in ways that have not always been appreciated by his successors, by its commitment to a non-cognitivist understanding of normativity.

IV. FURTHER OBSERVATIONS

In his book *H.L.A. Hart,* Neil MacCormick offers the following set of observations:

> [I]f in a constitutional state one criterion of rules binding on judges is that they be rules validly enacted by the legislature, the "validity" of a legislative act does not depend on the rule of recognition itself directly. Legislation is validly enacted if it satisfies the constitutional provision (a Hartian rule of change) governing the legislature's power. As such, it yields a valid or binding ground of judicial decision. This in turn implies a judicial duty to apply the constitutional provision. It does not follow that the rule of recognition makes the constitution "valid" in any other sense.[74]

These observations are interesting for the following reason. So long as a rule of change is in place whose legal status is not a matter of being recognized as valid by the rule of recognition—and I suggested in the preceding section that this will be true of most contemporary rules of change by virtue of a loose sense of customary acceptance—then legislation passed in accordance with that rule of change will give rise *directly* to a binding ground of judicial decision; there will be no need, in other words, to find a duty to apply the law in an independently existing rule of recognition.

Hart comes close to making a similar point when he says the following of Kelsen's theory of the basic norm (*Grundnorm*):

> It seems a needless reduplication to suggest that there is a further rule to the effect that the constitution (or those who "laid it down") are to be obeyed. This is particularly clear where, as in the United Kingdom, there is no written constitution: here there seems no place for the rule "that the constitution is to

73. Hart, *supra* note 1, at 41–42.

74. MacCormick, *supra* note 8, at 115.

> be obeyed" in addition to the rule that certain criteria of validity, (e.g. enactment by the Queen in Parliament) are to be used in identifying the law. This is the accepted rule and it is mystifying to speak of a rule that this rule is to be obeyed.[75]

If in this passage one replaced the phrase "the constitution is to be obeyed" with the phrase "the legislature is to be obeyed," then it becomes equally mysterious why we need an extra rule, in the form of the duty-imposing rule of recognition, to tell either subjects that they ought to obey, or judges that they ought to apply, the enactments of the legislature. To phrase the matter differently, it is possible to make the point that enactments of the Queen in Parliament are "valid law" without making any reference to an independently existing rule that supposedly imposes on judges a duty to apply those enactments.

Raz also appears to make a somewhat similar point—albeit one that is rather obscurely formulated—when he writes the following in *The Concept of a Legal System*:

> The fundamental reason which moved Hart to adopt his doctrine of the rule of recognition is expressed in the following sentence: "If the question is raised whether some suggested rule is legally valid, we must, in order to answer the question, use a criterion of validity *provided by some other rule*." It is this assumption that is questionable. It seems to me that to answer the question whether a certain law exists as law in a certain legal system one must ultimately refer not to a law but to a certain jurisprudential criterion. Ultimately one must refer to a general statement that does not describe a law but a general truth about law.[76]

Each of these passages, in quite different ways, appears to raise the possibility that, at least in cases where there is reason to say that a rule of change, say, exists within a legal system in a manner that does not depend on its being recognized as valid by an independently existing, duty-imposing rule, *there may simply be no need to suppose that there is, in fact, such an independently existing, duty-imposing rule*. We would not need such a rule either to identify the rule of change as law, or to make clear that the rule had normative (i.e., legal) force either for judges or for citizens generally. As an existing law the rule of change would of course have normative force, or at least it would do so according to the law's own understanding of itself as possessing legitimate authority. A similar point would hold for valid laws that had been enacted in accordance with the rule of change. If this suggestion is along the right lines, then a rule of recognition need not be, contrary to what Hart maintains, even the principal source of the courts' duty to

75. Hart, *supra* note 1, at 293.

76. Joseph Raz, The Concept of a Legal System 200 (1970), quoting Hart, *supra* note 1, at 107 (emphasis Raz's).

apply the law, let alone the exclusive source. In his contribution to the present volume, Jeremy Waldron explores a similar line of thought in a very interesting and illuminating fashion.[77] While I am quite sympathetic to his claim that neither jurisprudence nor constitutional theory requires a general rule of recognition in anything like Hart's sense, and that this is particularly so if the rule of recognition is, as Hart claims, necessarily constituted by social practice, it is not entirely clear that there is no room for at least a general default rule, to the effect that judges have a duty to apply a law where for some reason that duty is not apparent from the content or the character of the law itself.[78] At the very least, however, Waldron's discussion suggests that, contrary to Hart's own view of the matter, fundamental rules of change may take conceptual and normative priority over such a default rule of recognition.

Despite the doubts Raz expresses about the doctrine of the rule of recognition in the passage cited above, in *The Authority of Law* he essentially adopts Hart's own version of the doctrine, minus its noncognitivist dimension. He gives three reasons for doing so, the first of which is the claim that law-applying institutions, unlike law-creating institutions, "are a constant feature of law in every society."[79] But in contemporary times, and according to our modern concept of law, a political regime that lacked law-creating institutions would be, at best, a very marginal instance of a legal system.[80] Raz's second reason is that "since most legal systems recognize diverse sources of law, the only way to determine which are the lawmaking institutions and procedures is to establish which sources of law are recognized by the courts."[81] But surely it is too strong to claim that the *only* way to identify the existence of a lawmaking institution within a legal system is to examine the practices of the courts. Within the English legal system, for example, surely the legal status of Parliament as a body possessing the authority to make law is so deeply entrenched that it cannot be said to depend, either as a theoretical or as a practical matter, on the recognition of that status by the English courts.

---

77. Jeremy Waldron, *Who Needs Rules of Recognition?* (Chapter 12, this volume).

78. And there is of course always room, as Raz has pointed out, for ancillary (i.e., in Hart's terms, nonultimate) rules of recognition, which themselves take the form of valid law. Thus a legislature can pass a law that confers lawmaking powers on some other body or agency. *See, e.g.*, Raz, *supra* note 8, at 95.

79. *Id.* at 87–88. It should be noted that, strictly speaking, Raz presents his three reasons as bearing on a proper understanding of the relation between the existence and the efficacy of laws. It is, however, clear from his discussion that he has in mind the much more significant theoretical problem of which kind of institution, law-applying or law-creating, should have primacy in the identification of what is to count as a valid law.

80. *See supra* note 42.

81. Raz, *supra* note 8, at 88.

Raz's third reason is the following:

> [I]t is an essential feature of legal systems that they are institutional, normative systems. It is, therefore, reasonable to take the law to consist of those norms, rules, and principles, that are presented to individuals as guides to their behaviour by the body of legal institutions as a whole. When the actions of law-creating and law-applying organs conflict, the actions of the law-applying organs are those that affect the considerations of the law's subjects: they have final authority to declare what is law.[82]

It is indeed an essential feature of legal systems that they are institutional and normative in character, but surely the operative phrase in the above passage is that the law is presented as a guide to individual behavior *"by the body of legal institutions as a whole."* There is simply no good reason, either theoretical or practical, to focus exclusively, for purposes of identifying what is and is not a law, on either law-applying institutions or law-creating institutions. And it surely goes much too far to say that, as an empirical matter, it is *always* the actions of the law-applying organs that take precedence for the law's subjects when the actions of the two types of institutions conflict. It similarly goes much too far to say that, either as a legal matter within a given legal system or as a general matter of jurisprudential theory, courts always "have final authority to declare what is law." As a legal matter this would seem to be a question of law within the particular legal system, and as a theoretical matter there is no good reason to think that jurisprudence should offer a determinate answer to this question that would, as a matter of necessity, hold good for each and every legal system. For similar reasons, it goes too far to say that "the existence of the law is *logically* related to the practice of the law-applying institutions."[83] Raz remarks that, according to the doctrine of the rule of recognition, it is a necessary (although not a sufficient) condition of the existence of a law that it is (or under appropriate circumstances would be) recognized by the law-applying institutions.[84] Yet surely there are, in most legal systems, rules and principles that we would intuitively recognize to be legal in character, but that the courts either refuse to apply or are prohibited by law from applying. It seems simply to beg the question to label such rules and principles "political" and "not part of the law of the state."[85] Finally, to focus on the rule of recognition as being, principally, a solution to the problem of how to identify what is to count as a valid law from the perspective of guides for the behavior of individuals,[86] seems to treat the rule as, in essence, a list of criteria of validity. But to regard the rule of recognition in that way deemphasizes a crucial

---

82. *Id.*
83. *Id.* (emphasis added).
84. *Id.* at 87–88, 97.
85. *Id.* at 101.
86. *See supra* text accompanying note 82.

aspect of Hart's own view, which is that the rule is the principal (and probably the exclusive) source of the courts' duty to apply the law.

V. CONCLUSION

The core of Hart's doctrine of the rule of recognition is his notion of the internal point of view, and as was noted in Section III the internal point of view serves two important and related roles in his theory of law. The first is to specify one of the constitutive elements of the complex social practice that comprises a legal system, and the second is to explain the normative dimension of the meaning of such statements as "It is the law of Pennsylvania that everyone has an obligation to do *X*." Hart was absolutely correct to emphasize the importance to legal theory of the internal point of view, but he was wrong to characterize the internal point of view as simply a normative attitude. As Joseph Raz has constantly emphasized, one of the most fundamental attributes of both the concept and the practice of law, and an essential feature of law's nature, is that through its officials and its characteristic institutions law claims legitimate authority for itself, meaning that it claims for itself a legitimate moral power to change the normative situation of its subjects.[87] The internal point of view, properly understood, is the perspective of both those who make and those who accept the legitimacy of the law's claim to authority. Once we discard Hart's implausible semantic analysis of normative statements, we are free to acknowledge that those who accept the legitimacy of law have not simply adopted a certain normative attitude, but rather hold a certain *belief*, which could be either true or false, about the legitimacy of law.[88]

Although Hart was absolutely correct to emphasize the importance to legal theory of the internal point of view, his doctrine of the rule of recognition involves two related errors. The first is to conceive of the foundations of law as necessarily consisting of a rule that is simply *constituted* by a pattern of behavior and an associated normative attitude. Once we acknowledge that the internal point of view should be understood by reference to a belief and not simply an attitude, we are no longer committed to conceiving of the foundations of law as customary in Hart's strict sense of that notion (i.e., as consisting of at least one social rule). Nor are we any longer committed to the view that the recognitional community

87. The most important way in which a lawmaker might change the normative situation of its subjects is to impose obligations on them, but this is not, of course, the only way. *See, e.g.*, Stephen Perry, *Law and Obligation*, 50 AM. J. JURIS. 263, 266–76 (2005).

88. *See* JOSEPH RAZ, THE MORALITY OF FREEDOM 65 (1986). It should be noted that some scholars have rejected Raz's view that law claims legitimate authority for itself. Particularly noteworthy are the arguments offered by Himma in Kenneth Einar Himma, *Law's Claim to Legitimate Authority*, *in* HART'S POSTSCRIPT, *supra* note 8, at 271.

must consist of officials and officials only. It is a banality to say that law consists of a social practice that purports in some way to be normative, but it is perfectly possible that the relevant social practice is not best regarded as a rule or norm that is simply *constituted* by a Hartian custom, or by some related conception of a convention;[89] the practice may instead bear a much more complex relationship to the normativity (or potential normativity) of law. The law's basic claim of moral authority must rest on a belief that such authority is underwritten by a moral principle, but beliefs as to what that principle is could in principle vary quite widely. Thus it is perfectly possible that the foundations of law are most appropriately characterized by reference to what Dworkin once described as "concurrent" rather than "conventional" morality.[90] It is also possible, of course, that a conventionalist approach is the correct one, but that position must be argued for and not simply assumed. As Dworkin has often emphasized, a "concurrent" approach allows for much more disagreement about the content of law than does an approach grounded in some version of conventionalism. In his contribution to the current volume, Matthew Adler argues very persuasively that, in the all-important test case of American practice regarding constitutional interpretation, there is far too much disagreement to allow for a plausible Hartian understanding of that practice.[91]

The second, related error that Hart makes in propounding his doctrine of the rule of recognition is to emphasize the role of duty in the foundational arrangements of law, rather than the role of normative power. This leads him to further restrict the recognitional community so that it consists not of officials generally, but only of those officials who, like judges, have a duty to apply the law. There is, however, a much larger matter at issue here, which is that the law's claim to authority is precisely a claim to possess the normative power to change the normative situation of its subjects. As we saw in Section III, Hart himself repeatedly emphasizes the significance of the introduction into society of legislative powers.[92] Indeed, as we saw in Section IV, there is some reason to be skeptical about the very existence of duty-imposing rules of recognition in Hart's sense. Presumably Hart's failure to capitalize on his insight about the fundamental

---

89. See the helpful general discussions of conventionalism in law in FINNIS, *supra* note 27, at 134–60; LESLIE GREEN, THE AUTHORITY OF THE STATE 89–121 (1990); JULES COLEMAN, THE PRACTICE OF PRINCIPLE 74–102 (2001); Andrei Marmor, *Legal Conventionalism, in* HART'S POSTSCRIPT, *supra* note 8, at 193.

90. RONALD DWORKIN, TAKING RIGHTS SERIOUSLY 53 (1977). Dworkin wrote that "[a] community displays a concurrent morality when its members are agreed in asserting the same, or much the same, normative rule, but they do not count the fact of that agreement as an essential part of their grounds for asserting that rule. It displays a conventional morality when they do."

91. Matthew Adler, *Social Facts, Constitutional Interpretation, and the Rule of Recognition* (Chapter 8, this volume).

92. See, for example, HART, *supra* note 1, at 41–42.

importance to law of normative powers is due to his failure to offer an analysis of power-conferring customary rules that would parallel his analysis of duty-imposing customary rules. But once we abandon the idea that the foundations of law must be grounded in customary or conventionalist norms in Hart's strong, constitutive sense, the need for such a parallel analysis falls away, and other theoretical possibilities present themselves. There is no reason to think that the law's basic claim to moral authority must reside in anything like a single custom or convention (or in a set of customs or conventions), rather than in a more complex account of the relationship between normativity and social practice.[93] And once we abandon the idea that the foundational arrangements of law are simply *constituted* by Hartian social rules or some similar notion of conventionalist norms, we can allow for the possibility that both the existence and the legitimacy of law ought to take into account not just the actions, attitudes and beliefs of officials, but those of citizens as well. We reopen the door, in other words, to some version of "deep" popular constitutionalism.

One result of Hart's claim that every legal system rests on a duty-imposing rule of recognition is that many of his positivist successors have been almost obsessively concerned with analyzing the true nature of the rule of recognition, and with showing how it can, in fact, give officials obligations if we understand it, say, as a Lewis-style convention that solves a coordination problem,[94] or as an instance of Michael Bratman's notion of shared cooperative activity.[95] But interesting and important as these analyses are, they often simply sidestep the questions of whether and how the practices of officials might, by means of acts intended to be deliberate exercises of a normative power, give rise to obligations (or other changes in normative status) on the part of citizens generally. A related implication of understanding the internal point of view in cognitivist rather than attitudinal terms concerns the nature of law's normativity. Since Hart's analysis of normativity was noncognitivist in nature, he held the view, as we have seen, that all there is to be said about the normativity of law resides in the fact that those who adopt the internal point of view endorse its standards as obligatory; there is nothing more to be said about whether law, *as law*, gives rise to reasons for action.[96] Of course there might be prudential reasons to follow the law—or,

---

93. *Cf.* DWORKIN, *supra* note 90, at 57.

94. Jules Coleman, *Negative and Positive Positivism*, 11 J. LEGAL STUD. 139 (1982); Gerald Postema, *Coordination and Convention at the Foundations of Law*, 11 J. LEGAL STUD. 165 (1982). On Lewis-style conventions, see DAVID LEWIS, CONVENTION: A PHILOSOPHICAL STUDY (1969).

95. Scott Shapiro, *Law, Plans, and Practical Reason*, 8 LEGAL THEORY 387 (2002); Shapiro, *Massively Shared Agency* (manuscript on file with author). *See also* COLEMAN, *supra* note 89, at 95–102. On Bratman's notion of shared cooperative activity, see, for example, Michael Bratman, *Shared Cooperative Activity*, 101 PHIL. REV. 327 (1992).

96. Both Toh and Shapiro make this point, and observe that many legal theorists have criticized Hart either for assuming that social rules are inherently reason giving, or for

if a particular legal system can be assessed from the external point of view to have moral value, there might be moral reasons—but that is a different matter.[97] If, however, one adopts a fully cognitivist understanding of internal legal statements such as "It is the law of Pennsylvania that X," then one will understand them as asserting that a certain normative state of affairs obtains, rather than as expressing an endorsement of a certain kind. This does not preclude the possibility of understanding the foundations of law as consisting of conventionalist norms of some kind, but one will presumably try to do so, as Hart did not, in a way that shows these norms to be at least potentially reason giving.[98] This, I take it, is the project of Scott Shapiro and Jules Coleman in trying to extend Michael Bratman's notion of shared cooperative activity to enterprises in which, like law, some persons make claims of authority over others.[99]

Notice, finally, that once we abandon Hart's claim that the internal point of view in the attitudinal sense is one of the constitutive elements of the foundational arrangements of law, we are no longer forced to treat a political regime in which *no one* other than officials adopts the internal point of view as necessarily being a straightforward instance of a legal system.[100] The question of which

---

failing to give an account of how they could be reason giving. Toh, *supra* note 53, at 77; Shapiro, *supra* note 52. I have in the past been guilty of this sin myself. *See* Stephen Perry, *Interpretation and Methodology in Legal Theory, in* LAW AND INTERPRETATION: ESSAYS IN LEGAL PHILOSOPHY 97 (Andrei Marmor ed., 1995); and Stephen Perry, *Holmes versus Hart: The Bad Man in Legal Theory, in* THE PATH OF THE LAW AND ITS INFLUENCE: THE LEGACY OF OLIVER WENDELL HOLMES, JR. 158 (Steven J. Burton ed., 2000). Indeed, Raz himself makes this mistake in his early critique of Hart's "practice theory" of rules. *See* JOSEPH RAZ, PRACTICAL REASON AND NORMS 50–58 (1975). (It is worth pointing out that this work predates the articles in which Raz characterizes Hart as a noncognitivist.) Dworkin also made a similar mistake in his critique of Hart's theory of social rules in *The Model of Rules II, in* DWORKIN, *supra* note 90. However, once one realizes that Hart was really a noncognitivist, all such criticisms are immediately seen to be beside the point.

97. *Cf.* HART, *supra* note 1, at 107–09. Given that Hart understands legal normativity in partially noncognitivist terms, it is difficult to see why he would understand moral normativity any differently. Be that as it may, Hart clearly thinks that morality provides a distinct source of evaluative judgments that can be brought to bear, as an external matter, upon law.

98. I am here using the term "conventionalist" in a deliberately broad fashion; see the works cited *supra* note 89. In the Postcript to the second edition of *The Concept of Law*, Hart modifies his view of social rules in general, and of the rule of recognition in particular, so as to apply only to "conventional social practices." Social practices are defined as conventional "if the general conformity of the group to them is part of the reasons which its individual members have for acceptance." HART, *Postscript* to THE CONCEPT OF LAW, *supra* note 1, at 255. However, since Hart does not appear to be at all concerned with the ways in which the conventionality of a rule might further affect the reasons for action of those who accept the rule, this change in his view appears to be completely unmotivated.

99. Shapiro, *supra* note 95; COLEMAN, *supra* note 89, at 74–102.

100. HART, *supra* note 1, at 117.

participants in a legal system must make the requisite claim to authority, and which ones must accept it, in order to justify such conclusions as that a legal system exists in such and such a place may well simply involve a fairly narrow conceptual inquiry that has no larger theoretical ramifications. Raz is engaging in such an inquiry when, for example, he defines a de facto authority as an entity that "either claims to be [a] legitimate [authority] or is believed to be so, and is effective in imposing its will on many over whom it claims authority, perhaps because its claim to legitimacy is recognized by many of its subjects."[101] Our ordinary concepts of law and of a legal system do not make it a necessary condition of the existence of a legal system that political regimes in fact possess legitimate authority, but they do require that such regimes at least be de facto authorities in Raz's sense. No doubt it is a truth about our concept of law that the officials of a political regime that claims legitimate authority for itself must, for the most part, believe this claim to be justified if the regime can be said to have a legal system. But it may well also be a truth about our concept of law that at least some of the subjects of the regime must also hold this belief.[102] (As was noted in Section II, we are, at the very least, inclined to agree with Finnis that certain kinds of draconian political regimes are, at best, only marginal cases of legal systems.) How many might be a sufficient number to meet this suggested conceptual constraint? There is almost certainly no precise answer to this question. But because the internal point of view in the cognitivist sense does not, or at least does not necessarily, conceptually tie the existence of a legal system to the existence of a fundamental norm that is partly constituted by a shared attitude of endorsement, this fact could be regarded as essentially just a minor conceptual indeterminacy that has no larger theoretical implications.

---

101. JOSEPH RAZ, ETHICS IN THE PUBLIC DOMAIN 195 (1994).

102. Raz, following Kelsen, has made the very important point that it is possible to engage in the normative discourse of the law without actually accepting the law's moral authority, since it is possible to engage in such discourse by adopting a hypothetical or detached perspective. One can thus speak as though the law has moral authority while not actually accepting that it does, or while withholding belief on whether or not it does. *See, e.g.*, RAZ, *supra* note 8, at 137–43.

12. WHO NEEDS RULES OF RECOGNITION?

JEREMY WALDRON*

I. A WAY-TOO-FAMILIAR IDEA

The rule of recognition is such a central component of modern positivist jurisprudence that there is a danger of the phrase "rule of recognition" rolling too quickly off the tongue, allowing us to use it quite casually without proper reflection on its meaning.

In this chapter I would like to ask what a rule of recognition actually is, what it does, and what it is good for. I want to ask what its relation is to other sorts of secondary rules that we may find in a constitutional system, particularly rules of change. H. L. A. Hart introduced the idea of a rule of recognition, and he made it a key feature of modern jurisprudence; most legal philosophers since Hart have followed him in emphasizing its centrality. But from time to time it is good to question a prevailing paradigm. So let us pose this question: If we were not committed theoretically, as part of the basic ideology of modern legal positivism, to the centrality of the rule of recognition, what would we say about the importance of *recognition* in a modern legal system? So long as we have the modern positivist outlook, we just assume that there must *be* a rule of recognition, and that it performs a role that is absolutely central, foundational, and essential to every legal system. But just for a moment, let us not assume anything: let us look and see.

II. HART ON THE FUNCTION OF A RULE OF RECOGNITION

H. L. A. Hart introduces the term "rule of recognition" in a discussion of the ways in which the emergence of secondary rules might help remedy some of the inadequacies of a social regime consisting purely of primary rules.[1] He asks us to imagine a prelegal system consisting solely of primary rules of conduct. Such a system, he says, would suffer from a number of significant defects, one of which is *uncertainty*: "If doubts arise as to what the rules are or as to the precise

---

* University Professor, New York University School of Law. I am grateful to Matthew Adler, Ed Baker, Richard Fallon, John Gardner, Leslie Green, Alon Harel, Ken Himma, Matthew Kramer, Hans Oberdiek, Stephen Perry, Scott Shapiro, and Wil Waluchow for comments on earlier versions of this chapter.

1. H.L.A. Hart, The Concept of Law 91–99 (Penelope A. Bulloch & Joseph Raz eds., 2d ed. 1994).

scope of some given rule, there will be no procedure for settling this doubt."[2] The emergence of a particular kind of secondary rule—a rule of recognition—is supposed to be the solution to this difficulty. What exactly are people supposed to have been uncertain *about*? What uncertainty exactly does the rule of recognition dispel or mitigate? Or to put it another way: what does the rule of recognition recognize the rules that it recognizes *as*? What does it tell us about them? We should not say—as almost every legal theorist says—that it tells us they are *law*. For what does *that* mean? The rule of recognition is supposed to help us understand the idea of a rule's being part of the law, not presuppose it. Hart's answer to these questions is given a page or so later:

> The simplest form of remedy for the uncertainty of the regime of primary rules is the introduction of what we shall call a "rule of recognition." This will specify some feature or features possession of which by a suggested rule is taken as a conclusive affirmative indication that it is a rule of the group to be supported by the social pressure it exerts.[3]

I have two points to make about this, one small point and one big point. The small point is that we should assume charitably that, in this excerpt, Hart's phrase "the social pressure it exerts" refers to organized (institutionalized) social pressure including physical sanctions; otherwise the definition is way too accommodating. The positive morality of a group is no doubt supported by social pressure; yet I do not think Hart believes it is the function of a rule of recognition to recognize rules of positive morality just because the social group exerts "pressure" to uphold them. *Organized* social pressure has to be what we are talking about.

The big point is more troubling for those who want to regard the rule of recognition as the most fundamental rule of a legal system. On Hart's account, there are several kinds of fundamental secondary rules: rules of change, rules of recognition, and rules constituting institutions for enforcement. On the basis of the account given in the excerpt above, it looks to me as though the fundamental rule of recognition presupposes that rules of the third sort—rules constituting institutions for enforcement—are already in place. We have already constituted and institutionalized social rule-enforcing pressure, and the rule of recognition tells us how that organized apparatus will be used (in case there is any doubt or uncertainty).[4]

---

2. *Id.* at 92.

3. *Id.* at 94 (emphasis added).

4. This is similar to a point made by Kent Greenawalt, *The Rule of Recognition and the Constitution*, 85 MICH. L. REV. 621, 624 (1987) (reprinted as Chapter 1, this volume, at 4), that traditional accounts of the rule of recognition seem to presuppose that we already have an identifiable cadre of officials who practice it. But it is not the same point. Greenawalt's point is about who practices the rule of recognition; my point is about the work that that rule does.

The idea seems to be that the rule of recognition sorts other rules into two categories: (1) rules of the group that *will* be supported by the organized social pressure that the group exerts; and (2) other rules, which *will not* be supported by the organized social pressure that the group exerts. Category (2) may contain such things as rules of the group's positive morality that will not receive the full support of the group's organized social pressure, but will be supported by informal social pressure; objective moral rules that the group does not support with organized social pressure; rules that some members of the group wish were supported with the group's organized social pressure but that are not; rules that used to be supported by organized social pressure but are no longer; and rules that are *similar* to rules that *will* be supported by organized social pressure but that are understood by those who tout them in a way that is misleading about the extent of the group's application of social pressure (e.g., because the understanding of the rule that they convey is too wide or too narrow).

In these ways, it seems that the recognition/categorization function distinguishes between positive law, on the one hand, and, on the other hand, mere positive morality, critical morality, failed legal proposals, abandoned rules of law, and distorted understandings of legal rules.

III. HOBBESIAN RECOGNITION

Thomas Hobbes has given us a good account of the importance of a recognition function. We need a rule of recognition, on Hobbes's account, because there may be disagreement in the community as to what ought to be taken as law.

> Nor is it enough the Law be written and published; but also that there be manifest signs, that it proceedeth from the will of the Soveraign. For private men, when they have or think they have force enough to secure their unjust designes, and convoy them safely to their ambitious ends, may publish for Lawes what they please without, or against the Legislative Authority. There is therefore requisite, not only a Declaration of the law, but also sufficient signes of the Author, and Authority.[5]

Such signs, Hobbes says, will depend on accessible criteria of validity such as "publique Registers, publique Counsels, publique Ministers, and publique Seals."[6] On this account, the rule and apparatus of legal recognition is oriented to a compelling and substantive political end—namely, the end of ensuring that when someone faces what purports to be a legal demand, he knows that this demand really *is* playing the role that Hobbesian law aspires to play so far as the promotion of peace and the diminution of conflict are concerned. He can know

5. Thomas Hobbes, Leviathan 189 (Richard Tuck ed., 1988).
6. *Id.* at 189.

that only if he has some guarantee that the demand can be traced to a sovereign authority, which alone can provide a basis for social peace and order. If what we are looking for is Hobbesian peace, and the determinate principles of conduct and property that make peace possible, the last thing we want is people riding around parading their own favorite norms as sovereign commands. That is a recipe for reviving war, not peace, once more than one person starts to do this. We want some assurance therefore, before we defer to a putative law, that it really has been issued by the sovereign; we will want to check the seals with which a written rule has been embossed, its presence in an authoritative public gazette, and so on. An accepted rule of recognition gives us the basis for doing this. I shall call this the Hobbesian function of rules of recognition.

IV. LOW-LEVEL RECOGNITION OF VALID WILLS, CONTRACTS, AND SO ON

The Hobbes example operates at a pretty high level: the Hobbesian apparatus of recognition tells us how to reliably identify a sovereign command when we see one. But rules of recognition may operate at a lower level also. It is one of H. L. A. Hart's important contributions to jurisprudence to emphasize how many of the ordinary ground-level rules of (say) private law are not primary rules commanding or regulating conduct but secondary rules allowing people to change their legal position and keep track of the changes that they and others have made.[7]

A statute of wills is a fine example. It enables people to arrange for the postmortem distribution of their property, changing the default position that would obtain upon an intestacy. A typical wills statute requires that directions for the distribution of property be given in writing and signed by the testator, with two witnesses also signing to attest to the fact that it was really he who signed the will. If we like, we can think of the statute of wills as a little rule of recognition: it tells us how to discern a genuine will, with legal effect, from a pseudo-will that has no legal effect; it tells us how to recognize a valid will.

But there is another possible way of looking at the statute of wills. When he introduced the idea of secondary rules, Hart distinguished between a rule of recognition and a rule of change. The former has received much more attention in the philosophical literature than the latter; but it may be that the latter is as important if not more important. A rule of change is a secondary rule that empowers some person or institution to alter the law, either in general or in some particular respect, by following a certain procedure and conforming to certain requirements.[8] Plainly a statute of wills is a rule of change: it indicates

7. HART, *supra* note 1, at 27–42.

8. *Id.* at 93–94.

procedures and requirements that have to be satisfied if the actions of a property owner are to have the effect of changing the legally required postmortem distribution of his property. It provides a checklist—writing, signature, attestation, and so on—for a valid change. When a probate court recognizes the will, what it does is check that the steps required for a valid change have taken place.

If this is what we think is going on, we do not really need the idea of a rule of recognition to explain the "recognition" of a valid will. The rule of change is what does all the work; what the court does is ensure that the rule of change has properly been observed. If it has not—that is, if the procedures and requirements laid down in the rule of change have not been observed—then the change that the owner wanted to take effect will not take effect or the change that someone claims the owner wanted to take effect will not take effect. In this regard, the rule of change does all the work in determining the legal ordering. There is no particular role for a rule of recognition.

I think this is an important result, and I shall explore the implications of an analogous argument for constitutional law later in the chapter (in Section IX).

V. RULES OF CHANGE AND RULES OF RECOGNITION

Though H. L. A. Hart distinguished between a rule of recognition and a rule of change, it may be thought that it does not particularly matter which analysis we give of cases like the statute of wills. We can say (as I said in the final paragraphs of Section IV) that a rule of change is doing all the work; or we can categorize some of the work that is being done as recognitional. Certainly there is a removal-of-uncertainty aspect to some of the requirements for wills: attestation of signature, for example. Also, in some other private law areas, there does seem to be an independent recognitional aspect: some legal systems require certain donative promises to be given under seal, for example, and one might regard the seal as fulfilling a Hobbesian recognition function. (The requirement that contracts for the disposition of land be in writing might be another example.) So, in private law, I would not want to make too much of this point about the redundancy of the concept of a rule of recognition in light of the existence and operation of a well-functioning rule of change. It will be important, however, in the constitutional context.

Consider the example of legislation. In the Hobbesian case, there does seem to be a pretty clear distinction between the rule of change for legislation and the rule of recognition for legislation. The rule of change is that the sovereign may alter the rules by his command.[9] (Maybe there will be some procedures he has to follow, so we can distinguish his serious commands from his little jokes,

9. HOBBES, *supra* note 5, at 183–84.

musings, idle wishes, etc.) The rule of recognition enables us to keep track of the sovereign's commands by various devices. It might be thought that an expression of the sovereign's will does not count as a command, that is, as a basis for changing the law, unless the appropriate seal is affixed and the appropriate entry published in the gazette. But that need not be so. These devices need not be regarded as part of the legislative process; they may be seen as just an excellent idea for reducing public uncertainty.

Still, we can imagine cases in which engaging the apparatus of recognition comes to be regarded as an indispensable part of the enactment process: no one thinks the sovereign has actually made *law* or issued a command (in the appropriate lawmaking sense of *command*) unless the appropriate seal has been affixed. In that case it would be a toss-up whether we wanted to say that the rule of change does all the work, or whether we wanted to say that, besides the rule of change, there is independent evidential/confirmatory work being done by a rule of recognition.

VI. AN INTERLUDE ON RECOGNITION AS A SOCIAL RULE

In all of this, I am taking H. L. A. Hart at his word on some important points. First, I am assuming that secondary rules, even the fundamental rule of recognition, consist of social practices. The idea that secondary rules are to be understood as actual social practices is an important part of Hart's jurisprudence.[10] It gives his jurisprudence an earthy empirical, even sociological, flavor that is lacking in the positivist jurisprudence of someone like Hans Kelsen.[11] Though Hart notes certain similarities and isomorphisms between his idea of a fundamental rule of recognition and Kelsen's idea of the *Grundnorm*, we should accept what he says about the ontological differences between them. Whether a rule of recognition exists in a given society is, Hart says, ultimately a question of empirical fact about social practices in that society.[12] For Kelsen, by contrast, the *Grundnorm* is a theoretical postulate, presupposed in order to secure the basis of a chain of validation.[13] I will return to the relation between Hart's account and Kelsen's account in Section XII, below.

Second, I am assuming that the practice with which Hart identifies the rule of recognition is one of those practices that, on Hart's account, are rule-like.[14]

---

10. HART, *supra* note 1, at 110–17.

11. *Cf.* the account of the "purity" of legal science in HANS KELSEN, PURE THEORY OF LAW 1, 79 (Max Knight trans., 2002).

12. HART, *supra* note 1, at 292–93.

13. *Id.* at 292. *Cf.* the discussion of the basic norm (*Grundnorm*) in KELSEN, *supra* note 11, at 201.

14. There is a fine discussion in JULES COLEMAN, THE PRACTICE OF PRINCIPLE: IN DEFENSE OF A PRAGMATIST APPROACH TO LEGAL THEORY 78–84 (2001).

Not all social practices constitute rules. Some do; and when they do, the more or less convergent behavior that constitutes the practice will have an internal normative aspect. The existence of such a practice is compatible with people sometimes deviating from the rule, provided such deviations are treated in an appropriate way by the deviator and his peers—frowned upon, furtively concealed, regretted, and so on. I assume also that practices that we identify as rules have a nomological or universalizable aspect: they involve the application of *general* criteria to any one of an open-ended array of items. This distinguishes a *rule* from a widely accepted sense that something in particular ought to be done or deferred to. We will return to the issue of the rule-likeness of the practice of recognition in Section XII below.

Third, I am assuming that if there is a rule of recognition, it operates rather like a coordination convention.[15] It is not unlike the convention of driving on the right: each person most wants to drive on the same side as others, and the convention makes one side of the road salient, so that all can fulfill this desire. Similarly, we might say, each judge wants to be enforcing the same set of norms as other judges are enforcing, and a rule of recognition—which picks out a certain class of norms to be enforced—helps judges satisfy this want.

However, it is probably a mistake to think of a rule of recognition as operating *exactly* like a coordination convention. In the case of the rule of the road, no one has any particular view *ex ante* about what would be a good side to drive on; all they want is to drive on the same side as everyone else. But in the case of law, judges and officials *are* likely to have *ex ante* views about what would be a good basis for choosing norms to enforce: some of these will be content based, and some of them will refer to the process by which norms have been enacted. In the latter category may fall a judge's democratic convictions: he thinks it appropriate to enforce only rules that command democratic support in an elected legislature. But he does not want to be a lonely outlier in this. He prefers to enforce democratically supported rules, but he most prefers to be supporting the same rules as everyone else on the bench.[16] The structure of his relation to the other judges, then, is more like a "Battle of the Sexes" game than like a pure coordination game.[17] In *Law's Empire*, Ronald Dworkin questioned whether we should describe

---

15. *Cf. id.* at 78.

16. So he may not end up practicing the rule of recognition that he personally thinks would be best from a moral point of view. *Cf.* JOSEPH RAZ, PRACTICAL REASON AND NORMS 147–48 (2d ed. 1999).

17. *See* JEREMY WALDRON, LAW AND DISAGREEMENT 103–05 (1999). *See also* Jeremy Waldron, *Law*, *in* OXFORD HANDBOOK OF CONTEMPORARY PHILOSOPHY 181–86 (Frank Jackson & Michael Smith eds., 2005). See also the excellent discussion of the solution conditions for a "Battle of the Sexes" game in JEAN HAMPTON, HOBBES AND THE SOCIAL CONTRACT TRADITION 154–60 (1988).

legal conventions as pure coordination conventions or as convergent convictions.[18] (A convergent conviction would mean that a set of people reach the same outcome as a result of responding similarly to the same moral considerations.) I hope I have just shown that there is room in between these two descriptions. A rule of recognition might represent a compromise on the part of each judge of his substantive convictions with his desire to coordinate with other judges.

Fourth, I am taking Hart at his word that a rule of recognition and a rule of change are distinguished by the functions they serve: one provides a legal system with a measure of certainty; the other provides it with a measure of flexibility.[19] We should note, however, that in the Postscript to *The Concept of Law*, Hart appears to adopt a slightly different view: he says that promoting the certainty with which the law may be ascertained is *a* function, but *not the only function* of a rule of recognition; the need for certainty, he says, is not the be-all and end-all so far as the need for recognition is concerned.[20] Unfortunately, Hart does not tell us what the other functions of a rule of recognition may be. I suspect that some of them are actually functions supposed (in the body of *The Concept of Law*) to be served by the rules of change.

VII. RECOGNITION PROBLEMS IN COMMON LAW

Another area where there would seem to be a crying need for rule-based recognition is the area of common law. In his book *Of Laws in General*, in his great critique of "customary law" (aimed, with progressively less indirection, at the contemporary common law of England), Jeremy Bentham addressed himself to two central difficulties with this body of law: (1) the difficulty of extracting a rule from a decision by a judge in a single case, and (2) the difficulty of obtaining reliable and accessible versions of judges' decisions and the opinions that accompanied them. Both difficulties involve something like a problem of recognition.

Problem (2) is more like the problem of Hobbesian recognition: it is solved today by having officially certified law reports. These were not in existence in Bentham's time; reports of decisions were made by whoever wanted to make them, and their unreliability and incompleteness were notorious.[21]

---

18. Ronald Dworkin, Law's Empire 135–39 (1986).

19. *Id.* at 94–96.

20. *Id.* at 251–52.

21. Jeremy Bentham, Of Laws in General 187 (H.L.A. Hart ed., 1970): "In these reports taking them all together, about one third or one tenth or one twentieth or one hundredth part of the cases are made public which if they were equally known would be equally entitled to make law. . . . These reports are published by anybody that pleases. . . . If a lawyer who can get no practice happens to think of this method of making money: if the executor of a lawyer happens to find a manuscript among his papers; if either of these

Problem (1), however, represents a more basic problem. It is precisely a problem of uncertainty in Hart's sense, giving rise to "doubts . . . as to what the rules are or as to the precise scope of some given rule."[22] No clear rule of recognition had been supplied in Bentham's day to solve this problem, and it is arguable that no clear rule of recognition for this situation exists in common law systems even today. There are a few (often mutually conflicting) craft-principles among lawyers, telling you how to infer a rule from a given case or from a line of doctrine. But, as all lawyers know, the whole business is still haphazard and uncertain.

A large part of the difficulty stems from the fact that we are not in possession of clear, shared, and public rules of change, so far as changes in the law wrought by the judiciary are concerned. If we had such rules of change, we would have a basis for thinking clearly and sensibly about the recognition of common law norms; and, in my view, clearly understood rules of change in this regard would render the idea of a separate rule of recognition here redundant—just as they do in the type of case addressed in Section IV. We would just say (publicly): "Judges are entitled to change a society's law by enunciating new general rules and principles in the following form with the following procedure (and subject perhaps to the following constraints)." Then "recognizing" the new laws would just be a matter of checking to see that the procedures and forms (and constraints) prescribed in the rule of change were properly observed.

But of course it is no accident that we have no such rule. We are, as a society, profoundly ambivalent about judges' making and changing law. Actually we are publicly ashamed of it. The judiciary is not set up in a way that is calculated to make judicial lawmaking legitimate, nor are appointments made to the bench on the basis that this is a function that judges will be performing. On the contrary, when judges are nominated and confirmed, everyone goes around saying that it is of course out of the question that the person under consideration should be scrutinized as a potential lawmaker. Moreover the procedures that judges follow and the occasions for their decisions are not such as to amount to a sensible process of public lawmaking. As John Austin put it, judges appear to make law in fact, but theirs is an "oblique" form of lawmaking. The judge's "direct and proper purpose is not the establishment of the rule, but the decision of the specific case. He legislates *as properly judging*, and not *as properly legislating*."[23]

---

or any other such accident happens to throw a copy into the hands of a bookseller: the bookseller without being aware of it and without caring about it, becomes a legislator. Sometimes by commission from that high authority, a judge who had been dead and forgotten for half a century or for half a dozen centuries, starts up on a sudden out of his tomb, and takes his seat on the throne of legislation, overturning the establishments of the intervening periods, like Justinian brought to life again at Amalfi."

22. HART, *supra* note 1, at 92. *See supra* Section II.

23. JOHN AUSTIN, LECTURES ON JURISPRUDENCE 266–67 & 315 (5th ed. 1885) (emphasis in original).

A legislature, by contrast, is set up publicly as a place—as *the* place—for law-making and law-changing, and the secondary rules that it embodies to govern such changes are well known.[24]

Besides the two problems I have mentioned, Bentham leveled a third accusation against English common law. He complained that (3) it was inherently retroactive and that it therefore did not treat its subjects with respect. He called it "dog law."

> It is the judges . . . that make the common law. Do you know how they make it? Just as a man makes laws for his dog. When your dog does anything you want to break him of, you wait till he does it, and then beat him for it. This is the way you make laws for your dog: and this is the way the judges make law for you and me. They won't tell a man beforehand what it is he *should not do*—they won't so much as allow of his being told: they lie by till he has done something which they say he should not *have done*, and then they hang him for it."[25]

In principle, retroactivity or "dog law" is a separate problem from the ones we have considered. Even if problems (1) and (2) were solved, common law legal change would still be retroactive, at least as between the parties to the case in which the change takes place. But if problems (1) and (2) could be solved, maybe problem (3) would be manageable.

VIII. RECOGNITION OF RULES OR OF SOURCES OF RULES?

To the extent that Bentham's problems have been solved (which is not very much), they have been solved by the emergence of authoritative sets of law reports. Problem (2) is solved in this way. We now have rules that tell us how to recognize the judicial decisions and opinions that we are to regard as sources of law. Even though we haven't solved problem (1)—that is, even though we do not have determinate rules that tell us exactly how to infer rules from these sources—having an officially recognized set of sources is a huge advance.

This leads to the following question: why did Hart think it plausible to talk about a fundamental rule for recognizing *rules* of law, as opposed to a rule for recognizing *sources* of (rules of) law? I know of no good answer. I think it will be helpful to bear this question in mind when we turn finally—in Sections IX and

24. *Cf.* Jeremy Waldron, *Principles of Legislation, in* THE LEAST EXAMINED BRANCH: THE ROLE OF LEGISLATURES IN THE CONSTITUTIONAL STATE 15, esp. 22–23 (Richard Bauman & Tsvi Kahana eds., 2006).

25. This is from Jeremy Bentham's polemic *Truth versus Ashhurst, in* 5 THE WORKS OF JEREMY BENTHAM 231, 235 (John Bowring ed., 1843), *available at* http://www.law.mq.edu.au/Units/law420/LAW203S/Ashhurst.htm.

X—to think about the relation between the rule of recognition and the U.S. Constitution.

Ronald Dworkin seems to incline to the view that there may be a loose practice among officials of recognizing certain things as sources of legal rules (and standards and principles). His comments in *Law's Empire* on what he calls "the preinterpretive stage" of legal interpretation suggest something along these lines.[26] But he figures that this is quite a loose practice of recognition; he does not set a whole lot of store by it in his account of the objectivity of interpretation; and he certainly does not think of it primarily as a way of recognizing the rules that judges who engage in adjudicative practice are supposed to apply. It is at best a practice of recognizing the *sources* of the norms that judges will eventually apply to the cases that come before them. It does not guide the process of interpretation; at best, it tells us what to interpret.

Let us return to the solution of Bentham's problem (2): we now have a way of authoritatively recognizing certain decisions and opinions as sources of law. That is an advance. But are things not still screwed up (in the way that Bentham thought they were) by the lack of any agreed, established, and determinate solution to problem (1)? The answer is: no, because we have found that we do not need an agreed, established, and determinate solution to problem (1). We have a few vaguely shared ideas about how to proceed from source to rule or source to principle or standard. But we have found that things work better if we leave this unsettled and reasonably flexible. We have found that things work better if advocates and judges are free to experiment with new and unusual ways of extrapolating norms from decided cases, as well as tried and true ways. We do not need to be governed in this by any more determinate convention or rule.

I think this is an important point. Legal philosophers in the positivist tradition sometimes exaggerate our need for certainty in common law argument, in order to highlight the role that a rule of recognition has to play. But if we understand that legal argument proceeds in this area quite well without any great certainty about what follows or what does not follow from a given line of cases, we will see that this claim about the need for a rule of recognition in this area has been overplayed.

Personally, I believe that Ronald Dworkin gives a better account of this.[27] Instead of saying that judges and advocates are in possession of a rule of recognition that enables them to infer rules from lines of cases, he argues that judges and advocates are committed normatively to a principle of integrity that requires them to work with prior decisions, and to argue their way through to present conclusions that maintain some consistency with them. In order to do this, they

26. DWORKIN, *supra* note 18, at 63–64 & 90–91. See also discussion by Matthew Adler, *Popular Constitutionalism and the Rule of Recognition: Whose Practices Ground U.S. Law?*, 100 NW. U. L. REV. 719, 737-40 (2006).

27. DWORKIN, LAW'S EMPIRE, *supra* note 18, at 130–39 & 238–66.

need a sense of what the prior decisions are; that sense is given to them once Bentham's problem (2) is solved. With that in hand, what follows is normative argument informed by convictions about integrity, not the application of any rule of recognition. Judges argue normatively about what it is to keep faith with some previous decision(s), not about what it is to apply a rule to them.

One last point in this connection. It is sometimes said that a rule of recognition is necessary for us to discern the ways in which certain matters are settled authoritatively by the courts in a given legal system.[28] A decision by a court (such as the Supreme Court of the United States) might settle some controversial matter in two senses: (1) it might settle some outstanding issue as between the parties to a lawsuit (e.g., this petitioner is not to be executed after all), and (2) it might settle some general controversy in the society (e.g., no one is to be executed for offenses committed when they were children).[29] As to sense (1), it is of course important that there be in a community a shared way of ascertaining what the particular decision of the court is, and we may call this a rule of recognition if we like. As to sense (2), however, I am inclined again to doubt whether the legal phenomena require anything like a rule of recognition to explain what happens in this regard. What happens is that the courts decide a particular case in a way that indicates that, in the court's view, the decision is generalizable across a range of future cases. In light of this decision, it may prove very difficult to make a convincing argument for a contrary decision in a future case; our allegiance to the value of integrity may mean that any such argument will seem implausible. But not impossible: the law books are replete with examples of apparently well-settled precedents being overturned or unraveling in later lines of decision. When this happens, it is because integrity-based arguments (and other arguments, such as those based on reliance) for keeping faith with the original decision turn out to be not after all so peremptorily convincing. It is very difficult to give a simple account of what is going on in cases of this kind.[30] But one thing is clear to me: a good account will not have much of a role for anything like a rule of recognition, except to the extent that we need to be able to recognize what the decision is that integrity may command us to keep faith with. Rule-following is not what is involved in deference to precedent, even when the precedents seem

28. I am grateful to Matthew Kramer for suggesting that I deal with this line of argument, which is also represented in the contributions to this volume. *See* Larry Alexander and Frederick Schauer, *Rules of Recognition, Constitutional Controversies, and the Dizzying Dependence of Law on Acceptance* (Chapter 7, this volume); Kenneth Einar Himma, *Understanding the Relationship between the U.S. Constitution and the Conventional Rule of Recognition* (Chapter 4, this volume).

29. *Cf.* Roper v. Simmons 543 U.S. 551 (2005).

30. For a heroic attempt, see Kenneth Einar Himma, *Understanding the Relationship between the U.S. Constitution and the Conventional Rule of Recognition* (Chapter 4, this volume).

very strong indeed; what is involved is attention to an array of (defeasible) normative considerations, which may in particular cases seem to carry overwhelming force.

IX. THE CONSTITUTION: RULE OF RECOGNITION OR RULE OF CHANGE?

Bearing all this in mind, let us turn now to constitutional issues. How do Hart's categories apply in the constitutional context? What is the relation between the U.S. Constitution and the rule of recognition that supposedly lies at the basis of the system of U.S. federal law (as at the basis of every legal system)? Is there a rule of recognition in the U.S. constitutional scheme? Or does what we have said so far imply that it would be more interesting to focus on the role of a rule of change instead?

One possibility is that the Constitution actually gives us the rule of recognition. H. L. A. Hart, for example, says in the Postscript that

> in some systems of law, as in the United States, the ultimate criteria of legal validity might explicitly incorporate besides pedigree, principles of justice or substantive moral values, and these may form the content of legal constitutional restraints.[31]

It is difficult to understand this except as indicating that Hart is toying with the possibility that certain provisions of the Constitution might be or contain the rule of recognition (which Hart equates with the rule setting the ultimate criteria for legal validity).[32] I am not sure whether this is the view that Matthew Adler and Michael Dorf adopt in their essay "Constitutional Existence Conditions."[33] On the one hand, Dorf and Adler say in a footnote that positivists would resist any equation of the Constitution with the rule of recognition;[34] but on the other hand they seem to be willing to accept that the rule of recognition might in some way incorporate some of the criteria set out in the Constitution for determining when legislation has been validly enacted and when it is (at least presumptively) invalid on account of some issue about its content.[35] At any rate, it does seem to be Hart's view, or one strong possibility that he considers.

---

31. HART, *supra* note 1, at 247.

32. Hart also says of a constitutional system that "the system of course contains an ultimate rule of recognition and, in the clauses of its constitution, a supreme criterion of validity." *Id.* at 106.

33. Matthew D. Adler & Michael C. Dorf, *Constitutional Existence Conditions and Judicial Review*, 89 VA. L. REV. 1105 (2003).

34. *Id.* at 1130 n.53.

35. *Id.* at 1165.

So let us take this possibility seriously for a moment: the idea that the rule of recognition for U.S. federal law comprises a number of provisions of the U.S. Constitution, including (we might say) several of the clauses of Article I and a fair bit of the Bill of Rights. What should we say about this possibility?

One immediate point is that it is unclear why we should regard the constitutional clauses that authorize and limit the making of federal law as constituting this legal system's rule of *recognition*, as opposed to one of its fundamental secondary rules of *change*.[36] As we saw in the final paragraph of Section VI, above, these are different functions on Hart's account. Rules of change are remedies for the inflexibility of a simple system of primary rules, whereas a rule of recognition is a remedy for its uncertainty. It is the rule of change that sets up and authorizes a legislature, empowering it to make, alter, and repeal law. Moreover, when Hart discusses the importance of content-based constraints on lawmaking in a constitutional system like that of the United States, he actually says that these are best regarded as incidents of the rules of change:

> They are part of the rule conferring authority to legislate. . . . [L]egal limitations on legislative authority consist. . . of disabilities contained in rules which qualify him [the lawmaker] to legislate.[37]

If we regard these provisions as part of the system's rule of change, then how should we think about the role of a rule of recognition? Three possibilities suggest themselves. We might say (1) that, given the operation of the rule of change, there is no need for a rule of recognition. Or we might say (2) that a system with such a rule of change also needs a separate rule of recognition. Or we might say (3) that the rule of change *is* the rule of recognition, or part of it.

Possibility (1) is an analogue of what I said in Section IV about wills and contracts. To recognize a valid will, all a court needs to do is apply the rule of change—that is, the rule that specifies how a new will is to be made or an existing one altered. The court just runs through the checklist of valid procedures for this kind of legal change: signature, attestation, and so on. It does not need a separate rule of recognition. I personally do not see why this could not be a sufficient account of what is going on at the constitutional level also. There is at least one place where Hart seems to agree with this. Having said (as quoted above) that constitutional constraints "are part of the rule conferring authority to legislate," he goes on to remark that these constraints "vitally concern the courts, since they use such a rule as a criterion of the validity of purported legislative enactments coming before them."[38] The phrase "such a rule" must refer back to

---

36. Maybe the Article V provisions for the amendment of the Constitution constitute an even more fundamental rule of change; but the provisions for legislation are surely very important.

37. HART, *supra* note 1, at 69, 70.

38. *Id.* at 69.

"the rule conferring authority to legislate," and that means it refers to the rule of change, not the rule of recognition. Hart is saying that the courts use a rule of change as a criterion of the legal validity of the norms that come before them. That is quite different from what is normally said in Hart-ish jurisprudence—and quite different from what Hart himself says in the Postscript, where he implies that what the courts use to distinguish legally valid norms from nonlegal norms is a rule of recognition.[39]

In one place in the body of the book, Hart toys with possibility (2), which he distinguishes, though only barely, from possibility (3). He says this, when he introduces the idea of rules of change:

> Plainly there will be a very close connection between the rules of change and the rules of recognition: for where the former exists [*sic*] the latter will necessarily incorporate a reference to legislation as an identifying feature of the rules, though it need not refer to all the details of procedure involved in legislation. Usually some official certificate or official copy will, under the rules of recognition, be taken as a sufficient proof of due enactment.[40]

This seems to indicate that the rule of recognition is performing nothing much more than a sort of Hobbesian role (discussed above in Section III). It is really the rule of change that is the load-bearing item in the foundation of the legal system; the rule of recognition is just an ancillary certifying device.

Pretty soon, however, this delicate maneuvering disappears from Hart's account, and the idea of the rule of recognition simply takes over, with scarcely any further reference to the rule of change or to the relation between the two. So by the time we get to Chapter 6 of *The Concept of Law*, the rule of recognition has become the be-all and end-all of Hart's fundamental secondary rules. Hart says that in a simple legal society, like that of Rex I, "the sole criterion for identifying the law will be a simple reference to the fact of enactment by Rex I."[41] There is no reference to the fact that Rex I is empowered to enact law by something other than a rule of recognition. And in a more complex society, says Hart, reference to enactment will be one facet of the rule of recognition: in modern Britain, for example, "it is part of the rule of recognition that enactment by [the] legislature

39. Hart says in response to some argument by Dworkin: "I expressly state. . . that in some systems of law, as in the United States, *the ultimate criteria of legal validity* might explicitly incorporate besides pedigree, principles of justice or substantive moral values, and these may form the content of legal constitutional restraints." *Id.* at 247 (emphasis added). True, Hart doesn't directly identify the italicized phrase with "the rule of recognition," but the context makes this clear, as does his discussion of certainty and uncertainty in the rule of recognition's application a few pages later. *Id.* at 251–52.

40. *Id.* at 96.

41. *Id.* at 101.

is the supreme criterion of validity."[42] The rule of change that empowered Parliament to legislate no longer rates a mention.

This is a pity, because it encourages us to lose sight of the fact that the criteria of validity are given in the first instance by the rule of change. It encourages us to think that specifying the criteria of validity (in a rule of recognition) is something quite separate from and more fundamental than laying down a rule of change. But in fact the opposite is true. The rule of recognition gets its distinctive content from the rule of change; and it is still not clear to me that the rule of recognition actually does anything with that content that the rule of change has not already done.

X. POWERS, CHANGE, DUTY, AND CLOSURE

If we wanted to pursue possibility (2) from Section IX—that a system with a rule of change also needs a separate rule of recognition—what would we say that the rule of recognition might do, in addition to what a rule of change does? In his little book entitled *H.L.A. Hart*, Neil MacCormick says the following about the rule of recognition:

> What the rule of recognition does is to determine the criteria which settle the validity of the rules of a particular legal system. Whereas the secondary rules of adjudication and of change are power-conferring, the rule of recognition sets down duties; the duties of those who exercise public and official power, especially the power to adjudicate. If those who have power to act as judges are also duty-bound as judges to apply all and only those rules which satisfy certain more or less clearly specified criteria of validity, then the whole body of rules which those judges have power to administer has a relatively determinate or determinable content.[43]

Now, suppose we read this passage in the light of what has already been established—namely, that in the first instance, it is the rule of change that gives us the criteria of legal validity. What does MacCormick think the rule of recognition adds? It adds a *duty*, he says; a duty incumbent on courts to treat the results of the valid exercise of a power as law. All that the rule of change does is tell us how to exercise a power—the power of making law, for example, will be validly exercised if a bill has been bicamerally enacted, presented to the President for his signature, and either signed by him or voted on subsequently in a way that overrides the President's veto (provided that the bill is within the remit of Article I of the Constitution and not in conflict with the Bill of Rights). Professor MacCormick seems to be saying that the rule of change could do all this, but still

42. *Id.* at 106.

43. Neil MacCormick, H.L.A. Hart 21 (1981).

leave it open whether the courts were bound to apply as law a provision that passed all these tests.

But I do not see how this could be left open. The idea of a Hohfeldian power is not the idea of a change that leaves open what its impact on people's duties will be. The idea of a power *is* the idea of a capacity to change people's duties. So if the rule of change empowers Congress to legislate, it necessarily enables it to do something that will change the duties of other actors in the system.[44] That is what a power is. So a rule of recognition is not required as an additional factor to yield this result.

However, in addition to that, MacCormick suggests that the rule of recognition has one further task to perform: it imposes a duty on judges to apply *only* the rules that satisfy the criteria of validity. This goes beyond what the rule of change implies. The rule of change itself implies, as I said in the previous paragraph, that the courts must apply all the norms that satisfy the tests laid down in the rule of change. But now we are talking about an additional element: the courts must not apply any other norms. This is a closure principle, and it may be thought that the peculiar role of a rule of recognition is to enforce such closure (a role that I admit is not performed by the rule of change on my interpretation). I can imagine that some legal systems *may* have such a rule.[45] And sometimes some judges in existing legal systems act as though they were subject to such a rule. For example, in the antebellum period in the United States, judges enforcing the Fugitive Slave Acts were heard to say things like this:

> [W]ith the abstract principles of slavery, courts called to administer the law have nothing to do. It is for the people, who are sovereign, and their representatives, in making constitutions and in the enactment of laws, to consider the laws of nature, and the immutable principles of right. This is a field which judges can not explore . . . . They look to the law, and to the law only. A disregard of this by the judicial powers, would undermine and overturn the social compact.[46]

But, for one thing, other judges disagreed about this. Some did apply natural law considerations, directly or indirectly. (Part of the disagreement was whether "the

44. True, the terms of a given piece of legislation may not directly change the position of the judges (in the way that a law *about* judges might). But the legislation will change other people's legal position and thus indirectly affect the position of the judges, inasmuch as it is their role to say what the other people's positions (now) are.

45. And I suppose I should add that, to that extent, my account of the prominence of rules of change, compared to rules of recognition, cannot be presented as a necessary truth. I will say a little more about the modal status of my claims in this chapter in Section XIII. For now, it is worth noting that what I am responding to is the suggestion by Hart and his followers that, necessarily, a key role is played by a rule of recognition in every legal system. That claim I think is false, and it is falsified not just by some artificially imagined counterexample, but by our experience of actually existing legal systems.

46. Miller v. McQuerry, 17 F. Cas. 332, 339 (No. 9,583) (C.C.D. Ohio, 1853) (McLean J.).

law, and . . . the law only" defined a determinate set of norms and principles that (for example) did exclude principles of natural law or the law of nations or the moral principles widely believed to underlie the common law.) For another thing, notice that the judge in the passage cited above gives *a reason* for not looking beyond the constitution and legislation enacted under it (if indeed that is what he is confining himself to). He does not treat this restriction on his purview as a mere convention (though he may be treating it as one of those partial conflict coordination conventions I discussed in Section VI).

The most important thing to see in this example, however, is that the existence of such a rule in the antebellum United States was highly controversial: there were reasons put forward in its favor and reasons put forward against it. (These reasons and the controversy are traced in Robert Cover's book, *Justice Accused*.[47]) One reason in favor of having such a rule might be a reason that MacCormick mentions in the passage quoted above: if there is such a secondary rule, then "the whole body of rules which [the] judges have power to administer [will have] a relatively determinate or determinable content." That may or may not be thought desirable in a legal system. Some people may prefer a system of law that is more open than that. But it seems odd to build it into our very concept of a legal system that there must be a rule limiting what considerations can be appealed to in this way. Apart from anything else, that would imply that the judges and lawyers who criticized the view taken by Justice McLean in *Miller v. McQuerry* were making some sort of conceptual mistake about what sort of system they were in (or reflecting upon).

For reasons best known to themselves, legal positivists are interested in systems that do have this sort of closure. Normative positivists give moral reasons for this interest: they think that systems with this sort of closure rule are morally desirable.[48] And whether on conceptual grounds or normative grounds, positivists believe it is a good idea to understand the concept *law* as linked to this sort of closure. That may or may not be a plausible move in the philosophy of law. But there is some effrontery in saying, in addition to this, not only that law is to be understood as a closed system but also that the price of its being closed is that every legal system must be deemed to contain a fundamental rule that embodies the principle of such a closure. That is, there is some effrontery in the positivists' insistence that every legal system must contain a rule cast in terms that represent the positivists' own jurisprudential position!

Much of Ronald Dworkin's jurisprudence can be understood as the rejection of this sort of closure. First of all, he draws attention to features of our existing legal systems (e.g., in the United States) that show no evidence of such closure.

---

47. Robert Cover, Justice Accused: Antislavery and the Judicial Process (1975).

48. For "normative positivism," see Jeremy Waldron, *Normative (or Ethical) Positivism*, *in* Hart's Postscript: Essays on the Postscript to The Concept of Law 411 (Jules Coleman ed., 2001).

Secondly, he denies that such closure should be regarded as an advantage at the high levels of constitutional recognition and, incidentally, also at the lower levels of the recognition of wills and so on.[49]

XI. RAZ ON RULES (*PLURAL*) OF RECOGNITION

In *Practical Reason and Norms,* Joseph Raz argues that most legal systems have several rules of recognition of which no one is ultimate.[50] If this is the case, then no particular rule of recognition can contain the sort of closure clause that Professor MacCormick postulates. A given rule of recognition will say (at most) that all rules satisfying test φ are to be applied by the courts; but it cannot say that no rules not satisfying test φ are to be applied by the courts, since that would interfere with the operation of other rules of recognition in the same system.

Raz notes Hart's belief that this might give rise to conflicts and that we need an ultimate master-rule of recognition to sort this out. But Raz says that, whether or not this is thought desirable, it is plainly not definitive of a legal system: "there is no reason to believe that valid norms belonging to one system cannot conflict."[51] The most Raz is prepared to say, therefore, is that every system must have some rule of recognition; but since, as we have seen, the function of a rule of recognition (except this spurious function of closure) can be performed by a rule of change, we may not be able to get even that far.

Notice too, in this connection, that powers of change in a given legal system may also be plural and may also be more or less well-ordered. If they are well-ordered—that is, if there is a metanorm *N* saying that change through procedure α takes priority over change through procedure β—then I guess there is a question about how to describe *N*. Is it perhaps more like a rule of recognition than like a rule of change? Some of what Hart says in *The Concept of Law* might seem

---

49. This relates back to what was said in Section IV. Dworkin's early work on *Riggs v. Palmer, in* RONALD DWORKIN, TAKING RIGHTS SERIOUSLY 23 ff. (1977), can be seen as involving a denial that the existence of rules of change for valid wills entails anything in the way of a restriction on the types of considerations that can be admitted into determining the distribution of postmortem property. That a will conforms to the criteria for valid change indicates that it is to be taken into account in determining the disposition of the testator's estate. And normally it will be conclusive. But sometimes other provisions can impact on this as well: "family provision" legislation in certain jurisdictions, for example. And Dworkin shows that the class of other considerations is not closed in the way that a rule of recognition would suggest: hybrid moral/common law/law of nations ideas, such as the principle that no person may base any claim on his own iniquity, can also intrude, in ways we would expect a rule of recognition—on MacCormick's account—to prohibit. *See also* DWORKIN, LAW'S EMPIRE, *supra* note 18, at 15–20.

50. RAZ, *supra* note 16, at 146–48.

51. *Id.* at 147.

to suggest this.[52] But I see no reason to follow this suggestion: why not simply say that when there are multiple rules of change, it is desirable to have a metarule of change to sort out the priorities between them?

XII. THE *GRUNDNORM* FUNCTION

Maybe it is a mistake to identify the rule of recognition too closely with (certain provisions of) the Constitution. Some positivists may want to say that the function of the rule of recognition is not to do what the Constitution does, but to validate the Constitution as law. The Constitution then validates federal legislation as law by applying its own rule of change and (if you buy the MacCormick story) its own subordinate rule of recognition. But the fundamental rule of recognition is prior to and lies behind the Constitution. John Finnis, for example, says that "the rule of recognition . . . is the answer, ultimate for Hart's legal theory, to the question 'What is the reason for the validity of the highest rule of change . . . of this legal system?'"[53]

This more or less assigns the rule of recognition the normative function of Hans Kelsen's *Grundnorm*, with the difference of course that Hart regards it empirically, as an actually existing practice, whereas Kelsen is interested in it as a sort of logical postulate (albeit the logical presupposition of an empirically effective system of norms).[54] Some of what Hart says about the rule of recognition in a long endnote to the beginning of Chapter 6 of *The Concept of Law* supports this view. While noting the ontological and methodological differences between the terms of his jurisprudence and the terms of Kelsen's jurisprudence, he notes that his thesis that the foundation of a legal system consists in an ultimate rule of recognition "resembles in some ways Kelsen's conception of a basic norm."[55]

This is a very interesting alternative to the view explored in Section X. It is an odd analogy, however, for Hart or a follower of Hart to invoke. Kelsen's problem was that he wanted to find a way of applying the concept of validity to the foundational norms of a legal system even though (*ex hypothesi*) there were no norms to validate them. So he came up with this logical postulate of an ultrafoundational norm. One of the healthy things about Hart's account in *The Concept of Law* is that it avoids this problematic. Hart says in effect that the concept of validity simply does not apply to the fundamental secondary rules: as ultimate rules,

52. HART, *supra* note 1, at 95.

53. John Finnis, *On Hart's Ways: Law as Reason and as Fact*, 52 AM. J. JURIS. 25, 44 (2007).

54. *See* KELSEN, *supra* note 11, at 202.

55. HART, *supra* note 1, at 292.

they are presuppositions of validity, rather than valid in themselves.[56] To the extent that Hart identifies fundamental secondary rules with sociologically existent social practices, all we can say about the foundations of a legal system is that they *exist*. Now what exists, it seems to me, at the foundation of a legal system like the United States, is a practice of making and changing law according to procedures and criteria that are crystallized in articles I and V of the Constitution, along with the Bill of Rights. That's the practice that exists. It seems to me that a jurist proceeding in this spirit should not then try to conjure up some role for a rule of recognition to underpin these practices, assigning it a behind-the-scenes validating role that it was entirely the genius of Hart's contribution to dispense with.

No doubt the persuasiveness of what I have just said will vary according to a theorist's taste for metaphysics in his legal philosophy. But even if some want to persevere with something like the quasi-Kelsenian approach to Hart's rule of recognition, there are further embarrassing questions that have to be faced.

For one thing, notice that the quasi-Kelsenian account of the rule of recognition does not really treat it as a *rule*, in the sense of something nomological or universalizable in shape. It treats it instead as a particularized normative practice. It holds, for example, that the rule of recognition for federal law in the United States identifies the document crafted at Philadelphia in 1787, and ratified by the thirteen states, as law, and it separates that document from (say) the Declaration of Independence or the Articles of Confederation in this regard: the latter two are not recognized as law, the 1787 Constitution is.[57] So the task of the most fundamental "rule" of recognition on this quasi-Kelsenian account is just to *pick out one particular thing and distinguish it from a couple of other particular things*. It does not give us any sort of criterion for identifying things *of a kind*. The Constitution itself—once *it* has been recognized—puts into operation a practice of something like recognition that does operate in a rule-like way, identifying a potentially unlimited class of items by source-based and other criteria. (As I have said, the Constitution does this on the basis of the rules of change that it embodies.) But the fundamental rule of recognition does not, on the account presently under consideration. Of course, this may not be fatal to the quasi-Kelsenian positivist account. Those who take this approach may say that we should not be too exercised by the term "rule" in "rule of recognition." Nothing hangs on its rule-likeness. It may still be a normative practice—a widely accepted sense that something in particular ought to be done or deferred to, as discussed above in Section VI.

---

56. *Id.* at 107–10.

57. This of course leaves open the further question whether the rule or recognition, so understood, also has a closure function at this fundamental level; does it merely not recognize the Declaration of Independence as law, or does it lay an affirmative duty on courts to treat it as nonlaw, that is, not to ever take the Declaration of Independence into account?

But there is still another question to put to the quasi-Kelsenian account. If we do believe that there is a fundamental secondary rule or practice performing this crucial Kelsenian role "behind the Constitution," is such a secondary rule or practice more like a rule of recognition or more like a rule of change?

The analogy to Kelsen's account (partial though it is) suggests that the ultimate secondary rule or practice is better conceived on the analogy of a rule of change. In Kelsen's system the *Grundnorm* is supposed to give the impression that the framers of the historically first constitution had the right to do what they did. To the extent that it has content, that is what its content is: it empowers them; it authorizes their making the change that they did. It interprets what they did as a norm-creating act, as though there were a higher norm to validate their framing of this document. In other words, the fundamental norm is associated, in Kelsen's view, with *legal dynamics*—change in the legal system. This is absolutely essential in Kelsen's account, and I think it distinguishes any account like Kelsen's from jurisprudential theories that assign a key role to the static recognitional, rather than the dynamic transformational, character of the norm that is supposed to lie behind the constitution.

I know this is far from conclusive in our interpretation of Hart's theory. Hart is not Kelsen. But I think the points just made cast further doubt on the proposition that it is, specifically, a rule of recognition, rather than a rule of change, that lies at the foundation of a modern system of constitutional law.

XIII. CONCLUSION

It is not difficult to imagine a normative system in which something like a rule of recognition is crucial. John Gardner has suggested to me that the players of board games sometimes approach their juridical tasks with a fundamental norm that says (something like) "The rules of Monopoly can be found printed inside the lid of the box that contained the board, the cards, the money, and the playing pieces when they were purchased." In any disputes that break out among the players as to what the rules of Monopoly are, this secondary rule tells them where to look.[58]

It might be possible, at a stretch, to imagine a legal system that works just like this, or for whose workings this sort of example would offer a better analogy than the account I have offered, organized as it is around the central role of rules of change. Perhaps some systems of religious law are like this; they are organized around a basic secondary rule that says, "The rules for social life are those contained in the books of Exodus, Leviticus, and Deuteronomy." I suspect that in the

58. I am indebted to John Gardner for this example, offered verbally at the 2008 Annual U.K. Analytic Legal Philosophy Conference at University College, Oxford.

real world, systems of religious law are like this in some respects and unlike this in others. In some religious traditions, the relevant rule of recognition points to a holy book as a *source of law* rather than as a list of rules. And in all legal traditions, there is the additional role of argument, along the lines indicated above in Section VIII. As I said there, such argumentation does not itself require a rule of recognition to operate recursively upon its results. All it requires is a way of identifying the texts around which casuistry and interpretive argumentation will revolve.

To the extent that such legal systems are imaginable, one has to be very careful about making any claim that it is a necessary truth that rules of change, rather than rules of recognition, are fundamental to our understanding of law. But when we turn our attention to the real-life legal systems with which we are familiar, are they much like Gardner's Monopoly set and like these religious systems? I do not think so. Change is the key to a modern legal system. A well-organized system operates with settled rules of explicit formal change and also with rules that frame and facilitate informal change through argumentation. Neither set of secondary rules makes the recognition function fundamental. To the extent that it is fundamental, it is a function that rules of change are perfectly able to perform by themselves.

13. KELSEN, QUIETISM, AND THE RULE OF RECOGNITION

MICHAEL STEVEN GREEN*

Consider 17 C.F.R. § 205.3(b)(1), a regulation that requires attorneys practicing before the United States Securities and Exchange Commission to report evidence of material securities violations. Why is it the law? The reason is another law, namely section 307 of the Sarbanes–Oxley Act,[1] which authorized the Commission to establish minimum standards of professional conduct for attorneys practicing before it. Since the regulation was enacted by the Commission pursuant to the authorization in the Sarbanes–Oxley Act, it is the law.

But why is the Sarbanes–Oxley Act law? Here too the reason is another law. Congress was authorized under the Commerce Clause of the U.S. Constitution to "regulate Commerce . . . among the several States,"[2] and Sarbanes–Oxley was enacted by Congress pursuant to that authorization.[3]

But why is the Commerce Clause law? Is the reason, once again, another law, namely Article VII?[4] Is the Commerce Clause law because Article VII authorized any nine of the original thirteen states to ratify the Constitution (including the Commerce Clause), and the Constitution was indeed ratified pursuant to that authorization? Kent Greenawalt has argued that Article VII cannot be the reason that the Constitution is law. "[N]o judge or other official," he observes, "would presently be likely to countenance a legal argument that an original state purportedly

---

* Professor of Law, College of William & Mary. This chapter has benefited from helpful criticisms and comments by Matt Adler and the other participants in the Conference on the Rule of Recognition and the United States Constitution at the University of Pennsylvania Law School. Thanks also to Torben Spaak and an audience at the Faculty of Law of the University of Uppsala, Sweden.

1. 15 U.S.C. § 7245 (2002).

2. U.S. CONST. art. I, § 8.

3. *See* Implementation of Standards of Professional Conduct for Attorneys, Sarbanes-Oxley Act of 2002 Release No. 33-8185, 68 Fed. Reg. 6295, 6297 (Feb. 6, 2003).

4. U.S. CONST. art. VII ("The Ratification of the Conventions of nine States, shall be sufficient for the Establishment of this Constitution between the States so ratifying the Same."). For the Constitution's status as law to depend upon Article VII, Article VII cannot be part of the Constitution ratified. It must instead be a separate law specifying the means by which the Constitution may be made law. Article VII would be valid law not when the Constitution was ratified, but on September 17, 1787, the time of the unanimous consent of the twelve state delegations present at the Constitutional Convention.

bound to comply with the Constitution had not ratified it properly."[5] The Constitution's status as law is established, not by law, but by a social fact, namely "its continued acceptance."[6]

As we shall later see, I think Greenawalt is wrong about Article VII. It plays a meaningful role in validating the Constitution in our legal system.[7] But setting that issue aside for the moment, Greenawalt's argument provides a nice illustration of the application of Hart's idea of a rule of recognition to questions of constitutional law.[8] According to Hart, in every legal system officials use criteria to identify which norms are the laws of that system and so may be backed up by official power. Some criteria for law can themselves be identified as law by more fundamental criteria. For example, the Sarbanes–Oxley Act is identifiable as law because it was promulgated by Congress in accordance with the Commerce Clause. But eventually *ultimate* criteria are reached. These are the rule of recognition for the system,[9] and their use to identify

---

5. Kent Greenawalt, *The Rule of Recognition and the Constitution*, 85 MICH. L. REV. 621, 640 (1987) (reprinted as Chapter 1, this volume, at 18–19).

6. *Id.* (reprinted as Chapter 1, this volume, at 19).

7. *See infra* Section II, where I argue that the question of when the Constitution became valid law is answered by reference to Article VII.

8. In fact, Greenawalt's goal is *exploring* the consequences of the rule of recognition model for questions of constitutional law. He is skeptical about the adequacy of the model in a number of respects. Greenawalt, *supra* note 5, at 658–71 (reprinted as Chapter 1, this volume, at 35–46). My comments here are directed at the model itself, rather than Greenawalt's own views.

9. The term "rule of recognition" is ambiguous. In this chapter, I will use it in two senses. First, it is the propositional content specifying the ultimate criteria for law in the system. Hart uses the term in this way when he speaks of the rule of recognition of the English legal system as "what the Queen in Parliament enacts is law." H.L.A. HART, THE CONCEPT OF LAW 107 (Penelope A. Bulloch & Joseph Raz eds., 2d ed. 1994).

But Hart also uses the term to refer to the *social fact* that a certain rule of recognition, in the propositional sense, is *practiced* by officials—that is, that officials share a commitment to enforce only those norms that satisfy the propositional rule. *Id.* at 110, 292–93. On the distinction between these two senses of the term, see JULES COLEMAN, THE PRACTICE OF PRINCIPLE 77–78 (2001); Benjamin C. Zipursky, *The Model of Social Facts, in* HART'S POSTSCRIPT 219, 227–28 (Jules Coleman ed., 2001). Because disambiguation is awkward, in this chapter I will use the term in both senses in a manner that I believe will be clear from the context.

As a number of chapters in this volume have shown, Hart uses the term in still other senses. According to Hart, the purpose of rules of recognition is to reduce uncertainty about which norms are law, by identifying certain markers of legal validity. HART, *supra*, at 94–95. *Rules of change*, in contrast, solve the problem of the inflexibility of primary (especially duty-imposing) rules, by identifying means by which primary rules can be changed. *Id.* at 95–96. So understood, the criterion identified by Hart as part of the English rule of recognition ("What the Queen in Parliament enacts is law") looks more like a rule of change than a rule of recognition. Indeed, as Jeremy Waldron notes, it is

the laws of the system is justified, not by law, but by the social fact of official acceptance.[10]

In this chapter I will contrast Hart's approach with *legal quietism*. For Hart, when justification of law by law runs out, justification is still available by reference to social facts. For the quietist, *legal* justification exhausts the possible justification for law. If our judgments about the law are fundamental, in the sense that they cannot be justified by other judgments about the law, then they have *no* justification (which is not to say that they should be abandoned). There is, one might say, no legal epistemology—no possible account of why our fundamental legal judgments are justified.

My goal is not to show that legal quietism is correct. It is the more modest one of mapping the differences between a quietist approach and Hart's, and showing their consequences for fundamental questions of constitutional law. I also hope to inspire appreciation for, if not agreement with, Hans Kelsen's legal theory, for I believe that legal quietism is exemplified—if somewhat imperfectly—in Kelsen's writings.[11]

---

unclear why there need be a rule of recognition, rather than a rule of change, at the apex of a legal system *See* Jeremy Waldron, *Who Needs Rules of Recognition?* (Chapter 12, this volume).

Further ambiguity stems from the fact that Hart speaks of legal rules as either power conferring or duty imposing. Scott Shapiro and Stephen Perry argue that a rule of recognition should rightly be understood as imposing a duty upon officials to apply the rules that satisfy the criteria of legality in the rule of recognition in the propositional sense. I will ignore these complications in this chapter and use the term solely in the first two senses. *See* Scott J. Shapiro, *What Is the Rule of Recognition (And Does It Exist)?* (Chapter 9, this volume); Stephen Perry, *Where Have All the Powers Gone? Hartian Rules of Recognition, Noncognitivism, and the Constitutional and Jurisprudential Foundations of Law* (Chapter 11, this volume).

10. Hart, *supra* note 9, at 110, 292–93.

11. The following account cannot be understood as a comprehensive interpretation of Kelsen's legal theory, however. One reason is that Kelsen's views changed over time, making an interpretation of his legal *theory* (in the singular) impossible. *See, e.g.*, Stanley L. Paulson, *Four Phases in Hans Kelsen's Legal Theory? Reflections on a Periodization*, 18 Oxford J. Legal Stud. 153 (1998). The most notable change occurred in the early 1960s after the publication of the second edition of *The Pure Theory of Law*. In these later works, and particularly in Hans Kelsen, General Theory of Norms (Michael Hartney trans., 1991) (1979), it appears that Kelsen retreated from his Kantian approach. *See* Stanley L. Paulson, *Introduction, in* Normativity and Norms: Critical Perspectives on Kelsenian Themes xxiii, xxvii (Stanley L. Paulson & Bonnie Litschewski Paulson eds., 1998) [hereinafter Normativity and Norms]. I am primarily interested in the Kelsen of the first and second editions of *The Pure Theory of Law*.

Another reason that the following is not a comprehensive interpretation of Kelsen's legal theory is that I will ignore, and indeed express skepticism about, a number of core Kelsenian precepts (in particular, his notion of the basic norm (*Grundnorm*)). Nevertheless, I think the position I discuss is Kelsenian in spirit.

I will begin by describing the role that social facts play in justifying legal judgments for Hart. I'll then argue that such justification distorts our judgments about the law. Next I'll offer Kelsen's quietist legal theory as an alternative, and I'll end by exploring some difficulties that the quietist approach must face.

I. HART'S RULE OF RECOGNITION MODEL

Hart believed that in every legal system there is a rule of recognition, which sets out the ultimate criteria for identifying the norms that are the valid laws of that system. This ultimate rule exists by virtue of its general (although not necessarily universal) acceptance by officials as a guide for their conduct.[12] In contrast, a norm identified as law by the rule of recognition exists because it is so identified—even when it is uniformly rejected as a guide for conduct by those to whom it is directed. For example, the English rule of recognition (roughly, *what the Queen in Parliament enacts is law*) exists by virtue of its acceptance by English officials. The Copyright, Designs and Patents Act of 1988,[13] in turn, exists because it was enacted by the Queen in Parliament, even if the high level of copyright piracy in England indicates that it is not accepted as a guide for conduct by the English citizenry.

Although Hart did not believe that a conduct-regulating norm identified by the rule of recognition needed to be accepted by its subjects to be law, he did believe that a legal system cannot exist unless such conduct-regulating norms are *generally* obeyed by the citizenry.[14] (I shall describe this as the requirement that a rule of recognition be *efficacious*.) But, once again, the fact that an *individual* conduct-regulating norm is widely disobeyed will not undermine its existence as law.

Let us call the social facts that ground a legal system—that is, the existence and efficaciousness of a rule of recognition—*rule of recognition facts*. It would seem to follow from Hart's approach that legal judgments can be *justified* by rule of recognition facts. For example, if an English official doubted whether the Copyright, Designs and Patents Act of 1988 is the law, her doubts could be put to rest by pointing out facts about the beliefs, attitudes, and behavior of English officials and citizens.

---

12. This acceptance need not be moral, however. Official acceptance of the rule of recognition could be based on "calculations of long-term interest; . . . an unreflecting inherited or traditional attitude; or the mere wish to do as others do." HART, *supra* note 9, at 203. But simple fear of sanctions for disobedience would be insufficient for the rule of recognition to exist, although private citizens might obey the law solely from such fear.

13. The Copyright, Designs and Patents Act, 1988, c. 48 (Eng.).

14. HART, *supra* note 9, at 116–17.

Although I believe that this is indeed Hart's view, the matter is complicated by his distinction between *external* and *internal* legal statements.[15] An external legal statement (ELS) is made by an observer who need not accept the rule of recognition. Someone making such a statement merely "states the fact that others accept it."[16] Hart offered as an example of an ELS, "In England they recognize as law . . . whatever the Queen in Parliament enacts. . . ."[17] So understood, an ELS can clearly be justified by rule of recognition facts, since it amounts to a description of such facts.

In contrast, someone who makes an internal legal statement (ILS) accepts the relevant rule of recognition as a standard of conduct.[18] Hart offered as the simplest example of an ILS, "It is the law that . . ."—that is, a statement in which a participant identifies the valid law of her system.[19] But he made it clear that ILSs include other normative legal statements, for example, "You (legally) ought to . . ." or "You have a (legal) duty to. . . ."[20]

Although Hart believed that someone who makes an ILS accepts the relevant rule of recognition, he thought that such a statement *expresses* rather than describes this acceptance. As Kevin Toh has persuasively argued, Hart was attracted to this expressivist account of ILSs because of its ability to explain, in a naturalistic fashion, what Hart thought was the *reason-giving* character of ILSs.[21]

---

15. *Id.* at 102–03.

16. *Id.* at 103. Hart also speaks of an external legal statement (or a statement "from the external point of view") as describing only *regularities of behavior*, without considering the reasons the participants take themselves to have for their actions. But he makes it clear that the observer "may, without accepting the rules himself, assert that the group accepts the rules, and thus may from the outside refer to the way in which *they* are concerned with them from the internal point of view." *Id.* at 89. Thus, the external point of view may take a hermeneutic approach, rather than merely understanding its subjects behavioristically. Finally, there is a third sense of the external point of view that refers to a *practical* rather than a *descriptive* approach to the law—namely the approach of Holmes's "bad man," who is concerned only with the law insofar as there are sanctions for disobedience. On these three senses of the external point of view, see Scott J. Shapiro, *What is the Internal Point of View?*, 75 FORDHAM L. REV. 1157, 1158–61 (2006).

17. HART, *supra* note 9, at 102.

18. *Id.* It is important to distinguish an ILS from a statement made by someone legally empowered to create norms through a statement. An example of the latter is a justice of the peace uttering "You are husband and wife," thereby *making* it the case that the two are husband and wife. Those who make an ILS need not have any such legal power.

19. *Id.*

20. *Id.* at 57, 90; Kevin Toh, *Hart's Expressivism and his Benthamite Project*, 11 LEGAL THEORY 75, 76 (2005).

21. *Id.* at 81–105. Hart's account is expressivist because his semantic account of ILSs does not define the terms they use, but instead describes the mental state a speaker expresses when uttering them. His account is noncognitivist because the mental state expressed is noncognitive, rather than being a cognitive state like a belief. *Id.* at 78–79.

For example, if a judge makes the ILS that a certain statute is the law, she thereby takes herself to have a reason for action (in particular, a reason to adjudicate in accordance with the statute).[22] But for a naturalist this is a puzzle, since the world is motivationally inert: there is no noncontingent connection between the state of affairs a speaker might truthfully describe the world as possessing and the speaker's reasons for action.

Rather than concluding that ILSs are descriptive but false,[23] Hart concluded that they do not refer to states of affairs in the world at all. They are instead the expression of a noncognitive state—in particular, the speaker's acceptance of the rule of recognition.[24] An official who states that a statute is the law can rationally take herself to have a reason to adjudicate in accordance with the statute, because by making the statement she has expressed her desire to adjudicate in that fashion.

In addition to expressing acceptance of the rule of recognition, Hart thought that someone making an ILS *presupposes* rule of recognition facts. Once again, however, an ILS does not *describe* these facts. It is not *about* the beliefs, attitudes, and actions of officials and citizens. Instead it presupposes the presence of these beliefs, attitudes, and actions.[25] Indeed, Hart criticized the legal realists for treating ILSs as descriptions of rule of recognition facts:

> One who makes an internal statement concerning the validity of a particular rule of a system may be said to *presuppose* the truth of the external statement of fact that the system is generally efficacious. For the normal use of internal statements is in such a context of general efficacy. It would however be wrong to say that statements of validity "mean" that the system is generally efficacious.[26]

Because rule of recognition facts are presupposed, not described, by ILSs, Hart argued that someone who speaks of rule of recognition facts has ceased to talk about legal validity from within the internal perspective:

> When we move from saying that a particular enactment is valid, because it satisfies the rule that what the Queen in Parliament enacts is law, to saying that in England this last rule is used by courts, officials, and private persons as the ultimate rule of recognition, we have moved from an internal statement of law asserting the validity of a rule of the system to an external statement of fact which an observer of the system might make even if he did not accept it.[27]

---

22. This reason for action might be only prima facie—that is, it could be defeated by a reason for action that is stronger in that context.

23. For an error theory concerning ethical statements, see J.L. MACKIE, ETHICS: INVENTING RIGHT AND WRONG (1977).

24. *See* Toh, *supra* note 20, at 81–105.

25. HART, *supra* note 9, at 102–03.

26. *Id.* at 104.

27. *Id.* at 107–08.

To sum up, Hart's view was that an ILS *expresses*, rather than describes, the speaker's acceptance of the rule of recognition as an appropriate standard for behavior; and *presupposes*, rather than describes, rule of recognition facts—that is, that the rule of recognition is accepted by other officials and is efficacious.

That rule of recognition facts are presupposed when making an ILS does not mean, however, that they can play no role in justifying the ILS. Consider an English official who wrongly believes that the prevailing rule of recognition is *what Michael Green says is law*. She therefore refuses to assent to the ILS, "The Copyright, Designs and Patents Act of 1988 is valid law." Assuming that she would accept *what the Queen in Parliament enacts is law* as a standard of behavior if the relevant rule of recognition facts were in place, there seems to be nothing wrong, as far as Hart's legal theory is concerned, for someone to show her that the ILS is *justified* by appealing to the relevant rule of recognition facts.

This conclusion is supported by the two prevailing accounts of a linguistic presupposition. According to the semantic account offered by P. F. Strawson and Bas van Fraassen, a presupposition concerns the relationship between the truth values of sentences (or propositions): *P* presupposes *Q* if and only if the truth of *Q* is necessitated both by the truth of *P and* by the truth of not-*P*.[28] For example, "The President of the United States is male" semantically presupposes that one and only one President of the United States exists, because it follows from the truth of "The President of the United States is male" and from the truth of "The President of the United States is not male" that there is one and only one President of the United States. It is because its semantic presupposition is false that one feels uncomfortable about assigning a truth value to "The present King of France is bald."

Let us imagine someone disinclined to assent to "The President of the United States is male" because she is unsure whether there is indeed one and only one President of the United States. There would be nothing wrong with showing her that the statement is justified because such a unique President exists. By the same token, if an ILS semantically presupposed rule of recognition facts, someone reluctant to assent to the ILS could be shown that it is justified because the requisite facts are in place.[29]

---

28. Peter F. Strawson, *On Referring*, 59 MIND 320 (1950); Bas C. van Fraassen, *Presupposition, Implication, and Self-Reference*, 65 J. PHIL. 136 (1968).

29. Indeed, there does not appear to be anything seriously distorting in simply incorporating the semantic presupposition of a statement into its descriptive content, as when "The President of the United States is male" is reformulated as "There exists one and only one President of the United States and that person is male." The statement "The Copyright, Designs and Patents Act of 1988 is valid law" would be reformulated as "There exist rule of recognition facts identifying the Copyright, Designs and Patents Act of 1988 as valid law"—keeping in mind that the statement would also express the speaker's acceptance of the standard picked out by the rule of recognition facts. This is apparently how Joseph Raz understands Hart's semantics of ILSs. Joseph Raz, *The Purity of the Pure Theory*, 35

It is questionable, however, that ILSs semantically presuppose rule of recognition facts. It seems false, for example, that the statement "The Copyright, Designs and Patents Act of 1988 is valid law" *entails* rule of recognition facts about the English legal system. After all, meaningful use of an ILS is possible in the known absence of any relevant rule of recognition facts. For example, one might speak, using ILSs, of the valid law of past or hypothetical legal systems.[30]

Under the alternative *pragmatic* concept of a presupposition, offered by Robert Stalnaker, a presupposition is a propositional attitude on the part of *speakers*, rather than a semantic relation between sentences or propositions. Sentence *P* presupposes *Q* if and only if the use of *P* would normally be inappropriate unless it is commonly accepted that *Q*.[31] One presupposes a fact in this sense if he takes it for granted and assumes that others in the context do so as well.[32]

Kevin Toh has suggested, I think rightly, that Hart's understanding of a presupposition was pragmatic.[33] As Hart put it, "it would be generally *pointless*" to use ILSs in the absence of the relevant rule of recognition facts.[34] But only *generally* pointless: in a course on ancient Roman law, a teacher might speak of certain norms as legally valid, even though the relevant rule of recognition facts are not in place.[35]

But even if someone making an ILS pragmatically presupposes rule of recognition facts, it still does not follow that such facts cannot be used to justify the ILS, assuming that the justification concerns whether the ILS can be asserted in the *usual context*, when speaking about actual rather than past or hypothetical legal systems. Indeed, Hart himself admitted that "[i]f the truth of this presupposition [of rule of recognition facts] were doubted, it could be established by reference to actual practice: to the way in which courts identify what is to count as law, and to the general acceptance of or acquiescence in these identifications."[36] And he explicitly distinguished his approach from Kelsen's (in which, as we shall see, rule of recognition facts are justificatorily unrelated to legal validity),

---

Revue International de Philosophie 441, 448 (1981); Joseph Raz, *H.L.A. Hart (1907–1992)*, 5 Utilitas 145, 148 (1993).

30. Hart, *supra* note 9, at 104. I shall say more about such judgments, which Raz calls detached, later. *See infra* Section III.

31. Semantic presuppositions will also be pragmatic presuppositions. I would not normally say that the President of the United States is male except in a context in which it is taken for granted that one and only President of the United States exists. But not all pragmatic presuppositions are semantic. For example, it is a pragmatic but not a semantic presupposition of my uttering "My wife is either in the kitchen or the bathroom" that I don't know for certain that she is in the kitchen.

32. Robert C. Stalnaker, Context and Content 38 (1999).

33. Toh, *supra* note 20, at 86–87 n.21.

34. Hart, *supra* note 9, at 104.

35. *Id.*

36. *Id.* at 108. *See also id.* at 245.

on the ground that it "obscures, if it is not actually inconsistent with, the point stressed in this book, viz. that the question of what the criteria of validity in any legal system are is a question of fact."[37]

The only reason to doubt that rule of recognition facts can justify an ILS for Hart is his insistence that someone who describes such facts has ceased to speak from within the internal perspective. If any statement justifying an ILS must itself be an ILS—if such justification must always proceed through statements made within the internal perspective—then rule of recognition facts would be justificatorily irrelevant to legal validity. But Hart gives us no reason to think that this is the case.

In general noncognitivists have no problem with a normative statement being justified by a non-normative statement of fact. Let us assume that you have a positive attitude toward giving John $20 *if* you promised to do so. Your attitude is conditional, in the sense that it is directed at all possible worlds in which you give John $20, *provided* that you promised to do so in that possible world. I can show that you are justified in making the normative statement "I have an obligation to give John $20" by pointing out the non-normative fact that you made the requisite promise. To be sure, such justification will not satisfy you if you have no positive attitude toward promise-keeping at all. The justification of the *reason-giving core* of your normative statement—to the extent that such justification is possible at all—has to proceed through another normative (and so expressive) statement.[38] But assuming that you do have the appropriate attitude, non-normative statements of fact can have justificatory force.

Hart apparently treated ILSs as expressing a conditional attitude of acceptance of a rule of recognition. The speaker expresses a positive attitude toward all possible worlds in which the rule of recognition is followed, *provided* that the requisite rule of recognition facts are in place in that possible world. I see no reason, therefore, why Hart should not allow for the justification of ILSs—for people with the requisite attitudes—by ELSs concerning rule of recognition facts. Indeed, when an ILS is asserted in the usual context, in which the existence of rule of recognition facts is presupposed by the speaker, these facts *must* be justificatorily relevant to the ILS. If the facts weren't justificatorily relevant, there would be no reason to presuppose them.[39]

---

37. *Id.* at 293.

38. Compare Charles L. Stevenson, *Relativism and Nonrelativism in the Theory of Value*, *in* FACT AND VALUE 71, 89 (1963):

> A methodological inquiry, when it attempts to find the [reasons] that will justify a given [evaluation], does not stand apart from an evaluative inquiry but simply continues it, yielding ordinary value judgments that are expressed in a different terminology. The so-called noncognitive view, then, which we have seen to be nonrelativistic with regard to ordinary value judgments, is equally so with regard to justifications.

39. Thanks to Matt Adler for encouraging me to stress this point.

On the other hand, it is not clear that factual statements about a speaker's *acceptance* of the rule of recognition can be used to justify an ILS. As an analogy, consider your ethical statement "I have an obligation to give John $20." Although a noncognitivist would understand this statement as expressing a certain positive attitude, it does not follow that the statement can be justified by a description of this attitude. The reason is that the attitude expressed, although conditional in one sense (because it is directed only toward possible worlds in which you *promised* to give John $20), is *unconditional* to the extent that it is directed toward all possible worlds in which you keep your promise to John—including worlds in which you do not *want* to do so.[40] Since you would have a positive attitude toward a world in which you are forced to keep your promise, you would—expressing this attitude—say "I have an obligation to give John $20 even if I don't want to." You would not consider the presence of a positive attitude to be a factual condition for your obligation. For this reason, you would treat descriptions of your attitudes to be irrelevant to the justification of your ethical statement.[41]

Hart probably considered the attitudes expressed in ILSs to be unconditional in this sense, since such statements tend to attribute legal obligations to people whatever their attitudes. An American judge is likely to claim not merely that she has a legal obligation to adjudicate in accordance with the U.S. Constitution, but that she would have this obligation even if she did not *want* to adjudicate in accordance with the Constitution. And she would insist that other judges too have this obligation whatever *their* individual attitudes, unless the refusal to accept the American rule of recognition was so widespread that it undermined the presupposition that the rule of recognition is *generally* accepted by officials as a standard of conduct.[42]

---

40. *See* Derek Parfit, Reasons and Persons 151–54 (1984).

41. Simon Blackburn has helpfully described this form of noncognitivism as *quasi-realist*. Normative statements that sound realist, in the sense that they can assert the independence of value from desire (including the very desires expressed by the statements), are compatible with noncognitivism. Simon Blackburn, *Errors and the Phenomenology of Value, in* Morality and Objectivity: A Tribute to J.L. Mackie 1 (Ted Honderich ed., 1985); *see also* Jeremy Waldron, *The Irrelevance of Moral Objectivity, in* Natural Law Theory: Contemporary Essays 158, 164–71 (Robert P. George ed., 1992). The quasi-realist position can be found even among early noncognitivists. *See, e.g.*, Stevenson, *supra* note 38.

42. Kevin Toh has helpfully outlined Hart's somewhat muddled views on the categorical nature of ILSs. In *The Concept of Law*, Hart took the acceptance expressed in ILSs to be *full*. Kevin Toh, *Raz on Detachment, Acceptance and Describability*, 27 Oxford J. Legal Stud. 403, 415–16 (2007). Someone who fully accepts a norm considers it binding on all its subjects (whatever their attitudes). In contrast, someone who *weakly* accepts a norm considers it binding only on himself (presumably because of his acceptance). *Id.* at 415. Later, Toh argues, Hart came around to the view that the acceptance expressed in an ILS need be weak only, although Toh argues that Hart was wrong to make this change. *Id.* at 417–20.

In short, the descriptive fact that a speaker has the attitude an ILS expresses is justificatorily irrelevant to the ILS. To offer this descriptive fact as a justification for the ILS would be incompatible with the attitude the ILS expresses. To this extent, therefore, the internal perspective is isolated from (if not incompatible with) *some* of the external perspective, namely the perspective adopted when one describes one's attitudes and their relation to one's ILSs. But this separation of the internal and external perspectives is not complete. In the usual context, when rule of recognition facts are presupposed by a person making an ILS, such facts will be justificatorily relevant to the ILS. In such a case, there will be nothing wrong with showing that the ILS is justified through a statement from the external perspective about rule of recognition facts.

II. THE MODEL DISTORTS OUR LEGAL JUDGMENTS

In this Section, I will argue that Hart's rule of recognition approach distorts our legal judgments.[43] Consider the question *when* the U.S. Constitution became valid law. If the Constitution is currently law because of rule of recognition facts, it would appear that it became law when these facts were in place. And it is arguable (and I shall assume in this chapter) that this didn't happen until mid-1790—after the thirteenth state, Rhode Island, ratified.[44] After all, many officials may have thought that the constitutional experiment should fail, Article VII notwithstanding, without unanimous ratification.

But we know, without inquiring into the attitudes of officials at the time, that it is false that the Constitution became valid law in mid-1790. It became valid law on June 21, 1788, when the ninth state, New Hampshire, ratified it. This is not merely of antiquarian interest. In 1978, the Oneida Indian Nation sued the state of New York in federal district court to recover land purchased by the state on September 22, 1788—after both New Hampshire and New York ratified the Constitution.[45] The Oneida Nation claimed that the purchase was in contravention

43. For a similar argument, see Michael Steven Green, *Hans Kelsen and the Logic of Legal Systems*, 54 ALA. L. REV. 365, 381–89 (2003).

44. It took North Carolina until November 21, 1789, and Rhode Island (which failed to send any delegates to the Constitutional Convention) until May 29, 1790. HANNIS TAYLOR, THE ORIGIN AND GROWTH OF THE AMERICAN CONSTITUTION 218–19 (1911). For the pressures to ratify exerted by the new United States upon these two foreign nations in its midst, see David P. Currie, *The Constitution in Congress: Substantive Issues in the First Congress, 1789–1791*, 61 U. CHI. L. REV. 775, 834–37 (1994).

45. Oneida Indian Nation v. New York, 520 F. Supp. 1278 (N.D.N.Y. 1981), *aff'd in part, rev'd in part*, 691 F.2d 1070 (2d Cir. 1982). New York ratified the Constitution on July 26, 1788.

of the State Treaty Clause of the U.S. Constitution, which prohibits a state from entering "into any Treaty, Alliance, or Confederation"[46]

New York did not argue that the Oneida Nation should lose because at the time of the purchase there was no valid Constitution, since the relevant rule of recognition facts were not in place. Indeed, such a legal claim would be absurd. If true, it would threaten federal statutes enacted between June 21, 1788 and mid-1790. An example is the Judiciary Act, which was enacted on September 24, 1789, not only before Rhode Island's ratification but also before North Carolina's (on November 21, 1789).[47]

To be sure, the district court, following the Supreme Court's 1820 decision in *Owings v. Speed*,[48] concluded that the Oneida Nation should still lose, because the Constitution was not *effective* until March 4, 1789, when the first session of the new Congress began.[49] The issue in *Owings* was comparable to *Oneida*, namely whether a Virginia statute enacted in 1788 violated the Contracts Clause of the U.S. Constitution. Justice Marshall held that the "operation" of the Constitution "did not commence" before March 4, 1789, because after drafting Article VII the Constitutional Convention resolved that the old Congress of the Confederation should determine "the time . . . for commencing proceedings" under the new Constitution if it were ratified.[50] After the Constitution's ratification, the Congress of the Confederation chose March 4, 1789 as this time.[51]

It is clear, however, that *Owings* was not about when the Constitution became law, but merely about its operative effect. Just as a law may have retroactive effect on events that occurred before it existed, so it may have only prospective effect upon events occurring after its existence. Justice Marshall decided that the Contracts Clause had prospective effect only. Although it existed as law upon its ratification by the ninth state, it had effect on events only from March 4, 1789 onward. The *Oneida* Court came to the same conclusion about the State Treaty Clause.

In fact, as Gary Lawson and Guy Seidman have persuasively argued, *Owings* and *Oneida* wrongly decided even this narrow question of the Constitution's

---

46. U.S. CONST. art I, § 10.

47. Judiciary Act, ch. 20, 1 Stat. 73 (1789). Actually the matter is a bit more complicated, since subsequent acts applied the Judiciary Act to North Carolina, 1 Stat. 126 (June 4, 1790), and Rhode Island, 1 Stat. 128 (June 23, 1790). If a rule of recognition were established only after Rhode Island's ratification, and that fact validated the Constitution, the Judiciary Act would be valid law, but only with respect to North Carolina and Rhode Island.

48. 18 U.S. (5 Wheat.) 420 (1820).

49. *Oneida Indian Nation*, 520 F. Supp. at 1323.

50. *Owings*, 18 U.S. (5 Wheat.) at 421–23; *see* 2 THE RECORDS OF THE FEDERAL CONVENTION OF 1787, at 665 (Max Farrand ed., rev. ed. 1966) (1832).

51. 1 THE DOCUMENTARY HISTORY OF THE FIRST FEDERAL ELECTIONS 1788–1790, at 131 (Merrill Jensen & Robert A. Becker eds., 1976).

operative effect.[52] Consider provisions in the Constitution determining the proper means of creating the new Congress. These must have had operative effect before the new Congress was seated, or its creation would be a lawless event. There is no reason not to come to the same conclusion about provisions, like the State Treaty or Contract Clauses, that apply directly to the states and so do not require the existence of the federal government.

In short, we are committed, or at least can be committed, to certain provisions of the Constitution having operative effect at the moment of New Hampshire's ratification. Furthermore, we take these provisions to not be retroactive. We think they came into being as law at the moment of their operative effect, something that cannot be explained by Hart's rule of recognition model, which would treat them as coming into being with the establishment of the requisite rule of recognition facts. The problem cannot be solved by assuming that the American rule of recognition validates the Constitution indirectly, by validating *Article VII*, which in turn validates the Constitution—for the question remains when Article VII was valid law. Under the rule of recognition model, the answer is, once again, when the requisite rule of recognition facts were in place, which may have happened only in mid-1790.[53] But this misdescribes American law. Just as the Constitution was law at the moment of ratification, so Article VII was law, and the Constitution was legally amenable to ratification, *on September 17, 1787*—at the time of the unanimous consent of the twelve state delegations present at the Constitutional Convention.[54] Indeed, if *Article VII* did not become law until mid-1790, the Constitution could not have been ratified under Article VII at all.

One might argue, however, that it does not follow from Hart's model that Article VII or the Constitution became valid law only when a rule of recognition arose. After all, a statement about when a law became valid is an *ILS*. And it is possible that the only relevant rule of recognition facts that come into play in the

---

52. Gary Lawson & Guy Seidman, *When Did the Constitution Become Law?*, 77 NOTRE DAME L. REV. 1, 11–13 (2001).

53. Greenawalt, *supra* note 5, at 639–40 (reprinted as Chapter 1, this volume, at 18).

54. Since we would look to Article VII to determine *when* the Constitution became law, Article VII still plays a meaningful role in validating the Constitution. How then can we account for Greenawalt's observation, which is surely correct, that a judge would not now hold the Constitution inapplicable to an original state even if she were convinced that Article VII processes were not satisfied? One possibility is that she would conclude that such a state, although not in fact bound by the Constitution at the time of the failed ratification, is now estopped from challenging the Constitution's applicability. The estoppel argument would be very strong, given the great difficulty of disentangling the state's interests from those of the United States. How would we determine, for example, the state's interests in subsequent acquisitions, such as the Louisiana Purchase? If one adopted the estoppel approach, however, it would mean that Article VII is not the sole method by which an original state might become bound by the Constitution. The American legal system also contains a fundamental principle of ratification by estoppel.

justification of an ILS are *current*, not past, facts. If someone doubted the legal validity of the Constitution or Article VII entirely, because he thought that the American rule of recognition is *what the Queen in Parliament enacts is law*, reference to current rule of recognition facts could set him straight. But after that, all justification by rule of recognition facts ends. One can insist that the Constitution became valid law on June 21, 1788 (because that was when the procedures for ratification by Article VII were satisfied), whatever the rule of recognition facts on that date, since this ILS is justified by *current* rule of recognition facts.

This reading appears to be supported by Hart's discussion of a government returning from exile.[55] Upon its return, the question of the legal validity of certain norms during the interruption can arise. This question, Hart emphasized, "may *not* be one of fact"[56]—that is, it may not be a question of whether the rule of recognition of the returning government remained sufficiently in place during the interruption. Instead it may be a "question of law within the very system of law existing since the restoration."[57] So understood, it should be answered not by an ELS, but by an ILS. And Hart argued that there is no contradiction between the ELS that there were no laws of the restored legal system during the interregnum and the ILS that the laws of the restored system remained valid during that time. By the same token, there is no conflict between the ELS that the American legal system was not established until mid-1790 and the ILS that the Constitution was valid law on June 21, 1788.

But did Hart in fact believe that one can make the ILS that the laws of the restored system were valid *during the interregnum*? "[T]here is no reason," he argued, "why the declaration [that laws were valid during the interregnum] should not stand as a rule of the restored system, determining the law which its courts must apply to incidents and transactions occurring during the period of interruption." In other words, the statement that the laws were valid during the interregnum amounts to the claim that courts *after the restoration* should apply these laws when adjudicating events during the interregnum. The validity of the laws is "within the . . . system of law existing since the restoration."[58] It does not appear that Hart thought one could say, even from the internal perspective, that the laws were valid *during the interregnum*. For that would mean that officials during the interregnum were justified in making the ILS that the laws were valid. And given that the rule of recognition facts presupposed by such an ILS were not in place at the time, one cannot say that they would be so justified.

It appears, therefore, that Hart would understand the ILS that the Constitution became valid law on June 21, 1788 to mean only that *current* officials are obligated to treat the Constitution as valid law on or after that point. But when we say that

---

55. HART, *supra* note 9, at 119.
56. *Id.*
57. *Id.*
58. *Id.*

the Constitution was valid law on June 21, 1788, we can mean that it was valid law for the people *at the time as well*. We can be committed, in short, to a *categorical* ILS—one that is justified, not merely when made by us, but also when made by people at the time to which we refer. And Hart's theory has no place for such categorical ILSs.

Once again, the situation is different concerning the attitude of acceptance of the rule of recognition expressed in an ILS. As we have seen, a noncognitivist can allow for normative statements that speak of obligations that are independent of attitudes. I can say that I ought to keep my promises even if I don't want to, because the positive attitude I express in this statement is directed toward all possible worlds in which promises are kept, including those worlds in which I have an aversion to promise keeping. Hart therefore can explain ILSs that categorically speak of the independence of law from one's own (or any other individual's) acceptance—such as, "The Constitution would be valid law *even if I did not accept the American rule of recognition*," or "The Constitution was valid law in 1788 *even for an individual judge who did not accept the American rule of recognition*." An individual's attitudes are justificatorily irrelevant to the law's existence. But Hart cannot allow for ILSs that categorically state the independence of the validity of law from rule of recognition facts.

So far we have considered the problem of ILSs that are *temporally* categorical, by treating laws as valid when the relevant rule of recognition facts are absent. But there are also ILSs that are *spatially* categorical, by treating laws as valid in *places* where the relevant rule of recognition facts are absent. Consider two legal systems—the American and the Algerian—each with its own rule of recognition facts. Let us assume that, according to American choice-of-law rules, an American citizen currently living in Algeria is subject to a particular American law. According to Algerian choice-of-law rules, in contrast, she is subject to a different and incompatible Algerian law.

Assume that a participant in the American legal system makes the ILS that American law validly applies to the American. Hart cannot understand this ILS as the claim that the law validly applies *in the Algerian legal system*, in the sense that Algerian officials are legally obligated to apply the American law. After all, the requisite rule of recognition facts are missing—Algerian officials accept a different rule of recognition, in which Algerian law applies. Instead Hart must take the ILS to be about the obligations of *American* officials. The ILS must mean, for example, that an Algerian judgment that applies Algerian law to the American citizen should not be enforced *by American courts*. And yet it seems entirely possible that an ILS made by an American official might mean that *Algerian officials* are legally obligated to apply American law, not that American officials are obligated to treat them as if they were so obligated.

The problem of the temporal and spatial relativization of legal validity to rule of recognition facts under Hart's approach is even more serious than it might at first seem, because shifts in rule of recognition facts occur not merely between legal systems, but within what we would want to identify as a unitary legal system. As Matthew Adler has emphasized, governmental branches—or even smaller groups within a legal system—appear to have their own distinctive rules of recognition.[59] And yet a participant in a group might want to make an ILS that attributes legal obligations to members of other groups, not merely to members of her own group when dealing with members of other groups. Hart cannot explain how such an ILS is justified.

Furthermore, the fundamental criteria of legal validity accepted by American officials have changed in subtle and not-so-subtle ways over the last 220 years.[60] Each shift is a change in the prevailing rule of recognition facts. If Hart's approach is correct, these shifts would undermine the ability of current officials to attribute legal obligations to officials in the relatively recent past—for example, before the Supreme Court's revolutionary decisions in the 1930s and 1940s. And ILSs that attribute legal obligations to past officials seem possible.

Curiously, this critique of Hart looks very much like Hart's critique of Austin. Austin's reduction of law to the commands of a sovereign, Hart argued, could not account for legal continuity during changes in sovereignty—for example, when one sovereign succeeded another.[61] By looking to rule of recognition facts, this legal continuity could be restored. But Hart cannot account for legal continuity when rule of recognition facts themselves change.

What we need is an account of ILSs that treats rule of recognition facts the way Hart's model treats acceptance of the rule of recognition. Although acceptance is a ground for an ILS—in the sense that it is in place whenever an ILS is made—it is expressed in the ILS in a way that makes it justificatorily irrelevant to the ILS.[62] We need a comparable account of rule of recognition facts, in which such facts may be among the grounds for an ILS, but are justificatorily irrelevant to it. I believe that Hans Kelsen can be read as offering such an account. For this reason, his legal theory can accommodate categorical legal statements that assert the independence of legal validity from rule of recognition facts. But because

---

59. Matthew D. Adler, *Popular Constitutionalism and the Rule of Recognition: Whose Practices Ground U.S. Law?*, 100 Nw. U. L. Rev. 719, 745–49 (2006).

60. Greenawalt, *supra* note 5, at 644–45, 660–61 (reprinted as Chapter 1, this volume, at 22–23, 37); Frederick Schauer, *Amending the Presuppositions of a Constitution*, *in* Responding to Imperfection: The Theory and Practice of Constitutional Amendment 145 (Sanford Levinson ed., 1995).

61. Hart, *supra* note 9, at 62.

62. In speaking of rule of recognition facts as the grounds for ILSs, I assume that no ILS is made without rule of recognition facts in place in the group to which the speaker belongs at the time the speaker makes the ILS. But there is an even more extreme set of counterexamples to Hart's approach, offered by Matt Adler in this volume, in which even the speaker-specific rule of recognition facts are absent. I shall not consider these counterexamples here. *See* Matthew D. Adler, *Social Facts, Constitutional Interpretation, and the Rule of Recognition* (Chapter 8, this volume).

Kelsen modeled his approach after logical antipsychologism, in order to appreciate it we must make a brief digression into issues in the philosophy of logic.

III. LEGAL QUIETISM

Why are our logical principles justified? For some principles the answer is that they can be deduced from other logical principles through valid (that is, truth-preserving) inference rules. But eventually we will reach fundamental logical principles and inference rules for which no derivation is possible. What reason do we have to accept *them*? Why, for example, should we believe that all instances of the law of noncontradiction are true or all instances of *modus ponens* are truth-preserving?

Psychologism can be understood as the view that these fundamental logical principles are descriptions of our inferential dispositions.[63] So understood, the law of noncontradiction can be justified by psychological evidence—for example, that we have a disposition not to assent to not-*P* when we have already assented to *P*.

Although psychologism was dominant in the mid-nineteenth century, as the century progressed, a reaction arose. One perceived problem was that it relativized logic to psychological states, making it impossible to meaningfully condemn as mistaken a person who made different logical inferences. As Frege put it: "There would be no logic to be appointed arbiter in the conflict of opinions."[64] I would not be able to criticize someone who rejects the law of noncontradiction, except insofar as that person is not being true to his own inferential dispositions.

Instead of treating logical judgments as the description of our psychological states, Frege insisted that they are about abstract objects, namely the senses (meanings) expressed by sentences. And because logical truths are *necessary*, these senses cannot be in space and time—they must inhabit a "third realm" distinct from realms of the physical and the mental.[65]

Because he thought of senses as non-natural, it would appear that Frege was committed to a *Platonist* epistemology of logic, in which knowledge of logic is achieved through a mysterious form of metaphysical contact with the

---

63. *See* Richard R. Brockhaus, *Realism and Psychologism in 19th Century Logic*, 51 Phil. & Phenomenological Res. 493, 494–506 (1991). A possible example of psychologism in logic is J.S. Mill. *But see infra* note 69.

64. Gottlob Frege, The Basic Laws of Arithmetic 17 (Montgomery Furth trans. 1967) (1893).

65. Gottlob Frege, *Thoughts*, *in* Collected Papers on Mathematics, Logic, and Philosophy 363 (Brian McGuinness ed., Max Black et al. trans., 1984) (1918–19).

third realm.[66] But it is a distinctive aspect of Frege's antipsychologism that he rejected the very possibility of an epistemology of logic. His argument here was both simple and profound. An epistemology of logic would be a form of methodological syncretism, for it would seek to establish a relationship between two worlds that, by their nature, cannot be bridged. Our *judgments* about logic inhabit the world of psychology, which is in time and is subject to causal laws. But the senses about which these judgments are true do not exist in space or time and are not subject to causality. Because our logical judgments and their objects inhabit different realms, we can never say why it is that our fundamental logical judgments are justified:

> The question why and with what right we acknowledge a law of logic to be true, logic can answer only by reducing it to another law of logic. Where that is not possible, logic can give no answer. If we step away from logic, we may say: we are compelled to make judgments by our own nature. . . . I shall neither dispute nor support this view; I shall merely remark that what we have here is not a logical consequence. What is given is not a reason for something's being true, but for our taking it to be true.[67]

Logic can be justified only *from within logic*, that is, through fundamental logical judgments. Logic, as Wittgenstein put it, "must take care of itself."[68]

Indeed, the very attempt to justify fundamental logical judgments would undermine logic itself. Any attempt to show a connection between our logical judgments and their objects would threaten to treat these objects as empirical, since it is only by being empirical that they could have a relationship to our judgments. And that would undermine the necessity that distinguishes logical truths. The very possibility of logic depends upon *not* seeking such a justification. Frege, in short, was a logical quietist.

Frege arrived at logical quietism through *cognitivism*, that is, the view that logical judgments genuinely describe logical states of affairs. But there is an alternative noncognitivist (and indeed psychologist) route to logical quietism. Consider, once again, Frege's argument that psychologism leads to relativism. In arriving at this conclusion, he assumed that the psychologist would treat logical judgments as the description of (and thus as justified by) our inferential dispositions. But the psychologist might argue that logical judgments are the *expression*, rather than the description, of our inferential dispositions, and that these dispositions

---

66. For discussions of this problem, see Tyler Burge, *Frege on Knowing the Third Realm*, 101 MIND 633 (1992); Robert Hanna, *Logical Cognition: Husserl's Prolegomena and the Truth in Psychologism*, 53 PHIL. & PHENOMENOLOGICAL RES. 251, 251–53 (1993).

67. FREGE, *supra* note 64, at 15.

68. LUDWIG WITTGENSTEIN, TRACTATUS LOGICO-PHILOSOPHICUS § 5.473 (D.F. Pears & B.F. McGuinness trans., 1974).

would express themselves in judgments that assert the independence of logical states of affairs from our inferential dispositions themselves.[69]

If so, psychologism would be logically quietist. Fundamental logical judgments could not be justified, although they should not for that reason be abandoned. They could not be justified by other logical judgments, because they are fundamental. But they also could not be justified by our inferential dispositions, since that would be contrary to our dispositions themselves.

Kelsen modeled his legal theory on the logical antipsychologists' *cognitivist* approach.[70] He insisted that legal judgments were genuinely descriptive,[71] and that their objects were like Fregean senses in standing outside space and time. A legal norm, he argued, "does not exist in space and time, for it is not a fact of nature."[72] In particular, it is independent of social facts. Although a human act can generate a legal meaning, "[t]his 'meaning' is not something one can see or hear in the act *qua* external material fact, as one can perceive in an object its natural properties and functions, such as colour, rigidity, and weight."[73] The legal meaning of a social event is something over and above the event itself:

> People assemble in a hall, they give speeches, some rise, others remain seated—this is the external event. Its meaning: that a statute is enacted. Or, a man dressed in robes says certain words from a platform, addressing someone standing before him. This external event has as its meaning a judicial decision.[74]

---

69. *Cf.* Robert B. Brandom, *Semantic Inferentialism and Logical Expressivism, in* ARTICULATING REASONS: AN INTRODUCTION TO INFERENTIALISM 45 (2000). I think expressivism is certainly *a* theme in psychologism—for example, in the writings of Benno Erdmann. *See, e.g.*, Jack W. Meiland, *Psychologism in Logic: Husserl's Critique*, 19 INQUIRY 325, 331–37 (1976). For an illuminating account of J.S. Mill's psychologism that touches on these matters, see David M. Godden, *Psychologism in the Logic of John Stuart Mill*, 26 HIST. & PHIL. LOGIC 115, 138–40 (2005).

70. HANS KELSEN, ALLGEMEINE STAATSLEHRE, at vii (1925) (Kelsen's goal is "the passage from the subjective sphere of psychologism to the field of logical objective validity"). An important influence on Kelsen was the Neo-Kantian antipsychologist Hermann Cohen. Hans Kelsen, *A Letter to Renato Treves, in* NORMATIVITY AND NORMS, *supra* note 11, at 169, 171 (expressing his indebtedness to Cohen). I discuss the relationship between Kelsen and Cohen in Green, *supra* note 43, at 389–405. *See also* Geert Edel, *The Hypothesis of the Basic Norm: Hans Kelsen and Hermann Cohen, in* NORMATIVITY AND NORMS, *supra* note 11, at 195.

71. HANS KELSEN, PURE THEORY OF LAW 101–07 (Max Knight trans., 1965) (1960) (translation of the second edition).

72. HANS KELSEN, AN INTRODUCTION TO THE PROBLEMS OF LEGAL THEORY 12 (Bonnie Litschewski Paulson & Stanley L. Paulson trans., 1992) (1934) (translating the first edition of *The Pure Theory of Law*).

73. *Id.* at 9.

74. *Id.* at 8; *see also* KELSEN, *supra* note 71, at 2. Also like Frege, Kelsen insisted that the relations between the abstract objects described by our legal judgments are *necessary*. KELSEN, *supra* note 72, at 25; Hans Kelsen, *'Foreword' to the Second Printing of Main*

It is common to understand Kelsen as resisting sociological accounts of the law for much the same reason that Hart did—because they cannot account for the reason-giving character of legal statements.[75] Under this reading, Kelsen thought that legal norms cannot be reduced to sociological facts because there is no non-contingent connection between such facts and one's reasons for action. But if this were true, Kelsen would have no argument against an approach, such as Hart's, that uses expressivism to explain the reason-giving character of legal statements, while maintaining that legal statements can be justified by rule of recognition facts.

The truth is that Kelsen took the unusual (but I think very defensible) view that someone who makes a legal statement does not thereby take himself to have any reason for action: "Even an anarchist . . . could describe positive law as a system of valid norms, without having to approve of this law."[76] Kelsen understood legal statements to be, as Raz has put it, *detached*:

> A detached legal statement is a statement of law, of what legal rights and duties people have, not a statement about people's beliefs, attitudes, or actions. . . . Yet a detached normative statement does not carry the full normative force of an ordinary normative statement.[77]

In one respect, a detached legal statement is like an ELS: The person making it need not accept the rule of recognition as a standard of behavior. But it is also like an ILS, because it is formulated in the language of legal validity or legal obligation, not the language of social or psychological facts.[78] Detached legal statements are commonly made by lawyers, who often speak of valid laws without thereby expressing any attitude of acceptance.

Problems in the Theory of Public Law, *in* NORMATIVITY AND NORMS, *supra* note 11, at 3, 5; Green, *supra* note 43, at 375–81.

75. This is the reading provided in Joseph Raz, *Kelsen's Theory of the Basic Norm*, *in* NORMATIVITY AND NORMS, *supra* note 11, at 47, 59–60.

76. KELSEN, *supra* note 71, at 218 n.82; *see also id.* at 204–05, 218 n.83; Sylvie Delacroix, *Hart's and Kelsen's Concepts of Normativity Contrasted*, 17 RATIO JURIS 501, 512–18 (2004); Stanley L. Paulson, *The Weak Reading of Authority in Hans Kelsen's Pure Theory of Law*, 19 LAW & PHIL. 131, 136 n.19 (2000); Alida Wilson, *Joseph Raz on Kelsen's Basic Norm*, 27 AM. J. JURIS. 46, 53–55 (1982).

77. JOSEPH RAZ, THE AUTHORITY OF LAW 153 (1979).

78. Hart is quite clear that an ELS is a statement, from the external perspective, about people's attitudes and behavior, rather than a statement of legal validity. Someone making an external legal statement merely "states the fact that others accept [the rule of recognition]." HART, *supra* note 9, at 103. He offers as an example of such a statement, "In England they recognize as law . . . whatever the Queen in Parliament enacts. . . ." *Id.* at 102. It is for this reason that Raz insists that detached legal statements cannot be understood as ELSs. RAZ, *supra* note 77, at 153.

Because Kelsen understood legal statements to be detached, his resistance to sociological explanations of legal validity cannot depend on the idea that someone who makes a legal statement thereby takes himself to have a reason for action.[79] Kelsen resisted sociological accounts of the law for a very different reason—because he thought that we speak of valid laws as existing even in circumstances where the relevant rule of recognition facts are absent.[80] Kelsen's legal theory is, as he puts it, *doubly* pure: it is pure in distinguishing the law from morality (or, indeed, other forms of practical reasoning) *and* in distinguishing it from sociology.[81]

As we have seen, the ability of legal norms to transcend social facts is evident in the revolutionary beginnings of a legal system, that is, the point at which the "first constitution," as Kelsen put it, is created. The first constitution is the ultimate positive law in the chain of legal justification.[82] As we have described the

---

79. Torben Spaak has attributed to both Kelsen and Hart a strictly legal conception of the law's normativity, in which the existence of a valid legal norm entails only that legal and not moral reasons for action exist. Torben Spaak, *Kelsen and Hart on the Normativity of Law*, *in* PERSPECTIVES ON JURISPRUDENCE: ESSAYS IN HONOUR OF JES BJARUP 397 (Peter Wahlgren ed., 2005). But for Hart, someone who makes an ILS takes himself to have a practical (although not necessarily a moral) reason for action—namely the reason standing behind his acceptance of the rule of recognition.

80. Because Raz understands Kelsen's resistance to sociological accounts of the law to depend upon the law's reason-giving character, he has a good deal of difficulty explaining detached legal statements, since someone who makes such a statement need not take himself to have a reason for action. Raz offers two possible solutions to this problem. Under the first, the person making a detached statement speaks of the law in a *hypothetical* manner—she states what norms would be taken as valid *if* one adopted the perspective of the "legal man," that is, someone taking a truly committed perspective. Joseph Raz, *Kelsen's Theory of the Basic Norm*, *in* NORMATIVITY AND NORMS, *supra* note 11, at 47, 62–64. This would be going on when a lawyer says things like "*Under the law of Saudi Arabia*, practicing Christianity is illegal." But lawyers do not always make such hypothetical judgments. They sometimes make categorical claims about the validity of a legal norm—for example, "The United States Constitution is valid law," not "The United States Constitution is valid law *according to the American legal system*." According to Raz, lawyers make these categorical statements by adopting the point of view of the legal man, but solely in a "professional and uncommitted" manner. *Id.* at 65.

81. KELSEN, *supra* note 71, at 1; HANS KELSEN, GENERAL THEORY OF LAW AND STATE xiv (Anders Wedberg trans., 1945).

82. The first constitution need not be written. Kelsen argued, for example, that the first constitution of international law is that the custom of states creates valid law. *See* KELSEN, *supra* note 71, at 226, 323. Furthermore, this constitution was itself created through custom. *See id.* at 226. However, he argued that we cannot point to the first constitution of international law itself to show that the creation of this first constitution was an act of valid lawmaking. That would be vicious circularity. Neither can we simply identify the first constitution with the custom that created it, since that fails to explain why custom had constitution-creating legal power. In the end, a basic norm must be presupposed

American legal system, Article VII is its first constitution.[83] We cannot justify Article VII's status as law by other enacted laws. The Convention was not legally authorized to create a new method of constitutional ratification. Indeed the Convention's action was contrary to the amendment procedures in the preceding Articles of Confederation, which required consent by the Congress of the Confederation and the legislatures of all the states.[84] Because the Convention's creation of Article VII was a lawless act, rule of recognition facts had not yet coalesced around it. And yet, despite the absence of rule of recognition facts validating the Convention's actions, we now make the judgment that Article VII and the Constitution ratified pursuant to it were valid laws when created.

Indeed, we can put the point more strongly. Not only does valid American law precede the establishment of rule of recognition facts; there is also a sense in which American law is *timeless*. Consider the question when it was true that Article VII would be valid law if the Convention created it. We have no way of arguing that this point arose at a particular time—for example, when the relevant rule of recognition facts were in place—for that would mean arguing that the validity of Article VII depends on those facts, something our legal judgments deny. We seem committed to it always being true, even at the time of the dinosaurs, that Article VII would be valid law if created.[85]

Of course, Kelsen accepts that, as a psychological matter, we would not *say* that Article VII was valid when created if rule of recognition facts were not in place now. The first constitution is *treated* as valid, according to Kelsen, when there is efficacy, in the sense that the laws identified by the first constitution are largely obeyed by the population:

> A band of revolutionaries stages a violent *coup d'état* in a monarchy, attempting to oust the legitimate rulers and to replace the monarchy with a republican

---

under which custom was an authorized means of creating the constitution for international law. *See id.* On the role of the basic norm in Kelsen's thought, see *infra* notes 92–97 and accompanying text.

83. I ignore the fact that Article VII cannot exhaust the first constitution for the U.S. legal system, since a good deal of the valid law of that system (for example state law) cannot be traced to Article VII.

84. Bruce Ackerman & Neal Katyal, *Our Unconventional Founding*, 62 U. CHI. L. REV. 475, 478–80 (1995).

85. This can explain the seeming incompatibility between Kelsen's insistence that legal norms stand beyond space and time and his claim that they are brought into being by (although are not reducible to) social events. On the one hand, positive legal norms do not exist until concrete social events occur; Sarbanes–Oxley did not come into being until it was enacted by Congress. But the legal space within which these social events are acts of law creation has no beginning in time. It existed at the time of the dinosaurs. Indeed, in a certain sense, Sarbanes–Oxley existed at the time of the dinosaurs too, insofar as it was true at that time that it would be valid law if enacted by Congress.

> form of government. If the revolutionaries succeed, the old system ceases to be effective, and the new system becomes effective. . . . And one treats this new system, then, as a legal system, that is to say, one interprets as legal acts the acts applying the new system, and as unlawful acts the material facts violating it. . . . If the revolutionaries were to fail because the system they set up remained ineffective . . . then the initial act of the revolutionaries would be interpreted not as the setting up of a constitution but as treason, not as the making of law but as a violation of law.[86]

But this is merely a psychological claim about when we take the first constitution to be valid. We cannot understand the validity of the first constitution as justified by its efficacy. Indeed, at the time of its creation, it was not efficacious, and yet the initial act of the revolutionaries is interpreted "as the making of law."

We can put the same point in spatial terms as well. As we have seen, we cannot say that the spatial scope of American law is limited by rule of recognition facts, since we can speak of an American law as being binding upon Algerian officials who do not participate in the American rule of recognition. To be sure, American law might *not* apply extraterritorially in this fashion. But if that is so, it is not because American law is essentially limited by rule of recognition facts, but because it is limited by American law itself. Potentially, American law applies everywhere.

In a manner very similar to Frege, Kelsen insisted on a distinction between psychological explanations of why we take the law to be valid and justification of its validity.[87] Efficacy, he argued, is an "is-fact" that may not justify an "ought."[88] Rule of recognition facts are no more relevant to the justification of fundamental legal judgments than psychological facts about our inferential dispositions are relevant to the justification of the law of noncontradiction.[89] Indeed, Kelsen insisted that legal norms, being non-natural, cannot be efficacious at all. Only judgments about the law could influence people's actions: "One must therefore distinguish clearly between the *norm*, which is *valid*, and the *idea of the norm* [Norm-Vorstellung], which is effective."[90] To seek any relation between our judgments about legal norms and the legal norms themselves would be a form of methodological syncretism, for it would seek to establish a relationship between two worlds that, by their nature, cannot be bridged.

---

86. Kelsen, supra note 72, at 59. *See also* Green, *supra* note 43, at 401–02.

87. Green, *supra* note 43, at 402.

88. Kelsen, *supra* note 71, at 10–11.

89. The matter is complicated, however, by the fact that Kelsen takes efficacy to be a legal requirement under international law for the existence of a subsidiary legal system. *See infra* Section IV. Many of his comments about the relationship between legality and efficacy must be understood in this light.

90. Hans Kelsen, *Das Wesen des Staates*, 1 Revue Internationale de la Theorie du Droit 1, 7 (1926).

Rather than seeking to justify fundamental legal judgments through rule of recognition facts, Kelsen denied that they could be justified at all (which does not mean that he thought they should be abandoned). Just as the logical antipsychologists argued that logic can be justified only immanently, through fundamental logical judgments, Kelsen argues that all law *must be justified by law*: "To comprehend something legally can only be to comprehend it as law."[91] One can begin representing the law only by employing fundamental legal judgments. American law can be represented only when one accepts the creation of Article VII by the Constitutional Convention as the enactment of valid law, just as logic can be thought only once one accepts the law of noncontradiction. Law, Kelsen argues, must take care of itself.

As we have seen, Kelsen's route to legal quietism was through cognitivism about legal judgments. But there is an alternative route through an expressivist account, in which rule of recognition facts are treated in much the same way that acceptance of the rule of recognition is treated in Hart's theory. Kelsen admits that we make legal judgments when rule of recognition facts are present. We might understand legal statements, therefore, not as the description of abstract objects, but as the manifestation or expression of a mental state that depends upon rule of recognition facts. And just as our acceptance of the rule of recognition might express itself in legal judgments that assert the independence of legal validity from our acceptance, so the mental state that depends upon rule of recognition facts might express itself in judgments that assert the independence of legal validity from both the mental state and rule of recognition facts.

So far, I have spelled out Kelsen's theory of law without mentioning his doctrine of the basic norm (*Grundnorm*). And one might think that Kelsen's approach is not quietist, insofar as he thought that the validity of the first constitution can be justified by the basic norm, which Kelsen understood as a nonpositive norm that authorizes the first constitution's creators.[92]

There is an enormous literature on the basic norm, and I cannot do justice here to the many nuances of the idea and the varied roles that it played in Kelsen's legal theory.[93] But for our purposes it is enough to note that the basic norm could

---

91. KELSEN, *supra* note 72, at 11.

92. KELSEN, *supra* note 71, at 199–205.

93. In particular, Kelsen's idea of the basic norm is closely tied to the Kantian dimensions of his legal theory. *See* Green, *supra* note 43; Stanley L. Paulson, *Introduction* to KELSEN, *supra* note 72, at xvii. The basic norm, Kelsen argued, is a "*transcendental-logical* presupposition"—something *brought to* the law by the knower. KELSEN, *supra* note 71, at 201 (emphasis added). For examples of the (largely critical) literature on the basic norm, see Norbert Leser, *Die Reine Rechtslehre im Widerstreit der philosophischen Ideen*, *in* DIE REINE RECHTSLEHRE IN WISSENSCHAFTLICHER DISKUSSION 97, 101–02 (1982); Eugenio Bulygin, *An Antinomy in Kelsen's Pure Theory of Law*, *in* NORMATIVITY AND NORMS, *supra* note 11, at 297, 312–14; Stanley Paulson, *On the Puzzle Surrounding Hans Kelsen's Basic Norm*, 13 RATIO JURIS 279 (2000).

not have been understood by Kelsen as playing an explicit role in legal justification.[94] The basic norm of the American legal system, for example, would be a nonpositive norm authorizing the Constitutional Convention to create Article VII. And no such norm exists. It is simply false that the Convention was so authorized.

It is revealing that toward the end of his career, Kelsen spoke of the basic norm as a Vaihingerian *fiction* similar to a first cause.[95] One can best appreciate both the attractions and the difficulties of the basic norm by treating it as analogous to a first cause. On the one hand, it appears that there must be a first cause—a prime mover—to explain how the chains of cause and effect began. On the other hand, a first cause seems impossible. Everything is caused by something that is itself caused.

Kant described the conflict between these two arguments as an *antinomy* of pure reason.[96] And one can argue that there is a *jurisprudential* antinomy, in the sense that arguments exist both for and against the basic norm: On the one hand, it seems that the Constitutional Convention must have been authorized to create Article VII, or Article VII would not have the status of law. Indeed, the idea that the Convention was so authorized seems to reveal itself in our commitment to the fact that it was *always* true, even at the time of the dinosaurs, that Article VII would be valid if created. This seems to presuppose the existence of an eternal nonpositive norm authorizing the Convention to create Article VII. On the other hand, we are equally committed to the idea that the creation of Article VII was a *revolutionary* act, in the sense that when one follows the chain of legal justification, no such authorization can be found.

The basic norm plays no more of an explicit role in legal reasoning than first causes play in scientific reasoning. Like first causes, we are attracted to the basic norm only when reflecting philosophically on our judgments. As far as our actual legal reasoning is concerned, quietism is correct: we take the first constitution as valid *without justification*. Indeed, any attempt to provide such a justification—whether it is through appeal to rule of recognition facts or to the basic norm—will end up distorting our legal judgments.[97]

---

94. It is common to argue that if Kelsen had thought that the basic norm played an explicit role in legal reasoning, he would, in the end, have been a natural law theorist. *See* Iain Stewart, *The Critical Legal Science of Hans Kelsen*, 17 J.L. & SOC'Y 273, 296 (1990).

95. KELSEN, *supra* note 11, at 256; *see also* HANS VAIHINGER, THE PHILOSOPHY OF AS-IF (C.K. Ogden trans., 1935).

96. *See, e.g.*, IMMANUEL KANT, CRITIQUE OF PURE REASON A444–51/B472–79 (Norman Kemp Smith trans., 1965) (1781, 1787).

97. *See* Spaak, *supra* note 79, at 406 (arguing that the basic norm could be replaced with the observation that one judges the first constitution to be legally valid when enacted without any justification).

IV. THE UNITY OF LAW

Although I believe that legal quietism deserves to be taken seriously, it brings into focus an important tension in our legal judgments. Consider the fact that we make judgments about the valid law of multiple incommensurable legal systems—both legal systems in the past and the plurality of current legal systems that one finds as one makes one's way around the globe. To the extent that one thinks of these multiple systems as all containing valid laws, it would appear that one thinks of their validity as depending upon rule of recognition facts. If there are Algerian and American legal systems, each with valid laws, this must be because the validity of the laws of each legal system depends upon that system's own set of official practices. On the other hand, to the extent that we speak of legal validity as independent of rule of recognition facts, we appear to be committed to the existence of only one (timeless) legal system, similar to the logical quietist's timeless logical world.

But the idea that there is only one timeless logical world is acceptable because there is a certain *self-evidence* to fundamental logical judgments. And it is hard to see how the same can be said about fundamental legal judgments. There is nothing self-evident about the validity of Article VII, or the validity of the first constitution of any legal system (even the international legal system). Law seems contingent, not merely in the sense that positive laws depend upon contingent lawmaking acts for their existence, but *all the way down*, to the basis of the legal system. And yet the sociological accounts of law that can explain this contingency cannot seem to account for judgments that assert the independence of legal validity from social (and especially rule of recognition) facts.

How does Kelsen resolve this tension? He bites the bullet and insists that only one legal system can be thought.[98] This is Kelsen's doctrine of the unity of law, without which his legal theory cannot be properly understood. But Kelsen seeks to do justice to the fact that we speak of the valid laws of multiple legal systems, by arguing that we are actually speaking of *sub*systems (as individual regulatory regimes are subsystems within the American legal system) that are assigned by the law of the unitary legal system to govern different times and places.

Kelsen often seems to suggest that the unitary legal system is the *international* system, and that the laws of the domestic subsystems are valid to the extent that they are recognized under international law.[99] If that is true, then American law is fundamentally international law, since the American legal system is really a subsystem recognized by international law. But Kelsen generally claims to be agnostic about whether the unitary system is the international or a particular domestic legal system. All law might be, fundamentally, American law. If so,

---

98. Kelsen, *supra* note 72, at 111–25; Kelsen, *supra* note 71, at 328–47.
99. *Id.* at 336–38.

international law would be valid only because it is recognized by American law, and the laws of all other domestic subsystems would be valid only because they are, in turn, recognized by this American-based international law.[100]

It is important to see that, for Kelsen, the determination of the existence of subsystem law is a *legal* determination, not a factual one—although the legal conditions for the existence of a subsystem will of course *refer to* social facts, just as the legal conditions for creating a valid regulatory regime will refer to such facts. This is easiest to see if one assumes that the legal conditions for the existence of subsystems diverge measurably from what would be insisted upon by a rule of recognition model. For example, according to the law of the unitary legal system, a former French colony might remain part of France, even though, as a social fact, an independent Hartian legal system that does not refer to French law has established itself.

In fact, however, when Kelsen describes the legal requirements for the existence of a subsystem, they look suspiciously similar to rule of recognition facts. Kelsen argues that a subsystem is established, as a matter of law, when it is *efficacious*, in the sense that the norms identified by the constitution of the subsystem are largely obeyed by the population.[101] It is this *legal* doctrine of efficacy that makes it so often appear as if Kelsen agrees with Hart that legality can be justified by rule of recognition facts. But Kelsen is clear that this legal principle of efficacy "is, in itself, a positive norm,"[102] that is, a positive law of the unitary legal system. It is not the extralegal foundation of a legal system's existence, as it is for Hart.

Nevertheless, this legal doctrine of efficacy remains a serious mistake on Kelsen's part. First of all, Kelsen insists in other contexts that the content of positive legal norms is not something that can be determined in advance, since it depends upon the contingent choices of lawmaking organs.[103] Kelsen should no more know in advance the content of the positive law on the recognition of subsystems than he should know the content of Sarbanes–Oxley.[104]

More fundamentally, the legal principle of efficacy fails to account for the phenomenon Kelsen sought to explain, namely our judgments about the valid law of multiple legal systems. Assume, for example, that the French legal system is the unitary one, and that American law is valid because it satisfies the legal

---

100. *Id.* at 333–34. Curiously, American *subsystem* law would also reappear within the unitary American legal system, since American law as a subsystem would also be recognized by international law.

101. *Id.* at 336–39.

102. KELSEN, *supra* note 81, at 121.

103. KELSEN, *supra* note 71, at 198 ("[A]ny kind of content might be law.").

104. Efficacy is also arguably false as a principle of public international law. It ignores, for example, the rights of self-determination and other principles of international law limiting state sovereignty. *See* Tayyab Mahmud, *Jurisprudence of Successful Treason: Coups d'Etat & Common Law*, 27 CORNELL INT'L L.J. 49, 119–20 (1994).

principle of efficacy recognized under French law. This would mean that from the perspective of the unitary legal system the U.S. Constitution became valid law only when it became efficacious. And that, as we have seen, is an improper characterization of American law.

Indeed, unless it allowed for legal conflicts (something Kelsen rejected[105]), there appears to be *no* legal principle for recognizing subsystems that would not distort our legal judgments about the subsystems' laws. After all, the laws of subsystems *conflict*. American law claims applicability in Algeria in a manner that cannot be reconciled with Algerian law. Such conflicts are themselves substantial evidence of the contingency and plurality of legal systems.

V. CONCLUSION

My goal in this chapter has been to identify and discuss Kelsen's quietist observation that fundamental legal judgments cannot be justified by rule of recognition facts, and to explore its consequences for basic questions of constitutional law. I believe that Kelsen's observation is fundamentally correct. It is a different question, which I will not answer here, what conclusion to draw from this observation, given that it appears to force upon us a doctrine of the unity of law.

One possibility is an error theory. One might argue that our legal judgments, although descriptive, speak of entities that simply cannot exist. Such an error theory of law would be importantly different from an error theory of ethics, since the problem of legal norms would not be their *reason-giving* character but the conflict between their contingency and timelessness.

But it is possible that an error theory might be avoided by adopting the view that legal judgments, rather than describing legal norms, express mental states that depend upon the existence of rule of recognition facts. Such a position would treat rule of recognition facts in a manner similar to the way that Hart's theory treats acceptance of the rule of recognition. It is enough for our current purposes, however, that Kelsen has identified a weakness in rule of recognition theories like Hart's.

105. Kelsen, *supra* note 71, at 330–31; Kelsen, *supra* note 72, at 71–75, 117–19.

INDEX

Note: page numbers followed by an *n* indicate that the reference is to a numbered note on the designated page. For example, 17*n*51 would refer to note 51 on page 17.

B

C

S